www.palgrave.com/foundations/greetham

Palgrave Foundations

A series of introductory texts across a wide range of subject areas to meet the needs of today's lecturers and students.

Foundations texts provide complete yet concise coverage of core topics and skills based on detailed research of course requirements suitable for both independent study and class use – *the firm foundations for future study.*

Published
A History of English Literature
Biology
British Politics
Chemistry (third edition)
Communication Studies
Contemporary Europe (second edition)
Economics
Economics for Business
Foundations of Marketing
Modern British History
Nineteenth-Century Britain
Philosophy
Physics (second edition)
Politics (second edition)

Further titles are in preparation

Also by Bryan Greetham

How to Write Better Essays (Palgrave, 2001)

Philosophy

BRYAN GREETHAM

First published 2006 by
PALGRAVE MACMILLAN
Houndmills, Basingstoke, Hampshire RG21 6XS and
175 Fifth Avenue, New York, N.Y. 10010
Companies and representatives throughout the world

PALGRAVE MACMILLAN is the global academic imprint of the Palgrave Macmillan division of St. Martin's Press, LLC and of Palgrave Macmillan Ltd. Macmillan® is a registered trademark in the United States, United Kingdom and other countries. Palgrave is a registered trademark in the European Union and other countries.

ISBN-13: 978–1–4039–1878–9
ISBN-10: 1–4039–1878–3

This book is printed on paper suitable for recycling and made from fully managed and sustained forest sources.

A catalogue record for this book is available from the British Library.

A catalog record for this book is available from the Library of Congress.

Editing and origination by
Curran Publishing Services, Norwich

10 9 8 7 6 5 4 3 2 1
15 14 13 12 11 10 09 08 07 06

Printed and bound in China

To the memory of my father Robert Greetham – a quiet, kind and wise man. To Pat for all her support and unflinching faith in my abilities. And to Ken and Ellen Greetham for their interest in both me and my work.

Contents

PART I

Our Knowledge of the External World

PART III

Understanding Our Relations
with Others

Selected illustrations Tables

Biographies

Brief lives

Acknowledgements

I have many to thank for their help and encouragement not only in the writing of this book, but over the years as I have searched for ways to make myself a better teacher and philosopher. From my students to my teachers there are too many to acknowledge in this short space. So if I miss any out please forgive my oversight.

The biggest debt that I can never repay I owe to Patricia Rowe, my partner, who has been the one true constant in my life as we have journeyed around the world. Throughout all the difficult times she has kept up my flagging spirits with her indomitable optimism and faith in my abilities. I still marvel at the patience and forbearance with which she deals with my bouts of self-doubt and despondency.

Second, I owe a debt to the University of Newcastle in Australia for allowing me to take a year out to research and write large sections of this book. Among those at the university to whom I will always be grateful is David Dockrill, whose friendship, wise counsel and willingness to listen at any time helped me surmount many crises. I would also like to express my gratitude to my friend and colleague, Chris Falzon, for contributing chapters 13, 16 and most of 17. In my experience there are few who have a better grasp of continental philosophy and of the ideas of Foucault in particular.

Third, I must acknowledge my debt to the wider academic community, particularly to all those authors whose work I have read and who have taught me so much. We are all in your debt for contributing so richly to the community of learning. I just hope I have throughout treated your work with the respect it deserves and acknowledged sufficiently the debt that I owe you. The same also applies to all my former tutors and students. I owe a considerable debt to Professor John Burrow and Dr Joseph Mintoff for their wise and inspired teaching. To my former students you will see in this book traces of the many hours we spent together wrestling with these ideas. Thank you all for your patience.

Fourth, I must thank my editor and friend, Suzannah Burywood, who patiently let me get on with my work, although there were many months of silence from my end. Her gentle handling and patient treatment of me is a testimony to her skills and professionalism. In the same vein I would also like to thank my academic reviewers for their generous comments on the original text and for all their constructive and helpful suggestions. I owe them a debt of gratitude for bringing to my work quality and depth it would not otherwise have had.

And last, and far from being least, I would like to thank Aldous, my Airedale terrier and constant companion, whose insistence that I engage in long practice sessions improving his ball skills broke up many an hour of solitary toil.

Bryan Greetham

The author and publishers wish to thank the following for permission to use copyright material:

Getty Images, pp. 58, 72, 84, 131, 177, 208, 240, 260, 322, 347

Introduction

Palgrave's *Foundations* series has given us the opportunity of producing the type of introduction to philosophy that has been long overdue. As a student studying philosophy for the first time I can remember the discouraging experience of being faced with difficult, intimidating introductions that made you feel inadequate if you were unable to grasp the complex arguments and concepts it laid out before you. Using a strange, alien language without a phrasebook by your side, you were left despairing whether you would ever get to grips with this difficult and arcane subject.

But it doesn't have to be like this. This is an exciting, endlessly fascinating subject, which confronts and asks questions about the most important assumptions we make in our lives. And the language? Well, there *are* difficult concepts that we have to go through together, but carefully done without leaving you thinking that you've literally lost the plot, they become not a handicap but an essential means of opening up the fascinating issues philosophers explore.

And if you don't understand an argument first time around, that's normal. Difficult passages have to be read more than once if you are to process the ideas on a deeper level. Nonetheless there are things we can do. In this book I shall help you process these ideas in three ways, so that at each stage you can explore the ideas confidently and enjoy that rare excitement of seeing for the first time fascinating insights into the nature of things.

Most introductory texts in philosophy begin with the ideas that are to be explained. As a result it is this which dictates the form in which this is to be presented, rather than the needs of students and readers. In this book I have tried to avoid this by helping you to process these ideas in three ways, so that you can more effectively make them your own and use them in your work.

First, on the 'micro' level you need an introduction that will not only enable you to develop a clear understanding of the ideas, but presents them in a form you can use, so you can complete your assignments. We all learn better if we can process our ideas into clear structures. This gives our ideas organization, which means we are better able to recall and use them confidently when we need them in assignments and in class discussion. There are simple ways this can be done. In this book you will be given note structures in each chapter outlining clearly the structure of the more difficult arguments. But, even more important, you can download the note structures for the whole chapter from our website at www.palgrave.com/foundations/greetham. You can then adapt them to suit your own purposes as you would if you were taking notes yourself. And, of course, you will find them very helpful if you have them by your side as you read each chapter.

On the 'macro' level we all want texts that will show us how everything fits together: we want an intellectual map to help us navigate the territory. There is nothing worse than feeling lost, not knowing how it all fits together. As we read we are trying to synthesize movements in ideas, philosophers, and philosophical issues into a broad map that will allow us to see clearly how each fits into the whole. At key points in the book I will give you a time line, a structure showing the patterns of relations that link the various systems of ideas. These will include many of the key concepts in philosophy, concepts like empiricism, rationalism, idealism, materialism and so on. Once we have analysed these and you have understood them clearly they will help you to manage your ideas, see linkages between them and draw comparisons, all of which is likely to yield a wealth of interesting insights.

In my experience fitting these sorts of concepts into a time line, providing a map of the territory, can be quite an empowering experience. For the first time students realize what is possible in the subject: what they can do on their own to explore the territory. They realize they can generate their own insights unprompted and, as a result, begin to develop a real passion for ideas. They can explore imaginatively concepts like rationalism or idealism, with a greater sense of control over the subject.

The third thing this book does to help you process the ideas and make them your own might not be so practical, but it is nevertheless important. Throughout the text you will find not just a dry, academic account of theories, ideas and arguments, but also fascinating insights into the lives and ideas of philosophers, revealing just how they made their breakthroughs; how they went about defining the problem, asking the right questions and then, in many cases, summoned up the courage to overturn the weight of accepted opinion.

Although generally ignored there is an important place in an introduction to philosophy for these uniquely personal aspects of a philosopher's intellectual progress. It lifts philosophy to a level on which you can see the richness and excitement of the discoveries of those who have contributed massively to the way we think today. And, at the same time, you can see the simplicity of the original idea and, in many cases, the stuttering, stumbling attempts to get at the truth.

You will find this not only helps you understand these ideas, but is reassuring, particularly if you yourself are to learn to philosophize. And as you will see in the first few chapters this is an important goal of this book. You will be taught how to set about tackling problems and you will be shown simple techniques to develop your abilities to analyse concepts, synthesize ideas and evaluate arguments. Any introduction to philosophy must do more than give you the facts of the subject; it must teach you to think as a philosopher.

This book works on each of these levels, while at the same time explaining complex ideas and arguments in a way that is clear, interesting and insightful. It will not only enable you to learn the methods of philosophy, the skills and techniques to tackle philosophical thinking, and a sound understanding of the key issues and ideas in philosophy, but, hopefully, it will leave you with a passion for ideas, which will drive you to explore and chart your own intellectual development.

The Subject

CHAPTER 1

Key issues

▶ What is philosophy? How can we learn to philosophize?

▶ How can it teach us to be more effective thinkers; not just uncritical recyclers of the opinions of others, but people who can think for ourselves?

▶ Why do we search for ultimate answers? Why is it important to find the non-arbitrary explanation of things; the highest principles behind all things?

▶ If philosophical questions involve answers about the way things *had* to be, that they could not have been otherwise, how different is this from other forms of enquiry?

▶ Why should we learn to question all those assumptions we take for granted about the fundamental issues that shape our lives: about our knowledge of the world, ourselves and our relations with others?

▶ If we should, why stop there? Should we not question the very idea that philosophy is or can be the search for such foundations, perhaps even doubting whether they are there in the first place?

▶ Why are these questions even more relevant today?

Contents

■ 1. What is philosophy?

At the start of each year, as my mind turns to a new batch of students about to start their first course in philosophy, the same question comes to mind: 'What am I to say to them when they ask me "What is philosophy?"' And each year I try to answer with the same wide-eyed excitement I first felt as an undergraduate: 'This is a subject like no other that you have studied. You are about to embark on the most exciting experience of your academic lives. This will be a genuine voyage of discovery for all of us, me included. Together we will discover things that we have not seen or thought about before.'

This may seem wide-eyed and innocent, but it is the sort of excitement that drew most of us to philosophy in the first place. Like no other subject it places you at the centre of learning. We begin with the assertion that there are no right answers. You will see things from your own perspective that I have never seen before, as I will see things you have never seen. Both of our contributions are important and valuable. Of course it would be foolish to deny there are *some* right answers, but the key to this subject is not to recognize them as such. From the moment you do, the search for truth is ended, and in this subject the process, the search, is more important than the product. The twentieth-century British philosopher Bertrand Russell once said, 'To teach how to live without certainty and yet without being paralysed by hesitation is perhaps the chief thing that philosophy, in our age, can do for those who study it.' Unlike any other subject, then, philosophy asks you to accept doubt and uncertainty, and search beyond the narrow confines of accepted opinion. You are left free to make your own contributions and reveal your own insights.

These are the key ingredients of a genuine voyage of discovery. It is not an exaggeration to say that it is driven by the same insatiable search for answers that drove Columbus to set sail for the New World and the first astronauts to risk their lives. Philosophy shares the same sense of wonder and passion for the ultimate answers to things. Another British philosopher, A. N. Whitehead, once described philosophy as 'the product of wonder'. It is that persistent questioning of all those things we take for granted. Accepting nothing on trust, the philosopher asks what makes our assumptions rationally defensible. Even though we may think there is no need to question them, and even though our conclusions may make us uncomfortable, this is an unyielding quest to go beyond what we know and take for granted.

Stand anywhere on the Earth's surface, look up at the sky and everything you see will be moving – the stars, the moon, the sun – everything that is except the thing you're standing on, the Earth. All the evidence and all common sense should convince us that the Earth is the centre of the universe and everything else revolves around it. To doubt this should seem like the ravings of a madman. Yet this is exactly what Galileo and Copernicus did, despite the derision of all those who appealed to common sense and threatened them with prosecution to force them back into line. Indeed, so dangerous were these thoughts to the Catholic Church that Galileo was eventually forced to recant his beliefs in 1633 under the threat of excommunication.

Philosophy involves the same nagging doubt about all those assumptions we take for granted about the fundamental issues that shape our lives: about our knowledge of the world, ourselves and our relations with others. For example, we regularly use concepts like knowledge, truth, freedom, equality and authority, but rarely do we question what we mean by them. Yet they may contain implicit assumptions about us and the world which, unknown to us, shape and direct our views about life. And once we have examined them we may find we no longer want to retain these views.

Our understanding of the world around us depends upon concepts like 'knowledge' and 'truth'. When we say we 'know' something, this can mean different things, different forms of knowledge, about which we can have serious doubts. If we say we believe in God, what sort of evidence would we need to justify such a claim? We are accustomed to believe the word of scientists, but on what grounds do we base this trust? Indeed, it's worth asking whether we can, in fact, have genuine knowledge at all about anything beyond ourselves. We can be certain of our own existence, but can we be equally certain that anything else exists?

And yet even here, where we might think certainty about ourselves is easy to find, we can still have serious doubts about how we understand ourselves. We all ask ourselves whether we are doing the right thing, not just morally, but in terms of our personal goals. We might find ourselves pursuing fame, wealth, power or just pleasure, but when we stand back from our lives, we are bound to ask whether these are worth pursuing for their own sake, or whether they are worthless as goals, perhaps even dangerous. There may be other things of much more lasting significance and more deeply fulfilling. For our own happiness and fulfilment it's necessary to discover what these might be. As the ancient Greek philosopher, Socrates, says, 'The unexamined life is not worth living.'

But then even closer to home, what are we doing when we think about these things and come to our decisions? On what are they based and are we free to think what we will? Thinking, feeling, intending, believing, these are all part of our everyday experiences. But how do we understand these mental processes? Are they the product of a disembodied will, which we cannot locate within the physical body, or are they the results of physical changes in the brain, just blind biochemical responses? After all, we accept without any dismay that many people are increasingly using mind-altering drugs to influence their moods and govern their mental lives.

The same can be said about all those things that govern our relations with others: the political and moral issues that shape our daily lives. How should we conduct our moral lives? And how much power should governments have to restrict our rights and freedoms? Here most of us are more than willing to concede that there is almost endless room for doubt and difference of opinion.

For example, we might claim that democracy is the ideal form of government, or that we should always keep promises, or that we should never lie. But what sort of claims are these? Can we find an objective basis for political and moral judgements of this type, or are they all just a matter of individual opinion? If they are just a matter of opinion, is there any reason to prefer one opinion to another, or is it just a question of what the majority prefers, or perhaps even just a matter of taste?

■ 2. The relevance of philosophy

Nevertheless, despite their significance for the fundamental issues in our lives, we can still ask why these intriguing questions should be relevant to us *now*. What makes them any more relevant today than they were, say, 400 years ago, when modern philosophy began? The simple answer is that we all search for order, meaning and value in our lives: in our understanding of ourselves as individuals, of the world in which we live, and of our relations with others. We want our experience of life to make some sense, when all too often it appears fragmented and pointless. And most, if not all, of us find experience without sense intolerable. Psychologists and sociologists are frequently telling us that the rise in suicides among the young, the increased use of hallucinogenic drugs, and increased medication for depression are all signs of a growing sense of malaise, of alienation from a world that a growing number of us no longer have ways of understanding.

In pre-modern times, when societies were shaped, if not controlled, by their religious beliefs and the churches in which they worshipped, meaning and value was easy to find. Every daily activity was suffused in religious significance, from buying bread to planting crops. But since the seventeenth century, when the scientific revolution and the Enlightenment freed the individual from dependence upon the authority of the Bible and ancient texts, we have been dependent upon our unaided reason to uncover what we believe is the truth about ourselves, the world around us and our relations with others.

But this type of freedom comes at a price. The individualism born in the seventeenth century migrated from a dependence upon individual reason to uncover scientific truths, to our economic life in the nineteenth century with the triumph of *laissez-faire* capitalism, and to our political lives in the twentieth century with liberal democracy and universal suffrage. In the process it has laid waste to many of the traditional social mechanisms for creating meaning and value in our lives.

Indeed the achievements of the twentieth century were in many ways unique in marking the triumph of our attempts to create the means whereby each one of us can isolate ourselves within our own personal territory. Unlike the people of previous centuries, we acquired the capacity to draw tighter personal cordons around ourselves. With videos and television it is now no longer necessary to go beyond the home for entertainment and information. Most of us in the Western world spend at least four hours a day watching television. Within the family this process of individualization has gone even further, with children possessing their own televisions and video recorders in their own rooms, where they spend hours apart from the family under the influence of fantasies created by producers whose only concerns are sales and profits.

But even outside the home, where we're forced to confront other people on the streets or on public transport, the personal cordon can be maintained with technology, like the personal music player, that acts as a badge of privacy warning off all those who dare to intrude. And then there are even larger numbers of us who are happy to retreat from the real world into the safer confines of virtual relations on the Internet. As each generation passes we seem to be retreating further and further into the privacy and security of our own lives, spending more of our time passively observing the world through a screen.

Likewise in the West we demand as our right private access to those things we believe are essential to our lives: our own living space and forms of transport. Indeed in his book, *The Private Future* (1974), Martin Pawley points out that the equal distribution of population throughout the dwellings in any developed country would give every individual his own private room and still leave hundreds of thousands of rooms unused. A similar distribution in, say, Pakistan would result in each room holding nine people. In some developed countries, notably the United States, the entire population could be accommodated in private cars, none of them full. In India the same distribution would result in more than one hundred persons crowding around each car.

So, if we cannot get meaning and value from our contact with others or through religious authorities, or even through meaningful work in a mechanized society, where do we find it? The answer for most of us is in the worship of materialism, of possessions. We are what we own. We are the products of a new consciousness industry, buying not just goods, but identities. In the language of consumerism objects take on a magical significance. We buy cars, not only because they are a means of transport, but, perhaps more important, because they say something about us to the outside world. They are the advertising hoardings on which we etch our identities for those who look on. It leaves you wondering what might be the epitaph of our age, compared with the more noble achievements of previous ages, like the towering Gothic cathedrals of the twelfth and thirteenth centuries and the great engineering triumphs of the nineteenth century. As T. S. Eliot suggests in his poem 'The Rock', it might be something far more prosaic, like the asphalt road or thousands of lost golf balls.

Although this problem is not unique to the twenty-first century, it is probably more acute for us than it was for previous generations. While we are inclined to believe that technological progress and economic growth are good in themselves, bringing efficiency, prosperity and greater consumption, we are left without any sense that there is a global meaning to our civilization. And, on an individual level, the single-minded pursuit of wealth leaves most of us hollow, without any sense of having a personal meaning to our lives. Indeed, our need for this is probably more urgent today than in previous generations. Modern technology has given Western governments the means to exert their power over any part of the world and, significantly, a much greater capacity for good and evil. Some philosophers are fond of pointing out that technology is an amplifier; that each time we commit ourselves to some technology we are endorsing and reinforcing certain values that are inherent in it. So, we ought to be sure that these are the values that should have lasting significance in our lives.

Moreover, such technological change occurs at a rapid pace, leaving most of us without the time or capacity to think ethically about its effects. The prospect of human cloning confronts us before we have had time to discuss it. GM foods are now part of the food chain, consumed by millions of people, of whom only a small percentage have had the time to discuss it and even fewer who have had any influence over the decision making. The same can be said for stem cell research, organ donations and similar ethical problems. For many who protest, sometimes violently, globalization seems to go ahead at a pace and in search of goals dictated more by multinational companies than by the individuals who will be affected. Our knowledge seems divorced from our values: we have power, but without insight. Our wealth and technology always seem to be outstripping our wisdom.

All of this points to the importance of philosophy and for doing some serious thinking about these issues. Philosophy is this search for order, meaning and value. By thinking the unthinkable and asking the most difficult of questions we can rationally explore these and other fundamental issues. In this way we can form a consistent, systematic and coherent framework of beliefs, values and assumptions, which will help us interpret experience and find some sense in it all.

■ 3. Learning to philosophize

Given this need to create such a framework to negotiate the uncertainty of rapid, bewildering change, just how are we to begin to philosophize? The first thing we must do is to make clear what we're looking for: in other words what are these fundamental issues that we need to examine? What type of questions do philosophers ask that others don't?

Put simply, the questions philosophers ask are fundamental because they concern the principles, assumptions and beliefs that underlie all our other attempts to understand ourselves and the world: psychological, economic, sociological, political and so on. The truth of many other things depends upon our answers to these questions. They may involve questions about the meaning of the ideas and concepts we use, like 'freedom', 'justice' and 'responsibility'. Or they may be concerned about what we base our knowledge on and what we mean when we say that something is 'true'. They involve examining the standards we use when we arrive at judgements we believe to be sound. Other questions concern whether there is any meaning in life and, if so, how we are to reveal it. We are also concerned about the values we ought to hold and why, particularly in our relations with others.

As you can see, if you look at these questions carefully, they cannot simply be settled by calling upon evidence. They go beyond the findings of empirical science, which proceeds by way of experiment, testing each theory against the evidence. It explains one event, say the spread of influenza, by reference to other events, say, the spread of a new virus or changes in consumption habits that might weaken resistance to it. By contrast, philosophy doesn't confine itself to these secondary or 'contingent' factors (meaning that they might or might not have happened depending on the circumstances). Philosophers are concerned with the first causes that explain all contingent things. So, where scientists finish, philosophers begin. They will ask whether the methods employed in science are reliable; whether our observations of the world can be trusted or if they merely reflect our preconceptions; whether empirical evidence is the best indicator of the truth; indeed, whether the world as a whole is intelligible and, if it is, whether we can ever know it.

Questions like these are about fundamental issues, involving the search for ultimate answers. They are a search for the non-arbitrary explanation of things, the highest principles behind all things. We are rational creatures. We are not content with explanations that depend upon other explanations, and causes of things upon other causes, even though at times this is all we have. We search for the ultimate answer or cause of things. If we are told, 'Well, this is just the way things are!' we are inclined to go on asking 'Why?' until we get to the ultimate reason, where our explanation needs no further explanation.

As we all know, this sort of relentless questioning is most clearly seen in young children. For example, one morning last week as I took my dog for his usual walk I met my neighbours, who were taking their dog and their five-year-old son, Pearson, for a walk. As our dogs frantically chased each other around our legs tangling us up in their leads, Pearson interrogated me. Like many children of his age he asks 'Why?' questions with an unquenchable passion. Never satisfied with my answers, each one was followed by yet another:

'Where have you been, Bryan?' he asks.

'We've been for a walk around the reserve, Pearson,' I answer, already preparing myself for the next question.

'Why have you?'

'Because my dog likes to go out in the morning,' I answer, although I know it is not enough.

With crushing inevitability, he asks, 'Why does he?'

'Because he likes to see all the other dogs,' I respond, knowing that this will not settle it either.

Pearson ploughs on, 'But why does he like to see the other dogs?'

'Because he's very sociable,' I offer, hoping this might do it.

'Why is he?'

'Because all dogs are sociable,' I answer. And so the conversation goes.

Of course, in Pearson's case it was not a serious attempt to reveal an ultimate reason, but if we were in his position asking these questions, more than likely it would be. We set ourselves the task of uncovering the fundamental ground for believing what we believe. It's a search for reasons for things beyond which we cannot go. One explanation for something is more satisfactory if it explains more than the previous explanation: if it encompasses more, if it is more general. In Pearson's case he quickly reaches this point when I make the abstract statement that all dogs are sociable. At this point we are free of the actual circumstances: we have reached the general statement that applies to all dogs. At this level we may be able to discover the ultimate, non-arbitrary reason for things: the most satisfying explanation beyond which we cannot go; beyond which there is no further reason, no further explanation.

One further distinction may help in clarifying the type of question involved in philosophy. While the answers we give in subjects like history and the natural and social sciences are contingent, in that they depend upon the empirical evidence, which could have turned out differently, philosophical questions involve answers about the way things *had* to be: they could not have been otherwise. For example, in history and in the sciences we might find ourselves asking questions like, 'Were the Nazis responsible for setting fire to the Reichstag in 1933?', 'Was the fall in turnout at the last election due to the apathy of the electorate or to a revolt against all the established parties?', or 'Are the causes of global warming to be found in the increased emissions of carbon dioxide or some other factor?'

By contrast the questions philosophers usually ask are conceptual; they are in search of answers that are necessarily true. That is, their truth is not contingent upon the prevailing circumstances or available evidence, but by virtue of their very nature in all possible worlds. Having said that, of course, we may not always be able to produce answers that are necessarily true; we may just have to settle for answers that at this time are only just probably true. The point is, however, that the type of question we ask is designed to search out necessary truths, even though we may not always be successful and have to settle for something less.

As we will see in the following chapters, we will ask questions like 'What is knowledge?', 'What is truth?', 'Is there a God?', 'What is morally right?', 'What is meant by freedom?' The answers to all these questions do not depend upon particular times and circumstances: they are true in all possible worlds. We are not just asking about the truth of proposition X, but the truth of all propositions. What do we need to make *any* proposition true?

For example, you may ask the question, 'What is knowledge?'. This is not a question about a particular item of knowledge, nor is it asking for a scientific answer about the types of knowledge we possess and the methods we use to gather it. What we are asking is what it is to have knowledge: what distinguishes it from mere belief, a hypothesis or a rumour. What do we mean when we use the word 'knowledge'; what are we looking for that would make something knowledge? If you say that it is a condition of everything we regard as knowledge that it must be true, then this assertion is not just true, but necessarily true: it has to be true of all knowledge. It is not just true as a matter of fact for this or any other item of knowledge, but by definition. The very nature of knowledge dictates it.

From this you can see these are fundamental questions, for which we aim to find ultimate answers. Many philosophers describe the process as one in which we are in search of the 'foundations' of what we know about the world, ourselves and our relations with others. In the process this has generated a range of important theories and systems of thought, all of which we will examine in the chapters that follow; systems of thought like rationalism, empiricism, idealism, realism materialism and pragmatism.

However there is an important group of modern philosophers who challenge the very idea that philosophy is or can be the search for foundations, because, they argue, such foundations are not there in the first place. Loosely described as 'postmodernists', they start from the premise that philosophers cannot be divorced from the cultural context in which they work; a context structured by ideas, ideologies, values, assumptions, methods and aspirations. All of this shapes the way they function, how they go about their work and the goals they set themselves. The search for foundations, then, is inescapably determined by the culture in which it is pursued. Philosophers, they argue, are no different from other thinkers, in that they cannot think outside a frame of reference without at the same time adopting another. The best they can do, therefore, is to pursue a clearer understanding of the culture in which they work: its literature, its history, ethics, politics and so on. And in coming to such an understanding they are, in turn, themselves contributing to its evolution.

This is an important departure from the traditional way in which we see philosophers working. Indeed, it strikes at the fundamental assumptions of modern Western culture. Since the seventeenth century scientific revolution and the Enlightenment, we have assumed there is a single objective reality, and science and reason offer the most effective method of discovering it. In contrast the American philosopher Richard Rorty, in his now-famous book, *Philosophy and the Mirror of Nature* (1979), declares that 'we will not imagine that there are enduring constraints on what can count as knowledge, since we will see "justification" as a social phenomenon rather than a transaction between "the knowing subject" and "reality".'

So, according to Rorty, our search for foundations is more a search for understanding of the beliefs, values and assumptions of each of our cultures at a particular moment in history. He explains, 'the foundations of knowledge or morality or language or society may be simply apologetics, attempts to externalise a certain contemporary language-game, social practice, or self-image.' Truth, then, is merely 'what your contemporaries let you get away with.' As a result, he concludes 'no area of culture, and no period of history, gets Reality more right than any other.'

In fact, in terms of the search for foundations, he does not believe, as we are accustomed to believe, that truth can be pinned down in objective and rational conditions that must apply to achieve an

Richard Rorty (1931–)

Born in New York and educated at Chicago and Yale, he taught at Wellesley College, Princeton University, the University of Virginia and Stanford University. He has consistently argued against the idea of philosophy as the search for foundations. Indeed he has called for the over-throw of what he has described as the 'specta-torial account of knowledge' which has domi-nated philosophy since Plato and Aristotle. He holds that no statement is epistemologically more basic than any other and no statement is ever justified finally or absolutely.

So the search for foundations amounts to little more than an attempt to externalize our own contingent prejudices that find their roots in our own culture. Since Descartes invented the mind, traditional philosophy's attempt to uncover timeless foundations has been an 'attempt to escape from history'. Along the same lines he also rejects the idea that sentences or beliefs are true or false in any interesting sense other than being useful or successful in terms of present social practices. In Dewey, Wittgenstein and Heidegger he claims to have found philosophers who have developed, in what he describes as the 'edifying philosophy', alternatives to the search for 'grounding' of the intuitions and customs of the present. His pub-lications include *The Linguistic Turn* (1967), *Philosophy and the Mirror of Nature* (1979), *Consequences of Pragmatism* (1982) and *Contingency, Irony and Solidarity* (1989).

accurate representation of reality. Rather, it is merely what it is better in our interests to believe: 'the notion of "accurate representation" is simply an automatic and empty compliment which we pay to those beliefs which are successful in helping us do what we want to do', he declares. The rest is little more than 'a self-deceptive effort to externalise the normal discourse of the day.' There is no distinction between reason and persuasion, invention and discovery, theory and practice, even between litera-ture and philosophy. They all amount to just one thing: our attempt to present the beliefs, values and assumptions that rule our culture as reality.

Its critics see postmodernism as presenting a very real threat to the achievements of the last 400 years of modern philosophy. As the British philosopher Simon Blackburn points out,

'According to popular fears, they scoff at every-thing we hold dear, replacing truth, reason, objectivity, knowledge, and scientific method with fashion, rhetoric, power, subjectivity and relativism – thereby summoning our history and politics, literature and art, indeed western civili-sation itself, to its doom.'

Despite the exaggeration implied in these doom-laden fears, postmodern philosophers face serious criticisms, as Blackburn suggests. They have been charged with paradox when they say that there is not truth or that truth is relative, because if there is not truth they are in effect inviting you not to believe what they say. And, similarly, when they claim the fact that there are no absolute values justi-fies our tolerating all values, they are elevating toleration itself into an absolute value.

The conflict between these two sets of ideas will feature throughout this book as we examine each successive theme. Like all the other problems you will be presented with, you will have to decide for yourself where you stand on this.

■ 4. The method of philosophy

Nevertheless, despite the implications of this, when we study philosophy we are not simply tracking the footsteps of those who have gone before. This is your own voyage of discovery too. As the Austrian philosopher Ludwig Wittgenstein said, and we ourselves have already discovered, 'Philosophy is not a theory but an activity.' It is a method, involv-ing thinking skills, that lifts us above the simple and uncreative activity of merely reproducing the ideas of others, so that we are able to search for and discover answers for ourselves. In this lies, perhaps, its greatest value.

For some this comes as a shock, but for most it is a welcome liberation from the enthralment to facts that characterizes so much of our education. The problem is that we all grow up believing that education is largely about knowing things; that clever people just know a great deal. Each subject we study we assume has its own authorities, the teacher and the texts, and our role is just to sit quietly and patiently, learn the facts, memorise them, and then recall them on demand in examina-tions in order to trade them successfully for marks.

But by learning in this way we only exercise and develop a limited range of our intellectual abilities: the lower cognitive skills. It is often said that most of us use less than 10 per cent of our mind's potential. In other words, the most that we set ourselves to do is to understand what someone else is arguing and to recall it accurately on demand. These are important thinking skills, but that's not all there is to learning. Indeed, in learning this way, the most important part is left out: the ability to think. What's more, you have no opportunity to introduce and use your own ideas: they are seen as irrelevant and unimportant. So you don't experience the excitement of discovering something for yourself, some insight that is genuinely and uniquely yours. This may not be something you have experienced before in learning, but it is an essential part, a daily experience, in philosophy.

Although this is not a story that derives from philosophy, it is the sort of experience you should be having as you wrestle with your own ideas. To make sure it does happen try recording your insights and how your ideas develop in your own intellectual journal. In 1953 Francis Crick and James Watson together discovered the 'double helix', the structure of DNA, for which they were later awarded the Nobel Prize. In his account of his work with Crick, Watson explains how this unpredictable, inspirational thinker would suddenly be consumed by an idea that had been long fermenting in his mind. One day on a train journey to Oxford, Watson describes how Crick suddenly saw a key part of the solution:

> Soon something appeared to make sense, and he began scribbling on the vacant back sheet of a manuscript he had been reading. By then I could not understand what Francis was up to and reverted to *The Times* for amusement. Within a few minutes, however, Francis made me lose all interest in the outside world. … Quickly he began to draw more diagrams to show me how simple the problem was. Though the mathematics eluded me, the crux of the matter was not difficult to follow.

By the end of the hour-and-a-half journey, he explains, it was clear what they had to do.

As this example illustrates, decent thinking is a continuous, cumulative affair that goes on outside the classroom in your mind, your journal and your notebooks, producing sparks of inspiration and insights that are genuinely yours. This is philosophy, as it is any subject that involves genuine, serious thinking. We all see things from our own unique perspective, so we can all learn from one another. I'm convinced that I learn as much from my students as they do from me. Each time I examine a philosophical text or theme with a new group they help me to see things I have never seen before, because they see it with fresh eyes from a different perspective. You do have an important contribution to make. And this is the exciting opportunity that philosophy offers you.

Nonetheless, it does mean abandoning the easy, comfortable assumption that learning is just about accumulating facts. As we found out earlier, you cannot use your own ideas or develop the higher cognitive skills, like analysis, synthesis, criticism, evaluation and discussion, if all you are concerned about is to gather the facts and recall them. The German theologian Paul Tillich described the problem well when he said, 'The passion for truth is silenced by answers which have the weight of undisputed authority.' If you have a 'fact' there is nothing more to discuss, nothing to say, except to clarify details when they aren't clear. But you don't learn to think like a historian or a scientist by learning, respectively, historical and scientific facts. To learn to think involves suspending your judgement and accepting that there are doubts that need to be addressed. Only in this way can you develop the thinking skills that are so important to philosophy - the skills to analyse, synthesise, discuss, criticize, evaluate and use evidence.

And, of course, this is when learning gets interesting, because your own ideas count for something. You may think you know what a concept means; after all you have probably used it all your life. But now suspend your judgement and ask yourself, 'But what do we *really* mean by it?', and you are on your way to becoming a philosopher. Like a scientist testing a theory, you will have to think up your own borderline examples of its use to test the concept at its limits. This will allow you to see more clearly the assumptions you usually make when you use it, and reveal the interrelations it has with other ideas. In the process you will uncover the issues that are at the heart of the philosophical problem in which the concept plays a central role. This is an exciting process, but it means you must, as Russell says, learn to suspend your judgement and yet still function in a state of doubt.

Nevertheless, even though it draws upon your own ideas and insights, it doesn't mean that just *any* answer to a problem is satisfactory; it's not just a matter of opinion. Opinions may be a point of departure; they often are. But they have to result in the right answers: those that a rational person can accept as reasonable and defensible after careful thought. In this lies the method of philosophy.

In the next three chapters we will see what this method is exactly. When we consider a philosophical problem, indeed any problem, our first step is very often to gather the evidence from which we can devise a hypothesis or theory to solve the problem. But before we do this we must be sure that we have asked the best question, the one, that is, that gets at the heart of the problem and will allow us to answer it directly. To do this we must be sure that we understand the implications of the key terms, the concepts we are using.

We are concerned here with the logical analysis of language, the meaning of the words and concepts we use. Some philosophers argue that this is the main task of philosophy, indeed, its only legitimate function: to expose the confusion in our use of language that lies beneath the contradictions in our thinking. But, although this is centrally important and is often the point at which we discover the solutions to problems, it is not all there is to devising a solution. This involves both analysis and synthesis. Not only must we suspend our judgement and analyse the meaning and implications of the terms we often take for granted, we must also synthesise arguments and evidence to devise a possible solution to the problem.

Once we have this possible solution as our theory we need to test it. In the second step, therefore, our aim is to test for their validity the arguments, which make up our theory. We must be sure that our arguments are consistent, that there is no error in our reasoning. However, the validity of an argument is only concerned with its form, not its content. So, while an argument might be valid, in that it is quite consistent and makes no logical error, it still might be untrue, because its assumptions, its premises, are untrue. This leads us to the third step.

In this our concern is to test our arguments for their truth. It involves not just checking to see that our assumptions are correct, but, equally important, checking that our theory adequately answers the problem. Beyond this we must also look at the consequences of our theory. In particular we must check to see if it is consistent with other theories we might advance to answer other problems that are connected with this problem. Our aim is to create a coherent and systematic view of the whole. Each of the theories answering the problems we believe are important must create a coherent and consistent system of ideas.

So, to summarize:

1. Hypothesizing – designing a solution:

1.1 Asking the best question

1.2 Designing the best solution

1.3 Analysing the key concepts

2. Testing for validity – is our argument consistent? – are there any logical errors in our reasoning?

3. Testing for truth:

3.1 Are the assumptions correct?

3.2 Are the arguments true?

3.3 Is the theory adequate to answer the problem?

3.4 The consequences of our theory – does it make a coherent system of ideas?

■ 5. Conclusion

It should be clear from this that the study of philosophy brings to those who learn its method not just the excitement of genuine discovery, but benefits in the development of their minds that are not easily found elsewhere. It is sometimes said of philosophy that it detaches your mind from the real world: that it is concerned with speculative ideas that have no practical value. This may be true of some philosophers, but not of philosophy. Learning its method alone enlarges your view of the world and of yourself, liberating you from the fragile prejudices that your understanding may be built upon.

Learn well and you will likely become a more effective thinker, not just absorbing and reproducing facts uncritically. You will take less for granted, particularly the pronouncements of those we take to be authorities. You will be less willing to follow the crowd and be more prepared to doubt what seems obvious to everyone else. But, by the same token, your own beliefs will come in for the same critical scrutiny: you will be less willing to accept the ambiguities and confusions that lie at the heart of your thinking. In this way you are likely to become more aware of the limits as well as the justifications of your beliefs.

But still, this doesn't mean that you will become an inveterate sceptic unwilling to embrace any belief. Indeed, in many respects it's quite the reverse. Your thinking will not only have more depth, but more breadth. While you will be more likely to pursue your own ideas more deeply, freeing them from unexamined assumptions, implications and ambiguities, you are also likely to have a more open mind. You will develop the intellectual strength to tolerate and understand views different from your own. Not for nothing do parents often say to me that their offspring is not just more thoughtful, creative and inventive, but is, quite simply, just a nicer person.

■ Recommended reading

Blackburn, S. *Think* (Oxford: Oxford University Press, 1999).

Emmet, E. R. *Learning to Philosophize* (Harmondsworth: Penguin, 1968).

Nagel, Thomas. *What Does It All Mean? A Very Short Introduction to Philosophy* (New York: Oxford University Press, 1989).

Warburton, N. *Philosophy: The Basics* (London: Routledge, 1992).

The Method: Hypothesizing

CHAPTER 2

Key issues

▶ Before we search for answers we must have the best question, the one that gets to the heart of the problem. How can we learn to do this?

▶ Are you aware when somebody begs the question or uses loaded language in an argument?

▶ Can you recognize those assumptions you take for granted that seem so intuitively obvious?

▶ What factors should we take into account to design the best solution to a problem?

▶ How can we distinguish between different types of problem: normative, empirical and non-empirical?

▶ Can you analyse an abstract concept to reveal its implications? Learn a simple three-step technique.

▶ How can you distinguish open from closed concepts?

Contents

Philosophy is not the exclusive preserve of professional philosophers: we all philosophize in one way or another. You might be discussing with a friend an issue, which raises concerns, say, about freedom, equality or moral responsibility. At one point in the discussion you might find yourself stepping back to examine the way you are both using the concept, to see if you are both talking about the same thing, or if one or both of you are using it inconsistently, or whether you have clearly seen the consequences of using it in this way. At moments like this you are philosophizing.

■ 1. Asking the best question

If you have had these moments of self-conscious reflection about what you are doing, then you will have probably realized already that these problems usually emerge when: a) certain principles or beliefs conflict, and b) facts are interpreted in different, seemingly inconsistent ways. But even so, knowing this still doesn't prevent us from getting caught in discussions that seem to go round and round, and get nowhere. It's important, therefore, to be clear about why this happens and how we can avoid it.

The first thing we need to be clear about is not what we think might be the best answer to a question, but what is the best question. All too often our arguments go nowhere, because we have been presented with a pseudo question to start with. These come in various forms, but the most common are those that beg the question and those that employ loaded language.

We are all familiar with begging the question: it's when you accept as an assumption what you are supposedly arguing for as a conclusion. A friend might argue that she believes that sportsmen and women are fitter than those who are not involved in sports. In response you argue that you know plenty of people who play sports, but they also drink excessively, smoke, are overweight and, in general, don't take good care of themselves. But your friend refuses to accept this as evidence against her theory, arguing that these people are not 'really' sportspeople. In effect she is using a definition of sportspeople which already includes as one of its core elements someone who is fit. So, the very issue that is in dispute is begged by the definition. This underlines the importance of analysing the meaning of the concepts we use, which we will be doing in the second half of this chapter.

It also helps to take the sting out of loaded language: that is language that carries with it more than what it means descriptively, usually an emotional content, which manipulates our responses without us being aware of it. We may not want to support the argument, but, when it is used skilfully, loaded language pushes us towards a conclusion, which we have no choice but to accept. Some words have positive emotional implications, like 'democracy', 'freedom', and 'patriotism', while others have negative implications, like 'totalitarianism', 'hardliners', and 'extremists'. So, those who want to 'put a spin' on what they're arguing to encourage other people to accept it without looking at it too closely, are inclined to use positive words and associations.

For example, most nations today like to describe themselves as democratic. It reflects well on them and their status in the world community. There was a time when the overwhelming majority of the members of the United Nations were not democratic, but in the last quarter of the twentieth century the number more than doubled. Yet still for most countries their internal politics is no different. It's rather like someone trying to convince you not to worry about your overdraft at the bank, because after all it is in effect just a 'negative reserve'.

If, like me, you have wasted valuable time discussing a point with someone only to find that the whole argument was founded on a misunderstanding of the implications of the loaded language being used, you will know the importance of analysing clearly the terms and concepts we use. As an undergraduate I once spent an evening discussing with two people the contention that you cannot separate the economic and social implications of government policies. It wasn't until some time had passed that I realized we had been arguing at cross purposes: they had been using the word 'can't' to mean 'should not', whereas I had been using it literally and descriptively to mean 'it was not possible'. So, while they had been arguing the moral case against separating the two, I had been arguing whether it was in fact technically possible.

Yet even more deceptive are those assumptions *we* foist on ourselves: those things we take for granted because they seem so intuitively obvious that we fail to question them. To illustrate the importance of this I occasionally present students with the problem that, if a bottle and cork together cost ten pence and the bottle costs nine pence more than the cork, how much does the cork cost? I have never had a group in which the overwhelming majority does not argue that the cork must cost one penny. And most will take some convincing that their initial intuitive conviction cannot be correct.

Indeed, most of us would be surprised to learn just how much we habitually take for granted as fact: things we believe that are just too obvious to question. When Galileo argued that it is the Earth that is spinning around the sun and not the sun around the Earth, the religious authorities in the seventeenth century dismissed it as just fanciful speculation. All the evidence suggested it was us that were stable and the rest of the universe that was spinning. We can all produce our own personal favourites of things we have taken for granted as unquestionably true beyond all doubt, only to find that to our utter astonishment we were wrong. They all make the point that the first step in finding the right solution to a problem is to find the right question. For this we need to question those things we may have accepted to be beyond question, and to analyse the implications of the terms and concepts we use.

One of the ethical problems that modern businesses have to face is the action of whistleblowers. These are people who reveal practices and policies of the companies that employ them, because they think they present a danger to the public, say, an aircraft manufacturer that is cutting corners in its safety checks in order to meet a delivery date or to inflate its profits. Although there are some who do it for personal gain, those whistleblowers who do it simply to protect the public claim their concern is for the importance of truth, openness and public safety. But, at the same time of course, their behaviour amounts to a serious breach of trust. They owe the company, which employs them, their loyalty. So, how do you solve this problem, given that it involves for most of those who do it a sincere conflict of moral responsibility between loyalty and truth?

On the face of it this is a very difficult, perplexing problem, which easily evades each attempt we make to solve it. But step back from the problem and ask yourself how the business community as a whole could solve the problems that give rise to, and make necessary, whistleblowing, and the problem becomes more manageable. Clearly, in answer to this reshaped question, the answer would be to do two things. First they could make companies more transparent about their practices, particularly when it involves public safety. And, second, companies could introduce better internal systems through which individuals, who are concerned about their company's practices, can communicate these concerns to management without endangering their own careers and, therefore, without the necessity to reveal things to the press that could be damaging to the company.

Take another example, one that seems likely to call for a distinctively philosophical, rather than a purely practical, answer. Imagine that you are a microbiologist working for a small company that has employed you since you graduated twelve years ago. You're the head of your department, one of a number that make up the section working to bring about new methods of gene therapy. Recently your company has been taken over by a large multinational and, as a result, head office has appointed one of their senior accountants to run the section with the task of making sure that it achieves the returns to capital that the company gets from the other parts of the business.

Your department has been underfunded for some time and you believe you need a considerable injection of capital to fund the latest generation of equipment, if you are to keep pace with the other laboratories around the world that are now leaving you behind. However, your new boss turns down your investment proposal, arguing that he is not convinced you need this at the moment and that you can make do with the equipment you have. You protest that without this new equipment it will be impossible to keep pace, but he is resolute.

Privately you complain to one of your colleagues that your new boss knows nothing about this work. He hasn't been with the company more than a couple of months and, anyway, he's an accountant, not a scientist. You would like to go over his head, but your colleague warns you that your new boss has got all the power on his side: he has the authority to do what he likes. On the face of it your colleague seems to be right. But is this the question that will give you an answer to your moral problem? Is there a better question? Perhaps it is not so much that your boss has the power and authority over you, but whether he has the *real* authority. And before we can answer this we must make clear what we mean by 'power' and 'authority', and how they interrelate.

■ 2. Designing the best solution

We have now reached a point where we have a clearer idea of the problem and the questions for which we need answers. As a result we are more likely to come up with a hypothesis that could work as an effective solution. But beware: in this stage it's important not to doubt your own solutions just because they are yours and you suspect that others out there have better ones. This is not a contest. Even though you may feel your solution sounds naïve you would be surprised just how often the best solution does indeed turn out to be one that appears the most naïve, simply because it has taken less for granted. As a result it will lay bare and test the underlying assumptions that may otherwise have been ignored.

For example, say you have agreed to organize the annual tennis tournament for your local tennis club, and there have been 78 entries. The first thing you will need to know is how many matches there will need to be played, before you can then arrange the courts and the times at which they will be played. No doubt most of us would start with the 78 contestants, halve them, then halve them again, and so on, until we get to the number of games that will need to be played. But now turn the problem around. So far we have been concerned with the winners, shifting them on from one round to the next. But reverse this and think only about the losers and the problem becomes amazingly simple.

If there are 78 contestants that means there will be 77 losers and one winner, so the numbers of games that will need to be played are 77. The most effective way to a solution very often appears the most naïve.

2.1 What sort of problem is it?

The first thing we need to be clear about is what sort of problem it is that we are trying to solve: what sorts of claims are involved. This will determine where we should look for a solution. If we were to mistake, for example, an ethical claim for a factual one, as I did in the lengthy discussion I had with the two economists, we would find ourselves arguing at cross purposes getting nowhere. Nothing we might achieve in our discussion is likely to move along closer to a solution.

And it needs re-emphasizing at this point that this is not a contest: we are not seeking to defeat an opponent. This is a collaborative enterprise. In many cases we will have the advantage of picking up the baton where another person left off and building on their work so that we can edge even closer to the answer. There will, of course, be those who describe the work we do as an adversarial process, but it can never be this. This would reduce our task to stating an opinion and setting out to defend it at almost all costs. It would mean 'defeating' our opponent using carefully designed 'tactics', through which we only give away those things that support our case, while avoiding mention of those things that inconveniently conflict with it. The fact is our work is not adversarial in this sense. It is an open endeavour aimed not at winning a case, but approximating to the truth by suspending our judgement and exploring all the issues and evidence available, whether they support our argument or conflict with it.

2.2 Normative claims

So, with this caution in place, what sorts of claims should we be looking to identify? The first are those we have already mentioned: normative claims in which we say what *ought* or *should be* the case. These might be value judgements about art, politics or morality. They are not statements of fact; that is, they are not *descriptions*, but *prescriptions*. They may express value judgements about what we think is the right behaviour, attitude or action to take in a

particular situation. Although they are likely to convey some information, normative claims are primarily concerned with what we think we *ought* to do.

This means, then, that unless we can show the other person's judgement is based on inconclusive or contradictory evidence, or there is an inconsistency in their argument, ultimately we may be faced with a non-negotiable value judgement, a prescription, which is simply different from our own. That's not to say we cannot go further than this. As we will see in Part III of this book, normative claims have their own logic, which means they must meet the particular requirements of the normative language and concepts involved. This, then, gives us a way of revealing where weaknesses in the argument might lie and where we might find the solution.

Nevertheless, with the special requirements of normative claims to one side, all arguments contain two other types of claims: empirical and non-empirical. Most philosophical arguments contain one or more empirical claims that can be checked by observation and experiment, but every philosophical argument has at least one non-empirical claim and the truth of these depends upon what type of non-empirical claim they are. They may be the sort of claim that turns on a question of concept or they may be necessarily true from first principles.

So, to summarize:

What sort of problem is it?

1. Normative
2. Empirical
3. Non-empirical
   3.1 Questions of concept
   3.2 Necessary propositions

Although this traditional analysis of non-empirical claims is thought to be controversial by contemporary philosophers, it is a useful distinction when you first set out to study philosophy. For example, the case involving the microbiologist involved a question of concept. We found that a major part of the argument, if not the argument itself, depended upon what we mean by the concepts of power and authority. Later in this chapter we will examine a technique for analysing concepts like these to reveal the key elements of the argument. Alternatively, they may be the sort of non-empirical claim which is true 'necessarily' from first principles, in the same way that claims about triangles having three sides and bicycles having two wheels are necessarily true from first principles by definition. We must, therefore, draw a clear distinction between these sorts of non-empirical, and empirical, claims, if we are to recognize them and the particular problems that arise when we use them.

2.3 Empirical and non-empirical claims

In what follows I will use the words 'sentence' and 'proposition' to mean the same thing, whereas in fact they are different. A proposition is the meaning of a sentence. So, two sentences can be quite different linguistically, yet contain the same proposition. It's also worth being clear at this stage about the meaning of another term closely identified with these: the word 'statement'. We tend to use this quite ambiguously, either to mean the sentence that expresses the proposition, or the proposition itself. In fact a statement is what we do with the sentence and the proposition it conveys: we state it!

With that piece of housekeeping behind us, let's examine the nature of these two types of proposition: empirical and non-empirical. In Table 2.1 I have listed in the two columns the characteristics of each with the contrasting characteristic adjacent to it in the other column. Empirical propositions are those that depend for their truth on evidence of the real world, while non-empirical propositions depend upon reason alone.

So, empirical propositions are contingent; that is,

their truth depends upon experience, which could have resulted differently. It may be the case that the majority of speeding offences are committed by drivers between the ages of 18 to 35, but the evidence could have come out differently: there is nothing to say that it *had* to come out this way. If experience cannot falsify a proposition, that is, it cannot be proved true or false *a posteriori* (meaning that the truth 'comes after' we have consulted experience), then it cannot be contingent. Empirical propositions are also said to be synthetic in that they are formed as a result of pulling together different bits of empirical evidence. Unlike analytic propositions, they go beyond the terms that make them up to say something about the real world. For example, if I were to claim that the cat is sitting outside the door on the mat, I am saying something that we can only verify by getting up out of our chairs and opening the door to see if the cat is indeed sitting on the mat.

By contrast non-empirical propositions are necessary and analytic; that is, they are true by virtue of themselves alone; it is not necessary to refer to anything beyond their own terms. So, if I were to claim that a cat is an animal, we could verify the truth of this without getting up out of our chairs by just defining the terms that the proposition uses. Hence, this is an analytic truth: we only need to analyse the meaning of its terms to reveal the truth. Denying the truth of a proposition which is true analytically results in self-contradiction. If you were to say it is not true that a cat is an animal, you have made a logical mistake: you haven't understood the meaning of one of these two terms. But you can deny without contradiction the truth of a contingent proposition, because its truth depends

Table 2.1 Empirical and non-empirical propositions

	Empirical	**Non-empirical**
Logical distinctions: the meaning of the words	1. Contingent 2. Synthetic: transcends its terms	Necessary Analytic: self-referential true in virtue of its terms
Epistemological: the way we come to know the truth of the proposition	3. *a posteriori* 4. Evidence	*a priori* Intuition
	Evidence Can be denied or asserted without self-contradiction	***Reason*** Cannot deny a true proposition without self-contradiction

on the evidence, which could go both ways. Before we open the door to see if Tibbles is sitting on the mat waiting to come in, it is quite possible for you to think the proposition true and for me to think it is false without either of us contradicting ourselves.

This helps to explain the distinction between 1 and 2 on the one hand, and 3 and 4 on the other: the logical and epistemological distinctions respectively. Both *a priori* and *a posteriori* refer to the way we come by the truth of a proposition: whether or not it can be known to be true or false without consulting experience. This is an epistemological issue; that is, it is concerned with the theory of knowledge; with the nature and scope of knowledge, how we come by it, and the reliability of our claims to knowledge. Therefore, as we have seen, if something is *a posteriori* true, it must be true by virtue of something beyond its own terms: it must refer to experience.

By contrast, we come by the truth of an *a priori* proposition by means of reason or by some direct intuition, and not by consultation with the outside world. Indeed an *a priori* proposition is such that we can conceive of nothing that would count as evidence against it. We just know the meaning of the words 'cat' and 'animal', and this is all we need to know the truth of the proposition that 'a cat is an animal'. Such propositions are true by virtue of the constituent words that make up the sentence. In effect, they are true solely by virtue of what we decide those words will mean. We have decided that the word 'bachelor' will combine two ideas: unmarried and male. So, when I claim that a bachelor is an unmarried man, we both know without moving from our chairs that this is true.

Both of these, then, are epistemological distinctions, whereas the criterion for something being an analytic or synthetic truth has to do with its logical structure and the meaning of the words it uses. The logic of analytic sentences is self-contained. They are self-referential, whereas synthetic statements are not: they depend upon the way the world is. Similarly, propositions are true necessarily if they express beliefs about what must be the case, or what cannot be the case. If something is true necessarily it is a logical truth, whose denial, as we have seen, would involve a self-contradiction. In contrast, a contingent proposition is one which depends upon evidence that could go either way. It can, therefore, be denied or asserted without self-contradiction.

2.4 Synthetic *a priori* propositions

Having spent so much time drawing clear distinctions between mutually exclusive categories, it is time to muddy the water a little by introducing a type of proposition that bridges both categories. We will discuss this in more detail in Chapter 6, as we will the other distinctions explained here, but it is as well to understand what this is now.

A synthetic *a priori* proposition is not shown to be true merely as a result of the analysis of its constituent words or its logical form. It explains something about the world of experience, and yet is known to be true independently of experience. Consider the following examples:

> Every event has a cause.
>
> Parallel lines never meet.
>
> A straight line is the shortest distance between two points.

For each of these we need to have consulted experience to have discovered them, but we don't need experience to verify their truth. We don't need to gather as many examples as we can of straight lines before we can know the truth of this proposition. Its truth is independent of experience, because we accept no experience as a refutation of it. For example, we may not be able to find a cause for an event, but this doesn't lead us to claim it is uncaused. And yet, at the same time, the negation of a synthetic *a priori* truth is not self-contradictory: in other words, it is not analytic. For example, it is not self-contradictory to deny that parallel lines never meet.

We will examine synthetic *a priori* propositions again and explore their significance in the development of modern philosophy. For now, though, it is enough just to understand what they are and how they differ from other propositions. The point is that it is important to know the type of claims that are involved in a particular problem, so that you can design the most effective solution. It may be that you think the most effective solution lies with that part of the problem that concerns empirical claims, in which case you will probably need to gather more representative evidence to get a clearer idea of the actual problem. If, however, it lies with the non-empirical or normative claims, then you will have to analyse these claims to pin down exactly where the solution might lie.

■ 3. Analysing the key concepts

The same, of course, applies to those problems that largely turn on the meaning of a concept or principle involved. Always lurking just out of sight is that most insistent of all questions: 'But what do you mean by X?'. Although it's sometimes annoying to be halted by this sort of question as you build your argument with zest, it does have its value. We have to be sure that we are right about the ideas represented by a word or phrase. Do we need to change the words to carry the ideas more accurately? And if we stick with the word and the concept it carries, does this invalidate the argument? In the case of the microbiologist we found that the main problem was how to define the concepts of power and authority. With this, as with so many problems, we are likely to find that by analysing the key concepts involved we are able to reveal the underlying issues that need to be addressed.

Of course, at this point the temptation is to put your hands up in the air, appeal to those who have more knowledge than you and reach eagerly for the nearest textbook on the subject. But as we said in the previous chapter, your ideas and insights are as valuable as anyone else's. And by looking it up in a textbook or in a dictionary you will get in return only a picture of what somebody else thinks, or a mere snapshot, a still in the moving imagery, which records how the concept has, and still is, changing.

3.1 Open and closed concepts

Nevertheless, with some words, of course, that's all you need to do. They are what you might describe as 'closed concepts'. They usually have an unchanging, unambiguous meaning. Words like 'bicycle', 'bachelor' and 'triangle' each have a structure to their meaning, which is bound by logical necessity. We all agree to abide by certain conventions that rule the meaning of these words. So, if you were to say, 'This bicycle has one wheel' or 'This triangle has four sides', no-one would be in any doubt that you've made a logical mistake. When we use them according to their conventions we are, in effect, allowing our understanding of the world to be structured in a particular way.

But with 'open concepts' it tends to be the reverse: our experience of the world shapes our concepts. As a result, they cannot be pinned down just by looking them up in a dictionary. Their meaning responds to and reflects our changing experience: they change through time and from one culture to another. A dictionary definition, then, can only ever be a single snapshot taken in a constantly moving reel of images.

If you take concepts like 'aunt' and 'democracy', you can see that in some societies and at some times they have a fairly unambiguous, unchanging meaning. The concept of 'aunt', for example, in some societies has a narrow definition exclusively grounded in relations by blood and marriage. But in other societies it is more open, encompassing not just relatives in the strict sense, but also older, longstanding friends of the family.

This is likely to be a reflection of the social practices prevalent in different societies and at different stages in their development. A predominantly rural society with limited social mobility might use it in the narrow sense. In contrast, in a society undergoing rapid industrialization, with greater social mobility and less permanent communities, the concept is likely to be applied more loosely to close friends of the parents of a child. A young family, which has recently moved to a city some distance from their parents' homes, may seek to reconstruct the security of an extended family by including close friends as aunts and uncles to their children.

Much the same can be said for a concept like 'democracy'. We might all agree that it implies government in accordance with the popular will, but beyond this principle everything is open. Western liberal democracies, believing that democracy implies one-man-one-vote, regular elections, secret ballots, multi-party politics and freedom of expression, are just one adaptation of the principle, serving the needs of a particular type of society: a liberal society with its emphasis on the importance of individualism, competition, free trade and consumer sovereignty.

In other societies, under different cultural influences, democracy has taken on different forms where accountability, participation, multi-party politics, even regular elections and voter sovereignty, are much less important. More significant is the progress that is being made towards achieving democratic goals, like the eradication of epidemic diseases, alleviation of poverty, improvement in literacy, even industrialization. The achievement of these goals, rather than voter approval at elections, is seen as evidence of the democratic nature of government.

Just to complicate the picture a little, we can also argue that some open concepts are more open than others, in that it may not be possible to identify elements of the concept that are present in every example. In his *Philosophical Investigations* (1953), Ludwig Wittgenstein has this sort of concept in mind when he discusses what he describes as 'family resemblances'. He cites the example of games and finds as you move from one type of game to another some common features appear, while others drop out. Some involve competition, while others involve just one player. Some require skill, while others require just luck. He concludes there is no core set of characteristics, just 'a complicated network of similarities overlapping and criss-crossing'.

You may come across others like this, but most will have a core definition. To unwrap this you will need to consult your experience, so rely on your own insights and analyse the concept for yourself. Although most of us protest that we've never analysed a concept before, in fact we do it all the time. Yet still, we would be hard pressed to explain just how we do it. This, in itself, probably explains why most of us do it badly. And it's worth remembering that most philosophical problems begin with analysis, indeed a surprising number also end with it. Therefore, it's worth learning how to do it well.

Even with the briefest of acquaintances with a concept, after confronting just four or five examples of it for the first time, most people are quite clear about its core characteristics. Indeed, they can be surprisingly dogmatic as to what is and what is not an example of it just minutes after declaring they knew nothing about it and had no idea how to analyse it.

For example, in the following case the concept is represented by a number of unfamiliar abstract patterns. As a result we're freed from all those preconceptions that might otherwise have forced our thinking down pre-programmed routes. Nothing has been said about the concept to lead us to believe that those who are authorities in these sorts of matters think the concept has certain definite characteristics. The concept is ours to form without assistance from anyone else. Examine in turn each of the figures below. As you do this you will see a concept emerge. For want of a better name I call it an 'olic'. Not all of the figures are olics, so you will have to form your idea of the concept and then use it to distinguish between the olics and the non-olics. Identify those you think are olics and list three of their core characteristics. Then check your answers with those at the end of the book (page 404).

It's worth reflecting on what you've just done, so that you can get a better understanding of what's involved. Although I'm not suggesting that you have just worked your way through each of these stages, below I have explained a three-step technique, which will help you develop the skills you need to analyse thoroughly and imaginatively more difficult concepts. Try it for yourself, using the example of the microbiologist and his boss who had all the power and authority over him. Ask yourself, what do we mean by authority and how does it relate to power. If you find you use the concept of authority in more than one way, then you have a structure emerging: each way in which you use it needs to be explored and its implications unwrapped. I have done it below for you, but do it for yourself first by working through each stage as I explain it.

3.2 The three-step technique

Step 1. Gather your typical examples

First, spend some time gathering the evidence: in this case, examples of the way you use the concept in your everyday experience. With the olics I listed twelve for you; in this case list what you think might be five or six of the most typical examples of the concept. Try to make them as different as possible. In this way you'll be able to strip away their differences to reveal more clearly their essential similarities.

So, start by asking yourself, 'How do I use the concept – do I use it in more than one way?' Take the concept of freedom. We tend to talk about being free *from* things, like repression, constraints and restrictions of one form or another. I might say with some relief that I am finally free from pain having taken tablets for pain relief, or that a political prisoner has at last been freed from imprisonment. In both cases we're using the word in a negative way, in that something is being taken away, the pain or the imprisonment.

In contrast, we also tend to use the word in what we might describe as a positive way. In this sense the preposition changes from being free *from* something to being free *to do* something. We often say that, because a friend has unexpectedly won a large amount of money, she is now free to do what she has always wanted to do – to go back to college, or to buy her own home. Governments, too, use the concept in this way, arguing that the money they

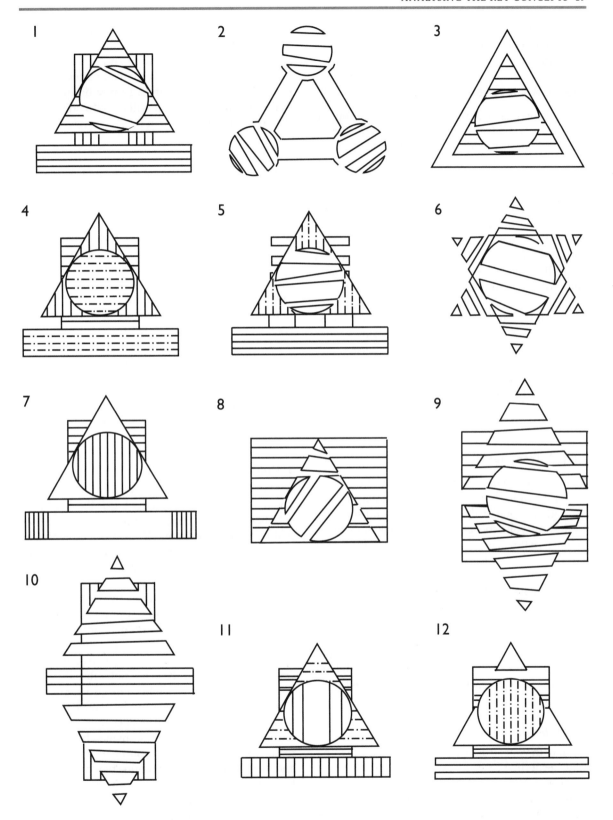

are investing in education will free more people to get better, more satisfying jobs and to fulfil more of their dreams.

Step 2. Analyse your examples

Now, using these examples, create your concept. In other words, analyse the common characteristics in each of your examples, isolating them so that you can then put them together to form the concept. This is one of those things we all know how to do, but most of us would be hard pressed to explain just how we do it. In effect it's simple pattern recognition. By recognizing the common pattern of characteristics that each example possesses, we visualise what the concept might look like that underlies all the examples. Sometimes you may find you have, say, seven examples, four of which have the same core characteristics, while the other three fail to match them in all respects. That's OK; in these cases you need to corral the four similar examples, using these to create your concept, and then use the remaining three to test it.

Once you have this, your hypothesis about what you think the structure of your concept might look like, you can move onto the next stage and test your hypothesis.

Step 3. Test your concept

In most cases you will find you have the overall structure right, but there may be details that are wrong, or subtle distinctions you haven't seen. So, by testing your concept you will shake out those characteristics that are essential and ditch those that are only accidental to it. In the process you will have sharpened up your understanding of the core characteristics. To test it in this way you need only take some simple, but quite deliberate steps. Our aim is to set up mental experiments to test our concept first against those examples that are borderline cases of it, then against those that are contrasting cases and, finally, against those that are doubtful cases. At each stage we will refine it until we have it right.

1. Borderline cases

First, with your structure in front of you try to think of a borderline case, an example of your concept that doesn't fit comfortably within your structure. It may lack features that are in your structure, or have other features that are absent from it. Then analyse

its characteristics to see if, in fact, it does fit after all. You may find there's more to this form of the concept than you first thought and it does, in fact, fit within the structure. Alternatively, after thinking through all the possibilities, it may become clear that it doesn't fit and you will have to adjust your structure to take account of it.

2. Contrasting cases

Either way, you will have confirmed important parts of your structure. As a result you will probably feel more confident that you have now got it just about right. So it's time to put this confidence to the sternest test you can find, this time by imagining an example that presents a clear contrast to your concept. Think of the strongest example you can find that clearly doesn't fit within the structure of your concept. The best examples fail to share one or more of the core characteristics of your structure. Again test your structure against this example to see if you need to make any adjustments to the components and the way they interrelate.

Once you have done this you will find that you have sharpened up your concept considerably. You will have shaken out one or more core characteristics that might not have been sufficiently clear in your original analysis.

3. Doubtful cases

Both of these two tests will probably have brought you to a point where you now know the core characteristics of your concept and the structure that defines their interrelations. If you are not this certain you will have to test it with one or more additional contrasting examples, but it will rarely take more than this. In most cases you will have shaken out the core characteristics fairly clearly by now.

If this is the case, it's time to move to the next stage and test the consequences of adopting these as your core characteristics. We need to imagine cases in which it would be difficult for you to accept these consequences. Either these are not, after all, examples of the concept, or we have missed something. Unlike the previous stages, in this one we are identifying neither core characteristics, nor others that we need to ditch because they are merely accidental to the concept. We have our core characteristics now and their interrelations that define the concept. So, in this stage we are refining the distinctions that were in our original analysis so that we get a clearer, sharper understanding of the core characteristics and their interrelations. As a result we inject more subtle shades of meaning into our distinctions.

As you can see, as we have worked our way through each of these stages we have deliberately asked awkward questions to test and refine the distinctions we made in our original analysis. By doing so we've not only revealed some important subtle shades of meaning, but in effect we have rehearsed some of the more complex arguments we'll develop when we come to use the concept in a discussion or in an essay. To make it easier for you to use this method routinely, I have listed the stages in Table 2.2.

If you have used the strategy on the problem of authority and power, you may have ended up with something like the following. Even though the examples we use will be different and we are likely to be more or less perceptive than each other, the concept and its core characteristics will be very much the same. If you want to follow this analysis there are notes at the end of this chapter.

Authority

Step 1. Gather your typical examples

In this problem the key concepts that have to be examined are 'power' and 'authority', and the relationship between them. Start, then, by asking yourself how you use these words. For this you need to summon up a few examples of situations in which both of these concepts might come up, say, in your family, in your local community or in the wider community, and in the schools and colleges you may have attended. These might involve figures of authority, like police officers, teachers, parents and other people who have the power and influence to get you to do what you might not otherwise want to do.

Step 2. Analyse your examples

From these examples you might conclude that the most obvious way in which we use the word

Table 2.2 The three-step technique

Activity	Objective
Step 1: Examples List five or six of the most typical examples that are as different as possible	To get material that will illustrate similarities and differences
Step 2: Analyse Pattern recognition: identify the common characteristics and their interrelations	To form the hypothesis: the prototype concept
Step 3: Testing *1. Borderline cases* Compare the concept with an example that either lacks features that are in our structure, or has others that are absent from it	To identify all those features in the structure that are merely accidental
2. Contrasting cases Compare the concept with an example that does not share one or more of the core characteristics of our structure	To identify the core characteristics and their interrelations
3. Doubtful cases Test the core characteristics by examining a case in which it would be difficult to accept the consequences of the core characteristics	To refine the distinctions in our analysis to get a clearer, sharper understanding of the core characteristics and their interrelations

'power' is to describe somebody as having force, the capacity to compel us to do something against our wishes. A police officer has this sort of power. In a similar way we talk about somebody being *in* authority, somebody like a police officer or a judge. In this case we might not respect the person or the reasons they may give us for doing as they demand, but we might respect the institution they represent, or we might just comply with their orders because we fear the consequences of not doing so. Police officers have powers at their disposal that can seriously affect us, even denying us our liberty.

Step 3: Test your concept

1. Borderline cases

Here you are looking for an example that either lacks features that are in your structure, or has others that are absent from it. For example, a mugger or a local gang leader can compel us to do things in the same way, through force or threats of force, yet they have no authority, although they still have this sort of power.

This, therefore, seems to lead us to the conclusion that authority doesn't simply amount to the possession of power alone: the gang leader has no authority, in the usual sense, to command us to do anything, unlike the police officer, who has been appointed by representatives to parliament or the local council, whom we have elected. In this sense the representatives and, in turn, their officially appointed officers are said to have democratic legitimacy.

2. Contrasting cases

As a result of this we have shaken something out which appears to be merely accidental to the concept: the appearance that authority amounts merely to the power to force others to do things they would otherwise not want to do. Authority seems to possess other qualities than mere power. To identify these qualities, which seem to be core characteristics of authority, we must compare our concept with an example that doesn't seem to share one or more of the core characteristics we have identified already. Take for example an experienced art collector. In her field she is an authority, so we are right to be persuaded by the arguments she presents because she knows what she's talking about. No force or compulsion is needed here. She

doesn't have the power to force me to do something against my wishes.

Nevertheless, she does have a certain 'power' and 'force' that she can bring to bear. We use phrases, like 'the power of persuasion', in which the force involved is the 'force of an argument', to describe the sort of power that such authorities possess. In the case of the art collector she has the ability to persuade us to do something we would not otherwise do, by giving us good and persuasive reasons for doing it. Through the force of her arguments and her power of persuasion, she has the ability to secure voluntary compliance to her way of seeing things without the use of threats or force in the other sense, because she has earned her authority.

We could say she has a 'right' to her authority, although it's a different sense of 'right' from that exercised by the police officer. It's the right that has been earned rather than been given. It's also different from the authority of the elected representative, although they can both be described as being 'an' authority. The difference is that the art collector's authority has been earned as a result of her study and devotion to her work, whereas the elected representative's authority has been earned as a result of putting himself up for election and campaigning for votes. Both have authority and exercise legitimate influence, because of the respect they have earned.

3. Doubtful cases

With this we seem to have identified our core characteristics and their relations to those we first identified. Now, to refine these distinctions and to get a clearer picture of their interrelations, we need to test these by examining a case in which it would be difficult to accept their consequences.

For example, there are some categories of people, like the elderly in our communities, who exercise the same legitimate influence, but who haven't earned their authority, either by being given it, as with the police officer, or having earned it, in the sense of 'an' authority, like the art collector. Nevertheless, we might argue that they, too, have earned their authority, only in a different way. The elderly in our communities have earned respect as a result of their years of experience and the wisdom this has brought. Others have certain personal qualities that have given them a reputation for integrity

Table 2.3 The three-step technique: authority question

Activity	Objective
Step 1: Examples List five or six of the most typical examples that are as different as possible	To get material that will illustrate similarities and differences
Step 2: Analyse Pattern recognition: identify the common characteristics and their interrelations	To form the hypothesis: the prototype concept
Step 3: Testing *1. Borderline cases* A mugger or gang leader can compel us to do things through force or threats of force, yet have no authority.	Authority does not simply amount to the possession of power; it also involves legitimate influence.
2. Contrasting cases An experienced art collector is *an* authority in her field, but she has no power to force me to do anything against my wishes.	She has the power of persuasion: the ability to secure voluntary compliance to her way of seeing things. As with the elected representative, our respect for her authority has been earned and is legitimate.
3. Doubtful cases Some people, like the elderly, exercise a similar influence without having earned their authority in the same way.	But have earned their authority through their years of experience and reputation for wisdom and integrity. There are good non-prudential reasons for following their advice.

See also the structured notes on the analysis of authority at the end of this chapter.

and honesty; people we might go to for advice and support.

We could say that we have good 'moral' reasons for complying with this sort of authority: that is, we have reasons that convince us to act in this way as a matter of our own free will. Whereas, when we comply with orders of those who are *in* authority, we do so not necessarily because we have any moral reason, that we respect them as individuals, but because we know that it would be prudent to do so. Otherwise we might suffer in one way or another as a result of the sanctions they can bring upon us. The threat of this is likely to force us, against our will, to comply with their orders.

In this sense we may be 'obliged' to obey, if the local gang leader or the mugger is threatening to harm us, but we have no 'obligation' to obey, because such threats are not backed by any right to

make such orders. Whereas the art collector has earned the right through many years of study, and the police officer, while he or she hasn't earned the same respect for themselves as a person, they have been given the 'rightful', legitimate authority by our elected representatives. In the same way, we could say that the elderly, with their years of experience to draw upon, have a similar authority and a right to exercise an influence.

Analysing carefully and imaginatively in this way the key concepts involved in a problem will reveal the central issues that you will have to take into account as you search for a solution. It will also help you to inject more of your own ideas into your work before you start to read those of others. You will, so to speak, have something to bargain with as you tackle the texts, rather than being taken over by their ideas.

Notes on

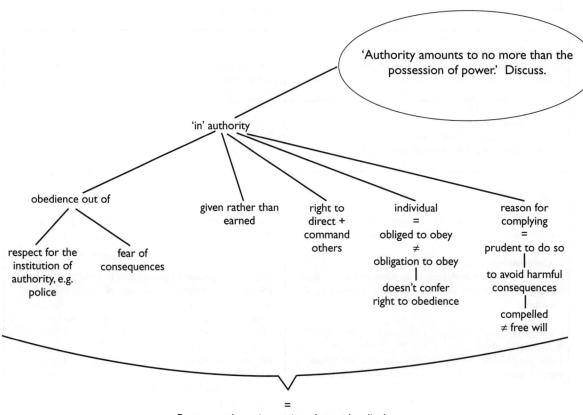

'Authority amounts to no more than the possession of power.' Discuss.

'in' authority

obedience out of

respect for the institution of authority, e.g. police

fear of consequences

given rather than earned

right to direct + command others

individual
=
obliged to obey
≠
obligation to obey
|
doesn't confer
right to obedience

reason for complying
=
prudent to do so
|
to avoid harmful consequences
|
compelled
≠ free will

=
Power to take action against those who disobey

obedience secured through threats/force – to make things worse for people

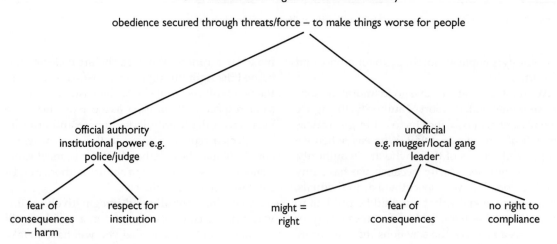

official authority
institutional power e.g.
police/judge

unofficial
e.g. mugger/local gang
leader

fear of
consequences
– harm

respect for
institution

might =
right

fear of
consequences

no right to
compliance

Power alone ≠ authority
Power alone without authority ≠ legitimate

authority

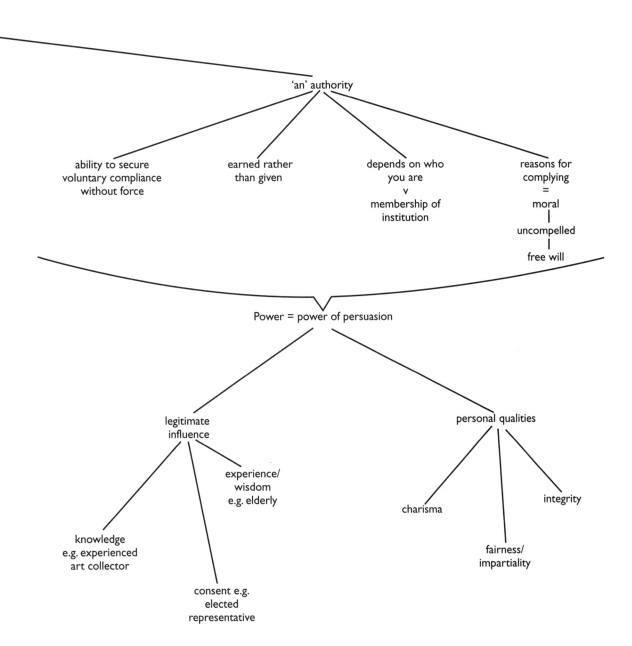

'an' authority

ability to secure
voluntary compliance
without force

earned rather
than given

depends on who
you are
v
membership of
institution

reasons for
complying
=
moral
|
uncompelled
|
free will

Power = power of persuasion

legitimate
influence

experience/
wisdom
e.g. elderly

knowledge
e.g. experienced
art collector

consent e.g.
elected
representative

personal qualities

charisma

integrity

fairness/
impartiality

■ 4. Conclusion

Now that we have a clear idea of the nature of the problem and the sort of arguments that will make up the solution, in the next two chapters we will check them for their validity and truth.

■ Questions

1. Which of the following statements are true (or false) (1) *a priori*, (2) *a posteriori*, or (3) synthetic *a priori*?

    1. $2 + 2 = 4$.

    2. Two trees plus two trees is equal to four trees.

    3. A straight line is the shortest distance between two points.

    4. Napoleon was an emperor.

    5. All men die.

    6. If A knows B, and if B knows C, then A knows C.

    7. If A precedes B, and if B precedes C, then A precedes C.

    8. It is cold at the top of Everest.

    9. No object can be red and green all over.

    10. A triangle is a three-sided figure.

    11. A man cannot walk on water.

    12. Every man has a mother.

    13. I am reading this sentence.

    14. Skyscrapers are tall buildings.

    15. Time moves forwards, not backwards.

    16. Something exists.

    17. A tomato is a fruit.

    18. My father's brother's son is my cousin.

    19. Your father's brother's son is my cousin.

    20. My bicycle is red.

2. Analyse the concept 'revolution', working through all the stages we did when we analysed the concept 'authority'.

■ Recommended reading

Ayer, A. J. *Language, Truth and Logic* (London: Gollancz, 1946).

Emmet, E. R. *Learning to Philosophize* (Harmondsworth: Penguin, 1968).

Flew, A. *Thinking about Thinking (Or, Do I sincerely want to be right?)* (London: Fontana, 1976).

Wilson, John. *Thinking with Concepts* (Cambridge: Cambridge University Press, 1976).

The Method: Testing for Validity

CHAPTER 3

Key issues

▶ What is the difference between truth and validity?

▶ Testing our theories for their validity. Are they consistently argued or are there errors in our reasoning?

▶ What is the difference between deductive and inductive reasoning?

▶ What is it that makes an argument 'sound'?

▶ How can we identify suppressed premises and equivocation in arguments?

▶ Can you identify the most common fallacies in arguments?

▶ How can we learn to use the different forms of syllogistic arguments?

Contents

We now know what type of problem we are dealing with and we've analysed the key concepts involved, so we know the likely hypotheses that might work as a solution. In the following two chapters we'll take the next step and test our hypotheses. In this chapter we'll test them for their validity, that is, to see whether the argument is consistent, whether we've made any logical errors. In the next chapter we will test them for their truth, whether they match up to the facts. Both of these tests touch on the two sides of modern logic: deductive and inductive arguments.

Unfortunately, it's the view of many people that philosophy unnecessarily complicates simple ideas: that philosophers are so preoccupied with the techniques of philosophizing that they lose sight of the important, enduring problems of our time and, as a result, have less and less influence on those around them. Nowhere is this truer than in logic. Many of us teach logic as a subject in its own right, rather than as a method which students can use, along with their other thinking skills, to help them critically evaluate their own arguments and those of others.

The result is that we fail to meet students on their own territory, instead dragging them into the alien and often arid world of symbolic logic, truth tables and quantification theory – OK for decoders at Bletchley Park cracking the German Enigma codes during the Second World War, but remote for anybody who wants to grapple seriously with the enduring problems of our time. Therefore, in these two chapters we will treat logic only as a method, as a means for you to evaluate the arguments you and others use, and for you to make better use of your own ideas and arguments. For those who want to pursue it as a subject in its own right there are a number of excellent introductions listed in the bibliography.

One way of distinguishing between deductive and inductive reasoning is to say that one is conclusive reasoning, the other inconclusive, respectively. Deduction is conclusive reasoning, because the conclusion never states more than is contained in the assumptions that make up the argument, whereas an inductive argument always does. In an inductive argument we start with singular observation statements that certain events, all similar in some important respect, have occurred, and then we derive a universal generalization that applies to all events of this type, observed and unobserved, past present and future.

For example, when Blaise Pascal, the seventeenth-century French philosopher and physicist, set about testing his law of atmospheric pressure he had his brother-in-law, Perier, carry the barometer up the Puy-de-Dome several times before concluding that the height of the mercury decreases as the altitude increases. So, his justification for his law that barometers fall as the altitude increases was a series of singular observation statements something like the following:

1. The first time the barometer was taken up the mountain (that is, the altitude increased) it fell.

2. The second time the barometer was taken up the mountain (that is, the altitude increased) it fell.

3. And so on until the nth time the barometer was taken up the mountain (that is, the altitude increased) it fell.

4. Therefore, barometers fall when their altitude increases.

In this case, even though we may know that 1, 2 and 3 are true, they do not guarantee the truth of 4. We can only possess a finite number of singular observation statements, like 1, 2 and 3, whereas in 4 we have come to an infinite, universal conclusion on the basis of them. We have gone beyond what our observation statements will allow. In *The Problems of Philosophy* (1912), Bertrand Russell cites the behaviour of a chicken that rushes out of its coop each morning to be fed by the farmer. On the basis of previous experience each day it confidently expects to be the same as the previous day, so it rushes out fully expecting to enjoy its breakfast. But then, on one day, it rushes out only to find that the farmer is ready to slaughter it for his dinner. As

Russell points out, the chicken lacked a sufficiently sophisticated understanding of induction and the relationship between past and future events to prepare itself for this eventuality.

To make the argument valid we would have to insert another assumption between the first three statements and the fourth to the effect that:

All unobserved cases resemble observed cases.

This is what's known as the 'principle of induction'. With this in place we can validly argue that 'All barometers fall when their altitude increases.' But, as you might have already realized, unfortunately this assumption suffers from the same problem: it is a universal claim for which we can only have finite evidence. So, we are caught in what's known as

Bertrand Arthur William Russell (1872–1970)

Best known for his public advocacy of causes from pacifism and nuclear disarmament to women's rights, Russell is beyond comparison as a philosopher who demonstrated the power of philosophy to bring about change. Born into the British nobility as the grandson of Earl Russell, the British prime-minister in the 1840s, his godfather was John Stuart Mill.

He is best known for his metaphysical doctrine, logical atomism, which strongly influenced logical positivism, and for his work in mathematical logic. In *The Principles of Mathematics* (1903) and *Principia Mathematica* (1910–13), which he wrote with Alfred North Whitehead, he sought to demonstrate that the whole of mathematics derives from logic. His later philosophical works include *The Analysis of Mind* (1921), *The Analysis of Matter* (1927) and *Human Knowledge: Its Scope and Limits* (1948). His *A History of Western Philosophy* (1945) and his three-volume *Autobiography* (1967–9) became best-sellers.

In addition to his teaching posts at Cambridge, he taught at a number of American universities, including Chicago and California. After the Second World War he led the world-wide campaign for nuclear disarmament. In 1961, at the age of 89, he was imprisoned for a second time for inciting civil disobedience. He received the Nobel Prize for Literature in 1950.

'Hume's vicious circle', after David Hume, the eighteenth-century Scottish philosopher, who pointed out that for the principle of induction to be true we would need the principle of induction to be true. We will examine this again in Chapter 10.

■ 1. Validity and truth

It follows from this that all inductive arguments must be invalid, in that the assumptions which make up the arguments can never justify the conclusions we derive from them. Even so, this is the best method we have for reaching general conclusions from the empirical evidence we can gather, and in the next chapter we will examine what we have to do to establish the truth of such conclusions. In this chapter we will be concerned with the validity of our arguments, which means we must examine the nature of our *deductive* reasoning and, in particular, what we must do to avoid errors and inconsistencies in it.

In studying logic we are concerned with the structure of reasoning. So, when we examine the validity of a deductive argument we are concerned with its form, not with its truth, the substance of the argument. Validity is a way of ensuring that if we do have true premises then we also guarantee that our conclusion is true. When an argument is valid it is not possible for its premises to be true, while its conclusion is false. It can have false premises and a false conclusion, but never true premises and a false conclusion.

But at this point we need to back up a little and explain what an argument is and what premises are. An argument is a set of sentences, one of which is the conclusion and the others, called premises, are offered as the grounds for the conclusion. The premises are said to imply or entail the conclusion. To illustrate this, look at the following argument.

1. All dogs are animals.
2. Aldous is a dog.
3. Therefore, Aldous in an animal.

This is what's known as a syllogism, one of the most common forms of deductive reasoning. Note how the argument moves from the most general premise (1), what's known as the major premise, to the particular premise about just one dog (2), which is known as the minor premise, and finally to the conclusion (3), which follows logically from the first two premises and forms a valid argument.

Major premise: All dogs are animals.

Minor premise: Aldous is a dog.

Conclusion: Therefore, Aldous is an animal.

The argument is made valid because of the way it distributes terms from the premises to the conclusion. A valid syllogism has three terms:

Middle term: dogs

Predicate or major term: animal or animals

Subject or minor term: Aldous

So, in all syllogisms the middle term (dogs) links the subject (Aldous) and the predicate (animal). Without the middle term, found in both premises, no conclusion can be drawn. Try it for yourself. Look at the following syllogisms and identify which are the valid and invalid arguments. In the valid arguments try to identify the three terms and notice how the middle term is distributed throughout, linking the subject and predicate.

1. Augustus was a Roman emperor.
   Julius Caesar was a Roman general.
   Therefore, Julius Caesar was the uncle of Augustus.
2. All successful diplomats are noted for their tact.
   Robert is noted for his tact.
   Therefore, Robert is a successful diplomat.
3. All metals are conductors.
   Steel is a metal.
   Therefore, steel is a conductor.
4. All composers are very creative.
   Elgar was a keen cyclist.
   Therefore, Elgar was very creative.
5. All native-born Americans are citizens.
   Jones is a native-born American.
   Therefore, Jones is a citizen.

Indeed, you can just as easily distinguish the valid from the invalid argument when you might not even understand the terms of the argument. Look at the following argument and decide for yourself.

6. All serial relations are transitive, aliorelative and connected.

    The relation 'greater than' is a serial relation.

    Therefore, the relation 'greater than' is transitive, aliorelative and connected.

But what is the significance of all this? Well, the most important thing to remember is that nothing can be drawn out by way of a conclusion that is not already contained in the premises. For example, while you can argue,

>   All bachelors are unmarried men.
>   John is a bachelor.
>   Therefore, John is an unmarried man.

You cannot argue,

>   All bachelors are unmarried men.
>   John is a bachelor.
>   Therefore, John is unattractive.

In the first argument the term unmarried was included in the first premise, so we can conclude that John is unmarried, but the property of attractiveness is not included in either of the premises in the second argument, therefore we cannot conclude that John is unattractive.

■ 2. Sound arguments

However, although this means that when an argument is valid the conclusion inevitably follows from its premises – that the conclusion is entailed by the premises – this does not mean that the conclusion must, therefore, be true. This occurs only when the premises are true. To say that a conclusion drawn from premises is valid is only to say that its truth is guaranteed *if* the premises of the argument are true. An argument of this kind is described as being sound. That is, it is sound if and only if it is a valid argument and has true premises. So, we can challenge the soundness of an argument either by criticizing it for being invalid, or by arguing that one or more of its premises are untrue. For example, the following argument is valid, but it is untrue.

>   All Australians have blond hair.
>   Colin is an Australian.
>   Therefore, Colin has blond hair.

The argument is valid, but it is unsound. It illustrates how a conclusion can be drawn from a valid argument, yet still be false. By contrast, in the following the conclusion is true and the reasoning is valid, but the premises are false.

>   All humans are dogs.
>   Aldous is human.
>   Therefore, Aldous is a dog.

What this means is that while we cannot be sure that the conclusion of a valid argument is true on the basis of knowing that the argument is valid, we do know that the conclusion of a valid argument would be true if all its premises were true. Just to make the point even clearer, let's consider two types of cases in turn: valid arguments with false premises and invalid arguments with true premises.

2.1 Valid arguments with false premises

Those in the first group have true conclusions, those in the second untrue. First check the validity of the arguments and then decide which premise, perhaps even both, is untrue.

True conclusions

A. All professional footballers earn large salaries.
    The managing director of IBM is a professional footballer.
    Therefore, the managing director of IBM earns a large salary.

B. All oboe players perform in rock bands.
    Mick Jagger is an oboe player.
    Therefore, Mick Jagger performs in a rock band.

Untrue conclusions

C. All American presidents take office below the age of 30.
    Richard Nixon was an American president.
    Therefore, Richard Nixon took office below the age of 30.

D. All golfers are less than five feet tall.
    Michael Jordan is a golfer.
    Therefore, Michael Jordan is less than five feet tall.

All of these arguments are valid, but this is not enough to know that their conclusions are true. However, what we can be sure of is that if we have a valid argument, the conclusion *must* be true if its premises are true.

2.2 Invalid arguments with true premises

True conclusions

E. All Stephen King's novels are very popular.
    The novel *Carrie* is very popular.
    Therefore, *Carrie* is a Stephen King novel.

F. All golfers are competitive.
    Tiger Woods is competitive.
    Therefore, Tiger Woods is a golfer.

Untrue conclusions

G. All Britons are citizens of the European Union.
    All Germans are citizens of the European Union.
    Therefore, all Britons are Germans.

H. All corporate lawyers are wealthy.
    Bill Gates is wealthy.
    Therefore, Bill Gates is a corporate lawyer.

If there is one important principle to take from all of these examples it is that two arguments may be alike in the truth of their premises and conclusions, yet differ in their validity or invalidity. The truth of the premises of E and F, for instance, does not guarantee the truth of their conclusions. Not all invalid arguments display their invalidity in the truth of their premises and conclusions: that is, not all invalid arguments have premises that are true and a conclusion that is false. Indeed, examples E and F have true conclusions and true premises, yet are invalid arguments.

So, it's worth remembering two quite simple methods of proving that an argument is invalid. First, describe a situation in which the premises would be true and the conclusion false, and then work out where the contradiction lies. For example, in F above we could change the conclusion to read 'Therefore Tiger Woods is a tennis player', which we know to be false. It now becomes clear that the argument is invalid because it rests on the assump-

tion that only golfers are competitive, whereas in fact those engaged in most sports are competitive, whether they are golfers, tennis players, footballers, or even tiddlywinks players, who I am reliably assured are intensely competitive. Using the same method on E above and you can see that we have adopted a similar assumption about Stephen King novels. The novel *Carrie* is very popular, but it doesn't follow that only Stephen King's novels are popular. It might have been written by another author of popular novels.

The underlying principle in this is that an argument is valid if and only if it is not possible for its premises all to be true and its conclusion to be false. So, if the first method fails to reveal the invalidity, try the second. In this case construct a different argument using the same logical form with true premises and a false conclusion. What we're testing here is the principle that an argument is valid only if there is no other argument with the same form, but with true premises and a false conclusion. If you can make the example from materials that are unfamiliar to you, so much the better. Freed from premises that you know all too well to be true, you may be able to see clearly where the contradiction lies.

So, to summarize:

Two methods for proving that an argument is invalid:

1. Describe a situation in which the premises would be true and the conclusion false, and then work out where the contradiction lies.

2. Construct a different argument using the same logical form with true premises and a false conclusion.

■ 3. Problems

While you test arguments in this way for their validity, it also helps to know the sort of problems and fallacies that you ought to look out for. Here are four of the most common problems that relate to what we have done so far.

3.1 Suppressed premises

When arguments are presented in the clear syllogistic form we have been considering, it is not difficult to see whether they are valid or not. But most arguments are not presented in this form. They may be clouded with all sorts of irrelevancies that you will have to strip away before you can get to the form of the argument beneath. More difficult to detect, however, are those arguments that leave out a premise or skip a stage, because those who argue the case are in a hurry or just assume you know and agree with the suppressed premise. The argument might, indeed, be valid, but you will only know this if you can discover the suppressed premise. Look at the following argument and see if you can identify the suppressed premise.

1. Aldous is a dog.

2. Therefore he is very loyal.

Clearly what would make this argument valid is the suppressed premise that:

All dogs are loyal.

That wasn't too difficult, but now try some simple one-liners whose form is a little more difficult to detect.

1. The customer can't expect much consideration from a multinational like XXX.

2. Why are you blushing? You have nothing to be ashamed of.

3. You should have no worries about buying this car, the engine's fine.

4. Intolerant? Well yes, of course he is. He's a racist.

3.2 Equivocation

Even in these arguments, where it's a little more difficult to reconstruct the syllogism, it's still quite straightforward to uncover the suppressed premises. But much more slippery and difficult to pin down is *the fallacy of equivocation*, where the terms used change their meaning or application throughout the argument. The problem is that many of the words and expressions we commonly use have more than one meaning; so that when we use them in two or more different ways in the same argument we can reach quite convincing though misleading conclusions. Take, for example, the following argument:

The loss of liberty makes men slaves.

I am denied the liberty of buying a beer outside licensing hours.

Therefore, I am a slave.

For the argument to be valid the meaning of the word 'liberty' must remain constant throughout. In the first premise liberty might have been spelt with a capital 'L', because it implies all of those basic human rights that free men demand and expect as part of their freedom. But in the second premise the liberty that is meant is liberty with a small 'l'. It is just one liberty and certainly not one of those we would list if we were to distinguish between the life of a slave and that of a free man. To be denied this liberty may be inconvenient, and at times frustrating, but we would not usually associate it with a condition of slavery, nor would we accuse those who denied it of being tyrants. Of course, if you were writing a commercial selling a certain brand of beer, in which you were trying to sell your product by linking it with the importance we attach to our rights and freedoms, then you might deliberately commit the fallacy of equivocation in the hope that the consumer will not see it and, therefore, attach the same importance to your beer.

An Australian advertisement promoting concern for the environment has the presenter surrounded by people planting trees. He is clutching a handful of soil, which he allows to fall gradually through his fingers, while he tells us that those who fought for this (holding up the soil), their land, in the two world wars would be deeply disappointed by our generation, if we fail to protect it. Those who wrote the commercial clearly sought to play on our inattention in not seeing that there is a difference between the 'Land' that we fought for, and the 'land' as in soil. By 'Land' we mean our culture, values and heritage, indeed our whole way of life, which might be threatened by an invading country. This is quite different from the soil in which we plant crops.

Two other forms of equivocation are worth noting, if only because they are so common. The first is *the fallacy of division*, which is committed whenever someone argues that something, which is true only for the whole, is also true of its parts taken separately. For example you might argue that,

Harvard University produces the best graduates in the country.

So, John Smith, who recently got his degree from the University, must be an excellent person.

But, although the graduates of the best universities are generally excellent, to infer that any particular graduate is excellent, merely because he or she attended one of these universities, would be an incorrect inference.

The converse of the fallacy of division is equally common. In *the fallacy of composition* equivocation occurs when we assume that what is true of the part is also true of the whole. For example, you might argue that,

> Players A, B, C, D, etc., are all top players in the game, so if we have these in our team we are sure to win the championship this year.

But the fact that you might have the best players around in your team does not ensure that you will have the best team. It will certainly help, but whether this is the best team will depend upon how well the players harmonize as a team and learn to work together, complementing each other's style, so that each player is able to play to his strengths and get the best out of himself.

However, that's not to say that in certain circumstances we're not right to reason from what is true of the whole to what is true of each part and vice versa. For example, you might argue,

> My computer is brand new, so all the parts of my computer are brand new.

> I have inspected each apple in this box and it is perfectly safe to sell each one of them to the public, so it is perfectly safe to sell this box of apples to the public.

Finally, there are two problems that relate to the way the terms used in our premises ought to be distributed, if the arguments are to be valid.

3.3 The fallacy of the undistributed middle term

We have seen that in a syllogism the middle term (dogs) must be distributed between both premises, otherwise no conclusion can be drawn. Usually it is distributed in the major premise by being general-ized ('All dogs are animals'). In this way the minor term (Aldous) can be included in the major premise. For example, we might argue,

> All accountants are businessmen.
>
> John is an accountant.
>
> Therefore, John is a businessman.

The major premise may not be true but the argument is still valid. The middle term, 'accountants', is distributed in the major premise: the word 'all' ensures that it is generalized so that no accountants are omitted. But now change it to read:

> Some accountants are businessmen.
>
> John is an accountant.
>
> Therefore, John is a businessman.

We have now committed *the fallacy of the undistributed middle term*. We have not distributed the middle term and, consequently, we can no longer validly deduce the conclusion that John is a businessman. He may be one of those accountants who are not businessmen.

3.4 The fallacy of the illicit process of major or minor term

In this fallacy it is not so much that the terms have not been distributed correctly, but that they have been badly processed. In effect, the conclusion asserts more than the premises will allow. Take the following argument that:

> All children are innocent.
>
> No grownups are children.
>
> Therefore, no grownups are innocent.

While you might agree with the conclusion, the argument is invalid. The conclusion cannot be deduced from the two premises, because the major premise does not exclude other groups from the category 'innocent', like animals and even some grownups.

In the next section we will examine 'conversion', the process of interchanging the subject and the complement of a sentence. In many cases it is quite valid to do this, but not in this. We have assumed in the argument that the premise 'All children are innocent' allows us to argue that 'All the innocent are children', which is an example of *illicit conversion*. Of course, this points to the way in which this argument could be made valid: by re-interpreting the concept of children to include all those people who appear to be ingenuous and unworldly, so that anybody who manifests these qualities of innocence can be legitimately described as 'children'.

So, to summarize:

A few simple rules about arguments

It may help to keep in mind the following simple rules when you come to consider the validity of an argument.

1. Check that you have all the premises in the argument: that there are no suppressed premises.

2. There should be no more than three terms.

3. There should be a middle term common to both premises.

4. Terms should not change their meaning or application throughout the argument.

■ 4. The forms of syllogistic arguments

Now that we're clear about arguments and how they work, all the rest is detail; not insignificant detail, but detail nevertheless. Therefore as we negotiate our way through this keep in mind that we are building on the structure we have already erected. The better we can process our ideas into clear organizing structures the more confident we feel about using them. In what follows, therefore, we will work through the different forms of syllogistic arguments, which we will organize in the following structure around the types of proposition that each syllogism contains:

A. Categorical propositions

B. Compound propositions:
    1. Disjunctive (alternative) propositions
    2. Conditional (hypothetical) propositions
        2.1 Pure hypothetical syllogisms
        2.2 Mixed hypothetical syllogisms.

This might sound complicated, but it isn't. Each

contains quite simple ideas; it is their pattern of interrelations that appears to complicate the picture. So, keep this simple structure in mind as we work our way through it.

A. Categorical propositions

Many of the syllogisms we use involve categorical propositions; propositions, that is, which assert relationships between two groups of objects or two classes of people or things. We have already used a number of these: 'All dogs are animals', 'All golfers are competitive', 'All corporate lawyers are wealthy'. One group or class of things, 'dogs', is contained in another, 'animals'. Similarly all 'golfers' can be included in another class of people, which we can describe as 'competitive', in the same way that 'corporate lawyers' can be seen as part of another class of people, who are 'wealthy'.

A.1 Universal affirmative generalizations

Each of the statements above was prefixed by the adjective 'all', making them universal generalizations. All of one class of things is contained in the class of another. A Venn diagram illustrates this well. All Xs are Ys, where X stands for a class of people or things that is wholly included in another class Y.

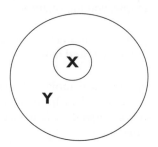

However, every generalization can be expressed in both a positive and negative way. Thus,

'All dogs are animals'

can be expressed as

'No dogs are non-animals.'

Of course, the meaning hasn't changed: to say that 'No Xs are non-Ys' is the same as saying that 'All Xs are Ys.' Similarly, to say 'No golfers are non-competitive' is the same as saying 'All golfers are competitive', as 'No corporate lawyers are not wealthy' is the same as saying 'All corporate lawyers are wealthy.'

A.1.1 Obversion

This form of the original proposition is known as the obverse and the process of changing it is known as obversion. However, in changing from the affirmative to the negative form it is easy to make a fairly common mistake and, as a result, to draw conclusions that are not justified. For example, from the generalization that

'All golfers are competitive'

someone might conclude that

'All non-golfers are non-competitive.'

Clearly this is invalid, as you can see from the Venn diagram. It's an example of illicit obversion. It doesn't necessarily follow that those who are excluded from the X class are also excluded from the Y class. The fact that someone is not a golfer doesn't mean they are non-competitive. There are many other sports that are competitive, along with many activities and occupations that call for people to be competitive if they are to be successful. The negative equivalent of 'All golfers are competitive' is, of course,

'No golfer is uncompetitive.'

We have already seen examples of how these sorts of generalizations are used in arguments; indeed there are, in fact, hundreds of valid and invalid forms of arguments, which we regularly use, that would illustrate this. You can probably think of your own examples, but here is one that illustrates the obverse form, which we haven't seen so far.

No golfer is uncompetitive.

John is uncompetitive.

Therefore, John is not a golfer.

It is worth noting here that the minor premise could have been another universal generalization or, indeed, a partial generalization, which we will come to in a moment. In the meantime, the following examples illustrate both of these forms:

A universal generalization as the minor premise

No golfer is uncompetitive.

All players who play for relaxation are uncompetitive.

Therefore, all players who play for relaxation are not golfers.

A partial generalization as the minor premise

No golfer is uncompetitive.

Some young players are uncompetitive.

Therefore, some young players are not golfers.

A.2 Universal negative generalizations

As we have just seen with obversion, syllogistic arguments are not just made up of universal affirmative generalizations. They can also involve universal negative generalizations, those in which all members of one class of things or people are totally excluded from another class. In the following Venn diagram, illustrating the generalization 'No Xs are Ys', you can see clearly that all the members of X class are totally excluded from the Y class. And you can probably work out for yourself that the affirmative equivalent of this is 'All Xs are non-Ys.'

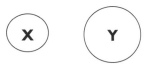

So, using universal negative generalizations we could argue that 'No oboe players perform in rock bands', or 'No corporate lawyers are poor.'

A.2.1 Conversion

The most interesting feature of this type of generalization is that the subject (X) and the complement (Y) can be interchanged; that is, the converse is also true. Thus, it follows from the proposition 'No Xs are Ys' that 'No Ys are Xs.' And the same goes, of course, for the affirmative equivalent of this. In other words, it follows from the proposition 'All Xs are non-Ys', that 'All Ys are non-Xs.' So, the important thing to remember here is that total exclusion is a reversible relation, whereas inclusion is not.

> Total exclusion is a reversible relation, whereas inclusion is not.

Given that 'No Xs are Ys', we can argue that 'No Ys are Xs.' But we cannot similarly argue that given 'All Xs are Ys', then 'All Ys are Xs.' A quick look back at our two Venn diagrams illustrating these two propositions will immediately confirm this. Indeed, to argue in this way would be an example of a very common mistake, that of illicit conversion.

At one time or another we've all found ourselves in the sort of endless discussion that seems to get nowhere. Very often the reason for this is that we have assumed that a universal statement about the subject makes a universal statement about the complement. Most forms of racism and discrimination begin with this mistake. Someone might hear or read about people being mugged in the street and every case appears to have been committed by members of a certain ethnic group. So they come to the conclusion that all muggings are carried out by members of that group. Then they convert the generalization, often without knowing that they have, and argue that all the members of that group are muggers. From arguing that all Xs are Ys, they conclude that all Ys are Xs.

If you're observant you won't have any trouble finding examples of this all around in the newspapers, on television and in discussion with friends. Indeed, you'll find so many that you might even begin to wish you had never read this passage. For example, during the Cold War, because it was found that many of those who were deemed to be unpatriotic were also pacifists opposed to nuclear warfare and the mass annihilation this would involve, it was illogically concluded that all pacifists were unpatriotic. Yet there were many people, including Quakers and many prominent war heroes, who were opposed to nuclear warfare, but through no stretch of the imagination could any of these be described as unpatriotic.

A.3 Partial generalizations

In this example a partial generalization would have been a more accurate representation of the situation. In other words we would be closer to the truth if we were to say that 'Some patriots are pacifists.' Most of us at times make the mistake of representing evidence inaccurately through our use of words, like 'all', when it would be more accurate to use words, like 'some', 'most' or 'few'. At other times we use the verb 'to be' in its strongest form 'are', when really we should be saying 'may be' or 'tend to be'. When we use partial generalizations to

say that 'Some Xs are Ys', we are stating that class X is partially included in class Y. Again, a Venn diagram displays the situation clearly:

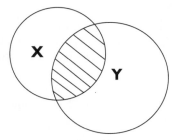

You can also see from this that partial generalizations are also convertible, in that while you can argue that 'Some Xs are Ys', or 'Some patriots are pacifists', you can also argue that 'Some Ys are Xs' and 'Some pacifists are patriots.' Before, when we examined propositions that were convertible, we found that while total exclusion was convertible, total inclusion was not. Now we can add to this that partial inclusion is convertible too.

Partial inclusion is convertible.

What's more, as with universal generalizations we can express the relation between the two classes involved either affirmatively or negatively. A partial negative generalization for the situation represented by the Venn diagram above would focus on the unshaded areas where we can conclude that 'Some Xs are not Ys' and 'Some Ys are not Xs.' By the same token we can conclude that 'Some patriots are not pacifists' and 'Some pacifists are not patriots.'

As you can probably see from this, given the number of combinations of universal and partial generalizations we can use in syllogistic reasoning there are hundreds of valid and invalid argument forms. However, in most of these you will be able detect which are invalid and which are valid simply by using Venn diagrams. The following examples seem complex at first sight, but once you have reproduced them in diagrammatic form it's not difficult to see whether they are valid or invalid.

Some As are not Bs.

All Cs are Bs.

Therefore, some As are not Cs.

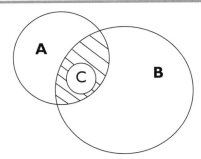

Wherever you locate the Cs on the diagram – whether in the shaded area of the overlap between As and Bs where Cs would be both As and Bs, or as some As and all Bs, or as just no As and all Bs – it is still going to be true that at least some As are not Cs.

The second example, too, looks equally complex until you reduce it to the diagrammatic form.

> Some As are Bs.
>
> Some Cs are Bs.
>
> Therefore, some As are Cs.

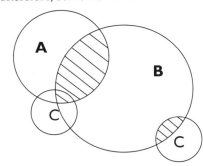

In this case Cs can be located in two types of position: one intersecting both the A and B circles where they themselves intersect and the other anywhere on the circumference of B where it doesn't intersect with A. Given this possibility it is invalid to argue that some As will be Cs.

However as a simple rule of thumb, when you've broken down an argument into its premises, ask yourself whether the premises could be true and the conclusion false. If you think this is possible then check it for yourself by converting the argument into diagrammatic form. For example you may find someone is arguing,

> Some pacifists are unpatriotic.
>
> Some members of the government are pacifists.
>
> Therefore, some members of the government are unpatriotic.

Clearly there's reason to believe that nobody becomes a member of the government if they don't love their country and want to do what they can to improve it. So, we have some reason to doubt the truth of this conclusion, even though the premises are known to be true.

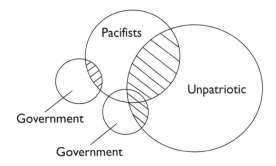

Now, looking at it in its diagrammatic form we can see that it's similar to the example above. The circle representing the members of the government can be positioned at the intersection of the circles representing pacifists and unpatriotic, but it can also be positioned anywhere on the circumference of the pacifist circle, which means that it is possible for members of the government to be both pacifists and patriotic, so the argument is invalid.

B. Compound propositions

So far all the propositions we have considered have referred to the qualities of people or things, the relations between them, or our judgements about them. But there is another group of propositions which allows us to move on from just noting qualities and characteristics to discovering the connections between things and people. This is an important step, because it allows us to explain events and, ultimately, to create hypotheses to explain the world around us through laws and theories. Quite simply, if you want to explain why something happened to you, or you want to explain why the world is as it is, you will have to bring two or more ideas together in these compound propositions. For example, if you try to explain to somebody what you think might be the reasons why you cannot get into your car, you will have to bring at least two ideas together: say, that you have mislaid your keys and that your keys have been stolen, one of which you think may be true.

B.1 Disjunctive (alternative) propositions

Disjunctive or alternative propositions bring these two ideas together in a very familiar way: in an 'either/or' relationship. So, as you attempt to force the lock of your car you might explain to a police officer, who is about to arrest you, that you can't get into it because,

> 1. Either I have mislaid the keys or they have been stolen.

In your panic to prove your innocence you might suddenly remember that you had in fact left them on the counter of a shop down the road. You might then argue with some relief that,

> 2. They have not been stolen.
> 3. (Therefore), I have mislaid them.

This would be a valid disjunctive syllogism. It takes the form,

> 1. Either X or Y.
> 2. Not Y.
> 3. Therefore, X.

It is valid only when a categorical premise (in this case, 'They have not been stolen') contradicts one of the disjuncts. Of course, we could just as easily contradict X to find that Y is true, but we must contradict, not affirm, one of the disjuncts. If we merely affirm the truth of one of them, this doesn't imply the falsehood of the other: both can in fact be true. If you were to remember that you last saw your keys at the bottom of your bag buried beneath some books, you might argue to the police officer with some relief that,

> 2. I had mislaid them.
> 3. Therefore, they were not stolen.

This would be an invalid argument, because it still doesn't exclude the possibility that your bag and the keys in it have been stolen. This occurs because of the *inclusive* sense of 'or', which allows both disjuncts to be true. It would be different if both disjuncts were *exclusive*. Then the argument would be valid, because both cannot be true. For example, you might argue,

> Either Alan plays football for England, or he plays for the USA.

In this case it is clear that it cannot be true that he plays for both nations, so to affirm one or the other of the disjuncts would be valid.

B.2 Conditional (hypothetical) propositions

Just as common as the disjunctive, another way of bringing two ideas together to explain an event is through the use of conditional or hypothetical propositions. Hypothetical propositions are marked by their distinctive 'if/then' structure. We might agree that people who are good at photography (one idea) are likely to take it up as a career (another idea). So, we might argue,

> If a person is good at photography, then she is likely to take it up as a career.

This is the distinctive structure of a hypothetical proposition. It has two parts, as you can see: the 'if' clause, known as the antecedent, and the 'then' clause, known as the consequent. In this case, if we were to use our hypothetical proposition as the major premise in a syllogism, we could argue,

1. If a person is good at photography, then she is likely to take it up as a career.
2. Jayne is good at photography.
3. Therefore, she is likely to take it up as a career.

The form of the argument, then, is

1. If X, then Y.
2. J is X.
3. Therefore, J is Y.

B.2.1 Pure hypothetical syllogisms

The last distinction we have to make concerns the way we use hypothetical propositions in syllogisms. Some syllogisms are pure hypotheticals, while others are mixed. Pure hypothetical syllogisms contain hypothetical propositions exclusively. For example, you might claim,

1. If an athlete takes performance-enhancing drugs, then he cheats.

You might then extend this by arguing that,

2. If he cheats, then he will be disqualified.

3. Therefore, if an athlete takes performance-enhancing drugs, then he will be disqualified.

As you can see this is a valid argument and you can probably also see that it has a fairly distinctive structure. If we look at this structure closely, we can uncover simple rules which will help us decide whether an argument which may adopt this form is valid. The argument takes the following form,

1. If A, then C
2. If C, then B
3. Therefore, if A, then B.

So, we can simplify this by setting out its structure in the following table:

1. A	C
2. C	B
3. A	B

As you can see from this there are three fairly simple rules that govern the validity of this type of argument:

1. The first premise and the conclusion have the same antecedent.
2. The second premise and the conclusion have the same consequent.
3. The consequent of the first premise is the antecedent of the second.

B.2.2 Mixed hypothetical syllogisms

As the name implies a mixed hypothetical syllogism has a hypothetical proposition as its major premise and a categorical premise as its minor premise. So, you might argue

1. If an athlete takes performance-enhancing drugs, then he will be disqualified.

2. Stephen has taken performance-enhancing drugs.

3. Therefore, he will be disqualified.

Like the pure form, the mixed hypothetical syllogisms have fairly simple rules by which we can decide whether an argument is valid.

B.2.2.1 Modus ponens *(Latin: 'mood that affirms')*

There are two forms of valid argument for mixed hypothetical syllogisms. The first is *modus ponens*, which means that to argue validly we must affirm the antecedent of the hypothetical major premise. This takes the following form,

1. If X, then Y
2. S is X.
3. Therefore, S is Y.

If we go back to our example you can see that the antecedent of the hypothetical premise was 'If an athlete takes performance-enhancing drugs'. We then affirmed in the second premise that 'Stephen has taken performance-enhancing drugs.' Therefore, it was valid to conclude that '... he will be disqualified.'

B.2.2.2 Modus tollens *(Latin: 'mood that denies')*

Unlike *modus ponens* this form, as you would expect, is valid because it denies the consequent. It takes the following form,

1. If X, then Y.
2. S is not Y.
3. Therefore, S is not X.

Using our example again, the consequent of the hypothetical premise was '... then he will be disqualified.' Our argument will be valid if, in the second premise, we deny that Stephen was disqualified, and then conclude that therefore he has not been taking performance-enhancing drugs.

As you can see from both of these forms of the argument there are quite simple rules to obey. An argument is only valid if you affirm the antecedent or deny the consequent. To help you, keep in mind the following simple table.

	Antecedent	**Consequent**
Valid	Affirm	Deny
Invalid	Deny	Affirm

B.2.2.3 *Problems*

By now the fallacies for the mixed hypothetical syllogism should be obvious. If the valid forms of the argument are to affirm the antecedent and deny the consequent, the fallacies are the reverse: to deny the antecedent and affirm the consequent.

Invalid forms:
1. To deny the antecedent.   2. To affirm the consequent.

Denying the antecedent

If we were to deny the antecedent our arguments would take the following form:

1. If an athlete takes performance-enhancing drugs, then he will be disqualified.
2. Stephen has not taken performance-enhancing drugs.
3. Therefore, he will not be disqualified.

Clearly this is invalid. Stephen may not have been taking performance-enhancing drugs, but this doesn't mean he will not be disqualified. He may have cheated in other ways.

Affirming the consequent

Similarly, if we were to affirm the consequent we would get a similar inconclusive and invalid result:

1. If an athlete takes performance-enhancing drugs, then he will be disqualified.
2. Stephen has been disqualified.
3. Therefore, he has been taking performance-enhancing drugs.

Again, Stephen could have been disqualified for many reasons; taking performance-enhancing drugs is just one of them.

This suggests one of the reasons we tend to make this mistake. In the proposition 'If X, then Y', we confuse the claim that X is a sufficient condition for Y with the claim that it is the *only* sufficient and necessary condition. We will examine the significance of necessary and sufficient conditions in the next chapter; for now it is enough to understand that if something is sufficient and necessary for the occurrence of something else, no other alternative reasons need be sought. If we were wrongly to assume this we would in effect confuse the hypothetical 'If X, then Y' with the proposition 'If, and only if, X, then Y.' In the case of the athlete, Stephen, we would in effect be arguing that 'If, and only if, an athlete takes performance-enhancing drugs, then he will be disqualified.' As you can see clearly, this means that no other reason will count as justification for his disqualification. So, if he is disqualified it can only be because he has taken the banned drugs.

Unfortunately this is a very common mistake to make, though it is not always as obvious as in this example. Even so the fallacy makes its appearance in the most unlikely places. A scientist arguing for the truth of Einstein's theory of relativity reasons,

> If Einstein's theory is true then light rays passing close to the sun are deflected. Careful experiment reveals that light rays passing close to the sun *are* deflected. Therefore Einstein's theory is true.

Perhaps an even more unlikely appearance occurs, not infrequently, in Arthur Conan Doyle's novels about Sherlock Holmes, who frequently takes great pains to convince the impressionable Doctor Watson and the hapless Inspector Lestrade that his success in detection is entirely due to his famed deductive method. In *The Boscombe Valley Mystery* (1891) Watson explains:

> It was about ten minutes before we regained our cab ... Holmes still carrying with him the stone which he had picked up in the wood.
> 'This may interest you, Lestrade,' he remarked, holding it out. 'The murder was done with it.'
> 'I see no marks.'
> 'There are none.'
> 'How do you know, then?'

'The grass was growing under it. It had only lain there a few days. There was no sign of a place whence it had been taken. It corresponds with the injuries.'

It appears the reasoning probably went as follows,

If the murder weapon was a heavy object, then we will find it with grass growing beneath it.

This stone was found with grass growing beneath it.

Therefore, this stone is the murder weapon

Holmes assumed there was only one reason why the stone was lying there, recently discarded, with grass growing beneath it: the murderer had thrown it away as he escaped from the scene. In other words, he assumed: 'If, and only if, it was the murder weapon, then it would be found with grass growing beneath it.' But, although this is a necessary reason for thinking the stone is the murder weapon, it is not a sufficient reason: we can think of a number of other reasons which would explain its discovery just as well. A boy returning from school might have picked it up to see how far he could throw it, or it may have been dropped by a gardener who was collecting stones to build a wall or a rockery in his garden.

■ 5. Conclusion

As you can see it is not difficult to understand the basic form of a syllogistic argument, and the ways we can check for validity and invalidity. The confusion more often occurs in the forms syllogistic arguments take, which are dictated by the types of proposition they contain, either categorical or compound. But as long as you keep in mind the quick reference structure (right) and the problems that relate to categorical and compound propositions, this should make it easier for you to identify mistakes as they occur in arguments.

■ Questions

In the following exercises the arguments are fallacious. See if you can identify what's wrong with them (answers can be found at the end of the book).

> **Quick reference**
>
> **A. Categorical:**
>
> 1. Universal affirmative generalizations – obversion and illicit obversion
>
> 2. Universal negative generalizations – conversion and illicit conversion
>
> 3. Partial generalizations
>
> **B. Compound:**
>
> 1. Disjunctive propositions
> 2. Hypothetical propositions:
>   2.1 Pure hypothetical syllogisms
>   2.2 Mixed hypothetical syllogisms
>   2.2.1 *Modus ponens*
>   2.2.2 *Modus tollens*
>   2.2.3 Problems
>   Denying the antecedent
>   Affirming the consequent

1. All successful diplomats are noted for their tact.

   Robert is noted for his tact.

   Therefore, Robert is a successful diplomat.

2. If a student cheats in an examination, he or she deserves to fail.

   But Colin did not cheat in the examination.

   Therefore, Colin did not deserve to fail.

3. If Lisbon is in Portugal, then it is in Europe.

   Lisbon is in Europe.

   Therefore, Lisbon is in Portugal.

4. If the battery is low, then the lights are dim.

   The battery is not low.

   Therefore, the lights are not dim.

5. The time has come for us to realize that our founding fathers had some mistaken ideas. For example, in the Preamble to the Constitution we read that 'all men are created equal.' But this is obviously false. Some are stronger than others. Some have more intelligence than others. Some have drives which lead to

success, whereas others seem to lack these drives. All men are not created equal.

6. Senator Snort can be trusted to do what is right, for he is a member of the majority, and the majority can be trusted to do what is right in the long run.

7. As creators, women are superior to men since men can only create works of art, science, or philosophy, whereas women can create life.

8. Improbable events happen almost every day, but whatever happens almost every day is probable. Improbable events, therefore, are probable events.

■ Recommended reading

Copi, Irving. *Introduction to Logic* (New York: Macmillan, 1978).

Flew, A. *Thinking about Thinking (Or, Do I Sincerely Want to be Right?)* (London: Fontana, 1976).

Lemmon, E. J. *Beginning Logic* (London: Nelson, 1965).

Mates, Benson. *Elementary Logic* (New York: Oxford University Press, 1965).

Salmon, Wesley C. *Logic* (Englewood Cliffs, NJ: Prentice-Hall, 1973).

The Method: Testing for Truth

CHAPTER 4

Key issues

▶ How can an argument be valid, yet still untrue?

▶ Is our theory supported by the evidence? How much evidence is enough?

▶ Why is it important to be able to distinguish between sufficient and necessary conditions?

▶ Argument by analogy: are the connections between our ideas reliable and credible?

▶ How can we avoid committing the fallacy of false analogy?

▶ Can you critically evaluate an argument? Learn a simple method to play devil's advocate.

▶ Is our theory an adequate answer to the problem?

▶ Is our theory consistent with other theories we might advance to deal with other problems that are connected with this problem? Together do they create a coherent and systematic view of the whole?

Contents

We began by examining the nature of the problem we wanted to answer. It might be why a particular event occurred or whether we are justified in holding a certain belief. We found that one important way of pinning down clearly the issues involved was to analyse the implications of the concepts we use to describe the problem. This gave us a much clearer idea of the sort of hypothesis that might give us the explanation we want. Armed with this we were able in the last chapter to test the validity of our arguments that make up our hypothesis or theory as to the probable explanation.

Now we are in a position to test our theory for its truth. To do this we must subject it to four tests:

1. Are the connections between our ideas true?

2. Is there sufficient evidence to support our theory?

3. Internal test: is it an adequate explanation?

4. External test: is it coherent with our other ideas?

We saw in the last chapter that to explain anything involves synthesising, bringing together, two or more ideas into a valid argument. But, while we now know that our argument is consistent, that we have made no logical mistake in putting these ideas together, we still have to be sure that the connections between them are in fact true. If they are not, then we have made unwarranted assumptions and we will either have to adjust our theory or abandon it altogether. Once we've sorted this out and we're clear about the connections between our ideas, we can consider in the second test whether there is enough evidence to support them.

With both of these tests done, you will no doubt believe that you've got the right answer. But before the sound of popping champagne corks echo around your study, you would be wise to subject your theory to just two final tests: the internal and external tests. In the internal test our concern is to check that the theory itself is adequate to answer the problem. We must be sure that it explains all we want it to. It is all too easy to lose sight of the adequacy of your theory as you work through the other stages, so checking it at this stage gives you the chance to narrow or broaden its scope.

Once you have satisfied yourself on this score, you can move on to the external test. While the internal test is confined just to evaluating the theory on its own merits, in the external test we turn our attention beyond the theory to its relations with our other ideas and beliefs. We have to be sure that it fits within a coherent system of ideas. If we find a contradiction with what we already believe, we will either have to change our theory to take account of this, or begin to examine our other ideas.

■ 1. Are the connections between our ideas true?

As we have already seen, you will often hear people attempt to clarify what is being said and the connections between ideas by asking whether what's being argued are sufficient or necessary conditions, or both, for the truth of our theory. It is important to determine which sense applies to the logical connection between two or more ideas, because it will shape the way we can evaluate the claims made.

1.1 Sufficient conditions

A condition is sufficient if its truth is all that is required for a belief to be true, or a certain event to occur. When an assumption is a sufficient condition

for a belief to be true, it is said to entail that belief. In other words, given the assumption, the belief necessarily follows, so that if the assumption is true, then so too is the belief.

That might sound complicated, but it's not, particularly when you have a simple example to illustrate it:

> A. Bryan is an Englishman.
>
> B. Therefore, Bryan is a man.

As you can see from this, the truth of B follows from the truth of A. When, given the truth of a proposition (A), another proposition follows necessarily (B), then the truth of the first proposition is a sufficient condition for the truth of the second. But it is not a necessary condition for the truth of the second proposition, because, as you can see in this example, it could be true that Bryan is a Frenchman, or a male of any other nationality.

Test your grasp of this on the following example:

> C. Ken is my father's brother.
>
> D. Therefore, Ken is my uncle.

As you can see, the truth of C is sufficient for the truth of D, that is, if C is true, then D must be true as well. But C is not necessary for the truth of D, because D might be true in other ways: he might be my mother's brother. So, questioning a theory's sufficient conditions is not necessarily effective in disproving it. There may be other conditions that are also sufficient for the truth of the theory.

1.2 Necessary conditions

An assumption is a necessary condition if it *must* be true in order for another belief to be true or an event to occur. When a proposition X necessarily cannot be true unless another proposition Y is true, then the truth of Y is by definition a logically necessary true condition for X.

> X. Cynthia is divorced.
>
> Y. Cynthia has been married.

When a proposition like this must be true for the theory to be true, it is said to be a *presupposition* of the theory. Necessary assumptions are entailed by the theory they presuppose, therefore, if you can show them to be false, you have disproved the theory. But a note of caution, you cannot reverse this relation: if you show them to be true, you haven't shown the theory to be true. Cynthia may be married, but this doesn't mean that, therefore, she must be divorced. You can see this clearly in the Venn diagram below. X is found in the Y circle making Y a necessary condition for X, but if you were to affirm that Cynthia has indeed been married we can plot her anywhere in the Y circle and not just in the X circle representing those who are divorced.

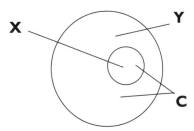

Another way of arguing this is to use the techniques we used in the last chapter to discover the validity of an argument. Questioning presuppositions may involve the *modus tollens* form of argument, 'If X, then Y', with the theory represented by X and the presupposition represented by Y. You will remember that we can validly affirm the antecedent and deny the consequent. Therefore, if we were to show that Y is false, denying the consequent, we will have validly shown that X is also false. But if we were to show that Y is true, invalidly affirming the consequent, this doesn't mean that X is also true. As we have said, even if Cynthia had been married, she might or might not be divorced.

1.3 Necessary and sufficient conditions: an example

The following example, illustrating both types of condition, will help you to see the differences between the two more clearly. Suppose I learn that my Uncle Ken has won the largest prize ever on the weekly lottery. As a result I can argue,

> 1. If Uncle Ken won the lottery, then he bought a ticket.

and 2. If Uncle Ken were the sole recipient of the largest ever prize in the history of the lottery, then he won the lottery.

In (1) the truth of 'he bought a ticket' is a necessary condition for the truth of 'Uncle Ken won the lottery', because, as the popular injunction goes, 'You've got to be in it to win it' and you've got to buy a ticket to be in it. But this is not a sufficient condition for winning the lottery: you need something more, in this case luck. In other contexts, like entering a chess competition, you would need skill and knowledge.

However, in (2) things are a little different. The truth of 'If Uncle Ken were the sole recipient of the largest ever prize in the history of the lottery' is a sufficient condition for the truth of the second part, 'he won the lottery.' In other words, if you were to win the lottery it would be sufficient to be told that you were the sole recipient of the largest ever prize in the history of the lottery. You would know that you had won it without anyone needing to say 'you won the lottery.' But it is not a necessary condition, because you can still win the lottery without breaking the record for the largest prize won.

1.4 Two general rules

Two general rules about the relations between necessary and sufficient conditions will help you in deciding what you must look for when you test the truth of any argument. As you can see the relations between the two conditions are reciprocal.

1. The truth of the antecedent of a true conditional proposition is a *sufficient* condition for the truth of the consequent.

2. The truth of the consequent is a *necessary* condition for the truth of the antecedent.

In the first conditional proposition about Uncle Ken's lottery win the antecedent A (below) is a sufficient condition for the truth of the consequent C, because, as we have already argued, it's not possible for him to win without buying a ticket. And, in turn, the truth of the consequent C is a necessary condition for the truth of the antecedent.

1. (A) If Uncle Ken won the lottery, (C) then he bought a ticket.

Similarly, in the second conditional proposition the antecedent A (below) is a sufficient condition for the truth of the consequent C. And, in turn, the consequent is a necessary condition for the truth of the antecedent, because unless he had indeed won he wouldn't have been the recipient of it.

2. (A) If Uncle Ken were the sole recipient of the largest ever prize in the history of the lottery, (C) then he won the lottery.

The only change to these relations occurs in the *biconditional* propositions we came across in the previous chapter, in which the two parts of the conditional proposition are connected by 'if and only if'. In this case the relation holds both ways: the two terms are said to be identical in that each part is a necessary *and* sufficient condition for the truth of the other. For example, we could say,

> (A) Patricia is Bryan's wife, (C) if and only if Bryan is Patricia's husband.

In this proposition A is not only a sufficient condition of C, but also a necessary condition. And, by the same token, the relation holds the other way: C is not only a sufficient condition of A, but also a necessary condition.

■ 2. Is there sufficient evidence to support our theory?

Now that we know the sort of connections that exist between our premises, we know what we must show evidence for if our theory is to succeed: the premises themselves and the connections between them. As you can see premises come as different types. The simplest to deal with are those that are true analytically; premises like 'All triangles have three sides', 'All bachelors are unmarried men' and 'All cats are animals'. These are true by virtue of what we agree to put into them in the first place. The fact that we agree the word 'bachelor' shall mean 'male' and 'unmarried' makes the sentence true. In the same way when we unwrap the meaning of other words, like 'triangle' and 'cat', we find that their meaning too links two or more characteristics in 'all' cases.

But we have more problems with those sentences that make claims about the real world, requiring us to find empirical evidence to establish their truth. Statements about a particular known group of things are the easiest to deal with. If you were to claim that 'I have ten coins in my pocket', or that 'All the people in the room are male', or even

that 'All the members of the party voted for Mr X as their candidate', it wouldn't be difficult for you to show the evidence needed to prove they are true. More difficult are those that rely on contestable evidence, like the observation reports of others. If a crime is witnessed, say, by 12 people you are likely to get witness statements which seem to describe 12 different events.

Nevertheless, difficult those these are, we do find ways of reconciling the differences between conflicting reports. But it is much more difficult to establish the truth of those statements that convey generalizations which are not concerned with single events or known groups of things, but with whole classes of things. To say that 'All heavier-than-air objects will fall to the ground if left unsupported', may seem like an incontestable truth, but like all inductive propositions it makes a universal claim for events in the past, present and in the future, for which it only has the limited evidence of past events. So for these we have to limit our aspirations: we have to give up our search for truth and settle instead for 'rational defensibility'. Few of us would doubt the claim made about heavier-than-air objects, but we can never collect enough evidence to demonstrate the truth of it.

As we discovered in the last chapter, unlike deductive arguments the truth of the premises of an inductive argument does not guarantee the truth of the conclusion, which always states more than is in the premises. From a limited number of singular observation statements we infer a general law or theory. As a result of observing many instances of unsupported objects falling to the ground we infer that 'all' similar objects will react similarly. And the more instances we observe, the more confident we become in our generalization being rationally defensible. Nevertheless, even if the premises are true, they can still only give a certain degree of probability to the truth of the conclusion.

So, one thing we need to have some idea of is just how much evidence would make our generalization rationally defensible. The other is to show not just enough evidence for the premises, but also for the connections between them. We have to establish credible connections between our premises that will convincingly explain why one event caused another or the reason why one thing should be included within a certain class of things.

For example, say I arrive at class one day soaking wet and you ask me why I am in such a wretched state. I explain that I had been marking student papers. The chances are that you would not be entirely satisfied with that explanation, because you know of no obvious connection between marking student papers and being wet through. However, I might try to make that connection by explaining that I had been busy marking and I hadn't noticed the time. When I did I rushed out without my raincoat only to get soaked on the way. You might now be happier with my explanation, because you know the connection I have made between the event and the cause is reasonable. You may have done similar things yourself and you know others who have done such things too.

2.1 How much evidence is enough?

Whether we have enough evidence largely depends upon the subject. If you are a scientist generalizing about the behaviour of some natural phenomenon, you will be confident about the regularity and constancy of what you observe. But if you are a psephologist examining the voting behaviour of an electorate, you will probably have to tread more carefully. Indeed your evidence may not only lack regularity and constancy; it may not be what it seems. Say you were to run a poll among voters to see what most affects their voting behaviour: the policies of each party or their images. You might get an overwhelming number saying that they are more interested in the issues and policies. But you know the way voters describe their voting behaviour may not reflect what they actually do: they may be happier describing themselves being influenced by issues and policies, than by mere images, yet still vote for the party presenting itself as the 'moderate' party.

2.1.1 Probability

Nevertheless, assuming that our evidence is reliable and constant, one way of judging how much evidence is needed to make a generalization rationally defensible would be to rely on statements of probability that accurately reflect the strength of our evidence.

However, this in itself may not be trouble free. In some cases it's true, probability statements can be dependably precise, particularly those that are simply a matter of logic and mathematics. If you were playing poker or bridge, you would know that there is a 1 in 13 chance of being dealt an ace. If

you were to get it wrong, it could only be that you have made an error in calculation.

But what is not possible to be precise about is the probability of the evidence on which these calculations are based being good evidence. You might roll a dice and know that you have a one in six chance of getting a six, but you cannot be so precise on the probability that the dice itself is not loaded and the evidence of each throw good. Go back to our example of the psephologist. The results of your poll would be clear: let's say 85% said that they would vote for a party on its policies and not on its image. But you can't know the probability that those who responded in this way did so because they like to present themselves as thoughtful rational voters, who weigh up the issues carefully. Our calculations are based on an analogy that each pack of cards and each dice will be regular and true. Even psephologists have to have an analogy of just how honest they believe their respondents will be.

2.1.2 Probability, soundness and truth

This has important implications for the way we view the truth and soundness of arguments. Unlike deductive arguments, which are either sound or unsound, inductive arguments only allow for *degrees* of soundness, with their conclusions being more or less likely on the evidence of the premises. While deductive arguments are general, abstract, involving necessity, inductive arguments are particular, concrete and subject to probabilities.

This points to an important distinction all too easily ignored or confused. It's tempting to view probability as if it is just an inferior type of truth. But truth is not something that admits to degrees. It is absolute: either a proposition is true or it isn't. A statement that is true is just that: it's not true dependent on a certain body of evidence. The proposition two plus two equals four is not true because we have gathered evidence of many instances in which it has been true. In contrast, probability is always a matter of degree. A statement which is probable is not just that: it is probable only in relation to a certain body of evidence. In other words we have to avoid thinking of statements having absolute probability independent of the evidence as we think of statements being true or false absolutely. Statements that are probable are always probable in relation to a certain body of evidence.

As a result the relation between truth and validity on the one hand is quite different from the relation between probability and soundness on the other. In the last chapter we saw that we could separate truth and validity: an argument may be valid, but its conclusion untrue; and it can be invalid, yet have a true conclusion. However, while truth and validity are separable, probability and soundness are not. We can define both in terms of the other. To say that the premises of an inductive argument support its conclusion is to say that if they are true the conclusion is probable. And, conversely, to say a statement is probably true is to say that an inductive argument can be produced to support it.

The significance of this should not be lost. Take one step away from the absolute truth of analytic propositions and deductive arguments and our statements are not just a vehicle conveying independent truth: they are inexorably bound up in a process of interpreting and processing ideas and evidence to get closer to what we believe to be rationally defensible. This may involve unstated assumptions about the quality of the evidence, as we have seen, and background assumptions about what in the context is likely to be accepted as probably true. In the chapters that follow we will look closer at the problems this presents.

2.2 Credible connections: argument by analogy

In turn, it is not difficult to see how important these thoughts are to our other concern in establishing the truth of our arguments: that the connections between our ideas are reliable and credible.

We have to be sure not only that we have *enough* evidence, but that it is *good* evidence. In a deductive argument it's not too difficult to check whether the connections between our ideas make for a valid argument. If we were to argue that all As are Bs, and all Bs are Cs, we can conclude that all As are Cs. But we cannot similarly argue, as in an inductive argument, that all known As have been Cs, therefore the next A will be a C. The cruel and unexpected treatment of Russell's chicken demonstrated the weakness of this argument. Logical inference in a deductive argument is abstract; it's not subject to the facts of the real world; it holds in all possible worlds. But inductive arguments are different. They have to take into account not just the quantity of evidence, which determines how probable the conclusion is, but whether this is good evidence in

that it establishes credible connections in our experience.

So what makes good evidence? Well, one way of arguing that the next A will be a C in the argument above is to find a cause or a reason for the connection. We will examine this in more detail in Chapter 10, but for now it's sufficient to point out that when we search for a contingent connection between things and events we are identifying a sufficiently stable pattern in our previous experience, which we think is reliable enough for us to conclude that given one event the other will follow with high probability. The larger the number of As that have been Cs and the fewer As that have not been Cs, the likelier it is that all As will be Cs, and therefore that the next A will be a C.

But it's not just a matter of finding the right *quantity* of evidence; it's also a question of the right *quality* of connection. It's possible to draw many generalizations from a given set of observations, but the connection we finally accept must allow us to make sense of the experience. In other words, it must simplify the experience for us and bring order to what is otherwise a confusing sequence of disconnected events. However, such stable and orderly patterns are not there ready-made just to be plucked from our experience without effort. This is not a mechanical process: we actively process experience in a highly selective way, imaginatively imposing our own order onto it. In effect, we read into it an order that is not plain to see.

Later in Chapters 10 and 11 we will examine more closely the way scientists form their conjectures and hypotheses, and how the process is justified by the fact that such conjectures are ultimately subject to testing and validation. But for the moment it is sufficient to note the important role that analogies play in the connections we form.

If I were to drop my pen and, just a fraction of a second later, we were both to look out of the window to see a car crash into a lamppost in the street below, it would not be convincing for me to argue that the first event caused the second, because we know of no law or uniformity in our experience in which the dropping of pens cause cars to crash. However, if I were to argue that the light reflected off the falling pen, distracting the driver, who then lost control and crashed into the lamppost, it would still not be as convincing as it should be for a satisfactory explanation, but it is on its way. The reason is that we have had analogous experiences in our own lives when people have been distracted in what they are doing by loud noises or bright lights, and this has led them to make mistakes or have accidents.

In this way we use the analogy to connect the premises to the conclusion. We assert that things which resemble each other in some respects (distractions like loud noise or bright light) will resemble each other in some further respect (making mistakes and having accidents). We might conclude from the fact that A, B and C all have characteristics x and y, and A and B in addition have characteristic z, that C too will probably have characteristic z.

A moment's thought will reveal just how deeply rooted this is in common sense. In our ordinary lives we do it all the time. A friend might ask you to fit a CD player into her car. You have never done this before, but you have fitted a radio into your own car, and you reason that the similarities are sufficient for you to adopt the same method of installation. What are you doing, if not using the analogy of fitting your own radio to get the job done?

Indeed, we would find it hard to communicate even on the simplest level without analogies. Our language would be impoverished without them. Each time we use a metaphor or simile we are using analogies. A metaphor occurs whenever we take a word out of its original sphere and apply it to new circumstances. Many of the words we use to convey mental perceptions, abstract ideas and complex relations have been drawn from their nearest physical parallel. When we use the word 'seeing' as in understanding an idea ('I see the point of that'), we are merely borrowing from the literal 'sight'. There are numerous examples of this in our language, many going back to Latin derivatives, like the verb 'to think', which is a metaphor from vine-pruning.

Nevertheless, like any powerful tool which we come to rely upon, there can be serious consequences from careless use. No two things are similar in every respect. Just because your friend's CD player is similar in certain respects to your radio it doesn't follow that it will be similar in others. So, while arguments by analogy are a very useful form of reasoning, on their own they cannot produce a valid argument, because their conclusions do not follow from their premises. We need, therefore, criteria for appraising them on whether they establish their conclusions with more or less probability.

As the example of the CD player makes clear, the usefulness of an analogy is directly proportional to the closeness with which the two or more subjects of the comparison are related. The more dissimilar they are the less reliable is the comparison drawn from the presumed likeness. In his well-known *Introduction to Logic* (1972) Irving M. Copi offers us six criteria against which to test the analogies we come across and use. I have rearranged them into three groups in the table below to make them more convenient for you to use routinely.

Table 4.1 Copi's six criteria for testing analogies

1. The numbers involved
   1.1 The number of samples used
   1.2 The number and variety of characteristics thought to be similar.
2. The relation to the conclusion
   2.1 The strength of the conclusion relative to its premises
   2.2 The relevance to the conclusion of the characteristics cited in the premises.
3. Differences
   3.1 The differences among the samples cited in the premises
   3.2 The differences between the samples cited in the premises and the one cited in the conclusion.

1. The numbers involved

1.1 The number of samples used

Up to a point, the greater the number of samples we can find among which the analogy is thought to hold, the more confidence we are likely to have in it.

1.2 The number and variety of characteristics thought to be similar

This, too, will increase our confidence in it. The *fallacy of false analogy* is often committed when we ignore differences and push similarities beyond what is reasonable. In the 1980s, for instance, in an effort to persuade us that cuts in expenditure were unavoidable, some governments seized on a useful analogy telling us that 'The economy is like a household budget', even though it was all too clear that despite its similarities there are significant differences. For one thing what you spend in a household budget doesn't usually generate new jobs in the household, thereby raising economic activity, reducing the costs of welfare and increasing revenue from income tax.

2. The relation to the conclusion

2.1 The strength of the conclusion relative to its premises

In the eighteenth century William Paley argued for the existence of God by using the analogy of the watch and the watchmaker. If you were to find a watch, he argued, taking into account how well it is carefully manufactured and designed to perform its task, you would quite reasonably assume there was a watchmaker who made it. Likewise, he argued, the world presents similar overwhelming evidence of design, of being carefully created, with all its delicate balance, order and harmony. So it is reasonable to conclude that it too has been created, only in this case by a perfect god. However, even if we allow the argument that the evidence of order shows that the world was created by a god, there are sufficient imperfections to suggest that we cannot go on to conclude that the creator was a perfect god. The strength of the conclusion goes beyond the strength of the premises.

2.2 The relevance to the conclusion of the characteristics cited in the premises

You might argue, for instance, that there must be life on other planets in our solar system. After all, they are similar to the Earth in so many ways: they revolve around the sun, their sole source of light; all are subject to gravitation; some revolve around their axis, giving them day and night like the Earth; and some have moons. With all these similarities, by analogy it is reasonable to assume they must be inhabited too. But despite this, these are not the most relevant conditions we would look for in a planet that could sustain life. Among others we would want to see a plentiful supply of water and a breathable atmosphere.

3. Differences

3.1 The differences among the samples cited in the premises

Usually the greater the number of differences between the instances used in the premises, the stronger is the conclusion. We are much more inclined to accept a conclusion if it is based upon instances drawn from many and different sources, rather than just one.

3.2 The differences between the samples cited in the premises and the one cited in the conclusion

Usually, the greater the number of differences the weaker is the conclusion. For example, a newspaper account of a speaker at a conference reported, 'He told the Conference last week that football hooliganism was exacerbated by press coverage. This was rather like blaming the Meteorological Office for bad weather.' It may indeed be true that in many cases newspaper reports had no influence on the activities of football hooligans, but the conclusion the report comes to differs in such significant and obvious ways as to make the argument untenable. As you can see the key difference which weakens the argument is that the weather cannot be influenced in its behaviour as football hooligans can by reading press reports of them and their behaviour.

With these six rules we are in a better position to check the reliability of the analogies we use and the extent to which they create convincing connections between the premises and conclusions in our arguments. With this, and having established that we have enough support for our premises, we can be confident that the quantity and quality of the evidence for our theory are convincing. This leaves just two final tests to check the truth of our theory: the internal and external tests.

■ 3. Internal test: is it an adequate explanation?

At this point you know that you have a theory that is consistently argued and for which you have convincing evidence. But we must be sure that it answers the question we set out to answer. It is all too easy to come up with an answer and develop an elegant, persuasive argument out of it, only to find that it fails to address all the important issues. So we have to check to see that it accounts for everything we want it to; that there are no exceptions.

To do this it helps to adopt a similar strategy to that which we adopted to analyse the implications of concepts in Chapter 2: that is to think about borderline examples that test the assumptions we have made. This allows us to see if there is any conflict with other ideas we might hold on this and related topics. We are likely to find that the truth of one assumption depends upon the truth of another, which we have taken for granted. This might be something which we have never had occasion to question, but there may be an unstated 'if–then' inference that connects it with one of the premises in our theory. We may suddenly discover that 'if' something is the case, 'then' something else is also the case and we are far from feeling comfortable with this as a consequence of our argument. This is a common experience for most of us: we commit ourselves to a position only to find, when we put it to the test, that there are unexpected consequences and problems which we will have to solve hopefully by simply adjusting our theory to take account of it.

At this point it's worth fortifying yourself against the temptation to be overly defensive. This is all too tempting for most of us. We have invested a great deal of time and effort into developing this theory, and we are pleased and excited with the results, so the last thing we want is to see it fail. But by putting it to the test in this way, it will become stronger and more convincing. Its success depends on how well it fits the cases to be interpreted, so look for borderline cases: examples that fit, but should not; and examples that should fit, but do not. You will need to play devil's advocate to give your theory the test it deserves. To help you in this, try working deliberately through the following steps each time you test yours or someone else's theory.

3.1 Playing devil's advocate

Step 1: Are there exceptions?

Even though you might have no obvious reason for doubting someone's arguments, play devil's advocate: ask yourself, are there exceptions to these?

For example, a politician might argue that 'All criminals come from socially deprived backgrounds.' If we were to think of an exception to this we could argue that we've all read in the newspapers about convicted criminals, who, on the contrary, have come from quite privileged backgrounds.

Step 2: If there are exceptions, are they general or specific?

2.1 Specific exceptions

If they are specific, then, while the politician can still maintain her claim, you've found sufficient grounds to justify qualifying it in order to take account of the special cases you've uncovered.

To return to our example, if the exceptions were just limited to one or two individuals from privileged backgrounds, she would have to qualify the original claim.

2.2 General exceptions

However, if you have found a general category of exceptions, then you will have to move onto steps 3 and 4.

Say you've discovered that most white collar and computer crime is, in fact, committed by criminals with university degrees. In this case the objection cannot be dealt with so easily: you will have to ask the following questions.

Step 3: Is the claim too strong?

If you have found a general category of exceptions you must first ask yourself: does this make the original claim too strong: more than the evidence can support? If it does, then the politician cannot maintain her claim: she must either rein it in, qualifying it in general terms, or abandon it altogether.

In our case the evidence can't support the claim, so, if she wants to maintain it, she must qualify it by excluding all white collar and computer crime. However, this might weaken and restrict it so much that it might be wiser to abandon it altogether, particularly when it leads you to suspect that you could probably find other groups, too, if you looked hard enough.

Step 4: Does it account for only part of the case?

Alternatively, if it can't be qualified, and there is sufficient merit in the argument to warrant not abandoning it, then the only thing she can do is to extend the claim to cover the general category of cases that is currently excluded. However, if this is possible, it is quite likely to lead to conclusions she either didn't see in the first place, or wouldn't agree with on the basis of her argument so far.

You might, for example, agree with the claim the politician has made, although question the notion that it is the 'socially' deprived who are the source of crime. You might argue that there are others responsible for crimes, who are deprived in different ways. They may never have been socially deprived, but they may not have had a stable father-figure in their lives: there may have been a family breakdown, or they may have been moved from one boarding school to another without ever being able to establish long-lasting paternal relations.

So, in this case the claim may be worth holding on to, but only in the extended form to cover this new category of deprivation. However, this may lead the politician either to conclusions she didn't foresee, or in a direction which doesn't serve the main purpose of her argument, which may have been to establish the claim that all crime can be identified with a particular social class.

Whichever is the outcome, whether you step off at steps 2, 3 or 4, you will have discovered for yourself that you have well-thought-out reasons for criticizing the theory and, if the theory is your own, you have uncovered ways of saving and improving it.

3.2 Saving theories

Of course, you may think that saving it in this way may just be an evasive strategy to avoid sacrificing a treasured theory which no longer deserves to be saved. In some cases this may be true, but, as we will see in Chapter 11 when we examine the way scientists deal with the problem, saving theories in some cases may be the only sensible thing to do, particularly if they are successful in explaining other things beyond the particular subject of dispute.

In these circumstances, inventing or adopting additional assumptions to take account of the borderline cases may be quite legitimate as long as two conditions are met. First, the additional assumptions should be testable, not couched in vague, indeterminate concepts that cannot be put to the test. For example, if we were to extend the concept of deprivation to cover the new categories of cases by defining it loosely as just all those who were not given emotional support at one time or another in their childhood, this may not give us the testable consequences we need to verify it. And, second, we may finally abandon the theory if it needs a large number of additional assumptions to save it, which leads us to believe there must be some simpler explanation.

■ 4. External test: is it coherent with our other ideas?

Finally, having assured ourselves that the theory itself is sound and answers the problem, we have to look beyond the theory to its relations with the other ideas we hold. We must check to see how it fits within the broad map of the philosophical ideas and systems of beliefs to which we find ourselves generally committed. In this we are no longer concerned with the theory's internal, but with its external, coherence: we need to ensure that it fits within a consistent and systematic body of ideas.

Let's say, for instance, that in your moral opinions you are a 'utilitarian', in that you believe your actions are right in so far as they tend to promote the greatest happiness of the greatest number. Now let's go one step further and say you are a 'preference utilitarian', in that you think the best way of achieving happiness is to satisfy the expressed preferences of people. This describes fairly accurately the position of the nineteenth century English philosopher John Stuart Mill, who argued that 'the sole evidence it is possible to produce that anything is desirable is that people do actually desire it.' Let's say you also hold another of Mill's beliefs, the importance of tolerance: that the individual should be allowed to exercise his rights and freedoms without interference from others who might disagree with him, as long as he does no harm to them.

Now you hear that a fascist group want to hire the local town hall so they can get their message across prior to an election. But you know that the preferences of the majority of local people are to prevent such racist propaganda. Thus you argue that the right thing to do is to prevent them using the town hall for their meeting. However, before you settle on this as the solution you must check to see if it is compatible with your other beliefs. When you do this you realize that you also have strong feelings against all those well-publicised cases in which individuals have been silenced because what they have had to say offended an intolerant majority. This means you must now re-assess your initial solution to see if there is a way of arriving at some sort of satisfactory compromise between your two commitments. Failing that, you may have to decide which in this case is more important.

No doubt you have experienced similar conflicts yourself, but it is all too easy to overlook the need to do this, particularly when you feel strongly about something. It's useful, then, in these situations to remind yourself of the *modus tollens* (denying the consequent) form of argument to check that you can live with the consequences of holding a certain view. Ask yourself, 'What if I am right, what follows?' If I am right that we should not tolerate opinions which the majority think are offensive, what are the implications? At this point use again our strategy of thinking up borderline, contrasting and doubtful cases – awkward cases that describe situations with which you would be unhappy.

First think of a borderline case. For example, you may be deeply offended by an advertisement, which you think should be withdrawn. However, this amounts to restricting the advertiser's freedom of expression: there is a conflict between this freedom and yours not to be offended. To resolve it you must look at both of these to see if one is more important than the other. You might conclude that while we all have the right to freedom of expression, we don't have a right not to be offended.

However, before you ditch one for the other, it will be wise to think of a contrasting case that helps you to analyse the concept of offence to see if there is a fundamental principle beneath it. In particular does offence amount to actual harm? If it does, you have a stronger defence of your right not to be offended, because this would amount to your right not to be harmed. You may want to argue that such offence causes you serious anxiety and stress, which, in turn, causes your blood pressure to rise to dangerous levels. Or the advertisement might target the social or ethnic group to which you belong, describing those who make up this group as lazy and untrustworthy, which makes it difficult for you and others to get jobs. In both these cases you can argue that a fundamental principle is involved, the freedom from harm.

Now you have a much clearer idea of the implications that lie behind the concept of offence, so apply it to a doubtful case in which it would be hard to accept its implications. Although you've discovered a fundamental principle this does not mean that it will prevail in all cases; it may come into conflict with other fundamental principles, which may be more important in that situation. So you have to be sure where the line is to be drawn; it may be that we have no right to be free from all harms that derive from offence. For example, in a democracy we place importance on the value of participation and freedom of expression. So, even though my blood pressure may rise to dangerous levels as I listen to a politician expressing opinions with which I disagree strongly, I have to accept this sort of harm.

As you can see in this example, many of the same strategies reappear when we ask ourselves the 'What if' type of question. We began by analysing the implications of the important concepts we use and we have finished with the same method as a check to see if our theory can fit within the coherent structure of our ideas. It may have seemed over the last three chapters that this is a complex system, but be reassured, it is not. The more you use it the more you will develop your skills and the more routine will it become. Nonetheless, it always helps to have a reminder of the stages pinned up in front of you. For this purpose I have listed below each of the stages as a simple reminder.

So, to summarize:

1. Hypothesizing: designing a solution
   1.1 Asking the best question
      - Pseudo questions: begging the question – loaded language
      - Questioning those things we take for granted
   1.2 Designing the best solution
      - What sort of problem is it?
      - What sorts of claims are involved?
      - Normative? Empirical? Non-empirical?
   1.3 Analysing the key concepts
      - The three-step technique
2. Testing for validity
3. Testing for truth
   3.1 Are the connections between our ideas true?
      - Sufficient and necessary conditions
   3.2 Is there sufficient evidence to support our theory?
      - Enough evidence
      - Credible connections – argument by analogy
   3.3 Internal test: is it an adequate explanation?
      - Playing devil's advocate
   3.4 External test: is it coherent with our other ideas?
      - Borderline, contrasting and doubtful cases

■ Questions

Analyse and assess the truth and validity of the following arguments.

1. 'Freedom of speech is obviously vital in a civilized community. But when a community is at war, and the basis of its civilization threatened, then freedom of speech has to be curtailed. We are a nation at war, and the war is the more insidious for being fought with words rather than bombs. Our most cherished institutions, church, family, and private property are under attack.'

2. 'Democracy must include not just the freedom to determine by one man one vote in elections every few years who governs the country, but also the freedom to determine how the resources of the country are distributed by how people vote to spend their money every day in the market place.'

■ Recommended reading

Carney, James, D. and Richard K. Scheer. *Fundamentals of Logic* (New York: Macmillan, 1974; London: Collier Macmillan, 1974).

Copi, Irving. *Introduction to Logic* (New York: Macmillan, 1978).

Russell, B. *The Problems of Philosophy* (Oxford: Oxford University Press, 1987), Chapter 6.

Skyrms, Brian. *Choice & Chance: An Introduction to Inductive Logic* (Encino and Belmont, CA: Dickenson, 1975).

PART I

Our Knowledge of the External World

If the cultural media is a reliable indicator, it seems we live in an age uneasy with certainty about anything. We seem more at home with complex accounts of simple things than we are with simple accounts of complex things. Gone are the vast expansive imaginations of people like Kenneth Clark and Jacob Bronowski, who charted man's achievements through the ages in TV series like *Civilisation* and *The Ascent of Man* respectively. Instead we seem more at home with a clever examination of simple things: a 20-part series on 'the telephone', 'war planes', or even 'office furniture'.

The same caution affects philosophy too. At times it may seem as if philosophers see themselves as gatekeepers to a difficult esoteric subject as they pursue complex technical examinations of seemingly insignificant details. At moments like this it's worth taking a step back and reminding yourself that this is a subject that draws its life blood from a plurality of visions, some analytical and sharply focused, others synthetic and expansive.

For instance, one moment in history when philosophers were possessed of this expansive vision and set aside their caution occurred in 1662, when the recently formed Philosophical Society in England was granted its royal charter to become the Royal Society. Its founding members boldly declared their intention, as sincere and honest witnesses, to share their ideas with open minds regardless of how unorthodox and shocking they might be.

Before this the world was seen almost exclusively through the lenses of traditional and religious authorities. But with the growing mistrust of these and the popular belief that modern humanity can progress beyond the ancients, philosophers set aside secular and divine authority and sought in their own reason and experience an alternative source of certainty.

This was the beginning of the Enlightenment which dominated European philosophy in the eighteenth century. With the decline of religious authority came a corresponding decline in the contempt for worldly things and an increasing determination to make the world a better place. The static conception of a divine immutable order, gave way to a new perspective in which societies were regarded as the products of the individual's free and creative will. With this came certain responsibilities: to gain a better understanding of the real world, to bring about greater individual happiness in stable societies, and to explore those factors that restrict the levels of individual liberty.

This called for a theory of certainty that relied not on traditional authority, but on individuals and their relation to the external world. Among other things it meant going back to ancient Greek philosophers, like Plato and Socrates, not for their answers, but more for the questions they posed as the starting point for modern deliberation. What was sought for was some test, a criterion of knowledge, by which we can evaluate our knowledge claims and extend our understanding. The central questions this raised concerned the role of reason and experience in generating knowledge, the relationship between knowledge and certainty, the possibility of universal scepticism, and the nature of truth.

Since the seventeenth century the answers to these questions have been found in a theory of the mind as a detached mechanism through which we can reveal truth either through our reason alone, or through its capacity to process experience. Uninfluenced by the context in which it works, it is the final arbiter, an honest broker of truth.

However, in recent times postmodern philosophers have emerged casting doubt on this account of knowledge as accurate representation made possible by certain uncorrupted mental processes. They ask not whether a theory is true, but what its cultural roots are. All knowledge, they believe, is socially constructed, all experience mediated by language and culture. Whatever the nature of the theory, whether it is science, history or religion, none is inherently better or worse than any other. Experience can only be evaluated by asking how interesting and edifying it is in terms of certain cultural agendas or how well it serves human needs, and not ranked in terms of a hierarchy of some supposed objective truth.

In the following chapters, these conflicting beliefs will be the background of our attempts to gain a better understanding of what we mean by knowledge and truth, and the role of reason and experience in developing accurate accounts of the external world.

You may find it helpful to have copies of the note structures for the following chapters by your side as you read them. These can be downloaded from our website at www.palgrave.com/foundations/greetham.

Knowledge

CHAPTER 5

Key issues

▶ What is knowledge?

▶ Is it justified, true belief?

▶ How are we to recognize when something is true?

▶ How can we be sure our true beliefs are not just inspired guesswork?

▶ What sort of reasons amount to justifications for our beliefs?

▶ Do we interpret experience and justify our beliefs through our own framework of ideas?

If we are to understand what knowledge is, we must begin from the same point as the philosophers in the seventeenth century. In other words, stripped of all our authorities to whom we might be tempted to go to answer the question for us, we must do exactly as we did in Chapter 2 and analyse the concept of knowledge. To do this, as we did then, we must conjure up examples from our own experience of how we use the verb 'to know', which will give us the material we need to answer the question, 'What does it mean to say you know something?'

Once you've done this you will no doubt find you have come up with examples like 'I know how to swim', 'I know Charlie Thomas from down the road', or 'I know you smashed that cup.' Each of these appears to be quite different. You learn to swim, as with any activity or skill, by continually doing it. But to know someone you only have to meet them once, unless that is we mean by this the altogether more exacting standard we imply when we say that we 'really know' someone. The same would appear to apply to the smashed cup, or any other event: assuming you know the meaning of 'cup' and 'smashed' you only have to see the event once to know that that is what has occurred.

But nonetheless, there may be a common denominator here. You might say that you have *learnt* to swim, but if, as a result, you say you *know* how to swim, this seems to suggest you can tell me how to do it. That is to say, you can give me certain propositions that you know to be true about swimming that will help me to learn to swim. The same goes for the second proposition, in that when I say 'I know Charlie Thomas' I mean that I know certain propositions about him to be true, and that once I have the evidence from the person in front of me confirming these propositions, I can say that this is, indeed, Charlie Thomas. As to the last example, this too appears to rely upon an unstated proposition, in this case that I know the proposition 'You smashed the cup' to be true.

If this analysis is correct, what we are looking for are the requirements we need to confirm that you know a certain *proposition* to be true. We will see later that Bertrand Russell in *The Problems of Philosophy* argues that we can in fact know things to be true by acquaintance immediately through our senses and not just as propositions. These he describes as 'non-mental' facts, because they have not been presented in the form of propositions at all, but in immediate, unprocessed sense data. We will look at this argument later in Chapter 8. For now we need to ask what knowledge amounts to in this propositional sense.

Rationalists place their primary trust in reason to reveal and justify truth. Genuine knowledge, as in mathematical and logical propositions, requires certainty. All such truths are derived deductively from a relatively small number of axioms and definitions known to be self-evidently true. This is what is generally thought to be the optimistic expectations of the three seventeenth-century philosophers most closely associated with rationalism: the German philosopher Gottfried Wilhelm Leibniz, the Dutch philosopher Benedict Spinoza and the French philosopher, scientist and mathematician René Descartes. Genuine knowledge about the world, they believe, can only be acquired through the application of reason in this way, and experience in the normal sense is at best misleading, if not irrelevant.

For a proposition to be true in this sense it must not only affirm its truth, but exclude the very possibility of it being false. When we first looked at propositions in Chapter 2, we found that this standard of truth could only be met by analytic propositions, which are true by virtue of their constituent parts. To understand the argument is to understand its truth. To understand the meaning of the proposition 'All bachelors are unmarried men', is to understand its truth, which lies in understanding the meaning of 'bachelors' and 'unmarried men', its constituent parts. However, empirical propositions cannot meet this standard: they cannot be known with logical certainty. So we need to ask ourselves whether we can really know these sorts of propositions to be true at all. That we do generally accept some empirical propositions to be true means that we must find an alternative criterion that will allow us to distinguish between those propositions that are true and those we regard as false.

One way of answering the question 'What is knowledge?' is to enquire into the state of mind of

Plato (c. 427–347 BC)

Born in Athens, Plato, along with his teacher Socrates and his student Aristotle, laid the philosophical foundations of Western culture. Plato is generally thought of as the creator of philosophical argument as we know it. After Socrates had been put to death in 401, Plato fled Athens and spent 12 years travelling. On his return he founded the Academy, for scientific and philosophical research, where Aristotle was one of his students. His fame rests largely on the *Republic* and the many dialogues, in most of which Socrates plays the role of a relentless questioner who systematically exposes as false the claims of his companions and students.

Plato developed a profound and wide-ranging philosophical system, subsequently known as Platonism. The key to this is his theory of forms. He distinguishes between the 'world of appearances', the object of mere opinion, where all our fleeting experiences belong, and the unchanging world of reality, the world of 'Forms' or 'Universals', the object of knowledge. This was not a world of contingency, but of ultimate and necessary truths. Knowledge, therefore, does not come from the world of appearances, but through recollection of the acquaintance we had with the forms before our immortal souls became trapped in our earthly existence.

someone who knows. This strategy was adopted by the ancient Greek philosopher Plato, who poses the question in *Theatetus*: what is the distinction between knowledge and true opinion or belief? One answer, he suggests, is that someone who knows, compared with someone who has true belief, has everything that the other person has, but something else as well. If you have knowledge you also have true belief, but the converse of this is not true: you might have true belief without having knowledge. You might simply have guessed correctly that something is the case, so you have in fact true belief. But you might not know until later; indeed, you might not even get to know at all.

In *Meno* Plato goes one step further by arguing that knowledge is 'true belief with an account'. And with this he makes what is thought to be the first reference to the traditional theory of knowledge as *justified* true belief. This means that John can only know X, if and only if,

1. John believes that X.
2. It is true that X.
3. John's belief that X is justified.

■ 1. Belief

Take a look at the first component of this trilogy. Belief you might describe as the subjective component. It's a psychological experience in that we have a conviction that something is the case without actually knowing it. For example, it is by no means unusual to hear the following type of dialogue, say, on your favourite TV detective series:

Detective: We know who did it. We just can't prove it. We've got no evidence.

Chief detective: Then how do you know he did it?

Detective: I just know. I have a feeling.

Like the detective we all believe a great many things which we cannot say we know. I might believe there is an afterlife, or there are other life forms in the universe beside us. But I cannot say I *know* these things. All that I can say is that I am convinced that this is true and as soon as I am no longer convinced that subjective conviction disappears. I cease saying that I believe it.

So, how important is belief to knowledge? As this is a subjective conviction it allows me to believe many things which I do not know to be true. Like the detective, I can believe that the suspect is guilty, although later the evidence might show he is in fact innocent. But the converse is not true: I cannot say I know things, which I don't believe. It would be odd for me to say, 'I know that, but I just don't believe it,' whereas I can ask 'I believe it, but do you really think it is true?'

It seems, therefore, if you go back to our discussion of necessary and sufficient conditions in Chapter 4, that belief that a certain state of affairs exists is a *necessary* condition for knowledge, but it is not a *sufficient* condition. There may be many propositions that I believe but don't know to be true, but none that I know but don't believe. Knowledge is not just a question of subjective convictions: it concerns an objective state of things. If that no longer persists, then what was knowledge ceases to be knowledge, regardless of what we might believe. This is what appears to lead the famous eighteenth century German philosopher Immanuel Kant to describe belief as 'a consciously imperfect assent'.

Even so, although this seems a perfectly sound analysis, it's worth testing it with a borderline example. Colin Radford, a British philosopher, gives us one that is familiar to us all. Say you are a nervous candidate in an exam. In the panic of the moment you produce all the facts you have been taught without actually believing the arguments you produce. To an observer you are producing exactly what you have been taught as the right answers, but can you be said to know them when you don't actually believe them? You have learned that these are the rights answers, so you produce them accurately, even though under the stress of the exam you cannot produce the grounds that might lead you to believe they are right.

This example certainly suggests you can know without believing, but there are a number of factors that weaken this interpretation. The most obvious is that there is at work here a rather curious idea of knowing. It suggests that by simply remembering things and spilling them out on paper you do in fact know them. Most students from an early age know that you can remember the most complex arguments accurately without understanding anything about them or having any reasons to believe them. To know something calls for more than remembering: it calls for justifications and judgements in terms of the relevance of the facts we remember to the wider network of our beliefs. Without this we might remember without being able to say genuinely that we know.

We might remember rightly that one of the causes for the rise in population in eighteenth-century Britain was the eradication of certain epidemic diseases, like the plague – the 'Black Death'. But we can only say we *know* this when we can show that our judgement, that it is a relevant cause, is justified by drawing upon our wider beliefs, like the plague periodically causing the death of 30–40 per cent of British and European populations during the previous 500 years.

What's more, in this case it seems the argument is that the candidate has only *temporarily* lost his normal beliefs, which have deserted him in the panic. By the same token, then, it would be reasonable to say that for the time in which he is temporarily deprived of his beliefs, he is also temporarily deprived of his knowledge. What he is left with is the simple task of remembering without relevance and justification. Even more interesting, it doesn't seem in fact that the candidate is totally without beliefs. He clearly believes these to be the right answers, although he may not believe they are convincing arguments that answer the questions satisfactorily. This experience is likely to be familiar to all examination candidates, who believe they know what the examiner wants, even though they are unconvinced by the answers themselves.

■ 2. Truth

This shows that believing is necessary to knowing something: it is a defining characteristic of knowing. But, by contrast, believing something is not a defining characteristic of something being true: we may believe something that is not true and something may be true even though no one in fact believes it. The proposition that the planet Neptune exists was true well before anyone believed it and, therefore, before it was knowledge.

And, of course, there are many other true propositions that we don't know to be true. Therefore, as with belief, truth is a necessary condition of knowledge, in that to know something is to know it to be true, but it is not a sufficient condition. That a proposition is true is not sufficient for us to *know* it to be true. The fact may be that we're just not in a position to know it to be true. Before the nineteenth century we simply didn't possess powerful enough telescopes to know that the proposition 'The planet Neptune exists' is true.

So it seems we can say that while belief is the subjective component of knowledge, truth is the objective component. At first, of course, this may sound odd; after all we hear all the time people saying things, like 'Well, that may be true for you, but it's not for me,' or 'In my opinion it's not true that most crime is the result of childhood deprivation.' However, comments like this can be misleading. Take the last one. When we hear people talk like this, in some cases it can be because they 'believe' the proposition is not true, but they cannot summon up good enough reasons to support their belief. So they confess to subjectivity as a way of saying, 'Don't ask me why I believe this, it's just my opinion.' It gets them off the hook of defending their opinion.

But the first type of comment raises a more interesting issue, in that it appears to confuse the *meaning* of what's said with its truth. We frequently make statements the meaning of which can only be fully understood by us from our own perspective, our own angle. So, for somebody else to understand our point of view they would have to try to see it from our perspective. But while the meaning of what's being said may be relative to the speaker, its *truth* is not. You might have made a personal statement about how you feel, the meaning of which is relative to you alone, but if it is true it is not just true for you, even though it is about you. You may describe to me the intensity of pain you feel and I may find this difficult to understand at all accurately, but if it is true that you feel this pain, then that is as true for me as it is for you.

Nevertheless, we do at times, and perhaps quite legitimately, say that we can see 'some truth' in a claim or an argument, which suggests that truth is not absolute and objective, but can be experienced partially and from a particular perspective. I suspect, though, that this only makes sense in those situations where we are presented with complex arguments composed of a number of integrated propositions, some of which we believe are true, but not others. So, in these circumstances it would be accurate for us to say guardedly that we see some truth in the argument.

What this means is that when we say truth is the objective component of knowledge, we are saying that a belief is true when it depicts things as they are, when its account of the world is accurate. So, beliefs are either true or they are not, and both alternatives apply equally and consistently to me and to you in any particular case. All philosophical accounts admit this much. But this still leaves us with the problem of how we are to recognize truth. And at this point differences begin to appear, both about the status of facts and how we are to know when we have portrayed the world accurately.

2.1 Certainty

One answer to both these problems is to say that we recognize truth when we are certain about the facts and that we have portrayed the world accurately. After all we hear people declare all the time that they know things with certainty. Unfortunately, as in so many cases, what is common use does not always make common sense. The word 'certainty' in such statements may only be used rhetorically, to give emphasis to the truth of what's being asserted. In terms of logic it adds nothing that is not already there. To say you know something is to say you know it to be certainly true. What's more, the word 'certainty' is not such a reliable benchmark. We can be certain about all sorts of things. We may have good evidence for a belief which we feel is certainly true, but which is in fact false. The problem here is that certainty is a subjective notion: we can have intense feelings of certainty about all sorts of things, which turn out to be far from certain. So, how are we to judge when our feelings are strong enough? About some things we may be totally convinced, while with others the scales may only have just tipped in that direction.

2.2 Rationalism

Unfortunately philosophers may not be of much help in solving this problem for you. They too have been divided about how strongly you must believe for it to count as knowledge. Rationalists, as we have seen, place their primary trust in reason to reveal and justify truth. Genuine knowledge, as in mathematical and logical propositions, requires certainty, and this can only be guaranteed through deductive reasoning from premises that are known to be self-evidently true. René Descartes, who is often described as the father of modern philosophy, is credited with having placed this epistemological question, 'How do I know?', at the centre of philosophy. Like the Enlightenment philosophers with whom we began Part I, he rejected the God's-eye view of the world, for one that was human-centred: the question worth asking was not 'What is the world like?', but how one could know what it is like.

His search for an answer had to have a foundation of absolute, unquestionable certainty, on which he could build all other truths. He found this in his awareness of his own self, in his famous 'Cogito ergo sum': 'I think therefore I am.' This is the foundation of his method of doubt, which we will look at more closely in Chapter 7. Descartes argues that even if I doubt my existence, in doing so I confirm it, because I have to exist to be able to doubt. With this immediate and indubitable data of consciousness as a starting point, he attempts to work out from this towards truths about the external world. If there is any way in which you can doubt what you believe, you don't really know it. The evidence must be so conclusive as to make it inconceivable that it be false.

2.3 Empiricism

In contrast, empiricists like the English philosopher John Locke in the seventeenth century, and Bishop Berkeley and David Hume in the eighteenth, accept that knowledge doesn't have to be absolutely certain in this way. Such certainty is restricted to limited areas, in particular mathematics and analytic truths. Beyond that our knowledge of the outside world depends on the evidence of our senses. Some empiricists accept that certain types of direct evidence of the senses have primitive authenticity: that is, they are immediately known to be true and certain, because they haven't been processed through our reason and imagination, which would make them prone to error. There are no grounds to doubt that your senses register a certain colour or smell. However, beyond this, empiricists accept that the general laws we derive from the evidence of our senses can only be justified inductively. For this, then, there can only be qualified assurance as we saw in Chapter 4.

Because of its close association with the scientific revolution of the seventeenth century and the continuing success of science, empiricism has tended to see the acquisition of knowledge in the same terms, as a cautious, piecemeal, self-correcting process which, like science, is limited by the possibilities of observation and experiment. In this context progress is made by building up our understanding from different perspectives, each one checking the other to avoid mistakes and to create a coherent picture of the world in which all the pieces fit together.

Obviously this calls for a more complex account of certainty measured against different competing criteria. In the next chapter we will analyse the implications of these for truth as measured in terms of certainty. One significant candidate, as we have seen, is coherence. We are likely to be more certain that a belief is true if it is consistent with our other beliefs. As a member of a jury you are more likely to believe what witnesses say if their evidence is consistent with that of other witnesses. If a witness relates a different story, which doesn't fit within the pattern already created, you are more likely to withhold your assent.

This becomes an even more compelling criterion if the coherent picture your beliefs create explains more than any alternative. In this case the belief that is more likely to be true is one that pulls your other beliefs together into a picture that explains the widest range of different phenomena. The Austrian philosopher Karl Popper explains that scientists prefer bold theories because they explain more and, therefore, can be tested more thoroughly. And, quite naturally, we're likely to have much more confidence in any theory that runs more risks of being falsified, and then subsequently passes those tests, than we are in a theory that explains less and doesn't run the same risks. Einstein's special theory of relativity was preferred to Newton's mechanics, because all the experimentally testable consequences of Newton's theory were also consequences of relativity, but not vice versa. For example, relativity predicts, among other things not predicted by Newton, that light rays passing close to a massive object will be bent.

Closely related to this is utility, the pragmatic criterion that if a belief is useful then we are more likely to believe that it is true. Obviously a bold theory which explains more is more useful than a weaker theory because it opens up new avenues of research and gives us greater knowledge of how to control the world for our own benefit. A belief that is true, say our belief in electricity, is likely to be one that helps us achieve what we want to, while a false belief, say a belief in magic and lucky charms, is one that doesn't have the same record of success.

However, although this seems quite compelling, it fails to account for a number of awkward borderline cases. We all know of beliefs that are true but are quite useless, while we also know of beliefs that are false but continue to be held because they are useful. It is in fact true that a snail can sleep for three years, that more people are killed by donkeys annually than are killed in plane crashes, and that women blink nearly twice as often as men, but it would be difficult to find any discernible use for such facts. Conversely we may in time find some way of demonstrating that the predictions of astrologers have no basis in fact, yet it would be difficult to deny their usefulness in easing the stress and anxiety of the many people who go to them for comfort and assurance.

■ 3. Justification

While this goes a long way to solving our problems over truth, we are still left with the question of justification. We can have beliefs that are true, but we still cannot claim to know on this basis alone. Belief and truth are necessary conditions of knowledge, but they are not sufficient. Something more is needed: we need to have some way of recognizing that our belief is true; we need to be able to show sufficient reasons for believing that it is true. Otherwise, it might be mere guesswork. At the weight-guessing competition at the local fête you might believe that the cake in question weighs five pounds fourteen ounces and you may be right, but you cannot say that you knew that. We need another condition to prevent such lucky guesses passing as knowledge. Either that or you have a certain skill that allows you to make these judgements with unerring accuracy. But in this case you would need to explain how you did it, the skills involved, which might then amount to the sufficient reasons you would need to claim this was knowledge.

For this to work, however, the reasons must support, or be evidence for, the truth of what you believe. They must have some connection that a reasonable person would accept. To return to an example we used in the last chapter, to convince you that the car we saw from my study window crash into the lamppost did so because I dropped my pen, I must establish a connection between the two events which you believe is reasonable if I am to claim that I know this to be true. By establishing such connections we explain to others why we believe these are good reasons. In the process they then have the opportunity to point out reasons why they are unconvincing.

Even so, this still leaves hanging the question about what we mean by 'good reasons'. What we seem to be looking to evaluate when we listen to the justification that others give for the truth of their beliefs is the quality and quantity of the evidence and reasons they give. In other words, on the one hand you want to know whether the connection I make between the light reflecting off the falling pen and the distraction this causes the driver who crashes into the lamppost is a reliable connection. Do we know of the same connection in similar events, when accidents have occurred as a result of people being distracted by sudden flashes of light? On the other hand, if we are content that this is a reliable connection to make, we must also ask how much evidence there is of similar accidents occurring. Although we might be able to imagine something like this occurring, it might never have happened before.

3.1 Quality

With the first problem concerning the quality of the connection I have made between the two events – whether it is reliable – we have to decide, even though I am sure of it, whether I am *entitled* to be sure. The British twentieth century philosopher A. J. Ayer explains that the difference between the man who knows the lottery numbers and one who is merely guessing is that 'to say that he knows is to concede to him the right to be sure, while to say that he is only guessing is to withhold it.' Usually we say that someone is entitled to be sure or that they have a right to know, after they have followed one of the accredited routes to knowledge, which involves them in meeting certain standards.

But what are these standards? As we saw in Chapter 3, in logic, and the same is true of mathematics, if you can give a valid proof of your argument, then you have met the standards necessary. This is the highest of standards, in which we argue that the reasons for my believing a proposition must *entail* the truth: that is, they must amount to sufficient conditions for the proposition to be true. But if *entailment* were to be the standard we need to reach, everything we take to be knowledge outside mathematics and logic would fail to meet it, including all of our empirical beliefs. They would not meet the standard of sufficient conditions for the truth of our beliefs, because to do so would exclude the possibility of them being false. And, as we have

already seen in Chapter 4, empirical propositions cannot exclude this possibility: they can only provide probable support for our beliefs.

We acquire our empirical beliefs from all sorts of sources, from our own perception, our own memory, from the testimony of others, including those whom we have never met, like historical sources, to scientific laws, which as we have seen may be based upon impeccable sources, yet cannot exclude the possibility that they are false. You might want to argue passionately that you have no grounds to doubt that you saw a ghostlike figure walk through the wall and into your bedroom, but even if you possess 20/20 vision, if the light was perfect that evening and you hadn't touched a drink in weeks, it might still be true that you don't really know. With past events, for which you are reliant upon your memory, the position is even less certain. We all like to claim that we have good memories, but when we are pressed for details like a witness in a courtroom we can easily be filled with reasonable doubt.

So, should we abandon our claim to know and call it something else – that it's reasonable to believe P, or that we are confident that P is probably true – and leave the sense of knowledge, meaning entailment, to logic and mathematics alone? In this weaker sense of justification, our evidence for the truth of P will not meet the standard of sufficient evidence, allowing, therefore, the possibility that P might in fact be false. What's more, we are no longer describing something objective, but merely describing our mental state, that we feel justified in believing something with varying degrees of assurance. However, although this more cautious approach might seem the most reasonable solution, it might exclude too much which we are quite willing to accept as knowledge.

For instance, there may be cases in which we know something, but we just cannot explain how we know it. At times we come across people with an impressive record of successfully predicting the outcome of sporting events. If they are sufficiently impressive at this we may say, 'She just knew it was going to win', even though she has reached her prediction by no recognized method. At times we're inclined to describe such success as resting on intuition, or in other circumstances as involving telepathy, but whichever way we describe it we are merely disguising the fact that we have no recognizable way of explaining it.

Take the well-known example of the chicken-sexer. There are apparently people who can identify with remarkable accuracy the sex of new-born chicks just by feeling them, but they cannot explain how they do it. Yet it is clear that when they decide one chick is male and another female we are inclined to say they 'know' this, because of their record of success. The question is, then, what standard are we to adopt? Are we to say they really don't know the sex of chickens, because they can't explain how they do it, or are we to say that given their incredible success rate they do in fact know it? In other words, should we say that someone has justification only if they can give an account of it, or should we say that all that is necessary for someone to know something is that there is in fact a justification regardless of whether they can explain it or not?

Ultimately this question may reflect an altogether unnecessary distinction between *what we know* and *what we know we know*. As the British philosopher Roger Scruton points out, 'if it is ever true that someone knows anything, it does not follow that he also knows that he knows.' We could say that the chicken-sexer is entitled to be sure, that he or she has the right to be, simply because of a record of success. In these circumstances, where there is no recognized usage we are free to decide ourselves.

3.2 Quantity

But that still leaves open the question of how much evidence we need to be justified in saying someone knows something. What rate of success do chicken-sexers need to achieve to be able to say that they know the sex of chickens and are not just guessing?

3.2.1 All the evidence

One answer would be to say that we need *all* the evidence, a complete account, before we can say we know something. This would exclude the possibility of guesswork, because we would exclude the possibility of falsehood entirely. In effect we would be saying that there is nothing more I or anyone can uncover that would cast the slightest doubt on the proposition. As long as there is any evidence I don't have that might contradict the proposition, then I cannot say I know it. So, on these grounds we would not be entitled to say that we know the sun will rise tomorrow, that when I see my wife next she will recognize me, or that when I drop my keys they will fall to the ground. If there is a possibility, however remote, that any of these propositions

could be contradicted by the evidence, we cannot say we know.

Of course the problem with this standard is that there would be very few propositions we could claim to know, even quite normal, everyday claims. Someone might ask you if they can borrow a book from you and you respond by saying, 'Yes, it's in my bookcase; I've just looked at it.' But, even though you have just looked at it, you cannot say you know it is there, because it is possible that while your back was turned someone might have removed it.

What's more, it's always possible to find more evidence for something, so we could never have *all* the evidence. To know that this is the book that you promised to lend to someone, you would have to view it from all possible angles. And as there are an infinite number of angles this would simply not be possible. In effect there would be no end to gathering the evidence you need to meet this standard. Yet, if we cannot hope to collect *all* the evidence and, therefore, cannot exclude the possibility of our beliefs being false, it seems we must conclude that we really don't *know* all of those beliefs we routinely use in our daily lives. Indeed, we would have to give up our claim to know anything outside of a small number of mathematical, logical and analytic truths.

3.2.2 All the evidence available

This standard seems too strong for the way we use the verb 'to know' in our ordinary lives. Normally we would accept a weaker standard that allows us to say we know something even though we don't have conclusive evidence for it. However, by adopting this we not only allow for the possibility that our beliefs may be false, but we cannot exclude true beliefs that are based on guesswork. So, our standard must be high enough to exclude as much of this as we reasonably can. One way to set a high enough standard might be to say we must have all the evidence *available*. But, as you can see, for this to work it must include one more criterion: it must set limits that are reasonably clear; we must know how much evidence is sufficient. Even if we had all the evidence available, this still might not meet even our weaker standard.

3.2.3 Adequate evidence

So, if it makes little practical sense to set our standards at *all* the evidence and it's too vague to seek *all the evidence available*, we are left demanding that we must have *adequate* evidence for us to know. The problem here is that this appears to be circular: knowledge, according to this, amounts to believing propositions to be true if we have 'adequate evidence that we know'. In effect we are defining knowledge in terms of what we need to know something. It doesn't get us very far. But as with all problems which appear circular it's worth unwrapping the concepts we use by asking that most nagging of all philosophical questions: 'But what do you mean by ...?' In this case, what do we mean by 'adequate'?

3.2.4 Probability

One way of answering this question, while avoiding the circularity of the last answer, which defined adequate evidence in terms of knowledge, is to add something to true belief to give us knowledge, which doesn't in itself presuppose knowledge. Defining adequate evidence in terms of probability might be one way of doing this. We might say that a certain amount of evidence is adequate because it makes the truth of a particular claim highly probable. This reflects what most of us do when we assess the sufficiency of the evidence we are presented with in our normal everyday lives. But, even so, we have to be clear what sense of probability we are using: statistical, inductive or absolute.

By the statistical sense of probability most of us mean some calculation of relative frequency. In this form probability statements tell us how frequently a given proposition or event occurs in a given class of things: how often cases of lung cancer occur in a group composed of smokers. But how does this help us define what we need to justify those of our beliefs that are true and are, therefore, knowledge?

If you know a certain proposition to be probably true in this sense, then you know that it is a member of a class of propositions a significant majority of which have a certain property, which means they are true. Given that it is a member of this group there is a high probability that your proposition too possesses this property and, therefore, is one that you can say you know to be true. But what is this property? It seems the only one that will work to answer our question is the property of being known to be true. But this doesn't get us very far. All we seem to be doing is begging the question: we are presupposing the very thing we're trying to find.

What about inductive probability then? We saw in Chapter 4 that probability in this sense refers to certain logical relations which hold between propositions. We also found that inductive arguments are invalid because they draw universal generalizations from only a finite series of singular observation statements: after viewing a thousand cases of black crows you conclude that *all* crows are black. But in this context this doesn't matter because we have already conceded that we can't be certain in the strongest sense. All we are claiming here is that propositions are related in such a way that given one, another is likely to occur rather than not.

For example, we could say the proposition 'John will die from lung cancer' is probably true in relation to 'John has been a heavy smoker for 30 years and a large majority of those who have been heavy smokers for 30 years die from lung cancer.' In other words, if it is true, the last proposition gives good inductive support to the first proposition. But this does little more than shift our problem on: now we have to ask what makes a good inductive argument, which we assume will also in turn make a good justification for our true belief.

Even so, this is closer to the sort of interpretation we generally place on the word probability in our normal lives, although more often than not when we make calculations of probability we usually do this implying the absolute sense of probability. In other words, when we say that 'In all probability it will rain tomorrow', we are saying that it is more probable than not in the inductive sense, *given all that we know to be true*. We know that certain signs are good indicators that it will rain and we know what the experts, like TV forecasters and professional meteorologists are saying. So, a proposition is probably true in this sense if it is probable in the inductive sense in relation to all these propositions we know to be true. But, as you can see, like the definition in terms of adequate evidence, this is circular: we have to use the concept of knowledge (those propositions we know to be true) to explain the concept of absolute probability. Given this, like the other forms of probability, we cannot use the concept of absolute probability to complete the definition of knowledge.

3.2.5 Good reasons

What we are left with, therefore, are the weak and strong senses of the verb 'to know'. We might have good reason for believing something, but we don't have sufficient reason: that is, although we have good reason, this might still be compatible with it being false. If indeed the proposition is false, then you didn't really know it in the first place. You might have believed it with good reason, but you didn't know it. So, while in the strong sense knowledge must consist of a true belief that is backed by absolutely conclusive evidence, in reality we are rarely, if ever, blessed with this. What we are left with, then, is the weak sense of knowledge: that is, true belief that is backed by, if not adequate evidence, then good reason. Even though what you believe to be true turns out to be false, you had a compelling good reason for believing that it was true.

This is familiar to all of us who have observed a courtroom scene. As a juror you might have good reason to believe the evidence of witnesses, but they could be lying or mistaken. Even though the evidence for the defendant's guilt is overwhelming, you cannot know this in the strong sense, in which nothing could be discovered that could make a difference. In the film *Twelve Angry Men*, juror number 8 holds out against all the rest who are absolutely convinced that the defendant is guilty. They cannot conceive how he could doubt the man's guilt, yet he does and eventually chips away at the evidence until they all come round to his way of thinking. If good reason is the answer to our question about justification, then something is justified if it survives our prolonged and persistent questioning. We can never know it to be true conclusively in the strong sense, but we can know it to be true in the provisional, weak sense.

However, this shifts our question onto slightly different ground. If a belief can be known to be true only after it has survived our prolonged questioning, we have to be able to say when we have questioned it enough, or at least distinguish between reasonable and unreasonable doubt. We can go on questioning long after we have carried out all the tests we could have asked for. The sceptic would say that by making this distinction between reasonable and unreasonable doubt we are assuming too much. We should doubt everything, they would argue, even the physical world. While scepticism is indispensable in challenging dogma and beliefs too easily accepted under the influence of authorities, there seems little point in scepticism for the sake of scepticism and not for the sake of truth. For people

who think this way doubting is a game, rather like the footballer who runs at defenders with amazing dribbling skills, but never passes to the other members of the team. Such players do it for the thrill of using their skills and not to win the game.

■ 4. Are the three conditions sufficient for knowledge?

Finally it's worth asking whether these three conditions (justification, truth, belief), even when they are fulfilled the best they can be, are sufficient to establish knowledge. In his famous 'Gettier examples', the American philosopher Ernest Gettier described a number of counter-examples where a belief was true and an agent was justified in believing it, but the justification did not relate to the truth in the right way, leaving it as relatively coincidental or a matter of luck that the belief was in fact true. If I see you driving a Porsche this might lead me to believe you own a Porsche. In fact you do, so my belief is true and justified, but on this occasion you were in fact driving a friend's Porsche, therefore I don't know that you own a Porsche, because this is only coincidental to my evidence.

The result of this has been a debate over the kinds of condition that might be substituted to give a better account of knowledge, or whether all suggestions would meet similar problems. Another American philosopher, Gilbert Harman, responded with the 'No false lemmas principle', arguing that the incorrect connection in the Gettier examples comes about as a result of the person's chain of reasoning passing through a false step. He argues that similar cases can be constructed in which there is no false step.

The problem with both of these arguments might lie in their dependence on the internal reasoning of the individual to account for when a belief is justified. Roger Scruton points out that we might be better adopting an 'externalist' perspective: that is we should cease thinking about knowledge in the first person, which leads us to confuse whether I know P to be true with the question whether I have adequate grounds for believing P. As he points out the concept of knowledge is designed to distinguish reliable from unreliable beliefs and is applied to endorse the epistemological capacities of the knower, rather than to evaluate his or her reasoning.

■ 5. Conclusion

Throughout this chapter our concern has been to check our beliefs against reality, so that we can identify when they amount to knowledge and not mere guesswork. This sounds simple enough: a matter of common sense. But it may not be so simple. We may be assuming too much. Postmodernists question how it is we can in fact have independent access to reality in this way.

Seen through the eyes of a modern observer, the medieval church in Bertold Brecht's play, *The Life of Galileo* (1943), seems rightly criticized for its refusal to accept the truth of Galileo's theory that the Earth, along with all the other planets in the solar system, revolved around the sun and not the sun around the Earth, even going so far as to force him to withdraw his theory in 1633 under the threat of excommunication. From our perspective they were wedded to a particular world-view, which prevented them from seeing the truth. But, by contrast, from their perspective the evidence for their world-view seemed overwhelming for anyone standing at any point on the Earth and looking skyward. And, of course, it was supported by all the authoritative opinion of the time. Yet, in fact, what was believed to be knowledge we now know was nothing of the kind, because it was untrue.

Even so, like the medieval scholars who believed that man was made in God's image, inhabiting the Earth at the centre of God's creation, we too accept a body of beliefs backed by experience and authority. Like them we are convinced that our beliefs satisfy the truth conditions we set and their objectivity is assured by procedures through which we can correct for all our subjective interpretations. But can we really be sure that we know any more than they did, or that our own beliefs are not the result of a similar over-arching frame of reference? As we walk along a windswept English headland and come across the crumbling remains of a Gothic church or abbey, we may look back 700 years and wonder at the superstition and ignorance symbolised in these remains. But who's to say that in 500 years time people roaming the same headlands will not come across the relics of our own civilization, the crumbling remains of a radio telescope perhaps, and wonder at our own superstition and false beliefs?

Of course, we assure ourselves that we can be confident in the openness of our scientific institutions and procedures, which allow for criticism and self-correction, unlike the unaccountable religious authorities of medieval societies. Scientific theories must submit to the possibility of falsification through experimentation and public scrutiny, so we're assured that we're not trapped by our beliefs as were medieval scholars. But still our openness doesn't threaten the structure of our beliefs, which remains undisturbed. We are confident that what we take to be knowledge, in the major theories that guide our research, is indeed knowledge.

As this suggests, knowledge needs more than facts: it needs a framework of beliefs and ideas through which we can interpret and make sense of experience. In medieval societies this meant a picture of an ordered universe arranged in a fixed system of hierarchies. Everything had its place in this great cosmic scene. E. M. W. Tillyard compares it with 'a gigantic game where everything is included and every act conducted under the most complicated system of rules.'

But we too depend upon a framework through which we can interpret experience and justify our beliefs by connecting them with other beliefs that we already accept. It is not so much that we are checking our beliefs against reality as against the framework of accepted beliefs. As we have seen the truth requirement is separate from our need to have good reason, so it is always possible that we may be no better off than our medieval predecessors. As the Nobel prize-winning scientist Sir Peter Medawar describes it, 'The purpose of scientific enquiry is not to compile an inventory of factual information. ... We should think of it rather as a logically articulated structure of justifiable beliefs about nature. It begins as a story about a Possible World – a story which we invent and criticize and modify as we go along, so that it ends by being, as nearly as we can make it, a story about real life.' The question then to ask is, is this an independent 'real life' or one inescapably bound by our own inventions?

■ Questions

1. Are we right in thinking that knowledge has foundations? If we are, what are they?

2. Outline one account of what knowledge is? What are the arguments for and against this account?

3. Can I think I know something?

4. Is knowledge a certain kind of superior belief?

5. Is there a difference between believing something and imagining it?

6. How can we be sure our true beliefs are not just inspired guesswork?

7. What sort of reasons amount to justifications for our beliefs?

■ Recommended reading

Plato. Theatetus. In Irwin Edman (ed.), *The Works of Plato* (New York: Tudor, 1927).

Plato. Meno. In *Plato: Protagoras and Meno*, trans. W. K. C. Guthrie (Harmondsworth: Penguin, 1956).

Ayer, A. J. *The Problem of Knowledge* (Harmondsworth and Baltimore: Penguin, 1990).

Phillips Griffiths, A. (ed.) *Knowledge and Belief* (Oxford: Oxford University Press, 1967).

Audi, Robert. *Epistemology: A contemporary introduction to the theory of knowledge* (London: Routledge, 1998).

 The note structure to accompany this chapter can be downloaded from our website.

Truth

Key issues

▶ How can some propositions be synthetic and true *a priori*?

▶ Are such truths evidence of an unchanging ultimate reality? Or are empiricists right that any talk of substance or ultimate reality is unintelligible?

▶ Is Kant right that knowledge begins with experience, but doesn't end there? That the *a priori* element is derived not from the world but from us?

▶ If something is true does that mean there is a correspondence between what we believe and an independent reality?

▶ Or is a statement true if it is coherent with others?

▶ Do we perhaps mean by truth that which is useful: anything which allows us to accomplish what we want to?

▶ How can we resolve the self-referential nature of the correspondence theory, which results in tautology and paradox?

In the last chapter we described truth as the objective component of knowledge, in that a belief is true if it depicts things as they are; when its account of the world is accurate. In this sense a proposition is equally true for you and for me, regardless of our subjective and differing opinions. Indeed, it is true even though *neither* of us believes it.

All philosophical accounts admit this much, but that is not to say that they all see a useful role for truth in our attempts to understand the world. Along with other postmodernists, Richard Rorty argues that we can usefully dispense with the notion of truth, which represents merely a lingering surrogate for the God we once worshipped. To fill the void, we have invented and now pursue the metaphysical fiction of truth, where once we pursued God. 'Truth', he argues, 'is what your contemporaries let you get away with ... no area of culture, and no period of history, gets Reality more right than any other.' On the other side there are those, like the twentieth-century British philosopher Bernard Williams, who argue that truth and truthfulness, and their twin virtues sincerity and accuracy, are indispensable to any human society. As we search for an answer to the problem of how we are to recognize truth, how we are to know when we have portrayed the world accurately, both of these perspectives will come sharply into focus.

1. Necessary and contingent truths

In Chapter 2 we drew the distinction between two different types of truth: empirical and non-empirical. In particular we explained the important distinction between necessary and contingent truths. A proposition that is necessarily true holds for all cases at all times: it is impossible to deny it without self-contradiction. In contrast a contingent proposition, if true, could have yet been false: it can be denied or asserted without self-contradiction. These we found were logical distinctions, in that their implications for the way we go about finding the truth of them depend upon the meaning of the words that make them up. In contrast, the epistemological distinctions, like *a priori* and *a posteriori*, denoted the way we come to know the truth, whether we verify it through intuition or experience.

This was made even clearer by the other logical distinction between analytic and synthetic propositions. This is a *semantic* distinction in that it denotes two ways in which the truth of a proposition is determined: by reference either beyond itself to the real world, or to the meaning of its constituent words. We found that the truth of analytic propositions is determined either by their logical structure or by virtue of the meaning of the words used in them, which guarantee their truth. Propositions like 'Either this is a pen or it is not a pen' and 'The head of paediatrics is the same as the head of paediatrics' are guaranteed to be true by their logical form alone: 'Either X or not X' and 'A is A' respectively. In contrast, the proposition 'A mother is a female parent' is true by virtue of the meaning of the words we use: all we are doing is exchanging synonyms – 'mother' for 'female parent'. If we were to replace 'female parent' with 'mother' we would transform it into a simple truth of logic: 'A mother is a mother'. The proposition 'All nieces are female' is similarly a truth of logic, although in this case the predicate, 'female', is only a partial analysis of the subject, 'nieces'.

In passing, it will not have escaped your attention that these propositions can seem empty and vacuous. When propositions say nothing about how things are in the real world and are true independently of the way things are, they are said to be *tautologies*. As you can see from the examples above, tautologies are true solely by virtue of the logical operators or the 'truth-functional connectives' ('and', 'or', 'if–then') used to construct them, rather than because things are in the real world as they are said to be in the proposition. They are not refutable because they are in fact trivially true. Whatever the content, and they may have no content at all, it is irrelevant to their truth, which is established by the logical form involved.

A representative of the Brewer's Association recently declared that, 'There's always been an association between drink-associated problems and drinking itself.' This cannot be refuted. Indeed it doesn't matter what you substitute for the words 'drink' and 'drinking'; as long as they are consistent with each other, the sentence will always be true. Daniel Taylor gives us another example where a newspaper correspondent explains group violence in terms of 'group psychological intoxication'. As he suggests, the explanation could probably never be tested because if there is no group violence doubtless there will be no 'group psychological intoxication'. It seems, then, that this is being used as a synonym for group violence and is therefore merely trivially true.

But beyond this, all propositions that are not analytic are synthetic; that is their truth or falsity cannot be determined by the meanings of their constituent words or by their logical form alone. To claim that a synthetic proposition is true is to claim that one of two mutually exclusive, but logically possible, states of affairs is actually the case. As we have said before, to deny or affirm a synthetic proposition is not self-contradictory. It could be both true and false that 'The head of paediatrics is a woman', that 'My mother has two brothers', and that 'Most deaths from lung cancer are the result of heavy smoking over long periods.'

2. Kant and synthetic *a priori* truths

Given this distinction between analytic and synthetic propositions, the obvious question is: if a proposition gives information about the real world how can we know it to be true, except by reference to the real world? In Chapter 2 we said a synthetic *a priori* proposition is not shown to be true merely as a result of the analysis of its constituent words or its logical form. It explains something about the world of experience (synthetic), and yet is known to be true independently of experience (*a priori*). And we cited examples like,

Every event has a cause.

Parallel lines never meet.

A straight line is the shortest distance between two points.

To these we could add others, like 'Whatever has shape has size', and 'You can't be in two places at the same time.' Their negation is not self-contradictory – they are not analytic – yet their truth is independent of experience, because we accept no experience as a refutation of them. As we said in Chapter 2 we may not be able to find a cause of an event, but this doesn't lead us to claim that it is uncaused.

That this sort of knowledge exists has troubled philosophers for centuries and it still does. We all know that appearances are deceptive; they cannot always be relied upon. And we're used to the idea that today's beliefs are likely to be proved wrong or inadequate as science reveals more about how the world really is. It's not unnatural, therefore, to suppose that at the end of this search lies an ultimate reality, a hard core of truth beneath the successive layers of mere appearance, similar to stripping away the successive layers of an onion until you reach its core.

This was a common enough assumption among pre-modern philosophers with the metaphor of the onion recurring again and again. Plato distinguishes between the 'world of appearances', the object of mere opinion, where all our fleeting experiences belong, and the unchanging world of reality, the world of 'Forms' or 'Universals', the object of knowledge. This was not a world of contingency, but of ultimate and necessary truths. For many, like Plato, this metaphysical world of reality could only be found in the next supernatural world, the properties of which could not be revealed, or only very dimly, in this world.

To the philosophers of the Enlightenment, however, such talk was deeply unsatisfactory. With their growing mistrust of traditional secular and divine authority, they sought a new theory of certainty in their own reason and experience, relying on the evidence of their senses and their direct relation to the world of appearances. Isaiah Berlin points out that for the Enlightenment philosopher, 'Propositions are either certain and uninformative or informative and not certain. Metaphysical knowledge which claims to be both certain and informative is therefore in principle not possible.' In other words, either propositions were necessary

and analytic but said nothing beyond their own terms, or they were contingent and uncertain but said something about the real world.

The questions that empirical philosophers like David Hume and John Locke asked of themselves were: what sort of material was it that the mind was supplied with and what use did it make of it? According to Hume the material consists of perceptions, which he divides into two types: impressions and ideas. Impressions, he argues, can be relied upon for their accurate representation of images of the external world conveyed through our senses, or of passions and emotions we directly feel. But ideas are fainter and weaker, because they come to us only as a result of reflecting upon the emotion, or the impressions of the object which is no longer present.

He concludes, then, that all 'objects' of human reason – the material – are naturally divided into two kinds: relations of ideas and matters of fact. Relations of ideas, the products of reflection, are intelligible because they express relations between ideas that we can see to be true, either intuitively or demonstratively – that is we can reveal their truth by formal proof as in mathematics or logic. As for matters of fact these are even more straightforward: they are intelligible because they can be tested by experience and observation. But beyond this no other concepts can be intelligible, because there is no way of testing their validity.

So, as for the ideas of pre-modern philosophers like Plato, and the metaphysical notions of ultimate reality and 'substance', which is supposedly the stuff of ultimate reality, these are simply unintelligible, because we're unable to define them in terms of something we know about. If our knowledge about the world is restricted to experience and the inferences we draw from it, we cannot possibly tell if there is any permanent structure to reality that exists beyond what we are aware of. And, conversely, if the qualities of immediate experience, like colour, taste, sound and smell, are excluded from being features of the world of substance, which supposedly exists independently of us, then we cannot possibly conceive of what it is like.

However this is a more disturbing thought than it might at first appear. If there is no unchanging ultimate reality all we are left with is the shifting sands of the world of appearances. Hume concludes that without some permanent metaphysical reality we cannot really be certain of the continued existence of the external world when we are no longer perceiving it. Indeed nothing in our experience suggests our impressions even belong to objects existing outside our experiences, although it might be convenient to assume that they exist. The individual cannot even confirm that he perceives a continuous 'something' that he can call 'himself', beyond a continuous series of impressions one replacing another in rapid succession. As for the existence of other people, they too are little more than 'a bundle or collection of different perceptions, which succeed each other with an inconceivable rapidity, and are in a perpetual flux and movement.'

So, if modern philosophers like Hume are right, how can we claim that anything is necessarily the case, beyond propositions that are analytically true? In other words, how can we claim that there are synthetic *a priori* truths, like the proposition that every event has a cause? After all, we cannot see a cause, only impressions of objects in the external world, or what we assume are objects. Indeed, for many this was the most disturbing of all Hume's conclusions: that all we see is one separate event following another, and if we see it often enough we assume out of habit or 'gentle custom' that the first event must cause the second. As a result of the 'constant conjunction' of two events occurring one after the other, we assume that the first causes the second. The necessary connection that we argue exists between a cause and effect is nothing more than the product of the mind.

Hume was a mere 18-year-old when this 'new scene of thought' came to him and he began his most famous work, *A Treatise of Human Nature* (1739–40). Described by A. J. Ayer as 'the greatest of all British philosophers', his disturbing influence was felt throughout Europe. Most notably it was felt by Immanuel Kant, a little-known German philosopher who had spent his whole life in the small provincial university town of Königsberg, where he pursued a routine life organized with such precision that we are told local housewives would set their clocks by him as he passed their windows on his afternoon walk followed a few paces behind by his old devoted servant, Lampe, carrying his umbrella in case of rain.

Then, in 1781, at the age of 56, after reading Hume's account of causation, he was awoken from his deep 'dogmatic slumber' to embark on his first significant work, *The Critique of Pure Reason* (1781), and so began a decade of philosophical work unrivalled in the modern world. Realizing that Hume was right, that necessity doesn't exist in the external

Immanuel Kant (1724–1804)

The son of a saddler, Kant was born in Königsberg, where he went to school and later to its university. After a number of years teaching privately he went back to take his master's degree in 1755 and was subsequently appointed an instructor at the university. He thereafter settled down to a quiet, routine life of study. He never married and never travelled more than forty miles beyond the limits of the town.

After he was appointed to the chair of logic and metaphysics in 1770 there began his 'critical' period. In the space of just ten years, after being awoken by Hume from his 'dogmatic slumber', he experienced what he described as his Copernican revolution and completed three critiques that revolutionised modern philosophy: *The Critique of Pure Reason* (1781), *The Critique of Practical Reason* (1788) and *The Critique of Judgement* (1790). The effect was to liberate modern philosophy on the one hand from enthralment to the empiricism of Berkeley and Hume, in which it appeared the only explanation for the apparent order in our understanding of the world was the habitual processes of the mind, and from Cartesian rationalism with its dependence upon clear and distinct ideas and the belief that we are all born with certain innate ideas.

world but is merely a product of the internal realm of thought, Kant experienced what he describes as his 'Copernican Revolution'. As Copernicus removed the Earth from the centre of creation, so Kant removed the earthly experience of our senses, making it peripheral to the active processing of the mind.

Kant agreed with empiricists, like Hume, that knowledge begins with experience, but, he argued, 'although all our knowledge begins with experience it does not follow that it arises from experience.' We understand the real world 'not through our perceptions but through our conceptions', not through our impressions but through our intellect. What is known is affected by the act of knowing, or as R. G. Collingwood describes it, '"knowledge" means both the activity of knowing and what is known.'

In arguing thus Kant was making the disturbing claim that the *a priori* element in our knowledge does not derive from the real world; it is of our own making; it's the way we come to know the world. We only know that things have certain properties and relations because we ourselves have put them there in the act of coming to know them. It would be like growing up wearing red spectacles and seeing everything in terms of varying shades of red. You could never know the world any differently, but only as shades of red. If you were a commercial fisherman trawling with a nine-inch net and you knew nothing else about fish but what you saw in your net, you would come to the conclusion that fish smaller than nine inches just didn't exist.

Synthetic *a priori* truths, then, are not true by virtue of their logical form alone, nor are they dependent upon empirical information for their truth. The equation $7 + 5 = 12$ is not true analytically, because more information is contained in the predicate (12) than is to be found in the concepts 7 and 5. In combining the two into one sum we process the information, creating something new in the conclusion: the sum of 12. The same can be said of other synthetic *a priori* truths. The concept of a straight line does not contain in itself the idea that it is the shortest distance, but the statement is, nevertheless, necessarily and universally true. And the same is true of the proposition that every event has a cause.

In this lies Kant's most strikingly novel insight, because we simply cannot know these true propositions in any other way. This is just the way the mind processes experience. So, what was for Hume

'gentle custom' was for Kant the unavoidable process of the mind. But for both there were two worlds: one knowable, the other not. The nineteenth century German philosopher Arthur Schopenhauer believed this was 'Kant's greatest contribution to philosophy ... the distinction he made between the real world and the phenomenal world.' On one side was the 'noumenal' world, the real world, consisting of 'things in themselves', which could never be known to us. And on the other was the 'phenomenal' world or the world as known by the mind, a product of experience and *a priori* conditions supplied by the mind. Experience provides the content, the mind the form.

But of what does this form consist? Kant argues that the mind is so constituted that everything we are presented with is processed through certain 'forms of intuition' and 'forms of understanding'. Forms of intuition consist of two types of *a priori* characteristics that we impose on what we process: temporal and geometric features, like space and time; and the truths of mathematics. Typically this includes judgements like A being larger than B, A preceding B, or A being north of B. Forms of understanding consist of those principles and concepts through which we organize data to create intelligible information. Kant identifies three types: quantity (all, some, many, none and so on); quality (positive, negative); and 'categories', through which we impose a general conceptual scheme on data to order and relate them. One category is causation so that events are presented to the mind in a net of causality (see pages 119/120).

As a result Kant sets the boundaries to valid thought beyond which lies only illusion and contradiction. There is no way of knowing whether this mental apparatus can be extended beyond the phenomenal world to build a bridge to the noumenal world. Any attempt to accomplish this he believes ends in error and confusion, what he describes as 'antinomies' or paradoxes: that is, conclusions that can be both proven and disproven. Any attempt to discover the world-in-itself, to prove the existence of God, or any other metaphysical goal goes beyond what we can know. Thus the pinnacle of our achievements is confined to discovering the conditions that regulate the phenomenal world.

Finally, one last thing worth noting before we leave the synthetic *a priori* is that the distinctions we have drawn here clarify some of the underlying conflicts between rationalists and empiricists.

While rationalists accept that there are synthetic *a priori* truths, empiricists believe true propositions can only be either analytic and *a priori* or synthetic and *a posteriori*. Indeed, some of the most interesting and perennial problems in philosophy find their source in this distinction.

■ 3. Theories of truth

Our search for an answer to the problem of how we are to recognize truth, how we are to know when we have portrayed the world accurately, now has the makings of a solution. Kant argues that although we cannot know the noumenal world, the phenomenal world at least conforms to the way the mind works. We therefore have a valid link between thought and reality because the world we think about is the product of our thinking and our experience of it. Reason has been enthroned as the judge of whether our representations of the world are right.

But that's not quite the end of the problem. When the Enlightenment faith in universal human nature began to wane in the nineteenth century, so too did faith in the validity of this link between the phenomenal and noumenal worlds. As a result we are now more willing to embrace the scepticism of Hume, that it is not reason but 'habits of the mind' that give rise to our ideas of the world; that reason provides neither a source for ideas, nor even a way of confirming we've got it right. Indeed in our postmodern world many are drawn to the relativist line that there are only different people with different perspectives each trapped within their own world-view.

3.1 The correspondence theory of truth

So, what are we to make of this? How are we to recognize truth? The most sensible place to start is with our everyday understanding of truth as agreement with the facts. We assume as common sense that truth involves a relation between two things: a reality composed of things and states of affairs, which forms the basis for truth; and our beliefs, which must portray these real things as they are if they are to be true. Truth, then, amounts to an agreement between what we believe and an independent reality. To make a true statement is to report accurately the way reality is: if we say we

believe 'Snow is white', this is true if and only if snow *is* white.

This view resembles the 'correspondence theory' of truth, in which a statement is true if it 'corresponds' to reality, to the facts. It is often described as an objective, *ontological*, or logical theory. Any argument can be said to be ontological if it infers that something really exists, in this case an objective independent reality. In contrast there are subjective, psychological or *epistemic* theories, which seek to define truth in terms of a subjective belief state: truth is the quality of our subjective convictions. Subjective/epistemic theories conceive of knowledge only as a special kind of mental state, or as a disposition, or as a special belief characterized by its history, or its relation to other beliefs. Therefore, they set out to produce a criterion of true belief.

As opposed to this, the correspondence theory is an account of what truth is. It is not about how we find out whether our beliefs are true or false, nor is it a procedure for developing true beliefs. This would be more like the question we considered in the last chapter: a question of justification – how we find out whether or not our account of reality is accurate. For the correspondence theory, beliefs are about the world: they portray it in a particular way. And they are true or false in so far as the world is like this or it is not. For those who want to make a sharp distinction between the knower and the known, the correspondence theory makes most sense.

But if we resort to our philosophical method again and do what we did in the previous chapter, we have to ask what is meant by 'correspondence' in this context. In what sense does a true statement correspond to an actual state of affairs? For example, one way we use the word 'correspond' is to say that a picture corresponds to a scene or a sketch to a person's face. We say that the artist has captured the likeness of the person, that the picture resembles her. Of course the most exact form of this sort of likeness is that of a photocopy of a document, but this isn't the sort of correspondence we are considering here. The correspondence between a statement and reality involves processing the evidence of our senses into words and sentences. The photocopy involves no processing of this type: it is simply an exact reproduction in the same form.

Maybe, then, it's like the sort of correspondence between a colour chart and the paint we choose for our home? Although exactly the same colour, it still involves some processing as we try to enlarge the

Table 6.1 Theories of truth

Objective or ontological theories	Subjective or epistemic theories
Correspondence theory	**Coherence theory** – truth as consistency. **Pragmatic/instrumentalist theory** – truth as usefulness.
Truth as correspondence with the facts.	Truth as a property of our state of mind or knowledge or belief.
The possibility of error or doubt implies the idea of an objective truth which we may fail to reach.	Truth is the quality of our subjective convictions. It is what we are justified in accepting in accordance with certain rules or criteria e.g. reliability, success, strength of conviction, inability to think otherwise. Therefore, the theory should produce a criterion of true belief.
Allows us to say the theory or statement may be true, although nobody believes it – and even though we have no reason to think it is true. A theory or statement may be false even though we have good reasons for accepting it, which would be self-contradictory from the point of view of the subjective or epistemic theory of truth.	Conceives of knowledge only as a special kind of mental state, or as a disposition, or a special belief, characterized by its history, or its relation to other beliefs. While coherence or consistency are no criteria of truth, since consistent systems may still be false, they do establish falsity.

small patch of colour and imagine it on our walls. But even this doesn't work. The colours, while they might not be exact, are still essentially the same sort of thing, whereas the evidence of our senses is transformed into words and sentences as we try to 'paint' an accurate picture. Words and sentences are not the same thing as the evidence of our senses.

Instead of resemblance, then, we seem to have in mind a more complex form of processing, the sort we refer to when we describe something. A fact has a structure which we represent in words and sentences. In his 'picture' or 'projection' theory, Ludwig Wittgenstein argues that basic statements representing the atoms of experience are a picture of reality combining components in the same relation as those in the fact they picture. Thus, a complex reality that combines objects related in a certain way is pictured by corresponding sentences in which nouns are related to each other through verbs, adjectives, prepositions and conjunctions.

Yet still the problem with this is that it involves correspondence between two quite different things: on the one hand features of the outside world, and on the other sentences composed of relations between words. A single unit of language corresponds to a discrete fact in the world. But it is far from obvious how this works. Our language is ruled by certain meanings and conventions, which determine the way we apply words and sentences to the outside world. We share certain assumptions in our language about the facts in the world and how we represent them. So, when we describe a situation, we are in effect carving up the world into identifiable facts: we are making judgements about it in accordance with the conventions that rule our language. So, not only are words not similar to the things they represent, when we use them we import all sorts of judgements about the thing we are trying to describe. If this is right, facts are not something external and independent of language. Indeed, they are bound up in language in a much more complex way than the correspondence theory suggests.

And even if we could assume that there was an independent reality, it's not at all clear how this correspondence would work in all cases. A sentence doesn't translate in this way into objects and relations in the real world. Indeed, words and sentences may change, but the meaning itself could remain the same. What's more, it seems this relationship works only with empirical statements. It doesn't, for example, work quite so well in cases where there are no simple existence statements. We know analytic truths are true *a priori*, but they don't seem to correspond with anything. The same is true of the type of claims made by historians, particularly counterfactual claims of the type 'If the Napoleonic Wars (1793–1815) had not occurred, the Industrial Revolution in Britain would have developed in an entirely different direction.' In these cases there is no reality to correspond with. So, not only does it seem that there is no such thing as a fact that can be picked out independent of the language we use to describe it, but there also seems to be no such thing as a statement that by itself is capable of corresponding with anything.

3.2 The coherence theory

If our common-sense understanding of truth as correspondence with an objective reality struggles to work, we may have to turn to subjective theories. You will remember that these set out to produce a criterion of true belief. They describe truth in terms of a subjective belief state that we must experience to know something to be true. As such they collapse one of the three characteristics of knowledge (truth) into another (belief), and in so doing they leave themselves open to the weakness common to them all, that it is possible to believe something, even fervently, and still for it not to be true. All of the staff of a bank may be convinced that Mr X was the man that committed the robbery, but it might be revealed later that he couldn't have done it, because he was at that time a thousand miles away undergoing an operation.

What this shows is that, unlike the correspondence theory, these theories appeal to all those who prefer not to make a sharp distinction between the knower and the known. The coherence theory, for example, argues that a statement is true if it coheres, or is consistent, with other ideas and beliefs. One idea is to be preferred to another if it coheres with a wider system of beliefs. So, for instance, idealists believe there is no independent reality. All we can know are ideas. Knowledge consists of ideas and nothing else. So there is no such thing as non-mental facts – facts that exist independently outside the mind. Consequently, the

only way we can recognize truth is not in relation to some independent objective reality, but in our ideas as they form a coherent system of beliefs with our other ideas. Our aim should be to discard all those ideas that fail to fit until we have pieced together the largest possible picture of the world, which we can then describe as reality, even though we cannot assume there exists an independent world.

'Absolute idealists' believe that anything short of the 'whole' can only aspire to degrees of the truth, sometimes described as 'degrees of the truth theory'. A single proposition can only be an approximation to the truth. Indeed Hegelian philosophers (named after the nineteenth-century German philosopher G.W.F. Hegel) believe that we cannot understand what any part is without already seeing how it fits into the whole. To understand something it is not enough to understand it in isolation: we must also know all its manifold and complex relations with other things.

As you can see, this does make a lot of sense. Part of the way we ascertain the truth of statements is to ascertain the truth of other statements and argue deductively or inductively for the truth of the original. Knowledge, then, does amount to statements forming a coherent complex of interrelated statements. But we have to be clear what we mean when we say that statements must be consistent with each other. If we mean they must not contradict one another, this may not be clear enough. With this meaning two statements can be consistent and have nothing whatever to do with each other. If I were to state 'there is a pen on my table' and 'George Bush won the presidential election', neither of these contradicts the other. And even if I were to discover that Bill Clinton had won instead, this would still make no difference to my statement about the pen. But at the other extreme, if we were to define consistency to mean that one statement entails (logically implies) another, as in 'I am a bachelor, therefore I am an unmarried man', this would seem to draw the definition too tightly.

A more convincing case may be made out for saying that statements are consistent if they don't contradict one another and are mutually supporting. One may not necessarily entail the other, but they just give evidence for each other. This is more like the criterion which scientists employ. As we saw in Chapter 4 we never have enough evidence to support the universal claims of a theory, so the only way to decide whether a theory might be true is whether it is coherent with what we already believe. A friend's personality may change overnight and he becomes sullen and incommunicative. Someone might suggest that this all points to him being abducted by aliens; after all, millions believe this is possible. But this conflicts with a vast body of scientific evidence which we have come to accept, so we search for reasons why that explanation is probably wrong: he's just been overworking lately; he's under stress; or we've just been imagining things. Scientists respond in the same way if their theories, backed by overwhelming evidence, are contradicted by new evidence.

Yet even so, this still doesn't meet the standard that we need for truth. Although all the witnesses in a murder case testify that they are certain the defendant is guilty, this still only *points* towards the truth; it doesn't *establish* it. It's still possible that they were all mistaken. In the history of science new theories have often struggled to be accepted in the face of established theories which most scientists prefer to believe. And this has been true even though they were later to be accepted, bringing greater coherence and explaining more than the theories that preceded them. In 1915, when the German meteorologist Alfred Wegener developed the theory of continental drift in his book *The Origin of Continents and Oceans*, most geologists of the time and, indeed, over the next 50 years, refused to believe it. For the previous hundred years or so, geologists had assumed that the continents were fixed in position, and they could not accept this new theory, even in the face of overwhelming evidence.

So, it seems, ultimately what makes the evidence statements of witnesses and scientists true is their correspondence to the facts. The very idea of error and doubt implies an objective truth, which in presenting our evidence we may fail to reach. Coherence can only *point* towards the truth, without it being what the truth of a proposition consists of. The defenders of the correspondence theory accept that coherence is a way of determining whether a statement is true, but deny that truth is *just* coherence. It is a necessary, but not a sufficient condition: for this coherence would have to exclude the possibility of a proposition being false. Indeed, we saw in Chapter 3 how an argument could be valid and, therefore, coherent, yet be false. In the same way two opposing systems of belief could both be equally coherent, but they cannot both be true.

If coherence is only part of the answer, we must look at other theories to see if they can provide a more complete account.

3.3 The pragmatic theory

One attempt to fill the void originates from the philosophical movement known as *pragmatism*. This is an almost exclusively American movement, most notably associated with Charles Peirce, John Dewey and William James. James believes that the truth of a statement can be defined in terms of the utility, the practical usefulness, of accepting it. Something is true if it allows us to accomplish what we set out to accomplish; if it helps us achieve our objectives. So, the theory of electricity is undoubtedly true because it helps us to achieve the many goals we daily set ourselves, whereas false beliefs are those, like the belief in lucky charms, which have a doubtful record of success. For example, James believes that belief in God is true because such a belief 'works satisfactorily in the widest sense of the word.' It's more likely to make us optimistic and happy about life, giving our lives meaning and purpose, which means it is a much more useful belief than those of an unbeliever, who is always uncertain about life.

Pragmatists, then, believe that an important indication of the truth of a belief or theory is its usefulness, that it 'works'. But what does it mean to say a belief 'works'? Things like appliances, cars and tools can be said to work, but it's not so clear what we mean when we say that beliefs work. We can test appliances to see how they work, but how can we test beliefs to see if they work? Of course, we might say a belief works because it is confirmed by the actual state of affairs, but this merely collapses the pragmatic theory into correspondence.

But perhaps the analogy with mechanical appliances is not a good match. More helpful might be other ideas we can be said to use, like 'programmes': exercise or diet programmes. Many of these are based on theories of what makes a good

> **Brief lives**
> **Peirce, Charles S**
>
> Dates: 1839–1914
> Born: Cambridge, Massachusetts, USA
> Best known for: Being one of the founders of pragmatism, although he also made important contributions to logic.
>
> Major works: *Collected Papers of C. S. Peirce* (8 vols 1931–58).

diet, and we all talk about these in terms of how well they work. The problem with this sort of talk, however, is that we are also inclined to say things like, 'That diet worked for me, but not for my friend.' This would suggest that it is true for me, but not for my friend. But if it is true it should be true for all. It would be odd to say that 'It's true for me that bicycles have two wheels, but not for most people.'

Nevertheless, despite these difficulties, in one sense we do appear to accept the usefulness of an idea as a key indicator of its truth. In science, as we have already seen, we cannot prove a theory to be true on the basis of evidence, because it makes universal claims for which we only have limited evidence. Yet we do accept theories if they have resisted all attempts to falsify them and, more important for this discussion, if they have greater explanatory power than their rivals. Kepler's theory of planetary motion was succeeded by Newton's theory of mechanics, and this, in turn, by Einstein's more inclusive theory of relativity. Their rivals also might have survived every attempt to falsify them, but if they are more limited in what they can explain, then the more inclusive theory with greater explanatory power will be adopted.

Yet although scientific theories replace one another in this way, this still doesn't show that truth is equivalent to usefulness. Some theories are false even though they are undoubtedly useful. For example, the Ptolemaic system of astronomy continued to dominate men's thinking right up until the sixteenth century, mainly because of its accuracy and usefulness. It was immensely successful as a method of preparing tables of the positions of the planets. Yet Ptolemy (AD 85–165) believed that physics was irrelevant to astronomy, so the physical reality or unreality of the planetary motions was beside the point: astronomy was a matter for mathematicians, not physicists. In his system the Earth was the immovable centre of the universe, with the sun and other heavenly bodies revolving around it in circular paths. Beyond the Earth and the planets was a crystal sphere to which were attached the 'fixed' or immovable stars.

The twentieth century, too, has seen false ideas being accepted as true within political ideologies because they have the practical value of promoting and protecting the interests of those in power. In the 1930s the Nazi government in Germany exploited the more extraordinary anthropological theories to lend weight to official state doctrines on the supremacy of the Aryan race over all others. And in the 1930s and 1940s, the genetic theory of the Russian agronomist Lysenko so suited the Soviet authorities' needs that they eagerly denounced the scientific establishment as obstructive and elevated 'Lysenkoism' to 30 years of supremacy with the most disastrous results. The theory that the characteristics acquired by parents through their own efforts could be transmitted to their offspring was thoroughly discredited in the eyes of reputable scientists long before Lysenko, but it was useful to the Soviet government, because through it they could claim that work to improve society is even more valuable than generally thought because it improves the heredity of future generations.

As you can see from this, the argument that truth can be defined as what works, what is useful, presents problems that are difficult to overcome. Probably for this reason modern pragmatists, like Rorty, have tended to sidestep the need to account for truth, concentrating instead on the origins and nature of our beliefs and their relations with emotions and needs.

3.4 The semantic theory

It is not difficult to see the recurring problem in each of these subjective theories: that in collapsing truth into belief we are no longer able to exclude the possibility that what we deem to be true may in fact be false. And any theory of truth needs to meet this standard. For this reason we have found ourselves coming back at each stage to the correspondence theory. But one of the most difficult problems preventing us from accepting the correspondence theory was that our sentences are composed of language, which is ruled by certain conventions through which we smuggle in judgements as we carve up the world into statements of fact. What we present for acceptance as the truth already contains assumptions of its adequacy as the truth. It is, in other words, self-referential. And any self-referential statement runs the risk of either being a trivially true tautology or a paradox.

The history of philosophy is full of many interesting and amusing paradoxes. A paradox is usually composed of a pair of statements, each with strong reasons for accepting them, but which cannot both be true. So an absurd conclusion appears to result from perfectly acceptable ways of thinking. One of the most interesting examples which has troubled philosophers for centuries is the 'Liar's paradox'. If someone were to say 'I am lying', then if what he says is true, he is lying and what he says is, accordingly, false. Therefore the statement is both true and false at the same time: if what he says is true, he is speaking falsely; and if what he says is false, he is speaking truly. Something clearly has gone wrong here. Some philosophers believed that this was neither true nor false, just ungrammatical, improperly formed and, thus, meaningless.

At the end of the nineteenth and early twentieth century there was a growing concern for this sort of paradox in philosophy; look only at the work of the Reverend C. L. Dodgson (Lewis Carroll), the author of the Alice adventures. Yet the concern for language went wider than this. With the democratization of society, greater social mobility and the emergence of popular culture, the rule of middle-class values began to wane. Novelists had lost their common currency of values in which to develop characters in the full expectation that the reader would understand their beliefs and reactions to situations. So, traditional characters disappeared and along with them the plot as a product of the interaction of characters. Without this common currency, a predictable sequence of events containing a confident blend of symbols, ideas and interactions was beyond the traditional novelist. The world became ultimately unintelligible, and novelists, painters and musicians retreated into the one possible source of certainty: their own inner world of emotions and feelings. The novel became an exploration of self, an emotional autobiography.

But if we believe that all we can ever really know is our inner personal states, then the outside world can only ever be a product of our own consciousness and this is incompatible with the public language we need to express it, whether in music, painting or literature. Any art built upon exclusively personal experience is in danger of having no anchor in a common, shared reality, its flotilla of symbols adrift with no charts. And with no common, shared reality, there can be no hard distinctions between what is real and unreal, what is true and false. As Samuel Beckett argues, in our world 'all reality, all language seems to have become disjointed, to fall apart, to empty itself of meaning'.

A similar concern for language and meaning preoccupied philosophers. Logical positivists believed that if language could be cleaned up and canons of meaningfulness could be established, not only would logical paradoxes disappear, but along with them many of the traditional metaphysical problems. Although Wittgenstein was not a member of the 'Vienna Circle' of logical positivists, he too shared similar ambitions: in his *Tractatus Logico-Philosophicus* (1922) he declares, 'The book deals with the problems of philosophy, and shows ... that the reason why these problems are posed is that the logic of our language is misunderstood. ... what can be said at all can be said clearly, and what we cannot talk about we must pass over in silence.'

Out of this concern in 1944 came the 'Semantic Theory of Truth' developed by the Polish-American philosopher Alfred Tarski. In helping us avoid the self-referential nature of the correspondence theory, some philosophers, including Karl Popper, have concluded that this is a version of the correspondence theory, but it is in fact quite different. First we ought to remind ourselves of the distinction between semantics and syntax. Semantics is concerned with the relations between the symbols we use and what they represent in the world, whereas syntax is only concerned with the relations between the symbols and can be dealt with independently of what they represent.

So, in order for us to avoid the self-referential problems of the correspondence theory and of paradoxes, like the liar's paradox, Tarski's method enables us to talk about two quite separate things in our sentence: statements, the meaning of which we must first understand, and the facts to which they refer. Having accepted that truth is synonymous with 'correspondence to the facts', he uses language to set up a correspondence between statements and the facts that our language picks out in the world. Whereas the correspondence theory accepts that

Brief lives
Tarski, Alfred

Dates: 1902–1983
Born: Warsaw, Poland
Best known for: Developing the semantic theory of truth as a solution to the problems raised by the correspondence theory.

Major works: *Logic, Semantics, and Metamathematics* (1956).

Ludwig Josef Johann Wittgenstein (1889–1951)

A lover of American movies and real-life crime magazines, this Austrian-born English philosopher is probably the most charismatic, if not, as many believe, the greatest philosopher of the twentieth century. After studying logic with Bertrand Russell at Cambridge in 1911 he wrote his most famous work *Tractatus Logico-Philosophicus* (1922), during the First World War, while a prisoner of war. The subject matter of empirical science, he maintains, is simple, unrelated facts. Thus, the purpose of language, which has a structural similarity with what it describes, is merely to state these by picturing them. All other uses of language, including metaphysics and ethics, are nonsensical.

However, despite his earlier belief that he had solved all the major problems of philosophy, during the early 1930s he abandoned the doctrines of the *Tractatus*, arguing instead that there are just different language games, social activities serving different purposes. Although he would allow none of his work of this time to be published during his life, it was later published in *Philosophical Investigations* (1953), along with *Remarks on the Foundations of Mathematics* (1956), *Philosophical Grammar* (1974) and *Philosophical Remarks* (1975).

the facts are already there independent of our language, Tarski's theory explains that it is language itself that sets up the correspondence between the two in the first place.

For example, to know that the sentence 'Seven plus five equals twelve' is true, we must first understand the meaning of each of the words in the sentence. Only then can we go on to establish whether it is true. In other words we must know two things independently of one another. In fact I couldn't even know what it would *mean* for the sentence to be true, unless I knew what the words in the sentence meant. In this case we do know the meaning of the words in the sentence, and we also know that the sentence is in fact true. But now consider what would happen if we were not able to separate these two things, as in the self-referential liar's paradox. If the very meaning of the sentence

depended on it being true we would be locked in a circular trap.

Tarski's way of presenting the problem is to box the sentence:

> This sentence is false

As we've just seen, before we can know what it means for this sentence to be true, we must know the meaning of the sentence. But the sentence merely means that it is false, and we have no way of knowing what it would mean for it to be true. For us to know what it would mean for this to be true (let alone whether it *is* true or not), we must first understand its meaning, but to understand its meaning we must first know what it means for it to be true. It is, therefore, meaningless, which accounts for the fact that we reach the paradoxical conclusion that if the boxed sentence is true, then it is false, and if it is false, then it is true.

To identify these two things and avoid this sort of self-referential problem, we need a language that can do two things: speak about the statement, and about the facts to which it refers that make it true or false. This is Tarski's 'metalanguage': a semantic language that can speak about both the statement and the fact, in contrast to a syntactical language, which can only speak about the statement. He argues that we must set up rules of 'satisfaction' in our language according to which our sentences become true or false. When we set out to establish correspondence, we are not just using language to create meaningful sentences, but to specify the relation of the language to the world, so that we can establish whether the sentence corresponds to the world and, therefore, is true or not.

So, let's be clear. A metalanguage does two things: it *identifies* in a sentence a class of things – say events, objects, states of affairs, 'facts' in general – and it also *identifies* which individual 'facts' in the world will 'satisfy' the sentence: that is, make it true. For example, the sentence '"John called" is true' belongs to a metalanguage, in that it sets up a correspondence between the sentence and an individual fact in the world (in this case an event), that 'John called'. In contrast, a syntactical language is only an object language: it can only speak about the object and not about the facts to which it refers.

Rather than identifying sentences and their parts, it merely *uses* them. For example, the sentence 'It is true that John called' belongs to the same language as 'John called'. So a metalanguage *identifies* both the statement and the facts to which it refers; a syntactical language merely *uses* them.

Clearly, as Popper suggests, there are distinct similarities between this and the correspondence theory: there is still something outside the language that makes sentences true. But the difference is that the semantic theory doesn't insist that this something already exists as discrete, identifiable parts of reality: it is itself defined through language in its stipulative role identifying those facts that make our statements true. Even so, there is work to be done in showing exactly how this stipulative role works.

■ 4. Conclusion

Throughout this chapter you have no doubt found yourself being swayed first by one account then by another. If you have ended up believing that truth is a special kind of belief that is well founded, you will have to come up with some kind of criterion of well-foundedness to distinguish between those beliefs that are well founded and those that are not. Alternatively you may agree with pragmatists like Rorty, who believe that we're not in the business of mirroring the world accurately at all; thought is for coping, not copying. Language is constantly adapting to allow us to do what we want to do, nothing more.

But if this is the position you adopt think about Simon Blackburn's argument that those who create maps indeed help us to cope, but they do so because they represent the world accurately. If we catch a train, the timetable enables us to cope because it is a correct representation of the times of the trains' departures. There is a special kind of success, he argues, in science, history, mapmaking and timetabling that goes beyond common agreement or finding something that works: 'there is such a thing as getting it right.' When scientists and historians work, there is a sense of discovery, a sense of making things intelligible by uncovering the truth about how things really are. But still could not this insight of intelligibility also be merely the subjective realization that what we have discovered fits with what we have already come to accept as true?

■ Questions

1. Can we argue that it is a necessary truth that something exists? Is there anything which necessarily exists?

2. What particular problems are there with the idea that there are synthetic *a priori* truths?

3. What is wrong with the argument that a belief is true if it corresponds with an independent reality? Why is it thought that this results in tautology and paradox?

4. Is Richard Rorty right, that what we accept as truth is nothing more than what our contemporaries allow us to get away with; a way of representing our own social practices as 'reality'?

5. Explain why coherence is a necessary but not a sufficient condition for something being true?

6. Does the concept of truth merely amount to that which is in our interests to believe, because it is useful in helping us achieve what we want to achieve?

7. Explain Tarski's solution to the problems posed by the self-referential nature of the correspondence theory.

■ Recommended reading

Kant, I. *Critique of Pure Reason* (1781) (London: Dent, 1993).

Hume, D. *A Treatise of Human Nature* (1739-40) (London and New York: Dent and Dutton, 1966).

Dancy, J. *Introduction to Contemporary Epistemology*, (Oxford: Blackwell, 1985).

Kirkham, R. *Theories of Truth* (Cambridge, Mass: Massachusetts Institute of Technology Press, 1992).

Rorty, Richard. *Philosophy and the Mirror of Nature* (Princeton, NJ: Princeton University Press, 1979).

White, Alan R. *Truth* (New York: Doubleday, Anchor, 1970).

 The note structure to accompany this chapter can be downloaded from our website.

Scepticism

Contents

Key issues

▶ How do you know you are not hallucinating or dreaming that you are reading this book?

▶ How do you know that you have not been abducted by aliens?

▶ Who is to say that we can in fact rely on our sense impressions from *wherever* they are derived, waking life, dreams or hallucinations? How do we know that what we take to be our waking experience is not part of another more inclusive and even more coherent dream?

▶ The question we face is not just 'what is the world like?', but 'how one could know what it is like?'

▶ Is your mind the only thing that exists?

▶ How can you be sure you did not spring into existence just five minutes ago?

▶ How do we know that our claims to know things are nothing more than what our contemporary culture accepts as knowledge? Or do we make these claims simply because they fit in with the rest of our beliefs?

We began Part I of this book by drawing attention to the importance of the Enlightenment in ushering us into the modern world where knowledge is empirical and its methods depend largely on observation and experiment. The principles that Enlightenment philosophers were applying were those developed by the supporters of the new scientific method in the seventeenth century. The starting point for the new sciences was a thorough scepticism about anything that wasn't based on experimental evidence.

The authority of classical texts, which had flourished during the Middle Ages, encouraged the application of *a priori* 'natural' principles to explain events without reference to empirical evidence; principles like the assertion that the 'natural' path of heavenly bodies, in their search for self-fulfilment, was necessarily circular. The work of the German astronomer Kepler, the Danish astronomer Tycho Brahe and Galileo all contradicted these 'natural' principles, in the process accumulating a mass of evidence to support their theories. They contributed to a process that ultimately saw the abandonment of the medieval world-view in favour of one built exclusively on the measurable aspects of the universe given through our senses.

This, of course, was not without its dangers, as Galileo discovered in 1633, when the Inquisition condemned him for teaching the Copernican system and forced him to recant his views on pain of excommunication. And the threat persisted despite the cautious and conservative approach of the new science. Its supporters hoped to reassure those in authority that modern science was grounded on simple truths that anyone could understand; that it harboured no preconceptions; and that it was not seeking to create a theory of the whole, an integrated account of the world. Indeed in terms of modern science, to develop such a theory would involve taking up a standpoint outside the world, which would render itself unintelligible to those in the world. Therefore the question of the whole of things was abandoned in favour of piecing together one by one beliefs that were supported by empirical evidence.

Nevertheless, even though the results were conservative, the real impact was to be felt in the revolutionary nature of the method, which deified the principle that individuals, through the solitude of their own reason and experience, were capable of discovering for themselves what was true. In this lay the real challenge to religious and secular authorities, who had been the traditional intermediaries bringing truth and knowledge. But equally, and with some irony, it extends beyond this to the new scientific methods themselves. For, once the genie had been let out of the bottle, there was no putting it back: if you could direct your scepticism at the ideas and principles advocated by traditional authorities, because they are not supported by the evidence of your senses, it could equally be directed at the evidence of your senses itself.

How do you know that such evidence can be trusted? At this very moment you believe that you are reading this book, but who's to say that you are not mistaken in this? You may be hallucinating or dreaming that you are reading this book. All that you have to rely on is the evidence of your senses, but when we dream our experiences can be just as real and vivid, so much so that we are convinced that they are real. Of course, we have certain common-sense checks to see if we are in fact dreaming, hallucinating or under the influence of some illusion, but these depend upon us being able to detect an inconsistency between one set of perceptions (those in our dreams) and another sort (those in our waking life). We assure ourselves that we can detect that our dreams are inconsistent with our experience of not dreaming, or that somebody

who is hallucinating is having a set of experiences that is inconsistent with normal, non-hallucinatory experiences.

But this is not so clear cut as we would like to believe; after all, according to some reports 3.7 million Americans believe they have been abducted by aliens at one time or another. So convinced are they that no amount of comparisons with waking life will shake them of their conviction that this really happened. What's more, we are rapidly moving towards a world in which a significant number in our societies will spend a considerable proportion of their daily lives in a virtual reality, in flight simulators or on computer games, which are so real as to leave uncertain whether we haven't actually experienced real events.

But even this doesn't answer the more significant underlying question, whether we can rely on our senses. We may or may not be able to distinguish between one set of perceptions and another, but who's to say that we can in fact rely on our sense impressions from *wherever* they are derived, waking life, dreams, or hallucinations? If we could not rely on them, we would be unable to establish whether what we take to be our waking experience is not part of another more inclusive and even more coherent dream. Unknown to Truman Burbank his everyday waking experiences were nothing more than a carefully orchestrated storyline in a 24-hour-a-day soap known as *The Truman Show*.

◼ 1. Philosophical doubt versus ordinary doubt

As you can see, it is not for nothing that the dream argument has been described as one of the most provocative and disturbing arguments in philosophy. Although most famously associated with the seventeenth-century French philosopher René Descartes, it also appears in Plato's *Theatetus* and today is more broadly construed as 'external world scepticism'.

In his *Meditations on First Philosophy* (1641), Descartes sets out in his 'method of doubt' to question all his beliefs, suspending judgement on each one until the truth can be shown. He begins with his sense experiences, which are the normal grounds for his beliefs about the external world. He demonstrates that the grounds for these are also compatible with them being false. In the past he has believed something on the basis of his sense

René Descartes (1596–1650)

Born in La Haye near Tours, Descartes was educated at a Jesuit college. In 1634 he was about to publish *Le Monde* when he heard of the condemnation of Galileo by the Inquisition for teaching the Copernican system as did his own thesis, so he quickly withdrew it. In 1637 he published *Discourse on Method* followed in 1641 by his most famous work *Meditations on First Philosophy*. In 1644 he did finally and cautiously set out his views on cosmology in the *Principles of Philosophy*. His method of systematic doubt has been his greatest legacy, but he has also left us with the problem of how we bridge the gap between mind and matter and, as the postmodernists point out, the assumption that ideas are purely mental entities that precede language.

In 1649 he accepted Queen Christina of Sweden's invitation to teach her philosophy in Stockholm. But Descartes was not used to the climate or to getting up to teach the Queen as she insisted at 5 am. This supposedly brought about pneumonia. He was treated by a German doctor who prepared to bleed him, but Descartes refused, telling him he would not shed a drop of French blood. By the time he agreed it was too late and he died on 11 February 1650.

experience and he has subsequently been shown to be mistaken, because he has dreamt it, or has been hallucinating, or has been deceived. So, he asks, how can he be certain now that he is not wrong and is not in fact only dreaming? After all, our experiences in dreams have the same order, connectedness and coherence as our waking experience. So what grounds are there for trusting the sense experiences of our waking lives?

It's not difficult to understand just how revolutionary and disturbing such a method could be, particularly to those traditionally held to be the source of authoritative opinion. But its significance extends beyond this, for it set in train a tradition of philosophical scepticism, which is the starting point for most modern philosophy. In our ordinary lives, even though we often express scepticism about beliefs or theories we hear others espouse, we accept without too much questioning all sorts of beliefs that we need for the practical necessity of living our lives. In contrast philosophical scepticism ends only when a belief is true beyond any *conceivable* doubt: that is, not just practical doubt, but any doubt that could be imagined. It sets out by identifying a set of beliefs which we accept as basic to our view of the world and whose truth we normally accept without question. Then it lays out all the possible grounds for such beliefs and sets out to show that these do not justify the beliefs.

Moderate scepticism is content to show that there are insufficient grounds to prove these beliefs conclusively. But extreme scepticism, an example of which we described above in doubting whether we could rely on our sense impressions from *wherever* they were derived, argues that whatever the grounds, they provide no reason for believing at all. This, more than moderate scepticism, has provided the greatest stimulus to philosophy, leading sceptics to doubt the existence of God, the past, other minds beyond one's own and objects when they are not being experienced or, indeed, any objects beyond our experiences themselves.

So, Descartes' 'method of doubt' has not only been a valuable way of probing our everyday assumptions, but it has placed the epistemological question 'how do I know' at the centre of philosophy. The question we face as a result is not just 'What is the world like?', but 'How one could know what it's like?' In what follows we will see that Descartes' abiding legacy is the belief that the only valid method of answering this question is to start from the immediate data of consciousness, which he described alone as 'indubitable', and then attempt to 'work out' from there to the external world. It has been said that, while Copernicus had taken man out of the centre of the universe, by virtue of this method Descartes had effectively reinstated him.

Descartes begins by setting himself the deceptively simple task of accepting only those ideas that are demonstrably true to him. They must be as certain as truths in mathematics and be established by a method that is equally clear and effective. He systematically calls into question every accumulated item of supposed knowledge, no matter what its source or the weight of authority behind it. Only when we have discovered a proposition that admits of no doubt whatsoever, he argues, will we have a rock on which to build knowledge.

Put yourself in Descartes' position, then, and think what sort of thing would this rock be made out of? Would it be scientific theories that have been so thoroughly tested over the years that there can be little doubt of their truth? Or perhaps the facts of history supported by overwhelming documentary evidence that certain events in the past did in fact take place? Or perhaps the evidence in your own life of events that repeatedly occur, which you have no doubt will continue to occur, like unsupported heavier-than-air objects falling to the ground or the sun rising everyday?

Few of us would entertain any serious doubt about these things, yet they all depend upon our feelings, thoughts and sense impressions. You believe the scientific theory because you have read the evidence and explanation. You accept the historical account of the fighting that took place on the Western Front in France and Belgium during the First World War because you have been there yourself to see the remains of trenches and the cemeteries full of headstones and crosses. And you know what happens to heavy objects when you drop then, because you have felt the cup slip from your grasp and heard it smash on the kitchen floor all too often. So ultimately the only thing you can be sure about is what happens in your own mind in the form of these feelings, thoughts and sense impressions.

But now take Descartes' step and ask yourself, how do you actually know these things are true? Even if you restrict yourself to just those things that you directly know and not through the second-hand testimony of others, like the evidence of a scientific theory of which you have only read reports, you still might not have the rock of indubitable propositions for which you

search. We are easily deceived by sense impressions. We put a stick in water and it seems to bend, or we appear to see a pool of water in front of us as we drive along a hot road only to discover it is a mirage. We recognize these as illusions and we correct our sense impressions to reflect the actual situation. But how do we know that our corrections are accurate and, even more, how can we tell when we are being deceived and when we're not? If we can never be certain of our sense impressions, we can never be sure of anything in the external world.

This would mean that all we could be sure about is that we are in fact *having* these experiences: that the only thing that is real is what's in our minds – the thoughts, feelings and sense impressions which we are experiencing. But if this were the case would it make any real difference? It might in fact make very little difference, if we can indeed be sure about these experiences. You might argue that you can't really be deceived that you feel a pain and hear a sound when you tap the table, or that you can at this moment see this book in front of you, but it is possible that all these experiences which we accept as real are just the product of a dream or hallucination, and in this lies the really disturbing force of Descartes' dream argument.

We normally assume that we have fairly reliable ways of distinguishing between dreaming and waking life: all sorts of things, people and environments occur in one that do not occur in the other. But dreams can mirror waking life with deceptive accuracy. You might say that you know when you are not asleep, but sometimes in dreams too we are convinced we are awake. You might argue that, unlike dreams, our waking lives are full of conscious and intentional actions, but again these appear convincingly in our dreams as well. Even the argument that our real lives are just sharper and more vivid doesn't hold up against the evidence of dreams that are all too vivid, often horrifyingly so. So, how can we be sure we're not dreaming at any given moment? Significantly, if we can't be sure of this, we can't be sure of anything we now experience and think. Unless we have some way of verifying that our waking-experiences are not dream-experiences, we have every reason to doubt even beliefs based on the most clear and vivid sensory impressions.

If it is possible that I am dreaming at this moment, it is possible that all my experiences come from a dream – that even my waking experiences are nothing but dreams. Indeed, how could I prove otherwise? If it is possible that all my experience is of dreaming with nothing outside it, any evidence I might use to prove that I am awake will come from the dream. I might rap the table in front of me and feel the pain and hear the noise, but this might just be another thing going on in my mind and therefore in my dream. I can't use this evidence to establish what's outside my mind.

Some philosophers have called this argument an 'undercutting defeater', because it counts against our beliefs in a way other than proving them false. It merely removes any grounds we have for postulating that our beliefs are true. Descartes himself describes it as 'hyperbolic doubt', in that it establishes doubt not by contrasting it with certainty, but by infecting every belief and certainty. It deprives us of the contrast we need between the known and the unknown, upon which our understanding of the world depends. As long as we think of knowledge as something that is left as a result of a process in which we eliminate all possibilities that may have counted against our beliefs, we cannot say we know that we are not dreaming.

1.1 The evil genius

Everything comes through the mind (sense impressions, thoughts, feelings, memories) and the mind might be caught in one long, continuous dream. And as the existence of anything outside your mind depends upon sense impressions, even your own body might simply be the product of a dream. I might argue that I know my car exists, because I can see it as I look out through my window. But this depends upon sense impressions, which can only be relied upon if we can rely upon what's inside our minds, and this is what we are doubting. To say that I know my car exists because I can see it is to say I know my car – which I know as a collection of sense impressions – exists because of my sense impressions. This is circular: I know my sense impressions exist because of my sense impressions.

But if we are only in direct contact with the ideas and representations in our minds, and not with the things they represent in the world, if it exists at all, they might be nothing like we perceive them. As Descartes suggests we might even have all our thoughts manipulated by some demon or 'evil genius', who places ideas directly into our minds and causes us to experience 'the heavens, the earth, colours, figures and sounds'.

The modern counterpart to this is the argument that Hilary Putnam tries to refute, which suggests that we might be nothing more than a 'brain in a vat'. A team of malicious scientists may have transplanted your brain from your head into a vat of fluid in which they are keeping it alive. They have made electrical connections with nerve endings through which your brain receives the same sort of electrical input it currently receives. In this way they are able to control your sense experience making you perceive all sorts of things that don't exist in the external world.

This is strikingly similar to the *Star Trek* episode, 'Ship in a Bottle', in which two holodeck characters, Moriarty and his friend from the Sherlock Holmes program, demand life outside the holodeck. Captain Picard convinces them that he has arranged this, but in fact all he does is to program the holodeck inside the holodeck. So, when Moriarty thinks he is contacting the bridge of the *Enterprise* as he travels across the universe, he is in fact merely contacting the holodeck, which he has never left. Reflecting on the broader implications of this deception, Jean-Luc Picard speculates as he looks around at the *Enterprise* and its crew, 'Who knows, our reality may be very much like theirs and all this might just be an elaborate simulation running inside a little device sitting on someone's table.'

If the evil genius argument is coherent it may be that there is no objective reality, just me and the evil genius. We could no longer rely on distinguishing between dreaming and waking, or between truth and illusion. The evil genius might simply produce in me experience that has all the characteristics I look for in what I believe to be true. He can allow me to operate in just the way I do, distinguishing between dreaming and waking experiences, between false and true perceptions, and creating a picture of the world I believe to be real, while all the time none of it could be set in objective reality – just a figment of his imagination.

Even if I am not a product of the imagination of an evil genius or a brain in a vat, it seems I cannot *know* I'm not, because, while I may believe I'm not, I have no *justification* for believing that, and, as we know, a belief requires justification in order to count as knowledge. Of course, you might argue that it's just common sense to believe there is an external world. But common sense is often proved to be wrong: it was once common sense to believe that the Earth was flat and that women could prove they were not witches by drowning in a ducking stool.

So, how are we to answer these doubts without falling into the circularity of arguing that I know objects, which are nothing more than a collection of sense impressions, exist because I have the evidence of my sense impressions? One answer, of course, is to say that you can't have both: if you don't like the circularity of this argument, then you must just accept that your mind is the only thing that exists. Commonly known as solipsism, this is the belief that only oneself and one's experience exists. Supporters of this view argue that once you accept that your sense impressions are mind-dependent it is difficult to argue validly for a mind-independent world.

Even so, there are problems with solipsism. If Wittgenstein's private language argument is valid, solipsism is incompatible with our having a language to express it. With solipsism, whatever seems right can only be decided by reference to our exclusive personal states. Given this, it follows that what seems right can only be expressed through a private language, the terms of which are defined by reference to our private sensations and whose meaning, therefore, can only be known to *us*. However, in *Philosophical Investigations* (1953), Wittgenstein maintains that a private language is not logically possible, because a language is designed to communicate with others, and this requires commonly accepted rules. In a private language there can be no such rules.

But beyond the practical problems of communicating ideas, solipsism simply goes beyond the evidence. To conclude that I am the only thing that exists is more than the evidence will support. The most I can say is that I don't know anything beyond the experience of my mind. There may or may not be an external world beyond me which is reflected accurately in the way I see it, but there's just no way of knowing that. As you can see, the problem with such radical forms of scepticism is that in order for them to be presented coherently they must assume their own falsity. To deny that things exist is to believe a negative proposition about the external world to be true. But if I am the only thing that exists I have no grounds to believe any proposition about the external world at all, positive or negative.

So it seems the agnostic stance is more reasonable: we simply don't know if the external world exists. But this too doesn't allow us to escape our problems. Indeed it allows us to usher in another radical form of scepticism which argues that you can only know what's in your mind *now*. If you can't be sure of the world outside your present consciousness, equally you cannot be sure of your past consciousnesses, which are also outside your present consciousness. All you have to go on are the thoughts in your mind at this moment, including your present memories.

Bertrand Russell presented this perplexing possibility by asking how we could know that we did not spring into existence, complete with 'memories', just five minutes ago. If, as the agnostic position allows us to argue, we are not sure that the world beyond us exists *now*, how can we be sure that we ourselves existed before now? You might argue that you just know how people come by their memories, but this in turn depends upon knowledge derived from the past. So, like the arguments before it, this too is circular: it relies upon the very justification you're trying to prove. As the American philosopher Thomas Nagel succinctly puts it, 'You would be assuming the reality of the past to prove the reality of the past.'

Like all the other arguments against scepticism, if we are to break out of this circularity and prove that there exists more than just the present content of our minds, we will have to use justifications that draw upon the belief that the external world exists beyond our minds. But, as we've seen, our sense impressions, which we depend upon to justify such a belief, cannot guarantee their own accuracy. We need some reason to trust them, which must come from elsewhere. Without it we cannot be sure, or even have good reason for thinking, that we're not being deceived. We need, then, something certain, a foundation on which to build, about which even the evil genius could not deceive us.

1.2 Descartes' answer

Strictly speaking Descartes was not a sceptic at all, but his 'method of doubt', developed in *Discourse on Method* (1637) and in *Meditations* (1641), was applied scepticism. He believed it drew upon the ethos and methods of modern science, starting from the assumption that we must accept nothing as true until we have been shown it to be true. He set himself the task of doubting anything that admitted of doubt to see whether there was anything left over that was immune from it. He explains:

Because I wished to give myself entirely to the search after Truth, I thought that it was necessary for me ... to reject as absolutely false anything as to which I could imagine the least ground of uncertainty. ... I resolved to assume that everything that ever entered into my mind was no more true than the illusions of my dreams.

However, in this, his own 'method of doubt', Descartes was to find his first certainty: the first stone in the foundations. For, in doubting his own thoughts and impressions, there was one thing about which he could be absolutely certain: that he was doubting. Even if he were to doubt that he was doubting, it would be true that he was doubting. My very doubt proves my existence as a doubter. And it follows from this that he could not also doubt that he was thinking, as doubting was a form of thinking. He could not doubt away his doubt or the existence of his thought. So, he reaches his first important certainty: 'I am thinking'.

From this followed another: 'I exist'. He explains, 'The fact of my thinking reveals to me something that thinks', and it was self-evident that nothing could think without existing. Even the most devious of evil geniuses could not fool you into thinking falsely you exist. Without you there would be nothing to fool. So the existence of self is Descartes' most important stone in the foundations; a certainty expressed in his famous formula, 'Cogito, ergo sum' – 'I think, therefore I am.' And, although this on its own does not give him any justification for the belief that the external world of physical objects exists, it does give him one thing; a principle to work with – that whatever I clearly and distinctly conceive is true.

One thing that characterizes Descartes' method is his principle that he would only accept those things that were self-evidently true, in the way propositions of mathematics and logic are true. These anyone could see were true through the clear light of reason. They were not just difficult to doubt, but intrinsically impossible to doubt: they were 'indubitable'. Now, in his own existence as a thinking being, he had found just such a proposition that was indubitable – a clear and distinct idea.

So up to this point Descartes has been successful in rejecting scepticism about his own existence and about the existence of his own thoughts, but he still doesn't know if the external world exists and if it corresponds to his ideas. He must, then, now turn his attention to the contents of his thoughts. And

remember, he can only rely on his own ideas – nothing else.

Nevertheless, in those ideas he finds, among other things, the idea of God – a perfect being. And he concludes that such a being must exist, for two reasons. First, he employs the ontological proof for the existence of God of the medieval Italian philosopher St Anselm, which we will examine more fully in Chapter 12. He argues that a perfect being must exist, otherwise it would not be perfect – it would lack the quality of existence. Second he argues, on the principle that the less cannot give rise to the greater, that only a perfect being could be the cause of the idea of a perfect being, which each of us has. Descartes argues that he himself could not have brought the idea into being, because he is imperfect, as shown by the fact that he is assailed by doubt, which is inferior to knowledge. 'For I see clearly', he explains, 'that it is a greater perfection to know than to doubt.'

And with the idea of God firmly in place, he can now use this to establish the possibility of knowledge of the external world. An all-powerful, benevolent God, he declares, would not deceive us into believing the external world existed if it really didn't. Only a limited, imperfect being has any reason to do this. Equally, God would not make us such that if we use all our faculties properly we would still make mistakes. If we are careful to think through our ideas and not to judge anything, until we clearly and distinctly understand it, we will not make mistakes.

We know the ideas we derive from sense impressions are not caused by our own minds, because they are not under our own control and are more vivid than ideas we imagine. What's more, we also clearly and distinctly understand the notion of causation, so that we know these ideas are caused by something. Given that God made us such that if we use our faculties properly we can avoid mistakes, there is no way of telling that we are mistaken in thinking the external world causes our sense impressions. We can, therefore, know that external physical objects cause our sense impressions and, thus, we can come to know general features of the external world.

1.3 Ordinary doubt

Of course, if we can't accept Descartes' reliance on the assumption of God, we must find some other means of proving there exists more than just the present content of our minds. Either we find external foundations to our thinking about which we cannot be deceived, or we might have to accept the extreme scepticism of solipsism.

However, we've already seen that such radical forms of scepticism, presented coherently, are self-contradictory: they assume their own falsity in arguing we can know that we cannot know anything. What's more, they make the very enterprise of knowing things impossible. Without Descartes' faith in God we have to concede that even our mathematical calculations and our logical reasoning correctly applied may even be false. To know anything, then, becomes an impossibility. Yet we do use the verb 'to know' to distinguish between justified and unjustified beliefs. So to accept the extreme sceptic's argument would mean we have adopted a criterion for the word 'know' which is inapplicable to any situation involving belief.

On the face of it this seems unreasonable. So we must adopt a more modest claim closer to the sort of doubt we accept in our ordinary lives and to the standards we employ when we ordinarily use the verb 'to know'. In these circumstances, when we say a statement is known to be true it must indeed *be* true, but even so we don't insist that it must be true beyond any conceivable doubt. In other words, we accept the possibility that we might be wrong to claim something is true, which might later turn out to be false.

No doubt one reason for accepting this is the success of modern science, which allows us to test our beliefs against the evidence by subjecting them to rigorous experimentation. In our ordinary lives we accept the findings of science as testimony not only to the fact that the external world exists, but also to what it looks like. After all, the scientific progress, medical advances and technological developments over the last 300 years have been based upon a method which has been astonishingly successful – indeed more successful than any similar enterprise in human history. People can now live to an age unimaginable in the past. As recently as the 1830s the average life expectancy of women in industrial towns in England was 34. Now it is more than twice that.

But still, the scientific advances that have provided the means for this improvement in the quality of our lives are based upon causal explanations and theories, which are still dependent upon our perception: they are still the product of our minds. So the question remains: how do we know this corresponds to the world as it is? Despite its predictive success, the way science characterizes the world may not be how it actually is. All manner of things may produce the same regularities and repetitions. Thus, the extreme sceptic can still argue we cannot be sure it's still not a dream, hallucination or an illusion.

Yet, like science, this argument too depends upon the assumption that we are able to check our perceptions and adjust them to identify and remove error. The arguments for dreams, illusions and hallucinations each assume the contrasting reality they need to exist. In other words, they each assume the very thing they are denying. A dream is a dream because we can compare it with the waking state. A hallucination is something which we later agree with others was not real. Otherwise, if there were no contrasting reality, the dream and hallucination themselves would become the reality. If we have no waking life to compare it with, then a dream *is* our reality. Therefore, like science, this argument is equally dependent upon the possibility of comparing our observations with reality to correct their mistakes. What we believe to exist is derived from what we can observe. And without the possibility of correcting our mistaken beliefs, the claim that our impressions of the external world are untrue would be meaningless.

Even so, philosophers like Norman Malcolm who have argued that to invoke a dream the sceptic must also invoke the idea of a world in which he is sometimes awake, are not entirely free from the persistent sceptic. Roger Scruton suggests that if there is a criterion for distinguishing between dreaming and waking, it is still possible to argue that I merely dreamed I had applied it or, indeed, dreamed of the existence of it in the first place.

Yet even though this could be true, extreme scepticism cannot avoid in its turn advancing its own knowledge claims, in particular that the external world does not exist and all that does is what's in the mind. And, like all knowledge claims, these need justification – for them to be true someone must observe the external world not to exist. Yet by arguing that there is no one to observe it, the sceptics are left with nothing but their own impressions which, like dreams and hallucinations, must become the reality. And, of course, they could never know it to be the reality because this would require, in turn, something with which to compare it. Such an argument would put us in the impossible position we described earlier: it would not be possible for us to claim we know any statement to be true.

Nevertheless, we are still left with the disquieting thought that what we believe to be the external world might be nothing more than what we have within our own minds. The sceptic argues that what exists is not the same as what we observe. Like dreams and hallucinations, we all have ideas for which there is no corresponding reality; in other words we cannot be sure they are anything else but just ideas. As we have seen, the only way we can try to prove otherwise gets us into a circular argument. This is what the American philosopher R. B. Perry once described as the 'egocentric predicament': that we are each confined to our own perceptual world.

Nonetheless, even though there might not be a completely successful argument against scepticism, and even though our beliefs about the existence of an external world might be false, in our ordinary lives we do in fact place limits on our scepticism. We accept that the consistency and coherence of our observations makes the belief in an external world a good bet, and we continue to say we 'know' propositions to be true, even though we cannot say that we know them to be true beyond any conceivable doubt.

■ 2. Doubt and the search for knowledge

Yet unfortunately we cannot just leave it there. As we go in search of knowledge in our ordinary lives, we need to find some explanation for how we justify our claims to know these things. How do we know they are not, as Rorty and others argue, nothing more than what our contemporary culture accepts as knowledge? Or maybe our search for knowledge is not an attempt to mirror or copy the world at all, just an attempt to cope with it by believing those things that help us achieve our goals?

To escape this dilemma we seem to need the sceptic's strong sense of 'know': that we cannot say we know when there is a chance that we may be wrong, when there might be evidence that refutes the claim. What we need to explore, then, is whether in our ordinary lives we are right to settle for anything less than conclusive proof, where there could be no conceivable doubt. To paraphrase Roger Scruton's argument, if somebody knows something, does it follow that she must also *know* that she knows, or is it enough just to concede the

possibility that refuting evidence *could* be produced, while not believing that it will be?

The moment you think about this you will realize there are very few propositions that we can actually claim to know in the strong sense. The most likely candidates are those we know intuitively to be true *a priori*: analytic truths (that all bachelors are unmarried men), or mathematical truths (that the sum of the angles of a triangle are equal to two right angles), or synthetic *a priori* truths (that the shortest distance between two points is a straight line). We know that nothing could exist that is incompatible with these; nothing the future could throw up which would count as evidence against them.

Less certain are the propositions we derive from our own reasoning: demonstrative knowledge. If we were to check and discover no mistakes in our reasoning and were sure that we had validly derived the conclusion from the premises, we might claim to know this in the strong sense. But still there is the possibility of flaws in our reasoning which we have not discovered. Unlike the strong sense of knowing it allows for the possibility of refutation. We cannot claim that doubt is inconceivable.

The strong sense simply doesn't allow for the possibility of error; it is simply not an open question. In contrast, many of the mathematical theories we learn at school, like the formula for the calculation of the area or the circumference of a circle, fall into this weaker class of knowing. We might not know the proof of the theory, but we accept its truth. However, if we were to be shown by a specialist in the field that the theory is in fact wrong, we might revise our beliefs in line with our doubts. So, we allow for the possibility, however remote, of a refutation of the theory, whereas the strong sense does not concede that anything could prove that we are mistaken.

Weaker still is the knowledge we gain directly from the evidence of our senses. Yet unless we have made a mistake in describing what we feel, see or smell, we could argue that we are less likely to be wrong about these things than we are about our deductive reasoning or our mathematical calculations. After all, what better authority is there to confirm the pain you feel as a result of twisting your ankle than you yourself? But the fact is we often do get these things wrong, either because we overreact in an emotional situation, exaggerating our feelings, or because we are easily deceived into thinking we see one thing when we really see another, like a mirage on a hot dry road.

Even so, this sort of direct knowledge is more reliable than descriptive knowledge. Bertrand Russell draws a distinction between this – 'knowledge by acquaintance' – and the more indirect 'knowledge by description'. If there are grounds for doubting the first, there are even more for the second. Although both involve a possibility of choosing inaccurate words to describe the evidence of our senses, Russell's 'knowledge by description' involves describing complex situations, events or memories, which leaves even greater room for mistakes. That we don't always trust this source of knowledge is shown by our eagerness to qualify our statements. We may be tempted to say categorically that the man who mugged the old lady was in his early twenties, white, six feet tall, thirteen stone in weight, and wore jeans and Nike running shoes, but we are more likely to prefix this with 'I think ...'.

Nevertheless, if we claim to know these things, it means we are prepared to submit our beliefs to the evidence and allow others to decide whether we are justified and whether we are competent observers. They would assess whether the conditions were good enough for us to see what we claim to have seen, whether our senses are good enough, and whether we ourselves were in a fit state to observe events accurately. And, of course, there is likely to be even more doubt about accounts involving memories of events in the distant past, or historical accounts of events drawn from a number of different sources.

Yet weaker still are the claims we make as empirical generalizations, and that is because they 'describe' events unseen by anybody – those in the future and, indeed, all possible events that are similar in important respects. They may be like Newton's universal law of gravitation that all bodies attract each other with a force proportional to their masses and inversely proportional to the square of their distances apart, or they may just be the traditional belief that cockerels and male mistlethrushes sing when a thunderstorm approaches. But they all have one thing in common: they extrapolate from a limited number of observed instances to make claims about *all* instances, including, of course, those that have never been observed by anybody and those that have yet to occur.

Even the most well attested scientific theory is only based on inductive inference from a limited number of individual instances. In the case of gravitation we are confident in claiming it as knowledge in that it is practically certain, but in other cases the most we may be able to claim is that we are reasonably confident, or just that there is a high probability, or even a mere possibility that it is true, in which case our claim to know may be tenuous indeed.

As you can see from this, if we were to use knowledge in the sceptic's strong sense to indicate only those things of which we can be certain, about which there can be no conceivable doubt, we would have to exclude most of what we claim to know. But to doubt that we know things, like scientific theories or everyday events, like the sun rising each morning, when these have passed every test that they have been set, seems to make certainty meaningless. Used in this way it would have very little application.

If you lived, say, within ten miles of Boston and you were a regular visitor, you might reasonably argue that you know Boston to exist. But, of course, it is a possibility that if you were to drive up the road you may find that overnight Boston has completely disappeared – there is nothing there! If this had occurred you would have been mistaken in saying that you knew Boston existed, and if you could have been mistaken, then, according to the sceptic's strong sense of know, you did not know Boston existed. But although it's possible Boston no longer exists, even though you might have seen it only a few days ago, this doesn't seem to show that you didn't know Boston to be there. All it appears to show is that, although you knew, you could have been mistaken.

If this seems like a contradictory result, it is so because you have your mind fixed on the sceptic's strong sense, one in which the very possibility that you could have been mistaken means that you did not know. We can only say we know a proposition to be true when we are certain, and certainty only comes after all the evidence is in. But this means that certainty has virtually no application at all, because for most empirical propositions, particularly universal scientific generalizations, *all* the evidence will never be in: they make claims about past, present and future events for which we can never have all the information.

So, to summarize:

Five categories of knowledge:

1. Intuitive
2. Demonstrative
3. Direct
4. Descriptive
5. Generalizations

The sceptic wants to describe as probable virtually every proposition we claim to know to be true. But this, of course, doesn't reflect the way we use the verb 'to know'. Whether you know Boston exists depends on whether you have grounds for your claim and the strength of these grounds. In this case you will without doubt claim you know Boston exists, because the probability is very high. But you cannot be certain, if that means there can be no conceivable doubt. The sceptic argues you are wrong to claim that you know. If he's right, we may have here nothing more than a verbal quarrel over how we use the words certainty and probability, and knowledge and belief. In this case we may have to devise alternative ways of labelling this distinction.

To decide, the key question that you must ask yourself is: are we to use knowledge to apply to only those propositions we can say we know that we know, or to the much larger group that we say we just know? Let me explain. The sceptic wants to argue that I can only say something is knowledge if I can reflect upon my claim to know and realize that there is no possibility of me being wrong. If I realize there is a possibility of being mistaken, then I now know that I don't know – I only believe. For me to have knowledge I must 'know that I know': I must believe that nothing could count as evidence against it. But much of what we describe as knowledge we don't know in this way – like the existence of Boston, we only 'know' it to be true, even though we cannot rule out the possibility that it might have disappeared overnight.

If we go back to our five categories of knowledge above (intuitive, demonstrative, direct, descriptive and generalizations), some philosophers argue that the last two, involving indirect empirical propositions, can never be anything more that provisional, mere hypotheses, because any empirical proposition whatever can be refuted by future experience. Indeed some propositions we only know as hearsay. We claim we know that saturated fats lead to a build up of cholesterol in our veins, which is likely to lead to heart disease. But we ourselves have no direct evidence of this. We have just read it in articles and books. And, of course, there is no logical absurdity to the most extraordinary things happening that would conflict with propositions that are backed by the strongest evidence. Yet even in these circumstances it might still be more reasonable to save a theory that has

been well attested by evidence, rather than ditch it on the grounds that we were mistaken to believe we knew it.

For example, suppose you were to return home from work late one night and as you walked down your street you were to see in front of you a driverless car parked by the kerb suddenly rise into the air. Unless you could find corroborating eyewitness evidence, you might be inclined to dismiss this, thereby saving the theory of gravitation, by arguing that you were tired, you had been drinking, or that somebody might even have been playing tricks on you. The point is that the evidence in favour of the theory of gravitation is so overwhelming that it might be more reasonable to dismiss this one event as unreliable, rather than the theory. As Hume argues, to believe in a miracle the weight of evidence for its occurrence would have to be greater than for the law of nature which it is supposed to have broken. To believe in it, it has to be more miraculous for it not to have occurred.

But even if it is more reasonable for me to say 'I know' in cases of empirical generalizations, when I cannot say 'I know I know', the case is stronger for our second and third categories: demonstrative and direct knowledge. If I were to be presented with a faultless proof for the formula for calculating the area of a circle, or if I were to consider the proposition 'My computer is in front of me', there is nothing that would prove to me I am mistaken in claiming I know both of these to be true. This amounts to knowing in the strong sense. But that's not to say that I cannot imagine that something could occur to prove me wrong, just that I do not *now* accept that any future development will do so. I am simply describing my present attitude to these things; I am not predicting what my attitude would be if things changed.

A claim to know something in the strong sense can still be disputed by another person. Just because I do not accept that anything can count as evidence against my claim that I know my computer to be in front of me, does not mean that I could not have made a mistake. I may make a claim to know something in the strong sense because I believe the evidence is irrefutable, but it doesn't follow that it is indeed irrefutable. We shouldn't assume that claiming we know something in the strong sense means that, like intuitive truths, it is logically and necessarily true. Synthetic, empirical propositions depend upon evidence and we have no undisputed criterion for judging when we have sufficient evidence to claim we know.

However, if I claim 'I know that I know', yet still accept that I may be proved mistaken if things change, it appears we can never know anything in an unqualified strong sense beyond intuitive truths. The fact that this seems to be the case may point to the importance that the notions of certainty and knowledge in the strong sense play in our thinking. To accept that something we thought was true is in fact false, we need to accept an alternative account as true. In other words, we must be able to say we know some things in the strong sense to have doubts about other things. One proposition about the external world turns out to be false only because we accept another as true. As Norman Malcolm argues, 'A conjecture implies an understanding of what certainty would be.'

Another way of perhaps saying the same thing is to argue that we call beliefs 'true' when they cohere with the rest of our beliefs. If we believe, as we seem to, that not every statement we make about the physical world could turn out to be false, then maybe we call beliefs 'true' when they cohere with the rest of our beliefs, and not by seeing how well they fit with those things Descartes imagines might be an illusion, a dream or a hallucination. This brings us back to the postmodernist objections to the line modern philosophers have taken since Descartes, in which they treat ideas as purely mental entities that somehow precede language, rather than being inextricably bound up with it and the cultural values it enshrines in the way Wittgenstein, Rorty and others maintain.

In a 1983 paper titled 'A Coherence Theory of Truth and Knowledge', the American philosopher Donald Davidson startled the philosophical world by pointing out that this way of thinking entails that most of anybody's beliefs about anything must be true. His point, as Richard Rorty makes clear, is that you have to have a lot of true beliefs about something before you can have any false ones. To say they are false is just a way of saying that we cannot make these beliefs cohere with the rest of our beliefs. Therefore, we have to know a great deal about what is real before we can call something an illusion, just as we have to have a great many true beliefs before we can have any false ones.

Rorty uses the film *The Matrix* to illustrate this. Even after the hero has been plucked out of his artificial environment he still has mostly the same beliefs as he did before. There are numerous common beliefs that make it possible for him to use the same language outside the Matrix as he does within it. As Rorty points out, 'He had been fooled about what was going on around him, but had never been fooled about what sorts of things the world contains, what is good and what evil, the colour of the sky, the warmth of the sun, or the salient features of beavers.' In the same way the images we form in dreams can only be composed of bits and pieces of real experience combined in novel ways. Therefore, although we have reason to doubt the surface perceptual qualities of our perception, we have no reason to doubt the properties we perceive as the basic components of our experience.

■ 3. Conclusion

To make scepticism plausible by treating the mind as some private inner space and all our ideas as mental entities that precede language, Descartes and the many modern philosophers who have followed his lead have, as Wittgenstein points out, taken language 'on holiday'. Ignoring the impossibility of a merely private language, they seem to have ignored the fact that our dreams, illusions and hallucinations each assume the contrasting reality they need to exist. These are the commonplace certainties we give expression to through a public language. Without this our dreams, illusions and hallucinations themselves become the reality. We need this strong sense of knowing in the form of these commonplace beliefs, if we are to have our normal doubts about what we believe we know.

■ Questions

1. Explain and examine critically the role played by clear and distinct perceptions in Descartes' attempt to arrive at certainty.

2. Is it possible that the whole world could have sprung into existence just thirty seconds ago complete with all its historical records, monuments, traditions, memories and the like?

3. Critically discuss the argument that some of our knowledge is innate.

4. 'All the world's a dream.' How can we be sure that it is not?

5. How could I convince you that solipsism was true?

6. a) What is the purpose of Descartes' method of doubt?

   b) Is this a reasonable method?

▓ Recommended reading

Descartes, R. Meditations and Discourse on Method. In *Discourse on Method and other Writings*, trans. F. E. Sutcliffe (Harmondsworth: Penguin, 1970).

Ayer, A. J. *The Problem of Knowledge* (Harmondsworth: Penguin, 1984), Chapter 2.

Chisholm, R. M. *Theory of Knowledge* (Englewood Cliffs, NJ: Prentice-Hall, 1988), Chapters 1, 2, 3, 10.

Pollock, J. *Contemporary Theories of Knowledge* (Totowa, NJ: Rowman and Littlefield, 1991).

Unger, Peter. *Ignorance* (London: Oxford University Press, 1975).

 The note structure to accompany this chapter can be downloaded from our website.

Perception: Rationalism and Empiricism

CHAPTER 8

Key issues

▶ If the world of appearances is so unreliable as a guide to the true order of things, how can we possibly know anything about what really exists?

▶ If all we can ever gather are just subject-centred experiences – different perceptions, different points of view from different perspectives – does this mean that no matter how many we gather we will only ever end up with different opinions, none any better than any other?

▶ How is knowledge of the external world possible? If it is, what tests should we insist upon and what assumptions should we accept or reject?

▶ Is Descartes right that we all have innate ideas, *a priori* knowledge from birth, rather than from experience?

▶ Can our perception of whole figures or patterns be construed as just the sum of their parts perceived passively or are we actively engaged in forming complete wholes which only have the meaning we bring to them?

▶ Is what we describe as 'real' nothing more than what is publicly confirmed by others?

Contents

In 1620 Sir Francis Bacon set about systematizing the body of practical thought that had developed out of the work of the early scientists, known then as 'natural philosophers'. In *Novum Organum*, the first account of the modern scientific method, he declares boldly we must go beyond the ancients: through modern science we must free ourselves of the dictates of the ancient Greek texts and the Bible, and explore the world for ourselves. His confidence in the potential of this nascent scientific methodology at times comes across more like missionary zeal. You might have thought that by rejecting traditional authorities in this way and declaring the sovereignty of the individual, he would be ushering in a world in which the individual would be freer than ever before. Yet in one respect it seems he was merely exchanging one gaoler for another.

Once freed from reliance on traditional authorities as to what is real, all we have to rely on is our own mind. But this does two things: not only do we experience the world through the mind, but the mind also tells us what it is right for us to believe about the world. This means all our experience is subject centred, and therefore we cannot escape our doubts about what our minds are telling us. In the previous chapter when we tried to refute the idea that the evil genius has simply staged all experience to fool us into believing a coherent, yet false, account of the world, all that we had to draw upon was the evidence of our minds, through which the evil genius' fantastic account was produced in the first place. As long as the mind is producing its own money in this way we are left with no independent authority to back its claims.

However, as you might imagine, this is not a new problem. In *Theatetus* Plato describes a discussion in which Socrates examines Theatetus' claim that whatever we perceive amounts to knowledge, a view that Socrates associates with Protagoras' argument that the individual is the measure of all things. He sets about trying to convince Theatetus that such an argument can only result in relativism, which would deprive knowledge of the objective validation it needs. He asks, 'Does it not sometimes happen that when the same wind blows, one of us is cold, and another not, and one slightly, but another exceedingly. ... Since, then, that which affects me is relative to me and not to another, do not I perceive it, and another not perceive it?'

As you can see, Plato held a very low opinion of perception. He classified the normal perceptual claims we make as just beliefs, not knowledge, because our senses often deceive us and we cannot be sure at any given time that we are not being deceived. Since knowledge must involve true claims, and truth must be unchanging, knowledge, he argued, cannot be based on sense perception, which is unreliable and continuously changing.

So, Plato wondered, if experience is so subject centred in this way, is it any more reliable than a mere shadow of reality, which it resembles only in broad outline. In Plato's *Republic*, Socrates compares mankind to prisoners in a cave, whose sense experience cuts them off from the real truth of things. He asks Glaucon to imagine an underground chamber some distance from the entrance to the cave, where men have been held prisoners all their lives. Since childhood their legs and necks have been chained, preventing them from moving and from turning their heads, so that they can only see in front of them.

Above and some distance behind them a fire is burning, and between the fire and the prisoners there is a raised road, along which all manner of people pass, carrying all sorts of things: containers of various types, statues and figures of animals made out of wood, stone and other materials. Some of them are talking, others are silent. And all of this activity is reflected by the fire onto the wall oppo-

site the prisoners, who see it all as shadows. Socrates explains to Glaucon, 'Like ourselves ... they see only their own shadows, or the shadows of one another, which the fire throws on the opposite wall of the cave.' The conclusion Socrates wants Glaucon to draw from this is that the truth for these prisoners would be 'literally nothing but the shadows of the images.' In other words, 'ultimate reality' is a world the senses simply cannot reach.

Like us, of course, the prisoners can distinguish between appearance and reality. If they have a dream or a hallucination which other prisoners don't experience, they can tell the difference: the 'real' is what is in the shadows, what is publicly confirmed by others. But, of course, if one of them were to escape and make it to the entrance of the cave, he would discover that it was quite different from what he saw reflected on the wall, or even what he was able to see directly by the light of the fire. And yet, while they are chained together, there is nothing unreal about their shared experiences, the shadows they see pass before them on the opposite wall. It's only the inference they make as to the reality this represents, the outside cause of it, which may be wrong.

For example, you might dream you are having a birthday party and your friends have played a practical joke on you. They've blindfolded you and told you that they are going to give you a present. Instead they have placed your hand in a bowl of cold custard. Like most dreams, this is so vivid that you are probably able to describe the experience in some detail: you can feel the wet, thick, cold liquid clinging to your fingers right up to your wrist. The point is, this is the same whether you are merely dreaming it or it has actually happened: you are still in contact with the same experience and you can describe it in the same detail. Even when you are dreaming, there is no doubt that you are, indeed, having this experience. The only difference is the inference you draw from the two experiences: in the case of a dream the inference that this is real is false, whereas if it has actually happened the inference is correct.

■ 1. Ultimate reality

If the world of appearances is so unreliable and deceptive as a guide to the true order of things, how can we possibly know anything about what really exists, and how can we possibly say anything about reality when all our experiences are confined just to the world of appearances?

As we continue to increase our knowledge and learn more about the way things are, it's natural to suppose that at the end of this search for truth we will uncover a hard core of reality lying beneath the successive layers of appearance. This was an assumption common among philosophers of the pre-modern era. Isaiah Berlin describes 'This craving for a metaphysical system' as 'one of the most obsessive of all the fantasies which has dominated human minds.'

Plato believed that since knowledge must involve statements that are true, and truth must be unchanging, knowledge cannot be based upon sense impressions, because these are unreliable and continually changing. For statements to be true they must be so in virtue of an unchanging 'reality', not by convention or agreement. In other words, such a reality could not be located in any particular place or time. It could only be found, he believed, in unchanging 'forms' or universals, pure ideas outside space and time, which could only be grasped by reason. While the senses could tell us all about the shadows, only reason could tell us about the causes of those shadows.

He believed that there were two kinds of information derived from two distinct worlds: the world of appearances and the world of forms or universals. In the world of appearances we gather 'sensible' information through our senses, but, as this is not indubitable, it can never constitute knowledge; it can only ever amount to mere opinion. As I look at the table before me I can only say that it *appears* to be of a dark brown colour with two short and two long sides and, as I cannot see its legs from here, it *seems* to be suspended in mid-air. However, by contrast, in the world of forms or universals we are presented with the source of 'intelligible' information from which knowledge is possible. In this lies the unchanging world of reality.

So, in the world of appearances all we can ever gather are just different perceptions, different points of view from different perspectives. No matter how many we gather we will only ever end up with different opinions, none any better than any other. Nevertheless, we do use general terms, universals, like 'table', which refer to something other than an item of our experience. They are a way of saying something *about* the experience, rather than just describing or relating it. We refer to a 'table', or a table 'leg', because we already

have an idea of this, waiting to apply it to the sense experience.

We must, then, have acquired these from some other source. We can't know them through sense experiences, because these are merely singular instances of them, which are always changing as we change our perspectives. Each time I move around the table it seems to change shape, assuming different forms of polygons. Additional legs appear as others disappear. So the world of appearances can at best only be a shadowy reflection of these forms, merely inaccurate reflections of them. Because of this, Plato believed we cannot 'know' them in the same sense that we can say we know forms.

If knowledge cannot come from our sense experiences, then it must come from reason. Plato argued that to acquire any knowledge we must first turn away from the sensible world, from reliance on sense impressions, and turn instead to the intelligible world, in which we rely upon reason alone to discover the forms or universals (like 'justice', 'smallness', 'beauty', 'redness') that are in our minds. In this way we can uncover, recollect, these ideas which have always been within us.

In *Meno* Plato describes Socrates' account of how we are to do this. And, in a passage that is music to the ears of both students and critics of modern education alike, he maintains that we cannot gain knowledge through learning. To learn anything involves acquiring the truth of something, which we didn't previously know. But, he argues, if this were the case, if we were unaware of it before we learnt it, we would have no way of recognizing it in the first place. It follows then that you can only tell something is true, if you already know it to start with. But this can no longer amount to learning, because you cannot learn something which you already know. Therefore, learning must be impossible – any knowledge that we can have we must already possess.

He concludes that we don't learn anything: we already have in our minds knowledge of forms or universals. All we do is to remember them. Our sense experience brings to our conscious attention information already in our minds, of which we may not have been aware. In effect we simply recollect information we were born with, which the soul acquired in a previous life, but forgot at birth. So the role of the educator is not to 'put into the mind knowledge that was not there before', but to help the mind see for itself: not to tell students what to think, but to help them think for themselves.

■ 2. Appearance and reality

It's not difficult to understand the resolve that has driven philosophers to search for this sort of certainty; what Berlin describes as 'one of the most obsessive of all the fantasies which has dominated human minds.' Once you have found it in the form of logical necessity and mathematical truths, it's a short step to believing the same could be found in a metaphysical system which would give us an account of the fundamentals of experience: something that would fix our understanding of experience in solid foundations and not in the shifting sands of appearance. And all of this is fuelled by the discoveries of modern scientists who, as if peeling an onion, appear to be stripping each successive layer of appearance away finally to lay bare the core of experience.

However the problem with such expectations is that we are not comparing like with like. David Hume argued that we can never get in the world of experience the certainty or logical necessity we find in closed systems like pure mathematics. Indeed, there's nothing very remarkable about this. The certainty we find in closed systems is there because we have put it there to start with. If you decide to accept that A precedes B, and B precedes C, then it follows necessarily that A precedes C. The necessity we derive from such arguments is there because we don't allow the assumptions to be informative: we don't allow them to have any more information than is necessary. In the last resort they are analytic statements, in that we decide what goes into them, which will determine what we can necessarily deduce from them. We all accept that the word 'bachelor' will mean unmarried man, thereby necessarily linking the two concepts: male and unmarried. Therefore, when we accept that John is a bachelor, we know that we can argue necessarily that he must be an unmarried man.

But as soon as we begin to deal with an open system, like the world of experience, we can never get the complete certainty, the logical necessity of a closed system. Of course, we are often entitled to have a high degree of certainty, particularly with the truth of propositions about things we see occurring regularly, like the sun rising each morning, or heavier-than-air objects falling to the ground when left unsupported. But these can never be as certain as the truth of those propositions, like $9 + 3 = 12$, that are necessarily true. As we saw in Chapter 6, Isaiah Berlin notes that 'Propositions are either

certain and uninformative or informative and not certain. Metaphysical knowledge which claims to be both certain and informative is therefore in principle not possible.'

So, it seems, even though this search for the hard core of reality is understandable, it is ill-conceived. Like the analogy of the onion, we may strip away all the layers of experience only to find that no core exists at the centre: there is just one layer of experience after another and nothing else. Those who have seen philosophy as essentially a search for 'substance', the ultimate reality they assume to lie beneath the layers of appearance, have really been asking an impossible question: what is this like *apart* from all the things we know about it and possibly could know about it? That is, what is it like apart from appearances? This means we can never know what this substance is, because whatever we can uncover will never *be* it, but merely *about* it. This seems to be ill-conceived because the nature of the question precludes any possibility that we may be able to answer it.

Given this, the only sensible thing we can do is to make sure we can distinguish between appearance and reality; not the ultimate reality of Plato and the Medieval philosophers, but the reality embedded in the world of experience. This is what modern philosophers like Descartes, Locke, Berkeley, Hume and Kant set about to do: to find the foundations of knowledge in the world of experience. In doing so they set in train a tradition which took as its starting point the mind as a special subject of study possessing all the elements and processes that make knowledge possible. Indeed, not until the twentieth century and the work of philosophers like Dewey, Wittgenstein, Heidegger and Rorty has this tradition been effectively challenged.

For any inference to add to knowledge, its premises must be known to be true. Therefore, in any theory of knowledge ultimately there need to be truths which require neither proof nor evidence. In recognizing this, modern philosophers like Descartes and Locke set about discarding entities and ideas in search of this ever diminishing area of certainty. Having accepted that we could be sure about the evidence of our senses, that it was not manipulated by some evil genius, their strategy was to stake out the territory where we could be certain of the truth of our conclusions and another where we knew our conclusions were only probably true.

With Descartes the area of certainty was restricted to his own existence as a thinking being and innate ideas inherent in the mind from birth. In contrast Locke declared, 'there is nothing in the mind except what was first in the senses': no innate ideas, just the mind as a clean sheet, a *tabula rasa*, upon which our senses write in a thousand ways. For Berkeley there was nothing but sensations and the ideas we derive from these, while Hume declared that the mind, like the body, was nothing more than what we perceive it to be: a series of ideas, memories and feelings which together *are* the mind.

Each of these represents an attempt to answer the question: how is knowledge of the external world possible? If it is, what tests should we insist upon and what assumptions should we accept or reject? Should we, for example, assume along with Descartes that we all have innate ideas, *a priori* knowledge from birth, rather than from experience? Although at the time this generated controversy, particularly about whether *a priori* knowledge was possible, it has been impossible to discover whether a newborn infant knows anything in the ordinary sense of knowing.

But if there are problems with *a priori* knowledge, there are equally problems with the assumptions we commonly make about *a posteriori* knowledge: that is, knowledge of the external world. It's easy to demonstrate the extent to which our most matter-of-fact observations are a matter of appearance, rather than reality. In *The Problems of Philosophy* Bertrand Russell shows that if I claim to see a table before me, I am making a claim to know something that commits me to more than is obvious. We might all agree that it is oblong, brown and smooth, but as soon as we begin to be more precise things are not so simple. Some parts of the table that are reflecting the light are a lighter colour than other parts, so I can't say any longer that it is 'really' the same colour all over. And if I move about the table the light changes and other parts become lighter, while the lighter parts go darker.

Of course I could argue that the reliability of such evidence depends on its analogy with similar cases of tables I've seen in the past. But in this lies an all too familiar danger: we can convince ourselves that we are seeing something that we're not, just because it is familiar and we have been conditioned to seeing that. Look at the triangles and read the familiar sayings.

So familiar are they that our minds selectively ignore and edit out the superfluous words as if we haven't seen them. But that's not the only problem.

We may in fact not be looking at a table, but at something for which we have no cases that we can use as analogies to interpret our subjective sense experiences. In these cases there is no past experience to build on: we are just trapped in our own minds.

You may be wondering, of course, why we don't just settle the matter by checking our experiences with other people who are experiencing the same thing. And this would, indeed, be the common-sense way of tackling it. But in doing this we take a lot for granted. We are assuming that they are having experiences that are the same as ours, but as Russell points out, 'if several people are looking at the table at the same moment, no two of them will see exactly the same point of view, and any change in the point of view makes some change in the way the light is reflected.' So what are we to do about these differences? You might think an average or consensus view of the colour of the table will settle the problem. But this is even more difficult to justify. It arbitrarily rejects most, if not all, of the experiences of the observers.

■ 3. The problem

The problem we have to solve is how we can move from our subject-centred experiences within our own inner world to statements we can justify about the external world. If you cast your mind back to the experience of having your hand in a bowl of custard, the same subject-centred experience works as the premise for an argument leading to the conclusion that you are dreaming as it does to the conclusion that you really do in fact have your hand in the bowl of custard. You are indeed having the same subject-centred experience; the only difference between the two is the final inference you make, that it is a dream or it is reality.

This was the problem facing modern philosophers once they had abandoned their reliance on ancient and biblical authorities. After the impact of Copernicus and Galileo, modern philosophers like Descartes abandoned the belief, typical of medieval philosophers, that the order of the world reflected God's purposes. Instead the world was depicted as a vast machine operating in accordance with God's constant laws. God became the clockmaker, whose role was not to intervene but just to keep the clock wound up and going. The traditional biblical picture failed to reflect the description produced by scientists like Newton of nature as a system of forces and mass in motion, obeying principles of mechanics and mathematics. The question Descartes and other philosophers had to address, therefore, was not just what was the world like, but how can we know what it's like. And in their answer they hoped to provide a satisfactory philosophical basis for the new science.

For Descartes the only valid method for answering this question, which he passed onto his successors, was to start with the immediate data of consciousness, which alone was indubitable, and work out from here to the external world. In what has become known as 'Cartesian dualism', Descartes argues that there are two and only two fundamentally different sorts of 'substance' or existing things: the 'thinking' and 'extended' substances, in other words mind and matter, between which there is a sharp division.

This gives us two ways of answering the questions what is the world like and how are we to know what it's like. First, we can adopt the traditional monist approach and simplify it by arguing that the world is composed of just one kind of substance, either mind or matter, from which all else flows. Idealists, like Bishop Berkeley for example, argue that the world is composed of nothing but ideas and mental states. We can, then, have no direct knowledge of physical objects and matter. Alternatively, materialists, in the same monist tradition, deny the mental or spiritual components of

Cartesian dualism and attempt to work out a more advanced mechanistic theory to account for the creation of ideas and spiritual states. Both of these we will examine in the next chapter.

However, the second way of answering these questions is the pluralist way: that is, to argue that there is more than one kind of ultimate constituent of the world – both mind and matter. Both Descartes, a rationalist, and Locke, an empiricist, argue in their conflicting ways for this method of answering the questions. Even so, this is a much more difficult path to take, requiring them to address three key problems. First, they must show how the two interact: how the mind influences matter and how matter influences the mind. Second, they must make clear the nature of the mind: what it includes. Does is include thoughts, volitions and desires, or just consciousness? Is it self-conscious to the extent that we know the 'self' in the same way we know the body? And third, they must address the problem of perception: can the mental part of us have knowledge of the physical world? If so, how does such knowledge enter the mind?

So, to summarize:

Questions:
    What is the world like?
    How are we to know what it's like?

Answers:
    1. Monist
        1.1 Idealism
        1.2 Materialism
    2. Pluralist: three key problems
        2.1 How they interact
        2.2 The nature of the mind
            What does it include?
            Is it self-conscious?
        2.3 Perception
            Can the mental have knowledge of
            the physical? If so, how does such
            knowledge enter the mind?

■ 4. Rationalism

In Plato's *Theatetus* Socrates argues that perception can only ever give us different perceptions from different perspectives, as Russell's observers of the table demonstrated. Thus, Socrates concludes, knowledge must come from some other source. Modern rationalists agree with this, arguing that the non-perceptual source of knowledge must lie in 'reason'. In contrast empiricists claim the ultimate source of all of our ideas is sense experience. At this point we must make clear that the word 'perception' in this debate is sometimes used confusingly in two ways: to mean just the passive reception of sense experience, or to mean the active thought process of creating understanding, as in our example of triangles above. In the argument above it is being used in the passive sense.

Rationalism is the belief that pure reasoning untainted by sense experience will yield incorrigible truths. Philosophers like Descartes, Leibniz and Spinoza believe that our reason gives us the ability to grasp certain general truths about nature and the structure of the universe. Knowledge, they believe, forms a single deductive system and everything can be made explicit by being brought within it: there is a fully ordered universe, perfect and immovable, as in the pure abstractions of physicists. In the seventeenth and eighteenth centuries, truths of syllogistic logic, Euclidean geometry, and the laws of Kepler, Galileo and Newton, all appeared to be necessarily true and to be discoverable by reason, which could grasp them independently of experience. Knowledge in this strongest sense consists of everything that is eternal and necessary: the truth of the proposition $2 + 2 = 4$ cannot be changed by any reference to experience, and no experience is necessary to know that it is true.

Indeed, experience is a hindrance. They maintain that what we know as certain by using our reason in this way is in fact 'reality' and not the world as we discover it through our senses, which is generally regarded as misleading, illusory and unimportant. In fact reality is masked by appearance; it's not presented to our senses. Only our reason gives us the capacity to penetrate to the true order of things. Indeed we already have within us, in the form of innate ideas with which we were born, certain knowledge independent of experience.

Critics of rationalism argue that the alleged certain knowledge may be nothing more than a few beliefs taken much too seriously. The advance of science has left many doubtful whether any ideas can be considered as absolutely certain and beyond refutation. Of course, Descartes and Plato might argue the work of science deals just with the world of experience in which nothing can be known with absolute certainty, whereas they are concerned with a different world of 'pure ideas', which never changes.

Nevertheless there have been conflicts among rationalists as to what is true about this world; the so-called self-evident truths, thought to be beyond any conceivable doubt, have in fact been shown to be open to considerable doubt. In the history of mathematics, a key source of clear and distinct ideas for Descartes, progress in our mathematical knowledge has forced us to reconsider some theories regarded as true. In the early nineteenth century doubts were raised about Euclidean geometry by those who showed that various systems of geometry could be developed and, in each, different theorems would be true.

■ 5. Descartes' rationalism

Descartes' rationalism is built around three central tenets: that the world is composed of two realms, the mental and the material; that we are members of the mental realm, in that we possess a 'substantial ego' or 'self'; and that there are causal interactions between the two realms, which we can see in our perception of material things and when we *will* something, that is, when we make up our mind to do something requiring bodily movement.

Take the first two tenets, that there are two realms and that we are members of the mental realm. Like all rationalists, Descartes has a preference for rational cognition over the senses. Our understanding of matter depends upon perception and our senses, which can deceive us, whereas the mind, he believes, has innate ideas, implanted by God and known for certain. In his *Second Meditation* (1641) he describes holding a piece of wax, which he places near a flame. As a result its taste and smell disappears, its colour changes, it loses shape and becomes hot and liquefied, too hot to hold. He asks, 'Does the same wax remain after this change?' He answers, we do indeed still conceive it surviving after all these changes in its sensible qualities. Therefore, he concludes, matter cannot be an empirical concept: *knowledge* of the external world must be knowledge of structure, not of that which fills out that structure: the unstable, changeable qualities we perceive through sense impressions, like taste, smell and colour. Thus, as structure he depicts matter as a geometric concept involving extension, in that it occupies space, and motion as its only physical nature. These are the only things left after all these changes in its sensible qualities.

He argues that the essential property of the wax is extension. Our senses and imagination are unable to picture all the possible shapes of the wax. Therefore it is only when we perceive it by the intellect extended in three dimensions that we get clear and distinct ideas of its geometrical properties. All other properties, like its colour, are not perceivable by the intellect and are not mathematical, quantifiable and *a priori*.

This sort of intuition is the key to rationalist thinking. It is the source of premises from which rationalists argue to their conclusions. While empiricists agree on the legitimacy of deductive reasoning, they differ on the source of their premises. For the rationalist, reason is more than the ability to reason consistently: it is the source of insights and *a priori* truths.

Descartes' innate ideas come not from experience or from our imagination; apart from the idea of a perfect being, they are usually mathematical, like the idea of a circle. They have properties not seen in experience. No circle in experience is perfectly round, but we can still think about perfectly round circles, as we can think about a perfect being, even though no human is perfect. We are finite and imperfect, yet have an idea of an eternal and perfect being. If such ideas do not come from experience they must be innate – implanted in us by some other being.

In contrast to the judgements we make about other things, when we come to think about clear and distinct ideas we are compelled to give our assent, to believe they're true. God forces this upon us and, as he is no deceiver, they must be true. However, we can withhold our assent to those ideas that are not clear and distinct. If we do assent to them God leaves it entirely up to our judgement. Consequently, there is no guarantee that they *are* true, because we are imperfect beings and we frequently insist upon using our faculties beyond their range of reliability. Once we have found just one clear and distinct idea – what Leibniz describes as a 'truth of reason' – Descartes thought we could use it to deduce all of our other beliefs about reality. This would be entirely a process of reason, involving an examination of our beliefs for their clarity and ensuring consistent, logical connections between them.

However, in this argument, as many of Descartes' early supporters soon realized, there is circularity; what has come to be known as the 'Cartesian circle'. In order to prove God's existence we must start from certain principles and axioms. But how do we know these to be correct? Descartes would argue that we clearly and distinctly perceive their truth. But, then, how can we trust our clear and distinct perceptions? Descartes' answer is that God is perfect and benevolent and wouldn't deceive us by giving us a mind capable of error if used correctly. But then we can't trust our clear and distinct ideas until we know God exists, and we can't prove God exists without relying on clear and distinct ideas.

Having introduced the evil genius Descartes has no way of getting rid of him. The evil genius undermines his confidence in reason as thoroughly as his confidence in God bolsters it. He even undermines any confidence we can have in the rules of inference Descartes uses to present his arguments, along with the core assumption he started with that he exists as a thinking thing. If these cannot come from God or from experience, from where do they come?

One line of defence is to argue that some clear and distinct ideas do not need God's guarantee, because they are self-guaranteeing, like the proposition $2 + 2 = 4$. However, this doesn't appear to get us far, because self-guaranteeing propositions of this kind are trivial and tautologous. It is too optimistic to hope that they will be rich and detailed enough to describe the complexities of the actual universe. If we want to go further than this, infallible guarantees vanish. We are presented with the dilemma Berlin refers to: either we begin and end with uninformative, yet certain propositions, or we advance to more informative propositions at the cost of losing certainty and necessity. And this, of course, as empiricists would remind us, is not the lost cause that rationalists claim. Although the propositions we derive from our senses are not immutable, this does not mean they are unreliable. The proposition that wax is hard at 10 degrees centigrade may be contingent on these circumstances, but this makes it no less true and unchanging.

As to the third tenet, even in his own time Descartes' idea of a separate substance of the mind was acknowledged as giving philosophers insoluble problems as to the causal interaction between mind and matter. Like the first two tenets, his explanation needs divine guarantees to certify any relation. He describes perception as immediate and unproblematic: the 'passive faculty ... receiving and taking knowledge of the ideas of sensible things'. (By 'ideas' he means anything that enters the mind, sense impressions, feelings, memories, ideas in the normal sense and so on.) But what these ideas represent in the external world cannot be known in this direct way. If material things can be known at all, they must be inferred from the ideas they cause in us: the 'causal theory of perception'.

But, he explains, there is another 'active faculty capable of forming and producing those ideas'. This cannot be in me, because these ideas are frequently produced in my mind without me contributing anything to them. At times they even come to me contrary to my will. As God is no deceiver he has given me a 'very strong inclination' to believe in the physical objects that produce these ideas. Even so, they are not exactly as we perceive them, because they are apprehended by the senses, which produce ideas that are 'obscure and confused'. Nevertheless, all that I clearly and distinctively conceive in them in terms of 'specula-tive geometry' really exists in the external world. About these there is absolute certainty. Whereas for all we know, all that is not clear and distinct, like smells, colours and sounds, may be nothing more than illusions, dreams and deceptions.

As you can see, Descartes adopts a similar argu-ment in this as he does in the first two tenets: he attempts to establish the reliability of our natural belief that there is an external world and that our experience consists of ideas derived from it. Since it is a natural belief, God would be deceiving us unless it were true. Since God is no deceiver, there must be an external world. As long as he can estab-lish the existence and honesty of God he is justified in inferring knowledge of the physical world from ideas. But the same circularity that undermines the first two tenets undermines this too.

■ 6. Empiricism

Empiricists, by contrast, are much less confident about the rationalist claim for the capacity of reason to reveal knowledge of the external world. *A priori* knowledge, they believe, consists of certain trivial propositions, whose certainty is not so much due to the intuitions of reason as to the fact that they exhibit certain relations between different ideas and words, the content of which we have already decided for ourselves. As Locke describes them, these are merely 'trifling propositions'. In logic and

mathematics *a priori* truths tell us nothing about the real world: they are trivial, derived from the mean-ing of the words and symbols in which they are stated. They tell us about the logical relations of ideas in concepts, like triangles and circles, but they cannot tell us that there *are* such things as triangles and circles. As for the laws of physics, these are empirical, not *a priori*. They are not known with certainty. As science progresses they are being rewritten to take account of new evidence.

Instead, empiricists place their faith in sense experience as the source of knowledge. Nothing enters the mind, they believe, except through the senses. Although these may sometimes be clouded, and though we might be the victims of deception and illusion, if we can only get at the evidence of our senses in its primitive form, it will provide the foundation of all knowledge – knowledge that is, which is not just the repetition of ideas or words. In the evidence of our senses, they believe, there is an essential trustworthiness, as there is in the simple observation statements which put that evidence on record.

We can, then, identify four key principles that empiricists are likely to believe. First, all knowl-edge, except purely logical relations, is based on experience: it is composed of matters of fact about evidence of the senses. Second, the evidence of our senses has primitive authenticity: that is, it can be trusted as the only reliable source of facts on which knowledge can be built. This can mean two things not entirely unconnected. It can mean that proposi-tions which accurately describe the evidence of our senses can be known to be unqualifiedly true in isolation. In other words, we don't have to know everything about the whole to know any particular part, as objective idealists argue. It can also mean, as some empiricists like Bertrand Russell believe, that there are non-mental facts in the external world: that is, facts which are what they are irrespective of whether some mind is aware of them. Not all empiricists believe this, as we will see. Berkeley, in particular, believes that such facts have to be in some mind, and ultimately in the mind of God.

Third, empiricists tend to believe the mind is, as Locke describes it, a 'tabula rasa', a blank sheet, on which nature imprints itself accurately. They would, then, not only reject the rationalist claim that it is possible to obtain by reason alone knowl-edge of the external world, but Kant's critical ideal-ism and his belief that the mind is already programmed with 'forms of intuition' and 'forms of understanding', though which it processes the evidence of our senses. And fourth, empiricists believe the only valid method of verification of the principles and theories we use to describe the external world is to subject them to empirical evidence. The truth of general factual statements can only be established through induction, even though this can provide only probabilistic support.

Empiricists, therefore, see experience as the one sovereign criterion for judging the truth of statements about the external world: it is authoritative and decisive. But this faith rests on two assumptions: the naturalness and inescapability of experience as we receive it through the senses, and the passivity and thoughtlessness of perception. They believe that the mind, like a mirror, should merely reflect accurately nature's image, and any thought of our own, like a smudge on the mirror's surface, will distort that image. So reason must be kept at bay in this process. Scientists must refrain from hypothesizing as they gather the evidence. As you can see there is in this the psychological theory that there is a sharp distinction between thought and perception as the passive undisturbed reception of sense impressions.

So, to summarize:

Four key principles:

1. All knowledge, except purely logical relations, is based on experience.
2. The evidence of our senses has primitive authenticity.
3. The mind is a *tabula rasa*.
4. The only valid method of verification is empirical.

■ 7. Locke's empiricism

Like all empiricists Locke rejects Descartes' belief that reason alone can reveal knowledge of the external world. Instead, in his *Essay Concerning Human Understanding* (1690) he sets out to show how knowledge is built up out of simple ideas from our sense impressions to form our most complex ideas.

7.1 Innate ideas

He begins by denying there are innate ideas 'born into' us prior to experience. We describe truths of

John Locke (1632–1704)

Born in Somerset, England, Locke entered Christ Church, Oxford, in 1652. In 1666 he met his friend and patron, Lord Ashley, later the Earl of Shaftesbury, whose turbulent political career and Locke's own radical liberalism set them at odds with the Stuart government. As a result they both spent long periods in relative safety in Holland. Following his return in 1688, after the accession to the English throne of William of Orange, Locke published his major philosophical works: *Essay Concerning Human Understanding* (1690) and *Two Treatises of Government* (1690). In his final years he also published *Some Thoughts Concerning Education* (1693) and *The Reasonableness of Christianity* (1695).

Although he draws back from the radical empiricism found later in the work of Berkeley and Hume, in *Essay* he adopts an anti-rationalistic position rejecting innate ideas and relying exclusively on sensations and reflection as the only raw materials of human understanding. His political philosophy, however, is more radical and explains the dangers that the Stuart government believed he posed. In *Two Treatises* he defends a doctrine of natural rights and the idea that political authority is both limited and held on trust on the condition that rulers use their power to serve the public good. This classic formulation of the principles of political liberalism influenced both the American and French revolutions and the Constitution of the United States.

this sort as innate, he argues, because we have simply forgotten when we first learned them. They are not to be found in all humans, like children or idiots, so to argue that they are in their minds when they have no knowledge of them makes no conceivable sense. He explains, 'To say a notion is imprinted on the mind, and yet at the same time to say that the mind is in ignorance of it, and never yet took notice of it, is to make this impression nothing.' Instead he argues the mind has no ideas; it is a *tabula rasa* upon which our senses write. All our ideas come from sensation and reflection: that is, from the evidence of our senses and from our capacity to reflect on what goes on in our minds ('remembering, considering, reasoning, etc.')

However, even Locke, as Leibniz points out, could not do without innate ideas in this argument, in that inference from experience itself needs principles that cannot be found in experience. Referring to universal or 'general truths' he explains:

if some events can be foreseen before any trial has been made of them, it is clear that we must here contribute something of our own. The senses, although necessary for all our actual knowledge, are not sufficient to give us the whole of it, since the senses never give anything except examples ... [which] are not enough to establish the universal necessity of this same truth.

So, if we argue that 'All heavier-than-air objects fall to the ground when unsupported', we must give something of our own to conclude that all of them do so, when we have only seen a limited number.

However, since Locke and Leibniz the debate has swayed first one way, then the other. Kant, as we saw in Chapter 6, argued that our minds are so constituted that to understand experience we impose forms of intuition and forms of understanding to create synthetic *a priori* truths and causal explanations. But since then modern anthropology seems to have supported Locke and Hume's explanation that we acquire the principles we need from oft-repeated experiences that lead us to create 'habits of association', through which we interpret experience by regularly associating one thing with another. The discovery of societies whose basic ideas are radically different from our own has shown how this can have a significant impact on our visual perception. Routine examples we take to be quite unproblematic are anything but for someone whose cultural ideas are significantly different. The anthropologist M. J. Herskovits explains the shock of discovering the extent to which our perception is ruled by conventional assumptions we take for granted. He explains:

even the clearest photograph is a convention; a translation of a three dimensional subject into two dimensions, with colour transmuted into shades of black and white. ... [A] Bush Negro woman turned a photograph of her own son this way and that, in attempting to make sense out of the shadings of grey on the piece of paper she held. It was only when the details of the photograph were pointed out to her that she was able to perceive the subject.

On the other side of the argument the twentieth century has also seen the rise of 'Structuralism', particularly through the work of Claude Levi-Strauss, the main argument of which is that beneath the superficial differences between societies there are certain basic structures which are universal and innate. Others, like Noam Chomsky, have argued that we all have certain capacities for language built into us from birth, which not only allow us to explain the similarities in human thinking, but our capacity to learn languages from a very early age.

7.2 Experience: the source of knowledge

Yet instead, rejecting innate ideas, Locke sets out an alternative empirical account in which the core component of knowledge is simple ideas, those which the mind receives passively both from sensation and reflection. These, he says, we can be sure represent something real because our minds are simply incapable of inventing them: they could not be created from the ideas the mind already possesses. They are immediate and unprocessed sensations, like the smell of a flower, the taste of sugar, the whiteness of snow, or the coldness of ice. Once we have experienced these, the mind has the capacity to store them up and, by reflection, reproduce them or combine them with other simple ideas to form complex ideas.

All simple ideas can be divided into two sorts: primary and secondary qualities. Primary qualities ('solidity, extension, figure, motion or rest, and number') are those that belong to the object, while secondary qualities ('colours, sounds, tastes, etc.') are not actually found in the objects, but just in their 'powers to produce various sensations in us by their primary qualities.' So, while size and shape are primary qualities, colour is not, because it is the result of certain conditions or 'powers' in the objects to act upon our minds in such a way that we see these colours, although the objects themselves possess no colour.

This is not unlike the distinction between our normal experience of an object and the account scientists give. And it suggests Locke saw the world as nothing more than a physical mechanism with the qualities that really are in bodies as those that are relevant to their mechanical behaviour. A scientist describes an object as a collection of electrons and protons producing light-waves that strike the retina of an observer activating nerve-ends, which results in changes in our neurological system producing an image we associate with the object. In this way the scientist dispenses with the secondary qualities, which Locke claims to depend for their existence on the mind of the observer, while accepting the objective existence of primary qualities as belonging to the object.

In Locke's causal theory of perception he makes use of the same mechanistic theory Newton develops in *Optiks* (1704), in which Newton describes light as composed of different sized particles each refracting at different angles as they pass through the denser medium of the prism to form the colours of the spectrum. Similarly in *Principia Mathematica* (1686–7), Newton's theory of mechanics, force is likewise the product of particles and masses in motion.

As you can see, Locke's theory is grounded on the assumption that the mind 'hath no other object but its own ideas, which it alone does or can contemplate.' This leaves him with real problems to overcome, particularly in our perception and knowledge of the external world. With *perception*, if all we can know is our own ideas, how do we know that these accurately represent the external material things that cause them? Locke's answer is that our ideas of the primary qualities do represent material things accurately, whereas those of secondary qualities are less reliable. But again, if all we can contemplate is our own ideas, it is not clear on what basis we can decide that the relations that hold between these and the external bodies are accurate. If we can't contemplate what they represent, we remain prisoners of our own ideas. Therefore it's not at all clear how Locke can confidently claim that bodies really do have some qualities, but only appear to have others. Indeed Berkeley argues on this basis we have no grounds for claiming anything external exists at all.

The same problem undermines our *knowledge* of the external world. If all we have to work with is our own ideas, that which we call knowledge might be just one person's opinion about what goes on in her own mind – just a product of her imagination without being anchored in reality. Locke argues that our knowledge of external things comes from the respect to which our ideas agree or disagree, or are related in some way. He explains, 'Wherever we perceive the agreement or disagreement of any of our ideas there is certain knowledge: and wherever we are sure those ideas agree with the reality of things, there is certain real knowledge.'

However, our knowledge of the agreement or disagreement in our ideas extends only so far as the ideas themselves, so how could we tell if it was about anything actually outside of ourselves? And if our ideas are all of the same type, it is difficult to see how we can distinguish between those that are the product of imagination and those that represent reality. As long as the only thing we can be 'immediately' aware of is our own ideas, what has been described as an 'iron curtain' falls between the observer and the external world.

Indeed Locke concedes as much when he says, 'It seems probable to me that the simple ideas we receive from sensation and reflection are the boundaries of our thoughts; beyond which the mind, whatever efforts it would make is not able to advance one jot, nor can it make any discoveries, when it would pry into the nature and hidden causes of these ideas.' Like Descartes, he believed we could know intuitively of our own existence and we could have demonstrative knowledge of God's existence, but beyond that we are restricted to 'sensitive knowledge', which only allows probable knowledge – 'degrees of assent'.

Yet despite the problems relating to knowledge and perception in Locke's account, there is still an equally serious problem raised by the distinction he makes between the two in the first place. The common-sense claim that sensory inputs are primary and unproblematic rests on the thesis which draws a psychological distinction between thought and perception. It is assumed that it is possible to recognize the external world in a primitive sense.

The 'primitiveness' thesis finds support within classical psychology, which distinguishes between sensation and perception. The former apprehends the qualities of an object (its size, colour, shape and so on), while the latter deals with the object itself; in other words, it involves recognition of *what* the object is. Sensation, therefore, is concerned with primary elements and fragmentary images, and perception represents a secondary level, which synthesises sensational elements into a coherent form.

Bertrand Russell, for instance, describes the language of objects, which we use to describe things like chairs and tables, as only shorthand for longer statements that go to describe what we receive through the senses. We call a table a 'table', but really we are referring to a particular, typical set of sense data, different colours and shapes, which we call a 'table'. Locke's 'atomistic theory of perception' is much the same: our understanding of what a table is is made up of isolated constituents of sense data, the whole being no more than the sum of its parts.

However modern Gestalt psychologists argue that such an atomistic theory of perception is quite untenable. Merleau-Ponty argues we can't isolate sensory atoms as the constituents of perceptual experience, because all perceptual experience includes structure and meaning. We necessarily interpret what we receive. As the nineteenth-century German philosopher Friedrich Nietzsche puts it, 'Everything that reaches consciousness is utterly and completely adjusted, simplified, schematised, interpreted.' Everything we perceive has a meaning we bring to it and points to something beyond it. Therefore our perception of whole figures or patterns cannot be construed as the sum of its parts. The French psychologist Jean Piaget argues,

> We do not nowadays believe in 'elementary' preliminary sensations of this kind. ... [P]erception exists immediately as a whole and sensations are therefore only *structured* and not structuring elements (and there is no difference of nature between the whole and its parts). When I perceive a house I do not see at first the colour of a tile, the height of a chimney, and so on, and finally the house. I perceive the house as a Gestalt straightaway, and only subsequently pass to a detailed analysis.

So, the distinction between sensation and perception dissolves. An initial apprehension of the world of objects cannot be depicted as a thoughtless process, whereby sensations imprint themselves onto a receptive and passive *tabula rasa*. Perception involves recognizing objects as objects and differentiating one from another. This is essentially an active, continuous process involving thought.

Recognition of the Gestalt character of perception also involves a rejection of the common-sense claim that our perceptual judgements are 'absolute' and 'objective'. For example, experiments have been conducted in which a person is strapped into a chair and the room is turned and tilted while the chair and the subject remain stable. Usually, the subject perceives the room to remain stable while the chair revolves. What is accurate in this report is the perception of the relative angular motion between the subject and the walls of the room. However, the interpretation given by the subject assumes that, because walls are normally fixed and upright, it must therefore be the chair which is revolving. This suggests that our perception of fixed and moving objects and our perceptions of up and down are fallible inferences based on comparative and not absolute data.

Similar conclusions have been drawn from experiments with inverting spectacles, which turn our retinal images upside down. Stratton and Kohler, who conducted separate experiments, both reported that objects appeared illusory and unreal initially, but that this strangeness disappeared within a few days of wearing them. Objects began to look almost normal again as the experiment continued, and the wearers were able to carry on with their normal day-to-day activities without any undue difficulty. Stratton concluded that, 'The different sense-perceptions ... are organised into one harmonious spatial system. The harmony is found to consist in having our experiences meet our expectations.'

■ 8. Conclusion

Nevertheless, if this is the case it leaves us with the problem of how our original perceptions organized experience into significant terms in the first place. In other words, where do these original perceptions come from? It would be a circular argument to claim they came from experience, so we may be compelled to return to Plato and Descartes and innate ideas, or forward to Hume and Kant as we will see in the next chapter.

■ Questions

1. a) What are the main differences between rationalism and empiricism?

   b) To what extent may Descartes be described as a rationalist?

2. a) What conclusions does Descartes draw from the example of the melted wax?

   b) How justified are these conclusions?

3. Could what looks green to me look red to you?

4. Do you agree with Locke, that you are able to

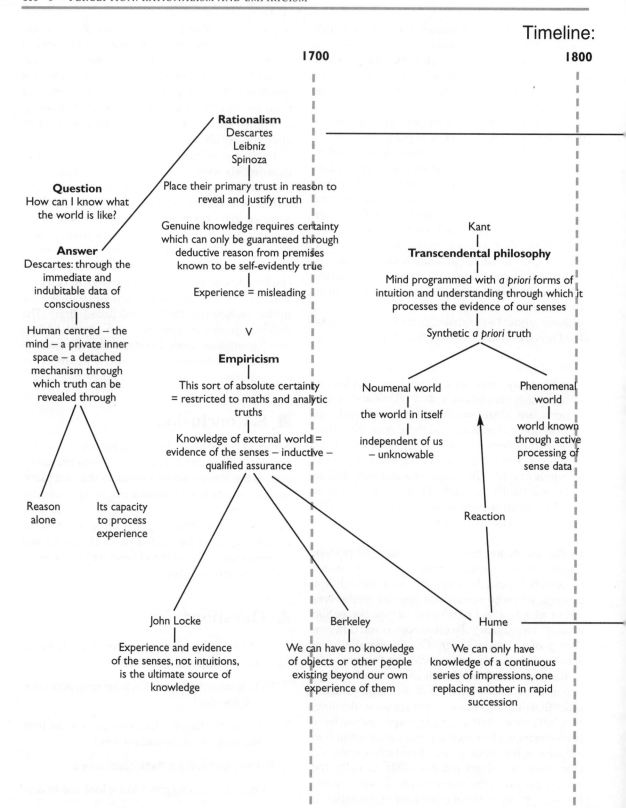

Timeline:

1700

1800

Rationalism
Descartes
Leibniz
Spinoza

Place their primary trust in reason to
reveal and justify truth

Genuine knowledge requires certainty
which can only be guaranteed through
deductive reason from premises
known to be self-evidently true

Experience = misleading

V

Empiricism

This sort of absolute certainty
= restricted to maths and analytic
truths

Knowledge of external world =
evidence of the senses – inductive –
qualified assurance

Question
How can I know what
the world is like?

Answer
Descartes: through the
immediate and
indubitable data of
consciousness

Human centred – the
mind – a private inner
space – a detached
mechanism through
which truth can be
revealed through

Reason
alone

Its capacity
to process
experience

Kant

Transcendental philosophy

Mind programmed with *a priori* forms of
intuition and understanding through which it
processes the evidence of our senses

Synthetic *a priori* truth

Noumenal world

the world in itself

independent of us
– unknowable

Phenomenal
world

world known
through active
processing of
sense data

Reaction

John Locke

Experience and evidence
of the senses, not intuitions,
is the ultimate source of
knowledge

Berkeley

We can have no knowledge
of objects or other people
existing beyond our own
experience of them

Hume

We can only have
knowledge of a continuous
series of impressions, one
replacing another in rapid
succession

Epistemology

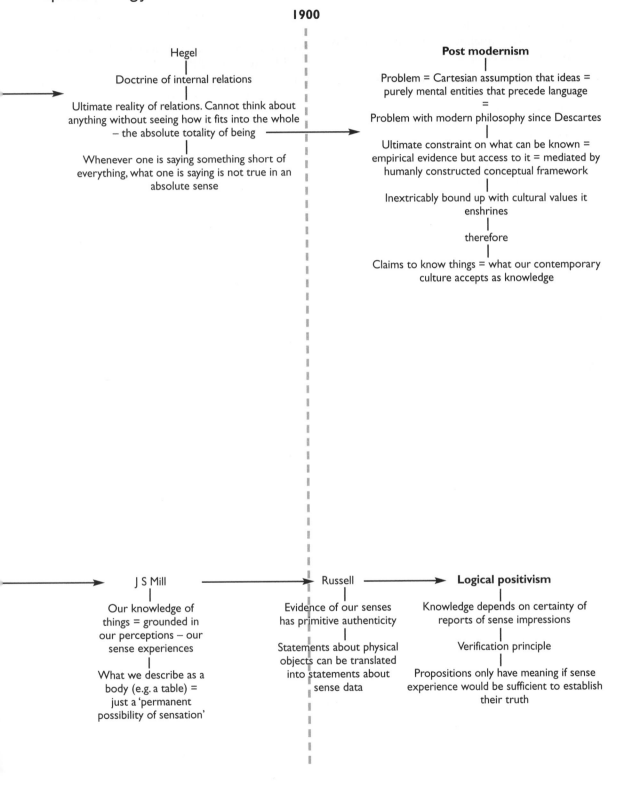

1900

Hegel
|
Doctrine of internal relations
|
Ultimate reality of relations. Cannot think about anything without seeing how it fits into the whole – the absolute totality of being
|
Whenever one is saying something short of everything, what one is saying is not true in an absolute sense

Post modernism
|
Problem = Cartesian assumption that ideas = purely mental entities that precede language
=
Problem with modern philosophy since Descartes
|
Ultimate constraint on what can be known = empirical evidence but access to it = mediated by humanly constructed conceptual framework
|
Inextricably bound up with cultural values it enshrines
|
therefore
|
Claims to know things = what our contemporary culture accepts as knowledge

J S Mill
|
Our knowledge of things = grounded in our perceptions – our sense experiences
|
What we describe as a body (e.g. a table) = just a 'permanent possibility of sensation'

Russell
|
Evidence of our senses has primitive authenticity
|
Statements about physical objects can be translated into statements about sense data

Logical positivism
|
Knowledge depends on certainty of reports of sense impressions
|
Verification principle
|
Propositions only have meaning if sense experience would be sufficient to establish their truth

form the abstract idea of redness in isolation from particular red objects?

5. Explain Locke's distinction between *primary* and *secondary* qualities. Do you think this distinction can be upheld?

6. Discuss the claim that statements about physical objects can be completely analysed into statements about sense-data.

7. 'The table… appears to be of different colours from different points of view, and there is no reason for regarding some of these as more really its colour than others.' (Russell) Discuss.

■ Recommended reading

Plato. *The Republic*, trans. H. D. P. Lee (Harmondsworth: Penguin, 1971).

Plato, Theatetus. In Irwin Edman (ed.), *The Works of Plato* (New York: Tudor, 1927).

Plato, Meno. In *Plato: Protagoras and Meno*, trans. W. K. C. Guthrie (Harmondsworth: Penguin, 1956).

Descartes, R. Second Meditation (1641). In *Discourse on Method and other Writings*, trans. F. E. Sutcliffe (Harmondsworth: Penguin, 1970).

Locke, J. *An Essay Concerning Human Understanding* (1690) (London: Fontana, 1973).

Ayer, A. J. *The Problem of Knowledge* (Harmondsworth and Baltimore: Penguin, 1990), Chapter 3.

Russell, B. *The Problems of Philosophy* (Oxford: Oxford University Press, 1987), Chapters 1 and 2.

Merleau-Ponty, M. *The Phenomenology of Perception* (London: Routledge & Kegan Paul, 1962), Preface and Chapter 3.

 The note structure to accompany this chapter can be downloaded from our website.

Perception: Idealism and Phenomenalism

CHAPTER 9

Key issues

▶ Is the search for foundations to philosophy necessary at all? Is it just a mistake that derives from Descartes?

▶ If the mind is not passive, if it actively judges and interprets experience, how can we know our knowledge is true independently of us?

▶ If we have no direct experience of physical objects, only the evidence of our senses, is Locke's assumption that our experiences are caused by physical objects unjustified?

▶ Are Hume and Kant right to believe the principles we accept as necessarily true about the real world are in fact of our own making?

▶ Is Berkeley right that the world is composed of nothing but ideas and mental states?

▶ Do tables and chairs cease to exist the moment I leave the room: the moment I am no longer perceiving them?

▶ Or is even the mind a mere figment, just a succession of impressions, separate ideas, memories and feelings with no bond between them?

Contents

In the last chapter we saw in the work of Descartes and Locke the consequence of rejecting the traditional metaphysical assumption of an unchanging ultimate reality (Plato's 'forms' or universals, for example; pure unchanging ideas outside space and time, which could only be grasped by reason). Independent of experience these were the source of our knowledge of the necessary truths about the world. By rejecting this I am accepting that I alone exist independently, with the outside world nothing more than the object of my consciousness. And once I concede that my immediate sense impressions are mind-dependent, it is questionable whether I can argue validly for the existence of a mind-independent world.

So, Descartes' dualistic theory of mind and matter has left us with the problem that our only starting point for knowledge of the external world is our own momentary conscious experiences. As these are private, they alone won't allow us to move from here to the public world of lasting physical objects. I cannot compare your experiences of these objects with mine, because I cannot know what your momentary private experiences are like. We cannot get beyond the ideas we take from our own senses.

The only solution, it appears, lies in the sort of assumptions any system of knowledge must be built upon, the truth of which we know without proof or evidence, like those we make about the predictability and stability of the universe, its harmony and order, and even the simplicity of the laws and systems governing it. However, this necessarily goes beyond the empiricist notion of the mind as a passive instrument receiving and reflecting accurately the impressions made upon it without interference. In this new role it is active, interpreting and judging experience on the basis of these axiomatic assumptions. Using concepts of its own making, the mind organizes experience, forming conjectures and hypotheses that go beyond present experience. Knowledge, therefore, has an element of us and our judgement in it. Indeed there appears no way of discovering order in experience without it. Yet, having imposed it we cannot then know it to be true independent of us.

In this chapter we will see how Hume and Kant negotiate this middle way between rationalism and empiricism. The mind, they believe, is not passive, as Locke assumed; it actively judges and interprets experience. And, unlike the rationalists' belief that pure reason alone can yield incorrigible truths about nature and the structure of the universe, they believe the principles we accept as necessarily true about the real world are in fact of our own making. This leaves us then with the concern for independent truth: that it should be built upon foundations that are objective and independent of us. In recent times philosophers have been keen to dismiss this concern, questioning whether knowledge needs this sort of foundation at all. We will see that they argue the search for foundations begun by Descartes has simply been a mistake.

1. Subjective idealism: Bishop George Berkeley

In the last chapter we saw there were two ways of answering the questions, what is the world like and how are we to know what it's like. The pluralist way of Descartes and Locke was to argue that there is more than one kind of ultimate constituent of the world: both mind and matter. In contrast the traditional monist approach was to argue that the world is composed of just one kind of substance, either mind or matter, from which all else flows. Idealists, like Bishop Berkeley, for example, argue that the world is composed of nothing but ideas and mental states. We can, then, have no direct knowledge of physical objects and matter. In later chapters we

George Berkeley (1685–1753)

Berkeley was born at Kilkenny in Ireland and entered Trinity College, Dublin, in 1700, where he became a fellow in 1707. By the time he visited England in 1713 he had already published *Essay Towards a New Theory of Vision* (1709), *Principles of Human Knowledge* (1710) and in 1713 the *Three Dialogues between Hylas and Philonous*. Thereafter he seems to have turned his back on his philosophical ideas in marked contrast to Locke whose main work did not appear until he was nearly 60. In 1724 Berkeley embarked enthusiastically on a project to set up a college in Bermuda for the Christian education of the colonial and indigenous people of America. Although his powers of persuasion and charm succeeded in getting promises of government support, this never materialized and the project collapsed. He returned to London from America in 1732 and was made Bishop of Cloyne in 1734.

The bold radical empiricism of his major work exactly suited Berkeley's temperament. He realized that once Descartes had opened up the gap between mind and matter it couldn't be bridged. He challenged the common-sense view that although the mind is different from matter it could still be in contact with the material world and know a great deal about it. Berkeley points out that once this separation is complete all we can ever know is our own minds and their ideas.

will compare this with the objective or absolute idealism of the famous German philosopher G. W. F. Hegel. We will also see how materialists like Karl Marx, in the same monist tradition, deny the mental or spiritual components of Cartesian dualism and attempt to work out a more advanced mechanistic and materialist theory to account for the creation of ideas and spiritual states.

For now we will concentrate on the ideas of Bishop Berkeley, whose most important works, *A Treatise concerning the Principles of Human Knowledge* (1710) and *Three Dialogues between Hylas and Philonous* (1713), were written in his early twenties while he was a fellow at Trinity College, Dublin. In contrast to Locke, whose major work was not published until he was nearly 60, Berkeley did little more thereafter than defend or explain his views; indeed in his later life he seems to have spent little time thinking about them at all. Instead, it is reported that one of his most fervent passions was the virtues of tar water as a cure for most human ills.

Subjective idealism is the belief that all we can know to exist are ideas in the largest sense (feelings, sense impressions, memories, ideas and so on), and other minds. Like Locke, Berkeley believed that all we can ever know of a thing is its sensible properties ('qualities'). So, as Locke argued, we can have no idea of ultimate reality or 'substance', and whether it exists, because it cannot be apprehended by the senses. But Berkeley was a more consistent empiricist than Locke: for him our knowledge of anything was just a bundle of sensations, beyond which we cannot go. The beer you enjoy each night at your local bar you might think is more significant than just a bundle of ideas, but in the final reckoning that's all it is. At first contact you have the sensations of sight, smell and touch, then taste, quickly followed by internal satisfaction and eventually light-headedness and, perhaps, inebriation. But that's all you know: the sensations it generates. It is just a condition of the mind. All we can ever know directly is our mind and our ideas.

1.1 Objects

So, Locke's assumption that our experiences are caused by physical objects is plainly unjustified: we have no experience of the objects, only their effects on us. It follows, then, that we must also reject Locke's distinction between primary qualities inherent in the objects and secondary qualities, which are not in the object, just in the mind. If we can only know ideas in the mind, exactly the same reasoning for secondary qualities applies to primary qualities. To think otherwise, Berkeley believed, can only lead philosophers to doubt 'those things which other men evidently know, and (believe) those things which they laugh at and despise.'

By creating a theory in which real things are different from sense experience, Locke was no longer a consistent empiricist. If he were, Berkeley argued, he would reject both the causal theory of perception, in which our sense experiences are caused by physical objects, along with the very notion of physical objects. A mental event cannot represent anything that is not an idea. If physical objects are different from ideas, we can have no way of knowing them. Ideas are ephemeral, fleeting and ever-changing, whereas physical objects are said to

be fixed and unchanging. We can perceive ideas, but we cannot perceive physical objects.

So, is there a sound when a tree falls in a forest, when no one is around? The fact that we can ask such perplexing questions, Berkeley believes, is due to the misleading 'doctrine of abstract ideas'. He asks:

> can there be a nicer strain of abstraction than to distinguish the existence of sensible objects from their being perceived, so as to conceive them existing unperceived? ... I might as easily divide a thing from itself. ... [I]t is impossible for me to see or feel anything without an actual sensation of that thing, so it is impossible for me to conceive in my thoughts any sensible thing or object distinct from the sensation or perception of it.

All that we can know are sense impressions at the moment of experiencing them. We have no reason to believe that they are related to one another or to anything else that has an existence apart from them. We have no reason to believe that the delicious taste of beer has any existence apart from our experience of it. This is not to say that physical objects are different from what they appear to be, just that all we can know about them are the ideas we have of them.

1.2 Mind and God

Nevertheless, this creates an obvious problem: what has become known as the 'perpetual annihilation and creation' problem. The position so far means that things like tables and chairs cease to exist the moment I leave the room, indeed, the moment I am no longer perceiving them. But things don't just disappear when we're not looking at them and, anyway, things appear with an order and regularity which is not of our own making, so what accounts for that?

Berkeley's answer is simple. With complete consistency he argues, if they are not perceived by me or anyone else, yet still exist, they must be perceived by some other mind – and this can only be the mind of God. In *Hylas and Philonous* he explains:

> seeing they depend not on my thought, and have an existence distinct from being perceived by me, there must be some other mind wherein they exist. As sure, therefore, as the sensible world

really exists, so sure is there an infinite omnipresent spirit, who contains and supports it.

He distinguishes between two types of ideas, those of sensation and reflection. The latter come from the operation of the mind, as we imagine and remember. They can be manipulated by the will and cannot, therefore, be relied on for their accuracy. But ideas of sensation are simply the passive effects of something. They are not the product of our will: as soon as we open our eyes we perceive them, whether we want to or not. You might prick your finger and feel the pain, even though you neither sought, nor enjoyed it. They are 'imprinted on the senses by the authority of nature'. What's more, they are more distinct and regular than those of our own making.

All this, he believes, points to the fact that the entire world of nature, its harmony and regularity, is nothing but the expression of the ideas in the mind of God. The natural world is presented to us as a kind of sign language by which we interpret the mind of God. Indeed the whole cosmos is composed of spirits or minds, some infinite, some finite, all active members. The passive effects in the form of the ideas that are regularly imprinted on our minds represent the permanence of the cosmos, in that it is constantly perceived by God.

The oddness of this idea has intrigued many, supporters and detractors alike, right up to our own day and our concerns about one hand clapping and unseen, unheard trees falling in forests. In 1924 this limerick, written by Ronald Knox, a Roman Catholic priest and translator of the Bible, appeared in the *Complete Limerick Book*:

> There once was a man who said 'God
> Must think it exceedingly odd
>   If he finds that this tree
>   Continues to be
> When there's no one about in the Quad.'

It provoked an anonymous response, clearly from someone who wanted to let Berkeley have the last word:

> Dear Sir, Your astonishment's odd:
> *I* am always about in the Quad.
>   And that's why the tree
>   Will continue to be,
> Since observed by Yours faithfully, God.

This, however, creates a problem, as you have no doubt already seen, since it assumes we have knowledge which doesn't come from our sense experience, in this case knowledge of the existence of God. Berkeley's response is to argue that in addition to ideas from sense experience we have other items, 'notions', in the mind, the most basic of which is our awareness of ourselves. We don't perceive ourselves in the same way we do chairs and tables, as a series or collection of sense impressions. On the contrary, we are aware of ourselves as active agents, who think, will and act. This awareness gives us other primary notions, the most important of which is the notion of God as an omnipresent spirit, who thinks and perceives all ideas.

1.3 Phenomenalism

The theory of perception developed by Berkeley has close affinities with phenomenalism, the view that denies that we must suppose that physical objects have an existence distinct from sensible appearances, ideas or 'phenomena'. Instead, as a theory of perception, phenomenalism argues that all statements about physical objects are logically equivalent to statements about sense data. The most useful slogan to remember is J. S. Mill's that a material thing is a permanent possibility of sensation, or even Russell's remark that a thing is the class of its appearances. As we have seen, Berkeley believes that what we ordinarily call physical objects are actually collections of ideas in the mind. In his famous phrase, the existence of things consists in their being perceived – *'esse est percipi'* ('to be is to be perceived').

We will see later, when we discuss logical positivism, that there are problems with this position, but for now it's worth noting that Berkeley's form of phenomenalism identifies a genuine problem with the common sense view that physical objects exist 'out there' and are responsible for our sensations. In Locke's and Descartes' account the things immediately perceived are ideas, which can only exist in the mind, whereas the common sense view, or 'direct realism', is that things immediately perceived are physical objects in the external world. While both Locke and Descartes believe that our sense impressions are signs of objects in the external world, they have no way of showing this. As a result, either we are driven into scepticism, doubting whether objects really exist, or into paradox: each time we ask what the object is really like, it eludes our grasp. We are bound to give an answer framed in terms of the very sensations and ideas we are trying to get behind. We seem to be imprisoned within the confines of our own sense impressions.

In contrast Berkeley argues that all our ideas come from experience, and if there are physical objects different from our ideas we can simply never know anything about them. In his theory real things are not only the sequences of ideas in my mind, but real continuously existing series of things, because the ideas I perceive are also the ideas of God. Hence my ideas are an accurate true picture of real objects, because they are in the mind of God.

Not only does this evade the problem of paradox that bedevils Locke and Descartes, but its strategy is similar in important respects to that of modern science. It is not in the world of material objects, but in sense experience itself in which science finds its source of data. For the scientist, material objects are useful concepts to postulate for certain practical purposes. And this is exactly Berkeley's point: it may just be very useful for us to postulate the concept 'apple' as a name for a group of experiences that are found together; 'A certain colour, taste, smell, figure and consistence having been observed to go together are accounted one direct thing, signified by the name "apple".'

But this is very different from concluding that external objects really exist 'out there' apart from our sensations, as Locke and Descartes do. If we have no way of proving their separate existence, the best, and perhaps the only, alternative is to deny it. Known as 'sensationalism' this is one form of phenomenalism, as a theory of knowledge, supported by philosophers like Hume, Russell and J. S. Mill, who maintain that nothing exists beyond appearances presented to our senses. Or, to put it another way, this is to argue simply that the object just *is* the name we give to a certain collection of ideas or sensations. Hume argues it is nothing else apart from these ideas: as Berkeley explains, 'In truth the object and the sensation are the same thing, and cannot therefore be abstracted from each other.' The alternative view of phenomenalism, supported by Kant and known as 'agnosticism', maintains that although we cannot infer the character of what lies beyond our sense experience we can at least infer there is something out there.

The importance of Berkeley's account in edging closer to modern scientific practice is also evident in his rejection of the traditional metaphysical notion of 'matter' as 'an inert, senseless, substance in which extension, figure, motion do actually subsist.' Matter could only be known through those qualities that subsist in it, like colour, hardness and shape. Take these away and there is nothing that could be perceived; it is unknown and unknowable. If 'to be is to be perceived', to assume the existence of something that can by definition not be perceived is a contradiction. Yet even more interesting, Berkeley abandons the metaphysical notion of matter not just because it could not be perceived, in line with modern scientific practice, but because it could not itself perceive. As 'there is not any other substance than spirit or that which perceives', matter – as an inert, senseless, unperceiving substance – could not exist. Nothing can exist but spirits or minds and the ideas, like colour, shape and hardness, that depend upon them.

To Berkeley's contemporaries his theory was fantastic and beyond belief. If you rejected the idea that God perceived everything, it seemed to end in the belief that everything was nothing but an idea in the mind with no real existence beyond. While visiting Dean Swift, the author of *Gulliver's Travels* (1726), Berkeley was left standing on the doorstep with the door closed in his face. Swift reasoned that if his ideas were correct, he would be able to enter through a closed door.

■ 2. Hume

Equally disturbing to its contemporaries was David Hume's *Treatise of Human Nature* (1739–40), thought by many to be one of the classics of modern philosophy. Although Berkeley's account has the consistency missing in Locke's and Descartes', it still doesn't pursue the logic of its assumptions to their conclusion. This was left to David Hume.

2.1 The mind

Extending Berkeley's account to its logical conclusion, Hume argues that we know the mind only as we know matter: only as a bundle of perceptions. So the mind or 'self' is as unclear as matter and we search in vain for an impression that would give us such an idea. All we have is a succession of impressions, separate ideas, memories and feelings, which flash before us like the separate images on a reel of film. There is no bond between them other than their similarity, succession and causation. Other than that the mind is a mere figment; like Berkeley's apple, it *is* the abstract name we give to a series of ideas. Hume explains:

> When I enter most intimately into what I call *myself*, I always stumble on some particular perception or other, of heat or cold, light or shade, love or hatred, pain or pleasure. I never catch *myself* at any time without a perception, and never can observe anything but the perception.

Therefore, he concludes, we are 'nothing but a bundle or collection of different perceptions, which succeed each other with an inconceivable rapidity, and are in a perpetual flux and movement.'

And with this Hume had effectively destroyed the concept of mind, as Berkeley had destroyed the concept of matter. Not only was there no divine mind, there was no individual mind: there was no substance, an organ that has ideas. But still, if the mind is a mere figment we create from a rapid succession of separate images, who or what is it that creates this? How is it that the series can be conscious of its own serial existence? At this point Hume 'pleads the privilege of the sceptic', conceding that the problem is too hard for him to solve.

2.2 Impressions and ideas

Such a cop-out, though frustrating, seems inevitable given the empirical foundations of his philosophy. Like Berkeley, Hume believes that everything we're aware of is just 'impressions' and 'ideas'. Impressions are what we describe as sensations, feelings and emotions, while ideas are thoughts. Impressions we receive with 'force and vivacity', while ideas are just faint copies of our impressions. Hume describes two types of impressions: primary impressions of sense 'from unknown causes', and secondary impressions of reflection, which arise as a result of our ideas. Say you enjoy the sensation of tasting chocolate. From that you develop the idea of enjoying it, itself a faint copy of the original primary impression. Then, after reflecting upon this, you develop the secondary impression of longing for it.

Ideas are also of two kinds: simple and complex. Simple ideas are just copies of primary impressions. So the idea of the taste of chocolate is an identical copy of the primary impression of tasting it. Hence all ideas, notably including Descartes' 'innate ideas', ultimately derive from experience. Complex ideas are combinations of simple ideas derived from impressions. These can be real combinations that we recall from memory, or imaginative combinations of things that have never existed, that is except in the minds of fiction writers, strange beings like the elves, goblins, hobbits and dragons in J. R. R. Tolkien's *The Lord of the Rings* (1954–5).

2.3 The principles and habits of association

Combining ideas in this way we use two faculties: the memory, which reproduces the fixed order of ideas as they were received, and imagination, which arranges ideas in any order. Nevertheless, even in imagination the mind organizes ideas into certain patterns. When we think of an idea we can think of a resembling idea, or one contiguous to it in time and place, or one related to it as cause or effect. These patterns, or principles of association, are, Hume believes, 'really to *us* the cement of the universe.'

Through them we are led to the fundamental principles that underlie our theory of knowledge, particularly the principle of the uniformity of nature. By inspecting two or more ideas for their contiguity and succession, we accumulate intuitive and certain knowledge. But we also develop psychological habits or customs of association. If we experience the constant conjunction of two events frequently enough, we come to believe that, given one event, the other will necessarily occur, and on this basis we fashion our causal and predictive explanations for events in the natural world. But we can never perceive causes or laws, just sequences of events from which we infer causes and necessity. A law is merely a summary of the sequences of events we have observed – a habit of association and nothing more.

No amount of observation will establish the truth of the principle of the uniformity of nature on which laws and causal relations depend. The most it will confirm is that nature has been uniform in the past, which has no bearing on what will happen in the future. But, as we will see in the next chapter, the habit by which one event is identified as the cause of another through 'constant conjunction', though lacking empirical justification, lies at the heart of scientific practice, particularly in its inductive methodology and its causal explanations. That modern science could be built upon unjustified habits of association shook the philosophical world, almost as much as Hume's refusal to believe in the existence of God, and did much to awaken Kant from what he described as his 'dogmatic slumber'.

2.4 Reasoning consists in discovering relations

From the material we gather from impressions and ideas we reason with one end in view: to discover the relations between them. This amounts to two things: discovering the relations between ideas, and the way things stand in relation to each other as a matter of fact. With relations of ideas we reason demonstratively to show what is conceivable and what is inconceivable. It is conceivable, for example, that ten is equal to two fives, and that the angles of a triangle add up to two right angles. But it is inconceivable, because it is self-contradictory, that a person could be a bachelor while being married, or that something could be a cat without being an animal.

In other words the truth of these propositions depends upon the nature of the ideas that are related and can be demonstrated through reason. In contrast all matters of fact relations could have been otherwise: something different, even the opposite, could be conceived without contradiction. That the French Revolution began in 1789, that Jupiter has 16 moons, or that London is 274 miles from Newcastle are all matters of fact – they could have been otherwise.

So, to summarize:

Relations:
1. Relations of ideas
2. Matters of fact relations

All else that contains neither demonstrative knowledge nor empirical reasoning about matters of fact is merely 'sophistry and illusion' and should be 'committed to the flames', Hume boldly declares. No other propositions can be meaningful, because there is no way of testing their validity. So, the key notions of metaphysics (substance, reality, mind, matter) are meaningless, because we are unable to define them in terms of anything we know. If our knowledge of the world is restricted to experience and the inferences we draw from it, we cannot possibly tell if there is any permanent structure to reality over and above what we are aware of. With qualities of immediate experience, like colour, taste, sound and smell, excluded from being

features of the material world, the world of substance, which supposedly exists independently of us, we cannot possibly conceive what matter is like. And, what's more, as Berkeley has shown, all the qualities metaphysics attribute to matter, like extension, motion, solidity, are just as subjective as those it excludes.

2.5 Physical objects

From this it also follows that we can have no knowledge of the existence of physical objects as relatively permanent things, distinct and independent of us. They cannot be known by our senses, nor can they by inference from effect to cause. For this we would have to be able to observe the sensation and the physical object separately, and clearly this is exactly the point at issue: can we verify its existence without sensations? Hence, as we can neither observe the cause, nor the two separately, Hume concludes physical objects must be considered an illusion, a fiction.

Nevertheless, he admits it is a convenient assumption we might have to accept:

> the sceptic ... must assent to the principle concerning the existence of body, though he cannot pretend, by any arguments of philosophy, to maintain its veracity. ... That is a point which we must take for granted in all our reasonings.

He turns his attention instead to the question why in fact we *do* believe in the continued and independent existence of physical objects and he concludes that our 'opinion must be entirely owing to the *imagination.*' We form the opinion of the continued existence of physical objects, because of 'the coherence and constancy of certain impressions.'

2.6 The complete sceptic

If Hume is right it seems we have little alternative but complete scepticism of ever knowing anything about the universe. All we're aware of are impressions unrelated to each other and, as far as we can tell, unrelated externally to physical objects and internally to the 'self' or mind. The only way we have of interpreting them is to use our own self-created mental habits to identify causal connections, external objects and some sort of thing inside us, a 'self', which holds our experiences together. The further we explore the bases for our beliefs, the more we realize how unjustified and irrational they are. Indeed, even Hume's belief in his own philosophical ideas was on this basis indefensible, the product of unjustifiable habits and customs, a matter of mere taste.

Nevertheless, as he himself realized, we cannot avoid believing. When he lifted his eyes from his work he couldn't avoid believing in the uniformity of nature, the existence of physical objects and in the continued existence of his own self. Hume, like most philosophers since, was burdened with the legacy of Descartes' metaphysical self, which was not only conscious of its own existence but capable of all manner of mental processing. Even though Hume had effectively dissipated this into the fragments of discrete, unrelated impressions, he was still left with the remains in the form of impressions and ideas, with which to try to recreate the world of common sense. With only the habits of association as the cement to bind the pieces together, no wonder he was left with such unremitting scepticism.

■ 3. Kant

At the beginning of this chapter we said the problem Descartes had left us was how to move from the subject-dependent world of private experience to the public world of knowledge. It seemed the only solution lay in the sort of assumptions that any theory of knowledge depends upon, the truth of which is thought to be known without proof or evidence. But in this the mind is no longer passive, a *tabula rasa*, but actively interprets and judges experience in the light of these assumptions. Knowledge has an element of us and our judgement in it: we cannot know something to be true independent of us.

With Hume our active judgement takes the form of the principles and habits of association. Though lacking philosophical justification they explain the way we make sense of the world through causal explanations and inductive generalizations. On reading this Kant was shaken from his 'dogmatic slumber' and in 1781, at the age of 56, embarked on ten of the most important years in the history of philosophy with his first major work the *Critique of Pure Reason*.

Like Berkeley and Hume he accepts there are two worlds: the 'noumenal' world, the world in itself, independent of us and unknowable in itself; and the 'phenomenal' world, which we know as a result of

our own active processing of sense data. Knowledge, he believes, begins with experience, as the empiricists claim, but this doesn't mean it *arises* from this. Our senses supply the content but not the form; this is a product of the mind and its synthetic *a priori* judgements. So, as for Hume, the mind is active in processing sense impressions into forms that yield understanding, yet not through habits of association, but through the very structure of the mind itself. Using the natural forms of 'intuition' and 'understanding', it processes experience, creating the necessary connections between events and ideas that Hume explains are the result of habits of association.

In the *Critique* Kant describes this as 'pure' reason in that it is independent of the senses and experience; it belongs to us, inherent in the nature and structure of the mind. He sets out to define its limits and possibilities, hence his term 'critical philosophy', and to explain the legitimacy of synthetic *a priori* judgements. This he also describes as 'transcendental philosophy', in that it transcends sense experience to study the inherent structure of the mind and the innate laws of thought. The problem with empiricists, he believes, is that they see only 'separate and distinct' events from which it is impossible to derive the necessity of invariable sequences of which you can be forever certain. This explains too why empiricists can only ever see a series of disconnected mental events and never the mind. Experience can never provide us with certain knowledge, because it is derived from an external world that can never guarantee regularity and predictability.

But, he claims:

Experience is by no means the only field to which our understanding can be confined. Experience tells us what is, but not that it must be necessarily what it is and not otherwise. It therefore never gives us any really general truths. ... General truths, which at the same time bear the character of an external necessity, must be independent of experience – clear and certain in themselves.

They must be true despite experience, indeed, *before* experience: that is, *a priori*. Like the truths of mathematics, they don't depend on experience for their truth; they are true absolutely and necessarily in the past, present and future. Indeed, it is inconceivable that they should ever be false. The source of such necessity, he argues, is the mind itself. It is inherent in the structure of the mind and the way it works. The mind is not Locke's passive *tabula rasa*, nor an abstract name for a series of separate impressions as Hume describes it, but an active organ, which moulds and coordinates sensations into ideas, into organized unity of thought.

3.1 Perception

The process of correlating our experience into knowledge, Kant believes, involves two stages, perception and conception, involving two faculties, respectively sense and understanding.

Experience ⟶ Knowledge

=

Perception(sense) ⟶ Conception(understanding)

In the first stage we coordinate our sensations by applying forms of intuition; two types of *a priori* characteristics that are present in any awareness we might have. These are temporal and geometric features, in other words, space and time, and mathematical truths. We organize our sensations, attributing them to an object or objects which are in a particular position in space and at a certain time in the past, present or future. Take Berkeley's apple, for instance: here we unite and group our sensations of taste, smell, sight, sound and touch around an object in space and time, so that we become aware of a specific object.

So, to summarize:

Perception =
    Coordinating sensations via forms of intuition
    = 2 types of *a priori* characteristics:
        1. temporal – space and time
        2. geometric – mathematical truths

In this way, using these various modes of perception, we give sense to our sensations. As Kant explains, our concern in what he describes as 'critical philosophy' is 'not so much with objects as with the manner of our cognition of objects, in so far as it is possible *a priori*.' All of our ordered experience involves and presupposes these *a priori* intuitions; indeed, it is inconceivable that we should ever have experience that would not involve them.

3.2 Conception

In the same way that perception organizes the unorganized data from our senses into organized sensation around objects and events in space and time, so conception organizes perceptions around concepts or 'categories', which make up our forms of understanding.

So, to summarize:

Conception = organizing perceptions via forms of understanding

This is a general conceptual scheme of four concepts, each divided into groups of three as the table on page 120 shows. Our perceptions are received into this structure, by which they are classified and moulded into ordered concepts of thought. They are raised from perceptual knowledge of objects into the conceptual knowledge of relationships, sequences and laws – the tools of the mind which refine our experience into scientific knowledge. For example, when we judge that A caused B we apply the general principle of causality that every event has a cause. And in applying this to our perception, the organized sense data of A and B, we synthesise the sense data with the *a priori* category of causality, part of the structure of our minds, to create a synthetic *a priori* judgement. This is not abstracted from some *perceived* necessary connection, because all we perceive, as Hume has already shown, is just the succession of events, which Kant accepted.

This astonishing insight, which Kant believed was one of the major contributions of his philosophy, came on the back of Hume's equally astonishing insight that we cannot see causes, that sensations have no necessary features, therefore we must create them ourselves. Woken by Hume from his 'dogmatic slumber', Kant compared it with Copernicus' revolutionary theory of the heliocentric nature of the universe. As Copernicus removed the earth from the centre of creation, so Kant removed the earthly experience of our senses, making it peripheral to the active processing of the mind.

By applying the categories to perception in this way we create an objective, or inter-subjective, reality, in which we can see physical objects as systematically organized perceptions capable of causal relations and interactions with other objects. Kant says, to be an object, as opposed to being merely a subjective impression, is to be the bearer of categories, to be capable of being changed by categories.

Table 9.1 General conceptual scheme

Quantity	Unity	Plurality	Totality
Quality	Reality	Negation	Limitation
Relation	Substance/accident	Causality/dependence	Community/interaction
Modality	Possibility/impossibility	Existence/non-existence	Necessity/contingency

In effect, this is what we *mean* by objective reality, which is only possible as a result of the connections between perceptions that the mind makes by means of the categories. They put order, sequence and unity into our perceptions. Kant says, 'Perceptions without conceptions are blind.' Things are known to us only through these laws of thought.

3.3 The phenomenal and noumenal worlds

As you can see, Kant's great achievement is to show that the empiricists are right that the external world can only be known to us through sensations. To that extent he, too, is a phenomenalist. But, like Hume, he goes beyond this, claiming that the mind is no mere passive *tabula rasa* on which impressions are imprinted, but an active agent selecting and reconstructing sense data into knowledge and understanding. We can only know the world, therefore, as a construction. It is made up of 'phenomena': objects we construct to have objective knowledge from sensations. An object is merely a bundle of sensations, as Hume thought, organized by our mental structures into perceptions, and perceptions into conceptions.

However, as we have seen before, any theory of knowledge built on assumptions about the mind and its workings is bound to be mind-dependent: it cannot know the world-in-itself independent of the mind. The object as it appears to us may be very different from the external object, the 'thing-in-itself', or 'noumenon'. Thus we can never know the noumenal world, things as they are in themselves. Kant says, 'It remains completely unknown to us what objects may be by themselves and apart from the receptivity of the senses. We know nothing but our manner of perceiving them.' He agrees with Hume that metaphysical knowledge of the general characteristics of ultimate reality is impossible. We can have no knowledge of things from beyond and independent of our mental processes: we can't have knowledge of things-in-themselves. The *a priori*

conditions and concepts the mind imposes are a set of rules for thinking within the phenomenal world and only for that.

Any attempt to go beyond what human beings can possibly know, to speculate about the nature of ultimate reality and attempt to build a bridge between the phenomenal and noumenal worlds, always ends in trouble. Kant showed how the typical claims made by metaphysicians ended either in elementary logical fallacies or in contradictory results, in 'paralogisms' or in 'antinomies'. The problems arise from taking the *a priori* conditions of pure thought, which apply only to the phenomenal world, as objective conditions of the universe, the noumenal world.

For example, if a scientist were to ask whether the universe had a beginning, this would result in an antinomy, something that can be both proven and disproven. Our thinking is locked within the modes of perception and conception so we can only understand within the structures of space, time and causation these impose. Thus we cannot conceive of any point in the past without feeling at once that there was some time before that. The same problem would arise if we were to ask whether there was a first cause that brought the universe into existence. An endless chain of causes is inconceivable, but so too is a first cause for which there is no cause.

Paralogisms, errors in our reasoning, result from the same cause: the mistaken attempt to use our modes of perception and conception to prove what lies beyond the phenomenal world. Among these are the attempts of religion to establish the existence of the soul, free will beyond the confines of cause and effect, and the alleged proofs of the existence of God, particularly the ontological argument that we came across in Descartes' theory. According to this we can prove the existence of God from the fact that we can conceive of the concept of God defined as the perfect being. For a being to be perfect it must have existence for without this it wouldn't be perfect. Kant dismisses this argument on the grounds that existence is not a predicate; it merely applies the concept of God to the real world.

So to prove his existence we need to have evidence from experience of the real world to establish that something exists that corresponds with the concept. We can't just define God into existence.

All of these dilemmas arise from assuming that our modes of perception and conception, like space, time and causation, are external and independent of the mind; features of the noumenal world. Whereas, in fact, they are the structure of our experience, the conditions that regulate our phenomenal world; they can never tell us if the noumenal world is similarly governed by space, time and causation. So the impact of Kant's theory was to restrict the proofs sought by science and religion to the world of surface and appearance. We can only *think* what cannot be perceived, we cannot *know* it. Thus not only had Kant set the limits to science, but perhaps he had, as Heinrich Heine observed, killed God and undermined the most precious arguments of theology.

■ 4. Logical positivism: phenomenalism in the twentieth century

In their search for the foundations of knowledge, we have seen that philosophers in the seventeenth, eighteenth and nineteenth centuries, from Descartes onwards, turned their attention to examining the human mind to see whether they could be found in its capacity to receive sense impressions or in its capacity to reason. Since all knowledge was possessed by some mind, they argued, by analysing the workings of the mind they could uncover the sources of certainty and the foundations of knowledge itself. In the twentieth century, however, the focus shifted. Now it was language that offered the best way forward. Since all knowledge is expressed in propositions, it was hoped the analysis of the language in which propositions are stated would yield a systematic insight into the logical structure and limits of knowledge.

This approach is most closely associated with logical positivism, also known as logical empiricism or scientific empiricism, which developed out of the work of the Vienna Circle founded in 1924 by Moritz Schlick. On his death in 1936 the Circle disbanded and its influence dispersed as many of its members emigrated to Britain and the US to escape Nazi persecution. Some of the most influential philoso-

phers associated with the movement were the German philosopher Rudolf Carnap, Ludwig Wittgenstein and A. J. Ayer, who at the age of 26 wrote his iconoclastic *Language, Truth and Logic* (1936), which not only introduced logical positivism to the wider English-speaking public, but still ranks as one of the clearest expositions of the subject.

As to Wittgenstein, though not strictly a member of the Circle, he knew many of its members and had a considerable impact on them through his *Tractatus Logico-Philosophicus* (1922), in which he argues that propositions are pictures of reality corresponding to the individual sense impressions and the structure of their relations. Like Kant, he attempts to draw a line between science and non-science, as the logical positivists drew a similar line between factual and nonfactual language. They set themselves the task of analysing the structure of scientific theory and language. This, they believed, would redefine the role of philosophy to that of eliminating its own problems by clarifying the language employed in framing them. Clean up the language and you remove many of the problems that traditionally have preoccupied philosophers.

Following the tradition started by Hume, they believed propositions are true either factually or formally: either they are empirically true, corresponding one-by-one to sensory experiences, or logically true, no more than an explication of their meaning. Ideas are direct or indirect copies of sense impressions, which means that knowledge is composed either of propositions about the internal relations between these ideas (Hume's 'relations of ideas'), as in logic and mathematics, or of those true by virtue of their content in the form of sense impressions ('matters of fact').

Propositions of logic and mathematics say nothing about the real world, because they have no content. Their only function is to state relations of equivalence or derivation between propositions. And, although if they are true they are necessarily true, this is only because they are true analytically, by definition. With factual propositions things are quite different. Experience, the logical positivists believed, is ultimately composed of immediate and incorrigible sensory observations. The structure of these is reflected in language, so that by logically analysing it we show that propositions can be reduced, like the experience of which they are a reflection, to elementary propositions corresponding one-by-one to items of sense experience.

4.1 The verification principle

But beyond these two sources of truth all else is sophistry and illusion. Meaningful statements can only be established either on formal grounds or factually confirmed by verification with sense experience. The cardinal principle for logical positivism, the 'verification principle', was stated in the well-known slogan, 'the meaning of a proposition is the method of its verification.' In other words, a proposition only has meaning if sense experience would be sufficient to establish its truth. It is grounded in the assumption that each thought is answerable to individual experience, thereby denying the truth of any proposition that is not verifiable in this way.

The chief casualties of this are the propositions of metaphysics and theology, which are clearly not formal, because they claim to inform us of things beyond ordinary experience. But on these grounds they are also meaningless or, as logical positivists described them, 'nonsensical', because, as they cannot be tested by experience, they are not propositions with any cognitive meaning in the sense that they are capable of truth or falsity. The same was said of ethics: that ethical judgements don't state ethical facts, but just the emotions of the speaker, perhaps with the purpose of inciting others to share ·the emotion. By contrast theoretical physics was seen as a highly systematic set of propositions resting ultimately on experimental evidence. As a result, because the relation between evidence and general theory is inductive, philosophers focused increasingly on the problem of justifying inductive inference from observation data to theoretical laws.

Nevertheless, the central claim that truth is either formal or factual inevitably pulled logical positivists back to the questions of language. Formal truths are true by virtue of their constituent terms. Likewise, as consistent phenominalists, logical positivists believed factual truths depend upon the certainty of the reports of sense impressions. So what is needed, as C. I. Lewis pointed out, is an 'expressive language', a private language for the individual to describe for herself her own sense experience. If, as Russell suggests, the language of objects we use to describe things like tables and chairs is just shorthand for longer statements that go to describe what we receive through our senses, we need another language to express accurately our private subjective reports of patches of colour, sounds, smell, and so on. And this must be a private language, if we are to avoid tainting our descriptions of our private sense impressions with the public ideas of tables, chairs and the like.

This, in turn, provoked a vigorous debate, with Wittgenstein arguing that such a language was in fact impossible because language is essentially a public inter-subjective means of communication. Without it we could not be sure what the other person was saying: we could not establish similarities between examples of the same thing we might each be describing. Since people *do* succeed in making these sorts of comparisons, some uses of a language to describe the world cannot depend upon what's inside our own private worlds, which, of course, is at the heart of Descartes' strategy of treating the mind as a private space.

It means that Descartes' attempt to shrink his world and find foundations in the incorrigible truths of our own private experience fails to show what lies at the bottom of our experience, because a public language is still necessary to describe it. Indeed without the public meaning of words there is no meaning left in this experience. As we will see this has been the source of a fierce debate in recent times about the search for foundations started by Descartes.

4.2 Quine and 'Two Dogmas of Empiricism'

The problem, of course, is that we all learn a public, not a private, language, so when we describe our sense experiences privately to ourselves we use a public language containing words that have the same sense on different occasions, no matter who uses them. Public rules of language and thought underlie private individual ones. Indeed this and the logical positivists' attempt both to ground scientific knowledge on incorrigible sense reports and set out a body of logical propositions that are true by definition famously came under attack from one of their own, the American philosopher Willard van Orman Quine, who was himself a student of Rudolph Carnap.

In his famous essay 'Two Dogmas of Empiricism' (1951), Quine rejects the two cardinal doctrines of logical positivism: the 'belief in some fundamental cleavage between truths which are analytic, or grounded in meanings independent of matters of fact, and truths which are synthetic or grounded in fact'; and the 'reductionist' doctrine that 'each meaningful statement is equivalent to some logical construct upon terms which refer to immediate

Willard van Orman Quine (1908–2000)

Quine is widely regarded as the most influential American philosopher of the second half of the twentieth century. Born in Akron, Ohio, he gained his doctorate in 1932 for his work on the system of logic of Russell and Whitehead's *Principia Mathematica*, after which he spent a year abroad on a scholarship. It was here that he came into contact with Rudolf Carnap, Alfred Tarski and logical positivists of the Vienna Circle. Returning to Harvard he later joined the faculty in 1936, became a full professor in 1948, and remained there until 1978, when he retired.

It was the collection of papers, *From a Logical Point of View* (1953), which brought wide recognition of the importance of his work. Though influenced by the logical positivism of Carnap and the Vienna Circle, his famous rejection of one of their cardinal doctrines, the analytic–synthetic distinction, was a significant turning point in a shift away from the logical positivist views about language. He argues there is just a seamless 'web of knowledge', stretching from observations, experiments and common sense to logic and the sciences. All are corrigible empirical statements we would be quite prepared to revise. His many books include *Word and Object* (1960), *The Roots of Reference* (1974), and an autobiography, *The Time of My Life* (1985).

experience'. He argues that no adequate account can be given of the notion that some propositions are true by definition, nor can we reduce scientific propositions to logical constructs of sense reports, as his tutor Carnap had argued. Philosophers had relied on inadequate theories of language and meaning. In particular he targets what he describes as an indefensible 'myth of meaning', which proceeded 'as if there was a gallery of ideas, and each idea were tagged with the expression that means it.'

Instead, he argues, we must give up the idea of a sharp division between knowledge that is certain and that which is open to doubt. There is just a seamless 'web of knowledge', stretching from observations, experiments, and common sense to logic and the sciences. All are corrigible: nothing is immune from revision. Even the fundamental laws of logic must be considered in no way necessary. They, too, are ultimately empirical statements, which we would be quite prepared to revise. Our willingness to do this depends upon our willingness to change

the rest of the 'system of science'. Our reluctance to revise propositions formerly regarded as analytic truths is not because they are immune from revision, but because they are central to our conceptual framework, which we want to protect as undisturbed as possible.

In a statement he credited to the French philosopher Pierre Duhem, which has subsequently become known as the 'Duhem–Quine Thesis', he argues that 'our statements about the external world face the tribunal of experience not individually but as a corporate body.' The totality of our knowledge, he declares, 'is a man-made fabric, which impinges on experience only along the edges.' He believes that our statements, even in science, are only 'deviously' connected with experience; indeed, whether in science or in common sense, they are merely 'cultural posits', determined more by cultural conventions than by experience. They are cultural myths at the heart of our culture in the same way that Homer's gods were at the heart of Greek culture: 'in point of epistemological footing the physical objects and the gods differ only in degree and not in kind.'

Knowledge, then, is a man-made fabric, a web of belief, its truth lying in its pragmatic usefulness as a manageable structure helping us understand what goes on around us in the flux of experience. This is more like the pragmatic picture of knowledge found in Rorty and the pragmatists like John Dewey and William James. From their perspective man is not Descartes' contemplative thinker, but practical and active. He seeks knowledge to satisfy his wants. His concern then is not to find absolute

Brief lives
Carnap, Rudolf

Dates: 1891–1970
Born: Ronsdorf, Germany
Best known for: Being one of the most influential members of the Vienna Circle, out of which developed logical positivism. He maintained that the terms and sentences that express assertions about the world are reducible to terms and sentences describing immediate sense data.

Major works: *The Logical Structure of the World* (1928), *The Logical Syntax of Language* (1937), *The Logical Foundations of Probability* (1950).

Timeline:

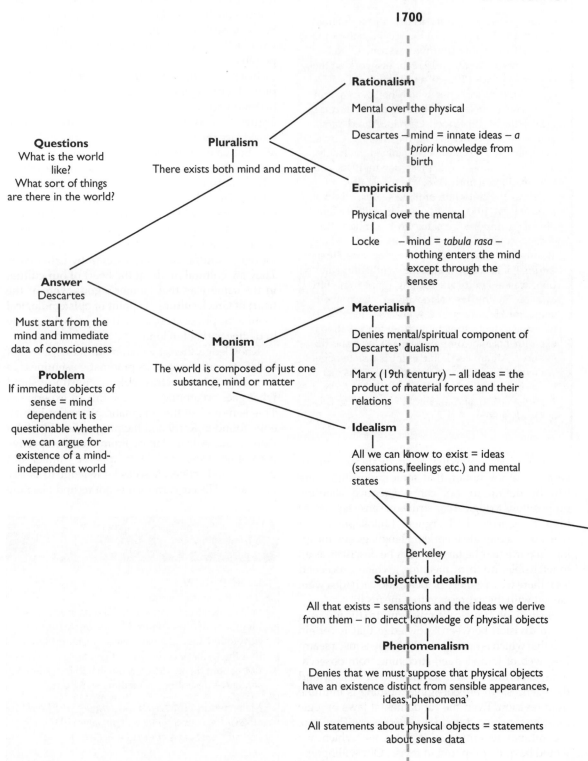

1700

Questions
What is the world like?
What sort of things are there in the world?

Pluralism
There exists both mind and matter

Rationalism
Mental over the physical

Descartes – mind = innate ideas – *a priori* knowledge from birth

Empiricism
Physical over the mental

Locke   – mind = *tabula rasa* – nothing enters the mind except through the senses

Answer
Descartes

Must start from the mind and immediate data of consciousness

Problem
If immediate objects of sense = mind dependent it is questionable whether we can argue for existence of a mind-independent world

Monism
The world is composed of just one substance, mind or matter

Materialism
Denies mental/spiritual component of Descartes' dualism

Marx (19th century) – all ideas = the product of material forces and their relations

Idealism
All we can know to exist = ideas (sensations, feelings etc.) and mental states

Berkeley

Subjective idealism

All that exists = sensations and the ideas we derive from them – no direct knowledge of physical objects

Phenomenalism

Denies that we must suppose that physical objects have an existence distinct from sensible appearances, ideas, 'phenomena'

All statements about physical objects = statements about sense data

Perception

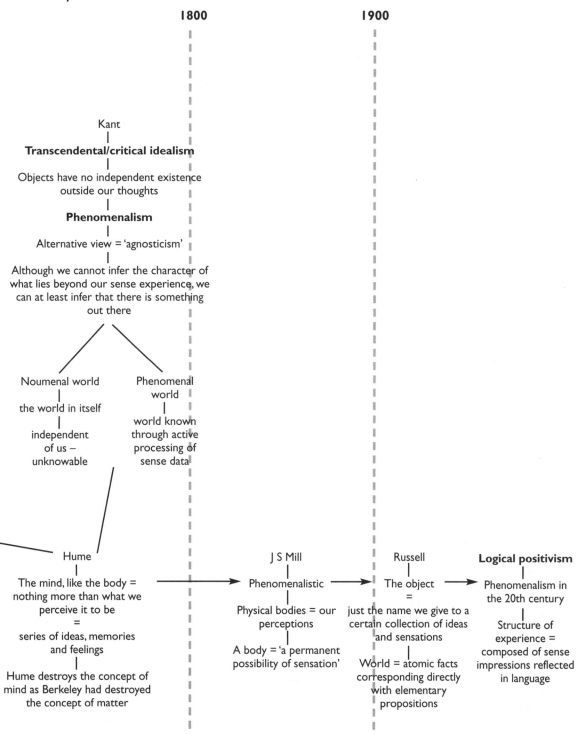

1800

1900

Kant

Transcendental/critical idealism

Objects have no independent existence
outside our thoughts

Phenomenalism

Alternative view = 'agnosticism'

Although we cannot infer the character of
what lies beyond our sense experience, we
can at least infer that there is something
out there

Noumenal world

the world in itself

independent
of us –
unknowable

Phenomenal
world

world known
through active
processing of
sense data

Hume

The mind, like the body =
nothing more than what we
perceive it to be
=
series of ideas, memories
and feelings

Hume destroys the concept of
mind as Berkeley had destroyed
the concept of matter

J S Mill

Phenomenalistic

Physical bodies = our
perceptions

A body = 'a permanent
possibility of sensation'

Russell

The object
=
just the name we give to a
certain collection of ideas
and sensations

World = atomic facts
corresponding directly
with elementary
propositions

Logical positivism

Phenomenalism in
the 20th century

Structure of
experience =
composed of sense
impressions reflected
in language

certainty: he is content with much less. He must commit himself to a course of action and proceed with what assurance is available.

5. Conclusion

This leaves us with a problem you have no doubt seen coming since Berkeley and Hume. If we cannot find foundations for knowledge in a mind that is passive, as Locke believed, if instead it actively interprets and judges sense data according to its own principles and concepts, then it appears anything goes. The idea of solid objects as just the product of sense data brought together in concepts of our own making seems subjective, lacking the guarantee of truth. But then the idea of solid objects composed of electrical charges and discharges from superinvisible components of unobservable particles seems no less detached from any guarantee of truth, yet still we willingly accept it as such. Perhaps this is just the price we pay in a world where the evidence of our senses is private and subjective, and the external public world is the creation of the mind's active judgement.

Of course, as Quine admits, 'The myth of physical objects is epistemologically superior to most in that it has proved more efficacious than other myths as a device for working a manageable structure into the flux of experience.' Unlike the myths of former cultures, if our theories about the world are refuted by experience we have to adjust them to take account of this; we cannot simply ignore it. However, as we will see in the next two chapters, we meet this demand on our own terms: the adjustments we make must be coherent with everything else we know; they must fit with our current beliefs. They cannot be made just *ad hoc*, because the effects are felt elsewhere. So, it seems, we are no longer involved in the same search for foundations begun by Descartes and Locke, but more in continually spinning a new, more comprehensive and coherent web of belief.

Questions

1. 'At the present moment, I have no doubt whatsoever that I am really perceiving the familiar objects, the chairs and table, the pictures and books and flowers with which my room is furnished; and I am therefore satisfied that they exist.' (A. J. Ayer). Is Ayer's belief naïve?

2. 'When I hallucinate a tree, what I am aware of is a mental image of a tree. There is no difference from the inside between hallucinating a tree and seeing a tree. So, when I see a tree, what I am directly aware of must be a mental image of a tree.' Discuss.

3. a) What does Hume take to be the contents of the mind?

   b) Critically discuss and evaluate his classification of these contents.

4. Explain Kant's distinctions between 'perception' and 'conception', and between the phenomenal and noumenal worlds. Why are they so significant?

5. a) What is the idealist account of the objects of perception?

   b) What are its strengths and weaknesses?

6. How did the search for foundations shift in the twentieth century from phenomenalism to logical positivism? Explain the importance of the verification principle.

7. Explain the significance of Quine's rejection of one of the cardinal doctrines of logical positivism, the analytic–synthetic distinction.

Recommended reading

Berkeley, G. *Three Dialogues between Hylas and Philonous* (ed. R. M. Adams) (Indianapolis: Hackett, 1979).

Berkeley, G. *A Treatise concerning the Principles of Human Knowledge* (1710). In T. E. Jessop (ed.), *Berkeley: Philosophical Writings* (Austin, Texas: University of Texas Press, 1953).

Hume, D. *A Treatise of Human Nature* (1739–40) (London and New York: Dent and Dutton, 1966).

Kant, I. *Critique of Pure Reason* (1781) (London: Dent, 1993).

Ayer, A. J. *Language, Truth and Logic* (1936) (Harmondsworth: Penguin, 1946).

Quine, W. V. O. Two Dogmas of Empiricism. In *From a Logical Point of View* (Cambridge, Mass.: Harvard University Press, 1953).

 The note structure to accompany this chapter can be downloaded from our website.

Explanations: Purposive and Causal Explanations

CHAPTER 10

Key issues

▶ What is it about explanations of the external world that leads us to accept some and reject others?

▶ What is the difference between a purposive and a causal explanation?

▶ Do all explanations simply reduce what is to be explained to what is familiar?

▶ What do we mean by saying one event caused another if there is nothing in the external world we can identify as a 'cause' in the same way we can identify chairs and tables?

▶ A good explanation is said to explain not just why something occurred but why it *had* to occur, but where does this necessity come from?

▶ Are scientific hypotheses invented or do they 'emerge' unprompted out of our observations?

▶ What is the role of observation and experiment in science?

▶ How do scientists establish the truth of their universal scientific laws, which are based on the finite evidence of observed cases?

Contents

In the last chapter we saw how even our everyday assumptions about the existence of solid objects might be little more than the product of sense data brought together in concepts of our own making. The public explanations we fashion to make sense of the external world are dependent on the private and subjective evidence of our senses. Given this, we must be clear exactly what it is about explanations that lead us to accept some and reject others.

■ 1. Purposive and causal explanations

So, what is it exactly that we are after when we ask for an explanation? The simplest answer, of course, is that we just want to be clearer about things. You may want to know exactly what happened in the French Revolution, so you want a clearer description of what happened and when. Or you may want to know how to sail an asymmetric sailing dinghy, so you are asking for an explanation of how you do it. In either case there's nothing unusual or difficult to understand about what's going on in such explanations.

But that's not to say we don't all make mistakes. You may ask for one type of explanation, a description of an event or an explanation of how something works, and instead someone gives you quite a different one. You may be walking home late one evening and you come across a group of people looking at a car with its bonnet buried in the smashed remains of a shop window. So, you join the crowd of onlookers and ask the nearest person 'What happened here?', and he tells you that the car came across the road, mounted the pavement and smashed through the window. Clearly this is an explanation, but it's not the one you are after. What you want to know is 'why' it happened.

But even if you get a 'why' explanation from someone, it still may not be what you want. Another onlooker might give you an explanation in terms of contractions of the driver's leg and arm muscles, impulses in his nerves, electro-chemical reactions in his brain, the injection of a richer petrol mix, acceleration, the steering wheel movement and so on, when really what you wanted to know was whether the driver meant to do it and, if so, why? Why did he want to smash the shop window? What did he believe would be the consequences? What were his reasons for desiring these consequences, and so on? Both explanations are relevant to answering the question why something happened, but they are quite different: one is causal in that it explains why something happened in terms of certain natural events, while the other involves giving reasons for believing something or for having certain purposes.

Take the last response, the purposive or reason-giving explanation. There are those who would argue that this is not an explanation at all. It doesn't tell us *why* an event occurred, it is only an attempt to *influence* us into believing that, given these reasons, if we are rational, it would be more probable that we too would hold these beliefs or that we too would act in the same way. If the driver had deliberately driven the car into the shop window, the sort of explanation we would be after would be in terms of his reasons: that he had been sold an expensive television by the shop owner, who refused to return his money when it broke down; or that he knew his wife was planning to leave him for the shop owner. Given certain evidence we may say that it was rational to believe what he did and, as a result, we can understand his purpose in driving the car into the shop window.

However, giving reasons for why we acted in a particular way may still not explain why we did it:

it might simply make it *more rational*, or *more understandable*. It may be just an attempt to influence the way others assess our beliefs and actions. It's like being a member of a jury. You are being given reasons why doing something is a reasonable, or at least an understandable, thing to do. For example, the real reason why the car driver drove his car into the shop window might have been that he was very insecure and couldn't face living without his wife, who had filled the void left by his mother. In other words, the actual explanation for our actions might lie in unconscious causes that we may know little about, like this man's insecurity, and not in the rationalizations we give for them.

The distinction we have drawn is between purposive explanations and causal or scientific explanations. We live in an age when we are not inclined to believe we have explained anything until we have given a causal explanation. But things were quite different before the seventeenth century, when lives had little meaning *without* purposive explanations. The seventeenth-century scientific revolution elevated the authority of modern science and with it a mechanistic concept of nature. The world was thought to be like a vast machine, no more than the sum of its parts. So to know the laws that control the behaviour of the most elementary parts was to know the laws that control the machine. Nature worked regularly and predictably according to certain natural laws. Today this mechanistic or atomistic philosophy still dominates the way we think about the external world.

Contrast that with the sort of purposive explanation that was common for the most ordinary everyday event prior to the scientific revolution and you begin to realize the change that was brought about in the seventeenth century. Today it is hilarious to see Basil Fawlty thrash his broken-down car with a branch from a tree as if the car had purposes of its own, obstinately deciding that day not to work. But before the seventeenth-century most societies had gods whose purposive behaviour explained everyday natural events, like this. The Mayan religion involved worshipping a number of nature gods, one responsible for rain, another for the sky, and complete trust was placed in their control of everyone's activities.

And still today we often find such purposive explanations far more psychologically satisfying than the mechanistic, causal explanations of science. As you look at the remains of the shop window, if someone had responded to your question by explaining in terms of the physiological laws describing the driver's reaction patterns and the physical laws relating to the mechanics of the car, you might still ask in more agitated tones, 'Yes, but *why* did it happen?', meaning what you really want to know are the driver's reasons for driving the car into the shop, his purposes.

Nevertheless, in many situations it is a causal explanation we want. You might ask me why there is sugar all over the floor and I might explain that I dropped the sugar bowl. This answers your question satisfactorily because it subsumes the event under a law of nature, a uniformity, which we accept as true. We know from our experience of dropping heavier-than-air objects that they fall to the ground. So the two events, letting go of the bowl and its hitting the ground, are linked by the universal law of gravitation which we accept as true. We only accept this explanation if we accept the law.

However you might reasonably ask if we can explain events by subsuming them under laws about purposes. On the face of it this is quite a reasonable expectation. But the problem is we often use the notion of purposes about things for which we haven't established laws that govern their purposes. We often hear people say the reason something happened was that it was God's purpose, but we know of no laws governing God's purposive behaviour. Similarly, I might explain the reason my dog always turns right when he comes in from his walk is that he wants a drink and he expects to find his water bowl there. But even though this sounds perfectly reasonable, we still don't have laws relating to the conscious purposes or expectations of animals. So, as sciences like biology have developed over the last 150 years, scientists have deliberately set out to exclude such purposive explanations which once were quite common in their work.

Nevertheless, in subjects like psychology, sociology, economics and history we do assume certain laws relating to the purposive behaviour of humans, which we accept as true. We accept that all humans are driven by a common purpose to maximize their own self-interests. This explains why we accept the laws of supply and demand, that given a shortage in supply the price will increase discouraging some potential buyers, for whom the price is too high, while encouraging more suppliers to enter the market with the purpose of reaping high profits. This will increase supply and bring the price down until it is in equilibrium, where a stable supply meets a stable demand. But this is not always the case. There are certain 'prestige' goods, like antiques and paintings, where as prices increase demand also increases, with more potential buyers coming into the market. Indeed this illustrates the problem with most laws relating to human behaviour in that they are rarely true without exception. So for them to be true they must be carefully qualified. The problem is that sciences, like psychology, are not yet sufficiently developed to give us true, exceptionless, universal laws about human behaviour.

Even so, there are still those who believe that science is doing nothing substantially different from what we all do when we give purposive explanations, in that both are reducing what is to be explained to the familiar. When I ask you why the car has smashed into the shop window, for your purposive explanation to be convincing you must cite a purpose that we can both understand as predictable, if not reasonable, behaviour. If you were to explain that the driver had just learnt that his wife was about to leave him for the shop owner, we can understand someone acting in this way under these circumstances. Similar feelings of betrayal may have made us react in this way too.

But then isn't science too explaining in the same way by reducing an event to a familiar class of events covered by the universal law? That I have dropped the sugar bowl explains why there is sugar all over the floor, because we have all dropped similar things ourselves. Likewise when scientists explain the behaviour of molecules by likening them to billiard balls, this too is an explanation that works by reducing unfamiliar events to the familiar. But this doesn't completely explain the effectiveness of causal explanations. For much of the time scientists are seeking explanations for both the familiar and the unfamiliar, and the explanation for the familiar often involves concepts that are completely unfamiliar, like quarks, DNA and membranes. What's more, familiarity is irrelevant to the validity of the explanation. You may be unfamiliar with 'membrane theory', but once it has been explained to you the explanation will be as valid for you as it is to the cosmologist who explains it to you.

However there may be one sense in which causal explanations work by reducing events to the familiar. By subsuming events under laws, by making them law-abiding, we make them predictable and less mysterious. The first time you saw a bottle cracked with frozen water in it this would have been mystifying. But as soon as someone has explained the law relating to the expansion of water molecules when the temperature of water falls below zero, you not only understand what happened, but the mystification has been removed because you can apply this to other events that the law predicts under similar circumstances, like the car radiator cracking and water pipes bursting. Indeed these things are no longer mysterious, even though we may not be able to understand the molecular physics that underlie them. The fact that they are a predictable, law-abiding part of nature is enough to make them familiar.

■ 2. Causation

However the explanatory power of causal explanation, which accounts for the phenomenal success of science over the last 350 years, lies in more than just its ability to make things more familiar. It does more than just show things to be reasonable or understandable by explaining why something happened: it also explains why it *had* to happen. In other words, the connection it establishes is a necessary connection: given A, B necessarily has to occur; given that I let go of the sugar bowl, it necessarily hits the ground. The two events are causally connected: A causes B.

But this raises important questions, many of which Hume saw with the sort of clarity no one else possessed. We need to ask ourselves, he insisted, what exactly we mean by this connection – what do we mean by saying one event 'causes' another? After all when you observe two events you see each event, but you cannot see a 'cause'. You see my fingers let go of the sugar bowl and you see it smash on the ground, but you cannot see the 'cause' that connects these two events.

We have no problem with using the term 'cause' in the context of animistic explanations, that is, to explain the behaviour of humans, animals, and even God. A man charged with robbery might protest, 'X was the cause of me robbing the bank, because he threatened that if I didn't I wouldn't see my family again'. Or someone might say that 'God has been the cause of all my happiness since I saw the light.' And often we attach a sense of moral responsibility to it. We might argue, 'The scratches on the front door were caused by the dog, he's to blame!'

But between events concerning inanimate objects things are not so clear, because we're no longer concerned with wilful behaviour, which we can understand through the purposes and intentions that motivate and explain them. When we use the word 'cause' we normally mean two things: first, an event or state of affairs that precedes another, and is said to explain it; and, second, that the first necessitates the second. And yet to say that one event necessitated another doesn't make the same sense as in the animistic explanations above. We saw in Chapter 2 that empirical propositions are contingent, that is, their truth depends upon experience, which could have resulted differently. So there is no necessity linking one event with another as there is in an analytic truth in which two or more ideas are linked by definition. This means that if we talk about event A causing event B, then either A and B are different events, in which case one can occur without the other, or it is impossible for them to occur separately, in which case they are not separate events at all. If these two events are necessarily connected so that one of them cannot occur without the other and vice versa, then they are in fact the same event.

Let's say, for example, that a friend of ours is so depressed that he decides to take his own life by taking an overdose of sleeping pills. If he were to die as a result we would have no hesitation in concluding that the overdose of sleeping pills killed him. Given event A (taking the overdose) event B (his death) occurred. A was the cause of B. But we cannot say that A is *necessarily* the cause of B, because if we were to get to him in time we could rush him to the hospital, where emergency treatment might save his life.

But if this is the case we cannot really be said to have explained what happened. A causal explanation means we not only explain what happened, but what *had* to happen; in other words, what necessarily happened. Unless we can exclude all possible contingencies we cannot be said to have explained the event. We may have got our friend to the hospital, but he still died because the hospital's equipment for pumping out his stomach was malfunctioning. This, then, becomes the cause, rather than the overdose, because in normal circumstances his life would have been saved. The only way to establish a necessary connection between event A and event B would be to make event A include event B. But then A would be no different from B: it would itself be death and the two events would no longer be separated by time in which other contingencies could intervene. But we know this cannot be true, because not all overdoses result in death.

Hume came to much the same conclusion. He rejected the notion that there were necessary causes in the contingent world. He argued it is quite conceivable that anything should cause anything else, and only experience teaches us that one thing is the cause of another. All that we can observe is 'constant conjunction': nothing but the fact that one thing has been regularly observed to be followed by another. And from this experience, he believed, we only *infer* that one thing causes another and that both are linked by a necessary connection.

Yet we have no evidence of either. All that anybody ever meant by necessary connection was that two events have been constantly conjoined, so that, when we see one, we automatically expect and predict the occurrence of the other. We see lightning and we expect to hear the thunder. We hit our thumb with a hammer and expect to feel the pain. He defines a cause as 'an object, followed by another, and where all objects similar to the first are followed by objects similar to the second' and as 'An object precedent and contiguous to another, and so united with it in the imagination, that the idea of the one determines the mind to form the idea of the other.'

According to Hume, therefore, a cause is nothing more than a habit of the mind. We get the idea that there is a necessary connection between two events as a result of repeated observations of seeing one event regularly follow the other. But is this all there is to it? Is constant conjunction on its own a necessary and sufficient condition to establish a cause?

In Chapter 4 we saw how important this sort of question is. Take sufficient conditions: can you think of examples in which one event regularly follows another, but we know that it is not caused by the other? Consider, for instance, traffic lights. The red light is regularly followed by the amber light coming on, and this is then regularly followed by the green light, and so on. But we know that each preceding light does not cause the next light to go on; there is an independent mechanism making each light go on in sequence. The same could be said for the regularly observed sequence of events that occur at 3 pm on Saturdays all over Britain, when whistles are blown and games of football begin. But, although we can regularly observe the

David Hume (1711–1776)

Scottish philosopher, historian and essayist, Hume has been regarded by many as the most important philosopher ever to write in English. Of all the empiricists he was the most consistent, refusing to accept any compromise. He was, therefore, a pivotal figure in the Enlightenment, not least because of the influence he exerted on those, like Kant, who sought to escape the implications of his radical empiricism.

At the age of just 18 he wrote *A Treatise of Human Nature* (1739–40), convinced that it was possible to bring the experimental methods of modern science to a study of the human mind to reveal the same order that Newton had discovered in the universe. With just ideas and impressions in the mind to work with he reconstructs and explains the way we come by our everyday thoughts about the world. If all we have are impressions, then causal connection and the self must be the products of our own inferences.

Of his other work, his *History of England* (1754–62) established his reputation as a man of letters, while *An Enquiry Concerning Human Understanding* (1748) and *An Enquiry Concerning the Principles of Morals* (1751), are generally regarded as an attempt to make more accessible the ideas in the *Treatise*.

sequence, we cannot argue that the whistle that is blown at St James' Park, Newcastle starts the game at Old Trafford in Manchester.

As for necessary conditions, as Hume accepts, any assumption of a necessary connection between separate events is a product of our minds and imaginations. But we think of causes as more than just the name for the generalization that two things regularly occur together. A generalization of this type must *explain*, not just represent, the regularity. This means that we must have reasons for thinking one thing caused another *prior* to knowing that they regularly occur together. Out of all the evidence of our observations we must have a reason to select these two regularly occurring events as causally connected.

This takes us back to our discussion of arguments by analogy in Chapter 4, where we said that if I were to drop my pen and, just a fraction of a second later, we were both to look out of the window to see a car crash into a lamppost in the street below, it would not be convincing for me to argue that the first event caused the second, even if we knew such events regularly occurred together, because we know of no law or uniformity in our experience in which the dropping of pens causes cars to crash. We need a reason to believe that one event could be the cause of the other, and only then do we begin to notice other events that resemble these in relevant respects.

Take one further, less fanciful, example. In our attempt to explain the rise in violence in Western societies we might find that 80 per cent of all those convicted of violent offences regularly watch violent programmes on TV. Such a correlation is very persuasive, but is it any more than this? Is it just a correlation or is it also the cause? We might also find that 80 per cent of those convicted also chew gum, but we're less likely to believe that this is the cause. So we must have something analogous between the two events, something that allows us to conclude that one might be the cause of the other, prior to identifying regularities. We know of no causal link between violence and chewing gum, so we probably wouldn't have looked for any correlation between the two, but we do have an idea that there exists a causal link between violent programmes and violent behaviour.

Without this, constant conjunction can only be a *description* of regularities, not an *explanation* of them. As a result, it alone cannot allow us to predict what will happen. If we only have a report that

event A is followed regularly by event B, we cannot predict that given A, B will necessarily occur. All we can establish from the report is that there is an accidental connection, and not a necessary connection between the two events. Like the correlation between chewing gum and violence, we have a report of a regularity, but no causal connection that will allow us to predict.

Without this we cannot test our explanation by predicting what will happen if we do certain things. So where do our causal explanations derive the assumption that there exist certain necessary connections between events? John Locke, realizing the seriousness of the problem, argued that it must come from God: from the 'arbitrary will and good pleasure of the Wise Architect', who sets laws of nature to work with regularity, so that 'causes work steadily, and effects constantly flow from them.'

Even Hume smuggles necessity in, having argued that there can only be constant conjunction. In the passage already quoted he says:

We may define a cause to be an object, followed by another, and where all the objects similar to the first are followed by objects similar to the second. Or in other words where, if the first object had not been the second never had existed.

Although he suggests that the second sentence is merely a restatement of the first, it is clearly different. The first describes the accidental regularity of constant conjunction, whereas the second implies necessary connection, that if the first event 'had not been', the second would 'never (have) existed'. With this we can extend our inferences beyond the present set of examples and make predictions about hypothetical cases. That is, it will support counterfactual and subjunctive conditionals. With counterfactual conditionals we mean particular instances that might have occurred, but didn't: 'If A had been the case, then B would have occurred.' With subjunctive conditionals we mean particular cases that might occur: 'If A should occur, then so would B.'

Nevertheless Hume is probably right in one respect, that necessary connection is a product of our own reasoning, rather than something we can find in the external world. Scientists, of course, do try to discover how events are connected, how the occurrence of certain events is necessary given certain facts. But they are not trying to discover *causes* that precede and necessitate their occurrence. Necessity in causal explanations comes from the form of the argument, what is known as the 'Covering Law Model' of explanation or the 'Deductive Nomological Model'. It is the effect of subsuming the event under a universal law within a deductive argument:

1. All As cause Bs.

2. S is an A.

3. Therefore, B.

The event that is to be explained (the 'explanandum' – 3) is deduced from the two premises that account for the event (the 'explanans' – 1 and 2). So if I were to explain why the sugar bowl and its contents are on the floor, my explanation would look something like this:

1. All heavier-than-air objects fall to the ground when unsupported.

2. The sugar bowl and its contents were heavier-than-air objects and were left unsupported when they slipped from my grasp.

3. Therefore, the sugar bowl and its contents fell to the ground.

Given premises 1 and 2, the event described in 3 *had* to occur. The necessity in the explanation comes from the deductive form of the argument.

For this to work we must have a major premise (1) in the form of a universal law, which explains more than just the one event, but a whole class of similar events – whenever an event of type A occurs, an event of type B occurs. In the case above the universal law was 'All heavier-than-air objects fall to the ground when unsupported.' To give an explanation of why an event occurred is to show how it is related to other events through a universal law: no conclusion can be deduced from just two particular premises. And the universal law must be testable. This is a hypothetical law, an empirical statement describing a uniformity of nature. But because it is connecting contingent events there is always the possibility that later events may turn out to prove it false, which means it must always be open to correction through testing and observation.

The second statement (2), the minor premise, is a statement of initial conditions, in other words a statement confirming that event A actually happened. And the conclusion (3), the explanandum, is a statement that event B, the event we set out to explain in the first place, actually occurred as a result of (1) and (2). So what necessitates (3) is not an event, but the truth of (1) and (2): given the truth of the universal law and the initial conditions, (3) must necessarily occur. The necessity derives from the fact that the three premises together form a valid deductive argument and, as we saw in Chapter 3, the definition of a valid argument is that if the premises are true the conclusion *must* be true.

The effectiveness of this explanation lies in the fact that the 'explanans', the universal law and the statement of initial conditions, together entail the 'explanandum', the event to be explained. In other words, the statement that the event occurred must be deducible from the statements giving the explanation. Otherwise we could not explain it. It is worth trying it yourself, to see if you can in fact explain one event by citing another without using a universal law. Try it with the following two events:

Event 1: As David was driving his car his steering column broke.

Event 2: David lost control of his car.

It is in fact only possible when both events are the same event; when all we are doing is revealing a definitional connection between them. For example, I might explain that 'Jonathan's sleeplessness was caused by his insomnia.'

Nevertheless, for the deductive argument to work we must still be able to extend the implications of the universal law to unseen cases. That is, it must support counterfactual and subjunctive conditionals. Without this it cannot serve as an explanation for anything, because it couldn't explain anything beyond the evidence from which it was first derived. I might find it is true that 'All the coins in my pocket were minted between the years 1975 and 1980', but this does not support the subjunctive that 'If I were to put another coin in my pocket it too would show it was minted between the years 1975 and 1980.'

And it's worth noting this is not simply a matter of how much evidence we have for the connection it makes between different types of events; it's more a question of form. It depends upon the type of connections that are made. We might claim that 'All dinosaurs, known as sauropods, are herbivorous', even though no such animal exists any longer. We are arguing not just that every sauropod is *in fact* herbivorous, but that if anything *were* a sauropod, it would be herbivorous. Similarly Newton's first law of motion states that a body remains at rest or moves with constant velocity in a straight line unless acted upon by a force. But there are no such bodies in the real world, because another of Newton's laws tells us that every body is interfered with by some force. Nevertheless, like the law about sauropods, this law supports unfulfilled conditionals, so that if there were such a body it would move in a straight line at constant velocity.

Compare that with accidental generalizations, like the coin example above, which cannot support counterfactual and subjunctive conditionals, even though they are universal generalizations. If I were to state truthfully that, 'All the cars in the carpark are Fords', I could not extend this to unseen cases by arguing, 'Therefore the next car to enter the carpark will be a Ford.' There is nothing in the laws of nature to preclude another possibility, therefore, it's not possible to extend it to other cases, or predict similar occurrences. To use William Kneale's famous example, 'From the premise that all the men in the next room are playing poker we cannot conclude that if the Archbishop of Canterbury were in the next room ... he would be playing poker.'

Consequently, even though they contain the universal quantifier 'All', accidental generalizations cannot provide a basis for explaining anything, because there is nothing analogous between the events being explained that would allow us to extend them to unseen cases. There is nothing analogous between the carpark and Ford cars that would allow us to extend it to the next car to arrive. Accidental generalizations are only logically, not empirically, infinite. It is a pure accident that this is the case, like the correlation between violent crime and the incidence of chewing gum. Neither can serve as the basis for an explanation.

This has led Kneale to argue that Popper and others, who argue that the necessary connection in scientific explanations is derived from the deductive form of the argument, are in fact wrong, because it comes from the particular form of the universal generalization itself. He argues we can only account for a law of nature's power to give rise to unfulfilled hypotheticals if we regard them as 'principles of necessitation'. Although we cannot demonstrate it,

we simply regard laws of nature as necessarily true. They determine what *must* happen and what is impossible. And from this we are able to draw counterfactual and subjunctive conditionals.

■ 3. The problem of induction

Nevertheless, whichever solution we accept to the problem of cause and necessary connection, it seems merely to have pushed the problem along. Now we need to explain our method of discovering and justifying these universal laws and the connections they make between different types of event. Although this is usually described as *the* problem of induction, there are, as you can see, two problems here: how we discover and then justify our hypotheses. And each throws a different light on the role of observation and experiment in the process of finding and testing universal laws.

3.1 Discovering hypotheses

Take the first problem: the way we discover our hypotheses. The traditional description of the inductive method in science, known as 'narrow inductivism', dates back to the seventeenth century and Francis Bacon, who believed that the new scientific method had to be conducted without any preconceptions, what he described as 'idols' of the mind that could distort the evidence. Nothing, he believed, should get between us and an accurate and honest representation of the evidence.

Today it's not difficult to find this represented in the way some scientists talk about their work. P. B. Weisz in *The Science of Biology* (1963) describes five stages in the scientific method. It begins with observation, which should be done without 'unsuspected bias' and 'unconscious prejudice'. After the evidence has been gathered we can move on to the second stage in which we define the problem. Then comes the stage of hypothesizing, when we guess at the most likely solution. In the fourth stage we experiment to test the hypothesis and gather evidence. And finally, after the hypothesis is shown to be reliable, we come to the fifth stage, in which we formulate a theory.

In his well-known book *Philosophy of Natural Science* (1966), the American philosopher Carl Hempel cites another scientist, A.B. Wolfe, who suggests a similar set of stages. This too begins with observation, when we record all the facts without selection. In the second stage the facts are 'analysed, compared, and classified, *without hypothesis or postulates*'. In the third stage we inductively draw generalizations from this. In the fourth and final stage we test these generalizations.

But in fact, even among scientists, the suspicion is that such rationalizations of the scientific method reflect less what scientists actually *do* and more about what they *think* they should be doing. Sir Peter Medawar, a Nobel Prize winning scientist, argues that such talk of inductivism in science is 'simply the posture(s) we choose to be seen in when the curtain goes up and the public sees us.' It only seems to be logical in character, because 'it can be made to appear so when we look back upon a completed episode of thought.' In fact, he argues, it is a much more imaginative and intuitive process than is reflected in the traditional narrow inductivist account.

Take each stage of A. B. Wolfe's account. Like Weisz, he begins with observation and the collection of all the facts. You have no doubt seen the problem here already: how can we possibly collect *all* the facts? There are an infinite number of facts out there, so, despite Wolfe's instruction, we have to have some means of selecting only those facts that are relevant. Otherwise, this method would be simply unworkable. But for this we need to know what the problem is and have a tentative hypothesis that will direct our observations. So, in fact, we do need preconceptions in the form of a hypothesis to start with. But the same problem shows up in the second stage too. Facts can be analysed and classified in many different ways, so here too we need a hypothesis which suggests ways in which the phenomena are connected. Otherwise, like observation, our analysis and classification would be blind.

In the third stage, like Weisz, Wolfe finally introduces a hypothesis in the form of an inductive derivation as if there were some well-documented procedure that would take us mechanically through to a hypothesis. The problem is there is no such procedure: there are no general rules of inductive inference, only imagination and intuition according to Medawar. As Einstein put it, 'A theory can be proved by experiment; but no path leads from experiment to the birth of a theory.' Scientific hypotheses are invented to account for the data, not mechanically derived from the facts. Karl Popper describes these as 'conjectures' and William Whewell in the nineteenth century thought they were just 'happy guesses'. Indeed, some scientists

appear to spend much of their time doing little else. James Watson, who, along with Francis Crick, won the Nobel Prize for the discovery of the structure of DNA, says of his collaborator that he was easily bored with experimentation and immersed himself for much of the time in theorizing.

This is not to say, of course, that just any theory will do. Wolfe's final stage of testing ensures that the theory is objectively valid. Not only is it a question of whether the theory is borne out by the facts already gathered, but by the new test implications that can be derived from it. Nevertheless, Wolfe's and Weisz's notion that there is some procedure of inductive inference that can be applied to facts collected blindly to reach a hypothesis seems to make little practical sense. The rules of induction, like the rules of deduction, seem more like canons of validation, rather than a method of discovery. They seem to describe the best way of justifying theories through experimentation, rather than a method of reaching theories.

So the narrow inductivist account appears to oversimplify the process. It assigns to the mind a passive and receptive role, what Karl Popper refers to as the 'bucket-theory of the mind', when in fact it seems to have a much more active role, inventing hypotheses that bring order and meaning to observational data. In this, the 'hypothetico-deductive' method, our hypotheses come first, forming the major premise in a deductive argument through which we deduce ways of testing the theory. There is a constant reciprocation between imaginative conjecture and critical evaluation. In describing William Whewell's view, Medawar explains, 'Scientific reasoning ... is a constant interplay ... between hypotheses and the logical expectations they give rise to: there is a restless to-and-fro motion of thought ... until we arrive at a hypothesis which ... will satisfactorily meet the case.' And this imaginative and inspirational process is not confined to the great discoveries of scientific legend, but enters into all scientific reasoning at every level.

This then, in turn, defines a different role for observation and experiment in science. Experiments are carried out more often to perform a regulatory role; to decide between conflicting possibilities, rather than to gather more evidence. The hypothetico-deductive method is more like a 'What if?' strategy: what if we vary this factor, or change that condition, what will happen? For example, in 'membrane theory' about a multi-dimensional world of parallel universes the cosmologists have a reputation for always being willing to try out almost any model of the universe to see where it leads. For much of the time this has been little but guesswork, but over the last decade, a new generation of telescopes and satellites has given them the sophisticated tools to test their theories and match their capacity for informed guesswork with actual data.

But how do we begin this process of forming hypotheses? How do we decide what is a relevant or significant factor or collection of factors, about which to form a hypothesis? The process is not illogical, it's outside logic: it's simply non-logical. Hypotheses come not from the apprehension of the facts, but from an imaginative preconception of what might be true – an informed guess, the willingness to take a view, to form an opinion. At least part of the art of hypothesizing lies in the ability to identify a stable pattern in the evidence you have collected in the past and part in registering that the indications in the evidence before you exhibit the same pattern. It used to be thought that there were definite rules for identifying such patterns. The greater the number of points of similarity between two things, the likelier it is that they are the same.

But it isn't just a question of the number of points of similarity or the number of examples that show them. There are an infinite number of generalizations that are possible from a set of observations. The American philosopher Nelson Goodman, in his famous book, *Fact, Fiction, and Forecast* (1955), showed that we need, in addition to the quantity of similarities, some reason for preferring some uniformities to others. Without this our claims about the uniformity of nature would be vacuous. In the 'curve-fitting problem' two independently measurable features are plotted against each other on a graph, resulting in a finite set of points. These may suggest a simple curve connecting them, but in fact they are compatible with many curves, and we need a reason for choosing one rather than another.

The pattern we identify that brings order and clarity to experience is not read mechanically from the evidence; it is imposed through our highly selective imaginations. One biographer of Stephen Hawking, the British cosmologist and theoretical physicist, observed that, even before the first signs of motor neurone disease, he had 'an astonishing ability to visualise solutions to complex problems, without calculation or experiment.' Later, when equations became difficult to write, he 'concentrat-

ed on the geometry of the universe, which he could picture in his mind.'

Try it for yourself. Imagine being in the position of William Smith, one of the earliest geologists at the end of the eighteenth century. You're clambering up and down mountainsides unearthing interesting fossils, known then as 'figured stones', which look uncannily like something which was once alive – sea urchins, shells, leaves and pieces of branches. But to declare that you think this is, indeed, what they are, risks public ridicule. How can once-living sea creatures be found half-way up a mountain? How would you set about explaining this? God working in mysterious ways to impress mankind? The effects of Noah's flood? Remember, you have none of the knowledge of modern geology: you know nothing about evolution. Take a look at Simon Winchester's fascinating book, *The Map that Changed the World* (2001), to see just how hypotheses to explain this got started.

And then put yourself in the position of Ignaz Semmelweis, a doctor working in the General Hospital in Vienna in 1847, where there has been a high mortality rate from puerperal or childbed fever among women in labour. The conventional wisdom has it that this is due to a 'prevailing miasma', which has settled over the hospital. But this doesn't explain why there are five times more deaths in the doctors' division of the hospital than there are in the midwives' division. How could a miasma settling over the whole hospital have such a strong differentiated effect? What is the cause? What facts would you look for and what sort of pattern would you impose on those facts?

Starting with the dissimilarities between the ways in which each division was run, he formed hypotheses based on each one and tested them one after the other. Maybe it was due to the different food served in each division, the different positions in which the women gave birth, or maybe it was something to do with the priest and his bellringer who walked through the doctors' division, but not through the midwives'? This rapid sequential evaluation of hypotheses seems typical of most scientists as they do their early probing before they settle on a theory. Much of Darwin's research was similar. Although close to the true Baconian method, in that his research was not theory directed, he still confessed that he could not resist forming a hypothesis on every subject. Indeed, Medawar believes the narrow inductivist method of working without hypotheses is so far from normal practice that 'if anyone working in a laboratory professed to be trying to establish Laws of Nature by induction we should begin to think he was overdue for leave.'

3.2 Justifying hypotheses

Nevertheless, the problems don't end there. Once we have a hypothesis that 'All cases of puerperal fever are caused by an infection of the blood', which seems to explain the phenomena, we still need to justify it. The problem is that we have to establish the truth of a universal statement, which is based on the finite evidence of observed cases. Yet we cannot infer from singular instances a statement referring to an infinite set. And so, since the evidence can never be more than finite, we cannot justify the truth of a universal statement based on evidence.

As we saw in Chapter 3, the solution appears to be to insert into this invalid inductive argument the 'Principle of Induction' – that in all cases unobserved instances resemble observed instances – in order to convert it into a valid deductive argument. So we then have the following:

1. All observed cases of puerperal fever have been caused by an infection of the blood.

2. In all cases unobserved instances resemble observed instances.

3. Therefore, all cases of puerperal fever are caused by an infection of the blood;.

4. S is a case of puerperal fever.

5. Therefore, it is caused by an infection of the blood.

But, as you have no doubt asked yourself already, how do we know the principle of induction is true? Hume saw this too, and in what has come to be known as 'Hume's vicious circle' he shows that the reasoning is circular. The only answer we can give is that it has worked in the past and, therefore, it will work in the future. But then this is the same inference we are making when we argue from some cases of puerperal fever to all cases. This, as Hume points out, is viciously circular. To know that the inductive methods of argument are correct we need to know that the principle of induction is true, but we can only know this to be true once we can show

we can rely on induction. It doesn't help to say that the past success of science shows how uniform and ordered nature is, since this is exactly the inference we are trying to justify. It begs the question: we have no evidence in support of the conclusion, which does not at the same time assume it. So, it seems, there is no reason for believing that inductive arguments are correct.

This means, therefore, that any attempt to confirm universal empirical laws is bound to be inconclusive. No matter how many confirming instances we might record they cannot guarantee that there are no counter examples lurking around the corner. And even if what we predict does actually transpire, it doesn't follow that the hypothesis from which we deduced them is true. After all in a valid argument false premises can always lead to true conclusions.

Confirmation also runs the risk we saw in Chapter 3 of committing the fallacy of affirming the consequent. In the conditional proposition 'If p, then q' this fallacy is committed by confusing the claim that p is a sufficient condition with the claim that it is the *only* sufficient and necessary condition of q. In other words, it confuses the conditional 'If p, then q' with 'If, and only if, p, then q.' We saw in Chapter 3 that Sherlock Holmes confused the conditional 'If the murder weapon was a heavy object, then we will find it with grass growing beneath it' with the conditional 'If, and only if the murder weapon etc.' But there could be many reasons, beside it being the murder weapon, to explain why it was found with grass growing beneath it: a schoolboy may have thrown it testing his throw or a gardener may have dropped as he gathered rocks.

It seems, then, that the only thing we can do that is conclusive is to attempt to falsify the hypothesis – to deny the consequent (*modus tollens*). As we saw in Chapter 3 deduction ensures that if our hypotheses are true, then so too will be the inferences we validly draw from them. So, if it leads to conclusions which turn out not to be supported by the facts, there must be something wrong. As we will see in the next chapter, this is the argument of Sir Karl Popper: that if a single falsifying instance is found, the theory must be discarded. He argues that there is a logical asymmetry between confirmation and falsification: no amount of confirming instances will establish the truth of a theory, but just one falsifying instance will succeed in proving it false. Francis Bacon must have had just this in mind when he argued 'the force of the negative instance is greater.'

◾ 4. Conclusion

Even so, we are still left with two problems. If the weight of confirming evidence is not the key to adopting a theory and only falsifications are of any value, we must find alternative criteria for deciding why some theories are more acceptable than others. Why do we choose to work with some hypotheses, rather than others, when they both might be unfalsified? We shall examine this in the next chapter.

And even if falsification is all that we can do in the light of the failure of the principle of induction, we are still dependent upon it. Invalid though it is, we cannot do without it. After all, if something is falsified, we are still assuming the principle of induction to be true, by assuming, on the basis of our past experience, that it will continue to remain falsified in the future.

◾ Questions

1. When two types of event are found to be highly correlated, how can it be shown that events of one type cause events of the other?

2. Discuss the argument that since there is no certainty that laws of nature will continue to hold, there is no guarantee that water will continue to freeze at 0 °C in the future. Therefore it would not be rational to expect to find ice-cubes in the fridge tomorrow.

3. Outline the difficulties involved in the problem of induction. What bearing do these have on the practice and claims of science?

4. Discuss the claim that although scientists think that they employ induction, they cannot, since it leads to paradox and contradiction.

5. 'If scientific observation is dependent on theory, scientific observation is not therefore neutral or objective.' Discuss.

6. How can we distinguish causal sequences from coincidences?

7. 'All swans are white.' 'All the coins in my pocket were minted in 2004.' Which of these is a law, and why?

8. An iron bar is very hot if and only if it glows white, and it glows white if and only if it is very hot. We say, however, that the heat causes the glowing rather than that the glowing causes the heat. Are we right, and, if so, why?

9. 'Whatever is the origin of scientific generalizations, it is not induction from particular instances.' (Karl Popper). Is this true?

◾ Recommended reading

Hempel, C. *Philosophy of Natural Science* (Englewood Cliffs, NJ: Prentice-Hall, 1966).

Chalmers, A. F. *What is this thing called Science?* (Milton Keynes: Open University Press, 1982).

Medawar, P. B. *Induction and Intuition in Scientific Thought* (London: Methuen, 1969).

Campbell, Norman. *What is Science?* (New York: Dover, 1952).

Hospers, John. What is Explanation? In A. Flew (ed.), *Essays in Conceptual Analysis* (London: Macmillan, 1956).

Nagel, E. *The Structure of Science: Problems in the Logic of Scientific Explanation* (London: RKP, 1970) (New York: Harcourt, Brace & World, 1961).

The note structure to accompany this chapter can be downloaded from our website.

Explanations: Confirming and Falsifying Theories

CHAPTER 11

Key issues

▶ If scientific theories cannot be conclusively confirmed, on what grounds should we choose one over another?

▶ Why are some theories pseudo-scientific and others not? How can we distinguish between a pseudo-scientist and a genuine scientist?

▶ Why should a simpler theory be preferred to a more complex one?

▶ Can scientists only ever seek to falsify theories, never confirm them?

▶ Is scientific progress as smooth and orderly as we learn in school, or is it characterized by a series of revolutions in which one theory overthrows another?

▶ Are feminists right that people from different backgrounds and sexes know the world differently and have different criteria for knowledge?

▶ Can a uniquely feminine perspective on the world produce knowledge that is more satisfactory than that produced by the normal standard methods?

▶ Do claims of this kind mean that the disinterested, detached, neutral scientist is lost forever? Can we no longer appeal to some neutral and objective set of appearances to correct our different interpretations as to what we observe?

▶ Do we, as Richard Rorty suggests, just appeal to agreed-upon criteria, which are culturally determined and not objective at all?

Contents

Buried deep in matter there are certain subatomic processes so strange and unpredictable that they strike at our most deeply held common-sense notions about the world, particularly our belief in its uniformity and predictability. The subatomic world is ruled by chaos. Nothing is predictable: atoms and their constituents move about in random order. Even a complete account of a situation cannot allow us to predict what a subatomic particle will do next. In his celebrated 'uncertainty principle', Werner Heisenberg, one of the architects of the quantum theory, explained that any attempt to reveal what's going on inside an atom is bound to fail. By probing one feature (say, its position) another (say, its motion) becomes uncertain. In a world resembling more a gaming table than traditional science nothing is certain; all is ruled by chance and statistics.

Even Einstein, whose boundless imagination had replaced other deeply held intuitions of absolute space and time with relativity, was unable to accept this. Nature, he believed, did not operate on chance. Gazing with 'rapturous amazement at the harmony of natural law', he was convinced that these theories must be incomplete. But his conviction was more a matter of faith, the expression of 'an inner voice', than of reason and evidence. He boldly declared 'God does not play dice.'

Although the past successes of science were good evidence for the uniformity and predictability of nature, Einstein knew such evidence was only relevant if we could already justify inferring from the past to the future. But, as Hume had already shown, we can only use evidence to justify this inference if we accept the inference itself. Einstein, and many philosophers and scientists since, have found this difficult to accept. Others accept that reason cannot justify itself and begin at that point to live with the consequences.

Two important consequences flow from choosing not to rely on the principle of induction and the uniformity of nature. First, scientific method can no longer be described simply as a method of gathering facts and compiling a comprehensive inventory of natural laws. No law can be conclusively confirmed if we cannot be sure that the principle of induction and the uniformity of nature can guarantee it will go on being confirmed. Science then becomes what Medawar describes as an imaginative and inspirational process at every level. We should think of it, he argues, as a logically articulated structure of justifiable beliefs, which begins as a story about a possible world which we 'invent and criticize and modify as we go along, so that it ends by being, as nearly as we can make it, a story about real life.' This is the method defined by the hypothetico-deductive system in which scientists invent hypotheses, and experiments are designed to help us choose between competing possibilities, rather than to increase our stock of facts.

The other important consequence is that if the testing of scientific theories is no longer decisive in confirming them, because we cannot rely on the principle of induction and the uniformity of nature to ensure that they will go on confirming them, we must be able to say why some theories are more acceptable than others. This is now a matter of meeting not so much certain logical conditions as certain subjective, psychological conditions. One theory might give us more confidence because it helps us make sense of more hitherto unexplained events or phenomena by bringing them all under a law or a unified network of interrelated laws.

■ 1. Theories

One obvious answer to the question why we find some theories just more acceptable than others is the quantity of evidence supporting a theory. However, this too relies on the principle of induction: on some analogy between known cases and the present and next case. If not the quantity then perhaps more important is the *type* of evidence. Evidence counts in favour only if other evidence could have counted against it. In other words, the theory must be amenable to objective testing, at least in principle though not necessarily at the time. Without this no empirical evidence can conflict or support the theory. It is a pseudo-hypothesis: questions about its truth or falsity make no sense. For example I might read tea leaves and make vague predictions, and then argue that what does in fact come about was what I meant in the first place. Nothing counts against the theory and everything counts for it.

Compare that with a theory that could only be tested in principle, but not in fact at the time. On 4 October 1971 an airliner made an around-the-world flight eastward carrying four caesium atomic clocks. The following week another airliner carrying the same clocks set off westward. Compared with similar clocks that remained on Earth, those carried eastward lost 59 nanoseconds (a nanosecond is a thousand millionth of a second), while those on the westward flight gained 273 nanoseconds. This confirmed the special theory of relativity, which Einstein developed in a paper in 1905. Although at that time there was no way of testing the theory, unlike the tea leaf theory it made predictions that could have gone either way.

So, as this illustrates, for a theory to be convincing it must not only have the type of evidence that could have gone either way, it must also have predictive power to guarantee that it is genuinely testable. In the Baconian method of narrow inductivism observation should always be conducted without preconceptions which would distort and mislead our observations. According to this method, then, experiments are merely a way of furnishing scientists with factual information out of which they can draw their inductions. However, with the hypothetico-deductive method experiments come into their own. They have a crucial critical role in discriminating between competing possibilities, rather than to enlarge our stockpile of facts. Watson and Crick, who between them discovered the structure of DNA, seemed rarely to do experiments, except at that critical moment when they needed to decide which of the alternative ways to go. Watson admits, 'The idea of Francis and me dirtying our hands with experiments brought unconcealed amusement.'

However, to achieve this sort of predictive power a theory must possess certain characteristics. First, it must use language that is specific. It must avoid the sort of literary traps that come from using vague words that could mean almost anything: words like 'affinity', 'tendency', even 'instinct'. We might explain that plants grow towards the light because they have an affinity for it. But for us to make any sense of this and to draw out predictive consequences to test it, we would have to ask further questions about what is meant exactly by 'affinity' and its predictable effects. Compare that with the concept of gravity, which we would also be hard pressed to define, and we can see that here we have clear and exact predictive consequences that apply to a wide range of distinctly different phenomena.

Second, as this illustrates, a theory must contain laws that explain more than one event or one type of event. You might wonder why you burnt your hand when you took the pan off the cooker. I might explain that it had a metal handle and all metals conduct heat. I could then go on to demonstrate with different types of metal. Although this is a perfectly good explanation, it still leaves you wondering why metals conduct heat and why other materials do not. Now compare that with one given in the previous chapter for the cracked milk bottle left out with water in it overnight in freezing weather. To explain this by using the law that all water expands when it falls below freezing seems much more satisfactory. It is probably more convincing, because it doesn't just explain why water that freezes in all sorts of bottles expands to break the bottle, but other different types of events as well. It explains why pipes freeze, radiators crack and lakes burst their banks.

A good theory, then, will deepen and broaden our understanding by explaining more than just one event or one type of event. It will present a systematic and unified account of diverse phenomena. If various empirical uniformities can be shown to be manifestations of the same theory, we are more convinced, because the theory has to pass more and varied tests to survive, and the more it

survives the more convinced we are likely to be that this is the right answer. This also explains why one theory might succeed another; why Kepler's theory of planetary motions was succeeded by Newton's mechanics and why Newton's was succeeded by Einstein's theory of relativity. Each successive theory had a wider range of application and therefore had to survive more tests. The earlier theories did not hold strictly and unexceptionally.

Not only does the new theory explain the old, but it predicts new regularities. Newton's theory of gravitation accurately explained the orbits of all the planets with the exception of Uranus. The slight differences from the predicted path of its orbit could only be explained by hypothesizing the existence of a more distant planet. On the basis of Newton's theory Leverrier and Adams did in fact predict this planet and, subsequently, Galle discovered Neptune in that part of the sky to which he had been directed. Other theories have had equally stunning successes. In his book, *Other Worlds* (1980), Paul Davies explains how the quantum theory at a stroke explained chemical bonding, the structure of atoms and molecules, nuclear reactions, the property of crystals and other solids, electric conduction, superconductors, the pressure inside collapsed stars and much else. It led directly to superconductors, lasers, electron microscopes, antimatter, and nuclear power.

So, it is not just the quantity of successful predictions that confirm the theory, but the range and variety of its predictions. This opens the theory up to the vulnerability of being falsified in different ways and contexts, many of them unexpected. And, as we saw in the case of Neptune, by revealing new evidence not initially predicted by the theory it demonstrates that it is not simply an arbitrary theory constructed to fit the facts.

Nevertheless, the theory must not explain everything, otherwise, paradoxically, it would explain nothing. John Hospers illustrates the point with the 'gremlin' hypothesis. Say we were listening to the radio and suddenly it were to go off. I might explain to you that this is because of gremlins. For good reason you would no doubt consider this an unsatisfactory explanation. It is not so much that gremlins are invisible, although it would help if we could see how they work: after all gravity and magnetism, too, are invisible. It is more to do with the fact that we know of no laws that will allow us to predict their behaviour.

You would no doubt be happier if I were to

explain instead that the plug had accidentally been pulled out of the socket, after all we can show what the radio and any electrical appliance would be like without the plug being in the socket. We could test the hypothesis on the fridge, the TV, the computer and so on. But we know of no similar laws by which we can demonstrate the behaviour of gremlins. By using them to explain everything that goes wrong with electrical and mechanical equipment we are left with no way of unplugging them in the same way. We need to be able to show the difference between cases in which the radio fails to work because of them and when it fails to work because of other reasons.

It is similar to the design argument for the existence of God that the evidence of God's existence is all around us in the exquisite design and order of the universe. But in explaining everything in this way it explains nothing, because for it to be effective it must show what the world would be like without God – we need to be able to unplug God to see what the difference would be. But like the gremlin hypothesis, as we can't do this we know of no laws that will give predictions by which we can test the hypothesis. Unlike scientific theories where predictions run the risk of error and falsification, these theories never run that risk – they can never be laid low by a false prediction. But as they can never be put to the test they can also never pass it. Whereas you might be forced to give up the plug hypothesis, when it is shown that the radio has malfunctioned for some other reason, nothing can force you to abandon the gremlin hypothesis. Because it doesn't predict future events, it cannot be falsified by them.

The third characteristic of a theory likely to promote our confidence in it is its relationship to the accepted body of knowledge. A theory gains strong deductive support from above if it can be shown to be implied by more inclusive general theories. This gives it independent evidential support. Indeed because of this theoretical support it may be accepted as a law even where there is no empirical confirmation of it. The theory of free fall was accepted, because it was implied by the universal law of gravitation, even though there were no instances of it – that is, until man stepped on the moon.

Conversely, of course, if the theory conflicts with a well-confirmed, established theory, then its credibility will be damaged. You might argue, quite reasonably, this sounds a little like scientists protecting their favourite theories, in which they have no doubt invested time and effort. But it is not so unreasonable to stay committed to a theory that has a successful track record and years of accumulated corroboration. The new theory may lessen your confidence in it, but its findings will have to be weighty and its experimental results repeatable to dislodge a well-established theory. And even if this is the case a well-established theory may still continue to be used in areas where it is not expected to result in problems. A large-scale general theory which has proved successful in many areas is not normally abandoned unless a good alternative theory is available.

The twentieth century threw up two such theories, both seemingly at odds with one another. Einstein's theory of general relativity contains laws that describe the large-scale universe to an astonishing degree of precision. But these are incompatible with the laws in the quantum theory, which describe the small-scale universe to an equally astonishing degree of precision. Both are so well confirmed that it seems almost inconceivable that either one must be wrong, or another even larger all-encompassing theory will somehow accommodate them both. In the meantime, they both survive together as scientists look for such a theory. The closest they have come is 'string theory', according to which the basic ingredients of the universe are not particles, but tiny strings vibrating in ten-dimensional space. Despite being still untested it has attracted a growing number of supporters, largely because of its impressive record in solving theoretical problems.

The fourth characteristic, probably even more controversial than the third because it appears to be little more than an intuition, is the belief that the simpler a theory is the closer it is likely to be to the truth. Carl Hempel explains, 'if a set of points representing the results of measurements can be connected by a simple curve, we have much greater confidence in having discovered an underlying general law, than if the curve is complicated and shows no perceptible regularity.'

This appears to exert a considerable influence on the thinking of most scientists. In 1821 John Herapath entered into his journal a description of his latest work on the kinetic theory of gases explaining that 'I took every opportunity of examining how far the other hypothesis ... agreed with phenomena, and was so well pleased with its simplicity, and the easy, natural manner in which the different phenomena seemed to flow from it ....' The work of

Watson and Crick was also driven by the same search for simplicity. Watson explains his admiration for the work of Linus Pauling because it relied on the simple laws of structural chemistry and was the 'product of common sense, not the result of complicated mathematical reasoning'. When Watson and Crick settled on the helix as the structure of DNA Watson justifies their decision saying, 'Any other type of configuration would be much more complicated ... our reasoning was partially based upon simplicity ... The idea was so simple that it had to be right.' And later they told each other '... a structure this pretty just had to exist.'

Nevertheless as a guiding principle we need something that is more objective: a criterion of simplicity. One key component might be the ease with which something can be understood. This, and the desire to avoid unnecessary complications, seems to be one of Watson's concerns. But what might seem uncomplicated and straightforward to you might be impossibly complex for me. Much depends upon our experience and abilities. We may have more luck with a more mechanical definition in which we define simplicity by the number of different variables or assumptions a theory might contain. But this too seems to promise more than it can deliver. We have to know what is to count as an assumption, after all we can always analyse each one into other simpler assumptions. And then, once we have identified these 'core' assumptions, if this is possible without some arbitrary judgement, we will have to have some method of assessing their relative complexity or simplicity. This, too, is not easy to do without resorting to subjective judgements.

One way of justifying simplicity, which might avoid these problems, is to see it as a methodological standard, a working principle. When we are presented with two hypotheses each with the same explanatory power, it might be more reasonable to choose the simplest. Watson appears to have this in mind at times. Again referring to their choice of the helix he argues, 'Any other type of configuration would be much more complicated. Worrying about complications before ruling out the possibility that the answer was simple would have been damned foolishness. Pauling never got anywhere by seeking out messes.' Each universal law is after all a compression of indefinite numbers of individual cases into a simple law.

But then this appears to rely upon the belief that ultimately nature is fundamentally simple, which is no more supportable than the principle of induction and the uniformity of nature. Even so, it might still be possible to justify this method of working on subjective and psychological, rather than logical, grounds. In other words, we may not have to justify our belief that nature is ultimately simple, if all we are doing is arguing that working this way we are just more likely to develop theories about which justifiably we can be confident. The argument is that the simpler a theory is the more vulnerable it is to falsification. It is not protected by a complex battery of limiting conditions, so it can be tested in innumerable ways. And, as we have already seen, the more tests it is forced to pass, the more confidence we will have in it.

So, to summarize:

A theory's predictive power depends on four criteria:

1. Its use of language must be specific.

2. A good theory deepens and broadens our understanding by the range and variety of its predictions.

3. Its relationship to the accepted body of knowledge.

4. Its simplicity.

■ 2. Karl Popper, falsification and pseudo-science

This argument is closely associated with Sir Karl Popper and his two most famous books, *Conjectures and Refutations* (1963) and *The Logic of Scientific Discovery* (1935). Popper argues that the simple theory inspires more confidence because it implies less simple theories and, therefore, explains more – it has more empirical content. As a result it simply forbids more things to happen, which means that it is more testable and more readily falsifiable. The best theory, then, is the bold theory: one that forbids more things to happen. The more it embraces and the more it forbids the better. It takes more risks and therefore has to pass more tests, and in so doing we have more confidence in it. Medawar explains, 'Popper takes a scientifically realistic view: it is the daring, risky hypothesis, the hypothesis that might so easily not be true, that gives us special confidence if it stands up to critical examination.'

So, a theory that is bold, in that it explains a great deal about the world, is preferable to one that explains less. For example, Einstein's special theory of relativity is preferable to Newton's mechanics, because all the experimentally testable consequences of Newton's theory are also consequences of relativity, but not vice versa. Relativity has greater empirical content, therefore it is more testable. And the more attempts to falsify it that it survives the more confidence we will have in it. This means that one theory is likely to replace another corroborated theory, if the new theory is simply more testable and contains the old theory. Kepler's theory was replaced by Galileo's, which was replaced by Newton's, which in turn was replaced by Einstein's. In this way science progresses as one theory that is more testable and bolder replaces another.

Nevertheless, greater simplicity in a theory is not always associated with greater empirical content. Popper assumes that the simpler theory always contains the more complex theory, because the latter is hedged in by all sorts of limiting conditions. But this is not always the case: different hypotheses might tell us as much and be equally falsifiable, but may not be as simple. What's more, simple hypotheses might simply be conjoined, resulting in a more complex theory, which nevertheless has more explanatory power.

But, even so, simplicity aside, we are still likely to have more confidence in a theory that forbids more things to happen and survives tests to falsify it than one that either doesn't forbid anything or is not so bold. Kepler's theory of planetary motion forbids planets to be in certain places at certain times, so we can easily test it. In contrast, an unscientific theory will forbid no state of affairs and will therefore avoid tests and falsification altogether. No possible observation could conflict with it and show it to be wrong: it could be equally true under any circumstances whatsoever. Popper controversially cites psychoanalytical theory as an example of such 'pseudo science', but we could also include astrology, reading tarot cards, telepathy, palmistry, flat earth theory, pyramid power and a number of others.

2.1 Experiments and observation

Popper's theory, more effectively than the traditional narrow inductivist theory, explains the importance scientists place on prediction. In doing so he rejects the assumption that the key role for experiment and observation is to provide inductive support for theories. He was persuaded by Hume's argument that we can find no justification for making inductive inferences from observed data to arrive at general theories. Hume was arguing not that we should stop doing it, just that we can find no logical justification for it. Popper thought the only solution was to abandon traditional inductive theory altogether and instead concentrate on falsification or 'refutation'. Just propose theories, 'conjectures', however you arrive at them, and then test them to see how well they stand up.

So the real function of experiments is to falsify, not to gather inductively support for theories. Scientific theories lie forever beyond any justification through inductive reasoning. All we can do is to try to falsify them. A good scientist, then, corroborates a general law; he doesn't assert it to be true or even probably true, just that it has passed severe tests. The only evidence in favour of a theory is the failed attempts to falsify it: predictions that turned out right, but could have been wrong.

Any theory, then, that attempts to 'immunise' itself against testing and the possibility of falsification must be 'pseudo-scientific'. A pseudo-scientist protects his theory from falsification, counting only the evidence in favour and arguing that his theory is well-supported, even though without genuine evidence we have no reason to believe it. Protecting theories in this way can take different forms. We can avoid making predictions at all and just explain the event after its occurrence. Psychoanalysts cannot predict a person will turn out with a certain set of neuroses, instead they explain after the event why things turned out as they did.

Of those pseudo-scientists who, unlike psycho-analysts, actually make predictions some collect and count only the favourable ones: fortune-tellers might tell you the number of times they have successfully predicted Derby winners or Wimbledon champions, but not how many times they have failed in this. Others make predictions but leave them vague, so that whatever happens they can argue this is what was meant in the first place. Medawar argues, 'The smooth facility of Freudian and the older evolutionary formulae exasperated those who were dissatisfied with them because, though explaining everything in general, they explained nothing in particular.' And, finally, the fourth strategy involves making predictions that are likely to come true anyway and then claiming this success supports the theory. Someone might predict that you are soon to come into money, knowing that pay day is approaching.

So, to summarize:

Protecting theories

1. Avoid predictions and just explain after the event.

2. Collect and count only favourable predictions.

3. Make vague predictions and claim this is what was meant in the first place.

4. Make predictions that are likely to come true anyway.

However, if the theory is conclusively falsified the pseudo-scientist still isn't done. According to Popper, while the good scientist will throw out the falsified theory, replacing it with another, which has not been falsified, the pseudo-scientist will cling to the old one and try to save it with excuses: *ad hoc* explanations of why the predictions have gone wrong and why the theory is still true. That's not to say that we cannot create new hypotheses to explain the unexpected failures of our theory, as long as our new hypothesis is testable. If a fortune teller unexpectedly failed to predict the Wimbledon champion she could still account for her failure by amending her theory that she can predict the future by claiming 'I can predict the future when the moon is in the third quarter.' This is, of course, testable.

However, if, after my failure to levitate as I had claimed I could, I now amend my theory to read 'I can levitate, except when I am surrounded by hostile, undetectable forces'; this would not do, because it is untestable.

At least a theory has to be testable in principle, if not in fact. As we have seen it was not until long after Einstein's special theory of relativity was published in 1905 that it could be tested. In the same year he published another paper, claiming that mass and energy were equivalent: the energy being equal to the mass multiplied by the square of the velocity of light ($E=MC^2$). It was not until much later that this could be tested in laboratory experiments and with it came the realization that converting mass into energy was the source of energy in the sun and the stars, and could be used for warlike and peaceful purposes here on Earth.

2.2 Falsification

So, Popper's solution to Hume's problem of induction, that we cannot derive general theories from singular observation statements, is simply to sidestep it, replacing induction with the irreproachable method of deduction. Nothing can justify induction and scientists don't need to use it anyway. Take the two problems of induction we discussed in the last chapter, discovery and justification of theories: that we have no method of discovering theories from singular observations, nor any method of justifying them. Popper argues we must start with a conjecture, a theory, if we are to undertake a systematic investigation. It is impossible to work without one: the narrow inductive method of beginning without preconceptions is simply unworkable. There is an infinite range of things we could be interested in and theories determine what is worth looking at. Anyway they will always sneak in: it is impossible to keep them out.

Then, with the theory in place, scientists should deduce conclusions, predictions, and set about trying to falsify them. The more tests it passes, the more confidence we have in it. If it's true, we cannot show it to be true or even probably true, whereas if it's false, we can conclusively falsify it. There is, he believes, an asymmetry between verifiability and falsifiability: '... an asymmetry which results from the logical form of universal statements. For these are never derivable from singular statements, but can be contradicted by singular statements.'

Scientists, therefore, must try to falsify, never confirm. It's a logical mistake to believe we can confirm a theory by amassing positive evidence.

Nevertheless, despite the sidestep, falsification still doesn't settle the matter. Popper's method cannot depend entirely on deductive inferences from the theory, which we then test. As we saw in Chapter 3 it is a matter of logic that any state of affairs is compatible with any future state of affairs. Yet Popper assumes once the theory has been falsified it will stay falsified. This, as you can see, is an inductive assumption about the uniformity of nature: that the laws applying today will apply in the future. Without this science would be impossible. We would have to continually repeat experiments to check that the laws haven't changed.

However, this is not the only problem, which suggests that whereas Popper may have been right about conjectures as an answer to the first of our problems of induction, about how we arrive at hypotheses from singular observation statements, he may not be right about refutations. When we test a theory a number of factors come together to affect the outcome and, if the test fails, it may be difficult to discover where the problem might lie. As Medawar explains, 'We could be mistaken in thinking that our observations falsified a hypothesis: the observations may themselves have been faulty, or may have been made against a background of misconceptions; or our experiments may have been ill-designed.'

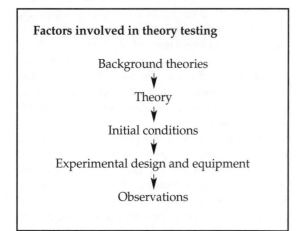

Factors involved in theory testing

Background theories
↓
Theory
↓
Initial conditions
↓
Experimental design and equipment
↓
Observations

As Medawar suggests the problem may lie with the background theories and assumptions we take for granted. Or it may be in our account of the

initial conditions, or in any of the other elements involved. But for falsification to be conclusive we must know that everything other than the theory we are testing is correct. We have to know everything about the world *except* the theory. In other words, we would have to assume there are no intervening forces, a hypothesis which, according to Popper's own theory, is not falsifiable. The point is the situation may not be as we think it is: there may be more objects or other influences we know nothing about, or qualities to those influences we *do* take into account, of which we are unaware. In such circumstances falsification is not only not decisive, but methodologically useless. It simply doesn't make sense to reject a theory in these circumstances, because the failure may be due to any of these other factors and not the theory at all.

And, of course, in this case where falsification is a reliable outcome, in that we know *something* is wrong – we just don't know what it is – then verification too is a reliable outcome. Indeed this appears to suggest that Popper's asymmetry between falsification and verification is in fact the reverse. If our predictions are continually falsified this can still get us nowhere near to falsifying the theory as long as we can't be sure there are no intervening influences. We may have no reason to believe the theory, but we certainly haven't proved it to be false. However, if our predictions are confirmed, then we confirm all the factors that have a bearing on the result: the background theories, initial conditions, the experiment and so on. Failed predictions cannot point one way or the other, but confirmation confirms everything, including the theory. It doesn't prove the theory to be true, but it does suggest we are approaching the truth.

In turn this suggests that some types of theories, fundamental theories about the ultimate determinants of the world, are by their very nature unfalsifiable, because they don't forbid anything without other theories. Kepler's theory of planetary motion, as we have seen, clearly forbids certain things from happening. By describing the path planets take it forbids them from being in certain places at certain times. It is, therefore, testable.

But Newton's or Einstein's theories are quite different. They describe the nature of things, the ultimate determinants of what happens in the world: that bodies are either at rest or move in a straight line unless acted upon by another body, or that energy is equal to the mass multiplied by the square of the velocity of light. On their own they forbid nothing, so they can only be tested if we can apply them using theories, like Kepler's, along with statements of initial conditions. But then, as we have just seen, if the test fails we cannot be sure where the problem lies: with the background theories, with our account of the relevant initial conditions, with the experiment, our observations, and so on. In effect it means that fundamental theories like these are not falsifiable.

2.3 Science and pseudo-science

If verification is in fact the only reliable outcome we can seek, this has serious implications for Popper's distinction between science and pseudo-science. It means that while he is right about the difference between a good scientist and a pseudo-scientist, he is wrong in putting it down to falsification. Newton's and Einstein's theories on their own are not falsifiable, yet they are not pseudo-scientific. Given certain initial conditions and other background theories we can predict what will happen.

So the distinctive feature between these and pseudo-scientific theories is not their falsifiability, but that they do say definite things about the world, that they are not vacuous. We would know a difference between a world in which they were true and one in which they were false. This is not the case with a pseudo-scientific theory, which, as we have seen, has no genuine content and cannot predict anything. If we were to prove that psychoanalysis is not pseudo-scientific, we would have to show that, given a complete account of the initial conditions of someone's life, we can predict that she will develop psychologically in a certain way. Of course, the problem is that this sets too high a standard: psychoanalysts can never be expected to compile a complete account in this way.

The difference, then, between a scientist and a pseudo-scientist no longer seems to lie in their willingness to falsify their theories, because verification is the only reliable outcome either can sensibly seek. Nonetheless, as we have already seen, those who only collect favourable outcomes, or make predictions that are vague or bound to be true anyway, are still not doing science. So, their difference seems to lie not in their willingness to falsify their theories, but in whether their confirmations are genuine or merely apparent. Genuine confirmations are those that could have gone the other way, whereas apparent confirmations come from pseudo-scientists only collecting evidence that is favourable where there is no chance of an unfavourable outcome, or from making predictions that are so vague that whatever happens will count as supporting evidence. In both cases nothing is allowed to count against the theory, so the evidence is worthless.

In turn, the unreliability of falsification also throws doubt on Popper's claim that whereas a good scientist will throw out and replace a falsified theory a pseudo-scientist will continue to cling to it, defending it with *ad hoc* assumptions. Clearly he is right to criticize those who cling to pet theories that have continuously proved to be wrong, but it's not unreasonable for a good scientist to search for reasons why her theory has failed as long as these yield additional test implications. Indeed Medawar argues that 'very few theories are utterly discredited ... Theories are repaired more often than they are refuted.'

It would be unreasonable to reject a falsified theory, when most theories cannot be conclusively falsified. If it fails we ought to ask whether the problem lies in the initial conditions, the background theory or elsewhere, rather than reject it. The anomaly in the orbit of Uranus seemed to falsify Newton's theory of gravitation, which could be used to predict accurately the orbits of all the other planets and much else besides. In these circumstances it would have been absurd to reject such a successful and useful theory. Rather, an explanation was found to account for the anomaly in the existence of a hypothetical distant planet. Eventually Urbain Leverrier and John Couch Adams both independently calculated where it could be found and Neptune was spotted on 23 September 1846 in just that part of the sky the theory had predicted.

It seems unreasonable, therefore, to expect the good scientist to reject a theory on this basis. The real problem lies in failing to realize that even though a theory cannot be conclusively falsified, if its failure cannot be explained, there are fewer reasons to believe it. To the pseudo-scientist this matters little: the mere possibility of accounting for failure leaves his theory as strongly supported as ever. Yet for a theory to be accepted in the long run it must demonstrate a record of successful predictions. The problem with Popper's account is that he assumes theory testing is relatively straightforward: it's all about what is forbidden to occur and what's not. In reality it seems a lot more complex.

■ 3. Thomas Kuhn and confirmation

Contemporary philosophy of science draws much of its inspiration from Popper and the radically different perspective presented in 1962 by the American philosopher Thomas Kuhn in his famous book *The Structure of Scientific Revolutions*. Kuhn challenges the traditional account of the linear progress of science accumulating one natural truth after another in an orderly advance towards a complete account of nature.

Instead, he believes that scientific progress is anything but smooth and linear: it is characterized by a series of revolutions in which one new 'paradigm' overthrows the existing paradigm for reasons not always entirely convincing. Relativity replaced Newtonian physics; evolution replaced special creation; and plate tectonics replaced a theory of geology in which continents did not drift. Yet the new astronomy of Copernicus was inferior to its Ptolemaic predecessor in its accuracy and predictions, and remained so for at least another century. Kuhn suggests that such scientific progress is not so ordered and rational as we are inclined to believe. It is governed by certain social constraints on how we order experience and on what we can and are willing to believe.

After each revolution science is dominated by a paradigm, a powerful theory, which sets the basis upon which research is to be conducted, defining its broad assumptions: its goals, the problems to be worked on and the methods to be employed. As Kuhn explains, it answers the sort of fundamental questions that a scientific community depends upon and takes for granted: questions like, 'What are the fundamental entities of which the universe is composed? How do these interact with each other and with the senses? What questions may legitimately be asked about such entities and what techniques employed in seeking solutions?' Without these it is impossible to know what kinds of questions to ask and problems to research.

Though they are not arrived at through conclusive confirmation – indeed, nor are they conclusively falsified when they are overthrown – paradigms are successful in explaining all sorts of things no previous theory could cope with. As a result a new paradigm quickly attracts supporters, who settle down to what Kuhn describes as 'normal' science. Accepting the theory, they make no attempt to falsify it. Instead they work to confirm it by concentrating on the questions it defines as relevant and which it guarantees to have a solution. But besides answering many unanswered questions, the new paradigm also points the way towards new questions that have to be asked, for which it can also guarantee a certain kind of answer.

In this way, from a state of comparative ignorance in which few people understood the paradigm, it gradually assumes a dominant position and 'a strenuous and devoted attempt' is made 'to force nature into the conceptual boxes supplied by professional education.' Few scientists in Europe understood Newton's *Principia* in the half century following its publication in 1686, yet by the second half of the nineteenth century so ingrained was Newtonian theory into the scientific explanation of the natural world that many scientists felt that in physics no serious problem remained to be solved.

Yet as normal science progresses inevitably a growing number of questions defy solution and, although tolerated for a while, they eventually become the focus for research. As the evidence mounts on a number of fronts a crisis develops from which eventually a revolution occurs. A scientist poses a resolution that lies outside normal science, challenging the paradigm. And if the problem cannot be disposed of in the context of the old paradigm a new paradigm will begin to attract supporters as those clinging to the old one are increasingly ignored. A new period of normal science sets in and the old paradigm fades away, unless assimilated into the new one as a special case.

A puzzling anomaly in the orbit of Mercury around the sun defied Newtonian theory. Eventually, after working outside the Newtonian

---

Brief lives
Kuhn, Thomas S.

Dates: 1922–1996
Born: Cincinnati, USA
Best known for: Arguing that science is a contingent social activity: that most 'normal' scientists do not construct theories on the basis of neutral facts, but solve puzzles based on paradigms.

Major works: *The Copernican Revolution* (1957), *The Structure of Scientific Revolutions* (1962), *The Essential Tension* (1977).

paradigm, Einstein published the theory of general relativity in 1916, which not only explained the anomaly, but much more besides. It laid down a new paradigm with a new set of assumptions and concepts through which we could view the world and interpret the results of experiments. Contrary to our common-sense experience Newton's absolute concepts of time and space were replaced by an understanding of them as merely sets of relations between objects.

3.1 Normal science

But is Kuhn's account true? Popper and Kuhn both agree that science must begin with theory. But whereas Kuhn argues they must compete to show which one is right – in other words we must seek to confirm one over another – Popper argues we must try to falsify them, accepting only that which survives. However, we have already seen that we cannot conclusively falsify fundamental theories, so it seems Kuhn's account is the only possible account: we have no alternative but to try to make promising theories work.

Nevertheless, Kuhn's normal science seems to share many of the weaknesses of Popper's pseudo-science. After all, Kuhn thinks testing stops altogether in normal science, because the truth of the paradigm is taken for granted. The aim of normal scientists is to answer specific questions about the world on the basis of the paradigm, which they accept without further question. Like the pseudo-scientist they don't appear to want to test the theory, only to work out its implications.

However, as we have seen, there can be no direct testing of the kind Popper wants of fundamental theories: failed predictions cannot show them to be false. And when some non-fundamental theories can be tested we also saw that it is equally possible to verify them. So it seems there is no alternative for most scientists but to work within the assumptions of a paradigm, accepting its laws and concepts, while they formulate new theories about the nature and arrangement of things. The work of Watson and Crick in discovering the structure of the DNA molecule was founded upon their acceptance of the ruling paradigm of atomic and molecular theory.

Moreover, even if theory testing were to be the sole concern of scientists, as Popper suggests, there seems to be no other way of doing it but to accept the paradigm and work within its ruling assumptions.

As an established theory it is already well supported: it has a good predictive record. So, to challenge it we would have to show its reliability was *in the long run* weak. No single failure will do because, as we've seen, we could never know where the problem lies – with the initial conditions, the experiment, the equipment and so on. Therefore only an accumulation of problems will show that the theory is probably wrong, and this is what Kuhn means by 'normal' science: a detailed demonstration of persistent problems.

3.2 Crisis and revolution

So whereas Popper believes a theory is overthrown when it is shown to have been falsified, even when these tests themselves are dependent on the theory, Kuhn believes it is only overthrown as a result of the gradual development of problems, which leads to the establishment of another theory that promises better success. A theory cannot be falsified by a single observation statement, but it can be confirmed if scientists can demonstrate that it has increasing reliability. And, by the same token, it can be overthrown by another theory, which can demonstrate more reliable predictive success. When the German geophysicist, Alfred Wegener, developed the theory of continental drift in 1915 in his book *The Origin of Continents and Oceans*, most geologists of the time and, indeed, over the next 50 years, refused to believe it. Yet it gradually showed itself to have a reliable record of predictive success as the theory of plate tectonics and geologists slowly abandoned the established theory that the continents were fixed in position.

Popper would argue that all those geologists who refused to criticize the established theory, Kuhn's normal scientists, were merely pseudo-scientists. To be a scientist means being a critical thinker, whereas the normal scientist, he declares, is merely 'a victim of indoctrination.' Yet that's not to say that Kuhn, like the rest of us, would not agree that Popper's pseudo-scientist is not doing genuine science. He can still argue that the normal scientist is in fact doing what Popper expects of a genuine scientist. She is being critical about her work, but only from within the paradigm against which her work is done, because she accepts she cannot falsify fundamental theories. All she can do is abandon them only when alternative theories arise with more long-term predictive success. If this really is the key distinction between Popper's genuine scientist and the pseudo-scientist, that one is critical and the other is not, then the problem with Kuhn's normal science disappears.

Popper and Kuhn both reject the traditional inductive methods: they both accept there is no straightforward route from singular observation statements to the discovery of a scientific theory. So a theory is necessary to give direction to research, otherwise we are just flailing around in the dark. Although not quite a pre-paradigm science it gives you some idea of the strange and bewildering territory of a pre-paradigm science, when you think of the work being done on parallel universes. This is a world where there are no objects in the normal sense – no matter, no particles, just multidimensional membranes wrapping around one another.

Nevertheless, a paradigm is more than just a theory. Indeed Kuhn believes that without a paradigm genuine scientific research can scarcely begin at all. In pre-paradigm science we have little idea what's worth studying and what will improve our predictive success. But with a paradigm we are clearer about what kind of investigation is likely to be profitable; we know the basic entities that we are researching and have an idea about their nature and arrangement; we know the sort of tests we need to devise and the equipment we need to carry them out. It defines the questions we may legitimately ask and creates the conditions in which we can achieve consistency in our predictive success. With all of this we are able to explore in more depth and with more care.

◼ 4. Feminist epistemology

As we have seen in previous chapters the idea that reality is mediated by our own conceptual frameworks is not new. Nevertheless, the empiricist view of an objective reality against which we test them to decide which we keep and which we reject still maintains a strong grip on Western thought. Even Kuhn fails to escape its clutches completely. He asks,

> But is sensory experience fixed and neutral? Are theories simply man-made interpretations of given data? The epistemological viewpoint that has most often guided Western philosophy for three centuries dictates ... yes! In the absence of a developed alternative, I find it impossible to relinquish entirely that viewpoint.

However, others have not been so reluctant. Kuhn's theory has attracted a much more radical relativistic interpretation. For example, feminists argue that different backgrounds and interests lead people to have different criteria for knowledge. People from different cultures or, in this case, from different sexes simply know the world differently. Many feminists criticize scientific objectivity on the grounds that it is an example of the masculine over-reliance on reason. Serious attention to the experiences of women would offer a more adequate account of human life. The question is, how personal is knowledge? Is it relative to the individual's cultural context and biology? If it is, then what counts as knowledge will differ from culture to culture, reflecting our national origins, religious backgrounds, and our social experiences and values.

If this is true, the underlying problem can be framed in political terms with an entrenched ruling elite and an oppressed majority who fail to share the same stock of experiences. Behind the mask of objectivity and neutrality feminists claim there is a system of power relations representing vested interests, dominance and subjugation. All the while traditional empiricists declare as their aim to produce knowledge that is free from androcentric (male-centred) and sexist biases, and class and race distortions, they are in fact speaking from deeply entrenched, androcentric positions. The particular focus for this attack is the Enlightenment concept of rationality, seen as a device for claiming mastery and control, a symbol of the male refusal to acknowledge that there are different perspectives and ways of understanding life and nature.

This seems to have implications both for the empiricist and the rationalist alike. Feminists argue that for the empiricist, if women do have different sense experience than men, they must have a different sort of knowledge. Likewise for the rationalist, they argue that if women have a biological nature which results in them reasoning in a different way than men, then again women are likely to have a different sort of knowledge.

As you can see feminist epistemology raises two distinct questions. One concerns whether there are different experiences and strategies of thinking with different emphases on logic and imagination, both of which shape the different male and female attempts to understand and theorize about the world. The other is concerned not just with the fact that this might produce radically different perspectives on the world, but different ways of establishing their truth and falsity. It is concerned with the claim that there might be different theories of justification: the way we validate our theories and hypotheses.

The answer given by many feminists to the first question is that we must recognize the specificity of knowledge; that only a value-laden empiricism aware of feminist ideology, a uniquely feminine perspective on the world, can produce knowledge that is more satisfactory than that produced by the normal standard methods. However, for many critics this violates the basic nature of empiricism. If we accept that we cannot escape the social and cultural influences of our time, we sacrifice the ideal of the ahistorical, abstract individual on which traditional empiricism has been built. What's more, on the same grounds are we also bound to accept other factors that influence our perspectives, like our particular capacities and training? Are these to count as much as gender in explaining how people acquire knowledge?

Those who are described as 'feminist standpoint theorists' are not only willing to accept that this does indeed undermine traditional empiricism, but see significant advantages in this. Western societies, they argue, derive their knowledge from the social experiences of a limited segment of the population, who are usually white, male, middle class and educated. Their experience alone provides the means of testing theory. But by knowing this, by being aware of their oppression, women can challenge the ruling male epistemology. They have, therefore, certain inbuilt advantages.

The feminist philosopher Uma Narayan argues that women can perceive and understand different aspects of the world in different ways that 'challenge the male bias of existing perspectives.' Mainstream theories are 'one-dimensional and deeply flawed, because of the exclusion and misrepresentation of women's contributions.' With women's contributions we will see a new perspective, a radically different picture, changing 'the very nature of these activities and their self-understanding.'

The challenge, then, for standpoint theorists is to undermine the abstract, rationalistic and universal image of scientific activity. Narayan maintains that to achieve this feminists must examine the contingent historical factors that have influenced scientific theories and practices, providing what feminists believe are sexist metaphors in which to conceptualize their work. They must also seek to reintegrate values and emotions into our understanding of our cognitive activities and challenge the traditional dualisms of western philosophical thinking on the grounds that they are sexist: dualisms like reason/emotion, culture/nature and universal/particular. While the first in each pair is traditionally seen as rational, scientific and masculine, the second is non-rational, non-scientific and feminine.

But still more important for standpoint theorists, such oppressed groups have a certain 'epistemic advantage' that derives from having their feet firmly placed in both camps: having knowledge of both the oppressor and the oppressed. As Narayan explains, because they are able to work in two different contexts with two different practices, this gives them access to critical insights as each perspective views the other critically. It means a woman must 'dichotomize her life' so that she has one framework for one side of her life and the other for the other side. She must try to acquire 'stereotypical male characteristics', like aggression, along with her female characteristics.

However, the question is whether sexes can appropriate characteristics in this way in the form of pre-conceived stereotypes. Can some characteristics be described as male and others as female? Indeed, arguing for stereotypes itself in this manner appears to be buying into the very male-dominated discourse of exclusive classifications of characteristics, some regarded as valuable, others not, which feminists themselves are targeting. In her ground-breaking book, *Sexual Politics* (1969), Kate Millett condemns the process of 'arbitrarily departmentalizing human qualities into two neat little piles' in which 'aggression is masculine, passivity feminine, violence masculine, tenderness feminine, intelligence masculine, and emotion feminine, etc. etc.' She warns, 'It is high time we began to be reasonable about the relationship of sexuality to personality and admit the facts – the present assignment of temperamental traits to sex is moronic, limiting and hazardous.'

Moreover, such an argument, that there are two mutually exclusive sets of characteristics, appears arbitrarily to exclude the middle ground. It might be just as plausible to argue that some people are more or less aggressive than others, male or female, on a continuum that stretches from the tolerant, compliant, pragmatic individual to the intolerant, inflexible dogmatist. Indeed some critics argue, that because in fact there is no single unified feminist perspective, in arguing this way standpoint theory ignores differences and, hence, fails by its own feminist standards.

We also need to ask, in what does this 'epistemic

advantage' reside? After all, despite its claims to 'inhabit two contexts critically', it is still located in some social reality, which means its perspective is as limited as any other. What's more, such epistemic advantages are not an exclusively female privilege. The 'double vision' and its epistemic advantage of having greater access to 'critical conceptual space', as Narayan describes it, is an experience all people have had if they have lived for any length of time in a country in which they were not brought up. For such people the 'double vision' is the creative experience of being at odds with the culture in which you are living.

Indeed, it is an experience which most great scientists and philosophers have had, whether that is Hume shaking the established ideas of his time with the publication of *A Treatise of Human Nature*, Kant with his 'Copernican Revolution', or Semmelweis, who, after his findings and publications were rejected, was finally dismissed from his post for refusing to accept the prevailing wisdom of his time and was left to live out the remaining years of his life in a mental hospital. And indeed, this is exactly what Kuhn seems to be describing as science progresses through a series of revolutions with an emerging paradigm overthrowing the established one, despite the latter having deep roots in the scientific establishment, dictating its concepts, methods and explanations.

As to our second question about the different ways of validating our theories and hypotheses, the answer is likely to be entirely Kuhnian. In *Science as Social Knowledge* (1990), Helen Longino presents the argument for 'contextual empiricism': that any reasoning about evidence is bound to be contextual, because we accept certain data as relevant on the basis of our background assumptions and hypotheses, which we accept as part and parcel of belonging to and working within a certain scientific community. It is an entirely social practice. Nevertheless, to accept that values and ideology play a part in enquiry does not in itself amount to indiscriminate acceptance of individual subjective preferences. Objective validation is a product of social criticism. As Kuhn argues, the community is the critic and arbiter in the justification of knowledge claims and in determining which projects gain recognition.

So, objectivity is socially produced: it's a mediated value. It is of course the product of attending to the evidence, but facts are not just what can be observed and recorded. They are recognized as such by a certain social criteria. The validation of knowledge claims is the product of intersubjective communal criticism. Those who claim to know are accountable as much to the community as they are to the facts. Feminist epistemologists, therefore, claim to be devising methods for analysing knowledge claims that are socially constructed, are shaped by the nature of the individual who makes them and are constrained by an independent reality.

As you can see the arguments of standpoint theorists and empiricists like Longino and others show how influential have been the postmodern critics of the epistemological thinking of the Enlightenment. However, the problem for feminists has been that indifferent tolerance for all perspectives robs them of any means of challenging the androcentrism and sexism of mainstream epistemology. If you accept that those who make knowledge claims cannot be free from the influence of their situation, this applies equally to the feminist as it does to mainstream epistemology. Lost forever is the disinterested, detached knowing subject, the neutral observer.

■ 5. Conclusion

The case for a feminist epistemology makes it even more important that we should distinguish between two radically different positions. The argument that, in order to explain how knowledge of the external world is possible, we must accept our own creative role in constructing our conceptual frameworks ought to be distinguished from the claim that the structure of appearances varies according to our theoretical commitments. The former involves the rejection of the notion that there is an unproblematic core of reports on experience: we may all be looking at the same reality, but through different lenses. The latter is much more radical. Not only does this suggest that appearances are often not what they seem, but that their interpretation by observers varies and cannot be corrected by appeal to some neutral and objective set of appearances on which they can all agree.

For example, Richard Rorty extends Kuhn's distinctions arguing that the traditional distinction between the search for objective knowledge and other discourses is nothing other than a distinction between 'normal discourse' and 'abnormal discourse.' Following Kuhn he explains that normal discourse is 'any discourse (scientific, political, theological, or whatever) which embodies agreed-upon criteria for reaching agreement: abnormal discourse is any which lacks such criteria.' Any attempt, therefore, to go beyond this and argue for 'objectivity' in terms of some notion of accurate representation amounts to no more than 'a self-deceptive effort to eternalise the normal discourse of the day.'

Creationists employ a similar strategy to attack the evolutionary argument. They claim philosophers of science have shown that science does not progress in an orderly manner accumulating objective truths about the external world. Rather they invent hypotheses, which they then set about testing. But the observations they make to do this are themselves dependent on the terms of the hypothesis, which in turn is dependent upon certain fundamental assumptions. Evolution is one of these assumptions: it is neither a hypothesis nor an observation, but in itself provides the basis for all practical and theoretical research. Therefore, as this research depends upon this fundamental assumption, it cannot provide the independent grounds for proving the theory true or false. In this, they argue, evolution is no different from creation: they are both alternative fundamental assumptions, neither of which is open to scientific proof or disproof.

The argument illustrates the distinction we made above between those who believe that our hypotheses can be tested and corrected by appealing to some neutral and objective set of appearances and those who suggest that not only are appearances often not what they seem, but their interpretation varies according to our theoretical commitments and cannot be corrected by such an appeal. The creationists believe that these fundamental assumptions are arbitrary, whereas the scientific community would defend itself arguing that scientists have reasons for choosing evolutionary rather than creationist assumptions, not the least of which is that they generate hypotheses that are rich in testable consequences.

This is an intriguing problem. In the next chapter we will look at whether the creationists and others are right in arguing that issues like this are better dealt with in the domain of religious belief, rather than in that of science. But for this we will have to be clear about what religion is, what claims it makes, and whether they are to be dealt with in a different manner to that of science.

 The note structure to accompany this chapter can be downloaded from our website.

■ Questions

1. If scientific laws go beyond experience, can they be justified by observation and experiment?

2. Discuss the view that scientific theories can no more be conclusively falsified than they can be conclusively verified.

3. 'If the scientific method is based on induction, scientific knowledge can never be certain knowledge.' Discuss.

4. Are we right to believe that, strictly speaking, there are no natural laws, only scientific hypotheses?

5. 'Scientific evidence is only as objective as those controlling it allow it to be.' Discuss.

6. Is Popper's view that 'the more falsifiable a theory is, the better it is' an adequate criterion of a scientific theory?

7. Is there a uniquely feminine perspective on the world? If so, does it mean we can no longer appeal to some neutral and objective set of appearances to correct our different interpretations of what we observe?

8. Are feminists right that there is a unique feminine epistemology or is this merely the result of 'arbitrarily departmentalising human qualities' as Kate Millett suggests?

■ Recommended reading

Popper, K. *The Logic of Scientific Discovery* (London: Hutchinson, 1968).

Popper, K. *Conjectures and Refutations: Growth of Scientific Knowledge* (London: Routledge and Kegan Paul, 1969).

Kuhn, T. S. *The Structure of Scientific Revolutions* (Chicago: University of Chicago Press, 1970).

Lakatos, I. and A. Musgrave (eds). *Criticism and the Growth of Knowledge* (Cambridge: Cambridge University Press, 1970).

Garry, Ann and Marilyn Pearsall. *Women, Knowledge and Reality* (Boston, Mass.: Unwin Hyman, 1989).

Harding, Sandra. *Whose Science? Whose Knowledge?: Thinking from Women's Lives* (Ithaca, NY: Cornell University Press, 1991).

Longino, Helen. *Science as Social Knowledge* (Princeton, NJ: Princeton University Press, 1990).

12 Religion

Key issues

▶ Do science and religion have conflicting and irreconcilable visions of the world?

▶ Are they founded upon radically different notions of truth?

▶ What is a religion?

▶ What do believers mean when they say there is a God?

▶ What sort of language is religious language? Does language function in a different way when we apply it to religious matters?

▶ If it does, how are we to understand and confirm its claims: how are we to distinguish between false and true statements about God?

▶ Does God exist?

Since the publication of Darwin's *Origins of Species* (1859) and *The Descent of Man* (1871) it has been difficult not to conclude that science and religion have two conflicting and irreconcilable visions of the world each founded upon radically different notions of truth. Yet, although scientists like Stephen Hawking expect to arrive at conclusions in their search for the origins of the universe that most modern religions will struggle to accept, there are many scientists who believe science and religion are not so different.

Indeed Einstein believed that serious scientists were the only profoundly religious people. It is their religious feeling, he believed, which provides the strongest motive in their pursuit of truth and it alone accounts for their willingness to devote themselves to their work and divorce their minds from the immediate realities of life. Above all their religious feeling shows itself in their deep conviction in the rationality of the universe, which sustains them through years of solitary labour despite countless failures. Indeed, Stephen Hawking, too, accounts for his own driving determination in just these terms. The conviction that guides and drives his work is the belief that the world is not simply a brute arbitrary fact, that there are certain well-defined laws, all of which in turn are part of some bigger law. He explains, 'So what we are trying to find out is whether there is some bigger law from which all other laws can be derived. I think you can ask that question whether or not you believe in God.'

But, as in science, in religion we have the same obligation to show that we are justified in what we say. And this in turn depends upon two things. As we saw in Chapters 2 to 4, we must be clear about what is actually being said: what do believers mean when they say what they do; what does it mean to say there is a God? In particular, what sort of language is religious language and how can we understand and confirm its claims? Once we have answers to these questions we can move onto the question we all want answered: does God exist?

1. What is religion?

But first we need to ask, what exactly is a religion? If you apply the method we described in Chapter 2, the first thing you will notice is that there is a rich diversity of meanings. Each culture has its religious tradition and each is as varied as the cultures that give them birth. Contrary to what we might first assume, some, like Buddhism, do not involve a belief in God. As for doctrines, beliefs, ceremonies and institutional organizations, there is as much diversity here as elsewhere. Many Christian Protestant sects believe that religion is an entirely private affair. The customary institutional organization with all its rituals and ceremonies leads worshippers, they believe, to worship the symbols and neglect what they symbolize. Quakers have eliminated practically all ceremony and ritual. Similarly, some religions have a priesthood, while others do not. In some divine revelation is important, in others not.

We may even question whether beliefs are important. It's true in the past that some, like Thomas More, have been sentenced to death for their religious beliefs, particularly during the Reformation and the Counter-Reformation. But it is not just a question of holding the appropriate beliefs and perhaps showing why you believe you are justified in holding them. Some who are able to explain and justify their beliefs might not be regarded as particularly religious. They may know the form but little of the spirit of their religion, while others, who might struggle to explain why they believe, might lead simple, devout and deeply religious lives.

But neither can it just be a matter of emotions: a feeling of absolute dependence on God and devotion to his word. This can lead us to abandon the spirit of religion as much as a highly intellectual approach. Just consider the experiences of Brian Keenan, John McCarthy, Terry Waite, Tom Sutherland and Terry Anderson, recalled in Keenan's remarkable book, *An Evil Cradling* (1992). All were held captive for years in hot, dusty, cockroach-infested cells in Beirut by Shi'ite militiamen driven by their devotion to God.

Perhaps the one element found in all religions is that it cannot be separated from the rest of one's life: it cannot just be turned on each time you enter the church, chapel or mosque. It must be felt, thought and lived as an everyday reality, translated into action. The Protestant pastor, Dietrich Bonhoeffer, who lost his life in a concentration camp, made the same point in a story he told to a fellow prisoner, who asked him how, as a Christian theologian, he could justify taking part in the resistance against Hitler. Briefly, under the eyes of the wardens, he explained with a story. If, as a pastor, he saw a drunken driver driving at high speed down a busy street, he did not consider it his only or his main duty just to bury the victims and to comfort the relatives. It was more important to wrench the wheel out of the hands of the drunkard.

But this on its own seems to allow us to include in 'religion' any system of beliefs to which we commit our lives. Political ideologies, like Marxism, fascism and nationalism, have been described as 'secular religions'. Many of those who are committed to them have been prepared to make the ultimate sacrifice. In return the beliefs and values of each ideology give individuals a means of making sense of their lives, giving them meaning and significance in ways similar to any religion.

Still, ideologies are not the sort of beliefs and commitments we would generally describe as religions. It seems, then, to suggest that the difference might be that a religion, as opposed to an ideology, gives 'spiritual' significance and meaning to our lives, which points to a reality that transcends our normal lives, whether or not that presupposes the existence of a God. We must, therefore, look at what religions mean when they talk about this reality.

2. Religious concepts: their coherence, meaning and justification

This is a good example of the type of work in which philosophers are generally engaged. The British philosopher John Hick, who served as the minister of a rural Presbyterian church before going on to teach at the universities of Cornell, Princeton and Cambridge, describes philosophy of religion as seeking to 'analyse concepts such as God, holy, salvation, worship, creation, sacrifice, eternal life, etc., and to determine the nature of religious utterances in comparison with those of everyday life, scientific discovery, morality, and the imaginative expressions of the arts.' So, we need to understand what we mean when we talk of our beliefs in a super-natural, spiritual reality, whether or not we call it God.

2.1 What does it mean to say there is a God?

We think of God (at least in the Christian, Judaic and Islamic faiths) as timeless, omnipotent, omniscient, immutable and supremely good. The Supreme Being is transcendent in the sense that he possesses powers greater than human powers, indeed greater than the sum total of all things found in the physical universe. He is not subject to the laws of nature, but stands above them as their creator. Indeed, he can even suspend them and intervene in events. He is, therefore, not only its creator, but he sustains the world; he is the ultimate answer, the final explanation of all things. At this point it's worth noting the distinction between deism and theism. Deism is the belief that God created the world and left it to run by itself, while theism is the belief that not only did he create the world, but he continues to exercise an influence over it. Most modern religions are theistic.

But the sort of influence we believe God exercises reflects our belief that, in addition, God represents a moral will: that he has a moral personality in many ways like our own. Indeed in Christianity God is made flesh as a result of the resurrection: he becomes a person and takes on the suffering of us all. In all modern faiths God has a personal relationship with us: he judges our conduct, he listens to us, forgives us our sins, shows mercy, and is both benevolent and wise.

By this stage you've no doubt already concluded that to talk in these terms is to talk about God in an anthropomorphic way: that is, to attribute to him certain recognizable personality traits found in humans, although to a lesser degree. God is a free and rational agent. He is pleased and displeased by our conduct. He has a personality in the sense that he forms reasons and preferences for doing things. He acts freely on his intentions and has a clear conception of the difference between right and wrong.

Such anthropological descriptions are probably inescapable. To talk of God as an 'it', an inanimate thing without a personality, simply doesn't work. While we might be able to conceive of God without a body, it is impossible to conceive of him without a mind. Even those who believe in some form of pantheism attribute to nature a benevolent purpose of regeneration and ecological stability. Consequently, as you will have already noticed, it is difficult not to give God a sex, although there seems no reason why we should not equally refer to 'she' as well as 'he'.

Nevertheless, although unavoidable, this doesn't mean that these anthropomorphic descriptions make any sense. How is it possible for God to desire something, when he has everything? Does it make sense to say that God changes his mind, or that he makes plans to achieve something, when he is omnipotent and can do it directly without adopting the means to achieve a certain end? For example, it is sometimes argued that God tolerates evil to achieve good, but why not just achieve good directly? And when we argue that God does certain things to glorify his name, isn't this, as John Stuart Mill once pointed out, attributing to God one of the lowest of all human motives?

Even our description of God as timeless makes little sense when events that God knows about occur in time. If God has a mind that thinks, judges and wills certain things to happen, all this is done in time. But if he is timeless, how can he know of these or any event that occurs in time? If he does know that an event has occurred, presumably there was a time when he got to know this. Of course, you might argue that he always knew of it, but this suggests that everything is predestined, which means I cannot claim to have free will and therefore be morally responsible for my actions. In this case it is God, not me, who is the real agent responsible for my evil acts.

And this, in turn, has a bearing on our description of God as omnipotent. If I have free will then God is powerless to prevent my actions, which means he is not omnipotent. J. L. Mackie describes this as the 'paradox of omnipotence'. If God can create a being he cannot control, then he is not omnipotent. Alternatively, if he cannot create such a being, then this too shows that he is not omnipotent.

The only way out, it seems, is to argue, as the mystic does, that to conceptualize at all about God is a mistake. It limits God, who is beyond description. Even to say he is limitless, or even that he exists, is to say something about him. Indeed, each time we use the concept God to refer to him we conceptualize him. So, it is better just to remain silent.

Even so, the mystic would still want to say these experiences I have are of God and not something else, and this is to say something definite about something beyond you. Even though you might have some revelatory experience, which is identical to the experiences of others, this is not to say it points to anything beyond you. It might merely be a sudden clarity of thought, the result of meditating to clear the mind. The method of Transcendental Meditation, as taught in the West by the Maharishi Mahesh Yogi, has been adopted by professional and government bodies around the world to teach people how to clear their minds and focus their creativity. But even though all those using the method each day report they are having the same experiences, there is still no reason to believe this points to a Supreme Being existing beyond them.

2.2 What sort of language is religious language? How are we to understand it and confirm its claims?

However, the mystic would argue that these problems arise because we are misusing religious language, which should not be taken literally, but symbolically. When we say things like 'Jack is a real terrier when it comes to tracking down the truth', we don't mean literally that he has a long hairy face with a large black nose and pointed ears. We mean it symbolically that he has the sort of temperament that never gives up on a problem until he solves it. In the same way when we say 'God is love' or that he is powerful, benevolent or that 'He is the unity of all things', these are not descriptions but symbols, like 'terrier', that reach for a truth that lies beyond our powers of description.

Nevertheless, although this seems to be something we all do, it should be troubling to us as philosophers. We are concerned to reveal the truth, so we must be concerned about the way we use language. We have to be able to distinguish between those statements that are meaningful and those that are not. But if such religious claims reach beyond our experience, how are we to do this? We saw in Chapter 9 from a strictly empirical position logical positivists would argue that statements can

only be meaningful if they can be verifiable either as logical truths or as empirical statements. Others argue this is too narrow: that we should also concern ourselves with metaphysical inquiry, including talk about God. F. C. Copleston argues that to talk meaningfully about God we must begin with human experience, with the world, and argue from this to its cause in God. And to do this we must use language analogically.

To settle the issue we must ask ourselves two questions. First, as Copleston suggests, does language function in a different way when we apply it to religious matters? And, second, if it does, how are we to confirm its claims: how are we to distinguish between false and true statements about God?

To answer the first question we need to be clear about the sort of meaning a language can have which describes the spiritual world using all sorts of anthropomorphic references to the body of God and to emotions, like jealousy and anger, which are drawn from human experiences. The mystic argues, as we have seen, that we shouldn't take these literally. They are merely gestures towards the nature of God using analogies and symbols. And this is not an unreasonable claim, after all much of our use of language is non-literal in the form of metaphor, simile, symbol and analogy.

For example, strictly, a metaphor occurs whenever we take a word out of its original sphere of use and apply it to new circumstances. In this sense all words are metaphorical when they no longer carry physical meaning. As we saw in Chapter 4, words expressing mental perceptions, abstract ideas and complex relations are all conveyed by means of the nearest physical parallel. When we use the word 'seeing' as in understanding an idea in the phrase 'I see the point of that', we are merely borrowing from the physical 'sight'. Indeed, as we saw earlier, there are numerous examples of this in our language, many going back to Latin derivatives, like the verb 'to think', which is a metaphor from vine-pruning.

But, nevertheless, some symbols are better than others in representing what we want to say, so there must be some affinity, some likeness, between the symbol and the inexpressible idea. When we use the verb 'seeing' to mean that we understand, we have in mind the affinity between this and seeing things in the physical world clearly and sharply. By the same token, when we use religious language to describe God we must have a concept of what we are trying to symbolize. We must know something about it, otherwise we would have no grounds on which to choose one symbol over another. If we know nothing, we must do as a genuine mystic would do and remain silent.

So, it seems, we are left with two unpromising alternatives. Either we can embrace the anthropomorphic view and accept that we *do* have a concept of God and our symbols are derived from human experience, or we can accept the full logic of the mystic's position and remain silent. In fact, however, there is a middle course, which most modern theologians choose: 'the doctrine of analogical predication'. Thomas Aquinas, the medieval Italian philosopher and theologian, argued that there is indeed a definite connection between the two uses of the word 'good' when I say that 'Pat is good' and 'God is good.' The only difference is one of quality: God's goodness is much greater and purer than Pat's could ever be. Nevertheless, despite its inadequacies, using such a word is still appropriate in conveying the quality God possesses. In other words, there is enough analogy between the two for it to be meaningful.

John Hick gives us the example of a dog that is 'faithful', a word we also apply to humans. There is a similarity between the two uses even though there is a difference in quality between the faithfulness of a dog and a human. He explains, 'There is a recognizable likeness in structure of attitudes or patterns of behaviour which causes us to use the same word for both animal and man.' It is the same character trait, but of a different quality. Similarly, Aquinas argues when a word, like 'good', is used for both God and man, it is not being used *univocally* (with exactly the same meaning) in both cases; nor is it being used *equivocally* (with completely different, unrelated meanings); but *analogically* in that, though there are differences, there is enough similarity for the term to be used in the two different contexts.

But still, in what ways are the properties of man and God analogous? Although we can argue that despite the fact there is an enormous difference between the goodness of God and that of man, the analogy works and we do get closer to understanding it by using these terms, we still need to know just *how* this works. One way is to say that the relation is simply proportional: that God's goodness is just so much greater than man's. This, however, is not without its problems. If it's just a matter of degree, God no longer appears so different from humans. And the closer we get the less room there

is to argue for the otherness of God. But if we go the other way and argue that God's goodness is quite different from that of humans, God becomes incomprehensible and we cannot have a concept of him that will allow the analogy to work.

The alternative might be to argue that God's properties are real, while human properties are derived. God is the source from which properties like goodness and wisdom flow. So we can only know of them as they are reflected in humanity, whose goodness or wisdom is analogous, but not identical to God's. It suggests the same distinction between an abstract noun and its application in the corresponding adjective: we might talk about 'beauty' in the abstract, but in contingent terms we can only talk about a 'beautiful woman' or a 'beautiful painting'.

Nevertheless, the flow of derivation is bound to go the other way: from man to man's conception of God, rather than from God to man. We are bound to derive from what we observe in man the properties we believe God possesses. The only other way to sustain the argument from analogy is to argue that God's and man's properties are quite different; then we could compare the two to see the analogy. But for this to work we would have to be able to observe both independently and, of course, we cannot do this. So, all we can do to speak meaningfully about God, whose properties are unknown, is to strike up an analogy between God and man, whose properties we do know. But then we are left with no independent concept of God, and if God is not conceivable independently, we have no idea of what would constitute proof of his existence. Even in the afterlife, how are we to know what or who is God if we don't have an independent concept of him?

This brings us to our second question: if language functions in a different way when we apply it to religious matters, as Copleston suggests, how are we to confirm its claims; how are we to distinguish between false and true statements about God? The ancient Greek philosopher Aristotle, who, along with Plato, has probably exerted most influence in the Western philosophical tradition, believed that all such non-literal uses of language amounted to little more than poetic ornament, which could easily be translated into ordinary language.

However, our limited understanding of reality frequently forces us into reaching beyond the limits of ordinary language, however inadequate our attempts to describe it might be. While we might argue that when poets use language in a non-literal way, they do so just to appeal to our feelings, isn't it also possible they expand our awareness, revealing new levels of reality by bringing things to our attention in a new and significant way? In contrast, scientific description is more limited and partial. Scientists are wary of hypotheses that cannot be tested independently in experiments and yield results that can be measured accurately. And they are more likely to be interested in those hypotheses derived from established useful theories, which not only have a record of successful predictions, but a capacity to explain a range and quantity of different phenomena.

But if we are to accept that such non-literal use of language offers us a unique access to a more inclusive understanding of reality, it must still show how it has a bearing on what we already know; it must be able to show how it makes a difference to the world. As Thomas Nagel points out, when we use words like 'mind', 'cause', 'exist', or 'nothing', we know the familiar conditions in which they operate: 'The minds we can talk about are revealed in what people with bodies do in space and time.' But when they are used in theological speculation 'they are being used in a way that tears them loose from these familiar conditions without supplying anything to take their place.'

So, if we are to do more than gesture to the nature of God through analogical use of language, we must show how it makes a difference to the world. For example, in 1950 James Stewart made the film *Harvey*, from the Pulitzer Prize winning story by Mary Chase. Stewart plays Elwood P. Dowd, whose constant companion is an invisible six-foot rabbit, named Harvey. The giant rabbit is, of course, a fiction, but if Elwood P. Dowd were to convince us that he was in fact real, he would have to show what difference he made to the world. He would have to show his effects on things around him. Otherwise, we could not perceive him and he could not exist. Indeed, this is what we mean by saying something exists: that we can perceive it.

The same must be demanded of those who argue for the nature of God. Yet, like Harvey, he too is not perceivable by the senses. Even so, there are many unobservable entities in science, whose existence we are still willing to accept: electrons, magnetism, quarks. Scientists believe they are justified in inferring their existence, because of certain observable phenomena. So can't we claim that the nature of God, likewise, can be inferred by his effects? Clearly, if God is unperceivable whatever evidence we could have would have to be indirect, like the evidence we have for electrons or magnetism. However, although we can't see magnetism, we know its effects on materials, like iron, cobalt, nickel and alloys of these. We can predict its behaviour. So what would constitute evidence for the effects of God? Without an answer to this no clear meaning can be given to the hypothesis.

And, of course, without this we are always free to reinterpret our hypothesis to fit the facts. If a disaster occurs, a famine in Africa or an earthquake that costs thousands of lives, this conflicts with our concept of God as benevolent and merciful. Yet in such circumstances, where there is no clear meaning to our hypothesis, we are then free to argue that God's plan is greater than we can understand; that he works in mysterious ways beyond human comprehension. In this way we save our hypothesis.

But, then, don't scientists, too, save their theories in a similar way by inventing auxiliary hypotheses to account for unexpected effects? The difference, of course, as we saw in the last chapter, is that such hypotheses, to be accepted, must provide independent test implications: they must predict new phenomena, not just account for the unexpected effects. They must put themselves to the test and allow themselves to be vulnerable to falsification.

So, it seems, although we are clearer about the nature of religious language and how believers understand it and set about confirming its claims, we are still left with the problem of whether there is any way of justifying these claims. In particular, we must examine the belief in which all other beliefs are grounded: that God exists.

■ 3. Arguments for the existence of God

As we saw in Chapters 2 to 4, to justify any proposition we must show it to be true either necessarily or contingently. If it is necessarily true, it is true *a priori* from first principles. It is true by reference to itself, so its denial would involve a logical contradiction. To say 'John is a married bachelor', or 'This bicycle has one wheel', is self-contradictory and you don't need to leave your seat to know this. But with propositions that are contingently true you do; we come by the truth *a posteriori*. If I were to say 'The dog is at the door', you would have to get up and open the door to verify the contingent facts. A proposition is contingent if, and only if, its denial and its confirmation could both logically be true. So, we need to consider whether the proposition 'God exists', is true in either of these two senses.

3.1 The ontological argument: a necessary proof

The earliest attempt to establish a necessary proof for the existence of God was the ontological argument, in which the eleventh-century priest and philosopher Anselm argued:

1. God is the most perfect being conceivable.

2. Existence must be a property of the most perfect being conceivable, otherwise it would not be perfect.

3. Therefore, God must exist.

Brief lives
Anselm, Saint

Dates: 1033–1109
Born: Aosta, Italy
Best known for: Being the author of the ontological argument for God's existence and the first systematic thinker of the Middle Ages. He became the Archbishop of Canterbury in 1093 and, like Thomas à Becket, became embroiled in disputes with the king over the independence of the church.

Major works: *Monologion* (1076), *Proslogion* (1077–8).

As you can see the argument rests on the idea that existence belongs analytically to the concept of God, in the same way that the idea of having three angles belongs analytically to the concept of a triangle. In each case the predicate is necessarily linked with the subject. Descartes, too, held the same opinion, arguing in *Meditations* that:

> existence can no more be separated from the essence of God than can its having three angles equal to two right angles be separated from the essence of a (rectilinear) triangle, or the idea of a mountain from the idea of a valley.

But Kant points out, *if* there is a triangle it must have three angles, otherwise it would be self-contradictory. And, likewise, *if* there is an infinitely perfect being, he must have existence. Both are necessarily and analytically true. Yet it doesn't commit us to self-contradiction if we reject the existence of God or a triangle altogether.

The idea of existence does not add anything to the concept of a particular thing or kind of thing, but merely *applies* the concept to the real world. To say that X exists is not to say that in addition to its various attributes it has the attribute of existing, but merely to say that there is an X in the real contingent world. Bertrand Russell makes much the same point when he shows that, although 'exists' is grammatically a predicate, logically it performs a different function. To show, for instance, that cows exist is not to show that they possess a certain quality, namely existence, but to show that there are objects in the real world to which the description 'cow' applies.

Take, for example, the argument:

1. Unicorns are horses with one horn.

2. Anything which is a horse with one horn exists.

3. Therefore, unicorns exist.

The conclusion is a trivially true statement of what is already entailed in the premises. But there is no attempt to apply the concept 'unicorn' to the real world. However, in contrast, the statement 'Unicorns do not exist' is equivalent to saying 'there are no Xs such that "X is a unicorn" is true.' It applies the concept 'unicorn' to the real world, concluding that there are no instances of it existing. So, while existence appears grammatically in the role of a predicate, it has quite a different logical function of asserting that a description applies to something in the real world.

It follows, then, that if existence is not a predicate, it cannot be a defining predicate of God, and the question whether anything in reality corresponds to the concept of the most perfect being conceivable remains an open question. A definition of God describes one's concept of him, but cannot prove the actual existence of any such being. By stating 'if and only if X is a bachelor, then X is an unmarried man', this does not establish the existence of such things as bachelors. If existence is not a logical predicate, either the ontological argument is an attempt to claim existence by definition, or it makes the trivially true claim that the concept of God would not be a candidate for anything if it did not exist.

3.2 Contingent arguments

It follows, then, that any proof of existence must be a contingent proof: it must possess causal properties in the real world. If we want to prove that something is real, we must be able to show how it makes a difference to real events. It cannot remain just an abstract concept. To prove God is more than this we must demonstrate how he functions within a temporal and spatial world.

3.2.1 The cosmological arguments

This means we must ask what aspects of our existence lend weight to the claim for the existence of God. Unlike the ontological argument, which focuses attention upon the *idea* of God and proceeds to unfold its inner implications, the cosmological arguments start from some general feature of the world and argue that there could not be a world with this particular characteristic, unless there was also an ultimate reality which we call God.

The 'first cause' or 'first mover' argument, first developed by Thomas Aquinas, the thirteenth-century philosopher and theologian, maintains that everything that happens has a cause, and this in turn has a cause, and so on in a series which must either be an infinite regress, or have its starting point in the first cause. Having rejected the possibility of an infinite regress of causes, Aquinas concludes there must be a first cause, and this is God. He explains in *Summa Theologica* (1266),

> whatever is moved must be moved by another. If that by which it is moved be itself moved, then this also must needs be moved by another, and that by another again. But this cannot go on to infinity, because then there would be no first mover, and, consequently, no other mover, seeing that subsequent movers move only inasmuch as they are moved by the first mover. ... Therefore it is necessary to arrive at a first mover, moved by no other; and this everyone understands to be God.

You might already see the two related problems such an argument faces: first, the arbitrary

---

Brief lives
Aquinas, Saint Thomas

Dates: 1225–1274
Born: Roccasecca, near Aquino, Sicily
Best known for: Developing a philosophy that reconciled Aristotelian teaching with Christian doctrine and for his five ways of proving God's existence.

Major works: *Summa contra Gentiles* (1261–4), *Summa Theologica* (1265–73).

---

rejection of the possibility of an infinite regress and, second, the contradiction in the premises: if everything has a cause this must mean that God, too, has a cause. If God is to be the ultimate cause, we have to avoid the demand to explain how he came into existence. God, in other words, has to be something whose existence requires no explanation: he must be something that couldn't not be. In his book *Why There is Something rather than Nothing* (2004), Bede Rundle dismisses this as incoherent on the grounds that it tries to employ the idea of an agent producing something, while withholding the two crucial conditions an agent would need: time and physical causation. If God were a non-spatio-temporal being, which he would have to be if he is the ultimate cause, he couldn't do anything.

Think about this for a moment. Scientific theories like the Big Bang can explain what goes on in the universe by revealing systematic, interconnected laws and theories, but science cannot explain the existence of the universe in this way. Science can only explain within the given context of time, space, energy and matter: it cannot explain how these came to be. To do this we need something that is not part of the universe; that is outside space and time, which can explain why there is something rather than nothing. If science were to identify an ultimate cause it would have to be part of the universe, the very thing whose existence we are attempting to explain. So God as the ultimate cause cannot be a cause as we ordinarily understand it, or perhaps could ever understand it.

As for the rejection of the idea of an infinite regress of causes, contemporary Thomists have attempted to dispose of this by interpreting the endless series not as a regress back in time, but as an endless and, therefore, eternally inconclusive, regress of explanations. Behind the complex of interrelating explanations, it is claimed, there must be a reality which is self-explanatory, whose existence constitutes the ultimate explanation of the whole. The only other alternative, if this reality does not exist, is that the universe is merely unintelligible. And in this lies the recurring problem for the first cause argument: how do we know that the universe is *not* merely an unintelligible fact? As long as the argument fails to convince us to reject the whole notion of an infinite regress, in whatever form it takes (a regress of causes or explanations), this argument appears also to fail.

Beyond this it also suffers from a view of causality that many philosophers and scientists would find difficult to accept today. The argument assumes that to indicate the causal conditions of an event is to render that event intelligible. This is not a view easily maintained in the face of modern theories of the nature of causality. Much of contemporary science assumes that causal laws state statistical probabilities and, as Hume argued, many of the causal connections we seem to observe between events represent merely observed sequences: 'constant conjunctions'.

3.2.2 The argument from contingency

However, Aquinas also argued for the existence of God from the contingency of the world. Everything in the world is contingent: it will die and be replaced by other things. Nothing is the source of its own existence. Indeed, each thing that exists might never have existed at all, or might have existed differently. If everything points beyond itself to other things, he argues, there must have been a time when there was nothing. But if this had been the case nothing could have come to exist, for there would have been no causal agency. But since there are things in existence, there must be something which is not contingent, and this we call God.

The problem is, as Bede Rundle points out, this is difficult to imagine. We can imagine the world being different, we can even imagine the universe not existing at all, but still we are left with an empty space, a vacuum; we are left with something. So to interpret this in a way that makes sense we must be able to think about there being nothing at all and not just a different state of affairs. I can imagine you not existing, but I am still left with a state of affairs

in which there is no you. But I cannot imagine me not existing, because to do so I must still exist. This is the parallel to imagining nothingness. As you can see it is self-contradictory: it involves the supposition that there might have been the case that nothing was the case.

The problem arises because this argument chooses to reject the possibility that there might be an infinite series of finite contingent events overlapping in the time sequence, so that no moment occurs which is not occupied by any of them. Modern Thomists have attempted to meet this objection by ignoring the original assumption that there was a time when no contingent world existed. In this form the argument is based upon the logical connection between a contingent world and its non-contingent ground. By use of the analogy of the workings of a watch, which remains inexplicable until we refer to something outside of it, which winds up the spring, it is claimed that in order for there to be a world of contingent realities there must be a non-contingent ground for its existence. Only a self-existent reality, containing in itself the source of its own being, can constitute an ultimate ground for the existence of anything else and this is the necessary being we call God. The concept of necessary being, it's claimed, is not concerned with a logical necessity, but rather with a kind of factual necessity which, in the case of God, is virtually equivalent to aseity, or self-existence.

However, again this suffers from the same weakness as the first cause argument. Both arguments contain the same dilemma that either there is a necessary being, or the universe is ultimately unintelligible. And as long as both arguments fail to rule out the second alternative they hold little force. Indeed this inability to exclude the possibility of an unintelligible universe prevents cosmological arguments in any form from acting as proof of God's existence.

The same can be said of their failure to meet the requirements of a satisfactory contingent explanation. If the explanation is to be convincing it must provide independent test implications and a set of facts, beyond those already used to form the God hypothesis in the first place, on which we can test it and demonstrate its claims. Without this it suffers from fatal circularity: it can only work if it breaks out from the facts from which it is derived and explains events and facts independent of them.

We are, therefore, entitled to ask if there is any other evidence for God's existence other than the evidence used to form the God hypothesis in the first place. But in view of what we say about God as the creator of all things, we have only one alternative: to find independent evidence outside the universe, which is implausible, if not senseless, in view of the fact that we can only ever have evidence within the spatio-temporal limits of the universe. Without this the argument is just a circular restatement of the facts.

The weakness here is that in trying to explain everything the God hypothesis actually explains nothing. As we saw in the last chapter, my explanation that every time a mechanical appliance breaks down it is due to mischievous gremlins deserves to be dismissed, because it provides no independent evidence, no predictions, on which to test the hypothesis. Yet if I were to point to the electrical plug that had fallen out of the socket as the cause for the radio going off we would be happier, because we can test this hypothesis on other electrical appliances to see if it works. We can see how the radio and other appliances behave with the plug in the socket and out of the socket.

The God hypothesis suffers in the same way as the gremlin hypothesis: unlike the plug we cannot show what the world would be like without God; we cannot unplug gremlins or God to see what happens. We must be able to identify experiences and demonstrate that they would not have happened without the influence of God. But as God explains everything we must go beyond the universe to discover such independent evidence. If we search for it within the universe, we move from one contingent argument to another, all disconnected in their assertions, as we gradually construct a whole scheme of hypotheses unrelated to one central explanation.

3.3 The teleological argument: the argument from design

One of the most popular of these is the argument from design; and one of the most famous expositions of this is that of the eighteenth-century English theologian William Paley. He argued that the natural world is as complex a mechanism, and as manifestly designed, as a watch. The rotation of the planets in the solar system, and on the Earth the regular procession of seasons and the complex structure and mutual adaptation of the parts of a living organism, all suggest design. Such complex

and efficient mechanisms, he claims, could not have been created by chance.

He extends his argument by adding certain comments concerning the analogy between the watch and the watchmaker, and the world and God. First, he argues, it would not weaken our inference if we had never seen a watch before (as we have never seen a world other than our own), and therefore did not know from direct observation that watches are products of human intelligence. Second, it would not invalidate our inference from the watch to the watchmaker, if we found that the mechanism did not always work perfectly (as may appear to be the case with the mechanism of the world). We would, he claims, still be obliged to postulate the watchmaker. And third, our inference would not be undermined, if there were parts of the machine (as there are of nature) whose function we are not able to discover.

As you can imagine his views were widely held until challenged by Darwin a century later. Nevertheless, even without Darwin, the argument rested on three questionable assumptions, as Hume was to show. First, the analogy between the world and a human artifact, such as a watch, is weak. The universe is not particularly like a vast machine. One could just as plausibly liken it to a great inert animal, or to a vegetable. And, if this were the case, the argument would fail, for whether inert animals or vegetables are or are not consciously designed, is particularly the question at issue. Only if the world is shown to be rather strikingly analogous to a human artifact, is there any proper basis to infer an intelligent designer.

The second criticism arises from the fact that even if we could validly infer a divine designer of the world, we would still not be entitled to postulate the infinitely wise, good and powerful God of the Christian, Judaic and Islamic traditions. From a given effect we can only infer a cause sufficient to produce that effect; so, from a finite world we can never infer an infinite creator. Equally, we cannot infer that this God *still* exists or even that there is just *one* God, given the world is full of diversity.

What's more, from the evidence we are not justified in inferring a wholly good and benevolent God, for there is evil, pain and suffering as well as good in the world. If we claim God is omnipotent and benevolent, we should expect there to be no evil in the world at all. Indeed, on these grounds we could quite rationally infer a god that is evil, and deal with the problem in reverse: explain the presence of good in the world. Given all this, the design argument is hard pressed to make its claim that God is omnipotent, omniscient and benevolent.

However, the main thrust of Hume's criticism lies in his third objection. Any universe, he argues, is bound to have the appearance of being designed, for there could not be a universe at all in which the parts were not adapted to one another to a considerable degree. The persistence of any kind of life in a relatively fixed environment presupposes order and adaptation, and this can always be interpreted as a deliberate product of design. The question, however, of whether this order could have come about otherwise than by conscious planning, remains to be answered. In an unlimited time a finite number of particles in random motion go through every possible combination, and will eventually result in stable order, Hume claims. The combination that has produced this stable order may be the orderly cosmos in which we find ourselves.

Hypotheses of this kind created the context from which Darwin arrived at his theory of evolution through natural selection acting upon random mutations in finite conditions. The Darwinian theory presents a more concrete account of the internal coherence of animal bodies, and of their external adaptation to the environment. According to Darwin, animals are relatively efficient organisms in relation to their environment for the simple reason that the less well-adapted individuals have perished in the continual competition for survival, and so have not perpetuated their own kind. The struggle for survival, operating as a constant pressure towards more perfect adaptation, lies behind the evolution of life into increasingly complex forms.

These arguments alone might be sufficient for us to abandon the design argument. But there are underlying differences between Paley's divine creation argument and the evolutionary arguments of Hume and Darwin, which point to still more important issues. While the arguments of Hume and Darwin rest on the notion of infinite time, the argument from design assumes that at one specific moment the world was created; that there was a time prior to which there was no time. As we have seen, such an idea struggles for plausibility. In terms of temporal priority it is always possible to think of a given date, for which there is a previous date, in the same sense that it is not possible to think of a number for which there is no greater number.

If time were merely an inference from memory and this were the only way in which we could justify our conception of it, the argument for infinite time would fall upon the same rock which has wrecked theistic explanations: there would be no independent criterion by which to justify it. But we do, in fact, have an independent criterion in that we are able to see states of things change, and thus we have direct experience of change within time. In the same way that we derive and then test through experience other concepts, like colours and sounds, by registering change we have immediate experience of time on which to test our concept of it.

From this we learn that there are always temporal precedents. Of course, we could argue that it is possible to imagine a situation in which there is no change. But this still assumes a viewer, one who surveys the unchanging scene, and this in turn smuggles in time. The sequence of experience is dependent on the viewer, temporally ordered as he perceives each object in turn. Time, then, is registered in the order of his perceptions. This gives us a justification for time in terms of causal experiences: there can be no time without change, the nature of our own experiences being temporally successive.

Still, isn't it possible to argue there was once a mass without any change and, therefore, in line with this concept of time there must have been no time? The prime mover and designer then created the world and time began. Yet, by arguing that there was once a mass in which no change occurred, we are logically committed to claiming that it was possible to have change, and in turn this implies time.

Even if the design argument could free itself from these objections, it would still be vulnerable to the problems that have struck down the other contingent arguments. If we argue the order in the universe is the evidence for the claim that God exists, and that God exists is the explanation for the order and the beginning of the universe, we are trapped in a circular argument. Failing this the argument seems little more than a picturesque way of accounting for the design in the world.

3.4 The argument from miracles and revelations

For obvious reasons our demand for independent criteria appears greater when it comes to the argument that evidence for God's existence can be found in miracles and revelations. As we have established we cannot by logic alone demonstrate any matters of fact; they must be known through experience. That we live in a spatial and temporal world of objects is a fact that could never be known independently of sense perception. So, if God exists, he is not an *a priori* truth but a reality outside us, and if he is to be known to us, he must manifest himself in some way within our experience.

However, when we reason about matters of fact this allows us only degrees of assurance. We are compelled to proportion the strength of our beliefs to the strength of our evidence. In the light of this Hume maintains we must balance conflicting evidence and where one side outweighs the other we should deduct the smaller from the greater to know the exact force of the superior evidence, and proportion our assurance to reflect this.

3.4.1 Miracles

So, in the case of miracles, when we are presented with evidence that such an event has occurred, we must set against it the evidence for its impossibility. A miracle, by definition, is a violation of the laws of nature, the evidence for which, Hume argues, is as entire as any argument from experience could possibly be imagined. Indeed there *must* be a uniform experience against every miraculous event; otherwise the event would not merit being described as such. Such a proof that exists for the laws of nature cannot be destroyed, and a miracle rendered credible, except by an opposite proof which is superior.

However, for laws of nature there is the strongest evidential support because they are regularly and consistently observed. In contrast, miracles by their very nature are isolated events, rarely observed. So, for the evidence supporting a miracle to be stronger than the evidence supporting the law of nature with which it conflicts, the miracle would have to be a regularly observed occurrence, in which case it could no longer be described as a miracle. No testimony is sufficient to establish a miracle, Hume argues, unless the testimony is of such a kind that its falsehood would be more miraculous than the fact which it endeavours to establish. But even then a mutual destruction of arguments would occur, leaving the superior argument providing us with only diminished assurance suitable to the degree of force which remains after deducting the inferior argument.

Given how unlikely it is for a miracle to occur, Hume warns, when anyone makes the claim we must consider the conditions affecting our valuation. We must consider the possibility that the person is either deceived or is deceiving us, or whether the event could really have occurred. We must weigh the possibility of one event against the other and, according to the superiority, reject the greater miracle. Invariably it is more rational to conclude that the person is deceived or is attempting to deceive. However, if the falsehood of the testimony is more miraculous than the event, then, and only then, can it command belief or opinion.

And even then, having met all the safeguards and reached this point of conditional belief, we still have problems. If our explanation of such a miracle was that God willed it to occur, we must provide some independent criterion to show that it was God who did in fact cause it. Otherwise such an explanation can be merely construed as another picturesque description of the event, and thus provide no basis for a rational belief in the existence of God.

3.4.2 Revelations

A further difficulty arises, however, when we come to consider the claim for God's existence on the strength of revelations, in that a system of beliefs is inseparably connected with this experience. In the strongest sense, to know means to be able to prove, yet the Bible makes no attempt to prove the existence of God. On the contrary, God is assumed to be an integral part of the ordinary affairs of life. God is known as a dynamic will, interacting with the believer's own will; a sheer reality and utterly inescapable. God is seen as an experienced reality, rather than an inferred entity. Indeed, the Catholic Church defines a revelation as 'the communication of some truth by God to a rational creature through means which are beyond the ordinary course of nature.'

So, any argument claiming that God manifests himself within human experience and that this is, therefore, a basis for believing that God exists, is handicapped by its inability to provide readily observable, objective evidence. At the heart of any argument for the possibility of a religious experience lies the belief that the person must be prepared, a receptive believer. Faith and subjective receptivity provide a bridge for the evidential gap. The position is best summed up by F. R. Tennant, when he observes:

> Belief is more or less constrained by fact or
> Actuality that already is or will be, independently

of any striving of ours, and which convinces us. Faith, on the other hand, reaches beyond the Actual or the given to the ideally possible, which in the first instance it creates ... and then by practical activity may realize or bring into Actuality.

Although scientists commit similar leaps of faith, when on limited evidence they present a theory explaining their findings, this is only the beginning. The scientific community will independently test it and, if it passes, will provisionally accept it. Religious faith, on the other hand, can hope for no such objective verification. Its evidence consists of inwardly satisfying and spiritually fortifying effects, and its verification the moral strength it bestows on believers to overcome adversity and achieve good works. This is more pragmatic and subjective: it cannot claim to prove God's existence with objective certainty, relying on unimpeachable objective evidence. The fruitfulness of faith in the moral and religious life is one thing; the reality and existence of what it assumes to exist is quite another. This seems to reduce religious belief and faith to some unverifiable hope.

4. Conclusion

In each of these arguments we have seen that many of the statements made about God are philosophically unimportant because the believer will not allow anything to falsify them: in effect they are not genuine assertions because they do not forbid anything to occur by which they can be independently tested. But attempts to provide a rational basis for a belief in God are not the primary point of religion. After all, when we reach the point of being able to prove something it no longer has the power to move mountains. Neither you nor I would make great sacrifices, let alone become martyrs, to prove 2 + 2 = 4. Once we believe something and can prove it we no longer need faith.

So the fact that the believer will not allow anything decisively to count against his belief in God is not the most important point about religious belief. Indeed Wittgenstein, who in the *Tractatus* (1922) famously attacked all language, including religious language, which failed to convey genuine meaning, concedes that religious language does not set out to make factual claims at all, but rather expresses an *attitude* towards the world.

In the next chapter we will see the importance of faith in its power to engage the whole being and to generate commitment that goes beyond normal objective reasons. In particular we will see the difference between the believer and the non-believer in their attitude to the world and what they expect to be the ultimate answer to life. Religious significance is found superimposed upon the natural significance of events in the believers' lives, their essentially receptive and creative response to events giving them a constant sense of God in their lives.

■ Questions

1. Does language function in a different way when we talk about God? If so, how does this affect our capacity to establish whether statements about God are true or false?

2. To what extent is our concept of God dependent on endowing the deity with human qualities?

3. Do you agree that the order we see around us could have come about only as the result of intelligent planning?

4. Explain and critically evaluate the 'first cause' argument for the existence of God.

5. Has Hume shown that a belief in miracles is always irrational?

6. Are the sincere statements that some people make that they have experienced God in their lives sufficient evidence for God's existence?

7. Is Anselm right in believing that the proposition 'God exists' is logically necessary?

8. Critically evaluate the argument that as everything is caused there is a cause for everything and this cause is called 'God'.

9. If we had a fully attested miracle, would this prove the existence of God?

■ Recommended reading

Kenny, A. *The Five Ways* (London: Routledge and Kegan Paul, 1969), translation, analysis and criticism of Aquinas' five arguments.

Anselm, *Proslogium*, trans. M. J. Charlesworth (Oxford: Clarendon, 1965).

Descartes, R. Meditations. In *Discourse on Method and other Writings*, trans. F. E. Sutcliffe (Harmondsworth: Penguin, 1970), particularly the third ('Of God; That He Exists') and the fifth (the ontological argument).

Hume, David. *An Enquiry Concerning Human Understanding*, (ed. L. A. Selby-Bigge), (Oxford: Oxford University Press, 1902), Section X, Of Miracles.

Hick, J. *Philosophy of Religion* (Englewood Cliffs, NJ: Prentice-Hall, 1963).

Davies, B. *An Introduction to the Philosophy of Religion* (Oxford: Oxford University Press, 1993), Chapter 6 on religious language.

 The note structure to accompany this chapter can be downloaded from our website.

Reason and Faith

Contents

Key issues

▶ What is the relation between faith and religion?

▶ What is the relation between faith and reason? Does faith begin when reason leaves off? Should we abandon all religious belief if we cannot justify it through rational argument or evidence?

▶ Is Kierkegaard right, that faith should be placed above reason as the highest thing to which we can aspire?

▶ If we were to abandon religion, does this leave us open to moral anarchy? Without God is everything possible?

▶ If God is omnipotent and good, why is there evil in the world?

▶ Is Marx right that religion is just the 'opium of the people': an attempt to make life bearable by promising in the afterlife salvation from the sufferings of this world?

▶ Or is Nietzsche right that human fulfilment requires the rejection of traditional values, including the Christian religion, which condemn all those vital energies that drive us to achieve a strong, vigorous, fulfilling life?

▶ Does religion just promote weakness and self-denial, a slave morality that turns weakness into a virtue?

■ 1. What is faith? Faith, evidence and knowledge

The various arguments that have been put forward for the existence of God are all attempts to provide a rational basis for religious belief. They try to prove religious doctrine, either on the basis of deductive argument, like the ontological argument, or through empirical evidence, like the teleological argument, the argument from design. But at the end of the last chapter we raised the question, what if none of these arguments are adequate? What if we cannot rationally justify religious beliefs? What then should our attitude towards them be? Should we abandon them, or are there other alternatives?

Here we are entering into some central questions in the philosophy of religion. First and foremost, what is the relation between faith and religion, between faith and philosophy? It is possible of course to argue that the question of the reasonableness of faith is irrelevant to having faith; that faith is by definition believing without sufficient evidence. Faith is a position we take towards a claim that is not demonstrable by reason, a belief in truths that are revealed through scriptures or the teachings of a church, or through special experiences of some sort. But reason is also a source of authority on which our beliefs can rest, something that plays an important role in our culture, and if we are unwilling simply to turn our back on rational considerations, the question of the relationship between faith and reason inevitably arises.

On this issue there have been a wide number of responses, ranging from the view that religious beliefs are largely compatible with reason, to the belief that they are completely irrational, or perhaps beyond reason. An example of someone who believed in the former is the thirteenth-century philosopher and theologian Thomas Aquinas. He stands at the high point of the great medieval attempt to reconcile Christian religion with reason known as scholasticism. Aquinas thought that certain 'preambles of faith', for example the existence of God, and some things about God's nature, could be proved by unaided human reason; although he also thought that other religious doctrines such as the Trinity and Incarnation are beyond human reason. These doctrines, the 'articles of faith', could only be known to humans because God has revealed them to us. They are matters of pure faith.

The alternative view, that faith is incompatible with reason, has become increasingly prominent in the modern period and is one of the features that characterizes our modernity. During the Enlightenment, which, as we have seen already, laid special stress on rational accountability, especially reason as exemplified in science and scientific method, there were various attempts from early on to formulate a 'rational religion', the doctrine known as deism. This would be a religion in which God's existence is rationally established through the argument from design, but where God's role is to do no more than set the great mechanism of the universe in motion. All additional trappings (including additional revelation, miraculous interventions, worship and prayer) would be dispensed with as superstition. But with God effectively reduced to an 'absentee landlord', there was little left of traditional religion in deism. And more and more as the century progressed, religion came under critical attack as failing the test of rational accountability.

However this leads to our second important question: even if we cannot justify religious belief rationally, what should our attitude towards it be?

For some it means that religious beliefs have to be rejected, or at the very least judgement has to be suspended. Many of the later eighteenth-century Enlightenment intellectuals were militant atheists, for whom even the minimal God of deism had to be dispensed with. Denis Diderot, one of the eighteenth-century French philosophers of the Enlightenment known as the *philosophes*, famously remarked that a deist was someone who has not lived long enough to become an atheist.

The empiricist David Hume, who, as we saw in the last chapter, offered a devastating critique of the argument from design in his *Dialogues Concerning Natural Religion* (1779), argued that belief in God could not be justified either through deductive reasoning or on the basis of experience. As such, he argued, we can make no judgement, either for or against, about God's existence. We have in other words to be agnostic about such matters. In fact the term 'agnosticism' was invented by Thomas Huxley in the nineteenth century to describe Hume's position.

At the end of his *Dialogues*, Hume says ironically that 'to be a philosophical sceptic is, in a man of letters, the first and most essential step towards being a sound, believing Christian.' But others have taken precisely this view. They have held that religious beliefs should be accepted despite the fact that they are irrational, or even because of it. It is not just that there is no rational basis for religious belief; there *ought* not to be. Reason is simply not appropriate for religious belief, for we are dealing with matters that go beyond the limits of human reason and understanding. This is the position known as fideism. Amongst others, the nineteenth-century Danish thinker Søren Kierkegaard can be regarded as a fideist, because he emphasizes the complete absurdity, from a rational point of view, of belief in God or doctrines like the Incarnation. We will come to Kierkegaard's position in a moment, along with a twentieth-century successor, Paul Tillich. First, however, let's look at another response to the view that religion cannot be justified through rational argument or evidence.

■ 2. Is it rational to believe in God? Pascal's wager

Writing at the dawn of the modern age, the seventeenth-century philosopher, scientist and mathematician Blaise Pascal rejected the arguments of the medieval thinkers, of Aquinas and others, by claiming that reason can neither affirm nor deny God's existence. In his book *Pensées* (1670) he argues that we cannot demonstrate through deductive reasoning that God must exist, because there is nothing logically absurd in denying God's existence; and also that what we know of nature is entirely compatible with God not existing. So to that extent, we have to be agnostic about the existence of God.

At the same time, however, Pascal also argued that even if there is no rational basis for belief in God, even if reason cannot tell us whether or not God exists, it is still in our interests to believe in God. If we calculate the benefits and costs of believing versus non-believing, it makes good practical sense for us to believe. If you believe, you will gain everything, eternal life and happiness, if you are right; and if it happens that you are wrong and God does not exist, you will not have lost very much. On the other hand, if you do not believe and God does exist, you will lose everything and suffer eternal damnation. So overall it is a much better bet to believe. You stand to gain everything if you are right, and you will lose very little if you are wrong.

Pascal does not think that you can choose to believe in God because of this kind of cost–benefit analysis. We do not believe things about the world just because it is in our interests to do so, or because of the possible practical benefits of believing. We believe things because we think they are true. However Pascal thought that we could use various means to get ourselves into the proper state of belief. We could go to church, associate with believers who would pass on their beliefs to us, and so on. Thus, on Pascal's account, religious faith is a matter of willing ourselves to believe, not through a single instantaneous decision but by choosing to undergo a process of 'conditioning'. In this way we would end up believing in God, and the wager argument has shown that to be the best thing to do.

Still, there are aspects of this argument that can be called into question. For a start, it depends on a certain view of what God is like, particularly the idea that God rewards those who believe in him. But what if God exists but cruelly punishes those who believe in him? If we cannot be certain whether God exists, we cannot be sure what God is like either, and so we cannot be sure of the possible practical benefits of believing. Moreover, Pascal is telling us that whether or not God exists, whatever the truth of the belief that God exists, we ought to hold this belief because it is in our interests. But is

it psychologically possible to believe in something without any evidence to justify it, any basis for thinking it true? We might come to have this belief by allowing ourselves to be conditioned into believing it, but this is now starting to sound like a form of voluntary brainwashing.

These considerations aside, Pascal's position is a fideistic one to the extent that he thinks we cannot justify our beliefs rationally, that reason is incapable of dealing with the most basic of religious questions, and that in order to believe we have to turn away from reason, from the search for knowledge through rational evidence. This view that reason is inappropriate for religious belief, that faith requires us to go beyond reason, reappears in the nineteenth-century thinker Kierkegaard, to whom we now turn.

■ 3. The leap of faith: Kierkegaard and subjective truth

For Kierkegaard, faith and reason stand in complete opposition. From a rational point of view, he argues, religious belief appears absurd. It is impossible to find a convincing argument for God's existence, and Christianity's central doctrine of the Incarnation is, rationally speaking, unintelligible. The union of two such different things, an eternal, infinite God and a historical, finite man, in the figure of Christ, is an extreme paradox for rational understanding. But for Kierkegaard there is no embarrassment in this. He places faith above reason. Faith is the highest thing we can aspire to, and only by attaining faith can we reach fulfilment as human beings, or in Kierkegaard's terms, 'become subjective'. To appreciate Kierkegaard's notion of faith, we have to say a little about his notion of subjectivity.

Subjectivity, human existence, has a central role in Kierkegaard's picture. He wants to restore the personal, the particular and the subjective, in the face of what he calls 'objective' ways of thinking that downplay or deny individual human existence, and which are becoming increasingly prevalent in moral, intellectual and religious life. Objectivity is the tendency to lose oneself in the crowd and the tyranny of 'mass opinion'; to live one's life in unthinking conformity with moral rules; and to engage in abstract, impersonal thinking.

Søren Aabye Kierkegaard (1813–1855)

Danish philosopher and theologian, Søren Kierkegaard is widely regarded as the father of existentialism. In 1840, after years of wasting his talents in superficial socializing, he became engaged and seemed to have settled for the respectable life of family responsibilities. But a year later, soon after completing his doctoral dissertation at the University of Copenhagen, he turned his back on this, breaking off the engagement to devote himself to his work and become a recluse.

Over the next ten years there was a constant flow of books and pamphlets including twelve major philosophical essays. Kierkegaard's work involves a shift from the objective world of reason and culture to the moral and subjective sphere. He rejected modern Christianity and Hegel's objective science of human spirit for obscuring the nature and importance of Christian faith. Instead he emphasized subjective truth and the partial viewpoint from which all human judgement begins and from which alone the questions that prompt faith can arise. Everything starts from human judgement, from the will and free choice unconstrained by reason and cause.

When he died at the age of 42 he had become an isolated figure of public ridicule and anger, because of his attacks on the state church. His major works included *Either/Or: A Fragment of Life* (1843), *Fear and Trembling* (1843), *Philosophical Fragments* (1844), *Concluding Unscientific Postscript* (1846) and *The Sickness unto Death* (1849).

In religion, it is evident in the reduction of religion to a series of doctrines to be learnt by rote, and rituals which can be participated in without feeling, commitment or inward transformation. In all these cases we lose what for Kierkegaard is most essentially human, our subjectivity, which is our capacity to make personal decisions, to commit ourselves passionately and deliberately to a way of life. The proper role of philosophy for Kierkegaard is to criticize the illusion of objectivity, to help us 'become subjective'.

This analysis extends to the notion of truth. In his book *Concluding Unscientific Postscript* (1846), he argues that truth is subjectivity. This sounds odd because we are used to thinking of truth 'objectively': as opposed to subjectivity it is impersonal

and valid for all. We think of it as correspondence between our belief and an actual state of affairs, requiring detached, disinterested observation and enquiry. Our personal emotions and interests are usually thought of as getting in the way of truth, something we need to rise above if we are to reach it.

For Kierkegaard, this notion of truth might be appropriate for a scientific context, but not for dealing with human existence. Truth here is a matter of something living up to its essential nature. For example we speak of a true friend, someone who exhibits all the essential virtues of friendship. And since for Kierkegaard, the essence of a human being is subjectivity, the truth of the individual is the state of being in accordance with the notion of subjectivity. The true human being is the subjective human being; or in short, 'truth is subjectivity'. This is not a truth which is impersonal, valid for all, but one individuals must attain for themselves, in the process of 'becoming subjective'.

As far as becoming subjective is concerned, reason has its limits. We can consistently and rationally apply an existing framework of values, but Kierkegaard is interested in the point where we have to choose the values themselves. We become subjective when we commit ourselves to a set of values, a way of life; and since we are choosing our guiding values, there is no guidance or justification for these choices. They cannot be made rationally, but only through a pure act of commitment, an irrational, passionate 'leap of faith'.

Kierkegaard also speaks of the task of becoming subjective as a process of 'transformation to inwardness', or the 'self-activity of personal appropriation'. What he has in mind here is that in becoming subjective, passionately embracing a way of life, I make it my own or appropriate it. And since subjective human existence is also true human existence, Kierkegaard speaks of truth as a matter of appropriation. My life is a true one to the extent that I have a personal, passionate commitment to it. Hence, as Kierkegaard puts it, whereas the objective accent falls on the 'what', the subjective accent falls on the 'how'. When the question of truth is raised in an objective manner, we are concerned with the object to which we are related, with whether it is as we say it is. When it is raised subjectively, we are concerned with how we relate to something, the passion with which we embrace it.

This brings us to faith. Kierkegaard thinks that the highest way of life, the most subjective and authentic form of human existence, is Christianity.

In other words, to become truly subjective is to become a Christian. We attain full selfhood when we freely relate ourselves to God. Why is this? Because Christianity involves the most intense subjectivity, the purest choice, and faith is the highest passion. Objectively, for disinterested reason, Christianity leaves a lot to be desired. As noted earlier, Kierkegaard holds that there is no rational justification whatsoever for faith or religious belief. It is 'objectively' quite unjustifiable. But this also means that faith has nothing to do with objective thinking or justification. It requires instead a completely subjective, passionate commitment. It is the most subjective choice or commitment one can make. In *Concluding Unscientific Postscript*, Kierkegaard says that in embracing a religious way of life, embracing the notion of God, 'an objective uncertainty [is] held fast in an appropriation process of the most passionate inwardness'. And this for Kierkegaard is what faith amounts to.

So Kierkegaard turns the lack of rational justification for religious belief into a virtue; it opens the way for faith, the passionate commitment through which we reach fulfilment as human beings. Yet as commentators have pointed out, there are costs to this approach. When faith is set in complete opposition to reason and 'objective' truth, it is difficult to see how we can say anything about the object of faith itself. All we can do is commit ourselves passionately, without knowing what we are committing ourselves to. Kierkegaard suggests this when he says that what is important for subjectivity and faith is not the 'what' but the 'how'. Yet it is not clear that we can commit ourselves to a God without having some idea of what we are committing ourselves to; and if we allow that, the sharp distinction between faith and reason will have to be abandoned; and then some kind of rational justification of religious belief will be required.

■ 4. God as the ultimate concern: Paul Tillich

Nonetheless Kierkegaard's view of religion has proved influential. His aim is to restore the meaning of religious belief for human existence. Religion is not a body of abstract doctrines to which we give rational intellectual assent, but something that demands a personal interest and commitment from us. This is what faith amounts to: a fundamental attitude that we need to adopt, which takes us

> **Brief lives**
> **Tillich, Paul**
>
> Dates: 1886–1965
> Born: Starzeddel, Brandenburg, Germany
> Best known for: His theory that God is the symbol of our 'ultimate concern' and no longer the transcendent judge of the scriptures.
>
> Major works: *Systematic Theology* (1951-63), *The Dynamics of Faith* (1957).

beyond rational thinking. And this view of faith continued to influence twentieth-century theological thinking. A representative here is the theologian Paul Tillich.

Tillich formulates his position in a number of books including *Systematic Theology* (1951-63) and *Dynamics of Faith* (1957). Like Kierkegaard, he accepts that it is impossible to demonstrate the existence of God in rational terms, but for him this similarly leaves room for faith, in the form of an 'original decision' made by individuals through which we fulfil ourselves as human beings. So once again, religious faith does not depend on impersonal rational considerations; it is something that is personal and 'inward'. In Tillich's version, faith is 'the state of being ultimately concerned'. Our ultimate concern is the thing or activity which determines our being or non-being in the sense of the meaning and aim of our existence. This can be a number of things: our personal success, status, our family, our nation and so on. Whatever we are ultimately concerned with demands our total submission, and promises total fulfilment; and we have an intense desire for the success of whatever it is that claims our allegiance. Our commitment to this ultimate concern, our faith, is an act that involves our entire personality: a fundamental act of will that is not an act of reason, an unconscious act or an emotional act, but a combination of all three.

However, concerns for things like our nation, family or personal success are not properly speaking ultimate concerns, only preliminary ones. These concerns are limited, transitory and finite. And faith in something which is not truly ultimate will be unsatisfying in the end. It will lead to what Tillich calls 'existential disappointment'. But it is possible, he thinks, to transcend these limited concerns in favour of a concern with something unconditional and infinite, in which we will find genuine fulfilment. This is the right kind of faith, the true state of being ultimately concerned; and what we are ultimately concerned with here, the 'unconditioned', is Tillich's conception of God. God here is not an object like other objects, a particular, finite being, but rather 'Being-itself', being in general, which transcends and contains all particular things. In the very act of existing, as Tillich puts it, we participate in Being-itself; and Being-itself is what grounds or supports our individual being. Thus to have true faith, to be ultimately concerned about God, is to express our true relationship to being.

One source of criticism of Tillich is that his conception of God as Being-itself is far from any Christian conception of God. It is unclear whether we should regard his account as a legitimate reinterpretation of the Christian position, or a distortion of it. Another area of critical concern brings us back to the problem that arose above in connection with Kierkegaard. Where Kierkegaard seems to reduce faith to a subjective attitude and make the object of faith unclear, Tillich claims that his conception of faith takes us beyond the distinction between subject and object. God is not an object 'out there', something that we can know; but nor is ultimate concern simply a matter of adopting a subjective attitude. Ultimate concern expresses our participation in that which grounds our being. Critics, however, have suggested that far from overcoming the subject–object dichotomy, Tillich's notion of faith shifts uneasily between the two, either identifying human beings with God as the ground of their being, or reducing God to that with which human beings are ultimately concerned.

■ 5. Morality and the problem of evil

We move now from the relationship between religion and reason to the relationship between religion and morality. For some, morality is simply impossible without religion, and to abandon religious belief threatens to open the way to moral anarchy. This is the view expressed for example by the character Ivan Karamazov in the novel, *The Brothers Karamazov* (1879–80), by the nineteenth-century Russian novelist Dostoevsky, when Ivan proclaims that 'if God does not exist, everything is permissible'. However, to try to make morality dependent on religion raises issues of its own, to which we can now turn.

5.1 God's will as the ultimate ground for our moral behaviour: the Euthyphro problem

On the religious view of morality, God provides us with our moral rules. In the Christian tradition God has fashioned human beings and the world for a purpose which is revealed through the scriptures and the church. According to these sources, in order to guide us in the right way of living God has formulated certain rules or commandments that we ought to obey. We do not have to obey these rules, because we have been created as free agents, and so we can know what is right or good and yet choose not to abide by it. Nonetheless, these rules tell us how we ought to live.

So on this view, moral laws are God's commandments. This kind of account has been spelt out by some theologians as the so-called 'divine command' theory of morality. The morally right thing to do is that which has been commanded by God, and the morally wrong thing is that which God forbids. To be moral is to obey God, and those who disobey God will be held accountable on the day of final reckoning.

However the idea that moral rules are an expression of God's will is not without its difficulties. First of all, this view of morality depends on a belief in God, and if this belief is undermined, morality is called into question, the circumstance that worried Dostoevsky so. But even if we accept the religious position, there is still a serious practical problem: how can we be sure what God's will actually is? How can we know what God commands? We may turn to the scriptures of course, but the scriptures are not always consistent, and they are open to varying interpretations. We may look to signs of God's will in the form of miracles, dreams and the like, for guidance, but such things are also notoriously open to interpretation. How can we know that our interpretations of these signs are not just mistaken, or in fact ways of rationalizing our actions, justifying them to ourselves?

These are practical problems, but there are also deeper problems that arise with the very way this kind of account formulates the notions of 'right' and 'wrong'. The problem is referred to as the

'Euthyphro problem' because it was first noted by Plato in his dialogue *Euthyphro*, written four centuries before the birth of Christ. In this dialogue there is a discussion about whether 'right' can be defined as 'that which the gods command'. Socrates questions this view, and asks for clarification. He wants to know: is conduct right because the gods command it, or do the gods command it because it is right?

We can ask the same question about the divine command theory. Is conduct right because God commands it, or does God command it because it is right? Both alternatives cause problems. If something is right because God commands it, then right and wrong become completely arbitrary. They are whatever God decides them to be. If he were to command us to murder, this would make murder the right thing to do. And we cannot say that a good God would never command us to do what is wrong, once again because it is solely God's commands that determine what is right and wrong. Alternatively, if the divine command theory means that God commands something because it is right, because God has the wisdom to know what is right and what is wrong, then this seems to make a religious conception of morality unnecessary. God himself is not required to make an action right or wrong, but has to obey moral standards that are defined elsewhere, independently of God's will. Thus, what is distinctively theological about this account of morality seems to disappear.

5.2 The problem of evil: God's omnipotence and goodness, and the existence of evil

If there are difficulties with the God-based, divine command conception of morality, we can go further and ask whether moral considerations might not actually call God's existence into question. Atheists and agnostics usually base their case on the absence of rational justification or evidence for God's existence, but there is also an argument for positively disbelieving in God, and this involves the 'problem of evil'. The problem of evil is a problem of consistency. If God is omnipotent or all-powerful, and also benevolent or good, why is there evil in the world? How can a benevolent, all-powerful God allow cruelty, pain, disease and suffering to go on? It is hard to reconcile the two, and for some, the presence of such evil represents an argument

against the very existence of God. A good, all-powerful God would not allow evil things to happen, and since evil things do happen, God cannot exist. Or in the form of the joke the nineteenth-century German philosopher, Nietzsche, cites in *Ecce Homo* (1888), 'God's only excuse is that he does not exist.'

Naturally from a Christian point of view a less drastic response to the problem of evil would be preferable. One might try to deny the presence of evil in the world, but one of the basic beliefs of the Christian tradition is that evil exists, both moral evil in the sense of things that people are responsible for, such as cruelty and war, and natural evil, all the terrible things that arise from nature such as disease and earthquakes. On the other hand, one might try to modify the way God is understood. One might argue that God is not good, but is perhaps an evil deity who enjoys the suffering of humanity. But this would be to abandon a significant aspect of the Christian conception of God. Similarly, to deny that God is all-powerful is to go against a central element in Christian theology, in which God is seen as being able to do anything (or in some versions, everything except what is logically impossible, such as making 2 plus 2 equal 5). In both cases the proposed modifications mean that the notion of God would be significantly damaged and diminished.

It would seem that if we are to avoid the argument from evil, and hold onto the traditional Christian conception of God, we have to find a way of reconciling an omnipotent, all-good God with the presence of worldly evil. The area of theology that tries to do this is known as theodicy. A classic attempt to reconcile the two, which goes back to St Augustine, is the 'free will' solution. That is, since God created human beings with free will, it is people, not God, who choose to bring evil into the world.

Yet this response is not without its problems. First of all, if God is omnipotent, why couldn't he have created us in such a way that we always freely choose the good? Another objection to the free-will solution is that it leads to the paradox of omnipotence. That is, if God created us with a totally free will, then he cannot be omnipotent since there is something, human free will, that he cannot control. And if he does have control but refrains from using it when people commit evil acts, then in what sense is he benevolent? Finally, resorting to free will would at best allow us to deal with moral evil, the evil that comes through human actions. It would not help us come to terms with natural evil, for example the earthquake that causes untold death and suffering. How could a good and all-powerful God allow such things to happen?

A more recent suggestion for reconciling God and worldly evil has been to supplement the free-will defence with the argument that what seems evil is for the best in the long run, because it makes it possible for us to perfect ourselves, to become good people. On this view, human beings are not fully completed creations but need to undergo a process of moral development, and for that to happen, there has to be evil in the world. If the Earth were free of suffering, pain and death, and nothing we did had any bad consequences for ourselves or others, we would not have any reason to try to be good, courageous, honest, loving and kind, or to take responsibility for our actions. This world might be pleasant, but there would be no possibility of character development. It is because the world is not like this, because we have to deal with evil, that we are able to develop moral character. Yet the critic might still ask why a good and all-powerful God allows so much evil, and does not step in to reduce it. Dealing with evil may be character-building, but the amount of moral and natural evil in the world seems far in excess of what might be required.

Overall, whatever strategies we might employ to lessen the conflict between the idea of a good and all-powerful God and the existence of worldly evil, the sheer amount of evil in the world remains problematic. The question remains: even if some evil can be accounted for, or even turn out to be required, why is there so much of it? Couldn't a good, all-powerful God have created a better world than this one, a world with a greater predominance of good over evil? Contemplation of worldly evil continues to raise questions about the existence of the Christian God. Indeed, the seeming imperfections of the world we live in are a key objection that Hume, in the *Dialogues Concerning Natural Religion* (1779), brings to the argument from design. That is, even if we could infer that some deity must exist in order to create the world, nothing in the world entitles us to think that this deity is anything like the Christian God. The world, with its many imperfections and unpleasantnesses, does not provide any evidence that the directing force is perfect, all-powerful or even moral.

■ 6. Critics of religion

All of this brings us back to the relationship between faith and reason. If modernity has been characterized by the demand that religion be rationally accountable, and the increasingly prevalent view that faith is incompatible with reason, one strand of thinking has been, as we have seen, to argue that reason has to make room for faith. Kierkegaard and Tillich carry this strand of thought into the nineteenth and twentieth centuries, and hold that only by attaining faith can we reach fulfilment as human beings. However for Hume and the Enlightenment *philosophes*, it is faith that has to submit to a rational critique.

There are also attempts to give a non-religious explanation of religion, to account for religious experiences, beliefs, practices or institutions in a way that does not rely on basic religious assumptions. And religion is now criticized because in various ways it fails to lead to human happiness and fulfilment, and indeed stands in the way of them. In the nineteenth and twentieth centuries, three prominent figures who engaged in this kind of critique of religion were Karl Marx, Friedrich Nietzsche and Sigmund Freud.

6.1 Marx versus Kierkegaard: meaning and value

Like Kierkegaard, Marx is fundamentally concerned with the concrete, individual human being and the possibility of human fulfilment. In Marx's case, however, the individual is understood in terms of the fact that he has to work with others, so that human beings can satisfy their needs and survive in the face of nature. And work for Marx is more than simply a means of survival; through work, human beings develop their 'essential powers' and find self-realization and fulfilment. Marx provides an extensive analysis of society in terms of its economic relationships, the way we as a society produce what we need to survive, and the way society is organized to bring about that productive activity, in terms of our relations with nature and with each other. Yet his concern is never simply with analysing the economic realm, but with the role and situation of workers under existing economic conditions, the extent to which they live a fulfilling life.

Much of Marx's work focuses on analysing the

nineteenth-century industrial society of his own time, and the picture he presents is a highly critical one, because of the situation of the workers within it. While modern industrial society is immensely productive and prosperous, the workers who have made this possible still live in terrible poverty, often working long hours in inhuman conditions. They do not produce for themselves in order to satisfy human needs, but for their capitalist overseers, those who own and make use of their labour to produce goods for profit. Marx's critique of capitalist society is motivated by the ideal of a more human life. Only in a society where forms of economic exploitation and oppression are overcome, where individuals can work cooperatively, and where they are able to control the conditions under which they labour, will they be able to find fulfilment and to live fully human lives.

Marx's focus is firmly on the economic realm, the 'material conditions' of society, and all other phenomena – political, cultural and intellectual – are to be understood on this basis. Our ideas and views of our place in the world are themselves the product of our economic needs and practices, reflecting them and also often providing a rationalization of them, a way of making difficult conditions palatable and thus preventing progress in overcoming those conditions. This is the general approach he applies to thinking about religion, which he sees as having entirely earthly roots. It is a reflection of the material situation of people, but a distorted reflection, and one that stands in the way of progress. As Marx famously puts it, in *Economic and Philosophical Manuscripts* (1844),

> Religious suffering is at the same time an expression of real suffering and a protest against real suffering. Religion is the sigh of the oppressed creature, the heart of a heartless world, and the soul of soulless conditions. It is the opium of the people.

In other words, religion kills the pain and suffering caused by oppression and exploitation. It does not do anything to solve the real problems, which come from the economic circumstances we find ourselves in. It is simply an attempt to make life bearable, because it promises that there will be salvation from the bondage, misery and suffering of the world in an afterlife; and that people will be rewarded there for their hard work and virtue. It thus provides a substitute for the happiness people are denied in

this world. At the same time, religion serves to justify the existing social order and the individual's place in it. It encourages those at the bottom of the hierarchy to accept their situation, and discourages any attempt to change conditions for the better in this world. Instead of confronting those who exploit them, it turns people's attention to an afterlife in which all suffering will cease and they will find happiness.

For Marx, then, religion is a bad solution to the problems of life. It helps to keep people in a degraded and imperfect condition. It must be abolished if there is to be any real progress. As Marx goes on to say, 'The abolition of religion, as the illusory happiness of men, is the demand for their real happiness.' Society has to be changed and social oppression overcome in order to bring about real happiness in this world. In the ideal society, there will be no more need for religion. People will have freed themselves from the kind of life that makes them take refuge in its illusions. Or to put this slightly differently, the yearning for happiness expressed in the illusions of religion will then find real satisfaction in this world. Heaven will be realized on Earth.

6.2 Nietzsche: the revolt against traditional values

Friedrich Nietzsche, working towards the end of the nineteenth century, argues that human fulfilment requires the rejection of traditional values, including the Christian religion. For Nietzsche, traditional morality and the Christian religion in particular stand opposed to a strong, vigorous, fulfilling life. Religion condemns strength and preaches hatred of our desires and instincts, the vital energies that drive us. It promotes weakness and self-denial, and offers us an impossible hope of fulfilment or salvation in the next life. We can only progress if we cast these ways of thinking aside and create new, life-affirming values to live by. Nietzsche differs from Marx in that Marx sees human progress as something to be achieved communally by changing society, whereas for Nietzsche self-perfection is the work of the solitary human being, the 'great individual'.

At the same time, in *The Genealogy of Morals* (1887), Nietzsche gives an account of traditional morality and religion that relates them to social circumstances, and provides us with a framework in terms of which all of history can be read. From

Friedrich Nietzsche (1844–1900)

The son and grandson of Protestant ministers, Nietzsche studied philology first at Bonn and then at Leipzig. At the age 24, before he had completed a doctoral dissertation, he was appointed professor of classical philology at the University of Basel. He became a close friend of Richard Wagner, but eventually broke with him in 1876. In 1879 mental and physical problems forced him to give up his post at Basel and he spent the next ten years a solitary, restless wanderer, living a frugal life on his pension, while continuing to write prolifically. His major breakdown in 1889 marked the virtual end of his productive life and he remained insane until his death in 1900.

He believed the motive power of all life is not the will to live, but the desire to grow, appropriate and gain in power, in short, the 'will to power'. Thus human fulfilment requires the rejection of traditional values, including the Christian religion, which condemn all these vital energies that drive us to achieve strong, vigorous, fulfilling lives. Christianity just promotes weakness and self-denial, a slave morality that turns weakness into a virtue. Among his best known works are *Thus Spoke Zarathustra* (1883-5), *Beyond Good and Evil* (1886) and *The Genealogy of Morals* (1887).

the beginning, Nietzsche thinks, there have been hierarchies in society, or in Nietzsche's terminology, 'masters' and 'slaves'. And 'good' was initially formulated from the perspective of the ruling class, the masters, where it was identified with their own attributes, their strength and nobility; while the weakness, fear and submissiveness of the lower orders were viewed as 'bad'. This is 'master-morality'. But the slaves developed feelings of envy and resentment towards their masters and took their revenge on them by devising a 'slave morality'. For this new morality, it is weakness and powerlessness that are 'good', and the strength and power of the master are considered 'bad'; a reversal of the master morality. The triumph of the slaves has been to get the master to accept a morality in which the master becomes reprehensible in his own eyes.

Religion comes in at this point, because for Nietzsche this reversal of values is above all the work of religion. For Nietzsche the priests planned and brought about the triumph of slave morality. They were the weakest and most impotent of all, and the most full of resentment. Religion was the instrument

of revenge, the means by which the values of slave morality could be imposed on the strong. The strength and vigour of the masters, expressed in strong, joyful, uninhibited action, became the object of religious condemnation, and what was celebrated instead were things like meekness, humility and submissiveness (to God). So for Nietzsche, the moral values bound up with religion are the values of slave morality; and he criticizes these values because they are life-denying, because they condemn the strong and turn weakness into a virtue.

Resentment is the first key idea to figure in Nietzsche's account of religion. The second is 'bad conscience'. Nietzsche traces the emergence of bad conscience also out of the confrontation between master and slave. The ruling group creates the state, the social order, the rules of society, through acts of violent imposition. Bad conscience is a reaction to the power of the masters by the ruled, the slaves. We have already talked of another reaction, resentment, the desire for revenge, through which slave morality develops. There, the slaves' feelings have an outward expression. In the case of bad conscience, the hostility and aggression of the slaves cannot find any external expression because the power of the masters is too great. It is thus internalized, turned inwards. We vent our hostility on ourselves, on our desires and instincts, which are regarded as base and evil. We suffer and feel guilty, and that is suffering from the bad conscience.

In Nietzsche's account, Christianity strengthens this instrument of self-punishment. It is not the origin of bad conscience, which lies in social power relations and reactions to them, but it intensifies humanity's self-hatred and self-torture to the point of madness. It contributes to this self-hatred because many claim that we stand to a God in the relationship of offspring to a father, and that whatever we have, we owe to God. That means that we are in God's debt, and this debt cannot be repaid without suffering. We must diminish and abase ourselves before God as far as possible. Religion then teaches the absolute goodness of God, and the baseness of human beings, who are nothing but unworthy sinners. In Nietzsche's account, religion is the instrument of self-torture, the means for the self-violation of the human self.

To progress we need to leave behind religion, which promotes weakness, self-denial and self-hatred. However it is important to note that Nietzsche's ideal is not a return to the unrestrained strength and mastery of the masters. Bad conscience, strengthened by religion, may be destructive and negative, but the phenomenon can take a different turn. We can overcome the bad conscience and relate to ourselves differently, in a life-enhancing way. For Nietzsche the greatest strength or power lies in 'sublimating' one's instincts and desires, disciplining and directing them without considering them evil or fighting them. Instead, we can take them up, organize, integrate and enhance them. So bad conscience is a stage we have to go through in order to get to a higher stage, the kind of positive self-control and self-perfection that for Nietzsche characterizes the 'overman'.

6.3 Freud: illusions and wish-fulfilment

Nietzsche's critique of Christianity anticipates Sigmund Freud's theory of religion. For Freud, the founder of psychoanalysis, religion is the product of constraints society places on the expression of our instinctual desires. It reinforces those constraints, as well as giving indirect voice to the desires that are denied. Like Nietzsche, he argues that we need to outgrow religion in order to progress. But Freud's account also resembles Marx's in that he thinks progress towards greater human happiness and fulfilment is possible through changing the social circumstances in which we find ourselves.

In *The Future of an Illusion* (1927), Freud locates religion in relation to the conflict between instinctual need and the requirements of society. Society works on nature to extract wealth and satisfy human needs. Because instinctual needs and desires exceed realistic possibilities for satisfaction, society imposes constraints on their satisfaction. They have to be restrained or in cases of extreme conflict repressed, pushed down into the unconscious portion of the mind. Each of us is required to undergo this process of 'instinctual renunciation' from very early on. The reality confronting the child and enforcing this denial is made up of the social institutions, rules and constraints that adjust people's relations with one another and distribute available wealth. These rules and demands are represented by the parents and internalized by the child in the form of the superego or conscience, the mechanism of self-control. There is much in common here with Marx's account, as both Marx and Freud start from the material relations of people with nature and with one another in their analyses of society.

Freud goes on to argue that forbidden, repressed desires and needs nonetheless find indirect expression in forms of substitute gratification. Freud speaks of the 'mental assets of civilisation', of 'illusions', which are the collective fantasies that compensate for the instinctual renunciation imposed by society. Ideologies such as nationalism provide a feeling of superiority over others; and artistic productions allow for the indirect expression of forbidden and repressed wishes.

But for Freud it is religion, in its various manifestations, that is the main cultural institution for compensating the renunciation of desire. Religion indeed plays a double role; it justifies social rules that demand instinctual renunciation, and it offers compensation for that renunciation. On the one hand, there are certain basic commands that are found in most religions, such as that one should not kill, or should love one's neighbour. On the other hand, religion offers compensation to people by teaching that there is a higher part, the soul, that will not die; and that whatever the deprivation and suffering individuals endure now, they will pass on to a higher state where there will be ultimate satisfaction and fulfilment.

For Freud, it is possible to examine religious beliefs rationally, for their truth or falsity. He rejects the idea that religion is above reason, which is to say, the fideistic view that religious beliefs should be believed because they are absurd or irrational. If that is so, he argues, we would not know which absurd beliefs to accept. Religious beliefs are not based on experience or reason because they are collective fantasies, informed by powerful human wishes and desires.

Nonetheless, the role of rational critique is not simply to dismiss religion, as merely a delusion which bears no relation to reality. Religion is an illusion, a belief motivated by the desire to see wishes fulfilled. The reality that religion reflects is that of human needs and wishes that have been denied. Freud does not think that we can ever do away with all social and moral restraints. But he does argue that at least some of the frustration and unhappiness that this causes can be alleviated. What is required is that we outgrow religion by developing more rational ways of constraining instincts, and where possible, by relaxing those social constraints so more needs and desires can find satisfaction within society.

■ 7. Conclusion

Over the last two chapters we have examined whether there are rational grounds for religious beliefs. In the process we have seen a number of writers argue that there are not, but that this is of no concern, because religious belief meets deeper needs; needs that can only be met by religious *faith*. This answers questions too deep and wide for rational scientific empirical methods; questions concerning the meaning of life and what we as individuals must do to be genuinely fulfilled in our lives. Whether these answers are grounded in illusions or not, as Marx, Nietzsche and Freud at least in part suggest, it does focus our attention on the ways in which we come to understand ourselves, rather than the external world, and this is the subject we will go on to examine in Part II.

■ Questions

1. What is religious faith? Is it just a form of knowledge or belief, or is it something quite different from these?

2. 'Faith in God is necessary only because knowledge of God is impossible.' Discuss.

3. Pascal called his belief in God a bet, saying 'If I lost I would have lost little, if I had won I would have gained eternal life.' Is faith merely a gamble?

4. 'Why does man need religious faith?' Discuss this question in the light of the arguments of one of the following:

   Nietzsche

   Marx

   Freud

5. Explain Kierkegaard's existentialist answer to religious faith and certainty. Do you think his response to those who demanded objective proof of God's existence was successful?

6. Given the fact that there are natural evils, like earthquakes, hurricanes and crop failures, does this not prove beyond doubt that there is no creator who is omniscient, omnipotent and perfectly good?

7. Is it true that if God does not exist, everything is permitted?

■ Recommended reading

Hume, D. *Dialogues Concerning Natural Religion*, (ed. J. M. Bell). (Harmondsworth: Penguin, 1990).

Freud, Sigmund, *The Future of an Illusion* (1927), trans. W. D. Robson-Scott (New York: Doubleday, Anchor, 1953).

Kierkegaard, S. *Concluding Unscientific Postscript* (1846), trans. D. F. Swenson (Princeton, NJ: Princeton University Press, 1941).

Plato, Euthyphro. In *The Last Days of Socrates*, trans. Hugh Tredennick and Harold Tarrant (Harmondsworth: Penguin, 1993).

Marx, K. and F. Engels. *The German Ideology* (London: Lawrence and Wishart, 1982).

Nietzsche, F. *On the Genealogy of Morals* (1887), trans. Francis Golffing (New York: Doubleday, 1956).

Tillich, P. *The Dynamics of Faith* (New York: Harper and Brothers, 1958).

Geach, P. T. *Providence and Evil* (New York: Cambridge University Press, 1977).

 The note structure to accompany this chapter can be downloaded from our website.

Understanding the Individual

In Part I we saw that the scientific revolution of the seventeenth century and the Enlightenment that followed brought with them a decline not only in religious authority, but in the contempt for worldly things, and with it a growing determination to make the world a better place for individuals regardless of their status. Those things that made life difficult for the individual could no longer be dismissed as just the will of God. Societies were the product of man's free and creative will. But to make the world a better place for individuals it was necessary for philosophers and scientists not only to have a clear grasp of what we mean by knowledge and truth and the methods we employ to uncover them, but to have a clear understanding of the individual himself without the intercession of religious and biblical authority.

This raised important metaphysical questions about the individual. The Bible saw man as made in God's image at the centre of the universe. Stripped of this, what was left? Was humanity any more significant than any other animal that walked the Earth? After all Copernicus and Galileo had already shown that man was not at the centre of the universe; just another living creature on a rather insignificant planet circling the sun. The one thing that seemed to distinguish him from other creatures was that he wasn't just matter, but he had a mind.

But what is the mind and how is it different from the body and other matter? In particular, in what way is it different from the brain? The brain is necessary for thinking, but it is not thinking itself: it is not the thing that *does* the thinking. Like the brain we say of a computer that it 'worked it out' or it 'solved the problem', even that it 'knew the answer', but we don't say that it has a mind. A mind implies something more than that part of the body that allows us to think: a mind is aware that it thinks; it is conscious. So it seems the problem of who we are and our self-identity begins with our awareness of our own consciousness. As Thomas Nagel points out, 'the fact that an organism has conscious experience *at all* means ... that there is something it is like to *be* that organism.'

Even so, there are still more problems lying in wait. Nagel wrote these words in an essay entitled 'What is it like to be a bat?' He suggests not only are bats and other animals conscious, but fish and even ants and beetles. This is not a view supported by those like Descartes. As we saw in Chapter 8, in the history of philosophy there have generally been two types of reply to the question 'what are the ultimate constituents of the world?' The monistic view is that it is composed of a single entity or 'substance': either it is composed of nothing but ideas and mental entities (idealism), or everything is ultimately explained in terms of matter (materialism), in which case the mind and mental states are nothing but physical states in the brain.

Descartes' answer was that there is more than one type of ultimate constituent or substance (pluralism). There is in fact a 'dualism', two kinds of constituents: mind or mental substance and matter or material substance; there is the physical organism and the 'soul', something purely mental. Descartes' explanation of mind as a separate substance marks the beginning of the long development in modern philosophy and science of what's come to be known as the 'bifurcation of nature'. Cartesian dualism allowed men to interpret the external world in mechanical and quantitative terms and put all other aspects of existence in the realm of the mind.

Most of the natural world came to be regarded as

just complex material systems. Descartes and the materialist Thomas Hobbes considered living things as just complex machines, arrangements of matter that operate in predictable ways in accordance with the laws of nature. So Descartes believed animals were not conscious. They might look as if they are thirsty or hungry or in pain, but their behaviour is explained by internal mechanisms. Only humans, he believed, have conscious experiences, which occur in a distinctly non-material type of thing – a mind or soul.

However, if there are two substances, mind and matter, the problem Descartes leaves us with is the relationship between them. Our normal everyday experiences suggest they constantly interact with one another. It would not be unusual to explain that 'Tom threw paint over his girlfriend's car when he discovered she had been cheating on him', or that 'Pat came down off the ladder because she felt dizzy.' But how can two things that are so different interact; how can an idea that his girlfriend had been cheating produce movement in Tom's arms so that he throws the paint, or the feeling of dizziness bring about movement in Pat's arms and legs so that she comes down off the ladder? In the next two chapters we will consider this and the problem of consciousness.

But beyond the relationship between body and mind lies the problem of self-identity. Easily stated, it's a problem that most of us confront each day of our lives. Each of us establishes our own identity through our own first-person experiences, to which only we have access, yet this is different from the way others know us. But we also acquire our identity by using as our reference point what we believe others think of us. We orientate ourselves as a person in the other person's scheme of things, which results in what R. D. Laing describes as 'ontological insecurity'. But what is the self? And what are its key features without which you could not claim to be you?

Is it consciousness? Descartes believes that all mental states are conscious by definition. The self and the mind are, therefore, one. The mind is essentially the self revealed to itself in an act of introspection. In contrast, animals have no self-identity. While they have mental states, in that they can feel, desire, even think, they are not conscious of these mental states as *their* mental states; in other words, they are not *self*-conscious.

But is the self ever the object of consciousness, or is it what is described as 'pure subject', or as

Edmund Husserl describes it 'transcendental ego': something beyond which our self-reflection cannot go? This means that it exists as observer, never observed. But if we can never observe it how can we be sure it can have no unconscious states, thereby robbing us of our confidence that we know ourselves, that we have self-identity? The nineteenth-century German philosopher Johann Fichte believes there can be no knowledge at all unless the self knows itself as object.

Then, once we have identified what is the self, how are we to account for continuous self-identity over time, during which the individual may have undergone extensive change – physical, mental and emotional – and be anything but the same individual? Are we to account for this by assuming that our identity is grounded in some unchanging essence? Criticism of this notion has seen the rise of existentialism in the nineteenth and twentieth centuries. Fuelled by novelists and philosophers across Europe, its followers believe that our self-identity is the product of our own commitments and experience alone; to use Sartre's famous phrase, 'existence precedes essence'.

As this suggests, if we cannot account for it in terms of some unchanging essence, a range of things can be ushered in as explanations. Does our self-identity originate in a belief in God, or in the social roles defined by the community, or in some definition of our abstract humanity? In the following chapters we will examine and compare those movements in ideas that set out to challenge the notion that our self-identity is grounded in some unchanging essence, theories like existentialism, Marxism, Freudian psychoanalytical theory, and structuralism and post-structuralism.

As you will see, at the heart of much of this discussion is the question whether self-identity is just a function, the product, of something greater than itself, say, social and cultural factors that determine what we are irrespective of our own choices, or whether we are genuinely free to choose our own identity. In the final chapters of Part II, then, we will examine the degree to which we can say we are genuinely free to make these decisions, and the equivalent extent to which we can be held responsible for who we are and what we do.

If we could not have done otherwise, because our decisions and actions were the result of factors beyond our control, we can hardly be held responsible. But we have already seen in Kant's 'forms of understanding' that we cannot understand any event except in the context of a complex network of causes. And if we cannot conceive an event for which there is not a cause, in the same way that we cannot conceive a time before which there was no time, how can we fairly claim that someone is responsible for her actions and decisions? If everything is caused, then so too are we and everything we do. This is not to say they are *predetermined*, just *determined* by forces beyond our control.

Yet we still do talk about people's moral, legal and political responsibilities: that we are responsible if our actions cause harm to others; that we are morally to blame if we break a promise or tell a lie; that we are legally responsible if we break the law. So what does it mean to say we are responsible, and how fair can punishment be if all our actions are the result of antecedent causes?

At the end of Part II we may not be convinced by one point of view or another, but in the process we will be clearer about the differences and the relationship between mind and body, the importance of consciousness, and those things that go towards giving us a sense of our own identity. In turn we will be better placed to answer the question whether we can genuinely regard ourselves as free and therefore responsible for our actions and choices.

You may find it helpful to have copies of the note structures for the following chapters by your side as you read them. These can be downloaded from our website at
www.palgrave.com/foundations/greetham.

The Mind and Mental Events

Contents

Key issues

▶ Is your mind something different from your brain, or is it the brain itself?

▶ If you feel happy or depressed are these just physical states – electrical impulses surging around your body and processed in your brain?

▶ Is there a difference between the sensation of a taste and the physical process that led up to it?

▶ Is the difference between a computer and your mind simply that the latter is conscious? And how is this affected by the fact that much of our mental activity is not conscious, but pre-conscious or unconscious?

▶ Have I any reason to believe that anyone else experiences pain; that like me they too are conscious?

▶ Or is there another way of describing ourselves without talking about bodies and minds; without arguing that we are one thing or the other?

The problem of who we are begins with the realization that we seem to be both mind and body, part of the mental and physical worlds – and this despite the fact that the two seem to be quite different. Scientific knowledge suggests the physical world is inanimate and purposeless, with things occurring in accordance with certain fixed laws of nature. The mental world, in contrast, is quite different, involving consciousness, planning, willing, desiring and feeling. Physical events are publicly observable, while mental events are experienced by just one person. Physical events occur somewhere in a spatial location, whereas mental events are non-spatial, so we cannot say where they occur. It's like asking 'Where is the concept "triangle" when you think of it?', or 'Where is the number 2?' Yet, though different, the physical and mental worlds appear to be connected, they interact with one another. We might say 'He damaged the car because he was jealous', or 'She came down off the ladder because she was dizzy.'

The obvious point at which to start in our search for an answer to the problem is to ask if your mind is something different from your brain, or is it the brain itself? When we are happy or sad, high spirited or depressed, nervous or calm, bold or afraid, are these mental states just physical states? And the same goes for our mental processes and activities: when we make decisions, or hope, or desire, or dream, are these different from the physical processes going on in the brain, or are they just complex physical processes themselves?

For example, you sip fresh orange juice and almost immediately you experience the strong taste of oranges – but what is this experience? Can we explain it as just a series of connected physical events? The orange juice sets off chemical reactions in your taste buds and these send electrical impulses along your nerves to your brain. Here another physical change takes place and finally you *taste* orange. But what is this *taste*? Is it just a physical event in your brain or something quite different? As many have pointed out, if we were to open up your brain as you sipped we would see no physical change.

It seems the taste is locked away within your mind and is not physical. In recent times advertisers have attempted to improve the effectiveness of their campaigns by monitoring the reactions in various regions of the brain to the stimulus of their advertising images. Known as 'neuro-advertising', although their techniques are as sophisticated as modern science will allow, all they know is that something is happening in specific regions of the brain, but they have no idea what that experience actually is.

It appears that at the end of this complex physical process something happens which is not physical: it's a sensation, in our case a taste sensation, but the same applies to sight, smell, hearing and touch. Indeed it also applies to those mental events not directly associated with sensations, like emotions, the perception of images or the recall of memories. Our physical explanation can go so far and no farther, and at that point we seem to experience an awareness, a state of consciousness. Thomas Nagel describes it as 'a kind of insideness that is different from the way that your brain is inside your head.'

Even so, the history of science is full of stories of quite normal events and processes having a kind of insideness quite different from what appears on the outside. From Watson and Crick's discovery of DNA to the changes at the subatomic level of protons, nuclei and quarks, they all have an insideness we cannot observe and from which we can only infer what goes on. In 1847 Ignaz Semmelweis suggested that microscopic particles entering the bloodstream were responsible for the deaths in pregnant women in the General Hospital in Vienna. Such a suggestion seemed ludicrous to his colleagues, who scoffed at it as not much short of witchcraft. But today we accept it as common sense. So who's to say that the mental processes we have described as culminating in a state of consciousness, an awareness, are little more than electrical impulses surging around our bodies and processed in the brain? Sooner or later we will discover the biological nature of these mental states and

processes as Newton discovered the nature of light in *Optiks* (1704) and Semmelweis took the first strides towards a developed understanding of bacteriology.

So we need to ask the question, is there a difference between the sensation of taste and the physical process that led up to it? Either they are the same event or they are two different events occurring simultaneously: one analysable, the other not; one occurring in the brain, the other in the mind. Perhaps the most striking consideration in this is that even though we can analyse exhaustively the physical processes that led up to the sensation, we are still left at the end with an unexplained mental event. Despite all our explanations of the physical processes going on they do not add up to this mental event, which is, in fact, quite different in itself from the physical event. There appear, therefore, to be two different events: one physical, which we can observe, and the other mental, which we can only experience for ourselves from the inside as conscious beings. And, as Nagel points out, 'This isn't true only of human beings: dogs and cats and horses and birds seem to be conscious, and fish and ants and beetles probably are too. Who knows where it stops?'

■ 1. The problem of consciousness

Still, we need to know what we mean when we say that something is conscious; what we mean by consciousness. A computer might be able to do all the things that a mind can do – beat you at chess, evaluate the symptoms of a medical condition, solve a problem, even translate from one language to another – but it has no awareness of itself doing this. It has no idea of what it is like to be a computer. It is not aware of itself solving problems and beating you at chess. Nagel argues that, 'an organism has conscious mental states if and only if there is something that it is like to *be* that organism – something it is like *for* that organism.'

This means that this is a necessary and sufficient condition for consciousness. That there is something that it is like to be a bat, a beetle or a bird means that each is conscious. And this is distinct from all the physical or psychological factors we can determine as necessary for something to have a conscious experience of what it is like to be that thing. To have these things is necessary but not sufficient for consciousness. For example, the brain is a necessary condition for thinking, but it is not thinking itself, or the thing that thinks. It is the equipment, the means. When I say I think, believe, hope or imagine I am not saying that my body or any part of it (the brain) is doing any of these things, even though I cannot do them without a brain. I mean that *I* am doing these things, or in some circumstances when I want to identify part of me I might say my mind is doing these things. I might say 'I haven't made up my mind' or 'I was going through it in my mind imagining what would have happened if the car had crashed.'

But what is consciousness and what is the difference between it and the mind? One thing that's becoming clearer from what we've said about experiencing what it is like to be a bat, a beetle or a bird, is that consciousness involves both a mental act and an object of consciousness, which we perceive in our own unique way. The object of consciousness is sometimes described as the 'intentional object': it is what your experience portrays and the way it portrays it. Our experience distorts the real world and the distorted appearance is the object of consciousness. Compare this with a camcorder recording two people walking down a road. We find it difficult, if not impossible, to imagine being the computer passively processing these images, because we have no experience of being a non-conscious computer. The way the computer processes these images is quite different from the way we do.

As this suggests, the difference between the way the computer processes information and the way we as conscious beings process it is that our processing is influenced by the complex background of factors of which we are conscious. As conscious beings we have pleasures, pains, desires, wants and aversions, and some of what we do is motivated by these factors. We have purposes and intentions which influence the way we perceive things. A material thing, like a computer, has no pleasures and pains, no desires and aversions, and experiences no frustration if its aims and purposes are thwarted. While we have values and standards by which we judge situations and actions, material things don't. They don't do things because they value or want to do them: their processing is an automatic function. For example, if you injure yourself, no doubt a computer and other diagnostic equipment can non-consciously report with a greater degree of accuracy than you can the extent of the damage, yet the doctor is still likely to ask you to describe the type of pain you feel: whether it is dull, sharp, deep and so on.

Nevertheless, while these different mental acts may *represent* different ways of being conscious, this is not to say we are always conscious of them. Usually there is more than one going on at the same time. At any one time we might be remembering, imagining, worrying, hearing, smelling and seeing. You might be reading a book, while you smell the fragrance of orange blossom through the window and feel an ache in your calf from your morning run. This distinction leads some to argue that, while animals like cats and dogs have mental states, they are not conscious. They desire and think things – they may want their dinner, think there is an intruder in the house and smell the scent of someone – but they have no awareness of the distinction between themselves and others. They never attribute these mental states to themselves as their subject.

Those who support this view argue that consciousness is a particular type of awareness: it is being aware of the relation between the perceiving individual and the object of consciousness. However, this may be arguing for more than is necessary. When we are aware that it is we who are conscious, we are more than just conscious, we are self-conscious. If the necessary and sufficient condition for consciousness is, as Nagel argues, that there is something that it is like to *be* that particular organism, there may be no reason to insist that, in addition, that organism should be self-aware. What's more, it seems we can't satisfactorily explain the experience of being self-conscious without some notion of the self: that personal identity that persists through various experiences and which make those experiences 'mine'. In Chapters 16 and 17 we will explore in more detail the wider implications of this.

For most people this may not be a problem. Although they find it implausible to argue, as Descartes did, that animals are just living machines, whose every action is mindlessly controlled by laws of nature, they still find it hard to prove that animals have minds, because they are wedded to the Cartesian view that the mind is essentially the self, revealed to oneself through an act of introspection. Descartes believed that humans are distinct from other animals because they possess reason, which is necessary for having a mind at all, leaving animals as just complex machines. Evidence of this rationality is easy to find in our abilities to evaluate evidence and arguments, solve problems, argue consistently, and understand language. But today complex machines like computers can solve problems, evaluate medical symptoms, prove theorems in mathematics, even beat you at chess and translate languages. Indeed they can perform any task that can be defined precisely. Yet such evidence of a capacity to reason is not enough for us to argue that they are conscious and have minds, let alone self-identity.

But, as we will see, this is not the only challenge to those holding the Cartesian view that the mind is set apart and distinct from the physical world: one conscious, the other unconscious. We may believe this and yet at the same time have no problem believing that the mind plays a real and active part in the physical world. Otherwise we could not attribute mental states to animals as we do, or explain a person's behaviour by referring to her mental state. If mental states are set apart from the physical world they cannot be the cause of behaviour, and if they cannot cause the behaviour they cannot explain it. Yet, as we have seen, we still do explain that 'She blushed because she was embarrassed', or 'He shouted at her, because he was angry.' Perhaps the most serious challenge to Cartesians, then, is how they are to reconcile their theory of the mind as a non-physical entity, revealed through introspection alone, with the view that the mind acts on, and is acted upon by, the physical world.

1.1 Incorrigibility

Of course, the main reason that the Cartesian account sets the mind apart from the physical world and sees it as the cornerstone of all certainty is that mental states can be known immediately and unproblematically: they are incorrigible, they are beyond correction. Every present mental state is immune from doubt; indeed it is self-confirming. You might be hallucinating or dreaming, and you might doubt what this is about, but nothing can lead you to doubt that you have had this experience. I cannot doubt that I am thinking or that I am in pain or having certain sense experiences. There is something about present mental states that puts them beyond doubt.

In contrast the things ideas represent in the physical world cannot be known in this direct way. You can doubt that you are speaking or walking, but you cannot doubt that you doubt. It suggests there is an 'ontological divide' between mental and physical states: mental states seem more truly a part of me – I have privileged access to them which guarantees the claim to knowledge – whereas physical states are prone to error. This leads Descartes to claim that I am essentially a thinking thing and only accidentally, contingently, a body.

But how far does this incorrigibility go? Descartes uses the certainty of the *cogito* as the cornerstone of what can be known and expands beyond that to include all things in the mind. But one of the unsolved mysteries of philosophy is how we can validate such things. Take pain statements. You might argue that even though modern technology might be baffled by your claim that you are in pain, nevertheless, if you *feel* pain, you *know* that you are in pain and this gives you 'epistemological authority' over any other source.

Yet, unlike the *cogito*, pain statements are not self-confirming. In the *cogito* it is self-confirming: if I say, I think, therefore I am. I can doubt this, but in doubting it I confirm it: I confirm that I think and therefore I exist. But in the same way, to doubt that I have a pain is not to have a pain, nor is it to give proof that I have one. It is not self-confirming like *cogito* statements. Yet some philosophers argue that sensations and similar mental states are 'incorrigibly known' and 'self-intimating': if they are present, I know that they are. And to most of us this seems true. Sincere pain statements appear to be immune from error. If I think I am in pain, then I am in pain; what's more, I know I am in pain.

So what we need to know is whether the truth of a sincere pain report can be overridden by other evidence. For example a doctor might point to an encephalograph (an X-ray photograph of the brain) and tell you that you cannot possibly be in pain. After all we often get other sensations wrong. We might enter a room and remark how hot it is, only to find that other people in the room are not hot at all. Indeed, a thermometer might show that it is in fact below normal room temperature. At this point, of course, you might argue that in fact what we're actually saying is that we *feel* hot, and we cannot be wrong about this, even though it might not actually be hot in the room. And, on the same grounds, we can argue that we cannot possibly be wrong about feeling pain. Indeed in such circumstances we are likely to argue that the encephalograph has simply got it wrong.

But say you misuse the word to describe your

pain, so that you misdescribe your experience. Richard Rorty presents a situation in which, say, children were taught the word 'pain' through an 'encephalograph-cum-teaching machine', which whispered 'pain' in their ear whenever the appropriate brain state occurred. In such circumstances we would have grounds for saying that someone has got it wrong, if he or she had failed to learn what 'pain' means and had misdescribed the situation. In this case, like the feeling of being hot and the thermometer, our inability to be mistaken about our feeling pain would remain, but our final epistemological authority on the subject would be gone, because there would be a standard procedure for overriding our descriptions.

If we accept this, we are left with the hardest case to settle, in which a person is neither lying nor misrepresenting the experience. Can they still be mistaken? Either you argue that if their description of the experience is not coherent with the physical evidence, then they must be wrong, or you argue that if the physical evidence is not coherent with the first-person reports, then it is the physical evidence that we must reject.

1.2 Freud and the unconscious

You have to keep in mind that incorrigibility is important to Cartesians. It not only serves as a definition of the mind as opposed to the physical, but also as a defence against materialism. To challenge it in any way, to limit its scope or to identify mental events which are unconscious, strikes at the cornerstone of the Cartesian account. And this is precisely the challenge posed by Freud's theory of the unconscious. In his psychoanalytic theory Freud argues that not everything in the mind is knowable and can be described incorrigibly. There are ideas (intentions, dispositions, experiences) that we know little about, let alone know for certain. Indeed there are things going on in the mind that we can be wrong about. You might be convinced you love playing football, but really hate it. Unknown to you it's just that it reminds you of all the happy times you spent with your father, whom you miss terribly.

However, this seems, not just to a Cartesian but to our normal manner of speaking, to be wrong by definition, which no doubt shows how much our thinking has been shaped by Descartes. We might well argue that if something cannot be known incorrigibly, then it cannot be known at all. Before

Freud it was widely agreed that the notion of unconscious mental experience was a contradiction in terms – a definitional mistake. Descartes describes all mental states as involving ideas (objects of consciousness) and conscious thoughts. He also conceives the self and the mind as one; therefore all mental states are conscious by definition. The only way of allowing the unconscious in is to describe it as non-mental or pre-mental, something like a physical condition that will in time become conscious and bring about a mental state.

The only significant exception to this prevailing Cartesian view was the argument advanced by Leibniz, who believed that much of our mental activity escapes consciousness, because it is just too rapid and small to be observed. As we mentioned earlier you may be reading a book, while you smell the fragrance of orange blossom through the window and feel an ache in your calf from your morning run, though you might only be conscious of the first of these. These are what Leibniz describes as *'petit perceptions'* that are so slight, so familiar, or just occur in a crowd of other perceptions that you are simply not aware of them at the time. You may be reading in your study unaware of the persistent drone of someone's lawnmower. Leibniz gives the example of someone who is unaware of the roar of a waterfall or the rumbling of a mill, if they have lived close by for some time. In contrast to Leibniz's time, since the publication of Aldous Huxley's famous book *Brave New World* (1932), we are all much more familiar with such 'subliminal' perceptions: those beneath the threshold of awareness which influence our behaviour unconsciously.

But Leibniz's unconscious states are limited to perceptions. Freud and his supporters, who talk about the unconscious, mean something quite different. Not only does it involve beliefs, desires, emotions and judgements, but they argue for something more deeply hidden; not just out of reach of consciousness, but not conscious at all. As one writer argued, this is not like an infection, an unconscious process acting on the body, running through the bloodstream unnoticed, of which we can never be aware consciously. They mean that there are mental objects and activity in the form of thoughts, beliefs, desires and feelings, which are before the mind, but about which we are not conscious. They believe these unconscious processes affect a person's behaviour without that person being able to report it. Dreams, even slips of the tongue, are concealed examples of unconscious content too threatening for the individual to confront directly.

Freud had discovered what seemed to be a type of mental phenomenon of which the individual was simply unaware. So, it was plausible to extend the concept of mind and mental acts beyond the Cartesian limits to include such unconscious phenomena, particularly when it was clear that we could become aware of its content through hypnosis or psychotherapy. Rather than the single concept of consciousness, Freud identified different levels. Activities in the immediate field of awareness, like reading a book or playing the piano, he described as conscious. Preconscious activity involves all that data we retain, which we may not be thinking about consciously, but which we can recall when we need it.

Other data that cannot be recalled immediately, but which you may be able to remember later are retained on an unconscious level. You may be unconscious of the fact that as a child whenever you were naughty you were locked in a cellar, which may account for the panic you feel each time you enter a damp, dark room. Under hypnosis, however, you may be able to recall the experience in all its vivid detail. Indeed, the origin of many neurotic symptoms is thought to depend on removing such conflicts from consciousness through a process of 'repression'.

1.3 Beliefs, abilities and qualities of mind

In the light of this it seems doubtful whether consciousness is a necessary condition of the mental. The subliminal *petit perceptions* of Leibniz and the vast store of unconscious phenomena revealed in Freud's different levels of consciousness suggest there is more to the mind and mental events than Cartesians acknowledge.

Indeed, in addition to the subliminal and the unconscious there is a wealth of familiar mental phenomena that do not consist of states of consciousness. You may be asleep or preoccupied in some other way, but you still retain your beliefs, your goals and intentions, and your desires, all of which continue to influence your behaviour and reactions to situations. You may admire someone deeply, but you don't stop admiring them the moment you stop thinking about them. Indeed, we

have all sorts of dispositions that affect our behaviour without us being conscious of them. We may be bitter or envious of someone, and while everyone else can see what's happening, we may have no idea what's controlling our behaviour.

Similarly, we have a sense of our own abilities, which for the most part is unconscious: we may know that we can speak different languages, that we're artistic and imaginative, or that we can do arithmetic or solve problems. And even though we're not conscious of them they influence the way we interpret and cope with our experiences. Knowing this we are not alarmed by one ability replacing another as we interpret experience. You may be watching a film and an episode triggers off in your mind a quite different scene, which replaces in your mind's eye what you are watching on screen. Aware of your ability to do this, it comes as no shock when one scene replaces the other.

Gilbert Ryle in *The Concept of Mind* (1949) makes a similar point, that a person might use her mind without the occurrence of a subjective experience or an inner state of consciousness. We describe people as exercising certain 'qualities of mind' – they may act thoughtfully, be witty, be sympathetic or cold-hearted, drive alertly or absentmindedly – but none of them are accompanied by inner states of consciousness. Indeed nothing is going on except a performance of a certain kind. He concludes, therefore, that subjective experience is not a necessary condition for being mental. To argue that it is a necessary condition is to make a 'category mistake': that is to 'represent the facts of mental life as if they belonged to one logical type of category ... when they actually belong to another.' The truth is, he argues, that 'to talk of a person's mind ... is to talk of the person's abilities, liabilities and inclinations to do and undergo certain sorts of things.'

Nevertheless, this is not to say that we are justified in concluding that subjective experience and states of consciousness are in no way involved in anything that is mental, nor even that those things we have discussed – the subliminal *petit perceptions*, the unconscious, the senses of our abilities, the qualities of mind, and all our beliefs, intentions, desires and dispositions – are not conscious at some point or can be made conscious. Leibniz's *petit perceptions* may have been conscious before we got used to them, and become conscious again when we are alone and our concentration is focused on an activity requiring silence. The same can be said of Freud's unconscious phenomena: we can be made conscious of the influence of being locked away in the dark, damp cellar. And the same is true of our beliefs and our abilities to be creative, logical, or good at languages: at one point we have no doubt consciously considered their importance in our lives and will probably do so again. Indeed it might be odd to argue that something which has *no* connection with states of consciousness could be mental.

■ 2. Privileged access: the privacy of mental events

Even so, the existence of states of consciousness in *others* is itself only an inference; one based on the slender evidence of our consciousness alone. We simply cannot have direct evidence of other peoples' states of consciousness. Gilbert Ryle argues,

> The mind is its own place and in his inner life each of us lives the life of a ghostly Robinson Crusoe. People can see, hear and jolt one another's bodies, but they are irremediably blind and deaf to the workings of one another's minds.

And, what's more, having a conscious experience is not in itself knowing about it: knowledge requires something more. Descartes argued that we know our conscious experiences only when we clearly and distinctly understand them. This involves understanding two things: the mental act itself and what the thoughts are about – the objects of thought, the ideas in the mind that represent things. That we alone experience these mental processes and ideas makes them available in a special way. As philosophers describe it, we have 'privileged access' to them; they are private. We can mentally observe the various features of our experience and when we are clear about them, we can claim to 'know' about the experience.

Knowing in this special way is an important mark of distinction between mind and body. Physical experiences can be publicly observed and validated, but mental events are private. You are not only the first, but the only one to know about your own mental events directly. You might have thoughts you want to keep to yourself or have done things only you know about. Nobody else need know, unlike things you might have said or done in public. A child might want a day off school. If he is wise he will choose his excuse care-

fully. If he were to fake a cold or a fever a doctor could check the symptoms and verify whether he is really faking it. But if he were to claim to have a stomach ache or a migraine, things are beyond verification. The mind is private with only privileged access; the body is not.

This in turn has an obvious bearing on the problem of self-identity, which we will examine in Chapters 16 and 17. If each of us establishes our own identity through our own first-person experiences, to which only we have access, this will necessarily conflict with the way others know us. We are social beings – we must interact with others to meet our needs. In doing so we find ourselves establishing our identity using as our reference point what we believe others think of us: we tend to orientate ourselves as a person in the other person's scheme of things.

It is a daily reality for us all, therefore, that we confront a schizoid situation, a dichotomy of two selves, which results in what R. D. Laing describes as 'ontological insecurity'. One self, that which we derive from our own inner consciousness, we are inclined to describe as our 'real', 'true' or 'inner' self. Divorced from all activity that is discoverable by others, it is quite different from our 'public' or 'false' self which we wear like a mask. Indeed, Laing suggests that such a persona will in fact consist of an amalgam of various part-selves; none fully developed into a complete personality and each a deliberately chosen impersonation.

However, the implications and significance of conscious experience elicits two contrasting reactions among philosophers. The materialists, whose ideas we will examine in more detail later in this chapter, deny there are conscious experiences. All that we are, they argue, and indeed all that we should be concerned about, are the inner causes of our complex behaviour. These are to be found in the physical and chemical characteristics of the human brain and nervous system. They are not some private experience to which only one person has direct access – they are physical, publicly verifiable phenomena.

In contrast, other philosophers accept the existence of conscious experiences, but believe we have no access to those of other people, which can only be known by the person who has them. I can only have knowledge of your conscious experience through inference. Say you twist your ankle; I can reliably infer from your behaviour as you wince, cry out and hold your ankle that you are in pain.

But when I twist my ankle I know my experience directly, by 'immediate acquaintance'. I can know about the inner causes of other people's behaviour: I can know that the ligaments in your ankle are twisted and perhaps torn. But I can't know whether these causes are conscious or how they are experienced. I can't distinguish between the inner, non-conscious causes – say those that take place within a sophisticated robot – and the inner, conscious causes. I can only infer from the evidence and from what you tell me that you have a pain.

What's more, I cannot check directly the validity of this inference. In most other cases when we make inferences from evidence we can check publicly that our inference is correct. If I were to look out of my study window and see people walking past in raincoats or carrying umbrellas, I would reasonably infer that it was raining. And I could verify this inference by going outside to check. But when I infer that you are in pain I cannot verify it by experiencing it independently of observing the symptoms as I can with the rain. It is logically and empirically impossible for me to feel your pain. It is logically impossible, because for me to verify the pain necessarily means that *I* must feel it, and for me to feel it, it must be *my* pain. I cannot feel a pain that is not mine. Knowing *that* you are having a feeling is quite different from me feeling it myself.

This points to the more general problem that I cannot know you experience pain and have certain emotions and feelings, except through what you tell me and the symptoms I observe. And, who knows, the rest of the world may be populated just by non-conscious robots. If this is the case and they are maliciously programmed to be deceitful and to mimic my own symptoms of pain, I have no reason to believe anyone but myself experiences pain. In *Star Trek: The Next Generation* 'Data' is a sophisticated android, who exhibits all the symptoms of having feelings without being able to have them. For example, he has friends, but is incapable of experiencing the feeling of friendship; instead, meeting a 'friend' is just recognizing a familiar sensory pattern. If you were like Data, a sophisticated android cleverly programmed to respond in all the human ways that suggest feelings and emotions, I would never know any different.

There are different and interesting ways of responding to this problem. First, some have suggested that one way around it is to say that when I talk about *my* pain I am really talking about pain, but when I am talking about *your* pain in fact I

am referring to your behavioural patterns that we associate with being in pain. But the problem with such a suggestion is that when we say someone is in pain we usually mean much more than this. When I say you are in pain I don't mean that you are behaving *as if* you were in pain: I mean you *are* in pain. It's not just that you are limping and each time you put weight on your ankle you wince and cry out, I mean that you have pain as I also have pain when I experience similar things. What I attribute to myself when I have pain I am attributing to you.

Second, I could just concede that I simply cannot know you are in pain because I can't feel it myself, so I should just give up making such claims. However this seems to interpret the concept of knowledge too narrowly. It would exclude as knowledge many of the things we normally say we know through inference. I have never seen gravity itself, only its effects. But few of us feel that we are not justified in saying we know gravity to exist. Indeed, we can legitimately argue that we know many things by inference.

Of course, and third, the resolute sceptic could still argue that even though you can point to the whole array of scientific evidence – all the neurophysiological evidence that shows your nerve-endings are stimulated, and the physical and chemical evidence of changes in the brain – you still don't know that this correlates to the experience of pain in others. You might only know that there is such a correlation in your *own* case, when *you* are in pain. We cannot know another person is in pain. Indeed, as we have already seen, it is logically impossible to meet this standard, because to do so we would have to be someone else. So, effectively we have no answer to the resolute sceptic.

But as the first sceptical argument interpreted the concept of knowledge too narrowly, this one sets the standard of evidence too high. We accept much less and still call it knowledge. Physicists have never seen quarks. All their knowledge is inferential. Yet we still accept their conclusions as knowledge. In effect we would be saying that despite the fact you are limping and each time you put weight on your ankle you wince and cry out, and despite the uniformity of natural processes showing that when I have similar injuries I feel pain and others describe a similar experience, there is still not enough evidence to describe this as knowledge.

Of course, the resolute sceptic is right: this is still an argument based on analogy and on the evidence of just one case: my own. I only have the direct evidence of my own mind and my own experiences that when I twist my ankle I feel pain. I can argue that you have the same physiological nature as mine: you have bones, tissue and nerve endings just like me. But still this is an analogy based on just one case.

Perhaps one way of answering the sceptic is to say that, just like scientific enquiry in other areas, we amass evidence of uniformity of behaviour: we see people interact with one another; we see them ask and answer questions, make jokes, respond to injuries, get frustrated, even angry when they cannot find solutions to problems; and we see them show affection, express emotions like joy, happiness, surprise and relief. And the best explanation of all this is that they have consciousness like me.

Even so, this is still only a hypothesis; albeit a well-justified one. And like most scientific hypotheses, we may need auxiliary hypotheses: we may need to assume that those we observe are not faking their behaviour or lying about their experiences. But given this, whether or not such a hypothesis is well-founded will depend, as we saw in Chapters 10 and 11, not just on the quantity of evidence, but on the variety of circumstances in which we test the hypothesis. If it passes all of these tests without being falsified – if, despite the number and different types of circumstances in which we see people react to pain, they react as I do – we are entitled to have more confidence in the hypothesis that they too have consciousness like mine.

Even though this seems a compelling argument, keep two things in mind. First, we still have the problem that Rorty raised earlier. Language is public, not private. For it to be private its terms would have to be defined by reference to our own private sensations, the meaning of which, therefore, can only be known to us. But, as Wittgenstein points out in *Philosophical Investigations* (1953), such a language is not logically possible, because a language is designed to communicate with others, and this requires commonly accepted rules. In a private language, where whatever seems right can only be decided by referring to the exclusive personal states of the user, there can be no such rules.

But we do in fact learn the meaning of words describing our inner states, like 'pain', 'anger', 'sadness' and 'joy', by hearing others, like our parents, friends and relatives, use them. And to use them correctly in the first place we didn't need to have felt any of these things, but just to use the word consistently to describe the same type of behaviour. In *Star Trek: The Next Generation*, in his

struggle to become more human Data learns to recognize a joke, pain, laughter, and friendship without having any inner experience himself. We, too, learnt to use the words in the same way, by analysing the occasions in which they are used and registering the behaviour of others. Of course, this is not to say you have no inner episodes that correspond with these words, just that you have to learn to associate these with the words that describe them by observing the behaviour that accompanies them.

The second thing to keep in mind is an objection, which derives from existentialist philosophers, like the French writer and philosopher Jean-Paul Sartre and the German philosopher Martin Heidegger, to this whole line of discussion. Other people's experiences, they argue, are not this sort of hypothesis at all. The consciousness of other people is as evident as our own consciousness. It is central to our interactions with others and to our whole understanding of ourselves. In *Existentialism and Humanism* (1946) Sartre talks about 'intersubjectivity' and the realization that your freedom is a reality that constantly defines and confronts my own. We evaluate ourselves partly in terms of how other people feel about us. We have no sense of feeling ashamed, proud, jealous or envious in front of our furniture, our piles of books, our computer or other possessions, but we do in front of other conscious beings. So the belief in the consciousness of others is not just a hypothesis for which there is or is not sufficient evidence: it is important to our sense of self – it is definitive of us.

■ 3. Materialism and the reductive fallacy

In the last section we examined the first of two contrasting reactions to the problem of conscious

---

Brief lives
Heidegger, Martin

Dates: 1889–1976
Born: Baden, Germany
Best known for: Being one of the most important influences in the development of modern existentialism and phenomenology.

Major works: *Being and Time* (1927).

experience. The second chooses the monistic answer, denying there is a problem at all. The idealists argue that there is no problem because everything is mental, so there is no need to account for the difference between mental and physical events and therefore the relationship between them. But this flies in the face of common-sense beliefs and scientific findings. We know that physical events do affect our mental behaviour: recreational and therapeutic drugs can transform our mental lives and modern surgical techniques can alter personality.

In comparison, the materialist case seems more plausible. Materialists deny there are conscious experiences. There are only inner causes of our complex behaviour that can be found in the physical and chemical characteristics of the human brain and nervous system. They are not some private experience to which only one person has direct access – they are physical, publicly verifiable phenomena.

3.1 The reductive fallacy

In our post-Enlightenment world it's not difficult to understand the popularity of this explanation. We all entertain expectations of a better future as science extends its mastery over the world, reducing diversity to identity. Yet the explanation harbours a fairly common fallacy that tempts us all. When two things always occur together, we are often tempted to reduce one to the other; to argue that one is nothing but the other. This is the reductive fallacy – the nothing-but fallacy. In a memorable passage from Aldous Huxley's essay 'Science, Liberty and Peace' he explains this 'nothing-but philosophy' arguing,

> Human beings, it is more or less tacitly assumed, are nothing but bodies, animals, even machines; the only really real elements of reality are matter and energy in their measurable aspects; values are nothing but illusions ... mental happenings are nothing but epiphenomena...; spirituality is nothing but wish fulfilment and misdirected sex.

Nevertheless there is no denying that our mental life is dependent on brain activity and if certain parts of the brain are damaged or removed then consciousness is simply not possible. But there is more to brain states, like the experience of pain, than certain physical events, like the stimulation of nerve endings. Conscious states may be dependent on the brain, but this is only to describe the conditions necessary for them to occur; it doesn't define them. The problem with definitions is that words only stand for the meaning their users choose to give them, and those committing the reductive fallacy assume that the word stands for one thing and one thing only. In effect they use a word to deny the existence of something in the world.

For example, we might explain that colours are just different wavelengths of light and nothing more. But this suggests it is senseless for painters and poets, indeed anyone who has stood breathless in the presence of a beautiful sunset, to try to describe the beauty of it. It is as if the only way to talk meaningfully about such things is to use the specialized knowledge and concepts of physics; all the rest is nothing but illusion. But we knew about such things long before Newton's *Optiks* (1704). No one denies that light waves and colours exist and there is a relation between them, but no amount of redefining can put either out of existence. And in this lies the fallacy of reduction, in that it is an attempt to deny the existence of something by using the word in a particular restricted way. In an age of science, perhaps not surprisingly, the fallacy is found most commonly in the form of materialism.

3.2 Materialism

Although there appear to be different definitions of materialism, and different people claiming they are materialists, strictly speaking a materialist is someone who argues that whatever exists is material and what is taken to be mental does not exist. It is not enough to say that a mental event is identical with something material, because this still harbours a belief in the existence of mental events. For example, some philosophers disagree with the traditional metaphysical assumption that the mind constitutes a substance distinct from matter, or that it is greater than the sum of mental events, but they cannot claim to be materialists, because they still believe in mental events.

However, for someone to deny there are mental events she would have to deny there is any form of consciousness – no thoughts, feelings, emotions or sensations. And this seems to be quite clearly self-refuting. How can a person think there are no thoughts? She must think that her thought exists. The materialist theory itself must be a mental event in somebody's life. And, of course, if the materialist is to be consistent she would have to argue that her theory is no different from any other so-called mental event: nothing but one more physical event in someone's brain. But then, likewise, any alternative theory too will be another physical event in someone's life. And this leaves us with the problem of how one set of physical events in the brain can be said to constitute the truth and others false. On what grounds are we justified in saying that one ought to be taken seriously and the other dismissed?

One way a materialist might deal with this is to argue that thoughts, feelings, emotions and sensations exist; it's just that they are physical in nature, not mental at all. The classic expression of this view comes from the seventeenth-century English philosopher Thomas Hobbes, who argues that all that exists is either a material object or some physical event consisting of some material objects in motion. Certain of these physical motions constitute what he describes as 'sense', which, he claims, is the source of all thought, imaginings, dreams and memories, and therefore the whole of the mental. So, he doesn't deny the existence of mental phenomena, but he reduces them to motion and, therefore, to material phenomena.

But if this argument is to hold up we must be clear about how we are using and defining 'physical'. If we use it too loosely it will lose its usefulness and the argument will lack precision. When we looked at the difference between mental and physical events before, we noted that for anything to be physical it must have a spatial location and be publicly observable. But mental events and processes are neither of these, so it is misleading to describe them as 'physical'. For them to be physical we should be able to locate them and gather physical evidence of the event. If we were to take off the top of your skull as you drink orange juice we should be able to see a physical event that *is* the taste of orange. But of course we can't. All we can do is trace the physical effects through your taste buds, electrical impulses along your nerves and chemical changes in your brain, but at that point the trail goes cold and we are still left with the sensation of taste unaccounted for in physical terms.

It doesn't seem to be true to say that every emotion, feeling, sensation, and memory is nothing but a set of physical events. They seem to be two quite different things. Even though physical events might be the cause of mental events, it still remains the case that they are distinct and distinguishable. As Nagel argues, mental events have a sort of 'insideness', an awareness that manifests itself in the form of knowing what it is like to be someone or something. This is different from a physical event, in that it is not open to direct inspection.

So, it seems, if the materialist argument is to succeed in its most consistent form it must achieve three things. First, it must successfully deny the existence of mental events: it must show that whatever exists is material. Second, as a result of this, it must show that there is no need to suppose there is a dualism and an interaction between the physical and mental. It must be sensible to accept that when we are talking about mental events we are mistaken and we should, instead, be talking about physical events. And, third, with these two in place it must avoid self-refutation, or if it cannot it must show why it is that one physical event can be taken as truth, as opposed to another which is false.

Failing this, most people fall back on the less consistent, though common notion of materialism, which doesn't deny the mental, but argues that mental life is dependent on certain physical conditions without which it would not exist. As we will see in the next chapter, in this form it becomes part of the argument for dualism and must provide some account of the interaction between the two. On the face of it this seems a more sensible line to take, after all much of our experience seems to support it. Recent progress in the treatment of mental conditions like depression, bipolar disorder, and mood swings, along with a range of biochemical drug

Brief lives
Hobbes, Thomas

Dates: 1588–1679
Born: Malmesbury, England
Best known for: His political philosophy, in which he argued for a system of government that has its origins in a social contract that gave absolute power to a ruler. He also developed a materialistic philosophy of nature which analysed everything in terms of matter and motion.

Major works: *De Cive* (1642), *Leviathan* (1651), *De Corpore* (1655).

treatments, shows a link between the physical conditions in the nervous system and the mental condition of the individual. Similarly, the development of artificial intelligence with sophisticated computers programmed to perform complex intellectual tasks, suggests that physical events, in this case in the circuitry of the computer, can resemble mental processes in human beings.

However, if this is the case, it has serious ethical implications, as we will see in Chapters 18, 19 and 20. If it is theoretically possible to explain our thoughts in the same way we explain events in the physical world, in terms of cause and effect, we may have demonstrated that, despite appearances, we have no free will, no real choice, and therefore no moral responsibility. We would, in effect, be explaining human behaviour not as we normally understand it, as a series of moral choices made on the basis of careful thought and evaluation, but in terms of certain inexorable physical causes and their effects. We would become mere automata, reacting according to a simple stimulus–response mechanism, thereby reducing moral choice to a mere fiction.

■ 4. Husserl, holism and intentionality

Finally, it's worth considering whether all the problems we're having are not due to the fact that we're trapped by the way Descartes and succeeding generations of philosophers have defined the problem. Perhaps Cartesian philosophers simply got it wrong and there is another way of describing

ourselves without talking about bodies and minds; without arguing that we are one thing or the other.

This is the question posed by Edmund Husserl, the German philosopher who founded phenomenology: the study of mental states as we consciously experience them. He suggests that perhaps we have just fallen into the Cartesian trap of talking about minds and bodies. He starts by focusing on the way philosophers use spatial metaphors literally to describe the mind. This, he argues, gives us all sorts of problems with consciousness, which we tend to see as some mysterious container in which we find things like ideas, thoughts, desires, sensations, feelings and emotions. But in fact consciousness is nothing like this.

He conceives consciousness as 'intentionality'. Minds and mental states or events are intrinsically 'about' something. Conscious experiences are always directed towards an object, what Husserl describes as the 'intentional object'. Therefore, we should not talk about conscious acts as if they were self-contained contents of our mind, which are somehow coordinated with our body. Conscious experiences involve two things: a mental act, an act of consciousness, which he describes as an 'intentional act', and the objects of these acts, 'the intentional object'. Mental acts cannot exist without their intentional objects; indeed, the 'aboutness' of mental acts may be necessary for most, if not all, mental things.

It is for these reasons that Husserl and his followers, particularly Maurice Merleau-Ponty, criticize those philosophers, like Locke and Berkeley, who developed their accounts after adopting the Cartesian dualism of body and mind. In Chapter 8 we saw the way Locke developed the atomistic theory of perception, in which he argued that primary and secondary qualities enter the mind through the senses simple and unmixed. Only then does the mind combine them like a mosaic, so that our perception of anything is just the sum of the perception of its parts.

But in the twentieth century more sophisticated neuro-physiology and Gestalt psychology have suggested that the unified whole, or 'gestalt', is greater than, or different from, the sum of its parts: it is a complete structure, which cannot be explained simply by analysing it into its constituent elements. Merleau-Ponty insists that one cannot isolate pure sensations in the way Locke suggested, because all perceptual experience necessarily includes structure and meaning. Everything we perceive has meaning we bring to it, which points to something beyond it. You can no doubt see the relevance this has for the debate over narrow inductivism and whether observation is always theory-laden. Objects of consciousness are dependent on certain 'descriptions'. An intentional object only has the characteristics the mind ascribes to it and these are dependent on the way the mind portrays or describes it.

Similarly, Husserl's realization that conscious experience is always about things and always involves the intentional act and the intentional object led him to criticize Berkeley's idealistic account of perception. You'll remember Berkeley argues that all we can know to exist are ideas. This leads him into solipsism from which he can only fashion his escape by drawing on the assumption of God: that things must still exist when he is not thinking about them because they are in the mind of God.

But Husserl argues that Berkeley has this problem because he confuses our act of experiencing with the object experienced, and many of the attributes of an act don't apply to the object. Most importantly the object is not private, unlike the act: only one person (me) can perform my act of seeing, but many can see the object I am seeing. Berkeley assumes they are the same, so that I must conclude that I can only know the existence of ideas and when they are not in my mind they cannot, therefore, exist. Therefore, in order to explain how things do continue to exist when the idea of them is not in my mind he draws upon God in whose mind they can always be found.

In contrast, Husserl and his supporters reject the traditional way of dividing up body and mind, although in order to study mental states as we consciously experience them – the work of phenomenology as Husserl defined it – it was necessary to adopt a method similar to Descartes'. As Descartes doubted everything he could not prove, Husserl, in *Cartesian Meditations* (1931), 'bracketed' everything that was not given to consciousness. So, for example, at work your boss might complain about everything you do, but this might have nothing to do with the quality of your work. He might just be worrying about the business or he might have reached that age when he is getting depressed because he's wondering about what he has done with his life, and this leads him to take it out on you. Thus, in Husserl's phenomenological 'reduction' you and your work must be bracketed as not belonging to his mental state, leading to the isolation of the pure mental content – the mind's 'essence'. Indeed, it goes even further, abstracting from the thinker himself, leaving only pure consciousness, the 'transcendental ego'.

In *The Structure of Behaviour* (1942) Merleau-Ponty likewise rejects the idea of a distinction between mind and body, arguing instead that there is just a dialectic between them. The body is not a 'self-enclosed mechanism', nor the mind a distinct entity in some mysterious relationship with it. There is just a single entity: 'There is not a duality of substances, but only the dialectic of living being in its biological milieu.' Consciousness, he explains, is 'the meaning of one's body'. The body is not just alive, but in an important sense also conscious; it is aware of itself. He insists, my body and myself are essentially one and to try to separate them is to make the relationship between 'me and my body' into an unnecessary mystery.

■ 5. Conclusion

Despite this, Cartesian dualism has had a sustained influence on modern philosophy and science. In this chapter, in addition to the problem and nature of consciousness, we have explored the beliefs of idealists and materialists who reject the very idea of dualism in favour of a monistic account. In the next chapter we will examine the ideas of those who, while they accept dualism, either reject the notion of causal interaction between the two or account for it in ways they believe answer many of the problems we have identified in this chapter.

■ Questions

1. Can sense be made of the idea that people have thoughts and feelings of which they are unaware?

2. Is thought a physical process?

3. How can a mental event, like deciding to pick up a glass, have physical effects, like movements of one's hand?

4. Can we be sure that what you call 'pain' is the same kind of experience I call 'pain'?

5. What problems are involved in arguing from analogy with ourselves to the existence of other minds?

6. a) Explain and illustrate how solipsism is possible.

    b) Discuss and evaluate the solutions to the problem of other minds.

7. a) Explain what role you believe the idea of an *unconscious* mental state can play in any account of human behaviour.

    b) Discuss the particular philosophical problems involved in supposing that a mental state might be unconscious?

■ Recommended reading

Churchland, P. M. *Matter and Consciousness: A Contemporary Introduction to the Philosophy of Mind* (Cambridge, Mass.: Massachusetts Institute of Technology Press, 1988).

Nagel, T. *Mortal Questions* (Cambridge: Cambridge University Press, 1991), Chapter 12 'What is it like to be a bat?'

Merleau-Ponty, M. *Phenomenology of Perception*, trans. C. Smith (New York: Humanities, 1962) (London: Routledge and Kegan Paul, 1962).

Rosenthal, D. (ed.) *Materialism and the Mind–Body Problem* (Englewood Cliffs, NJ: Prentice Hall, 1971).

Ryle, G. *Concept of Mind* (Harmondsworth: Penguin, 1990), Chapters 1, 2 and 5.

Sartre, J-P. *Existentialism and Humanism* (London: Methuen, 1946).

 The note structure to accompany this chapter can be downloaded from our website.

The Problem of Dualism

Key issues

▶ If there are two substances – mind and matter – how are two such different things connected? How do things as different as feelings, ideas, sensations and desires result in physical movement, when they cannot touch any physical particles in the brain to stimulate them?

▶ Do we need to redefine our notion of causation, or are the laws governing the relation between mind and body ultimate laws that are just inexplicable in terms of anything else?

▶ Or are mental and physical events different aspects of one and the same thing: expressions of one higher substance generally conceived to be unknowable to human beings?

▶ Alternatively are they independent, running in parallel and keeping exact pace with one another?

▶ Perhaps the mind cannot causally affect the body at all and we are just 'conscious automata'. Indeed if this is the case, would the entire course of human history have been exactly the same even if minds had never existed?

▶ Or do both terms represent different ways of talking about the same thing, so that when we talk about thoughts we mean certain brain processes?

▶ Maybe the mind is like the software of a computer, just an elaborate program?

In the last chapter we saw that the traditional view of metaphysics was that the world was made up of two substances: two underlying realities that support certain qualities or properties. One was matter, an extended substance, in which resided certain physical properties like shape, size and weight. The other was mind, a non-spatial, conscious substance, in which resided mental properties like the capacity to think, perceive, remember and imagine. Traditionally, also, the mind and body were connected, although the mind (the soul) was distinct from the body: its mental properties were not dependent on the body and, therefore, a continuing mental life was thought possible after death.

◼ 1. Cartesian dualism and causal interactionism

However our problems begin when we try to pin down exactly the nature of this connection. Clearly there is a close connection between the two. After all we perceive the world through our sense organs – we feel pain, pleasure and tension in our bodies – and we act to fulfil our intentions or desires by using our bodies and their powers. Descartes' solution is to argue for causal interaction, that they causally affect each other, even though, as we saw in the last chapter, this is more difficult to understand in view of the mind's lack of extension, its 'privileged access' and the 'incorrigibility' of mental claims.

But even with these problems, the weight of evidence from our normal lives seems to support this view. Few of us have any problem accepting that physical changes influence our mental outlook: drinking coffee stimulates us, drinking alcohol relaxes us, and if we have a blow on the head we are likely to lose consciousness. Similarly there seems little doubt that our mental experiences affect our bodily processes: resistance to disease is affected by our mental outlook, worry may lead to ill health, and anger may lead to high blood pressure.

However, the problem is finding some way of explaining how it is that these entirely distinct substances can affect each other in this way: how something as different as feelings, ideas and sensations can interact with the nervous system and brain cells. We can understand a causal relation between a change in the brain or nervous system and a muscular movement, but a causal relation between an idea and a physical movement is difficult to comprehend. There seems to be something wrong with the mind–matter interaction. They both seem to be independent and self-sufficient.

It is the same problem we saw in the last chapter, when we discussed how we can have the sensation of tasting orange juice. How does a sensation emerge from a complex network of neurological reactions going on in the brain? There is something non-physical coming from a physical process. You twist your ankle and you feel pain. But how does the final brain event result in a mental event, which cannot be spatially located? And the converse too: how can a desire result in physical movement, when it cannot touch any physical particles in the brain to stimulate them?

It seems no matter how far our knowledge develops we are still faced with this mysterious gap between the last known neurological occurrence and the sensation itself, or, in the other direction, the idea and the physical movement. One answer to the problem worth considering is that perhaps we have conceived the notion of causation rather too narrowly. From the moment Newton conceived of light as made up of different-sized molecules each refracting at different angles as they passed through the denser medium of the prism and splitting light into its seven different colours, we have tended to adopt a mechanical concept of causation. One thing has to physically act on something else for the effect to occur, which makes it difficult to see how non-spatial, mental things can act on spatial, physical things.

But perhaps this is just one type of causation, after all we accept other forms of causation, like 'action at a distance' to explain the gravitational pull of the planets. This involves no actual physical contact and yet without it we would be hard pressed to explain the orbits of planets, the regular emergence of comets and other events in the universe. Without knowing how this occurs in terms of the narrow concept of causation, we accept that the evidence is sufficient for us to believe it does in fact occur.

For example, scientists have recently discovered another black hole in our galaxy. But in terms of black holes this one is comparatively small – only about 1,000 times the size of the sun. And, of course, because of what it is, there is very little direct evidence of its existence. The gravity of black holes is so great that nothing, not even light, can escape from them. So, scientists can only claim to have found them by inference from the effects of their influence at a distance on all those objects and gases around them. One way of detecting them is through gas falling towards them, which becomes so hot that it emits X-rays.

Modern scientific explanations of this type seem to have outgrown the simple, narrow concept of causation that drew heavily on analogies from our everyday experiences. To explain the molecular nature of light or boiling water in terms similar to the behaviour of billiard balls gives us an immediate sense of understanding the phenomenon. But not all phenomena fit so easily into explanations constructed around familiar analogies. So, perhaps we just have to accept that this is the way things are. It might just be a brute, arbitrary fact, an 'ultimate law' that we cannot explain by breaking it down into familiar terms or by using other laws. To explain anything involves subsuming the event under a law. In turn these laws are then explained by subsuming them under a more basic law or theory. But eventually there must come a point when we reach an ultimate law: a law that cannot be explained in terms of more basic laws. It is a brute, arbitrary, inexplicable fact.

Perhaps the laws governing the relations between the mental and physical are ultimate laws. We are not aware of any other law or theory in terms of which we could explain them, nor are there any familiar analogies that would give us an idea of how they work. Like the gravitational pull of the planets and black holes, we can only assert that there is a uniformity in their behaviour, which suggests that a causal interaction takes place. Indeed, this is not a new idea. In the nineteenth century J. S. Mill in *A System of Logic* (1843) suggested exactly this, that all laws stating a correlation between physical states and states of consciousness are basic or ultimate laws.

Nevertheless, even though this might seem compelling, we are still left with the problem that the causal interaction involves two radically different types of things. The causal explanation of black holes sucking in matter all around them involves just physical phenomena as both cause and effect. But in the interaction between the mental and physical, it doesn't seem enough to argue that changes in the brain or nervous system resulted in an idea or a sensation, or that the formation of an idea or desire resulted in physical movement. An idea or a sensation is something quite different from the physical causes that might be said to produce them. Indeed Descartes was attacked on just these grounds both by his immediate followers, particularly Spinoza and Leibniz, and by the empiricists. Different substances, they argue, cannot interact. Only physical bodies can causally interact and not anything as different as physical bodies and minds.

■ 2. Accept dualism, but reject interactionism

Logically there are three ways of responding to this. First, we could accept dualism, but reject interaction, finding some other explanation for the way they both function. Second, we could accept dualism and accept interaction, in which case we must come up with an account of the interaction which answers the problems we've identified above. Or, third, we could reject dualism entirely, and with it the problem of interaction. If there are only minds or only bodies we have no problem to solve.

One simple solution to the problem is to deny there is a problem at all by arguing that there is no interaction in the first place. Some accounts of dualism refuse to accept Descartes' description of the

position, describing a different relationship that attempts to eliminate some of the difficulties. All these accounts amount to attempts to subordinate both mental and physical events as expressions of one higher substance. They don't interact with one another: they are just manifestations of the same independent thing. They are either both expressions of this substance or they are coordinated to occur together in parallel.

2.1 The dual aspect theory

The seventeenth-century Dutch philosopher Benedict Spinoza found that the problem with Descartes' account is the complete separation of mind and body, and the total separation of both from God. Instead, he argues that they are both aspects of an infinite substance he calls God or nature. This is known as 'the dual aspect theory'. Neither mind nor body subordinates the other, indeed there is no relation between them at all. For everything that occurs in one there is a corresponding event in the other, because the physical and mental worlds are just two ways of looking at the same thing: God or nature. So, when the glass I have dropped smashes on the floor and I hear it smash these are two different aspects of the same thing – two different ways of looking at the same thing as it occurs in God or nature.

Both mental and physical experiences are two aspects of an underlying reality that is generally conceived to be unknowable to human beings. It appears as an expression of the mind when we experience something from the inside or subjectively, and as body or matter when we view something from the outside or objectively. Although our mental lives go on in our brain, our thoughts, feelings, desires

Brief lives
Spinoza, Benedictus de

Dates: 1632–1677
Born: Amsterdam, Holland
Best known for: Being a rationalist who believed in pantheism and the uselessness of human struggle in a determined universe.

Major works: *Tractatus Theologico-Politicus* (1670), *Ethics* (1677).

and emotions are not just the product of certain physical processes in the brain: although it is the seat of consciousness, conscious states are not just physical. The brain with its billions of nerve cells is not just a physical object; it has a mental side too. When you drink a glass of orange juice I might be able to monitor all the physical and chemical changes and all the electrical activity in your brain, but the taste is a mental event that is yours and yours alone. This is what Nagel means by 'insideness': it cannot be reached or monitored by an observer.

Although as a pantheist Spinoza regarded all reality as divine and God as present in all nature, the dual aspect theory need not be an account of the 'one substance' metaphysics that he presents it as. In the twentieth century Bertrand Russell presented a similar theory without reference to substances and their 'attributes', arguing that mental and physical events were just different aspects of one and the same 'something'. Our experiences and ideas are just one aspect of events and activities, of which the various chemical reactions in the brain were another. Again, as in Spinoza's account, they are just two aspects of the same thing, rather than two separate things. Hence the problem of interaction no longer arises.

But still, with both accounts we are still left with this mysterious 'something', of which mind and body are just aspects. In attempting to solve one mystery we have embraced another – and one that we have no means of solving. If it is neither physical nor mental, but something more, we can have no means of discovering what it is. What can we say about something that is neither brain nor mind, but both? It remains a substance with which no one has any acquaintance, or any knowledge. It is the same distinction Kant drew between the 'phenomenal' and the 'noumenal' worlds, which we examined in Chapter 6. While we can know the phenomenal world or the world as known by the mind, we can never know the noumenal world, the real world, consisting of 'things in themselves'.

2.2 Psychophysical parallelism

In contrast, the seventeenth-century German philosopher Gottfried Leibniz was able to sidestep this problem by arguing that mental states run in parallel with physical states without interacting with them. He explains that God has programmed them so perfectly that they are exactly coordinated.

Brief lives
Leibniz, Gottfried Wilhelm von

Dates: 1646–1716
Born: Leipzig, Germany
Best known for: Devising an elaborate metaphysical system composed of small immaterial substances known as 'monads', each of which is a reflection of the entire universe. He discovered differential calculus independently of Newton. He was a military strategist and the inventor of a primitive computer.

Major works: *Discourse on Metaphysics* (1685), *The New System* (1695), *Theodicy* (1710), *Monadology* (1714).

Minds and bodies are like two finely made clocks running together, keeping exact pace with one another. Yet each proceeds on its own way quite independent of the other. In more modern terms it is like the visual and sound tracks on a film: both have been created independently of one another, but they occur in perfect coordination as we watch the film.

For example, the glass that I drop smashes on the floor and at the same time I have the mental event of hearing the noise of the glass smashing into pieces. Yet the mental event has no causal impact: it is nothing more than a running commentary. What's more, the physical event does not cause the mental event: physical events can only cause other physical events as mental events cause other mental events. While there is a one-to-one correlation between the two events, with the mental event occurring simultaneously, a complete causal account can be given of the event in physical causes alone. And although a complete *description* of the event would include such mental events as my decision to pick the glass up, this, the supporters of parallelism argue, had no causal impact on the event.

In his metaphysical works, such as *The Monadology* (1714), Leibniz argues that every entity, mental or physical, is independent and constitutes a 'monad', the individual properties of which determine each thing's past, present and future. Everything that can possibly happen to a monad is fixed by its nature, by its essential qualities, and not by any external influence. Nevertheless, although they can exert no influence on each other, God has created such a perfect pre-established harmony between monads that events occurring in one will be harmonious with events occurring in others. So, when the glass smashes, at that very moment I hear the sound of it smashing.

Although this relieves us of the problem of accounting for a mysterious 'something', of which mind and body are just aspects, as in Spinoza's theory, to accept Leibniz's account we still have to accept the metaphysical and theological supports it rests on. What's more, the mind appears to be reduced to the status of mere spectator. Indeed this account appears to make the mind irrelevant in the great evolutionary and physical struggles of mankind, when in fact most of us believe the mind has an important part to play. In terms of our day-to-day lives we all realize the importance of reflective thinking in helping us avoid wasting our time and energy. But in the broader context of history and the progress made by civilizations, we know their capacity to survive and prosper has been dependent on the influence of great minds in science, the arts, medicine, politics, even ethics and philosophy.

In response, the 'parallelists' reject the charge that they reduce the mind to the status of mere spectator, arguing instead that, although the mental event is not in the causal chain, nevertheless the eventual outcome would not have occurred without it. Unless I had decided to pick up the glass it wouldn't have smashed on the floor. Therefore, while it is not a cause, it is a necessary condition and part of the account of sufficient conditions for the event to have occurred. All they are insisting is that it was events in the physical world that did the actual work: not the mental events, but their representatives in the physical world.

Even so, as you can no doubt see, what we have now is what appears to be a verbal difference – a difference of language. We need to know what difference there is between calling something a necessary condition and calling it a cause. The parallelists and the interactionists both agree that physical events are part of the sufficient conditions for a mental event to occur and mental events are part of the sufficient conditions for a physical event to occur. But, while parallelists are not prepared to describe mental events as a cause of physical events, the interactionists are.

So, where does the difference lie for parallelists to refuse to call necessary conditions causes? In our normal lives we don't share the same reluctance. If you were to ask me why the glass smashed on the floor, I would have no hesitation in giving you a causal explanation that begins with the explanation that I decided to pick it up and goes on to explain that it was wet and it slipped from my grasp and smashed on the floor. My decision to pick it up is a necessary condition, one of the contributing causes of the glass smashing, without which the event would not have occurred.

It is not difficult to imagine that perhaps one reason for this reluctance might be the narrow mechanical concept of causation that we came across earlier. You will remember that this involves the assumption that for one thing to have caused another it has to physically act on the other thing for the effect to occur, which makes it difficult to see how non-spatial, mental things can act on spatial, physical things. In other words, we can only talk about the notion of cause in those cases when one physical event acts upon another. Since physical contact is not possible with something mental, the mental event cannot be described as a cause. But, as we saw previously, perhaps this is just one type of causation, and we should accept a broader concept, including 'action at a distance' to explain those cases in which there is no actual physical contact. Without knowing how this occurs in terms of the narrow concept of causation, we still do seem to be willing to accept this as a type of causation. Once we have acknowledged this and accepted it as a definition of cause, any difference between the parallelists and the interactionists is removed.

■ 3. Accept dualism and interactionism: epiphenomenalism

If this is the case, and we accept this notion of cause, parallelism does appear to collapse into interactionism. We are then faced with the challenge of not just accepting the dualism of mind and body, but explaining what sort of relation there is between them. Rather than rejecting one of these components outright and sidestepping the problems created by Cartesian dualism, we must attempt to deal with them. One theory that attempts to provide the answers is epiphenomenalism.

Like Leibniz, epiphenomenalists believe the mind cannot causally affect the body, but unlike

Leibniz they believe the body can causally affect the mind. Mental events are merely some kind of by-product of certain complex physical processes in the brain and nervous system. Consciousness is an 'epiphenomenon', literally an event which occurs 'after' the physical process.

This, then, is a one-way causal model: it allows bodies and changes in bodies to cause mental events, but mental events have no causal influence in the other direction, or even on other mental phenomena. It is like the petrol gauge in your car – it reflects the way the car is functioning, but the car itself can work equally well if the gauge fails. In the same way each time a physical situation comes about in the brain a thought also occurs, as smoke occurs when there is a fire, or your body casts a shadow when the sun comes out. The conscious thought represents the brain state, but is causally impotent. Consciousness is just a side effect of certain physical processes.

This leads T. H. Huxley, the British biologist and supporter of Darwin, to describe humans as just 'conscious automata'. So, for example, if you were to cut your finger on a sharp knife the awareness of the pain would produce a conscious thought that you should take your finger away from the knife. But it is the C-fibres that do the real work; they represent the pain in the physical world, affecting your efferent nerves, which lead you to pull your finger away.

As you can see this overcomes some of the problems faced by materialists. It is not forced to adopt the implausible position of denying that the mind exists; instead mental events are accounted for as merely the insignificant by-products representing brain states. But, like Leibniz, it achieves this at a cost: it fails to do justice to our mental life and the importance we attach to it. Of course, we could be wrong about this. Although we look at the great minds of the past and marvel at the immense contributions they have made to our development – people like Leonardo da Vinci, Martin Luther, Isaac Newton, Charles Darwin, Albert Einstein, Stephen Hawking and many others – perhaps the entire course of human history would have been exactly the same even if these minds had not existed and only the material events in the brain had occurred.

All that the epiphenomenalist is arguing is that consciousness is not causally necessary to the process. The immense contributions that these and others have made to our development could only have come about as a result of the immensely complex activity of cells in the human brain. All the rest that consciousness creates is merely a running commentary, nothing else. When we say that the mind affects the body, what we really mean to say is that events going on in the *brain* affect the body. But the problem with this argument, of course, is proving it. We would have to find some way of splitting the brain event from the corresponding mental event.

Even so we are still left with the nagging feeling that there is more to it than this. The great achievements of mankind – works of art, music and literature, architecture, science, politics and philosophy – all suggest the world is different because of minds. Even though we agree that none of it could have been achieved without the complex physical activity in the brain, it is still part of the body that seems unpredictable, over which for much of the time we seem to have little control. The work of most artists and scientists seems at times to be quite inexplicable even to themselves. Their work takes a radically different direction, or assumes a new form which has no precedents, or a solution appears from a direction least expected. There are novelists who say the plot and characters simply take on a form of their own and dictate the shape of the novel; and artists who confess that the music simply takes them over and it is not them any more.

In this there is the underlying and recurring question of Part II: what is *you*; what is the self that underlies our actions and gives us a sense that we are free agents making decisions? Is this just the product of the physical processes of the brain, the unpredictable creativity of the mind, the results of social conditioning, or maybe the will of God?

■ 4. The rejection of dualism

Of course, the simplest way of dealing with the problem of mind and body is just to deny there is a difference between them and, therefore, that there is no problem of interaction at all. But as we saw in the last chapter, when we examined the problems of monism, particularly materialism, to reject dualism and argue that there exist only minds or only matter seems to suggest that both have the same meaning, which fails to explain the apparent distinctions between them. If matter is all that exists, we would have to endow it with the properties we ordinarily associate with minds and this would stretch the meaning of matter beyond its normal limits.

Nevertheless, many philosophers believe that the mind is not a substance distinct from matter. Increasing evidence shows that everything mental depends on a properly functioning brain and nervous system. Every type of mental event or capacity is affected by the brain. If we damage it we are likely to lose many of these capacities. We might impair our memory, our capacity to recognize others, or our capacity to restrain our emotions or desires. If it is so dependent upon matter, the mind doesn't appear to be a separate substance.

But one way round the problem of stretching the meaning of matter beyond its normal limits is to argue that although the mind is not a substance distinct from matter, there are mental *properties* that are distinct from physical *properties*. Some philosophers believe that a normal brain has both material and mental properties. Yet the mental properties are distinct in that they are emergent properties: that is, they emerge out of the complex organization of the parts of the brain. In the same way that the identity of a university, a football club or a charity is greater than the sum of its parts, mental properties are emergent in that they are more than the organization of the parts of the brain. And in particular they possess the distinctive characteristic of being conscious.

So, in place of a dualism of substances we have substituted a dualism of properties. However, while this is still a rejection of Cartesian dualism, it is now no longer a rejection of dualism as such. Therefore it has to deal with all the problems faced by those who accept dualism and accept interaction. In particular it has to explain whether our mental properties cause any part of our behaviour. For example, we need to know whether our desires and intentions are the product of brain events or whether they are at least partially caused by our conscious experiences.

4.1 The identity theory

One of the more obvious ways of meeting this problem is to argue that mental and bodily events are in fact the same. This is the view of identity theorists, who believe that mental events are identical with certain processes in the brain and nervous system. Although it is sometimes presented as a contemporary form of materialism, unlike materialism

identity theory doesn't deny the existence of mental events, only that they have no independent existence – they are just certain bodily events. Mental events, like feeling pain and experiencing sensations, do exist, and terms like 'believe', 'want', 'feel' and 'desire' do refer to some mental state, it is just that at present scientists are unable to give a detailed neurological description of the process that produces them. In time they will be able to show that certain bodily events produce certain mental events.

The key feature of this argument is that identity theorists are not merely saying that physical brain states and mental states are correlated with one another, so that whenever there is a brain state there is a corresponding mental state, but that they are in fact the same event. They are asserting a monistic position that eliminates dualism entirely and with it the problem of interaction. There are no longer two things to interact. There is just a single event: a mental-neurological event that can be described using two quite different languages.

On the face of it this seems like a very obvious suggestion, that all mental experiences are identical with processes taking place in the brain. But it is testimony to the influence of Descartes that only comparatively recently have philosophers discussed this. Since Descartes philosophers have tended to define the mental in terms quite incompatible with the physical. So, to say that the mental is physical would be paradoxical, perhaps even logically contradictory. Working in the shadow of Descartes, a mental event was seen as private and incorrigible, allowing privileged access only to one person. It would be impossible then to describe this in terms of a physical event, which is public and without the privileged access to clear and distinct ideas.

But once we have left behind the Cartesian analysis of body and mind, the identity theory offers some clear advantages over the other theories we have examined. For one thing it's a more convincing way of rejecting dualism, while at the same time accepting the obvious influence of mental events on our lives. It answers the problem we raised above, whether our consciousness has causal influence. Unlike parallelism and epiphenomenalism, it allows mental states a causal role – decisions really do result in actions. Therefore it has a better chance of doing the sort of justice to our mental life that reflects the importance we attach to it. Moreover, the identity it seeks to establish between brain and thought processes is an empirical identity, one that must be established through experiment and the methods of modern science. It is not just claiming that there is a logical identity between mental and brain events grounded in certain linguistic conventions, which allow us to claim merely that 'brain process' and 'thought' are synonymous – that one means the other.

Nevertheless this argument hasn't freed itself completely from the Cartesian analysis. It faces one significant problem. As Jerome Shaffer points out, if mind and brain are identical they ought to share the same properties. But they do in fact have different properties: brain processes, like all physical processes, occur in a specific spatial location, but thoughts and consciousness have no spatial location. A brain process, at least in principle, is a publicly observable event, but a thought or a sensation of pain is a private event. Nobody can have your pain or thought but you. If somebody were to say they feel your pain, it is no longer yours but theirs. And it is not enough just to say that consciousness is *dependent* on the brain. For it to be the same it must be found *in* the brain. If it is not to be found in the same space it cannot be numerically identical with what *is* in that space, in other words the brain.

So, identity theorists must be clear about exactly what they mean by claiming that brain processes and thought processes are 'identical'. Normally when we use this word we mean that there are two things that have exactly the same properties, except for their spatio-temporal properties. You might know a pair of identical twins. They are exactly the same, except that one is in New York, the other in London. Otherwise, if they were to have the same spatio-temporal properties, there would be only one person. Alternatively we can mean that they are indeed one and the same thing, in other words that they are numerically identical, and this is what identity theorists want to claim: mental-states and brain-states are literally the same thing. As J. J. C. Smart describes it, 'When I say that a sensation is a brain process or that lightning is an electrical discharge, I am using 'is' in the sense of strict identity.'

But, then, whether or not they are the same, when we describe brain processes and thought processes we are describing two different sets of characteristics. If I were to describe the sensation of seeing a pan of boiling water I would be describing quite different characteristics from those I would describe if I were to give a molecular description of what was happening. C. D. Broad makes the same point by drawing the distinction between describing what it is to see something red and describing the molecular movement in the brain that corresponds to it. He explains these are two different explanations of two different sets of characteristics: 'There is a something which has the characteristic of being my awareness of a red patch. There is something which has the characteristic of being a molecular movement.' Conscious states have different qualities from physical states, and if the conscious state has just one quality which the physical state does not have, they can hardly be described as identical.

Nevertheless, identity theorists can quite reasonably argue that the meaning of each description might be different, but what they denote is the same thing. Their identity is empirical, not logical. They are not saying that mental words *mean* the same thing as physical words. They are just two descriptions that denote the same thing. Two descriptions can refer to the same thing and at the same time have different meanings. The word 'lightning' doesn't mean the same thing as 'electrical discharge', although every flash of lightning is in fact an electrical discharge. I can know this person in front of me is the Archbishop of Canterbury without knowing that he is the head of the Anglican Church, yet the same person can be accurately described in both ways. The two descriptions have the same denotation, although different meanings. So when I look at a patch of red I have the sensation of redness without knowing that at the same time a certain molecular process is taking place. But this is still the same thing; only the meanings of the words are different. Modern scientific research tells us that pain is numerically identical with the stimulation of C-fibres: they are one and the same thing; we cannot have one without the other.

The denotation argument that the identity is empirical not logical, grounded in the meaning of words, is a convincing rebuff to the critics of identity theory. Yet the one key question you must ask is whether it successfully addresses the point made by Jerome Shaffer, that if two things are to be numerically identical they must share the same characteristics, otherwise, like the pair of identical twins, they would be two things. And for this to be the case they must be located in the same place. As Shaffer says, 'If it is not there it cannot be identical with what *is* there.' Of course you might argue that in time modern physiological research will be able to show that they do indeed both take place in the same place in the brain.

But though we might know that both processes take place in the same location, is this enough to establish they are the same thing? It seems that no amount of scientific research will show brain processes to be the same as thought processes. Although research has shown that certain brain processes correlate with certain thought processes, this is far from establishing identity. The new generation of 'neuro-advertisers' believe they can locate the area in the brain that is activated when the mind is stimulated by certain commercial images, but they cannot tell what you are thinking or what form this stimulation takes. In time science may indeed be able to go farther and identify exactly which brain state correlates with each sensation or feeling, but this is not to say they are the same thing: correlation is not identity. To *know which C-fibres* are active when you have a particular feeling is not to *know the feeling*. Even if I *know* what you are thinking, this is not the same as *having* your thought. I might know you are in pain, but this is not to have the pain myself. I might know that the pain is the stimulation of C-fibres, but this says nothing about the sensation itself, the awareness of the pain.

In his influential book *Naming and Necessity* (1973), the American philosopher Saul Kripke asks what God would have to do to make the identity theory work, say in the case of heat and molecular motion. First, he says, God would have to create molecular motion, then sentient beings to ensure the molecular motion produces the sensation in them. But to do this he would have to create the C-fibres capable of producing the appropriate type of physical stimulation. But even then something would still be missing: 'He must let the creatures feel the C-fibre stimulation as *pain*, and not as a tickle, or as warmth, or as nothing.' In other words, what's missing is what Nagel describes as 'insideness': the inside view from the perspective of the person having the feeling, sensation or thought as opposed to the scientist's view from the outside. We must know what it *feels like* to have the experience. As Nagel says in *The View from Nowhere* (1986), 'The strange truth seems to be that certain complex, biologically generated physical systems, of which each of us is an example, have rich non-physical properties.'

4.2 Behaviourism

Of course there is a simpler method of dealing with the problems of dualism and interactionism, and that is the positivist approach: to argue that we can only have genuine knowledge within the bounds of science and observation. If we cannot observe the mind, talk about it is metaphysical speculation not knowledge. This is the sort of position held by most of those who support behaviourism. Although often thought to be the counterpart to materialism, unlike materialism it doesn't deny the mental, only that we cannot claim genuine knowledge of it. Beyond this position it's possible to distinguish between two types of behaviourism: methodological or psychological behaviourism and logical or metaphysical behaviourism.

4.2.1 Methodological behaviourism

Methodological behaviourism is more accurately characterized as a method employed in psychology, in which practitioners refuse to accept any introspective evidence of one's own mental state as material for arriving at laws or theories in psychology. As a form of science it involves a refusal to accept any evidence of events that cannot be publicly witnessed. Behaviourists, like John Watson and B. F. Skinner, believe that introspective reports are far too misleading to be reliable. Any talk of the 'mental' is likely to embroil us in a hopeless tangle of confusions, which we cannot sort out through experiment, because only one person can observe the results. And, anyway, we are only tempted to postulate the existence of abstract, unobservable entities like the mind as a result of certain kinds of observable behaviour. Why go beyond such reliable evidence to make such metaphysical claims, when it is much more sensible to study the behaviour itself and not burden ourselves in this way?

Although behaviourists exclude mental events as a legitimate object of study, they need not deny their existence. All they are saying is that we should not define 'behaviour' in such a way as to include consciousness, which we cannot observe and publicly test, nor should we identify behaviour with the consciousness that goes with it. So, they are able to give a complete account of me seeing something in behaviourist terms – a full account of all my bodily reactions – but this would leave out any talk of the sensation I have in seeing it. They can study my reactions, but not the sensation within me. They can guess at my thoughts, feelings and emotions by studying my reactions, but the experience itself is beyond them. This is similar to someone administering a polygraph test. She can record all the changes in heart rate, blood pressure, pulse, respiration, body temperature and the electrical conductivity of the skin, but she cannot know what the subject is thinking. All she can conclude is that the subject's responses to certain questions are different from those she knows he has answered truthfully.

Nevertheless, many behaviourists have gone beyond their own empirical methodology and ventured into the very metaphysical arguments they refuse to condone in others by denying that there can be mental events. John Watson has argued that belief in consciousness merely reflects the thinking of pre-scientific ages, when we believed in superstition and magic. The only test for concepts like consciousness or the 'soul' is whether someone can experience them, but 'no one has ever touched a soul, or seen one in a test tube, or has in any other way come into relationship with it as he has with the other objects of his daily experience.' And, he concludes more like a metaphysician than a scientist, that there is no such thing as consciousness and no rational person would believe in it.

4.2.2 Logical or metaphysical behaviourism

In contrast, metaphysical behaviourism is concerned about what we mean when we talk about minds or mental events. Hence its concern is with the logical implications of the way we use these terms; what we mean by them. This is a doctrine about reality which starts from the assumption that mental events are just complex tendencies to behave in certain ways. There are no inner episodes, conscious mental events, just behaviour. Likewise there are no non-material minds or mental properties. All the talk about people's minds and mental properties is just about their behaviour and dispositions to behave. This line of thinking has taken two forms: the 'instrumentalists', most notably the American philosopher John Dewey, and the logical or 'new' behaviourists represented by Gilbert Ryle.

In *The Quest for Certainty* (1929), Dewey rejects dualism and with it the notion of the mind as a noun in favour of it as an adjective describing a kind of activity, a certain kind of behaviour. Rather than something in and of itself which has a capacity for thought, the mind is the way in which we respond to doubt and uncertainty. It is a problem-solving activity through which we move from a situation of uncertainty to the security of finding a solution. We are presented with a problem, we define the nature of it, and we then form an idea of how we could solve it. In the process we move from doubt to certainty. Our minds and our thoughts are functional responses to problems: they represent the way we interact with natural events. The mind is not, as he describes it, the 'mystery of a power outside of nature and yet able to intervene within it.'

Ryle, too, targets the same problem, what he describes in *The Concept of Mind* (1949) as the 'official doctrine', the traditional 'dogma of the ghost in the machine': that the mind represents another world parallel to or beyond the ordinary world. This is Descartes' mistake, to see the mind and its events as some strange mysterious private thing behind our behaviour. Ryle explains:

> My destructive purpose is to show that a family of radical category mistakes is the source of the double-life theory. The representation of a person as a ghost mysteriously ensconced in a machine derives from this argument.

Following suggestions made by Wittgenstein, Ryle set about establishing a new form of behaviourism. The mind, he argues, is not something distinct from the body and matter; it is the way a person behaves. To believe that it is distinct is an example of a 'category mistake': in other words, it makes the mistake of talking about the facts of something as if they belong to one logical type or category when in fact they belong to another. He illustrates this with the

John Dewey (1859–1952)

A prolific writer of books and articles, Dewey was a pioneer in functional psychology, a leader of the Progressive movement in US education and one of the leading exponents of pragmatism. He received a PhD (1884) from Johns Hopkins University and taught for ten years at the University of Michigan before moving to the University of Chicago, where he remained for a further ten years before moving to Columbia University. His enormous influence is due partly to the fact that he synthesized the views of Charles Peirce and William James to develop pragmatism as a theory of logical and ethical analysis.

He developed an instrumentalist theory of knowledge that conceived of ideas as tools for the solution of problems encountered in a specific environment. Seeking out solutions, therefore, is a self-corrective process undertaken under certain specific social and cultural circumstances. For this knowledge requires no foundation in certainty: it is only what is required by the enquiry. Convinced that the experimental methods of modern science provided the most promising approach to social and ethical problems, he applied this view to studies of democracy and liberalism, arguing that democracy provides citizens with the opportunity for maximum experimentation and personal growth. Of his many published works probably the most important is *Experience and Nature* (1925). Others include *Reconstruction in Philosophy* (1920), *Human Nature and Conduct* (1922) and *The Quest for Certainty* (1929).

example of a foreign visitor who is shown around Oxford or Cambridge universities. He sees the colleges, the libraries, the playing fields, the museums, the scientific departments and the administrative offices. And then, having seen all this, he asks 'But where is the university?' He has made a category mistake in that he has assumed that the university is an entity over and beyond what he has seen, when in fact it is just the way in which all that he has seen is organized. It is, explains Ryle, 'as if "the University" stood for an extra member of the class of which these other units are members.' He has mistakenly allocated the university to the wrong category.

Philosophers make the same mistake when they represent the facts of mental life as if they belonged to one logical category when in fact they belong to another. This, he describes as, 'a philosopher's myth': the mistake that is made when they try to think abstractly about the mind. When Descartes thinks abstractly about the mind, he believes it is some strange, mysterious, private sort of thing behind our behaviour, whereas in fact it is the pattern of our behaviour, not behind it at all. When we use 'mentalistic' terms, like 'believes', 'thinks' and 'feels', we are describing certain 'dispositions'. Framed in the hypothetical form, 'If A, then B', they describe certain tendencies for something to happen given certain conditions.

Therefore, the difference between methodological or psychological behaviourism, and Ryle and Wittgenstein's logical behaviourism is that theirs is not a theory about behaviour and its causes: it's a theory about the language of the mind; about what we mean by mentalistic terms, like 'believes', 'thinks' and 'feels'. When we use these terms it is the logical equivalent of saying that a person will have a disposition to act in accordance with a certain pattern of behaviour.

There are, as you can see, obvious advantages in this account, the most important of which is that we can now eliminate the mysterious entity of the mind by translating all our terminology describing it and its events into statements about behaviour, not inner states. So, if I said of my teenage son that 'David loves Newcastle United Football Club', I would be merely describing a disposition to act in accordance with certain patterns of behaviour. I expect him to buy a Newcastle United football shirt, to go to as many games as he can, to become a member of the supporters' club and so on. The problem of dualism between mind and body has disappeared in translation. And the causal interaction between the two has been recast as a causal connection between a physical state (a disposition to behave in a certain way) and the actual consequent behaviour. The causal relationship described in the statement 'David will buy a Newcastle shirt, because he loves the Club', no longer poses the same metaphysical problems, any more than saying that 'The glass broke, because it slipped out of my hand.'

Nevertheless, it seems we mean more than this when we use these mentalistic terms. If a person has a certain disposition, as David does, this seems to suggest that he has certain feelings for the Club that amount to love. This is an inner episode, which, in itself, is not behaviour, although it is usually the cause of behaviour. In this case fans that are passionate about their club usually buy their replica shirts, go to as many matches as possible and become members of the supporters' club. It seems, then, that the inner episode, the feeling of love for the Club, is an indispensable part of the causal process.

> **Brief lives**
> **Ryle, Gilbert**
>
> Dates: 1900–1978
> Born: Brighton, England
> Best known for: His view that the main function of philosophy should be to correct the misunderstandings arising from 'category mistakes' and for 'logical behaviourism' – that to talk about the mind is to talk about behavioural dispositions and abilities.
>
> Major works: *Philosophical Arguments* (1945), *The Concept of Mind* (1949), *Dilemmas* (1954), *A Rational Animal* (1962), *Plato's Progress* (1966), *The Thinking of Thoughts* (1968).

As with many of the behaviourist arguments, this seems to work better the more distance you can place between yourself and the mental state. For example, it acts as an important reminder to scientists, particularly biologists, not to identify so closely with animals that we assume they have the same mental processes as we do, which can lead us to describe their behaviour in ways that suggest they have minds and a capacity for decision-making. To say that 'The mouse figured out how to get the cheese' or 'The rat decided he would rather search for the water than find a way out of the maze', involves a level of mentalistic theorising about animal behaviour that suggests intentions, a capacity to weigh up and evaluate alternatives, and other inner states.

But while it works in describing someone else's behaviour, it doesn't work quite so well in describing your own. When I say I am in pain, I am not describing what I do. Or at least it is not the whole story. To describe my behaviour may be the way *someone else* gets to know I am in pain, but it is not the way *I* know that *I* am in pain. When I tell you I am in pain I am not describing what I do, I am describing how I feel.

Although Ryle is right that behaviourism is important as an antidote to the all too easy assumptions we make about our minds being just containers of ideas inhabited by ghostly entities and processes, we are still forced to confront Nagel's 'insideness': that sense of knowing what it is like to be that living thing; an awareness, a state of consciousness. Not everything can be described from the outside. And, indeed, as we saw in the previous chapter with materialism, you cannot consistently argue that you never think, but just act in a certain way. By arguing the case, you are denying it. You are forced to confront the hard rock of Descartes' *cogito*: the ultimate acknowledgement of the mental, that there is something that thinks existing beyond the patterns of behaviour.

4.3 Functionalism: the mind as computer

Perhaps it is as natural for us in the age of computers to think about minds and brains as computers as it was for Newton in the seventeenth century to think about light as molecules acting and reacting like billiards balls. But the questions that have been raised by the analogy are not so much whether the mind could be a product of the brain, but whether mental processes could be based on physical processes that are not brain processes.

Functionalism, a modern successor to behaviourism, claims that minds are the product not so much of particular kinds of material, but rather of the relations of their parts. In other words, the mind might just be a function of the patterns of neurological activity in the brain. Like the software of a computer it might just be an elaborate program, the product of immensely complicated patterns embodied in the physical workings of the brain. And if this is the case, that the mind is not that different from a computer, could it not be possible for mental processes to be the product of a computer and its complex network of chips and circuit boards?

Most psychologists have recognized that the traditional structural approach to the mind as simply a product of the brain is inadequate. Function and human activity are particularly important. The notion of man as a purely rational animal needs to be modified to take into account the importance of impulse, emotions, habit and custom in explaining his behaviour. The functionalist argues that all of these, our perceptions, beliefs, thoughts, desires, interact with one another as part of a system of inner causes, all partially defined in terms of their relations and interactions with one another. We might perceive something, which causes us to have a certain belief, which in turn leads us to form other beliefs as a result of thinking about it. This might then interact with our desires and cause in us intentional action to meet those desires.

The functionalist, therefore, attempts to form a systems account of psychological states, events and processes. Mental states can be explained in terms of a system of inner causes. Functionalists argue that we can define them by three types of relations: those that cause them, what effects they have on other mental states, and what effects they have on behaviour. Though not a form of materialism, in that it doesn't say in what sort of thing this system occurs, nevertheless, it is not inconsistent with materialism. The system may be formed out of nerve cells that make up the brain, although it could as easily be formed out of non-material features of the mind.

Even so, the analogy with the computer has clear limits. John Searle, the American philosopher, argues that we have consistently exaggerated the capacity of computers to develop an intelligence that would threaten human intelligence. Indeed it may not be the case that the mind works anything like a computer. It is quite conceivable that it works on different levels in parallel in a vastly more complicated and faster manner than any computer.

■ 5. Conclusion

At times this may have seemed an obscure topic to examine, what with talk of substances, monads and God's pre-established harmony. But, although we may not be able to define adequately the relations between mind and body, like self-identity it has a significance that reaches beyond us to what we expect and hope from others. Our capacity to think and feel, and to have ideas and values, is central to individuality, personality and a sense of self. It gives meaning and value to our lives. If we are just 'automata', as T. H. Huxley argues, there can be no more meaning to our lives than there is to a leaf falling from a tree in autumn or to any natural event. Whether or not we get our university degree is not something we can alter; it is already determined by genetic and other factors for which we can claim no credit. Of course we may try to convince ourselves that our achievements are significant, that they have meaning and value, but we cannot claim any responsibility ourselves. And by the same token, nor can we be held morally responsible for our actions. If we are mere automata, the product of forces beyond our control, we have no free will.

Beyond our own sense of value and identity it matters, therefore, whether we are a mind with powers to make decisions and take genuine control of our lives, or whether we are merely fooling ourselves. Plato's influence on western life has left us with the optimistic notion of the mind as the seat of reason through which we can control our lives and passions. But in the twentieth century Freud painted a very different picture. Man is ruled by his 'id', the source of his passionate nature which is largely beyond the control of reason. His ego, representing his rational and reflective side, is weak and too easily dominated by his passions and the outside world.

Whichever account we accept determines just what we think man is capable of by exercising self-discipline and control. In 1930 Freud published *Civilization and its Discontents*, in which he examines humanity's need to create illusions, like God, to comfort them in the face of their helplessness. Reflecting on the horrors of the First World War, his conclusions are pessimistic as to whether man can control his aggression and his urge to dominate. In 1937 he expressed this pessimism ironically in a comment to a friend made after the burning of his books in Berlin: 'What progress we are making,' he reflected. 'In the Middle Ages they would have burned me. Now they are content with burning my books.'

■ Questions

1. What in your view are the strengths and weaknesses of behaviourism?

2. If human beings have minds and bodies, dualism must be correct. Do you agree?

3. a) Explain the theory of interactionism.

   b) What in your view are its main strengths and weaknesses?

4. 'No version of behaviourism can account successfully for the fact that an inner life exists and it has no behavioural manifestations.' Discuss.

5. Outline and illustrate the main criticisms of dualism.

6. Explain and critically evaluate the mind-brain identity theory.

■ Recommended reading

Descartes, R. 'The Passions of the Soul' (1649) and 'Principles of Philosophy' in *The Philosophical Writings of Descartes*, trans. J. Cottingham, R. Stoothoff and D. Murdoch (Cambridge: Cambridge University Press, 1985), Vol. I., for his classic statement of dualistic interactionism.

Leibniz, Gottfried, *The New System and Associated Contemporary Texts*, (ed. R. S. Woolhouse and R. Francks) (Oxford: Clarendon, 1997), for parallelism.

Spinoza, B. *Ethics*, trans. A. Boyle (London: Dent, 1993), for the dual-aspect theory.

Dewey, J. *The Quest for Certainty* (New York: Minton Blach, 1929).

Huxley, Thomas. *Animal Automatism and Collected Essays* (New York: reprinted Greenwood Press, 1968), for epiphenomenalism.

Ryle, G. *The Concept of Mind* (Harmondsworth: Penguin, 1990), Chapters 1, 2 and 5.

Searle, J. R. *The Rediscovery of the Mind* (Cambridge, Mass.: Massachusetts Institute of Technology Press, 1992).

 The note structure to accompany this chapter can be downloaded from our website.

The Essence of Self

Key issues

▶ What are the qualities that characterize someone as an individual?

▶ What is it that distinguishes you from someone else?

▶ How do you identify someone as being the same individual over time?

▶ What is it about you without which you wouldn't be you?

▶ What are the essential features of the self? Is the body even part of our selves?

▶ Can the self be separated from the body, or even from the wider social context in which we find ourselves?

What are the qualities that characterize someone as an individual, and distinguish them from other individuals? How do you identify someone as being the same individual over time? What is it about you without which you wouldn't be yourself? These questions relate to who we are, to the nature of our selves, and many philosophical accounts have sought to address these questions, to explore the self and ask who we are.

■ 1. The meaning of identity

Who we are is by no means a straightforward question with an obvious answer. The self is not simply 'me'. We often think of the self as something within us, as that which is most central or essential to who we are. In this spirit, we might talk of our true self, our identity, our soul. Even quite normally there are times when we want to say that our behaviour does not express 'who we really are', that we 'weren't ourselves' when we said or did what we did. That is, we want to say that not all of our behaviour expresses our true selves or nature, only what might be called our 'authentic' behaviour.

But it is then that questions arise about what the self is, what are the features that characterize it, what aspects of our existence are not essential to it. Is the body even part of our selves? A number of philosophers have thought of the self as something immaterial or spiritual, distinct from the mere physical body. Others have insisted that the self cannot be separated from the body, or indeed from the wider social context in which we find ourselves. In this and the following chapter we will look at a number of philosophical accounts of the self, which will take us from medieval religious thinking to twentieth-century post-structuralist philosophy.

■ 2. The essence of the self

2.1 The religious conception

The medieval religious view of the self reflected the wider understanding of the world current at the time: the medieval world-view as constructed by the Catholic church and combined Christian doctrines and ancient Greek science. The world was seen as an ordered and meaningful cosmos, created by God and expressing his will. All the elements of nature, including human beings, had their proper place in God's grand scheme of things. This account made use of Aristotle's 'teleological' view that things in nature exist for a purpose or *telos*. You could explain everything in nature by working out what it was for, what purpose it served. For the Christian thinkers, the purpose things have is a God-given one. God created the world, and everything has a role or purpose within God's overall plan.

Against this background, we can understand the medieval notion of the self. Human beings also have their proper role or purpose within the God-given order. To understand the world is to grasp this order, along with one's proper place within it. The self here is defined in terms of its role in the greater scheme of things. Being your self, being a subject, means bringing yourself into harmony with this order, conforming to your place in the order of things

The thirteenth-century philosopher and theologian Thomas Aquinas provides a good example of this way of thinking. It is he above all who brings together Christian doctrine and Aristotle's thinking in the vision of the universe as a meaningful cosmos, with each element having its proper role or function. Human beings in particular have their role or purpose built into their very nature. When we comprehend this purpose in our nature, this tells us the kind of life we ought to lead. Aquinas makes this the basis of his moral theory, his account of how we ought to act. Some ways of behaving are said to be morally right because they are natural, in conformity with our nature and its purposes, and others to be wrong because they are unnatural, not in keeping with human nature. We can also say that living properly is a matter of 'being ourselves', conforming to our nature and hence to our place in the God-given natural order. Thus the self here is defined, and also limited, by an essential purpose, bound simply to realize an intrinsic nature or purpose given to us by God.

In the sixteenth and seventeenth centuries, however, this religious world-view came under increasing attack. The key impetus for this was the rise of modern science: the new scientific way of thinking that develops through thinkers like Bacon, Descartes and Locke, and is legitimized by the scientific successes of Galileo and Newton. The world that comes into view with the science and philosophy of the modern period is no longer imbued with purpose, meaning or divine will. Scientific thinking, based on experience, empirical observation and the mapping of mathematical regularities, calls into question the whole idea of the universe as a meaningful order. In the course of what is sometimes called 'demythologization' or 'disenchantment', nature is stripped of any inherent purpose or significance. It is reduced to no more than a collection of material bodies or particles, mechanically interacting.

Now, there is no room for the Christian-Aristotelian kind of explanation of the behaviour of things in terms of purposes, what Aristotle called final causes. The behaviour of things is now to be explained in terms of what Aristotle called 'efficient causes', in which one thing brings about a change in another. Everything that happens is as the result of the mechanical interactions of particles, interactions governed by universal natural laws which can be formulated mathematically, working blindly and without purpose. And with the destruction of the religious view of nature, and the revised view of external nature as meaningless, disenchanted matter, a new kind of selfhood or subjectivity emerges. Now, the self is no longer understood in terms of an essential, God-given purpose. We do not define ourselves in terms of conforming to a larger order. Rather, we have to look within ourselves to find out who we are, the purpose and meaning of our existence. As Charles Taylor puts it, the modern self has to become a 'self-defining subject'.

2.2 Descartes and the 'soul'

This modern view of the self finds expression in the work of René Descartes, who, as we said earlier, is sometimes referred to as the father of modern philosophy. In his account, the self is no longer part of some larger meaningful order of nature, but rather a non-physical subject of experience, essentially distinct from the body and from nature more generally.

Descartes arrives at this conception of the self in his *Meditations on First Philosophy* (1641), the project of which is to find certain foundations of knowledge. As we have seen, to this end he pursues his method of radical scepticism or doubt, questioning all his beliefs to see if there are any that cannot be doubted and are thus certain. By this method he quickly arrives at the conclusion that the only thing that is certain is that I exist. I can doubt the evidence of my senses, the existence of the external world, even the existence of my own body, but I cannot doubt that I exist. When I am doubting, I am thinking, and if I think I must exist in order to do the thinking.

But Descartes then proceeds to a more controversial conclusion: that what I essentially am is a thing that thinks, a thinking thing, and that this is all I am. If I can doubt the existence of my body, then my physical characteristics cannot be essential to who I am. I could be myself without my body. Thus, the self is essentially mental. And if I am essentially a thing that thinks, I am only accidentally connected to my body. My self is essentially disembodied.

In this manner Descartes establishes the self as a thinking thing that is distinct from the material world, including its own body. And since the self is separate from a larger natural order, we no longer define ourselves through conformity with a larger order, but must find our purpose and meaning within ourselves.

As we saw in the last chapter, Descartes' account of the self involves a dualistic picture of the human being. Overall, the human being is made up of two very different kinds of stuff, or 'substance': mental or spiritual substance (mind or soul), and physical or material substance (body). While the body is a physical substance with properties like having mass and occupying space, the mind is a non-material substance, the seat of consciousness and mental states like thinking and experiencing. Being non-physical, it is a ghostly kind of entity that does not have mass or occupy space. More important for our purposes in this chapter, for Descartes I am essentially my mind, a spiritual or mental being. It is possible for the mind to exist separately from its body, and even if I were to lose my body I would still be me. The body is not essential to who I am.

What follows from this is a particular kind of account of personal identity. The general question of personal identity is: what makes me the same me, what makes someone the same self or person, over

time? The answer we give to this question depends very much on our conception of what the human being is. As we've seen, given Descartes' dualist view of the human being, I am essentially my mind, a spiritual or mental being, and not my body. So what is essential for me to be me over a period of time is to have the same mind. This means that I would be the same person if I were, say, reincarnated in a different body, or if my body died and disappeared entirely, just as long as my mind continued to exist.

The idea of the self as a non-physical substance distinct from the body is an appealing picture since it allows us to think of our selves as something spiritual, rising above our coarse physical bodies, and providing the basis for our 'higher' capacities like thinking and reasoning. As we saw in the last chapter, however, it is more problematic when we consider how two such utterly different entities as mind and body can interact, as they seem to when we are physically hurt and then feel pain, or when we decide to do something and then physically act on it.

And while we have access to our own minds, we are completely disconnected from the minds of others, which causes problems for personal identity as well. Usually we would feel quite confident in claiming that someone is the same person we saw yesterday, because they have the same physical appearance and ways of acting. However on the dualist view we can never be sure. Someone is the same person only if they have the same mind, and this is something that another person cannot possibly observe.

2.3 Locke and memories

By contrast, the English philosopher John Locke offered a different account of the self, using an approach that differed significantly from that of Descartes. Whereas Descartes thought we could establish important truths about the world and ourselves, our existence and nature, through our reasoning ability alone – the 'rationalist' approach to knowledge – Locke saw knowledge as being based on careful observation and experience – the empiricist approach. He offers a reflective analysis of how we experience our self in our everyday existence. In the chapter entitled 'On Personal Identity', in his *An Essay Concerning Human Understanding* (1690), Locke argues that a person is 'a thinking intelligent being, that has reason and reflection, and can consider itself, the same thinking thing, in different times and places; which it does by that consciousness which is inseparable from thinking, and, as it seems to me, inseparable from it.'

So Locke's definition of a self or person emphasizes reason, consciousness and self-consciousness. A rational being is conscious, able to think; and self-consciousness is inseparable from thinking because for Locke it is not possible to do something consciously, such as thinking or perceiving, without also being conscious of doing so. So consciousness is always accompanied by self-consciousness. And this self-consciousness is central to personhood. A person has a sense of themselves, and of their continuity and identity over time as the same person. When we see, hear and so on, we know that we do so; we have self-consciousness. As Locke puts it, 'by this [self-consciousness] everyone is to himself what he calls a self.'

From this, Locke's notion of personal identity follows. A person is aware of themselves, and personal identity – the sameness of a rational being – is a matter of continuing consciousness. That is, as long as we have the same consciousness we have the same self, the same person. Personal identity extends as far back in time as this consciousness extends. So as far as I can remember being the same person, doing and thinking certain things and so on, then I am that person. What makes me the same person as the child playing in the schoolyard is that I can remember myself as a child playing in the schoolyard. That is, I don't simply remember someone playing in the playground, but I have the memories of myself playing. We can put Locke's account of personal identity another way and say that, for Locke, memory is the criterion for personal identity, since this awareness of past actions is a matter of my being able to remember being the same person, doing and thinking certain things.

On this account, a person is not the same thing as a human being, a certain kind of living biological being. Selfhood here is tied not to particular bodies but to consciousness. So if for example I find I have memories of a previous life or previous actions, say as Julius Caesar, then I am the same person as Julius Caesar, even though our bodies might be completely different. At the same time, Locke distinguishes his view from that of Descartes. For Descartes, what you are most essentially is your mind or soul, where this is understood as an unextended, immaterial, non-physical

substance, distinct from the body which is an extended material substance. You could lose your body and you would still be you. As long as there is the same immaterial substance, you are the same you. Locke does think that there has to be a substratum, a substance, which does the thinking, perceiving and so on, but for him there is no reason why it should be an *immaterial* substance. Perhaps a material substance can also think. Even if we do in fact have an immaterial soul substance, Locke argues that personal identity does not depend on the continuation of such a substance, but only on continuity of consciousness. So even if your immaterial soul substance changed, you would still be you as long as you had the same consciousness.

One question that immediately arises from Locke's view of personal identity is that if this is purely a matter of continuity of consciousness, what holds this consciousness together to form one whole person? The difficulty arises because, as Locke himself recognizes, there are breaks in this consciousness. We forget things that we have done; we do not necessarily think of things we have done even if we are capable of remembering them; and during sleep, we do not have any consciousness, thoughts or memories at all. So the question is, at these times, am I the same consciousness, the same self? And does this mean that if I forget things I have done, I am no longer the person who did them, but a different person? Or that if I do something while I was drunk or sleepwalking, but have no recollection of doing so, that it was not me who did these things?

Locke's account does seem to commit us to this kind of view. And there are important moral implications here. Locke himself holds that to be a person, a rational, thinking being, is also to be an agent capable of living in accordance with moral laws and requirements, and capable of taking responsibility for what he does. So there is an important moral dimension to his notion of personhood. Persons are responsible for what they do, and can be rewarded or punished accordingly.

But if personal identity is created by sameness of consciousness, by sameness of memory, then this would imply that without consciousness of doing something, without memory of doing something, then it was not me who did it. I would not be responsible for whatever it was that was done. And hence, to punish me for something I did in my sleep, when I was out sleepwalking, would be unjust; since I have no memory or consciousness of the act, it was literally not me who did it. Likewise, the sober man is not responsible for what he did when he was completely drunk, or the sane man for acts committed when he was insane.

This does indeed appear to be Locke's view, that if I cannot remember doing something then I literally did not do it, and am not responsible for the action. And on the face of it, this is not very plausible. Locke's account also leads to difficulties like those pointed out by the eighteenth-century Scottish philosopher Thomas Reid, who posed what has become known as the 'brave officer' paradox. Imagine a brave officer. As a boy, he steals apples; as a grown man, he is an army officer, decorated for heroism; and as an old man, he becomes forgetful. Now suppose the army officer can remember stealing the apples. The old man can also remember stealing the apples, but cannot remember being the brave officer. It would seem then, on Locke's criterion of personal identity, that the brave officer is the small boy, and the old man is the small boy, but the old man is not the brave officer. This seems absurd, and goes against our ordinary way of thinking.

2.4 Hume and the idea of the self as a fiction

Now compare Locke with Hume, who continued in the empiricist tradition, holding that direct experience is the only genuine source of knowledge. As we have seen, for Locke your self is not tied to any particular underlying substance, but depends on your consciousness of it. Using the same empiricist view that knowledge depends on experience, Hume ended up with an even more radical account of the self. In the same consistent way in which he argued that through experience we cannot discover a 'cause', but only 'constant conjunction', he argues that if we examine our reflective experience of ourselves, we discover that we have no self.

Hume discusses the self in 'On Personal Identity', in his *Treatise of Human Nature* (1739–40). First of all he completely rejects the substance view of the soul or mind, which originally appears with Descartes, who argues that the mind is essentially an immaterial, unextended substance distinct from the body which is an extended material substance. Locke also thought that there must be a spiritual substance underlying the operations of the mind, but by this he simply meant a substance that thinks. It was not necessarily a non-material substance;

perhaps a material substance could also think. Some immaterial substances might be associated with some material things in a way not clearly understood.

But are claims about an underlying substance, material or non-material, consistent with empiricism? Logic may demand that there must be something which has these mental properties of thinking, feeling and so on, but empiricism holds that our claim to know something must be based on experience (what Hume calls 'perceptions' or 'impressions'). So if we are to talk meaningfully of an inner, spiritual substance, we should be able to find it by looking into ourselves. But as Locke admits, we cannot do this. And Hume agrees, only he is more consistent in his empiricism. For Hume, we could only claim that there was an underlying spiritual substance if we could look inward and observe it. But because we find no such entity within us, because we have no experience of it, Hume rejects the idea of an underlying spiritual substance.

The question now is, if there is no substance, how exactly are we to understand the self and personal identity? Hume notes that our idea of self or person is of something that is a constant point of reference, to which all our perception and ideas are supposed to be related. And Hume's position is that if we have any clear idea of such a self, it must be derived from a constant experience of it within us. However, when Hume looks within himself, he can find no constant perception of the self, and as a result, there is no such idea. All our perceptions are distinct and separate from each other, and we can discover no self apart from or underlying those perceptions. Here there's a famous passage where he describes his failure: 'For my part, when I enter most intimately into what I call myself, I always stumble on some particular perception or other, of heat or cold, light or shade, love or hatred, pain or pleasure. I never catch myself at any time without a perception, and never can observe anything but the perception.'

Hume's conclusion then is that the mind is a kind of theatre where various distinct perceptions appear, mingle and glide away. There is no identity here, no self to tie these perceptions together. In the end, says Hume, there is 'nothing but a bundle or collection of different perceptions, which succeed each other with an inconceivable rapidity, and are in perpetual flux and movement.' This is sometimes referred to as the bundle theory of the self. There is just a collection of different perceptions, in perpetual movement.

And yet we still take ourselves to be continuing selves. This is our common-sense belief. So Hume now gives an account of why we believe that we are continuous selves, why we tend to attribute identity and simplicity to the mind. This is his account of personal identity, and it is a psychological account. It involves the attribution of a fictitious identity to the mind. We do this, in Hume's account, with objects in general. We also experience the world as a succession of distinct perceptions; but we come to see some as experiences of the same thing by ignoring interruptions or minor changes in what we experience, and by coming to see the parts we experience as related to each other. Thus we ascribe sameness or identity to things without strictly speaking observing it. In other words, it is the mind's work that constructs identity, not anything real corresponding to identity in the objects themselves.

Hume thinks that a similar process is involved when we ascribe identity to the mind. That is, we make the same errors about ascribing identity with regard to ourselves as we do with objects around us. Strictly speaking, as we've seen, with the mind all we experience is a multiplicity of distinct perceptions. If we are to think that all these perceptions constitute one mind, it cannot be because of some real connection we observe between these perceptions, for there is none. We attribute identity to our minds only because of the effect that these different perceptions have on the mind that is contemplating them, because the mind comes to see these separate perceptions as related to each other. Finally, according to Hume, to justify ascribing identity to a multiplicity of perceptions in this way, we may go so far as to invent a uniting principle here, a permanent self distinct from our perceptions. This is what philosophers like Descartes have tended to do, to invent something that remains unchanging throughout the successive changes, something that is not directly accessible to observation. They call this substance, or in the case of the person, soul or self.

It is worth noting that the account that Hume gives is completely counterintuitive. It is hard to believe that the mind is just a succession of different perceptions, a bundle. This seems to fly in the face of common sense. The common sense view is that we are in some way a continuing, identical self. This is where a Cartesian substance theory of the self might seem to have an advantage over Hume's bundle-theory. A substance theory of the self fits in with this idea of ourselves as an enduring, unitary self. Hume however doesn't care that his account is counterintuitive. He produces an account of why we ordinarily think of ourselves as enduring and unitary, and hence why we would, of course, find his philosophical view counterintuitive.

Interestingly enough, Hume himself came to have doubts about his account of personal identity, which he expressed in the appendix later added to the *Treatise*. One possible explanation for these doubts is that Hume came to see his account as involving a vicious circle. That is, in his account, we get the idea that we have a unitary self because the mind comes to see the distinct perceptions it has of itself as related, and thus comes to consider this series of perceptions as a continued view of the same mind. But in order to relate these perceptions in the first place, it seems that these perceptions must have appeared constantly in that person's mind. So it seems that we must have a continuing mind in order to explain personal identity. In other words, to explain personal identity, we have to appeal to personal identity, to a continuing mind or self, which leaves us in a vicious circle. It seems that even if we can say that our notion of personal identity is constructed out of various perceptions, there must be something distinct from these perceptions, something that has not been explained, which is responsible for that construction.

2.5 Kant: the self as transcendental

We saw in Chapter 6 how Hume's radical empiricism awoke Immanuel Kant at the end of the eighteenth century from his 'dogmatic slumber', only to see Kant in turn introduce a revolution into philosophical thinking. The same occurs here, too: he introduces a new way of thinking about the self. In the face of empiricists like Hume, Kant argued that we do not experience the world as a stream of disconnected sensations. Rather, we perceive an organized, orderly world of objects. This is the world that we know. Experience is still vital for this knowledge. Kant agrees with the empiricists that knowledge needs to be anchored in experience. So experience is a necessary component of knowledge. But he does not think that experience is sufficient for knowledge. In the introduction to the *Critique of Pure Reason* (1781) he announces that 'there can be no doubt that all our knowledge begins with experience [but] although all our knowledge begins with experience, it does not follow that it arises out of experience.'

As we saw earlier, what is missing from the empiricist picture, for Kant, is the mind's contribution, the contribution of reason. For Kant, the orderly world that we are familiar with, the world of things existing in space and time, interacting causally with one another, is the result of both reason and experience. We have experiences, but by itself experience is a meaningless confusion of impressions. The orderly world that we know only emerges when the mind or reason organizes these experiences.

The role of reason, for Kant, is to order and organize our experience, and it does so in terms of various general forms or principles which, as we saw in Chapter 9, Kant calls 'categories'. We do not have to learn these principles; they are *a priori* or pre-given ways of organizing and relating our impressions. As we saw in Chapter 6 Kant calls this his 'Copernican Revolution'. Like Copernicus, who turned our thinking about the universe on its head, so too does Kant turn thinking about knowledge on its head. He rejects the empiricist view that we passively receive experience from the world, in favour of the idea that we actively organize our experience, constructing the orderly world that we know.

But how does this relate to Kant's notion of the self? In fact, the self is fundamental to Kant's account, because it is the self, the mind, that actively organizes experience, in terms of the basic forms or categories. It is a necessary condition for knowledge. We could not have any experience of knowledge if there was no self that had these experiences, and it is through this self that experiences are organized into a meaningful whole.

But what is the nature of this underlying self? It is not the human being that we can know through experience or can study through science. This is the self that is a certain age, has brown hair, blue eyes, a certain physiology, and so on. This is what Kant calls the 'empirical self', ourselves as an object of experience, part of the knowable world of space, time and causality. The Kantian self, properly speaking, is not an object of knowledge at all, but the active subject that, by organizing and unifying experience, makes knowledge possible. As such, it transcends sense experience, and Kant refers to it as the 'transcendental self'.

So for Kant, Hume went wrong because he was looking for the self in the wrong place. He examined the contents of his mind and could not find his self, because the self is not an object of experience. It is the transcendental activity that organizes experiences into an intelligible whole. Kant's conception of the self is closer to that of Descartes. Like Descartes, he sees the self as the starting point for knowledge. But for Kant, the self is much more active, organizing experiences and constructing an orderly world. It should be stressed that he is not saying here that the self constructs the world itself. What it constructs and organizes is our experience of the world, producing the orderly world that is the only world we can know. Of the world as it is outside of our experience of it, the 'noumenal world', the world as it is 'in itself', there is nothing we can say.

Now it might seem that we cannot say very much about this transcendental self either, since it too lies beyond what we can experience. But Kant in fact has quite a lot to say about it, especially in connection with his moral thinking. The transcendental ego is not only the source of the organizing principles of knowledge, the knowing subject; it is also the source of 'agency', of the will behind our actions, and in this capacity it is central to Kant's account of morality.

In his account of knowledge, the self, through its rational activity, imposes principles upon the world of experience. In his moral theory, the self, through its rational activity, imposes principles on itself. That is, it shapes its will, determines what ought to be done, in accordance with principles it rationally formulates for itself. Here, the rational principles being imposed are moral principles, understood as general laws laying down what we ought to do. It is important to note here that in Kant's moral theory, rationality is not reason in its theoretical, cognitive function, but practical reason, reason understood as capable of determining the principles by which we ought to live, what we ought to do.

So Kant's conception of the active rational self, the transcendental self, plays a central role in his moral theory too, as we will see in Chapter 22. And here also we find a distinction between ourselves as objects in the world and as active subjects. It is only in so far as we are active rational subjects that we are moral agents. This means that as moral agents, we have to stand apart from the natural world, including our own natural makeup, our physiological and even our particular psychological makeup. This includes our ordinary desires, inclinations, passions and feelings. In so far as these hold sway over our behaviour, we are nothing but objects, determined by external forces.

So to be moral agents, we have to exclude all natural desires, inclinations and feelings, and act purely out of rational motivations. This exclusion of all non-rational, natural influences also plays a part in Kant's notion of freedom. In being moral, in acting in accordance with our reason alone, we are radically free. The moral self is radically free in that it is not determined by nature and its causal laws, even by its own natural makeup, but rather determines itself, by rationally formulating its own moral laws. It is rationally self-determining, or to use Kant's term, autonomous. This stands as one of the most powerful formulations of the modern conception of the self as a self-defining subject.

■ 3. Conclusion

What is noticeable, however, is that the Kantian self is extremely abstract. It is not only understood as being independent from desires, inclinations and feelings, making the self a highly rational but also austere and rather inhuman entity. It is also taken to be independent of all social and historical circumstances and influences. For Kant, the social and historical realm belongs to the realm of the scientifically knowable, and the human being as a rational subject must necessarily stand apart from this realm.

As a result, however, Kant's rational subject comes across as isolated, asocial and ahistorical, standing apart from social relationships, cultural traditions and historical circumstances. Some of Kant's nineteenth-century successors, like Karl Marx, argued that the subject can only exist in the midst of society and history, and is necessarily conditioned by its social and historical circumstances. We will come to Marx in the next chapter. But first we will turn to the influence Kant had on subsequent thinking about the self which takes as its central concern the individual and individual self-determination.

■ Questions

1. What does Descartes take the essence of the self to be? How well do his arguments support his conclusions?

2. What is it to be a person and have self-identity?

3. Is Kant's transcendental ego a satisfactory answer to the problems that Hume raises?

4. 'Kant's account of the transcendental ego deals exclusively with the form, rather than the empirical content of the Self.' Discuss.

5. 'Persons change from moment to moment; they really only exist momentarily. The idea that they individually survive for many years is a convenient fiction which makes social relations and social organization possible.' Discuss.

■ Recommended reading

Descartes, R. *Meditations of First Philosophy* in *Discourse on Method and Other Writings*, trans. F. E. Sutcliffe (Harmondsworth: Penguin, 1970).

Locke, J. Of identity and diversity, in *An Essay Concerning Human Understanding* (1690) (London: Fontana, 1973), Book 2, Chapter XXVII.

Hume, D. Of Personal Identity, in *A Treatise of Human Nature* (1739–40) (London and New York: Dent and Dutton, 1966), Vol. I, Part IV, Section VI. (Hume himself came to have doubts about his account of personal identity. Read the appendix later added to the *Treatise*.)

Kant, I. *Critique of Pure Reason* (1781) (London: Dent, 1993).

Copleston, F. C. *Aquinas* (Harmondsworth: Penguin, 1967).

 The note structure to accompany this chapter can be downloaded from our website.

Creating the Self

Contents

Key issues

▶ Are we free of all natural and social forces to determine our own selves?

▶ How can women be genuinely self-defining subjects, when social and cultural influences around them appear to constitute much of their oppression? Does their best chance of freedom lie in being more like men?

▶ What does it mean to exist as a particular human being? How are we to live and what are we to do with our lives?

▶ Is it impossible for us to answer these questions in terms of our conscious desires, intentions and wishes, when our unconscious drives shape much of our behaviour?

▶ Or is it the position we occupy in the social and economic system that determines our consciousness of self?

▶ Alternatively, has the meaning we create little to do with us as conscious subjects? Is it more the product of the language through which we express it?

▶ Or perhaps what we regard as our intentional behaviour as subjects free to create our selves and shape the societies in which we live is nothing of the sort. Perhaps it is the product of structured systems with their own rules of combination and transformation, which, unknown to us, determine the meaning of social and cultural phenomena?

Kant's vision of the autonomous, self-determining individual appears in a number of recent philosophical contexts. One of its strongest expressions in twentieth-century thought is in the movement known as existentialism, which flourished in France in the 1950s, particularly through the work of Jean-Paul Sartre.

■ 1. Existentialism: inventing the self

Existentialism holds that human beings are above all free, choosing subjects. In their choosing they are not determined by natural forces, or by social circumstances. They are completely free to make themselves, to choose the sort of person they are to be. So existentialism presents a picture of the self as a completely self-defining subject. Indeed it is a picture that is even more radical than Kant's, because existentialists hold that our choices of ourselves are not even determined by rational considerations. We choose ourselves without any guidance or rules whatsoever. And it is only in so doing that we acquire a self in the sense of a certain character, essence or identity. In so far as we have a self, a determinate character, it is one that we have invented for ourselves, through our free choices.

1.1 Sartre: existence precedes essence

In his 1945 lecture 'Existentialism is a Humanism', published later as *Existentialism and Humanism*, Sartre formulates his radical conception of the human being as a self-defining subject, using the terminology of 'essence' and 'existence'. What Sartre calls the 'first principle' of existentialism, that 'existence precedes essence', amounts to the assertion that human beings are absolutely free to choose themselves. For Sartre, a thing's essence is what can be expressed about it in a definition, what determines its purpose or function, and what makes it behave in a certain way. Its existence is simply the fact that it happens to be a particular item in the world. In these terms Sartre makes a sharp distinction between human beings and other things in the world. For all things except human beings, 'essence precedes existence' – they have an essence that determines their purpose and behaviour, and sums up what they are.

The claim that for human beings 'existence precedes essence' means that human beings have no pre-given essence, character or function that defines them or determines their behaviour. It is only by first existing and then exercising our freedom in choosing and acting that we come to acquire an essence, to be a certain sort of person, to have a character. As Sartre puts it,

> man first of all exists, encounters himself, surges up in the world – and defines himself afterward. If man as the existentialist sees him, is not definable, it is because to begin with he is nothing. He will not be anything until later, and then he will be what he makes of himself.

It is because we lack any pre-given essence that we are free, free from prior determinations, and free to make or create ourselves through our own willpower. And we are not even bound by the definition, the self, that we choose for ourselves. Whatever self we try to become, we can always

Jean-Paul Sartre (1905–1980)

A philosopher, novelist and playwright, Sartre became the symbol of the committed intellectual in the twentieth century. When he died over 50,000 attended his funeral and still today the stream of people visiting his grave each day never dries up. Born in Paris he studied at the Sorbonne, where he met Simone de Beauvoir, who became his lifelong companion and intellectual collaborator. He studied in Germany in the 1930s with Husserl and Heidegger. He spent the war years in Paris where he completed his major philosophical work *Being and Nothingness* (1943). Although a central figure of the French left and an admirer of the Soviet Union, he was an outspoken critic of the crushing of the Hungarian uprising in 1956.

In *Being and Nothingness* he places human consciousness, or nothingness, in opposition to being, or thingness; consciousness is nonmatter and thus escapes all determinism. In his postwar lecture, later published as *Existentialism and Humanism* (1946), he argues this radical freedom carries with it the responsibility for the welfare of all. If we attempt to escape this burden, disowning our responsibility on the grounds that our actions are determined, we resort to bad faith. We act 'in' ourselves as if we were a mere thing, rather than 'for' ourselves in which we make ourselves through our own choices. Sartre, therefore, locates the essential nature of human existence in our capacity for choice.

choose ourselves differently. Human existence is a constant striving to acquire a self, a determinate essence or character, that is never ultimately successful.

Sartre does not deny that there are determined aspects of our existence. Physically or biologically, it's true, human beings have a pre-existent makeup or essence. But morally, as a person in the full sense, our existence remains to be determined by the exercise of our free will. There are certainly limits to what we can make ourselves be by the exercise of this freedom. There is a human 'situation', within which the exercise of our freedom takes place, which includes not only our biological makeup but also the natural environment, social structures and so on, within which we exist.

But these limits do not determine our behaviour

as the essence of non-human objects determines their behaviour. Rather, human beings freely determine themselves in relation to these limits. Sartre's example: I am a sexual being, able to have relations with a being of the other sex and able to have children. This is part of my situation. But this situation doesn't determine what I will choose to do. Whether I'll choose to remain single, marry without having children, or marry and have children, is entirely up to me.

Sartre distinguishes his position both from Kant's account and from the older religious picture of the self. The dictum that our existence precedes our essence figures in Sartre's rejection of Christianity. For an object like a penknife, its essence precedes its existence; so the knife-maker can have an idea of the essence of the knife prior to the actual existence of the knife. It is this kind of conception, Sartre argues, that Christians rely on when they declare that human beings have an essence or a predetermined purpose and function.

For Christianity, there is a conception of what a human being is which dwells in the divine understanding, and which is realized when God creates human beings. Made by God to a formula, human beings automatically have certain values and pursue certain goals. This is Aquinas' view, for example. Human beings have a proper role and function that reflects their God-given nature. Sartre rejects this conception of humankind and all that accompanies it, in particular the idea that we have a God-given purpose, a divinely grounded set of values or morality. On similar grounds he also rejects eighteenth-century attempts to introduce the notion of 'human nature' as the basis for rules about how we ought to act, along with Kant's attempt to make reason the basis for morality. For Sartre, these are dishonest attempts to find a substitute for God.

To believe that my values, purposes and goals are simply given to me by God, a human nature or my rationality, or for that matter to suppose that my behaviour is determined by my biological makeup or by society, is for Sartre a form of 'bad faith', an attempt to evade my responsibility for myself, to deny my freedom. Certainly, having to define ourselves entirely is a heavy burden and the source of much anxiety. Bad faith protects us from the anguish of freedom and gives us a sense of security. But for Sartre it is a form of cowardice in the face of our freedom and a denial of what is central to our humanity.

Existentialism seeks to shatter the illusions of bad faith, to remind people that they are above all self-defining subjects. For Sartre, a properly human life is one which is lived 'authentically', in the awareness that we are free selves, responsible for our values and goals. It involves a heroic acceptance of our complete responsibility for what we are and what we do.

1.2 The feminist self: Simone de Beauvoir

However for modern feminists this may seem to have a hollow ring about it when all around them social and cultural influences define women in ways not of their own making. It was this challenge that Simone de Beauvoir took up. Like Sartre, with whom she had a lifelong association, she was an existentialist. Her most famous work, *The Second Sex* (1949), was a landmark text in the rise of modern feminism. It became a worldwide bestseller, raising feminist consciousness by arguing that the liberation of women was liberation of men too. Nevertheless, as an existentialist she had to explain how women could be genuinely self-defining subjects free of the illusions of bad faith, while acknowledging the social and cultural influences around them that constituted much of their oppression.

The problem can be best illustrated by the distinction between gender and sex. Gender is whatever there is to being male or female which cannot be attributed to innate bodily differences. In other words, it is socially created, whereas sex is what we believe to be biologically given. The difference finds its roots in Descartes' theory of the relationship between the mind and the body, on which feminists believe Western ideas of the self have largely been founded. This is a disembodied, autonomous self, free of all contextual constraints and in every instance the same as every other self. According to Descartes' model of the mind–body distinction, gender is the product of the mind free to be what it wants to be. The mind and consciousness transcend the body. As a result, humans, unlike animals, are not merely a product of their biology: on one side there is indeed the passive influence of nature, but on the other is the autonomous human will.

However, so influential has this model of the mind–body distinction been that many feminists believe society has learnt to accept the 'masculinity' of the mind and the 'femininity' of the body. In

**Brief lives
De Beauvoir, Simone**

Dates: 1908–1986
Born: Paris, France
Best known for: Being a founding theorist of
modern feminism and, along with J-P Sartre, a
key figure in French existentialism.

Major works: *The Second Sex* (1949).

other words, the self has become consciousness or
mind, smuggling into our understanding of the
very notion of human nature a sexist interpretation.
In her aptly titled book *The Man of Reason* (1979),
Genevieve Lloyd argues that when philosophers
talk about the 'Man of Reason' they are in fact not
talking about idealizations of human beings, as
might be thought, but about ideals of manhood.

Like many feminists, she traces this association
of reason with masculinity back to Descartes, who
argues, as we saw in Chapter 7, that all knowledge
is the result of self-evident truths (clear and distinct
ideas) and deductive reasoning. If we break down
what is complex and obscure into simple and self-
evident truths, we can then recombine them
through deductive reasoning to give us knowledge
of the world.

The structure of the outside world is identical
with the order of thought itself, with the very structure of the knowing mind. And even though we can
systematically doubt this, thereby opening up a gap
between our ideas and the material world, between
the structure of the mind and the structure of reality, the gap is immediately closed the moment we
accept, as Descartes does, that God is a truthful god,
who will not deceive us this way. Therefore, introspection into the nature of thought in an individual
mind gives us access to universal reason: 'God
given and God guaranteed.' The structure of reality,
according to Cartesian rationalism, is identical with
that of the mind. As Lloyd points out, this gives
reason a 'quasi-divine character'. Man is made in
God's image.

But the key to man's ability to reason and to gain
access to the structure of reality is his ability to shed
'the sensuous' from all thought. The 'fluctuating
testimony of the senses' tends to obscure our clear
and distinct ideas if we let it. Out of this, Lloyd
points out, there develop those common polariza-

tions that structure modern Western thinking: intellect as opposed to emotions, reason to imagination
and mind to matter. Before Descartes these were
contrasts within the rational, but afterwards mind
and matter were sharply distinguished.

Women became associated with matter and the
body. They were seen as impulsive and emotional,
lacking in rationality. Their special area of responsibility was the sensuous world of emotions and
imagination, while man, Lloyd argues, was to be
'trained out of his soft emotions and his sensuous-
ness ... because that is precisely what it is to be
rational.' Man was made in God's image, with
woman his companion. The separation of functions
based on Descartes' model of the mind and body
distinction was complete.

To illustrate the degree to which this might have
influenced the way we interpret gender differences
consider the very interesting question that Sherri
Ortner asks: is there anything that would lead all
cultures to place a lower value on women, as they
all appear to do? The answer she finds in the
contrasting notions of nature and culture. Put
simply, 'nature' is something every society seeks to
subdue and control in its own interests through
technology and other products of its own 'culture'.
So, culture is broadly equated with the notion of
the mind and human consciousness, the products
of which provide humanity with the means of
controlling and exploiting nature for its own ends.

But now, if we have all come to assume that
'mind' is masculine and 'body' feminine, this might
explain the pan-cultural second-class status for
women. If they have become identified with nature
and men with culture, as culture seeks to subsume
and transcend nature, so men seek to subordinate
and oppress women. Although Ortner in fact
defends the weaker thesis that women seem merely
to be closer to nature than men, she argues that
women still represent a lower order of being, less
transcendent over nature than men.

Given the problem, how should feminists
respond? They appear to face a dilemma. If they
argue that gender has little to do with sex, that it is
a socially created concept that transcends natural
distinctions, then femaleness is no longer distinctive, just one aspect of being human which coin-
cides with its opposite in socially created maleness.
Men and women simply have male and female
sides to their characters. Alternatively, if they argue
femaleness is distinctive, drawing it closer to sex
and arguing that there are differences between the

ways in which the sexes think, this appears to reinforce existing social stereotypes by making them natural.

Of course, to escape the dilemma feminists can argue that there is indeed a distinctive femaleness, but that the stereotypes are simply wrong: that femaleness not only has distinct characteristics, but that these are in many ways superior. Alternatively, for many of those who insist that gender transcends sex, a different concept is more important – that of 'personhood', which transcends both sex and gender. This allows them to argue for equality of the sexes; that regardless of gender we are rational people who are neither sexed nor gendered. Such an argument turns back the Cartesian clock, while at the same time explaining why so many postmodernist criticisms of Enlightenment assumptions have such resonance with feminists.

This brings us back to Simone de Beauvoir, who addresses the same issues by employing, in existentialism, what appears to be one of the most promising ways of responding to the social and cultural influences that have contributed to these gender distinctions. As we have seen the non-essentialist ideas of existentialism insist that there is nothing biological, social or cultural determining our self-identity. We are free to invent ourselves: free from all deterministic forces. All excuses we use to explain why we do not invent ourselves through our own commitment and choices are acts of bad faith.

De Beauvoir starts from these existentialist assumptions and sets out to address the problem of woman as the 'second sex', the 'perpetual Other' of man. By virtue of their humanity women have as much need for their freedom and autonomy as men. But by being culturally relegated to the status of mere 'Otherness' they are forced to endure forms of dependency and subordination that are incompatible with any notion of genuine freedom. She argues that while biological differences do not necessitate the oppression of women, 'the peculiarities that identify her as specifically a woman get their importance from the significance placed upon them.'

However, this signals an important departure from Sartre, in that de Beauvoir argues that a women's oppression means that she cannot experience in the first place the consciousness of freedom in existential philosophy, which is necessary if she is to be able to overcome all forms of servitude which are not voluntarily entered into. Significantly, this means two things: first that the freedom of the individual can be limited by social conditions; and, second, that it is not necessarily an example of bad faith for women's consciousness to be affected by such conditions. De Beauvoir seems to have been more aware than Sartre of the central weakness of *Being and Nothingness* (1943) in its neglect of the social context in which actions are taken and commitments made. Some even suggest that in this respect it was de Beauvoir's influence that led to the shift in Sartre's work from a 'philosophy of consciousness' to the more Marxist perspective of his later work.

Nevertheless, this does leave existentialism with problems, in that it cannot easily embrace the significance of such social, political and cultural influences, like patriarchy, to explain women's oppression without allowing in other factors that might explain what appears at face value to be cases of bad faith. Why not let in economic and social factors like class and race discrimination? It significantly blurs the argument, making it less clear that the individual is indeed free to invent herself and all excuses why she hasn't are merely examples of bad faith.

However, this is not to say that de Beauvoir believes women are incapable of transcending their situation, although the way they are to achieve it does not attract universal approval from modern feminists. Like Sartre she expresses a misogynist view of women, who are condemned by their biology and socialization to emotional dependence. Therefore, in order to realize themselves, to have more influence on affairs and enjoy the same freedom as men they must become more like men. Unlike men they must repudiate part of their nature, their 'Otherness', their femininity. In other words, women are oppressed by virtue of being feminine.

This contrasts with contemporary feminists, including those most influenced by postmodernism, who are more likely to assert the importance and value of femininity and the unconditional and irreducible 'difference' women present to a male-dominated society. Theirs is an unreserved celebration of the difference of women, who lack nothing – they are neither deficient nor subordinate. Where de Beauvoir saw liberation in women becoming more like men, their fight is against patriarchal oppression which devalues female qualities, depriving them of any power in a male dominated power structure.

1.3 Kierkegaard and Nietzsche

Although existentialism is best known as a twentieth-century movement, there are a number of nineteenth-century thinkers who can be seen as forerunners. These include the Danish philosopher Søren Kierkegaard, and the German philosopher Friedrich Nietzsche. During their lifetime both were lonely figures, not really understood by their contemporaries. However they have had a great deal of influence on twentieth-century existentialist thought, especially by turning the philosophical focus onto what it means to exist as an individual human being, and the idea of the self as an achievement, something we have to actively produce.

Turning first to Kierkegaard, who has been called the first existentialist, because his philosophy makes central the question of individual human existence, what it means to exist as a particular human being. And he argues that central to individual existence is our subjectivity, where subjectivity is characterized by freedom: the freedom to choose, to commit ourselves and to take responsibility for what we choose. Kierkegaard thus introduces the characteristically existentialist emphasis on the individual, and in particular the focus on the individual self as a free, self-defining subject.

His aim is to remind people of what it is to be an individual, what it is to be a free subject. He seeks to rehabilitate the notions of the personal, the particular and the subjective, and to do so in the face of what he calls 'objective' ways of thinking and acting, ways of thinking which downplay, deny or forget individual human existence – for example, to lose oneself in the crowd and the tyranny of 'mass opinion'; to live one's life in unthinking conformity with formalized rules; to engage in abstract, impersonal thinking; to stand apart from our lives rather than living them. In Sartre's thought, there is a similar rejection of ways of thought that forget or deny our subjectivity, the forms of thinking Sartre calls 'bad faith'.

For Kierkegaard, the proper role of philosophy is to criticize the illusion of objectivity that is so prevalent, and to convert people to subjectivity, to help us 'become subjective'. In line with this project, Kierkegaard articulates a conception of the 'essentially human', which is subjectivity, and this can be understood as our capacity to freely choose our own way of life, to choose the kind of person we are going to be, to define ourselves. Subjectivity is our capacity to make personal decisions, to commit ourselves passionately and deliberately to a way of life. Objectivity, in all its forms, is a way of avoiding subjective decision and commitment, by relying on external props – conforming to mass opinion, to the dead rituals of institutionalized religion and so on.

Some general points can be made about Kierkegaard's conception of human existence. Firstly, as noted already, Kierkegaard is concerned with what it means to be a particular human individual, the individual subject. He makes this individual the point of departure for his thinking. It's true that many modern philosophers have started with the individual subject. Descartes begins modern philosophy by making his own existence the starting point. For Descartes, 'I think, therefore I am' is the first thing that we can know with certainty. What Kierkegaard disputes, however, is the kind of subject involved here. For Kierkegaard, philosophy in the Cartesian tradition tends to define the individual self in impersonal terms, as a detached, disinterested knowing subject. In this view, what is merely individual about us, our personality, passions, interests and so on, is peripheral to what we are. They are 'merely subjective' interferences that have to be suppressed if we are to attain objective knowledge. Kierkegaard stresses what the Cartesian philosopher downplays. For Kierkegaard, human beings are essentially particular, subjective, passionate individuals. Human beings are not primarily detached, disinterested, knowing subjects, but ethical subjects, moral agents who have to live, to make choices, commit themselves and act.

The second point to note is that Kierkegaard, in describing the 'essentially human', aims to articulate what human beings ought to be, what they ideally can be. In a sense, we don't have to work at being human. Physically and biologically, we already exist as human beings, with the characteristics distinctive of our species. Even if we are just mindless conformists, part of the unthinking crowd, we are still, in this basic sense, human beings. But for Kierkegaard, this is a very uninteresting sense of 'being human'. When Kierkegaard talks of 'being human', he wants to describe how human beings ought to be, what it is to live a fully human life, a kind of existence proper to human beings in which we become ourselves. He is describing what he thinks is 'authentic' human existence. And being authentically human for Kierkegaard means 'becoming subjective', becoming a moral agent, choosing your values and committing yourself to a way of life. So to be human, to exist authentically, to become subjective, is for Kierkegaard a task and an achievement. Indeed for Kierkegaard it is the 'highest task' facing a human being.

But now for Kierkegaard, as far as being subjective, being authentically human, is concerned, clear reflection, understanding, or reason, have their limits. We can consistently and rationally apply an existing framework of values; do things which are consistent with it. But what Kierkegaard is most interested in is the point where we have to choose the framework itself, the ultimate values in terms of which we conduct our lives. Kierkegaard's denunciation of objectivity is also a rejection of the security of pre-existing value systems, of living our lives in conformity with ready-made rules handed down to us by others. 'Becoming subjective' means that we don't just thoughtlessly conform to a set of already existing values, but choose our values, commit ourselves to a way of life. And since we are not making such choices on the basis of a set of values, but choosing the values themselves, there is no guidance or justification for these choices. We can't make these choices rationally. They can only be chosen through a pure act of commitment, an irrational, passionate 'leap' of choice.

Where twentieth-century existentialists like Sartre most diverge from Kierkegaard is in rejecting the theological elements of his position. For Kierkegaard, the highest way of life, the most subjective and authentic form of human existence, is Christianity, because Christian belief, being utterly unjustifiable in rational terms, requires the most intense subjectivity, the purest choice. In the main, twentieth-century existentialism has been atheistic. What it primarily takes from Kierkegaard is the concentration on the category of the individual, on concrete individual existence; and the emphasis on personal, free choice as central to an authentic human existence.

In fact, dropping the Christian theme serves to intensify these features, this emphasis on the individual, because it throws us even more decisively on our own individual resources. More than ever, it is necessary for us to choose our way of life, to exercise our subjective capacity for choice. There is nothing outside ourselves which can serve to show us the way. For twentieth-century existentialism, 'God is dead.' There is no final escape from the anguish, the burden of choice, into the arms of a benevolent God who can tell us how we are to live

our lives. Indeed, religiosity itself comes to be considered by people like Sartre as a way of denying your subjectivity, of trying to hide from your freedom.

This also lies at the heart of Nietzsche's influence on twentieth-century existentialism, which is best reflected in his famous slogan 'God is dead!' Nietzsche insisted that the God of traditional religion was dead, which is to say religion was no longer an important cultural force in European society, and no longer had any role to play in the lives of serious people. Instead, human beings have to create a meaningful world, to establish values they can live by, through their own will.

At the same time, Nietzsche is a fierce critic of many aspects of modern philosophy, and he directly attacks the notion of the self as the indivisible, immaterial soul. As we have seen, this is how Descartes understood the self, as an individual substance with the properties of thought and rationality. For Descartes, although the soul is in fact joined to a body, the body is not essential to the self. It's the soul that is essential to the self. On this view personal identity is not affected by changes in the body; as long as the soul remains the same identical substance through time, we are the same self or person. However Nietzsche rejects the idea of the self as an immaterial soul, and along with that, this idea of personal identity. For Nietzsche, personal identity is not attached to a substantial individual soul that each of us has.

Nietzsche doesn't think that we should get rid of the soul altogether. Rather we need to rethink it. As he puts it in *Beyond Good and Evil* (1887), the self needs to be understood as a 'mortal soul', a 'subjective multiplicity', and the soul as a 'social structure of drives and affects'. The idea of the mortal soul means that the soul isn't to be understood as an entity distinct from the body in Nietzsche's account. The notions of subjective multiplicity and the social structure of drives indicate two things. Firstly, the self as Nietzsche understands it is the effect of a number of forces, and secondly, these forces are largely unconscious drives.

So for Nietzsche, the self is not primarily a conscious, rational entity. What we see as a unitary, autonomous, rational self is in fact the effect of a multiplicity of unconscious drives. Nietzsche also tells us about the nature of the social structure of the drives. He says that each drive wants to be master over the others. So the self is not a chaotic multiplicity of drives, but a structured one. And the nature of this structure is explained in terms of the most basic drive, what Nietzsche calls the 'will to power'. This is behind all the other drives and forces. So, given that the self is an effect of the multiplicity of forces and drives, we can say that the self is a product of the will to power.

The self, then, for Nietzsche is not a unitary soul substance, but the effect of a multiplicity of forces. Nonetheless, he acknowledges that most people, and not just philosophers, believe that the self is a unitary entity. But like Hume, Nietzsche sees this unitary self as a fiction, and he tries to explain how this fiction comes about. There are good reasons for developing it. In order to perform activities like making and keeping promises, we have to link our future to our present and past. Making promises assumes that I will be the same person in the future, the one who keeps the promise, as the one in the present who makes the promise; and that the one who keeps the promise is the same person who made the promise in the past. To relate our present to our future, and our present to our past requires us to create this fiction of one and the same self that persists through time.

This fiction of a unitary self is useful because life in society would be impossible without it. Life in society involves making promises, and more generally, anticipating future eventualities as if they belonged to the present. It requires that human beings be 'calculable', reliable, and this fiction of a unitary self is important for making human beings reliable and responsible. So the development of the notion of a self-identical subject is socially induced, according to Nietzsche, because human beings need to become reliable in order to function in society. Only if I think of myself as having an identity that goes beyond the present into the future am I suitable for social life.

Also, we need to see ourselves as the cause of our actions, for otherwise we cannot be held responsible for them. In other words we need to see ourselves as a subject or agent. This means as far as the issue of personal identity is concerned, that self-identity is the result of an interpretation of ourselves as unitary selves, which is induced by society. In adopting this fiction, we've become reliable, calculable, regular, rational. But it is still a fiction. While we may believe in a unitary self, and function as though we were unitary agents, we are not unitary beings but a multiplicity of forces.

Through the socially induced fiction of personal identity, human beings have become what Niet-

zsche calls herd animals – predictable, calculable creatures who conform to social requirements, submit to the customs and interests of the community. But while it makes social life possible, this also means depriving individuals of their independence and individuality. Herd animal thinking, dominant in European society, regards all that expresses strength and independence, everything that elevates the individual above the herd, as a danger. It condemns the strong, independent individual and fosters equality and conformity.

Nonetheless, although the transformation of human beings into personal identities is socially induced, it makes possible a further transformation according to Nietzsche. That sort of personal identity is the foundation for what Nietzsche calls the 'higher man', the 'overman'. At the end of the process emerges the sovereign individual, 'liberated again from the morality of custom, autonomous and supramoral'. The overman has the task of self-creation. He is the individual who dares to be individual and different.

The overman is he who 'overcomes himself'. That is, through hard work and a long process of self-disciplining, the overman transforms himself by organizing and directing his drives and instincts in a way that integrates and enhances them. He thus creates himself as an autonomous individual, living independently of the ideals of the majority of people. The personal identity of such an individual is not to be understood in terms of the notion of a spiritual substance, which is a fiction. The united, disciplined self of the overman is not a fiction but a genuine achievement. However at the same time, for Nietzsche, the socially induced belief in the unitary self is a necessary step in the creation of the overman. It is necessary, in order to make the further transformation possible.

Returning to existentialism, there are many aspects of Nietzsche's account that are taken up by Sartre and the existentialists. Both Nietzsche and the existentialists see the important philosophical question as being what it means to exist as a particular human being, how we are to live, what we are to do with our lives, rather than abstract, impersonal considerations concerning knowledge and truth in general. Moreover, like Nietzsche, existentialism emphasizes the idea that we create ourselves, that the self is not simply something that is given to us but something that we have to invent or make. It is individuals who give order and meaning to their lives through their self-creating activity.

At the same time there are many aspects of Nietzsche's thought that the existentialist would not adopt. The idea of an absolute and universal will to power is absent, for example. There is no concern with underlying, largely unconscious drives and forces. For Sartrean existentialism, what remains central is the conscious, choosing self. And unlike Nietzsche, the existentialists typically insist that each human individual has a unique capacity which they call absolute freedom, the freedom to consciously define themselves. This is much closer to the Cartesian tradition, and to Kant's view of the self-defining subject.

Nietzsche himself is part of this tradition in modern thinking to the extent that he holds that, in the absence of God and a God-given order, we have to define ourselves. But he departs from it in questioning the centrality of the conscious, rational self, and stressing the importance of unconscious drives and forces, which we can only shape and define through hard work and long discipline. As we will see, this aspect of Nietzsche's picture, his questioning of the Cartesian-Kantian notion of the self, is something that becomes increasingly prominent in twentieth-century thinking.

■ 2. Psychoanalysis

In our own time it has become a commonplace that this questioning of the primacy of the conscious, rational self should be dominated by psychoanalysis and the role of psychotherapy in identifying our most repressed unconscious drives. The most important influence in this, of course, has been Sigmund Freud.

2.1 Freud and the unconscious

Just as Nietzsche's account points to underlying drives beneath consciousness that provide the 'real motives' for our actions, the distinctive feature of Freud's psychoanalytic account is that it looks to the unconscious as the basis for understanding human action. We cannot account for our behaviour solely in terms of our conscious desires, intentions and wishes. There are also unconscious desires and wishes, largely unknown to our conscious selves, and these provide the basis for much of our behaviour.

For Freud, this unconscious realm is very different in character from the conscious self. The unconscious contains all the basic instinctual drives, including sexual desire, and aggressive and self-destructive drives, as well as traumatic memories, childhood fantasies, and thoughts and wishes that are forbidden by society. Our instinctual drives seek immediate gratification, immediate satisfaction, regardless of the demands that our environment places on us, and the restrictions it imposes on their satisfaction. They are governed only by what Freud called the 'pleasure principle', the goal of fulfilment at all costs.

While the goals of the conscious self are ultimately the same as those of the unconscious – the gratification of basic bodily needs – the conscious self seeks to satisfy them in a different way, through realistic transactions with the environment. It seeks to take into account the realistic demands of the situation, to organize behaviour in ways that are rational and appropriate to the external environment. In short, it is governed by what Freud calls the 'reality principle'. As such, the conscious self is in the position of having to control the constant pressures coming from the unconscious self, to balance the conflicting demands of the primitive instinctual drives for immediate satisfaction, and the constraints imposed by external reality.

While the unconscious self is hidden from the direct view of the conscious self, it shows itself from time to time in behaviour that the conscious self finds mysterious and difficult to understand – slips of the tongue, dreams and, most importantly, in pathological, neurotic behaviour. In particular, Freud sees neurotic symptoms as being caused by repression, the pushing of unwanted, shameful desires, wishes and memories into the unconscious. When these rejected, repressed desires and wishes find an outlet in unexpected ways, the result is neurotic symptoms. So in Freud's account, these symptoms are not seen as an expression of the person's conscious self, but rather the outcome of these psychic mechanisms, the processes of repression and the reappearance of the repressed.

This is the picture that emerges prior to the 1920s. Later, Freud came to revise his model of the self, to move away from the straightforward division of conscious and unconscious. In his writings of the 1920s such as *The Ego and the Id*, (1923) Freud divided the self into three parts: the ego, the rational 'I' which deals with the outside world; the superego or moral conscience, containing social standards of behaviour acquired during childhood; and the id, containing the instinctual drives that are constantly seeking immediate satisfaction. Although the id is similar to the unconscious, being the reservoir for the primal instincts, the ego and superego have both conscious and unconscious aspects.

The new model, for Freud, offered the prospect of more clearly delineating the conflicts within the personality. For Freud, the primary conflict we face is between the superego, the moral conscience, allied with the ego, and the desires of the id. The ego strives to balance the conflicting demands of the id for desire-satisfaction, the moral rules of the superego, and the constraints of external reality. Where there is extreme conflict between instinctual impulses and moral standards, the denial of instinctual satisfaction demanded by morality is achieved through repression; and if the repression is too severe, the denied desires find indirect expression in various neurotic symptoms.

Overall, Freud offers a picture in which we do not fully grasp the nature of our motivations, where much of our motivation is hidden from us. Powerful instinctual drives that we are unaware of, rather than deliberate and rational decisions, play a large role in determining human behaviour. The conscious self is in the grip of these powerful forces, not only when we are in the grip of pathological symptoms, but even when we are 'normal' or 'healthy'. Thus the conscious self is no longer at the centre of things, as it was in Descartes, Kant and Sartre.

At the same time, while Freud does not think that we can ever restore the straightforward sovereignty of the conscious, rational self, he does think that the conscious self can gain a degree of control over the personality. The purpose of psychotherapy is to control the power that the unconscious has by bringing repressed thoughts and wishes into consciousness, facing them and obtaining a conscious grasp over the unconscious wishes. The ego can at least be strengthened so that it is more in control of the influences affecting it. Nonetheless, for Freud, there are limits to this; there will always be an irrational core of instincts we have to contend with.

2.2 R. D. Laing: existential psychotherapy

One response to Freud's thinking has been to try to restore the primacy of the conscious self. This is a feature of the so-called existential psychotherapy inspired by Sartre's existentialism, and involving people like R. D. Laing, Victor Frankl, David Cooper and Anthony Storr. As we have seen, existentialism rejects all accounts which would reduce human beings to mere material objects, determined by external forces. It seeks to remind people that they are free subjects, that they are responsible for the direction, value and significance that their lives have. It is this determination to treat human beings as free subjects that is taken up in existentialist psychotherapy. Very broadly, in treating people with psychiatric disturbances, existentialist psychotherapy aims to do so not by approaching them as objects, as broken mechanisms, but as conscious, free subjects. It aims to cure by getting disturbed people to adopt a new way of seeing the world – a perspective which gives central place to the patients' freedom, and their freedom to help themselves.

So, existential psychotherapy sets itself up in opposition to psychological theories which would see human behaviour in terms of causal mechanisms; and it considers the classical Freudian type of explanation to be a 'mechanistic' theory of this sort. In Freud's model, neurotic symptoms are caused by the repression of wishes, drives and so on to the unconscious level, resulting in the emergence of neurotic symptoms. These symptoms are seen not as an expression of the person's conscious self, but of psychic mechanisms. For example, an unfaithful woman's inability to perform a sexual act would be explained in the Freudian model in terms of the repression of the woman's guilt feelings about the infidelity at the unconscious level, resulting in her inability to perform the sexual act on the conscious level.

Sartre and the existential psychotherapists reject the notion of the unconscious, regarding the self as a unified, conscious being, all of whose acts are conscious ones; and they reject the idea that psychic mechanisms control or determine behaviour. According to their model, the woman is in bad faith, lying to herself, distracting herself. Her inability to perform the sexual act is a refusal to do so on her part: in other words, it is understood as an intentional, conscious act, rather than as the outcome of causal mechanisms. She deliberately chooses to distract herself from the sexual act in order not to face up to her infidelity.

Thus, the alternative model to the Freudian one for explaining certain disorders makes reference not to the underlying cause of neurotic symptoms, but rather to what the person intends or means by his or her behaviour. This in turn allows the use of notions like 'bad faith', 'distraction', 'pretence' and so on in explaining certain psychological states. It is this sort of model which has been exploited in the writings of psychiatrists like R. D. Laing, who go so far as to explain even disorders like schizophrenia in these terms.

To sum up, existentialist psychotherapy underplays the notion of the unconscious, and emphasizes the person as an autonomous, conscious being, the author of his or her own actions. It doesn't look for causal processes, scientific laws and so on to understand what's going on. Instead, it concerns itself with the meaning and value kinds of action have for the person involved. It asks – what does the person 'mean' or 'intend' by this behaviour, why did this person choose this course of action? In short, in the face of Freud's 'decentring' of the conscious, rational self, existential psychotherapy seeks to reformulate psychoanalysis in a way that restores its sovereignty.

■ 3. Marxism

Freud suggests that individual consciousness and behaviour can only be understood in terms of the obscure, less than rational workings of the unconscious mind. But he is not the only figure to call into question the primacy of the conscious, rational self. Another blow to the self's sovereignty comes from the work of the nineteenth-century German thinker Karl Marx. In Marx's theory of ideology, individual consciousness (beliefs, attitudes and moral values) reflects the position that individuals occupy in their social and economic context.

3.1 Marx and false consciousness

Marx's account is distinguished by its 'materialist turn'. This means that he turns his attention away from individual consciousness, in favour of the 'material conditions' of society. His emphasis is on the economic conditions under which we live, the way society produces what we need to survive (our relations with nature), how it is organized to bring about that productive activity (our relations with each another). Marx's starting point, then, is not the individual, conscious self, but embodied human beings who have to work on nature in order to eat,

Karl Heinrich Marx (1818–1883)

Born in Trier, Marx studied law at the University of Bonn (1835) and history and philosophy at the University of Berlin (1836-41), where he came under the influence of the radical Young Hegelian movement. He moved to Paris in 1843, where he met Friedrich Engels, who became his lifelong collaborator. During this time he began to develop his own unique revolutionary theory, most notably in *Economic and Philosophical Manuscripts* of 1844, *Theses on Feuerbach* (1845) and *The German Ideology* (1846).

In his theory of alienation he distanced himself from the Young Hegelians, challenging the accepted notion that inequality is a natural fact, rather than the product of particular social conditions and arrangements. However, he also distanced himself from 'mechanistic materialists', like Feuerbach, who believed individuals and their ideas were a passive product of social conditions. Marx believed individuals were not only the product of circumstances that shape their consciousness, but the potential changers of those circumstances. His evolutionary theory of historical materialism explained the way different forms of human societies evolve in response to underlying contradictions between different social classes.

Expelled from France and Prussia he finally settled in London in 1848, where he lived for the rest of his life, often in considerable poverty, producing his most famous works, *The Communist Manifesto* (1848) and his major undertaking *Capital* (3 vols, 1867, 1885, and 1893).

drink and survive. In the course of working on nature, they also transform themselves. That is, to work on nature effectively, human beings have to organize themselves. Specific forms of social organization thus emerge, which Marx calls the relations of production. This is the division of labour in which productive tasks are distributed between different social groups. Some labour directly on nature, and others direct the labour process. There is always a hierarchy of some sort.

So particular forms of social relations emerge, and along with them social classes, the groups who play different roles in the productive process. And in the course of working on nature, the successive forms of class society emerge – slavery, feudalism and most recently, capitalism, in which the labour of the workers is owned and directed by the capitalist class. Moreover, along with these relations of production, there emerge all the other features of social life. These include legal structures and forms of political organization; and also what Marx calls forms of consciousness, various ways of understanding the world – religion, philosophy, ethics and so on. These are the ideological forms of thought, kinds of false consciousness which are reflections of the material conditions of society, products of our economic needs and practices, which serve in turn to rationalize and justify the prevailing social and economic conditions, to make those conditions palatable or at least bearable.

On this view, it might seem that individuals are completely subject to their economic circumstances; their very consciousness is conditioned by their material conditions. Just as Freud sees the conscious self as largely determined by the forces of one's unconscious, Marx seems to see individual consciousness as largely determined by one's economic interests and class position. The conscious self seems to have entirely lost its primacy. However, just as Freud holds out some hope that the conscious self might be able to recover at least some of its sovereignty, Marx also leaves open this possibility. Human beings are not merely the products of their social world. They make the social world through their productive activity; but at the same time they are its alienated authors. That is, they have become subject to oppressive social and economic arrangements that have taken on a life of their own – the successive forms of class society. And these circumstances prevent human beings from living fully human lives, which is to say, human beings are alienated from themselves.

The idea of alienation itself presupposes an essential nature or self from which one is alienated, and for Marx this essential nature takes the form of what in his early writings at least he calls *gattungswesen*. This refers to what the human being is ideally and essentially, a communal or species-being. What is essential to human beings is that they engage in labour or productive activity, they produce collectively, and they produce on the basis of conscious, intentional activity. However under class society, and particularly under the most recent, capitalist form of class society, none of this is possible. Workers produce, but rather than this productive activity being under their conscious control, their labour and its products are owned and directed by their capitalist overseers; what they produce is sold for profit rather than being for the satisfaction of human needs; and they labour in separation from one another. If class society, above all capitalism, prevents human beings from being themselves, the overcoming of those oppressive social and economic arrangements promises the overcoming of alienation and the attainment of a fully human life.

Indeed, this will be the final phase of history. Capitalism may bring about the most extreme alienation of humanity from itself, but the enormous productivity it makes possible means that the workers are in a position to overcome the division of labour; it is no longer necessary to submit to an oppressive system in order to survive. It is now possible for labouring human beings to overcome class society once and for all, through the revolutionary overthrow by the workers of their capitalist overseers.

The result will be not another class society but the classless society of communism. This will also mean overcoming the ideological distortions of class society, and the attainment of true consciousness. The fully human life here is one in which human beings will make their social world collectively and consciously. So we can say that Marx, although he wants to move away from the individual conscious subject, reformulates the conscious self as a collective subject. For Marx, human beings can be, and ought to be, the collective, rational producers of their way of life. It is the modern conception of the self as self-defining subject writ large.

3.2 Marcuse: one-dimensional thinking

Some of Marx's twentieth-century successors focus on the idea that economic circumstances shape other aspects of society, and see Marxism as a deterministic theory in which human beings are mere objects, entirely determined by their social and economic circumstances. Others reject this reading of Marx, and instead take up and develop his notions of alienation and ideology. As such, they also develop the notion of the self that Marx formulates, the notion of human beings as, at least potentially, the collective, conscious authors of their way of life.

One important figure here is the twentieth-century German philosopher Herbert Marcuse,

Brief lives
Marcuse, Herbert

Dates: 1898–1979
Born: Berlin, Germany
Best known for: His belief that under the influence of advanced capitalism individuals have surrendered their intellectual and spiritual freedom in return for the blandishments of consumer society, a process he described as 'repressive desublimation'.

Major works: *Reason and Revolution* (1941), *Eros and Civilisation* (1955) *One-Dimensional Man* (1964), *Counterrevolution and Revolt* (1972).

whose best known works are *Eros and Civilisation* (1955), and *One-Dimensional Man* (1964). There are three features of his account worth stressing. Firstly, Marcuse holds that capitalist exploitation has become more intense since Marx's time; secondly, there is a particular focus on the role of ideology, socially produced false consciousness which in its modern form Marcuse calls 'one-dimensional thinking'; and thirdly, Marcuse's account incorporates insights from Freudian psychoanalysis.

First of all, Marcuse adopts Marx's conception of human societies as systems for the production of goods necessary for survival; and of contemporary society as characterized by the capitalist organization of this productive activity, in which workers are subject to exploitation. At the same time, he thinks that this exploitation has become more intense since Marx's time. In the twentieth century, the development of technology means that we have a much greater capacity to produce goods for the satisfaction of human needs, but exploitative economic relationships have become stronger. In the eighteenth and nineteenth centuries the owners of labour were typically individual capitalists; now they have been replaced by more powerful agencies, large corporations. Their productive activity remains tied primarily to making profit, rather than the satisfaction of real human needs. Workers' lives remain subordinated to the requirements of profitable production.

However, Marcuse augments this account with psychoanalytic insights, particularly Freud's account of the relation between the individual and society. Freud, as we have seen, introduces the key

notion of unconscious desire, particularly of sexual interests and drives. He articulates a conception of human being in which the basis of much human thinking and behaviour can be traced to instinctual forces. This conception figures in Freud's account of the relation between the individual and society. For Freud, the child comes into the world as a creature of untamed instinctual desire, desire which demands immediate gratification. What the child promptly runs up against are the rules and constraints of organized, orderly society – social rules and expectations, represented most directly by the parents. This is the reality which the child must adapt to in order to survive. That is, the child has to learn that it cannot satisfy all of its desires at once, or immediately. It has to learn to restrain its desire for immediate gratification.

In the beginning such restraint is imposed externally, by parental authority, punishment and so on. As we grow up, social rules and expectations become internalized. A superego or conscience takes shape, which requires the observation of social rules from within. We acquire a set of internalized parents and learn how to restrain ourselves. In this manner we learn to give up the immediate gratification of our desires, and to deflect our instinctual energies into socially useful and not immediately pleasurable activities, such as work. And for Freud, civilization in general is a system of self-preservation in the face of external nature. The continuing existence of civilization requires that individuals be forced to repress their instincts, to forgo immediate satisfaction, and redirect their energies into productive labour, into the work required to provide the necessities of life. So the renunciation of sexual desire is seen by Freud as a condition of civilization itself, and thus a feature of all societies.

Freud's view can easily be incorporated into standard accounts of capitalism. Under capitalism, worker's energies and desires are not to be squandered in pleasure but redirected into productive activity, work, which is itself directed not towards the satisfaction of their wants but profitable exchange. So capitalist domination enforces the repression of biological needs, along with frustration and resentment. And Marcuse adopts this psychoanalytically coloured account of capitalism. However he also departs from Freud, because he argues that the repression so far characteristic of human societies need not always be required. The more productive a society becomes, the more goods are produced, the less it needs to be repressive. And capitalism is a highly effective form of economic organization. Through the development of productive forces and technological capacities, we are removing the need for society to enforce instinctual repression. This is increasingly becoming what Marcuse calls 'surplus repression', repression that is not essential for society to keep going.

This is why Marcuse says at the start of his introduction to the *Essay on Liberation* that technological development has 'utopian possibilities'. It makes possible a substantial release of our instinctual energies, energies hitherto tied up in hard work. It opens up the possibility of what Marcuse calls a 'qualitative transformation' of life, a new society characterized not by repression and pleasureless toil but by play, pleasure and the satisfaction of human desires. Marcuse argues that automation promises to put an end to any need for human labour at all, and this means that people would be free to engage in work that has itself become play, a means of pleasure and gratification. And this would also be a society characterized by a genuine human community. Marcuse holds that our instinctual drives seek to create ever-greater unities in life, and so provide an instinctual foundation for human cooperation and solidarity. In this way, he draws on Freudian psychoanalysis to reformulate Marx's notion of the essentially human, the idea of species being, and to articulate a new vision of human self-realization.

So far, however, this promised self-realization has not happened. The reason for this, Marcuse argues, is that, despite the development of the productive forces, despite the increasing ability of society to satisfy all human needs, the capitalist system persists, and real human wants and needs continue to be denied satisfaction. This is because in the contemporary context our instinctual energies are no longer simply repressed, but manipulated and distorted in the service of the prevailing system. Capitalism continues to produce goods for profitable exchange rather than human needs. Workers remain subordinated to the system, rather than controlling it and turning it to the satisfaction of their real needs. And increasingly their needs themselves are harnessed to the system.

This is part of the ideological power of the present system, the way it distorts and falsifies our wants and needs themselves. Through advertising, mass media, films and so on, we are encouraged to desire and find pleasure in the commodities the existing system produces, to be avid consumers of the goods produced by the system. Here we will find satisfaction and fulfilment. But for Marcuse what's being satisfied here are the false needs inculcated in us through external agencies. In satisfying these needs, we simply perpetuate the system that continues to deny our real needs.

For Marcuse, the very notions of what counts as desire, pleasure, satisfaction, fulfilment and happiness have thus been manipulated so that individuals are entirely content with the existing system. In a fundamental way, people have been incorporated into the existing social system. They internalize, or as Marcuse puts it, 'introject', the prevailing conceptions of what is desirable and valuable. As such, their instinctual nature has been obscured by what Marcuse calls a 'second nature', a socially produced nature and set of needs that functions to maintain the existing system. People thus reproduce, through their own aspirations and satisfactions, the very system that exploits them and denies their real needs.

In the end Marcuse is not as confident as Marx that human beings will be able to overcome distorted, ideological forms of consciousness and work to overcome existing social arrangements. In his account, society enters very deeply into the workings of the individual self. Our instincts themselves have been co-opted into the system. But it is also to these instinctual needs that Marcuse appeals as a basis for opposing the system: that is, to genuine human needs as opposed to the false needs that are implanted by the system. Despite the corruption of needs themselves, Marcuse holds out hope that here there remains a biological basis for revolt, for the rejection of the prevailing system. Since power corrupts and falsifies our needs, such revolt requires a qualitative change in our wants and needs themselves – a rebellion grounded in the very nature, the 'biology' of the individual.

It's interesting to note that while Marcuse draws on a number of psychoanalytic insights, especially the notion of instinctual drives, he does not see them as reducing the self to a mere plaything of powerful unconscious forces. Rather, they are basic to who we are, fundamental needs that have been distorted and falsified by an oppressive society. They also provide a basis for standing up against a social system that seems to be on the verge of completely corrupting the individual. And they point towards a better, more rational society, one that would be designed to satisfy real needs and allow for genuine human self-realization. Marcuse thus in effect incorporates the instincts into the Marxist notion of the conscious, rational self, the vision of human beings as, at least potentially, the collective, conscious authors of their way of life.

■ 4. Decentring the subject

Both Freud and Marx can be said to 'decentre' the conscious, rational self, which is to say they point to influences that undermine its primacy – in the case of Freud, the forces of instinct, and for Marx, the conditioning effects of society. However they do not dethrone it completely. They also leave open the possibility of restoring its sovereignty, at least to some extent. The aim of Freud's psychotherapy, and Marx's revolutionary action, is to overcome these influences and give people some degree of conscious control over their existence; and some of their followers, such as the existential psychotherapists and Marcuse, are able to formulate their positions in ways that seem to reinforce this possibility.

However with more recent movements like structuralism and post-structuralism we have a more radical decentring of the self, a recognition of the various forces that go into the making of the self, which does not entertain any hopes of recovering sovereignty later on. Some have gone so far as to declare the traditional subject dead. Nietzsche declared that God is dead, and some now want to say that the self has gone the same way.

4.1 Structuralism and the self

An important source for the structuralist way of thinking, which flourished in the 1960s, is the structural linguistics of the Swiss linguist Ferdinand de Saussure. He argues that language exists as a structured system of signs. Speakers can only say or mean something by making use of a language that already exists before they speak, and this means that the meaning of what they say cannot be explained in terms of the subject's conscious intentions, in terms of what they intend to say. Far from being created by subjects, meaning is a product of the language as a whole. Any particular sign is meaningful because it is different to other signs. For example, the meaning of a term like 'cat' depends on the particular contrasts with other signs that the language allows. A cat is whatever is not a dog, a bat, a rat and so on. So speakers can only mean something with what they say because there is a

pre-existing, structured system of oppositions embodied in language.

The movement known as structuralism extends this structural approach beyond language to social and cultural phenomena more generally. The more general claim being made is that we should not treat these phenomena as the intentional products of human subjects, but as structured systems of elements with specific rules of combination and transformation. It is these structured systems that now determine the meaning of social and cultural phenomena. The anthropologist, Claude Levi-Strauss, applied this approach to society. He argued that society cannot be understood simply by examining the will and intentions of individual social agents. Rather, each element in the social system is explained in terms of its position within the overall system of society. Indeed, the French Marxist, Louis Althusser, went even further. He applied this approach to the Marxist account of society, developing an influential strand of structural Marxism. In this account, history itself becomes the rule-governed transformation of impersonal structures.

For any structural account of society, there are limits to the extent to which social phenomena can be explained in terms of the will and intentions of individual actors. Individuals act within arrangements or structures that exist prior to their actions. Indeed it is sometimes suggested that agents are completely determined by the roles given to them within various structures. In these extreme structuralist accounts, the sovereign self disappears entirely. The self is completely reduced to a function of external, impersonal structures. One of the difficulties that such an account poses, however, is that it seems to make any attempt by human beings to change their society impossible. To put this slightly differently, how can we account for political practice, resistance and struggle, without resorting to some notion of the subject, to the deliberate choices of actual historical agents?

4.2 Post-structuralism and the self

The post-structuralist movement emerged in France in the 1970s, and includes people like the French thinkers Jacques Derrida and Michel Foucault amongst its representatives. It rejects the idea that language, and more broadly social and cultural phenomena, can be completely accounted for in terms of structured systems governed by specific rules. This does not, however, mean a return to the traditional notion of the subject. Both Derrida and Foucault see the subject as having a peripheral status. They do not deny that there is a subjectivity, but they do deny that it is autonomous and sovereign, as traditionally conceived. And they aim to give a new explanation of subjectivity, one that gives the final blow to those traditional accounts that give the subject a central and autonomous status.

For example, Derrida in his essay 'Differance', argues that the subject is a product, an effect. For Derrida, the subject is a product of the play of textual structures, of language. We can only relate to ourselves, our thoughts and feelings, through the medium of signs, in other words through language. I have to use signs to articulate what I am thinking, feeling and so on. But Derrida claims that the identity of each sign depends on being different to all other signs. This is similar to Saussure's view, but where Saussure claims that language is a closed structured system, and signs have a fixed, final meaning in this context, for Derrida language is an open-ended totality of signs. Because each individual sign only has its meaning through its relation to an open-ended totality, this means that no sign can have an entirely fixed meaning or play a precise identifying role.

It follows that I can have no fixed notion of what I am either, because signs have no ultimate, precise meaning, including the signs through which I relate to myself, my thoughts, feelings and so on. And what this means is that there is no author or subject if we mean by that someone who produces meaning, who determines and fixes it. What we call subjectivity is just an effect of those differential sign-relations – or to quote Derrida: 'subjectivity is produced by the structure of the text.'

A related though different approach to Derrida's concerning subjectivity is that of Foucault, who argues that the modern subject emerges not out of the interplay of signs but of social forces. This interplay gives rise to forms of control and regulation, bound up with forms of classification and knowledge. In his account, developed in *Discipline and Punish* (1977) and *The History of Sexuality* volume 1 (1979), forms of social control and regulation have emerged which make use of classifications such as sane and insane, healthy and sick, law-abiding and delinquent, sexually normal and perverted, and, most broadly, normal and abnormal. What we call the subject is for Foucault the product or effect of this regulation and classification. They work precisely by turning human beings into certain kinds of subjects: that is to say, by bringing them to act in accordance with certain standards of normal behaviour, a certain identity.

Foucault thus develops the idea that modern forms of subjectivity or selfhood reflect social power relations, forms of social control and regulation. Moreover, individuals participate in this 'subjectifying' kind of regulation, to the extent that they try to seek to determine who they are in terms of these classifications. To seek to know yourself, to discover your true self or soul, is to identify yourself with these socially constructed forms of normal selfhood, and bring your own behaviour in line with them.

At the same time, in post-structuralist fashion, Foucault does not want to argue that individuals are wholly determined by these forms of classification and regulation. They also resist them and seek to modify them in turn. In other words, for Foucault, although social forms condition what individuals can do and be, individuals can in turn modify the social forms and what it is possible for them to do and be. To use the analogy of language, you can certainly describe a language as a set of linguistic structures which you are constrained to obey. To speak English, you have to conform to certain structural rules as to what constitutes a grammatical sentence. But these rules don't constrain absolutely what it's possible to say or how it's possible to say it. English has evolved over time, and it does so as a result of the way individuals use and introduce modifications in language. So there is an interaction, an interplay, between individuals and language. Similarly, people may be subject to certain social forms, but these forms can be changed, and they change at least partly as the result of the actions of individuals.

For Foucault, then, social forms and relations come to be transformed over time, and it is people's resistance within social relations that is a key feature of that change. So, to take an example, the forms of social relations between men and women have changed over the years, and a feature of that has been the resistance of women to the traditional kinds of gender relations in a patriarchal society. This resistance is not only to social forms but to the kinds of subjects it is possible to be within these forms. That is, resistance includes resistance to the roles traditionally allotted to women, the forms of identity deemed appropriate for women (housewife, mother) by society, and the development of different forms of selfhood.

So Foucault rejects the idea, found for example in Marxism, that resistance is a matter of discovering our true selves and asserting who we are, in the face of a society that prevents us from being ourselves. Rather, it involves 'refusing ourselves', resisting socially imposed forms of selfhood that serve to limit what we can do or be, in order to create new ways of being. This capacity to resist, including resistance to constraining forms of identity, and to create ourselves anew is for Foucault at the heart of what we are. We might say that this capacity to break away from ourselves is what the self has become in Foucault's post-structuralist account.

■ 5. Conclusion

In the last two chapters we have seen how philosophers have sought variously to define the self as some sort of predetermined essence of human beings; as some detached consciousness, a 'thinking thing'; or as the product of social forces beyond our control. In the process we have seen the conscious self radically affirmed by the existentialists, dethroned by Freud and Marx, and entirely dismissed by the structuralists, only to see it restored to some extent by the post-structuralists.

Your head may very well be spinning, and at times you may have thought this seems an arid debate of no practical importance. But, of course, it is in at least two important respects. If we are to have a clear idea of who and what we are, we must start at this point to decide how much of our personal identity we have chosen for ourselves and how much we accept unconsciously and without protest. Our wants and needs may indeed be, as Marcuse says, the product of advertisers and the mass media shaping our desires in order to sell the goods our society produces. And this indicates clearly the second respect in which this has practical importance, which we will explore in the next three chapters: we may talk about being free to choose and we may accept responsibility for the consequences of our choices, but our freedom may in fact be systematically constrained by forces beyond our conscious control.

■ Questions

1. Explain what Sartre means by 'bad faith' and consider its importance for existentialism in the light of Simone de Beauvoir's arguments

suggesting Sartre's neglect of the social context and the reason for the shift in his later work towards a more Marxist perspective.

2. 'If we are free from all influences, free to "invent" ourselves, all ethical choices must be groundless. We can have no reasons for preferring one thing to another. Therefore nothing can, rationally, be preferred. 'Is the position Sartre describes an ethical lottery as this suggests?

3. Sartre maintains that for human beings, 'existence precedes essence'.

   (a) Explain why he believes this means that there is no such thing as human nature.

   (b) Critically discuss this claim.

4. (a) Sartre believes that 'man is responsible for what he is'. What does he mean by this?

   (b) Discuss the arguments for and against this view.

5. Does freedom for women ultimately lie in being more like men?

6. Who do you believe is right? Do we 'invent' ourselves as Sartre contends? Do our unconscious drives shape much of our behaviour as Freud insists? Or is it, as Marx argues, the position we occupy in the social and economic system that determines our consciousness of self?

■ Recommended reading

Beauvoir, S. de *The Second Sex*, trans. H. M. Parshley (1949) (Harmondsworth: Penguin, 1972).

Glover, J. *The Philosophy and Psychology of Personal Identity* (Harmondsworth: Penguin, 1991). A useful introduction.

Lloyd, Genevieve. *The Man of Reason: 'Male' and 'Female' in Western Philosophy* (Minneapolis: University of Minnesota, 1984).

Marcuse, H. *One-Dimensional Man* (London: Sphere, 1968).

Perry, J. (ed.) *Personal Identity* (Berkeley, Calif.: University of California Press, 1985) A collection of classical and contemporary readings.

Sartre, J-P. *Transcendence of the Ego* (New York: Noonday, 1957).

West, D. *An Introduction to Continental Philosophy* (Cambridge: Polity, 1997).

 The note structure to accompany this chapter can be downloaded from our website.

Determinism and Freedom

CHAPTER 18

Key issues

▶ If we believe that every event has causes, how can we believe that we are free to choose?

▶ If we are not free to choose, this negates the possibility of moral judgement, so how can we be held responsible for our actions? And why do we praise or blame people, congratulating or punishing them, when they are not the cause of their behaviour?

▶ Who's to say that our enduring sense of freedom is not simply due to the fact that we're always looking forward into an unknown future waiting to be shaped by each decision we make? If we were to look back at the causes of our actions, we might see just how much each action and decision was caused by forces beyond our control.

▶ Is our unwillingness to abandon the idea of freedom merely due to the fact that it is tied to consciousness? If so, does this contribute anything which allows us to argue that we are genuinely free?

▶ Is it just that determinism works well enough to explain how physical causes produce physical movements but cannot be applied to human actions, or do we only *appear* to be free because we don't yet know the causes of our actions and choices?

Contents

It seems there is no other experience so deeply woven into the daily reality of our lives than that of being free to choose and decide what we will do. It's obvious to us that our deliberations, and the decisions and choices we make as a result, do make a difference to our lives. And, although we choose to do one thing, we know, in fact, that we could have chosen to do something quite different. Our behaviour is quite unpredictable. Having weighed up all the points for and against doing something, I might find one course of action seems overwhelmingly sensible, yet at the very last moment I might just decide to do the opposite.

And yet, with equal conviction, we all believe that things don't just happen: they happen because they are caused. The sugar bowl slips from my hand and smashes on the kitchen floor, because my hands are wet, because of the law of gravity, because the bowl is made of brittle clay and because the floor is made of hard tiles. The glaciers are melting in the Antarctic because of global warming, which is caused by the accumulation of carbon dioxide emissions and other greenhouse gases. You may disagree with the causal explanation, but you don't disagree with our shared belief in the Principle of

Universal Causation: that every event has causes that are sufficient to bring about that event. Otherwise we would just have to accept that there is simply no reason why the car will not start when only a moment ago it was working fine, or why I have been struck down with a cold today, when yesterday I was well. As Paul Edwards and Arthur Pap argue,

> If the doctor had merely said that he had never come across this kind of illness before and that he knew of no cause for it or that the cause had not yet been discovered, we would not necessarily consider his statement absurd. We are ready to admit that there are illnesses whose causes are unknown. We are not ready to admit that there are illnesses without a cause.

Indeed, few things have had such a powerful influence on modern philosophy as the Principle of Universal Causation, particularly since Newton. The eighteenth-century French philosopher Pierre Simon de Laplace had such faith in it that he argued if he knew the location and motion of every object in the universe and the laws governing their movements, he could predict the location and motion of every object at any time in the future.

But this leaves us wondering how we can ever entertain a belief in our own ability to choose. If everything we do is determined by circumstances that precede our actions, it seems we couldn't have done otherwise, even though we feel as though we are making a free choice. For an act to be completely free it would itself have to be a cause, but not an effect: it would have to be beyond the causal sequence and universal causation. Determinism, then, appears to leave no room for free will. This is the philosophical doctrine which holds that every event, mental as well as physical, has a cause, and that, given this cause, the event invariably follows.

Note that this is distinct from predestination: the doctrine that whatever is to happen has been unalterably fixed by God from the beginning of time, regardless of human choices. Nor is it the same as fatalism: the belief that some, perhaps all, events are irrevocably fixed. Whatever happens, the end is inevitable and no human effort can change it. Unlike these, determinism involves a conditional claim – 'If A, then B.' No event is inevitable. It depends upon certain antecedent conditions being fulfilled. Only then can we be certain that the event will occur. Given the accumulation of carbon dioxide and other greenhouse gases, the Earth's atmosphere will increase in temperature and the ice cap will begin to melt. There is nothing to say this was inevitable from the dawn of time, nor that it is inevitable now, that it is beyond our control and fated to happen. There are still things we can do to prevent it.

All that the determinist is arguing is that all consequences have necessary antecedents, but not all antecedents have necessary consequences. You might put all you possess on Wonder Horse running in the 2.30 pm and you might have an impressive list of fulfilled antecedent conditions that convince you that she cannot lose: she has won over the same course and distance, the going will suit her, she has the most successful jockey riding her and she comes from the best stable and trainer in the country. But, sadly, this doesn't make it inevitable – these antecedents don't have necessary consequences. However, if she does win, you will be able to explain this consequence by using all these antecedents to create a convincing causal explanation, and in the process convince others they should trust your judgement in future.

Nevertheless, if the determinists are right, this has far-reaching consequences. If all events, including an individual's thoughts and actions, are determined by forces beyond her control, this leaves no room for freedom and choice. And to deny someone's ability to choose a course of action seems to negate the possibility of moral judgement, without which she cannot be held responsible for her actions. No matter how much we think a person should be praised or blamed for her actions, it makes no sense to do either, when she has no responsibility for them and no power to alter her behaviour. In turn this has important implications for social and political policies, particularly those to do with punishment. It makes no sense to say she deserves to be punished, when she is not the cause of her behaviour. Like praise and blame it would be irrelevant and superfluous and, moreover, unnecessarily cruel and vindictive. It would be like blaming the sugar bowl for acting according to the law of gravity and smashing on the kitchen floor.

Correspondingly, if you do well in your exams you cannot be praised for that, even though the difference between your result and your friends' was due largely to your willingness to study every night, when they went out to the bar. Your strength of will is no credit to you, because it's the result of factors beyond your control: heredity, the environment in which you were brought up, the experiences which have shaped your attitudes, your desires and so on. In fact you cannot be praised for anything you achieve or be blamed for your failures.

So, there we have it: a set of very strong arguments for believing that free will can have no place in the universe and an equally strong conviction derived from our own experiences of the reality of our own freedom to choose, which leaves no doubt that free will does in fact exist.

◼ 1. Causes and compulsions

Of course, we must be sure that each of these convictions is referring to the same thing. Using the method we described in Chapter 2, think of examples of borderline, contrary and doubtful cases. As soon as you do you will be struck by the difference between the type of case in which, for example, you are willing to forego the delights down at the bar so that you can work to get better grades in your exams and, say, a mugger accosting you late one night and forcing you to hand over your money. Even though we could give causal explanations for both, the first appears to be done voluntarily out of your own free will, while the second is done because you are compelled to do it.

This suggests that part of the problem might lie in the confusion of a cause with a compulsion: that if an action is caused this necessarily means that it is compelled and cannot, therefore, be done voluntarily with free will. This seems to derive from the fact that we use the notion of 'cause' in two different contexts with two different meanings. In a scientific causal explanation, to explain something we must be able to say 'if and only if A, then B has to occur'. In other words, given that we have A, the necessary and sufficient conditions for B, we can say that B necessarily had to occur. But as we saw in Chapter 10 this necessity in causal explanations comes from the form of the argument. In the deductive nomological argument the necessity is logical; the effect of subsuming the event under a universal law within a deductive argument:

1. All As cause Bs.
2. S is an A.
3. Therefore, B.

The event that is to be explained (the 'explanandum' – 3) is deduced from the two premises that account for the event (the 'explanans' – 1 and 2). So if I were to explain why the sugar bowl and its contents are on the floor, my explanation would look something like this:

1. All heavier-than-air objects fall to the ground when unsupported.
2. The sugar bowl and its contents were heavier-than-air objects and were left unsupported when they slipped from my grasp.
3. Therefore, the sugar bowl and its contents fell to the ground.

Given premises 1 and 2, the event described in 3 *had* to occur. The necessity in the explanation comes from the deductive form of the argument.

But when we describe something being compelled, the necessity is altogether different. When the mugger compels you to hand over your money the necessity does not derive from subsuming the event under a universal law, but from his threat to do you harm and your calculation that to avoid this is worth more to you than the little cash you have on you. This is what R. G. Collingwood describes as the original sense of cause as necessary connection: the animistic sense of the influence one individual has on another. We see people each day attempting to influence the behaviour of others, using a range of strategies from pleading with them or offering them inducements, right up to actual compulsion. So it is not surprising when we think of causality in scientific explanations to think of it in this animistic sense in terms of the way we regularly see people compel others to do what they want them to do.

But an act may be caused though not compelled. If you decide to forego the delights of the bar, preferring instead to study, although we could account for your decision causally, nothing compels you to act in this way. Once you have made your decision we can explain causally why you did so, but even though it is caused this is not to say it is compelled. Indeed, you might have decided to give yourself the evening off and go to the bar, or not to go to the bar and watch TV instead. Whichever decision you make could be explained causally, but this is not to say it is compelled. While it is true to say all actions that are compelled are caused, the converse is not true: it is not the case that all actions that are caused are compelled. This suggests that an act can be caused, yet be free and voluntary, but it cannot be compelled and remain the same.

It seems, then, from this that what makes an act voluntary is that you have some sense of what you're doing and consent to it. Aristotle argues that 'an act is compulsory when its origin is from outside, the person compelled contributing nothing to it.' He maintains that an action may be involuntary for either of two reasons:

1. that someone is ignorant of what he is doing, say, a cigarette smoker who is unaware of the dangers of smoking to his health;

2. or that someone acts under compulsion from an external influence that denies him the opportunity to contribute anything.

The first seems straightforward enough. After all, if you don't know that smoking is a danger to your health, you don't even know you have a choice to make at all on these grounds. You may make it on other grounds, but as far as your health is concerned there is no choice to make. But the second is more difficult. Aristotle argues that a captain of a ship blown off course by the wind is compelled to go in that direction. He has no choice. He has no opportunity to contribute anything to this change in direction.

But not all cases of threats and unusual circumstances that 'force' you to do something that you would not normally do are clear cases of compulsion, because in some cases you do have it in your power to resist or ignore them. Aristotle cites the example of the passengers of a ship in distress who have to throw their possessions overboard to save themselves and the ship. Like the case of you having to hand over your money to a mugger, this is not a clear case of compulsion, because you do have it within your power to resist or ignore it. Ultimately what is done is chosen or willed. Even so, it would be absurd to deny that in cases like these, though you do have a choice, the degree of voluntariness is negligible. The more force or compulsion exerted the less we can argue that you have consented to it. Nevertheless, we can no longer talk about a clear distinction between compelled and voluntary acts, but more accurately about degrees of voluntariness.

Equally interesting is Aristotle's distinction between internal and external influences. If you were to leave the country to go on holiday, you would be doing so voluntarily of your own free will. But if you have to leave because the government is expelling you, this is involuntary because you are being forced to leave. Both are caused, but the first is done freely because the cause is internal: you simple desire to go abroad on holiday. Whereas

Aristotle (384–322 BC)

The son of a court physician, Aristotle was born in Stagira in northern Greece. His ideas effectively shaped the course of Western intellectual history until the seventeenth century. At the age of 17 he entered Plato's Academy, where he stayed until Plato's death in 347. Between 343 and 340 he was the tutor of the young Alexander the Great. In 335 he returned to Athens and set up the Lyceum, where he undertook research into many subjects.

He wrote prolifically, but the most famous philosophical works that have survived include the *Organon* (the logical works), *De Anima* ('On the Soul'), *Physics, Metaphysics, Nicomachean Ethics, Eudemian Ethics, Magna Moralia, Politics, Rhetoric* and *Poetics*, along with other works on natural history and science. His concern was to present as full an account as possible of the many different facets of the world in which we live. Nowhere is this seen more clearly than in his ethical theory, which still exerts considerable influence today, particularly his account of ethical virtues and of human flourishing ('happiness'). He also invented the study of formal logic, for which he developed the syllogistic system of analysis.

the second is involuntary, done in response to force exerted externally by the government.

But this doesn't always work quite so simply. Some inner influences can be compulsive. Certain inner psychological factors, like cravings or mental illness, force people to act and remove their ability to choose. We can argue that someone addicted to heroin consents to take it, but he is not able not to consent. He has no freedom of will, because his desires and cravings control him. He is, therefore, not responsible, if we mean by responsibility that he could choose not to take it.

These are key issues for those who commit themselves to any of the three positions normally associated with the problem of determinism and freedom. Hard determinists accept determinism, but reject free will, which they believe is incompatible with determinism. Indeterminists, likewise, believe that free will and determinism are incompatible, but reject any form of determinism, believing instead that while the inanimate world is determined, universal causation does not apply to human actions and decisions. In contrast to both of these soft determinists, or compatibilists, as this name implies, believe that while all actions are caused, this is compatible with free will, because among the factors that determine our actions are our own choices and desires.

So, to summarize:

	Determinism	Free will
Hard determinism	Accepts	Rejects
Indeterminism	Rejects	Accepts
Soft determinism	Accepts	Accepts

■ 2. Hard determinism

Hard determinists believe that all events, including human actions, are caused or determined by antecedent conditions: the present is determined by the past. Indeed, if we knew the laws of nature and the antecedent conditions, we could predict what will happen. If this were not so, the world would be incomprehensible: events would occur inexplicably and we would be left hostages to fortune, unable to predict or understand even the most normal event in our daily lives. This would, indeed, be a frightening place, where one unconnected, unpredictable and completely incomprehensible event follows another without end.

This is not the world as Spinoza saw it. His was one infinite, rational cosmic vision, with unity, order and necessity everywhere, excluding all chance and spontaneity from nature. Men think they are free merely because they are conscious of many of their acts, but the presence or absence of consciousness is neither here nor there. Their decisions and actions are determined by their impulses whether or not they are aware of them. In *Ethics* he paints a dispiriting picture:

> the infant believes that it is by free will that it seeks the breast; the angry boy believes that by free will he wishes vengeance; the timid man thinks it is with free will he seeks flight; the drunkard believes that by a free command of his mind he speaks the things which when sober he wishes he had left unsaid. ... [A]ll believe that they speak by a free command of the mind, whilst, in truth, they have no power to restrain the impulse which they have to speak.

While men believe themselves to be free, in fact they know nothing of the causes by which they are determined. They think they are free, but in reality they 'dream with their eyes open'. All events in our moral and mental lives and in the physical universe are explained as a result of causes and effects. Therefore terms like 'ought' and 'should', and 'praise' and 'blame', have no real place in the world. No matter how much we think people should be praised or blamed for their actions, determinism leaves no room for freedom, so there can be no choice and no responsibility for our actions.

2.1 Physical determinism

Modern expressions of this argument take one of two forms: physical or psychological determinism. In Chapter 15 we saw a form of physical determinism in epiphenomenalism, the belief that the mind and mental processes were nothing more than brain processes and mental events some kind of by-product of certain complex physical processes in the brain and nervous system. And as all brain processes are physical processes caused by antecedent physical factors, which are governed by certain natural laws of the physical universe, human action is likewise the product of the same physical laws. In Arthur Koestler's *Arrival and Departure* (1943), he suggests that bravery might be nothing more than an overactive thyroid gland. Making a decision, then, is causally determined by mental states, which are dependent on certain brain states caused by antecedent physical factors. You may believe you are free to make up your own mind, but in effect all such mental events are the product of physical determinism.

So, for example, an individual who habitually settles disputes using violence may not be entirely responsible for his decisions. Anthony Storr, in his book *Human Destructiveness* (1972), points out that 40–50 per cent of those in US penal institutions have serious drinking problems. Indeed a study of homicides in the Philadelphia area revealed that in nearly two-thirds of the cases either the offender or the victim, or both, had been drinking. Hypoglycaemia, alcohol and certain other drugs, including amphetamines, have the common effect of reducing the amount of serotonin in the brain. Serotonin, a neurotransmitter, is an important component in the neural mechanism inhibiting aggression. Before drug-related offences became common less than 20 per cent of murders were committed by strangers. Now drug-related street murders exceed domestic murders. In fact certain diets do the same. Periods of famine and general protein and carbohydrate malnutrition have historically been associated with great increases in criminality and violence. Diets with more than the average corn consumption have been shown experimentally to result in low levels of serotonin.

2.2 Psychological determinism

In contrast, psychological determinists believe that all psychological states and events are caused by antecedent psychological states and events. So, antecedent psychological facts in combination with psychological laws determine everything a person might think, decide or do. However, for this to succeed the determinist has to explain how our emotions, needs, desires, values, our moral conscience and other similar factors influence our decisions and actions. The determinist answer is to argue that everything about us, our current psychological profile, our mind, personality and character, has been caused by the interaction between certain hereditary characteristics and our environment – the external forces to which we are all exposed, like our upbringing. So, not only is every action and decision of ours the product of antecedent factors, but so too is our mind, personality and character, which determines our emotions, values, needs and so on.

2.3 Freedom as an illusion

This forms the basis of the hard determinist case and leads to the conclusion that what we experience as freedom is nothing more than an illusion. We may be able to give very plausible reasons that justify our actions, but, unknown to us, our every utterance, act or desire may be the result of a compulsion no different from the compulsive behaviour of a smoker who lights up a cigarette without knowing that she has done so or the compulsive eater who stares forlornly into the empty giant bag of crisps and wonders where they all went. Indeed, our enduring sense of freedom may be due to little more than the fact that we are always looking forward into an unknown future waiting to be shaped by each decision we make. If we were to look back at the causes of our actions we might see just how much each action and decision was caused by forces beyond our control.

And yet, although we can understand life backwards, it has to be lived forwards, which leads the compatibilists to reject this account on the grounds of our daily experiences of being free. We have a constant sense of being able to decide between several alternatives. Both before and after we have made a decision we have a sense of having made it without it being forced upon us by antecedent factors. For the most part we seem to be free of the sort of psychological compulsions suffered by the smoker and the eater. Indeed the fact that it is 'suffered' suggests it is pathological, a disease not shared by a normal healthy individual. And even though you may be a smoker, you are still no doubt free of the same kind of compulsive behaviour in the rest of your life.

Here your decisions are driven by your intentional states (your hopes, desires, beliefs and so on), which 'determine' your actions without being compulsive. We may have certain hopes, fears and desires in a certain situation, yet still not act on them, and this is what we regard as free will: the power to detach ourselves from our inner motivation and choose from the alternatives. In choosing we give expression to the person who made the choice. While we must take these motivational factors into account, we are not causally determined by them. It's up to us to decide which we will allow to be effective in any situation. Although we may not be able to describe exactly what's happening when we use our free will in this way, we are able to recognize when we are using it and when we're not.

Like Aristotle's, this argument rests on the distinction between internal and external influences. It's a form of compatibilism, in that it accepts we are determined, but by inner causes in the form of rational thought processes. When they make a difference our actions are free; when they don't, they're not. But still, can't we argue that these rational processes themselves are determined? We might still *describe* ourselves as free, but we're not in any significant way. It's just the customary way of describing these things, like saying as we travel on a bus that we saw the Opera House go by, when we all know it was us who went by not the Opera House. Maybe what we mean when we say we are free is that our actions and decisions are determined by a particular type of cause: our rational thought processes.

At least this argument evades the problem we noted earlier: that for an act to be completely free it would itself have to be a cause, but not an effect: it would have to be beyond the causal sequence and universal causation. It would amount to cordoning off an area of life from causality, which nevertheless still possesses the ability to interfere with the causal order of nature. This would seriously challenge the way we understand the world.

2.4 Consciousness

Perhaps the reason we are so unwilling to abandon freedom of the will, as the American philosopher John Searle suggests, is that it is tied to consciousness. We only attribute freedom to conscious beings. For this reason we are unwilling to regard as free even the most sophisticated computer or robot. Critics of hard determinism insist we are more than just physical bodies: our minds are not just the by-product, the epiphenomena, of our brains and we are not just 'conscious automata'. So the questions is, once we have accounted for ourselves in terms of the laws of the physical universe is there something left? And if this is consciousness, as it seems, does it contribute something distinctive, which means we can genuinely describe ourselves as free?

It may be that there is nothing left; that the physical laws that determine our bodies account for everything and what we call consciousness is just an illusion through which we vainly convince ourselves we are conscious and free. It may just be a running commentary on events with no power to affect anything. As we've seen this is roughly what Spinoza believed, along with some of the early Stoic philosophers. Everything is determined by the laws of nature and it makes no sense to resist this or to dress it up in a way that convinces us that we possess freedom of will. Consciousness is itself part of the determinist process. It can be explained by physical processes: the product of the brain and

Brief lives
Searle, John

Dates: 1932–
Born: Denver, Colorado, USA
Best known for: Being a proponent of the 'speech-act theory' in the philosophy of language and for his criticisms of cognitive science and the idea of the mind as a computer.

Major works: *Speech Acts: An essay in the philosophy of language* (1969), *Minds, Brains and Science* (1992), *The Rediscovery of the Mind* (1992), *The Construction of Social Reality* (1995), *Mind* (2004).

nervous system. We might not be able to explain the complex pattern of causal antecedents that produce our conscious experiences, but this doesn't weaken the argument.

Even if we were to concede that consciousness was part of the causal pattern – just one of the causes along with physical causes – we would still be left with consciousness, like other causes, being themselves determined by other causes. As soon as we let it in as a causal factor, like all the others, it too is determined. No matter what we decide our decisions are already determined by antecedent conditions. For example, you might leave work with a friend, who asks you to go for a drink. You decide to go and it seems this decision determines whether or not you go. But if we knew enough about you we could probably explain that you could not have decided otherwise. It had been a hard day and you needed to relax. You were thirsty. You had spent the day quietly in front of the computer and you needed to unwind and socialize. Your decision was determined by these and other causal antecedents. You only *appear* to have made a choice.

So, hard determinism appears to win both ways. Either consciousness is part of the deterministic scheme, in which case it cannot be free, or it is not part of it, in which case it cannot have any possible effect on our actions. The logic of cordoning off an area of life from causality, in which free acts are a cause, but not an effect, doesn't appear to be plausible.

Nevertheless, as we saw in the mind–body problem, there is a limit to scepticism, which ends at Descartes' *cogito* and Nagel's 'insideness'. If it seems to me I am conscious, then I *am* conscious. We cannot discover that we don't have minds and that they don't contain conscious, subjective intentional states. To discover anything is to have a mind. And it follows from this that we cannot apply determinism to our own case without changing it. We can consider other people's decisions to be causally determined, but not ours. To apply causal psychological laws to your own decision making you would have to know both the psychological laws and the antecedent factors causing your decision. But once you *know* these, a new factor (you knowing) has been added: it is no longer the same situation. Moreover, you may be determined to preserve your free will by making the laws no longer applicable to the new situation. For each situation, what is known as 'active agency' adds another factor making it a new situation *ad infinitum*.

So, to think at all is to have a mind, and to have a mind is to have consciousness, which is part of the causal process and, therefore, contributes something distinctive. We can, then, genuinely describe ourselves as free. But it is not just any consciousness. It has to be active consciousness, involving the ability to control our thinking and our desires, emotions and other inner motivations. If you were unable to move or control the course of your own thinking, yet were able to observe passively and receive sensations, we would not be inclined to describe you as having free will. The key to our conviction that we have free will is consciousness in the sense of the experience, as Searle describes it, of 'voluntary, intentional human action'. It is not even enough to show we are able to come to a decision as a result of engaging in rational thought; it must be consciousness in the sense that we experience the possibility of alternative courses of action.

Whenever we decide to do anything we are immediately and throughout conscious that we can act differently, and without this there can be no consciousness of freedom. What's more, it implies active agency. There is a difference between being conscious that something is happening to you, as in the sense of observing an event or perceiving a colour, and the sense that you are making something happen, which carries the implication that I could have chosen to make something different happen. Whether we are right to believe that we are free to do something else, this is the source of our unshakeable conviction in our own free will.

Searle describes this as involving an 'intention-in-action'. When we act intentionally we have the experience of freedom. This is an essential component of any case of acting with an intention. The intention-in-action of a compulsive eater or smoker, or someone addicted to heroin, is totally unconscious. Searle explains: 'The options that he sees as available to him are irrelevant to the actual motivation of his behaviour.' It is as if he were acting in response to someone else's movements, like a puppet, without any experience of freedom. So, as long as we engage in intentional activity we cannot give up the experience and conviction of being free. We can be convinced by evidence and explanations to give up other conceptions – like seeing the Opera House go by in the bus, when we know it has not moved an inch, or talk about the sun setting when we know from Copernicus it does no such thing – but not this one: we cannot give up the experience of freedom as long as we engage in intentional activity.

This suggests that not all of our behaviour is psychologically compulsive as long as we have the experience of voluntary action that we could have done otherwise. That's not to say physical determinism is also false. Indeed, as we will see, psychological libertarianism (the belief that our free will is not constrained by psychological factors) is compatible with physical determinism in a modified form of compatibilism.

■ 3. Indeterminism: libertarianism

Of course, this is not a conclusion that the hard determinist and the indeterminist would accept. Like the hard determinist, the indeterminist believes that free will and determinism are incompatible, but accepts free will as a reality and rejects determinism in human affairs. They argue not every event has its sufficient natural causes. Some are uncaused, which leaves room for free will. While the inanimate world is mechanistically determined by laws of nature, universal causation does not apply to human actions, making them predictable in the same way. Our actions may well be influenced by physical and psychological conditions, but they are not predictable, because we possess choice. Although conditions may predispose us to do Y, we can always do X.

Some indeterminists anchor their arguments in the reality of our experience of freedom as we described it above. Nothing, they argue, can be more certain than what is given in immediate experience. This gives us intuitive certainty that is far more reliable and trustworthy than trusting in some complex justification for determinism. Our experience of our freedom of choice is immediate: it has intuitive certainty that sets the limits to scepticism.

Others reject determinism on the grounds that, despite Spinoza's arguments, there does indeed exist novelty, spontaneity and creativity. The world, they maintain, is far more open and unpredictable than the closed world described by materialists handed down from the Enlightenment. William James, the nineteenth-century American philosopher who first coined the term 'indeterminism', focuses his most telling criticisms on the determinist view that as the past determines the future it cannot have within it any indeterminate or ambiguous possibilities.

In fact, he argues, the universe has a considerable amount of 'loose-play' in it. Not all things are causally connected. There is genuine pluralism in the nature of things; genuine possibilities that exceed the actualities in many situations. It is not that *any* imaginable action is possible for *any* person, just that among two or more mutually exclusive choices more than one is possible. Without this, James argues in *The Dilemma of Determinism* (1884), the determinist is forced into ethical indifference, where judgements of regret and blame are not only inappropriate but foolish. In a telling passage he maintains this is beyond the limits of our normal comprehension:

> I cannot understand the willingness to act, no matter how we feel, without the belief that acts are really good or bad. I cannot understand the belief that an act is bad, without regret at its happening. I cannot understand regret without the admission of real, genuine possibilities in the world.

The case the indeterminist presents, therefore, accepts that determinism works well enough to explain how physical causes produce physical movements, as if like some reflex, but it cannot be applied to human actions. These involve intentions,

---

Brief lives
James, William

Dates: 1842–1910
Born: New York City, USA
Best known for: Developing the philosophy of pragmatism. He argued that the truth of ideas consists in their usefulness in that they either accurately predict experience or promote valuable behaviour.

Major works: *The Principles of Psychology* (1890), *The Varieties of Religious Experience* (1902), *Pragmatism* (1907), *The Nature of Truth* (1909).

---

motives, desires and so on. This is a context that goes beyond mere movement. And the case for determinism cannot be made by describing such things as mental causes for our actions, because they are not separate states or events at all. They are features of our actions providing them with a form of classification. For example, when we describe an action in terms of a motivation, like greed, we are not identifying its cause, but describing its nature by giving it a classification. For something to be a cause of something else they must both be two separate things, but desires, intentions and motivations are not sufficiently independent to be causes.

As James explains, a context defined by things, like desires, motivations and intentions, presents considerable 'loose-play': genuine possibilities between which we have the freedom to choose. Although our personalities are empirical, the products of causal factors like heredity and environment, and although this limits the choices we might make, there is nothing inevitable about the choice we actually make. Moreover, it excludes the 'moral self': an ethical side of ourselves that operates in situations of moral choice. As John Stuart Mill describes it, the moral self manifests itself in the feeling 'of our being able to modify our own character *if we wish* ... the feeling of moral freedom which we are conscious of.' C. A. Campbell makes the same point, arguing that if the individual is conscious of acting 'against the line of least resistance, against the line to which his character as so far formed strongly inclines him', then the self, the source of moral freedom, is distinct from our formed character and its desires and inclinations. He explains:

> if the self is thus conscious here of combating his formed character, he surely cannot possibly suppose that the act, although his own act, issues from his formed character? ... the 'nature' of the self and what we commonly call the 'character' of the self are by no means the same thing. The 'nature' of the self comprehends, but is not without remainder reducible to, its character; it must, if we are to be true to the testimony of our experience of it, be taken as including also the authentic creative power of fashioning and refashioning 'character'.

The formed habits of our character are far from being the masters of the situation, but we are theirs. These are causally undetermined choices. We can subdue causal factors, and resist temptations and desires, through the force of our will. We can choose to do something not out of self-interest, but out of duty. In so doing the individual becomes morally responsible for what he does and in this, the indeterminists argue, lies the distinction between men and animals.

3.1 Why isn't our moral self determined?

But, if our character is determined by heredity and environment, why not our moral self too? Critics argue that the indeterminists not only assume free will without giving any evidence of it, but without reason they restrict it to one set of choices. If a person is free to choose in moral issues, why are they not free to choose in others?

The indeterminist generally has three overlapping responses to these charges. First, as we have seen, they will appeal to the overwhelming evidence of our experience of having moral choice, of being self-determining and creative. Even when our choices are restricted we all have an immediate experience of having the freedom to choose. Thus, although there are limits to freedom, we still have sufficient experience to sustain the general belief in the existence of free will.

Second, the fact that we make decisions all the time demonstrates that we all have free will, because we can only make decisions if beforehand we could have done or chosen otherwise and if it's in our power to do what we're planning to do. In other words, for someone to make a decision they must believe they have a real choice. Since we all do often make decisions, we must all believe we can make choices – we must all believe we are free. Just the universal experience of decision making is enough to reject determinism.

But, even so, we may *believe* we have free will, but this is not to say we *are* free. To this the indeterminist responds, thirdly, with a simple contingent argument. In the contingent world error is always possible, so the question is not can I be deceived by experience, in this case of my freedom to choose, but whether the possibility of deception means that I cannot accept these experiences as sufficient evidence for the truth of my beliefs. The evidence we have for contingent propositions may not be enough to meet the requirements of a necessary truth, which excludes the very possibility of error. But this is not a standard we ordinarily expect from any contingent proposition. Science and all empirical research accept a much lower standard, which includes the possibility of error. And the empirical evidence of our experience of choosing freely is

more than sufficient to meet the requirements of a contingent truth. It may be based on corrigible evidence, but it provides more than is necessary to be accepted beyond a reasonable doubt.

If the experience of our deliberating and choosing freely must be rejected as evidence of free will, because it could deceive us, then any evidence based on experience must be rejected on the same grounds. But this can lead only to total scepticism. Alternatively, indeterminists argue, if this evidence is to be accepted, the overwhelming weight of it is enough to establish grounds for rejecting the theory of determinism.

3.2 We only *appear* to be free because we don't yet know the causes

However, the determinists insist we only have the appearance of being free because we don't yet know the causes that determine our actions. As science steadily advances these causes will be revealed as they have been in other areas and we will piece together a picture of a stable universe each part of which functions predictably according to certain universal laws of nature. We might think that phenomena like free will escape this universal system of laws, but, like telekinesis and the paranormal, they will eventually be explained and shown to be predictable, law-abiding phenomena.

Up until the twentieth century this view of science may have seemed to provide a compelling argument, but the results of twentieth-century physics, in particular the development of quantum theory, has left us with serious doubts about the traditional mechanistic picture of the universe functioning predictably according to certain laws. Many physicists agree that the notion of cause does not apply to certain subatomic particles: not every event has its sufficient natural causes. But if it is not caused, it is not determined and its behaviour is not predictable. And if not every event in the universe has its sufficient natural cause, perhaps human action, too, is undetermined.

In fact what physicists like Max Born, Werner Heisenberg and Max Planck found was that the behaviour of subatomic particles involves an element of chance. In any given situation there is more than one thing that an electron, the basic particle of matter, can do. Whether one quantum event or another will occur is not strictly determined by antecedent physical factors. In his famous 'Uncertainty Principle' Werner Heisenberg revealed that we cannot know both the location and the momentum of a subatomic particle. Our attempt to ascertain one makes it impossible to ascertain the other.

Of course, you might argue that while this may be true at the micro-level of the quantum theory no one is suggesting it is also true at the macro-level of everyday events. We can still predict all the normal events in our lives: the phases of the moon, when the sun will rise and fall, that heavier-than-air objects will fall when unsupported and so on. But this is not the point that many indeterminists are arguing. They argue that the old Newtonian mechanistic view of causation in the universe is seriously flawed: that, as William James argued, there is more plurality, more 'loose-play' in the universe than is allowed for in the mechanistic notion. The physicist, Henry Margenau, argues that while the mechanistic view allowed no freedom, the new view 'rescues man's destiny from the fateful web of physical determinism' and brings to light uncertainties that may harbour freedom.

3.3 Freedom is impossible if indeterminism is true

However, if everything is in fact undetermined, two things result. First, we cannot be free because we cannot predict with any certainty: everything is unpredictable, random and capricious, and we are forced to live like hapless inmates in a prison of uncertainty.

And second, we cannot be free because we cannot convert our actions into effective results that bring about what we intended. If actions are uncaused and random, we have no power to cause actions. Nothing we do can have any predictable outcome; all events are random. To be free means two things: that I have the opportunity to make free choices about what I should do and that once I have made my decision this has a predictable outcome. For example, if friends were to invite me out to a restaurant, for me to be free I must not only have the opportunity to choose, but I must know that my muscles and limbs will work to get me to the restaurant. If true, indeterminism, by making everything uncaused, random and unpredictable, would mean that I could not know this. I could never know that I could do what I might choose to do. It would rob me of my freedom just as surely as would determinism.

If this is the case, the problem for determinists and indeterminists alike is that we can't be responsible for our actions, whether determinism is true or false. If it's true, antecedent circumstances are responsible; if it's false, nothing is responsible. If *nothing* can determine an event, then *I* cannot determine it. For an action to be something I have done, it has to be the product of a certain type of cause in me. It has to be determined by my desires, intentions, beliefs, character and so on. If it is not, if it is one of those things that just happened without explanation, it is difficult to see how this could be *my* doing. If this in fact is the case it implies mere chance and randomness, and usually we mean more than this when we talk about free will. We mean not just that it wasn't determined in advance, but that *you* determined what you would do by *doing* it. It didn't just happen, nor was it determined in advance. *You* did it and you could have done otherwise.

■ 4. Soft determinism: compatibilism

It seems, then, that determinism is necessary if we are to make any sense of the notions of freedom and responsibility. But for an action to be something *you* have done, it must be the product of a certain type of cause *in* you – it must be *your* cause. Determinism by itself doesn't threaten freedom, only a certain type of cause. For an act to be free it has to be caused by a familiar type of psychological cause found in our desires, beliefs, fears or intentions. It is possible for us to give a psychological account of our actions in all cases; otherwise they wouldn't be *our* actions. And although it seems odd to think that everything we do is determined by our circumstances and psychological conditions, for us to be responsible for our actions it doesn't make sense if they're not determined. As Nagel points out, 'It's not clear what it means to say *I* determine the choice, if nothing about me determines it.'

Thus, the compatibilists believe the argument that free will and determinism are incompatible rests on a confusion over what we mean when we say we're free. Freedom is incompatible with fatalism, but not with determinism and the theory of universal causation, because among the factors that determine our actions are our own choices and desires. Hume, for example, argues that actions we praise or blame are those determined by the person's character. This, he believes, is the key to solving the problem we started this chapter with: that we accept with equal conviction the reality of choice in our daily lives and at the same time that all things are caused. This, he maintains, is just a verbal dispute concerning the concept of liberty and he asks what we mean by liberty when applied to voluntary actions:

> We cannot surely mean that actions have so little connection with motives, inclinations, and circumstances, that one does not follow with a certain degree of uniformity from the other. ... By liberty, then, we can only mean *a power of acting or not acting according to the determinations of the will.*

We can only make sense of voluntary action if there is a uniform, causal connection between what we do and our motives, inclinations, circumstances and characters. Whether someone is acting freely, therefore, depends on Aristotle's distinction between external and internal causes. A person acts freely and responsibly not because their actions are uncaused, but because they are not compelled by external causes.

4.1 Character

Freedom, therefore, lies in being able to do what you choose to do. You are free if you could have done something else had you chosen to. There are still antecedent factors that cause someone to choose certain alternatives and these are to be found in our character, desires and beliefs: they are part of the person. Thus, the compatibilist contends that we are free as long as the decision is caused by the person we are. We are not free if we act in response to external forces that leave us no choice. Our actions can be caused by outside forces and still remain free as long as we are still free to choose.

Remember Aristotle's example of the passengers who threw their possessions overboard to save the ship. They still had room to make a decision, even though this was limited, unlike the captain whose ship was forced to go in the other direction than he wanted to go by forces beyond his control. If the ship had foundered on a reef to the loss of all onboard, the captain would not have been found responsible in a subsequent enquiry. But if it were shown that there was something that could have been done and he chose not to do it, then he would have been found responsible. In this case what he did would have been of his own choosing and freely undertaken. It is not that this decision was undetermined, but that he had the ability to act on the basis of self-chosen ends.

We could still show that his decision was the result of his experience, beliefs, thoughts, motives, desires and needs. In other words, for someone to be responsible for their actions they must derive from his character. It was precisely because the captain was the character that he was that caused the ship to founder and made him responsible for his action. In cases where there is no causation from this as the determining antecedent factor, there is no basis for responsibility. And, of course, the more we know about our character, particularly our abilities, needs and desires, the more freedom we have. We can accept it and yield to its demands, or reject it and counteract it. Indeed, John Stuart Mill argues that if we know the motives and inducements bearing on an individual and his character and volitions, we will be able to predict his conduct with the same unerring precision as we can physical events. Nor does this full assurance conflict in the least degree with our feeling of freedom. Indeed, he argues, we would resent it or at least feel disappointed if our close friends did not know us well enough to predict accurately what we would choose to do.

However, the notion of character doesn't solve all the problems. Indeed it brings with it certain problems of its own. If nothing is undetermined, then character is itself determined, which still leaves us wondering whether the individual's actions are caused or compelled. If she is compelled to have the character she has, it can hardly be said, except in some malicious sense, that she is responsible for her actions and decisions. In all the influences that go to shape a person's character, say her education, upbringing, social class, national origin, gender, maybe even height and weight, to what sense can we say that she has been able to intervene and choose her own character?

For example, in the light of this what sense does it make to condemn serial killers for what they do? In his award-winning book, *Killing for Company* (1985), about Dennis Nilsen, who confessed in 1983 to killing 15 homosexual men, Brian Masters cites the portrait of serial killers that Dr Robert Brittain published in 1970. In it Dr Brittain describes an introspective, withdrawn figure with few associates and usually no close friends. He involves himself in solitary pursuits, is uncommunicative and feels different, isolated and insecure. Except when he is killing, he feels inferior and is, therefore, at his most dangerous when he suffers a loss of self-esteem.

Brian Masters comments that Nilsen fits this so exactly that 'it takes one's breath away.' But what made Nilsen into this figure? Did he make himself or was it circumstances? Nilsen was brought up cut off from a small fishing community itself cut off on the east coast of Scotland. The only person with whom he was able to establish a bond was his grandfather, who died at sea when Nilsen was six. This blighted the rest of his life, leaving him with a vacuum, which he was thereafter always attempting unsuccessfully to fill. He blames this for his disordered personality and its numbing effect on his moral sensibilities. It seemed to the young boy that both his father and grandfather had walked out on him, leaving him with an intense feeling of worthlessness from which he retreated into privacy.

The greatest fear for serial killers is humiliation, which they equate with the position of being loved, because at any time that love might be withdrawn, leaving them convinced they are unlovable. So, extreme hostility ferments. Fearing vulnerability, they retreat into a fantasy world, where they won't be emotionally dependent and won't risk disappointment. Here they can compensate for this with disproportionate power and superiority. Dr Brittain argues that this world is more important and more real than the ordinary world. Consequently, they place diminished value on the real world and on ordinary people. Emotionally flat and without remorse, they have no pity for their victims, who step into their fantasy world. Nilsen, who had a rich and active fantasy life, says,

> The need to return to my beautiful warm unreal world was such that I was addicted to it even to the extent of knowing of the risks to human life. ... It was a great and necessary diversion and escape from the troubled reality of life outside. ... The pure primitive man of the dream world killed these men. ... I have been my own secret scriptwriter, actor, director and cameraman. ... I took this world of make-believe, where no one really gets hurt, into the real world, and people can get hurt in the real world. ... These people strayed into my innermost secret world and they died there.

It's difficult to argue convincingly that people like Nilsen are responsible for the characters they end up with. As a result, driven by compulsions that they have few means of controlling, they retreat into a fantasy world where they play out their relationships and kill.

This in turn raises an equally important concern. So far we have argued that a person acts freely and responsibly not because their actions are uncaused, but because they are not compelled by external causes. But this has ignored those internal causes that might be compulsive. The most obvious case is brainwashing, where even a person's character is changed. Subliminal advertising has a similar effect

implanting messages unconsciously to control a person's behaviour. But the most common compulsions take the form of neuroses and addictions, say, to drugs or alcohol. We can argue, of course, that those so addicted are still responsible for deciding to take drugs or alcohol in the first place. But this is not relevant to those normal physiological conditions that are not self-induced, like menstruation or clinical depression. Nor is it in those cases where individuals, under the influence of others, are brought to a state where their actions are taken under extreme stress or strong emotions they cannot control.

Today we are more aware of the defence of 'protracted provocation' in cases involving killing, which, although done after deliberation, is the result of extreme emotional provocation. But this was not the case in 1955 when Ruth Ellis, the last woman to be hanged in Britain, was executed for the murder of her boyfriend David Blakely. For two years he had taken malicious delight in making her jealous, reducing her life to a living hell. So desperate had she become that she valued neither her own life, nor his. Finally, she got herself a revolver and shot him at point-blank range outside a pub in Hampstead, then turned and asked onlookers to get the police. Even though the British public sided with her *en masse*, collecting 50,000 signatures on one petition, it was to no avail.

But things were different in 1988 when June and Hilda Thompson were convicted of the murder of their father, Tommy Thompson, at Liverpool Crown Court. For 20 years he had violently abused and tyrannized the two girls and their mother. They were forced to wash the dishes in absolute silence, knowing they would be severely punished if even one dish were to touch another. His cup had to be placed a stipulated distance from the edge of the table, and the curtains drawn at precisely 7.35 pm – not a minute sooner or later. From early adolescence to their mid-30s the two girls had to submit to him sexually. In the evenings a mere twitch of his head was enough for one of them to leave the TV programme they were watching and go upstairs and wait for him. Then, after he was done, they would return to finish watching the TV. Finally, when they could take no more, they shot him as he lay sleeping on the couch. But, despite the fact they killed with deliberation and planning, the judge declined to give a custodial sentence, telling them he believed they had served their sentence prior to their offence.

4.2 The moral self

This suggests, even though our actions come from our character, still they may not be free and we may not be responsible for them, not only because we have little influence over the character we end up with, but because our actions may be driven by internal compulsions over which we have little or no control. As you can see, this is to measure freedom by the degree to which we can reasonably be held responsible. But to measure it accurately we have to consider two factors. First, we have to know the degree of determination and ask the question, are the forces so great that we could not expect a reasonable person to act morally? And, second, on the other side of the equation, our concern is not so much about whether the act was caused, but whether we have a sufficiently strong moral self.

This, then, becomes our new measure of free will. It is no longer a matter of whether our actions were done in response to external forces or internal ones from within our character. Recognizing the problem that at least initially we end up with characters not of our own making, the problem becomes do we have a strong enough moral self to change our character. In *A System of Logic* John Stuart Mill describes it as the 'grand error' to assume our characters are formed by circumstances and there is nothing we can do to change this. He argues, although our characters are formed *for* us, they are in part formed *by* us. A person's character is 'formed by his circumstances ... but his own desire to mould it in a particular way, is one of those circumstances, and by no means one of the least influential.' In the same manner that our parents and teachers placed us in certain circumstances that would have a beneficial effect in forming our character, we can likewise place ourselves under the influence of other circumstances: 'We are exactly as capable of making our own character, *if we will*, as others are of making it for us.'

According to Brand Blanshard this involves a different kind of causality from that operating in the realm of physical bodies. There are different causal levels with the higher level supervening on the lower levels. The causality brought into play by reflection and choice on the higher level is different from the mechanical causality of the physical world. Possessing self-consciousness the individual is capable of personal initiative and of responding to events. He is creative and, within bounds, can reshape the external world, himself and his relations with others. The self, as the centre of creativity, is free to choose to respond to stimuli, and the more we learn about ourselves and the world the more choices and the more freedom we have.

It appears, however, that in Mill's argument the words 'if we will' gives the argument away, because the will to alter your own character is itself given to you by circumstances. It seems to lead us to the conclusion of the German philosopher, Arthur Schopenhauer, that 'A man may surely do as he wills to do, but he cannot determine what he wills.' We seem to be moving from character to moral self to will in what appears to be an infinite regress as we discover each one is determined by forces beyond the individual.

And yet, Mill has no problem in conceding that the will is indeed formed by our experience: '... experience of the painful consequences of the character we previously had; or by some strong feeling of admiration or aspiration, accidentally aroused.' But here's the rub. As he points out, to argue that we have no means of changing our characters, or that we shall not use our power to change unless we have the desire are two different things. Unlike the former, the latter accepts that we can change it, if only we have the desire. And this feeling of being able to modify our character is the moral feeling – a feeling of moral freedom. Lo and behold freedom resolves itself in the moral individual. He argues,

> A person feels morally free who feels that his habits or his temptations are not his masters, but he theirs; who, even in yielding to them, knows that he could resist; that were he desirous of altogether throwing them off, there would not be required for the purpose a stronger desire than he knows himself to be capable of feeling.

Of course, we still cannot claim genuinely to have this freedom unless we have formed our own character: unless we have converted our consciousness of freedom into actual freedom, or at least know that in a case of conflict we can conquer our character. And this leads him to the epiphanic insight that 'none but a person of confirmed virtue is completely free.'

So, perhaps as Hume pointed out earlier, what the compatibilist presents us with is a verbal dispute. We accept both determinism and freedom. The problem is: what do we mean by freedom when applied to voluntary actions? And, like Mill, Hume concludes it is 'a power of acting or not acting according to the determinations of the will...'. The verbal dispute is resolved by defining freedom as the will to impose our moral self on our character. By this means, it seems, the compatibilist

> **Brief lives**
> **Schopenhauer, Arthur**
>
> Dates: 1788–1860
> Born: Danzig, Prussia
> Best known for: Advocating the importance of intuition, creativity and the irrational in philosophy and for arguing that our inner awareness of ourselves gives us knowledge of reality as it is in itself.
>
> Major works: *The World as Will and Idea* (1819).

has brought us to the destination we predicted earlier. We have cordoned off an area that is uncaused: the will is a cause, but not an effect.

■ 5. Conclusion

If you think this is an unsatisfactory conclusion, then you will have to decide what it is that gives us this 'power of acting' according to the will and for this you may have to make up your mind on what you consider to be a satisfactory explanation of human actions: what explains why we do what we do. For the hard determinist human action is no different from events in the natural world, explained with deductive necessity by subsuming events under universal laws. The compatibilist, while not denying causation, does reject this sort of mechanical causation. Universal laws are unnecessary: they add nothing more. All that is required to explain why we will as we do is a 'reason explanation': the cause of our willing lies in our reasons, in our motives and purposes. All that is necessary is for the explanation to show, not that our actions were inevitable, but merely that they were reasonable: what a reasonable person would think justified in the circumstances.

In the next two chapters we will examine what these reasons might be and the bearing they have on how we decide the degree of someone's responsibility for wrongful actions and what punishment they should receive.

■ Questions

1. If every event has a cause does this exclude the possibility that someone could have acted otherwise had he or she chosen to do so?

2. Is it logically possible for you to predict today with certainty what you will decide tomorrow without thereby deciding it today?

3. If I were to act on the basis of my own decision, does this mean that my action can be both free and caused?

4. 'As we have not chosen our characters we cannot be held responsible for actions that result from them.' Discuss.

5. Am I right in thinking that if determinism is true, nobody can be blamed for anything?

■ Recommended reading

Berofsky, Bernard (ed.) *Free Will and Determinism* (New York: Harper and Row, 1966).

Hook. S. (ed.) *Determinism and Freedom in the Age of Modern Science* (New York: Macmillan, Collier, 1961).

Kane, Robert. *The Significance of Free Will* (New York: Oxford University Press, 1996).

Mill, J. S. *A System of Logic* (London: Longman, 1965), Book IV, Chapter 2.

O'Connor, D. *Free Will* (London: Macmillan, 1972).

Watson, G. (ed.) *Free Will* (Oxford: Oxford University Press, 1982).

 The note structure to accompany this chapter can be downloaded from our website.

Freedom in Context

Contents

Key issues

▶ If society is just a loose collection of isolated individuals and we are free of all social, religious and cultural influences, how are we to make sense of the world and create meaning and value in our lives?

▶ If neither society nor religion mediates between the individual and the world, how can we know that our reality *is* reality, or what we believe to be morally right *is* morally right?

▶ And without the mobilizing force of faith in some divine purpose how are we to relate thought and action, such that if a person believes something this will induce them to act?

▶ Is the individual's reason alone sufficient to generate answers to such questions? And if it is not, how are we to explain the individual's actions, and depict social relations and processes within different societies? If not individual reason, what is it that drives these societies: what are the laws of social development or progress?

▶ Are the structuralists right when they claim that all human life can only be made intelligible through their relations?

We saw in the last chapter that, if we are to measure freedom by the degree to which we can reasonably be held responsible, one of the things we must know is whether the degree of determination is so great that we could not expect a reasonable person to act morally. We also saw that one way compatibilists argue for the freedom of the individual is to cordon off an area in which actions are uncaused: they are themselves a cause, but not an effect.

In this chapter we will see the extent to which this view is sustained by philosophers who take their inspiration directly from the Enlightenment, and is challenged by a different tradition that has its roots in the nineteenth and twentieth-century philosophers, whose vision placed the individual squarely in a community, the subject of a rich pattern of interpersonal influences. These philosophers 'collectivized' and 'historicized' the individual: that is, her actions were seen to be influenced both horizontally by the community in which she lived, and vertically by the historical process that culminated in this community with all its institutions and traditions.

■ 1. Centring the subject

The Enlightenment emancipated man from the unquestioned acceptance of religious authority. In its place philosophers erected the sovereignty of individual reason. As Descartes founded knowledge on the certainty of self-consciousness, so the subject was given privileged status in modern western philosophy. But this was not without its problems. First, how was the individual to create meaning and value, if not through a religious interpretation of events and the world? If there were no divine mediator between the individual and the world, how can she know that her reality *is* reality, or what she believes to be morally right *is* morally right? And, second, without the mobilizing force of faith in some divine purpose how are we to relate thought and action, such that if a person believes something this will induce them to act? How are we to ensure the political obligation of individuals to a society without divine endorsement? The relation between knowledge and the will to act, between thinking and being, Marx describes as the 'great basic question of all philosophy'.

This last problem we will examine in Chapters 24 to 27; for now we need to consider the first. Philosophers in the Enlightenment tradition see individual reason alone as responsible for our beliefs and values, and the decisions we freely take on the basis of them. Reason is the ultimate validation, leaving us alone responsible for our undetermined choices.

1.1 Kant

The most important advocate of this view is Kant, who maintains that if we are right to believe we are free to choose and be responsible for our actions, we need an area that is free from determinism. Morality by its very nature involves choice, so no obligation can be imposed on the individual from outside her own will, nor can it be internally imposed as the expression of some compulsion or need, some inner desire that craves for satisfaction. In all such cases the individual's rational will, the ultimate determinant of right and wrong, would be unfree. As Aristotle argues, a moral person acts voluntarily, and is not the slave of her passions.

Yet, as we noted earlier, Kant was also an enthusiastic supporter of Newton, modern science and the concept of universal causation. In the *Critique of Pure Reason* he argues:

Actions of men are determined in conformity with the order of Nature, by their empirical character and other causes; if we could exhaust all the appearances, there would not be found a single human action which would not be predicted with certainty.

The explanation for this apparent contradiction lies in the different standpoints we adopt. When we adopt the theoretical standpoint, we seek to understand the natural world through science and determinism. Every event, including human actions, is determined: we can show why it occurred by producing sufficient natural causes. But this is distinct from the practical standpoint. When we act or arrive at a decision, we ought to consider our own acts of will and our decisions as sufficient causes of our actions. We can't just trace back the origins of our actions, showing how these turn out to be caused.

At the heart of this lies Kant's two-world view, in which the world is divided between humans and other creatures or mere 'things'. For humans, no matter how much you might know of the causes of your actions, even if you could predict accurately what you would do, you would still be deciding freely that this is what you will do. It is this freedom that distinguishes man from other creatures or from mere things. The behaviour of other creatures in the 'sensible' world is determined by laws of nature that are beyond their control. They are driven by desires, needs and inclinations over which they exercise no choice. In contrast man, as part of the 'intelligible' world, is free to choose, but this does not mean that, in contrast, he is free from laws. Freedom is not the absence of laws, but acting according to self-imposed laws. In this lies the importance of reason: man's capacity not just to impose laws on his own behaviour, but to act for reasons that are implicitly universal.

At this point we ought to slow down and explain this carefully. At the heart of Kant's theory is this difference between mere 'things' and humans. Humans are distinct by virtue of their reason, their capacity to choose self-imposed laws that will govern their behaviour. The behaviour of mere things is the product of causal forces both internal, in the form of desires and inclinations, and external. That we can live according to self-imposed laws means we have 'dignity', that is, man is an end-in-itself.

But to say that individuals are ends in themselves by virtue of the fact that they live by self-determined laws, the product of their own reason, is also to say that these laws are universal. As we saw when we discussed the synthetic *a priori* in Chapter 6 the mind imposes a form, which is pure, free of all taint of desire or inclination. The closest analogy is that of nature and natural laws in science. Our perception of the external world yields empirical information about what *does* happen, whereas laws tell us what *has* to happen. The element of necessity and universality is pure, the *a priori* contribution of the mind. The same is true of moral reasoning: the will, our practical reason, imposes a pure form on the given, our desires. Desires, like perception, are the passive products of experience, the source of our maxims, whereas the universal and necessary features of the laws we impose on ourselves are the formal product of reason.

This means that by imposing my own rational laws on my own will, I do so only on the basis that the same laws should also be imposed on all other rational natures in the same circumstances. Indeed, the only way we can be sure that our will is in fact determined by itself is whether our maxims are universalizable. We transform our maxims into universal laws through the application of our reason. If they are not universalizable, then either they are determined by others who treat us as mere means to meet *their* needs and inclinations, or they are subjective: done as a result of *our* inclinations, our needs and desires determined for us by nature. These are natural, rather than rational laws. Thus, a rational will can only be free and self-determining if it acts on universalized maxims. This is Kant's first formulation of his famous categorical imperative: 'Act only on that maxim through which you can at the same time will that it should become a universal law.'

1.2 Individualism

Beyond Kant into the nineteenth century the influence of the Enlightenment was felt systematically in different forms of political, social and moral theory. Faith in the atomistic scientific method of breaking the whole down into its elementary parts, and analysing the behaviour of each part to reveal the laws governing the whole, focused attention on the individual as the ultimate source of validation of political values and principles of government. The whole it was thought was no more than the sum of the parts, and society no more than a loose collection of isolated individuals. As each one was rational and driven by an overwhelming need to maximize his own self-interest, he knew his interests best. Thus, it followed that society should allow the individual the freedom to organize his affairs without interference; the state's role should be limited to removing those obstacles that restrict the individual's pursuit of his own self-interest.

If the individual were to be given as much freedom as possible to maximize his self-interest, it was believed that the best of all worlds would result. Manufacturers would be free to produce cheaply and competitively, maximizing their profits, extending their markets and generating jobs. If workers were free from the interference of governments or trade unions to negotiate with employers, they too would be able more effectively to maximize their interests. In summary, as Thomas Jefferson maintained, 'That government is best that governs least.' In his essay 'On Liberty' (1859), John Stuart Mill argued that interference in the affairs of the individual should be restricted only to those occasions when his actions are likely to cause 'harm' to others. And, of course, the reasons justifying our acceptance of our political obligation to obey the laws of such a system of government were ultimately not to be found in a belief in God or in our rulers as God's lieutenants on Earth, but in our own self-interests which are served best by accepting the conditions it guarantees.

With moral values, too, it was thought the sole and sufficient arbiter of our beliefs and values was to be found in the individual and his capacity to reason. In utilitarianism, the theory that actions are right in so far as they promote the greatest happiness of the greatest number, the ultimate validation was in the individual's capacity to reason prudentially to maximize his own happiness. In any situation the individual is capable of calculating the balance of pleasures and pains, to reveal what action is most likely to maximize his pleasure. This alone was sufficient to reveal what it was morally right to do. Alternative moral theories suggested the ultimate validation of moral values was to be found in the individual's intuition or in his emotions.

1.3 Existentialism

Nevertheless, while this was compatible with the new materialism of the Industrial Revolution and the capitalist culture it brought with it, there were many who saw in this a threat to individual liberty, not least those whose work promoted existentialist ideas. Nineteenth-century materialism fostered the belief that if human actions can be causally explained, determinism would exclude the possibility that the individual can be both free and responsible. But instead of denying that causal explanations entail this kind of determinism, the existentialist goes further to deny the probability of causal explanations of human action.

Choice is unavoidable, they believe. All my actions imply choice. Even when I don't choose explicitly, as I may not do in the majority of cases, my action bears witness to an implicit choice. I can choose to do something, choose not to do it, or choose not to choose. But whichever option I take I cannot avoid choosing. If any single principle constitutes the doctrine of existentialism it is that freedom and choice are central facts of human nature. Take, for example, Viktor Frankl's account of his experiences at Auschwitz concentration camp in *Man's Search for Meaning* (1946). There cannot be many places on Earth or many times in human history that would convince us more that in such circumstances man is unfree. Yet, despite his horrifying experiences, Frankl maintains,

> Man is not fully conditioned and determined; he determines himself whether to give in to conditions or stand up to them. In other words, man is ultimately self-determining ... every human being has the freedom to change at any instant.

1.3.1 Kierkegaard

In the nineteenth century it was the Danish philosopher Søren Kierkegaard who took up the process of individualism begun by the Protestant Reformation in the sixteenth century and Martin Luther's assertion of the importance of individual conscience, rather than the authority of the priests, as the criterion of what is right and most likely to secure salvation. But Kierkegaard lived in a time of mass production and rapid change, where individuals were fast becoming mere spectators and machine minders, condemned to perform repetitive meaningless tasks. In the 1840s, in *The German Ideology* (1846) and *The Communist Manifesto* (1848), Karl Marx was attacking capitalist production for alienating man and robbing him of the means to create meaning and value in his life. Capitalism had transformed man from an end to a means, from a person to the instrument of an impersonal process, which subjugates him without regard for his needs or desires.

While the 1840s brought Marx to the realization that the solution lay in historical materialism and the culmination of the class struggle, Kierkegaard was brought to the conviction that the solution lay in the reality of the individual's moral commitments and choices – in existentialism. For Kierkegaard the leading edge of reality was the individual's own choices: man makes himself through his actions and his commitments. The modern state, Kierkegaard accepted, was thoroughly secular: it no longer promulgated official religious doctrine. So the problem of meaning and value was not going to be solved by the social order. Christianity, therefore, was forced back to its original starting point in the individual's will and conscience. It was the 'how' rather than the 'what' of religion that mattered. The individual's religious faith was an act of pure freedom, a commitment, and all commitment brings the individual back into the forward movement of life. Only in this way can the individual create meaning and value in the world. For Kierkegaard choice is everything. Perhaps you can understand life backwards, but it has to be lived forwards.

So, as Marx was to do later, Kierkegaard sought to reverse the traditional relationship of knowledge and action in western thought. Reality is a process of becoming: action comes first. But, whereas Marx had seen this as cooperating with historical forces, for Kierkegaard the leading edge of reality itself is nothing else but our own personal decisions. The choices we make settle what we become and what kind of world we're going to find ourselves in. Existentialism is a philosophy of action, a will. Life's chief task is to become an individual.

1.3.2 Sartre

The relevance of this became even clearer during the Second World War, when the optimism of the nineteenth century was replaced by dictatorships that threatened both material and spiritual destruction. The confidence in democracy and industrialization to stride ineluctably towards societies that distributed wealth more equally, cared for the weak and ensured social justice, seemed badly misplaced. Existentialist writers were driven to depict a different situation, one which involved serious instability and risk to human life and freedom. The individual, they believed, was 'thrown into the world': abandoned to deterministic forces that could at any moment frustrate his initiatives. His freedom was conditioned and threatened by forces beyond his control.

The loudest clarion calls came from the French writer and philosopher Jean-Paul Sartre, particularly in his trilogy of novels set in the years 1938-40, *The Roads to Freedom* (1945–9), and his most notable philosophical works, *Being and Nothingness* (1943) and *Existentialism and Humanism* (1946). Sartre argues that, even in such threatening circumstances, man has absolute freedom: he must 'invent' himself.

Drawing the same distinction Kant does between 'things' and humans, he insists that 'existence precedes essence'. The individual has no *a priori* essence, a core nature that determines what he will do. There is nothing within him or outside him that he can depend upon to make the decision for him. He is without excuse: there is no God, no good *a priori*, no given human nature, and no determinism. 'Man is free, man *is* freedom.' He is 'condemned to be free.'

Although he didn't create himself, from the moment he is thrown into the world he is responsible for everything he does. In *Being and Nothingness* Sartre says, '... man being condemned to be free carries the weight of the world on his shoulders.' He must create himself through his own commitments. No causal explanation can obscure our need to decide in any situation. We are nothing but a freedom which reveals itself, invents itself, in its choices.

Moreover, at every instant our actions and decisions are examples for everyone to follow. As Sartre explains, 'Everything happens to every man as though the whole human race had its eyes fixed upon what he is doing and regulated its conduct accordingly.' Given this responsibility we seek some means of escape through 'bad faith' or self-deception from the anguish this creates. We ask, 'Who ... can prove that I am the proper person to impose, by my own choice, my conception of man upon mankind?' We can refuse to make a decision and act as though the decision has been made for us by forces beyond our control, or we can refuse to believe we have a decision to make at all. But even here we are making a choice: we are choosing not to choose. We can abandon ourselves to the situation, indifferent to any possible outcome, or we can project ourselves into the future. As Sartre says, 'it

amounts to the same thing whether one gets drunk alone or is a leader of nations.' We choose and in choosing we invent ourselves.

Our responsibility extends even to choosing in those situations in which we don't seem to have any choices, when we even appear to be victims, as in a war. He argues,

> If I am mobilized in a war, this war is *my* war; it is in my image and I deserve it. I deserve it first because I could always get out of it by suicide or by desertion.... For lack of getting out of it, I have *chosen* it.

If I argue others are to blame because they declared the war, this is only true in a judicial sense, not in a moral sense. And in this sense there is no compulsion: 'the peculiar character of human-reality is that it is without excuse.' I cannot distinguish the choice I make about the sort of person I am from the choice I make about the war. I cause the situation of war to come about along with the sort of person I am who chooses the war. 'To live this war,' he argues, 'is to choose myself through it and to choose it through my choice of myself.' I make the war mine day by day as I make myself day by day. The point is we have been born into certain conditions (genetic, economic, social and so on), but it is up to us entirely what we make of them. In making a decision we can make no appeal to determinism: whatever is theoretically determined, in practice we must choose. A coward or a hero is not made a coward or a hero by his nature, but by what he has made himself.

Sartre, like most existentialists, distinguishes between beings that exist *for* themselves (*pour-soi*), which have consciousness and freedom, and those that exist *in* themselves (*en-soi*), which are simply things that live according to their predetermined natures. For existentialism all the important possibilities of human life are bound up with the fact of human freedom. Those who seek to live *en-soi*, according to what they perceive to be their own nature and inner necessity, are guilty of bad faith, self-deception.

Even within the constraints of a concentration camp, where it seemed no individual had the freedom to choose and everything was determined, even here inmates were free to choose their own moral attitude to their loss of freedom. They were free to 'invent' themselves, as Sartre describes it. Viktor Frankl, and Primo Levi, in *If This is a Man*

(1958) and *The Truce* (1963), both describe three familiar types of inmate.

There was the inmate who chose not to choose by submitting to the morality of the camp. With pitiless determination he accepted that to survive he must steal, trade, seize every opportunity, and make the most of every advantage he had to make sure he had as much food as he could get, the warmest clothes, the most comfortable shoes, and the best job. But this was not without its personal costs. Levi argues, he had to 'throttle all dignity and kill all conscience, to climb down into the arena as a beast against other beasts...'

At the end the ferocious life of the camps had left him only half a man, peering out from behind a thick insulation of insensitivity through empty eyes that saw only life without value. As Frankl describes him, he had 'lost the feeling of being an individual, a being with a mind, with inner freedom and personal value ... his existence descended to the level of animal life.' Worse still, he was left with an experience that had happened to him, but had never been a part of him and, as a result, was unable to deal with it successfully. He wanted nothing more than just to forget, although the torment of recurring nightmares never allowed him to do so. The experience was for him extraneous, devoid of meaning.

Although different, the second type also refused to make choices, but in this case by refusing to adapt, insisting instead on conducting himself according to the traditional values he brought into the camp from a society and circumstances radically different. This left him vulnerable to a system that worked by identifying and eliminating all of those who failed to adapt. But that was only one of the dangers. The worst came from within. The constant anxiety and stress of trying to negotiate with a system of values that not only didn't work, but left him vulnerable every moment of the day, led him to seek shelter in the past, to live retrospectively. With no goal to aim for, no future, he robbed the present of all reality, overlooking the opportunities to make something positive of camp life. He treated his existence within the camps as unreal and lost his hold on life. This type of prisoner was a common sight. With no faith in the future he would let himself go mentally and physically.

In contrast, the third type, while possessing the flexibility to adapt to his surroundings and to survive, chose to retain the strength of conscience and inner resources to see beyond the present moral vacuum of the camp. He retained a clear vision of the possibility of recreating civilized moral values and it is this that sustained him, giving meaning and value to his sufferings. Despite the conditions, he had respect for human dignity, freedom and integrity. He saw not just things, but men, for whom he could still have empathy and moral sensitivity. Thus, as Levi says, he was able 'to avoid that total humiliation and demoralization which led so many to spiritual shipwreck.' Afterwards, in contrast to the other two, this experience remained an important part of his moral development; it was part of the core meaning of his life and his moral awareness. For him remembering was a moral duty, indeed, for many it was the one thing that secured their survival.

All three types illustrate the pivotal claim of the existentialists that despite all the determining circumstances there is always the possibility of choice. As Frankl argues,

> everything can be taken from a man but one thing: the last of the human freedoms – to choose one's attitude in any given set of circumstances, to choose one's own way. ... Every day, every hour offered the opportunity to make a decision, a decision which determined whether you would or would not ... become the plaything of circumstances, renouncing freedom and dignity.

Even in circumstances where most of us would assume the individual bore no responsibility for the sort of person he became, what he became was ultimately the result of an inner decision.

■ 2. Decentring the subject

Nevertheless, those who centre the subject and cordon off an area in which actions are uncaused, except by the undetermined sovereignty of individual reason, leave us without any means of measuring someone's responsibility. If, as Sartre maintains in *Existentialism and Humanism*, the individual is free to 'invent' herself, without excuse from heredity, passion or social and economic conditions, then we have no means of relating her actions to consequences. We cannot live in a world without causes, yet at the same time cause things to happen. In a world of indeterminism it would be impossible to measure the influence a person's actions have on others, nor the extent of her free will and, therefore, her responsibility. For there to be responsibility there must be deterministic factors by which we can measure the extent of the individual's free will. And normally, as we saw in the case of June and Hilda Thompson, we have no problem in recognizing and accepting diminished responsibility and crimes of passion.

Equally important, particularly for those in the nineteenth century who began to doubt the Enlightenment strategy of centring the subject, this indeterminist account undermines and dissipates the notion and influence of the interpersonal: communities both past and present, which shape our lives. Napoleon was the heir of the Enlightenment. As French forces dominated much of Europe, they brought with them standard forms of government, legal systems and even education. The traditional institutions and customs of nations that had developed out of their unique histories were threatened by a form of rational universalization. Not surprisingly, then, thinkers across Europe ignited new interest in the origins of European nations, their folklore and their languages. In the process they contributed to a romanticist revolt against standardization wherever it was found, most particularly in mass production that was rapidly reducing individuals to mere machine minders.

In particular the search for an understanding of the individual and her relation to history and society took a different turn. As we said earlier these philosophers 'collectivized' and 'historicized' the individual: that is, her actions were seen to be influenced both horizontally by the community in which she lived, and vertically by the historical process that culminated in this community with all its institutions and traditions. In his reaction to the French Revolution and the rationalism of the Enlightenment that had swept away values and cultural heritage represented in traditional institutions Edmund Burke railed against the idea that the individual could be abstracted from her community and its traditions. These, he believed, civilized the individual, shaping not only the institutions that govern public life, but her moral understanding of how she relates to others.

Through the process of history, society threw up an elite of natural leaders who had soaked up the accumulated wisdom of the ages. Yet even these were not expected to govern in accordance with their unencumbered reason. In Burke's account theirs is not to reason, but to follow the precedents set by previous generations of natural leaders before them. After all, he argues in *Reflections on the Revolu-*

tion in France (1790), it is better to rely upon the accumulated wisdom of the many past generations of natural leaders, than to depend just upon the slender stock of wisdom of the present generation:

> We are afraid to put men to live and trade each on his own private stock of reason; because we suspect that this stock in each man is small, and that the individuals would do better to avail themselves of the general bank and capital of nations, and of ages.

2.1 Historicism

Burke's influence was significant, particularly on German nineteenth-century social thought, of which historicism was the dominant paradigm. It shared with conservative thinkers, like Burke, the belief in an organic concept of society that has grown and developed through time in response to its own unique history. In contrast to the Enlightenment's mechanistic concept of society as a loose collection of isolated individuals all with their own universal rights motivated by their own rational assessment of the best way to maximize their own self-interest, the organic concept envisaged more complex bonds of social cohesion through hierarchies, customs and traditional institutions. But it was bolder than the conservatives in its belief that each nation possessed a spiritual identity and destiny that revealed itself through history according to its inner laws of development. This holistic concept of society growing organically according to its own inner necessity promoted an eager search for national identity.

2.1.1 Dilthey and hermeneutics

In addition to carving out a distinct subject matter in the unique history of nations, historicism also advocated new methods of how these phenomena should be explained. It rejected the positivist notion of scientific explanation through laws and uniformities, which were thought to be inappropriate to unique historical events and national histories. Historical understanding is unique, requiring 'identity' with, and 'hermeneutic understanding' of historical agents. The observer must empathize with the past, vicariously experiencing the feelings, values and intentions of historical agents.

This contained implications for the status of the scientific observer and his 'historicity': his inability to free himself from his own values relative to a particular time and society. Without a methodology different from science all history would be nothing more than contemporary history seen through the eyes and values of the present, or the history of nations would be seen through the perspectives of other national cultures and traditions. But it was not just the subject matter that was thought to make the objective detachment of the scientific observer impractical. His lawlike explanations were charged with oversimplifying the complex mixture of feelings, emotions and unconscious as well as conscious intentions in historical situations.

The German philosopher Wilhelm Dilthey was the first to make a significant contribution to hermeneutics and its concern with the nature of understanding and interpretation of human behaviour and social traditions. To understand any text or utterance, he maintained, indeed to reveal the original intentions or meaning of any individual, can only be achieved through knowledge of the broader cultural and linguistic context. To understand the part it is necessary to understand the whole. If we are to understand why someone chose to do something, it is not enough to understand it just from his individual perspective. The meaning of his action in terms of his beliefs and values is not undetermined. His intentions are the product of horizontal influences from the society in which he lives and of the vertical influences in the form of history and tradition.

**Brief lives
Dilthey, Wilhelm**

Dates: 1833–1911
Born: Biebrich, Nassau, Germany
Best known for: His opposition to the attempt to transform the humanities and social sciences by bringing their methods more into line with those of the natural sciences. He argued their subject matter could only be grasped through 'hermeneutic' understanding as it manifests itself in language, literature and history.

Major works: *Introduction to the Human Sciences* (1883), *Ideas Concerning a Descriptive and Analytical Psychology* (1894), *Formation Structure of the Historical World in the Human Sciences* (1910).

2.1.2 Hegel

However, if the individual's beliefs and values were so determined by the social context in which he lived and not by his own private reason, and if rational conduct in pursuit of self-interest is not enough to explain his actions, how are we to depict social relations and processes within each of these societies? And, with even wider implications, if not individual reason, what is it that drives these societies: what are the laws of social development or progress?

Both questions impinge on the degree of freedom the individual has and on how he can guarantee that freedom. The German philosopher Georg Wilhelm Friedrich Hegel gave perhaps the most influential answer to these questions; indeed so influential was he that much of modern philosophy is depicted as a series of revolts against him and his followers. He maintains that all life and each stage through which the nation, the historic community, goes is a manifestation of the 'Spirit' (*Geist*) or 'Mind'. It is the march of God through history – that is if, as many believe, this is what he meant by 'Spirit'.

In *Phenomenology of Spirit* (1807) Hegel traces the development of the Spirit both logically and historically in the process of world history. History is the rational unfolding of the Spirit. Although on the surface of things there appears to be nothing but confusing disunity, Hegel believes beneath this the world is intelligible: reason lies at the heart of things. The Spirit, a rational force, manifests itself in the material universe and in man. Unlike Kant's two-world view, Hegel argues that nothing external to man is different from him: the external world is part of us and we are part of it. Nature is our other self, our objective self as opposed to the conscious self.

Thus to obtain truth and freedom we must not only view the external world from the standpoint of our inner selves, but our inner selves from the standpoint of the external world. That is, we must regard ourselves with complete objectivity as our opposite or 'antithesis'. Every condition of thought or things leads to its opposite, then unites with it to form a higher more complex whole, a 'synthesis'. When we can regard ourselves with complete objectivity we are ready for the highest synthesis known to human experience, where we are liberated from our petty prejudices into absolute freedom. Leaving behind our imperfect consciousness we achieve a higher consciousness, indeed the perfect consciousness of

Georg Wilhelm Friedrich Hegel (1770–1831)

Hegel is widely acknowledged as one of the most influential of all western philosophers. Some say that the history of philosophy since Hegel can be represented as a series of revolts against him and his followers. Born in Stuttgart, he was educated at Tübingen and taught in Jena, Nürnberg, and Heidelberg before succeeding Fichte as professor of philosophy at the University of Berlin in 1818. Here his influence was at its highest, particularly on those known as the Young Hegelians, including Marx. In all he published four major works: *Phenomenology of Spirit* (1807), *Science of Logic* (1812–16), *Encyclopedia* (1817) and *Philosophy of Right* (1821).

In contrast to the scepticism of Hume, he argues that the world is ultimately intelligible. Beneath the bewildering disunity on the surface, he insists reason lies at the heart of things. Even if we cannot understand it through our senses we can nevertheless understand it through our reason. There are things beyond the senses that have an equally real existence. The key to Hegelian philosophy is the notion of freedom, found not in the mere licence to do as you desire, but in living self-consciously within a rationally ordered state. All history he sees as progress towards this to the point where we are aware not just of phenomena but reality itself as knowledge of the Absolute.

Self, where our consciousness of nature and our self-consciousness become one in freedom.

A familiar battle-cry of the Hegelians was 'The real is the rational.' Hegel believes all that exists must be mental: one thinking substance or agent. Thus, as our reason is dictated by certain necessary laws and processes, history too is a process that follows necessary laws. Moreover, unlike the atomistic and mechanistic theories, he rejects any philosophy that denies the ultimate reality of relations: any one that sets out to understand the parts distinct from the whole. It is not possible to 'know' anything in isolation from the whole. The notion of things-in-themselves, he maintains, is unintelligible: 'The true is the whole.'

So, any proposition or system of propositions that is less than the complete system will turn out to be self-contradictory. Since one cannot adequately think about any particular fact without inflating it into the absolute totality of being, whenever one says anything short of everything, what one is saying is not true in the absolute sense. We can't understand what any part is without already seeing

how it fits into the whole, which means already knowing something about the whole. Otherwise our understanding would be incomplete, irrational and self-contradictory. And without full knowledge and consciousness, we cannot have complete freedom.

The progress of history, then, follows necessary laws towards complete knowledge as the rational Spirit progressively reveals itself in human history, and with this comes complete or absolute freedom. The individual must surrender himself and his particular, partial notions of self-interest to this process: the march of Spirit through history as it reveals itself in more complete forms. Different outlooks correspond to different states of mind, different stages in the development of the Spirit. None are true or false, just more or less developed. As long as any system of propositions is incomplete it will be self-contradictory, which will drive on the dialectic of thesis, antithesis and synthesis. Indeed, the complete system does not so much correspond with reality, it *is* reality. As all the possible forms of consciousness develop a point is reached when an awareness becomes possible, not just of the phenomenal world, the world we know through our sense impressions, but reality as it is in itself, the 'noumenal' world that Kant claimed we could never know. This is knowledge of the absolute, when 'mind' finally knows itself.

Thus, freedom lies in the recognition of necessity, in accepting determinism in the progress of history. We must surrender ourselves to the state as the latest and, therefore, the most complete manifestation of Spirit. The individual, he declares, must sacrifice everything to his 'better self', the state. One suspects that it was not for nothing that Hegel was the favourite author of Bismarck, who, later in the nineteenth century, set about building Prussia into the most powerful state in Germany.

Freedom is not to be found in the rational deliberations of the individual. This would be like the trivial freedom enjoyed by a prisoner who is free to crawl eastwards on a boat travelling westwards. The dialectic takes place behind the backs of individuals. History Hegel describes as the 'cunning of reason', which fulfils the aims of the Spirit as unintended by-products of the actions of individuals, who can only be free by surrendering themselves to the unfolding of the Spirit through the dialectical progress of history.

2.1.3 Marx

However, it is perhaps not without some irony that out of such conservative idealism develops its opposite in Marx's revolutionary materialism. In fact, although Marx himself was a Young Hegelian up until the early 1840s, Marx and Hegel were opposites in more ways than one. Hegel pursued the quiet life of research on excellent terms with the reactionary and absolutist Prussian government, whereas Marx moved from one European country to another, expelled from Paris and pursued by German spies until he finally took refuge in London in 1848.

Although in Marx's theory there is the same dialectical development through which man gains his freedom, Marx, as he claims, turns Hegel upside down: it is not ideas that determine the shape of material forces, but material forces in the form of social and economic factors, like production, that shape society, social relations, the individual, his beliefs and values, and the extent of his freedom. The industrial revolution had brought a system of production that was reducing the individual to a mere machine minder, a spectator, whose only

contribution was his labour power as a mere factor of production. He was no longer an end-in-itself, but just a means.

In Marx's theory the individual has no fixed, unchanging nature, nor does he develop in accordance with the progressive unfolding of some spiritual essence. There is a dialectical relation between his nature, as determined by his conditions of life, and the practical transformation of those conditions. He is not only the product of circumstances that shape his consciousness, but the potential changer of those circumstances. Material circumstances, notably the mode of production, condition us, leading us to believe that the present mode of production and the political system and ideas developed from it is not only inevitable, but the most just system: the only way of guaranteeing the maximum freedom of the individual.

In capitalism the system of competition, private property, the unequal distribution of wealth and human exploitation are promoted as the only just and effective way of securing freedom. Unlike Hegel, Marx believes it is not ideas that are the motive force behind the dialectical development of history, but material forces. Man creates ideas merely to serve his own material needs, making idols of them, which he then bows down before and worships. He makes a 'fetish' out of them. Although alien to all former political systems, man created the idea of private property to serve his material need to accumulate private wealth. He then enshrined it in the constitution as an inalienable right. As for the exploited worker, engaged in meaningless repetitive tasks, to assuage his alienation the ruling ideology promotes 'commodity fetishism' or consumerism. This gives some meaning or justification for such alienating work as the means towards the one all-consuming goal of accumulating consumer goods. This in turn, of course, promotes production, profits and, ironically, the means of perpetuating the workers' own exploitation and alienation.

As you can see in each stage of Marx's theory of history, or 'dialectical materialism', there is a ruling class, whose interests are served by the means of production. But to secure the stability of such an unequal and exploitative system it is necessary to create an ideology, a ruling class ideology, which promotes and protects the interests of the ruling class by guaranteeing the acceptance of these false idols. In other words, it creates stability by generating 'false consciousness' among members of the exploited classes. The ruling class ideology sets out to legitimize in the consciousness of workers the social relations that develop out of the mode of production through which the ruling class maximizes its interests.

Thus, unlike Hegel's account, in which the state is the ultimate guarantor of freedom and the manifestation of Spirit in history, in Marx's account it is merely the means of oppression of one class by another. It does this not only by securing all the levers of power, but by generating all that can be thought and said through the ruling class ideology. As Marx says in the *Communist Manifesto*, 'Law, morality, religion, are for him (the proletarian) so many bourgeois prejudices behind which lurk in ambush just as many bourgeois interests.' And Engels, Marx's long-time collaborator, makes much the same point when he says in *Anti-Duhring* (1878):

> As society has hitherto moved in class antagonism, morality was always a class morality; it has either justified the domination and the interests of the ruling class, or as soon as the oppressed class become powerful enough, it has represented the revolt against this domination and the future interests of the oppressed.

So, it is not the Spirit, a rational force working through history, that determines man's freedom, but economic and material forces. These are the basic causes of every fundamental change, whether in the world of things or in the life of thought. Change these and the objective social relations that develop out of them also change. In turn the problem of restoring value to human life is solved. To bring this about and achieve his freedom the individual must promote and contribute to the dialectic so that it moves through all its stages until it culminates in the communist stage of classlessness. As the dialectic is driven by class conflict it will cease in the communist stage where there are no classes. And, by the same token, as the state is the means of oppression of one class by another, the communist stage will be stateless. Individuals will be freed from the state and its oppressive rule into true consciousness and freedom, able to live their lives according to self-imposed laws.

For Marx, then, history is a process through which the human mind grows in consciousness and freedom. Both Marx and the Young Hegelians believed that the human mind has the inveterate tendency to project out its own creations, make idols of them and then fall under their sway. The cure for this 'fetishism' was critical analysis to expose false gods, combined with revolutionary action to topple them in religion, politics and economics. In the *11th Thesis on Feuerbach*, written in the 1840s, at a time when he was transcending his sources and developing his own original theory in response to the forces of industrialization that were changing European society dramatically, he wrote: 'The philosophers have only *interpreted* the world, in various ways; the point is to *change* it.'

In contrast to the Enlightenment, understanding is part of a process of bringing about change in the world, not standing back and analysing it into its atomic parts. As with Kierkegaard, it's essentially a process of engagement, of commitment, not abstraction. But with Marx this engagement is with the community in which you live and with the objective tendencies of the environment to create conditions essential to ensure respect for human dignity, which can only be secured in conditions of social freedom.

From Marx's historicist view old-style religion disappears and the historical process itself becomes the sole redeemer. Nothing beyond history is invoked and what the individual believes and does is no longer of cosmic importance: only the objective process counts. Unlike the atomistic theories of the Enlightenment, Marx's thinking comes down to concrete social relations. Social and economic conditions come first, and only if they are first put right can everything else come right. The individual doesn't exist apart from his society: it has created him. He is what it has made him and his freedom ultimately depends upon getting it right.

2.2 Freud: undermining consciousness

As you can see the strategy of establishing the freedom of the individual by centring the subject and cordoning off an area in which actions are uncaused, except by the dictates of individual reason, was undermined by those who sought to 'collectivize' and 'historicize' the individual. But it was just as effectively undermined from within by those, like Freud, who challenged the notion of free choice that undetermined reason seemed to guarantee.

As we saw earlier the theory of psychoanalysis, first developed by Freud in the 1890s and pioneered as a method of treatment by Josef Breuer, Wilhelm Reich, Melanie Klein and others, challenges the status of the conscious individual. It suggests that individual consciousness and behaviour can only be understood in terms of the less than rational or less than transparent workings of the unconscious. Not only does consciousness give us a distorted and partial view, but it may amount to little more than an attempt to rationalize our actions, justifying them by carefully selecting reasons after the event. In this way it may obscure the real origin of our behaviour, which may have more to do with certain deep-seated traumas and unresolved emotional conflicts that can be traced back to childhood experiences. As a method of treatment psychoanalysis seeks to reveal these long-buried events and to understand their significance to the patient. By linking aspects of the patient's past with the present, the treatment aims to free the patient from specific symptoms and from irrational inhibitions and anxieties.

In the light of this it seems implausible to argue that anyone can be responsible for their behaviour. If the criminal has no idea what's going on nor any means of preventing it, he can hardly be punished for his actions. What he says of his crimes and the attitudes he expresses are little more than the symptoms of an unconscious mind riven with conflict and anxiety. John Hospers expresses it well when he says:

> The poor victim is not conscious of the inner forces that exact from him this ghastly toll; he battles, he schemes, he revels in pseudo-aggression, he is miserable, but he does not know what works within him to produce these catastrophic acts of crime. His aggressive actions are the wriggling of a worm on a fisherman's hook.

If the psychoanalysts are right, the individual cannot be certain of 'knowing his own mind'. We may believe we are free to make up our own minds and choose what we think we should do. And, given this, we may believe criminals make choices for which they can be reasonably held responsible. But, as in Marx's theory of historical materialism, where the individual is just a product of a particular stage in the development of the dialectic, in psychoanalytic theory we are just the product of certain unfathomable unconscious forces that we don't understand and can do little about.

2.3 Structuralism and post-structuralism

But psychoanalytical theory was not the only challenge in the twentieth century to the strategy of centring the subject. As we saw earlier, in the post-war period structuralism challenged the dominant influence of existentialism and its belief in the autonomous human subject. Inspired by the work of the Swiss linguist Ferdinand de Saussure, structuralists believe that the key to understanding observable phenomena is the underlying structures and systems of social organization. Phenomena should be analysed as systems of relations, rather than as positive entities. The movement's influence has been felt in areas such as linguistics, anthropology and literary criticism, but it was not until the 1960s that it had a significant impact through the influence of French thinkers like Jacques Lacan, Roland Barthes, Louis Althusser and Claude Lévi-Strauss.

The underlying theme in all this diverse work is that human life can only be made intelligible through people's relations; that behind all local variations in the surface phenomena of each society there lie constant laws of abstract structure. Different societies have different customs, myths and practices. They have different beliefs about marriage, child-bearing and the status of the elderly; they have different ways of giving expression to their culture in arts and crafts; and different folklore and myths are handed down from one generation to another; but behind all these differences there lies one common pattern or structure. So, in contrast to existentialists, like Sartre who argues that man makes himself, he 'invents' himself, the structuralist argues man is the product of structures that are beyond his conscious will or individual control. Linguists argue that it is not man who speaks language, but language that speaks man.

This means that to understand the different social and cultural phenomena within any society we can neither think of them as the intentional products of human subjects, nor as the unintentional by-products of history. But, rather, they are the products of structured systems composed of elements with specific and irreducible rules for combination and transformation. We cannot reduce these systems atomistically into their elementary particles to discover the laws that govern the behaviour of each part and from there to the laws governing the whole as in traditional science. The whole is more than the sum of the parts. Structuralism is a form of 'holism'.

For example, Ferdinand de Saussure, describing 'structural linguistics', maintains that language cannot be explained in subjective terms – its meaning cannot be attributed to individual subjects – because speakers can only say something by using a language that already exists. In contrast, those who start with the subject begin with Descartes' *cogito* and work out from there, as the phenomenologists do, to argue that meaning can be understood in terms of the individual's conscious intentions.

Echoing a similar argument to Saussure's, Claude Lévi-Strauss argues that, like the rules of language, the patterns of social organization are reproduced each generation without being deliberately chosen or, indeed, consciously understood. Likewise, each part cannot be understood by examining the intentions or actions of individuals, but only in terms of their position within the overall system of society as it exists at a particular time. And all social life should be understood as structured systems composed of elements with specific and irreducible rules of combination and transformation. He claims that it can be shown that the diversity of human societies and cultures derive from a single underlying structure, a structure of structures, which is common to all humanity.

Such an anti-historicist account was bound to attract fierce criticism, particularly from Marxist scholars, but it was its deterministic implications that generated the most concerted response in the form of post-structuralism, which again attracted prominent French philosophers like Michel Foucault, Jacques Derrida and Julia Kristeva. While they accept the structuralist case that words mean what they do as a result of their relations with each other, rather than with some extra-linguistic reality, they have an additional concern for their origins in relationships of power or in the unconscious. For example, Foucault, in his work on Western attitudes to the insane, had a significant influence by showing that what might be described as progressive and humane improvements in treatment is one aspect of increasing social and political control.

But more generally post-structuralism's focus is on the scientific claims of structuralists that different social systems obey structural laws, which are yet to be discovered. Like other forms of postmodernism it rejects all concepts of objectivity, reality and truth. In particular it rejects the search for scientific objectivity. Derrida and the deconstructionists challenged the claim to have uncovered the hidden unconscious structures behind surface meanings, arguing instead that language is irreducible, involving a multiple play of meaning. Rather than reducing human behaviour to certain laws or generalizations, the sort associated with deterministic systems like Marxism, the post-structuralists emphasize instead the spontaneous, the formless and subjective.

■ 3. Conclusion

Whatever the answer to these complex problems it seems we are unlikely to find it by assuming that we can cordon off an area in which actions are uncaused, except by the undetermined dictates of individual reason. This ignores the social, economic, political and psychological influences, leaving us without any means of measuring someone's responsibility. In the next chapter we will examine in what sense we can hold someone responsible for his or her actions and how this should influence what we regard as suitable punishment.

■ Questions

1. (a) Explain why Sartre believes our responsibility is so great.

    (b) Are we as responsible as he believes?

2. Is our reason alone sufficient to create meaning and value in our lives, or do we need the mediation of religion, culture and social norms?

3. How much does history shape the present?

4. If society is just a loose collection of isolated individuals, isn't it just every person for themselves?

5. Are the structuralists right that all human life can only be made intelligible through people's relations?

■ Recommended reading

Hegel, G. W. F. *Phenomenology of Spirit*, Trans. A. V. Miller (Oxford and New York: Oxford University Press, 1977).

Marx, K. and F. Engels. *The German Ideology* (1846) (London: Lawrence and Wishart, 1982).

Paton, H. J. (Trans.) *The Moral Law: Kant's Groundwork of the Metaphysic of Morals* (London: Hutchinson, 1948).

Sartre, J-P. *Being and Nothingness* (1943) (London: Methuen, 1984).

Sturrock, J. *Structuralism* (London: Fontana, 1993).

West, D. *An Introduction to Continental Philosophy* (Cambridge: Polity, 1997).

 The note structure to accompany this chapter can be downloaded from our website.

Responsibility and Punishment

CHAPTER 20

Key issues

▶ If our choices are constrained by forces beyond our control, how are we to view the punishment of those who have committed criminal offences? Are they criminals or patients?

▶ Are we all under pressure to conform to the prevailing social beliefs and values for fear of being thought insane, criminal, or just not 'normal'?

▶ To what extent can we be blamed for our actions when they are influenced by movies and the media? Can we excuse the violent criminal because he has seen too many acts of violence on television?

▶ Even if I can say my decisions are my responsibility, can I be responsible for the person I am, when heredity and the early parental environment in which I grew up are mostly responsible for my character?

▶ Or is it much simpler than this? Perhaps people just commit criminal offences because they like it: they just enjoy the excitement of rape and stealing?

▶ How should this affect our attitude to punishment? What should be our main aim: vengeance, retribution, to deter, to rehabilitate or just to protect society?

Contents

If the conclusion of the last chapter is right, it seems we are now at the point where we have to accept that the problem of free will is not just an extension of the mind–body problem: a question of whether our decisions are in fact brain events, the result of physical and psychological laws of nature operating within the individual. Those who argued against centring the subject placed the individual in a collective and historical context with her actions and choices shaped by external forces beyond her control, indeed perhaps even beyond her comprehension. But if we cannot view the issue of freedom and responsibility as if we lived in a world which is just a loose collection of isolated individuals, each of us free to make up our own minds, then the problem of deciding how responsible someone is for their actions and how we should respond to it in the form of punishment or treatment becomes a lot more complicated.

■ 1. When is an act compelled?

This argument that there are external forces beyond our control that compel us to act is similar to Aristotle's conception of compulsion. You will remember he argues in *Nicomachean Ethics* that 'an act is compulsory when its origin is from outside, the person compelled contributing nothing to it.' Someone is literally pushed into acting by someone or something outside, like the captain who is powerless to prevent his ship being swept off course by a strong wind. But from what we've seen this can take various forms and we must be sure which we are willing to allow into our calculations of someone's responsibility.

1.1 External compulsion

Physical compulsion is easy to recognize, except in cases, say, of ADHD and other behavioural problems which may be caused by the additives and preservatives commercial food companies use in their products. Of course, you may argue that it is we who choose to buy these foods. If we know of the dangers and we are told what is in them, the choice is still ours. But this depends upon us knowing and it is here that Aristotle casts the net wider to include anything of which we are ignorant. And this means we must include a much wider range of influences, all those that affect our beliefs, values and preferences without us knowing.

In the second half of the twentieth century we became much more aware of the impact of promotional advertisers, movie makers and political campaigns on our beliefs, values and behaviour. At the extreme ends of the compulsive spectrum the term 'brainwashing' was used for the first time, meaning a process in which a person is subjected to systematic indoctrination to make them confess to a crime or change their views or behaviour. In the film, *The Manchurian Candidate*, a soldier returns from the Korean War having been conditioned as a result of sleep and sensory deprivation to act in certain predetermined ways, even though on the surface his behaviour appears to be voluntary. Similarly, in George Orwell's novel, *Nineteen Eighty-Four* (1949), Winston Smith is conditioned by being threatened with the thing he fears most, in his case, rats. To avoid this he betrays his girlfriend, Julia, and denies his doubts about the state's propaganda, and even that 2 + 2 = 4.

But, of course, these are fictional cases and few of us are subject to such harrowing methods. Even so, most of us live in societies in which the legitimacy of governments is maintained by a political ideology that is both pervasive and powerful. We are enjoined by the most subtle methods to love our country, promote its status in the world regardless of what it may do and conform to prevailing attitudes and values that are described as 'American', 'Australian' or 'British'. To do otherwise is to suffer the worst of fates: to be labelled 'un-American' or 'un-Australian'. Barry Humphries is reported to have said that he always knows when he is getting close to Australia on his flight home, because of the sound of millions of his fellow countrymen patting themselves on the back. Some of the worst forms of this could be found in the 1950s during the Cold War. In the United States the perceived threat of communism was so great that anyone or any organization that was even mildly egalitarian in its attitudes was vilified and condemned as unpatriotic, un-American, even un-Godly.

If you had been brought up in the southern states in the USA in the 1950s and 1960s during the time of segregation, you would have been imbued with the ideas of the racial inferiority of blacks and with the importance of upholding segregation on buses, in restaurants, in public facilities of all kinds, even on public park benches. No doubt even to the most reasonable person this would have seemed beyond any sensible challenge and it would have taken an immense effort of will and considerable courage to risk serious social alienation to think otherwise. Yet even the influence of more benign societies and cultures imposes upon us a similar clamp of conformity. Indeed it is a mark of the effectiveness of such influences that if we were that person looking back at our years growing up in the southern states during segregation, we could no doubt look back with incomprehension at how we could have held such reactionary ideas that supported such socially unjust practices. So effective in exactly the same way is the influence of the benign times in which we now live.

Indeed for some philosophers it raises the serious question of what we regard as 'normality'. Not to think in conformity with prevailing social beliefs and values may be thought to be not normal; in some societies even insane or mad. R. D. Laing has suggested that, as a result, the terms 'sanity' and 'madness' have become ambiguous and psychiatry has been used as a means of social control by removing from society those who are 'different' from the majority.

Michel Foucault, in *Madness and Civilization* (1965), argues similarly that human knowledge and subjectivity are dependent upon specific institutions and practices, which change through history. In particular, he targets the conventional assumptions

**Brief lives
Foucault, Michel**

Dates: 1926–1984
Born: Poitiers, France
Best known for: His major concern was the use of science and reason as instruments of power particularly in the treatment of the insane. He explored the codes and concepts of society, particularly the 'principles of exclusion', like the distinction between the sane and insane. He was one of the early victims of AIDS.

Major works: *Madness and Civilization* (1965), *The Order of Things* (1970), *The Archaeology of Knowledge* (1972), *Discipline and Punish* (1975), and *History of Sexuality*, 3 vols (1979–88).

about 'social deviants' – the mentally ill, the sick, and the criminal – who, he believes, are oppressed by the approved knowledge of the period in which they live. In the Soviet Union it was more likely to be dissident intellectuals who were identified as abnormal 'social deviants'. Hundreds, including the nuclear physicist Andrei Sakharov, were confined to insane asylums usually for actions considered subversive to the regime.

So the fact that an individual thinks or behaves in a certain way may not be of her own choosing, but the result of the society in which she lives and the need to conform, to feel normal. The realization that the alienation felt in modern societies leads to such cravings for conformity unites philosophers as diverse as Marx, Kierkegaard, Nietzsche, Heidegger, Freud, Tillich and Sartre. Laing describes the individuals of modern industrialized societies as 'bemused and crazed creatures, strangers to our true selves, to one another, and to the spiritual and material world.'

But in practical terms, what does this alienation and the craving to conform mean in terms of the degree of responsibility we have for our actions? Those who fail to conform and slip through the social bonds that might tie them to 'normal' behaviour, of course, might turn to drugs, where they can escape the alienation they feel, or to a life of crime, where they can in some way satisfy their need for self-esteem. The search for self-esteem lies behind much of what we do. When we're successful in our search we're more content, with a

sense of achievement and stability in our lives. When we're unsuccessful this may lead to bitterness, hostility and resentment. In his famous and influential work, *Motivation and Personality* (1954), Abraham Maslow outlines a hierarchy of needs from physiological needs (food, drink, etc.), to security (order and stability), to social bonds (social fulfilment, love, friendship and sexual fulfilment), to self-esteem (praise, achievement, acknowledgement and status) and finally to self-actualization in which we reach our full potential. Although most of us don't meet this last need, we all need to achieve the first four.

Yet in large impersonal societies, where alienation is more likely the norm, any sense of self-esteem from the acknowledgement of your achievements by others is difficult to come by. The resulting resentment might all too easily lead to crime and violence. Maybe it's for this reason that the motiveless criminal seems to belong exclusively to the twentieth century. In the early 1960s when the Boston Strangler, Albert De Salvo, was convicted of a series of brutal killings it was thought that this was a killer without parallel. Yet since then we have become almost inured to the horrors of such killing by a succession of gruesome murderers who have far exceeded De Salvo's crimes. In many of these cases, it seems, their killing only occurs when there are no social bonds around them through which they can maintain human contact. In a depersonalized environment, where the individual is anonymous, resentment at the lack of recognition of them and their achievements can no longer lie undisturbed. In his journal Dennis Nilsen writes: 'In any domestic situation where I had constant contact with people or a person, these things could never have occurred. They were the products of a lonely empty life and the mind therein.'

Indeed, as long as he had a flat-mate and maintained human contact his destructive tendencies remained in check. But when his flat-mate left and his isolation was complete the killing began. As Brian Masters writes, 'Feeling defeated and humiliated on all sides, and unwilling to blame himself for his misfortunes, resentment grew like a cancer and others had to pay the price.' Murder, he argues, is a creative act for these people, a form of self-fulfilment, rendering them admirable and achieving in their own eyes.

But if this analysis of the serial killer is correct, it hardly seems right to argue he is responsible and should pay the highest price. We should more likely treat him as a patient, not a prisoner, because the problem is ours as a society, rather than his as a lone individual trying to cope with a situation not of his making. Indeed, Anthony Storr in *Human Destructiveness* argues,

> Competitive, capitalist, industrial societies have not begun to solve, or even to address, the problem of making the less gifted and the less competent feel valued or wanted. If that problem could be solved, we can be sure that the prevalence of violent behaviour would be substantially reduced.

But so far we have considered just those who fail to conform and slip through the social bonds that might tie them to 'normal' behaviour. What about those of us who learn to conform, who respond like everyone else to influences on us, how much freedom and responsibility can we be said to have? The American behavioural psychologist B. F. Skinner argues in his influential book, *Beyond Freedom and Dignity* (1971), that certain forces, like education, moral discourse and persuasion, work in our democracies in such a way that they are not perceived as the forms of control they really are. He writes: 'Through a masterful piece of misrepresentation, the illusion is fostered that these procedures do not involve the control of behaviour; at most, they are simply ways of "getting someone to change his mind".'

Yet, he maintains, they are still as much a form of control as any form of physical coercion or threat of force. For example, in education a history teacher can control a student's behaviour as effectively by the way he presents the facts as he can by suppressing them. In Nazi Germany students were taught that Jews were the enemy within, the ultimate threat to the 'ancient decency of the Volk'. Lurid tales were retold of supposed Jewish sexual crimes and 'ritual murders'. And more recently the war in Iraq could be presented either as a war fought for the control of oil or for the liberation of people from a cruel dictator. Whichever alternative we choose to present, we limit the opportunities for students to make up their own minds. Skinner quotes Ralph Barton Perry, who argues,

> Whoever determines what alternatives shall be made known to man controls what that man shall choose *from*. He is deprived of freedom in

proportion as he is denied access to *any* ideas, or is confined to any range of ideas short of the totality of relevant possibilities.

Even so, we accept influences, like education and persuasion, because they are only partially effective in controlling behaviour. Nevertheless they still have an effect on our behaviour for which we are held responsible. Civil rights lawyers, in particular 'First Amendment' lawyers in America, argue we should be free to influence others regardless of the effects. Movie makers can associate violence with pleasure in violent movies, even though this might result in increased violence. Indeed, feminists maintain that advertisers, movie makers, pornographers and others in the media routinely portray men's treatment of women as violent. And most official monitors have recorded a significant growth in the amount and intensity of explicit violence and sex in the big blockbuster movies. For example, Oliver Stone's film *Natural Born Killers* features 52 brutal murders.

In these circumstances some have argued that scenes of violence seen over and over again are likely to leave us desensitized to the suffering of others, while those who defend the media maintain that, although there may be a correlation between screen violence and actual violence, there is no causal connection. Nevertheless a select committee of the British House of Commons found that there are more than 1,000 academic studies which establish a 'causal connection' between viewing violent or sexually explicit material and similar behaviour being acted out in real life. One of these studies, 'Video Violence and the Protection of Children', conducted by Professor Elizabeth Newson, Emeritus Professor of Child Psychology at Nottingham University, found that a connection can be made between the availability of videos and the increase in violent behaviour in children. Referring to the savage killing in 1993 of two-year-old Jamie Bulger by two ten-year-old boys who were familiar with violent videos, she says, 'It is desensitization that makes children behave in this way, and enjoy it. It took a long time to kill Jamie Bulger, and they would not have sustained their attack had they not been desensitized.'

However, while this may be an explanation for the rising incidents of child violence and killings, can the same causal connection be established between violence in the media and adult violence? Can we really excuse the violent criminal for his acts on the grounds that he has seen more graphic acts of violence than anyone from a previous generation? It may be that some individuals simply haven't got the ability to process the images effectively so that they don't result in such desensitization. Yet even this suggests that some individuals, for no fault of their own, are not able to cope with the graphic imagery from which they have no means of escape. Moreover, in one way or another, we might all be affected, although most of us are fortunate in that it doesn't result in criminal behaviour.

Most 'adult material' is designed to exploit our imagination, to evoke emotions like hate and loathing, along with the desire for revenge and the need to control and dominate others. In the 1930s and 1940s in Germany the same range of emotional reactions were systematically evoked against Jews, along with authoritative pronouncements from scientific authorities that biologically Jews were inferior and damaging to the German nation. That ordinary intelligent people should willingly acquiesce in this and stand by, indeed help, in the persecution of their Jewish neighbours whom they had lived among and counted as their friends, posed serious and difficult questions. If this could be done so effectively in Germany there was no reason why it should not be done elsewhere in other democratic countries, albeit for different ends.

In his ground-breaking research in the 1950s, published as *Obedience to Authority* (1974), Stanley Milgram examined why most people surrender personal responsibility for their actions, if those actions are dictated by an authority figure. In particular he explored the capacity of ordinary, decent people to carry out horrendous acts of cruelty. The subjects were told they were taking part in a study to understand the effects of punishment on learning. They were to teach a 'learner' a list of word pairs. If the learner made a mistake, they were to administer a painful electric shock, the intensity of which was to increase with each mistake. In fact the learners were actors and there were no electric shocks, although the subjects of the experiments were not aware of this. They were simply given instructions by an authority figure: a scientist dressed in a white laboratory coat.

The majority administered severe shocks, some forcing the hands of learners onto the metal shock plate, even after being told they had a heart condition. Despite agonized protests and desperate pleas a substantial proportion (28 out of 40) continued to administer the shocks right up to the highest level of 450 volts, when they knew they were causing severe distress, even endangering the life of the learner. These were just ordinary people doing the jobs they were given, without any particular hostility, yet they became agents of a terrible, destructive process. And they were the norm: most people agreed to take part in the experiment, with only a few refusing.

1.2 Internal compulsion

In view of this, then, perhaps we should argue that a person is responsible as long as he is free to decide what to do, which follows directly from his character alone. As long as he is free from external influences that might induce him to do something he would not otherwise have done; has a fairly accurate understanding of the circumstances; and follows his current desires, then he is responsible for his actions. His decision is caused by the person he is, by his character. Thus, responsibility rests on our freedom to act on the basis of self-chosen ends, influenced by our own experiences, thoughts, motives, desires and needs.

But even here I can argue that my decisions are dictated by influences over which I have little or no control. There are various forms of internal compulsions we know little about, and even when we do learn about them we have limited or no means of resisting them. Someone suffering from a neurotic condition, say, anxiety, depression or hysteria, and, even more, someone suffering from a psychotic disorder, like schizophrenia, cannot be said to be in control of their decisions and can only manage their conditions with constant treatment in the form of drugs, analysis and, in the worst cases, electroconvulsive therapy. In earlier times such people were described as being 'possessed', their actions dictated by forces beyond their control. This seems to match perfectly what Aristotle means by ignorance: something that controls or influences a person's behaviour without her knowing.

Similarly, we all know the effects of stress on a person's behaviour, leading them to act in ways we normally describe as 'out of character'. It might lead them to do things without adequate reflection, driven by motives of revenge or when they believe they are desperate, 'at the end of their tether', and they have no other choice. In Chapter 18 we saw, in the cases of Ruth Ellis, and June and Hilda Thompson, examples of 'protracted provocation', where individuals killed as a result of extreme and prolonged emotional provocation. Equally serious today are all those acts of violence and killing done by those addicted to alcohol or drugs. Although we might argue that they are still responsible for having taken them in the first place when their decision was free of compulsion, very often there is a prior need that drives them to seek solace in this way.

And in this is the underlying problem: how can anyone be responsible for his actions, since they grow out of his character, which has been shaped and moulded and made what it is today by influences, some hereditary, but most stemming from his early parental environment, that were not of his own choosing? Even if we have the ability to change, to overcome the influence of our early environment by taking on board rational considerations, the will to overcome these early disadvantages is of no credit to us. We are just lucky, because the strength of will to overcome our early environment is itself a product of that early environment. We can no more blame others for their inability to change than we can congratulate ourselves for our ability to do so.

Indeed our behaviour is likely to be the result of the coming together of a number of different factors: our genetic inheritance, our education, social class, gender, family life, childhood experiences, national origin, even the time we were brought up in. If you were brought up in the 1920s, 1930s or 1940s, when there was war or the constant threat of it, you are probably more likely to hold strong patriotic feelings and have an abiding respect for authority. If you came of age in the 1960s with the rise of the 'counter culture' and political activity that questioned authority over issues like the Vietnam War and nuclear weapons, it would not be surprising to find that you have a pronounced tendency to question what you're told and to take nothing on trust.

As we have seen John Hospers believes that all our actions are compelled; they are all influenced by determining factors over which we have no control. Of these heredity and our early parental environment are responsible for forming our character. So the aggressive criminal is as much a victim of these forces as those who are caught up in his violence. Hospers argues: 'His aggressive actions are the wriggling of a worm on a fisherman's hook.' He asks what if we were to find that a man commits a murder only after eating a certain combination of foods, say, tuna salad, peas, mushroom soup and blueberry pie; wouldn't it be foolish, pointless, indeed, immoral to hold someone responsible for their crimes?

In contrast, the psychologist, Hans Eysenck, while agreeing that criminality is largely determined by inheritance, rejects the notion that it has anything to do with family background and social environment. Even with the same social factors, people react differently to similar situations. He suggests that most delinquents and criminals are extroverts, who, in contrast to introverts, are resistant to conditioning and less likely to incorporate the normal social restraints on aggressive behaviour. Indeed this finds some support from the research of Leon Radzinowicz and Joan King quoted in Anthony Storr's book *Human Destructiveness*. In their study of Danish children adopted at birth, they found that their criminal records were likely to resemble those of their natural fathers, rather than their adopted fathers.

Whatever you think has the most influence on a person's behaviour, the fact remains that the more we know of the causal factors leading to a person's behaviour, the more we tend to exempt him from responsibility. If he is not responsible for A (a series of events in childhood), then neither is he responsible for B (a series of things he does as an adult), if B follows unavoidably. We don't have to show that it follows necessarily, just that it was unavoidable. Such an argument is common among defence lawyers.

Perhaps the most famous example occurred in 1924 when two youths, Nathan Leopold and Richard Loeb, kidnapped and murdered 14-year-old Bobby Franks. The two killers were wealthy and intelligent. They were the youngest graduates of the universities of Michigan and Chicago. To demonstrate their contempt for society and its conventional morality, the two planned what they believed was the perfect crime. But it went wrong and they were quickly caught and confessed. At their trial, the death penalty was demanded, which prompted the most celebrated lawyer of his age, Clarence Darrow, to plead for mercy in a summation to the jury which lasted over twelve hours. In it he argued,

> Nature is strong and she is pitiless. She works in her own mysterious way, and we are victims. We have not much to do with it ourselves. Nature takes this job in hand, and we play our parts .... What had this boy to do with it? He was not his

own father; he was not his own mother; he was not his own grandparents. All this was handed to him. He did not surround himself with governesses and wealth. He did not make himself. And yet he is compelled to pay. ... If there is a responsibility anywhere, it is back of him; somewhere in the infinite number of his ancestors, or in his surroundings, or in both. ... [U]nder every principle of ... right, and of law, he should not be made responsible for the acts of someone else.

In the event Darrow was successful in his plea and the defendants were sentenced to life imprisonment.

But now set against that arguments of a quite different kind. The American psychologist Stanton Samenow argues that stealing and raping are exciting, and criminals commit crimes because they like to. In his book, *Inside the Criminal Mind* (1983), he argues 'Criminals cause crime – not bad neighbourhoods, inadequate parents, television, school, drugs, or unemployment.' Criminals are just quite different from ordinary, responsible people. They know the difference between good and evil, and prefer evil. Their entire way of life is predicated on the view that the world is there to suit them and if things don't go their way they take matters into their own hands regardless of whether this harms others or breaks the law. Whether it is an uneducated criminal off the streets or a corrupt business executive, they 'regard the world as a chessboard over which they have total control and they perceive people as pawns to be pushed around at will. Trust, love, loyalty, and teamwork are incompatible with their way of life.'

Starting out a Freudian, after working for years with the criminally insane he was turned 180 degrees and came to view inmates not as sick, but as brilliant manipulators of the legal and psychiatric systems. Their mental life is a rich dreamscape of depredations and, rather than reform under classical therapy, they learn to fool their Freudian therapist, playing the psychiatric game by mouthing insights. In contrast, under the Samenow theory, the therapist begins by holding the criminal completely accountable for his offences. There are no excuses, no hard-luck stories; at the heart of the treatment is the premise that he is free to choose between good and evil. Samenow explains, there is 'nothing in the programme to make (him) "feel better" about himself. ... Rather, in order to change he would have to grow intensely fed up with

himself.' Gradually the therapist teaches the criminal how to 'deter' criminal thinking: how to think of something else when he sees a women and thinks of rape. In short, he says, 'the change process calls for criminals to acquire moral values that have enabled civilisations to survive.'

To summarize, then, on the one side we have a set of arguments that set out to convince us that our acts are determined and we have no real responsibility for them. Supporters of this view argue that an act is free if one of its causes is a decision we make, but if the decision itself is caused, then it's not really a decision at all. Alternatively an act is free if it flows from our character, but then, as we saw in Clarence Darrow's summing up, if our character is no more within our control, then we cannot be responsible for any act that issues from it. All that is left after both of these arguments is simply the view that an act is free if we could have done otherwise. But then, given the first two arguments, all this means is that the act would have been different if the circumstances had been different, or if the person had been a different person, neither of which count because neither were in fact different. On the other side, however, is Samenow's argument that we can in fact choose between good and evil. Like Sartre, he argues that we are ultimately responsible for the choices we make. All the rest is nothing but rationalizations and excuses.

■ 2. Responsibility

In practical terms, then, assuming the person is not ignorant of the nature of the situation or of the effects of her actions, what conditions do we require to be fulfilled to hold her responsible for her actions? In his paper, 'What Means This Freedom?', John Hospers offers five contrasting criteria we should consider.

In the first he suggests whether or not someone is responsible is determined by *the presence or absence of premeditation*. This is a familiar distinction, one we meet almost without fail whenever we watch a cop movie or serial on TV. In the United States first-degree, as opposed to second-degree, murder requires proof of premeditation. Under British law murder, as opposed to manslaughter, is committed only when the killer acts with malice aforethought, that is, intending either to kill or to cause serious injury, or realizing that this would probably result. In both legal systems the difference being struck is between someone who murders impulsively without thought of the consequences and someone who deliberately sets out to kill another with thought and planning.

But, as Hospers points out, there are problems with this criterion. Some acts are not premeditated, but are responsible, while others are premeditated but are not responsible. You might put your own life at risk as you grab a child who is in danger of being hit by a speeding car. Afterwards you might describe your actions as quite impulsive, that you never thought about the dangers to yourself, you just acted. Yet, though this was like a reflex action, it was still a very responsible thing to do. Indeed, it is just this type of habitual response that Aristotle has in mind from a confirmed moral character. A virtuous act should be performed as if it is by instinct, confirming that you have integrated this sort of behaviour so well within your character that you no longer have to make the effort each time the relevant situation arises. R. M. Hare in *Moral Thinking* (1981) makes a similar point: that as a result of being brought up well we learn certain moral intuitions, so that without having to think through what it would be best to do in most situations we simply act intuitively.

However, we can also argue the reverse: that some actions are premeditated, but are not responsible. They may just be the result of powerful unconscious motives. With or without premeditation we would have acted just the same. Indeed, all our premeditation simply serves to camouflage the fact that our behaviour was nevertheless compulsive. For example, even though June and Hilda Thompson deliberately, with premeditation, killed their father after more than 20 years of his cruelty and abuse, as the judge recognized, it is difficult to argue that these women, severely damaged emotionally, were responsible for what they did. Indeed the fact that they would have deliberated for years before committing the act is a mark of the strength of their moral character. Despite all their deliberation, the overwhelming impulse was no doubt as compulsive as it can be.

The second criterion Hospers suggests we should consider is that we can say we are not responsible for our actions, unless we can *defend them with reasons*. But this seems to get us no farther forward. No doubt you've already come to the conclusion yourself that there are some people, like those we might describe as intellectuals, who are just better at finding reasons for what they do.

This would mean that this type of person is more responsible than those who, while acting out of moral conviction, do not implement these convictions through a process of reasoning. And this doesn't seem to square with our experience of moral responsibility.

We don't believe that a certain type of person, who can give reasons for acting as she does, is likely to be more morally responsible than those who act morally without reasoning. A person who accepts her responsibility to help the poor acts no less morally if she acts from her own conscience, her moral convictions, than one who reasons before she acts. Indeed, as we found with the first criterion, reasons may be no more than a mere camouflage of unconscious motives of which we might know nothing. It seems to represent only a greater facility for rationalizing our motives. As Hospers argues: 'one's intelligence is simply used in the interests of the neurosis – it is pressed into service to justify with reasons what one does quite independently of the reasons.'

Nevertheless, in one sense this does accord with our experience of moral responsibility. You might argue that someone who can give you reasons for why they acted as they did is more aware of the implications of their actions and therefore consciously takes these onboard when they act. They have thought it through and weighed the reasons on either side. As a result of this they carry a heavier moral load and, therefore, more responsibility. Whereas someone who doesn't think the consequences through and acts on a less developed understanding is not so aware and, therefore, is not so responsible.

But now this is beginning to sound like our first criterion. The problem might be that Hospers appears to be using the word 'reasons' in this criterion to infer 'justifications' for our actions, whereas in the context of the first criterion 'reasons' suggest that we have gathered up all the moral facts before we act – the consequences for acting, the harm to others, our motives and so on – and then weighed them all, deliberating carefully before we act. Clearly someone who has done all this is more aware of the significance of their actions and the responsibility they shoulder.

Hospers' third criterion might be thought to be the negative of his second, in that he suggests a person is responsible unless his actions are *the result of unconscious forces of which he knows nothing*. Now we are no longer talking about a person being conscious of reasons he had for acting, but about being unconscious of forces which explain why he acted as he did. This is the criterion that is perhaps more generally accepted by psychoanalysts. But for the rest of us it excludes a great number of actions from the domain of responsibility, for which we normally think it appropriate to praise or blame people. Whether we are selfish or unselfish, whether we keep our promises, pay our debts, or tell lies, even whether we can exert our own willpower to change our behaviour – all these may, and often do, have their source in our unconscious life. If this is the criterion we ought to adopt to measure responsibility, we will have to give up praising or blaming people for all these things and many more.

Perhaps to avoid these implications Hospers suggests a more narrowly defined version of this as his fourth criterion. In this a person is responsible unless his actions are *compelled by unconscious causes inaccessible to introspection and which nothing can change.* Although similar to the third criterion in that we cannot be held responsible for unconscious forces of which we know nothing, it does exclude all those we can change through introspection. In this narrower compass it means we cannot be held responsible as passive victims for the consequences of situations in which we were placed as an infant: for the compulsive actions occurring in adulthood that are the inevitable consequences of those infantile situations. And psychiatrists and psychoanalysts agree that actions fulfilling this description are characteristic of all people some of the time and of some people most of the time. Hospers argues, once the infantile events have taken place, their occurrence is inevitable, as an explosion is inevitable once the fuse has been lit – there is simply a more delayed action in the psychological explosions, than there is in the physical ones.

Once Dennis Nilsen's grandfather had died – the only person to have established a bond with the boy – he was left with an emotional vacuum which he spent the rest of his life trying to fill. Convinced that both his father and grandfather had walked out on him, he struggled with an intense feeling of his worthlessness. But as long as there were social bonds around him through which he could maintain some human contact, his destructive tendencies remained in check. Once these were lifted and his isolation was complete, the killing began. The only way he had of dealing with his sense of worthlessness was to retreat into privacy and into a fantasy world, where he was no longer emotionally dependent on others, no longer at risk of disappointment and where he could generate some sense of self-esteem.

As Hospers maintains, once these infantile experiences had shaped Nilsen and others like him, once the fuse had been lit, it seems the explosion was inevitable. The question is the extent to which such behaviour can be avoided once the infantile patterns have been set. If there are things Nilsen could have done to prevent it, then he is responsible. If there are things society could have done, then it is responsible. Moreover, if this criterion is the one we choose, we will have to revise those things and others listed in the third criterion which we normally praise or blame. If the causes of this behaviour are inaccessible to the individual through introspection and beyond change, then we would have to give up praising and blaming them. Only those that can be changed by the individual can they be held responsible for.

This brings us to Hospers' last and preferred criterion, that our responsibility for our actions can be measured in the degree to which the act can or could be *changed by the use of reasons.* We saw earlier that Stanton Samenow's treatment of criminals is predicated on a similar assumption that they know the difference between good and evil, and just *prefer* evil. They are not sick, but just brilliant manipulators of the legal and psychiatric systems. Given then that, like the rest of us, their behaviour is the result of making certain rational choices, in this case preferring evil rather than good, the therapist teaches the criminal how to change his behaviour by making certain reasons more prominent than others. The therapist gradually teaches the criminal how to 'deter' criminal thinking: how to think of something else when he sees a women and thinks of rape.

But this still leaves us with the question of the extent to which changed beliefs result in changed behaviour. If it does, then the person is acting responsibly; if not, he's acting compulsively. We can *believe* we ought to do something, but not *desire* to do it, as we can *desire* to do something, yet *believe* we ought not to do it. You might believe that you ought to go to the dentist to have an aching tooth removed, but you don't want to. And you may want to smoke a cigarette, but you believe you ought not to. So with this criterion it is not so much the use of reasons, but their efficacy in changing behaviour that is being made the criterion of responsibility. In neurotic cases, say where a person obsessively washes his hands for hygienic reasons, if we give him reasons that convince him that this belief is groundless, the test of his responsibility is whether this changed belief results in changed behaviour. In genuine neurotic cases no such change occurs. Indeed, as Hospers argues: 'this is often made the defining characteristic of neurotic behaviour: it is unchangeable by any rational considerations.'

So, to summarize:

Hospers: On what grounds should we hold someone responsible?

Suggestions:

1. The presence or absence of premeditation.

2. If we can defend our actions with reasons.

3. Unless our actions are the result of unconscious forces of which we know nothing.

4. Unless our actions are compelled by unconscious causes inaccessible to introspection and which nothing can change.

5. To the degree to which the act could be changed by the use of reasons.

■ 3. Punishment

But now, how should this affect our approach to punishment? If we are to justify it, what do we need to do in the light of these criteria? To make the job just a little easier, this is not a question that involves using only one of these criteria to the exclusion of the others. Even those with extensive knowledge of psychiatry may use a conjunction of two or more at once.

As we normally understand it, punishment implies two things: first that penalties are inflicted upon the offender in the form of deprivation or distress;, and second that these penalties are imposed by a group of people empowered to do so through some generally recognized, legitimate procedure. The first implication is important in that it allows us to distinguish between treatment and punishment, and between the patient and the prisoner. While both treatment and punishment may have the same aim of rehabilitating the individual, treatment seeks to avoid distress as far as possible. The second implication, too, is important in that it distinguishes between the official acts of authorized bodies and those who use the term to describe the unauthorized and illegitimate acts of groups, some criminal, who aim to bring their members and others into line through force or the threat of force.

3.1 Vengeance

Broadly we can distinguish five major theories used to justify punishment: vengeance, deterrence, retribution, rehabilitation and protection. The first is perhaps the simplest and easily stated. It is the view that all forms of legal punishment amount to some form of controlled revenge. Authorities take on the role, rather than those who are harmed, of gaining revenge for the harm done. In this way, while the desire for revenge is satisfied, society avoids the continuing feuds that are likely to result if those harmed, their relatives or friends seek satisfaction through their own hands. Equally important it is seen as a more effective way of ensuring that the punishment is not too excessive: that it fits the crime. Nevertheless, it does seem odd to describe punishment in terms of the impersonal community taking revenge. Usually vengeance is personal, associated with those who are harmed, but are not authorized to act.

3.2 Deterrence

Vengeance, then, seems more like a justification based on the rights of those harmed, rather than an attempt to reduce the incidence of crime. It could, of course, result in a reduction, but more likely it would lead to resentment and continuing incidence of crime as the offender attempts to get back at those who punished him. By contrast, the theory of deterrence sees punishment as a way of discouraging actual and potential law breakers. It is a consequentialist theory in that its only concern is to ensure a reduction in crime. And as a consequentialist theory it usually takes a utilitarian form: that is it judges whether a certain form of punishment is good or bad in terms of the principle of utility, whether it increases the sum total of happiness. Jeremy Bentham, the English philosopher and legal and social reformer who is often described as the founder of utilitarianism, argues in his major work, *Principles of Morals and Legislation* (1789), that the

Dates: 1748–1832
Born: London, England
Best known for: Being one of the founders of modern utilitarianism and for developing the 'felicific calculus', a method of calculating the amount of happiness that will result from any given course of action.

Major works: *An Introduction to the Principles of Morals and Legislation* (1789).

object of all legislation should be 'the greatest happiness of the greatest number'. He argues an increase in the penalties for offenders is justified if it leads to the prevention of crime and, therefore, an increase in social happiness and security.

Even if some things are determined in advance under this theory, it would still make sense to condemn a bad action and praise a good one. The criminal might do it again, so by blaming or punishing him you are attempting to change the deterministic factors that led to the action. This is like our attitude to a pet who has just chewed up our favourite pen or eaten through a new pair of shoes. If we blame or punish him it doesn't mean we hold him responsible, because he probably couldn't have chosen to do otherwise. It is just that we're trying to influence his behaviour, so that he doesn't do this sort of thing in the future. And even if it doesn't deter actual or potential offenders, Bentham argues punishment is still justified if it has an 'incapacitative' effect of removing people from society, thereby protecting society by making it impossible for them to repeat the offence.

However, the problem with such a utilitarian justification, indeed with all consequentialist justifications, is that it can and often does have a highly corrosive effect on all those rights and principles we hold to be inviolable. If it can be shown that excessive punishment is likely to increase social happiness and security, say by sending out a message to potential offenders that we mean to get tough, this is justified even if it results in disproportionate punishment for the one offender who just happens to be in the spotlight of attention.

Similarly, it allows for the punishment of innocent individuals or those who have not been charged or found guilty of any offence. Detention without trial of suspected terrorists, who may have important information, would be justified if it kept dangerous individuals off the streets or yielded valuable intelligence. Bentham argues, similarly: 'When security and equality are in conflict, it will not do to hesitate a moment. Equality must yield.'

3.3 Retribution

For these reasons the theory of deterrence is often combined with the third theory, retribution: in other words, with a theory of proper punishment for crimes. At the core of the theory of retribution is the principle of justice that only law breakers should be punished and it should correspond to the severity of the crime. This excludes a policy of imposing brutal punishments in order to deter law-breaking. Offenders should receive no more than what they deserve.

Thus, unlike the deterrence theory, retribution is backward looking. Rather than looking forward to the consequences of punishment, it looks back on the crime in an attempt to weigh up someone's guilt and responsibility by assessing how far his free will was limited in the circumstances by factors beyond his control. With the focus fixed here it is not concerned with how to prevent the crime occurring again. It has no concern about whether punishment does any good for the offender or society. Indeed, it may very well have bad consequences, reducing the amount of good to society. For example, a successful prosecution for crimes against humanity of a doctor who conducted experiments on unwilling inmates at a Nazi concentration camp might result in the closure of a clinic he has created and maintained over the last 40 years in a poor, developing country whose level of health care is very low.

But we must also distinguish retribution from any form of punishment based exclusively on vengeance. Whether or not anyone seeks revenge, this theory holds that the lawbreaker deserves punishment. As the name implies the offender must 're-tribute', repay the community for the harm done. It is not uncommon for those who hold this view of punishment to quote the Old Testament principle of 'An eye for an eye and a tooth for a tooth.' Supporters of the death penalty argue that when someone commits murder he should pay society back by forfeiting his own life in turn. On the same principle in medieval England any minter of the King's coinage who reduced the metallic content of the coin to line his own pocket paid for his crime by mutilation, usually losing the hands that were responsible for stealing from the king. Under Islamic law, or *Shari'a*, retribution allows the family to exact equal punishment, and *diyat*, blood money, is payable to a dead person's family as compensation. However, as you can see, the simple calculation on which this principle of repayment is based can militate against the other element of retribution: to weigh up someone's guilt and responsibility by assessing how far his free will was limited in the circumstances by factors beyond his control.

3.4 Rehabilitation

It also makes it difficult to achieve any measure of rehabilitation, our fourth theory of punishment. Like deterrence, this too is a consequentialist theory. As we saw in our examination of responsibility, much of the discussion was not just about how responsible a criminal was for his actions, but, given that much of his behaviour was the product of infantile events over which he had no control, about what treatment he can be given to free him of this. Even Stanton Samenow, who does not regard criminals as sick, believing they are ultimately responsible for their criminal behaviour, nevertheless works to rehabilitate them by getting them to make certain reasons more prominent than others, to 'deter' criminal thinking.

Nevertheless, rehabilitation is generally grounded in the assumption that the offender is sick rather than guilty, a patient rather than a prisoner, and a judicial system can bring about changes in his behaviour. This is not just something that is good for the offender, but good for society too, making it safer for individuals and their property. Not surprisingly, therefore, when the rate of recidivism is high, thoughts turn either to more effective forms of punishment and rehabilitation that would bring this down or to locking prisoners away for long periods to protect society. At present the reoffending rate among ex-prisoners is around two-thirds of those released, which is thought to be higher than the rate among those not imprisoned. Indeed, among some classes of offenders, like petty burglars, prison is regarded as a training ground for those who want to pursue their criminal careers when they get out. Locked up for long periods with other criminals

without the opportunity to acquire vocational skills that would allow them to take another course when they get out, this leaves them few options other than to continue where they left off.

However where rehabilitation is employed it can take different forms, each raising difficult ethical questions. The first modern prisons in England developed as collection points for those sentenced to transportation to the colonies, a policy which began in the seventeenth century. From this it was soon realized that such a practice had the beneficial side effect that prisoners could serve several years' hard labour in prisons. In the nineteenth century the Protestant work ethic justified these long sentences on the grounds that such hard labour, like the dull and monotonous work sewing mailbags, was effective in inculcating strong moral sentiments; the longer the sentence the more effective the cure. Today methods of rehabilitation are more sophisticated, involving not just education and training to equip offenders with vocational skills they can use on the outside to pursue a life other than crime, but the more contentious methods, like psychotherapy and behavioural conditioning, to change their attitudes and behaviour.

Predictably this raises serious objections, of which three are worth noting. The most common complaint is that by 'treating' offenders in this way prison sentences no longer have sufficient deterrent effect. The result of concentrating on the habitual offender and on ways of rehabilitating him within society is that the system will then have to treat more offenders, who no longer fear the deterrent effect of prison sentences. Prison will have become a pleasant place to rest up and gain some additional skills, rather than the harsh regime feared by actual and potential offenders. Nevertheless there is still a considerable deterrent effect in a prison sentence. You are denied your freedom of movement to see your friends and family, and your every hour is controlled by timetables imposed on you. What's more, whether you like it or not you are required to undergo a programme of 'treatment', involving education, training and some form of therapy.

A more significant objection is that there is no longer a correlation between the length of the sentence on the one hand, and the degree of responsibility of the offender and the seriousness of the crime on the other. The length of the sentence must equate with the time it takes to cure the offender. But in many cases the less serious offender is more difficult to cure than the more serious. Most offenders who commit murder are unlikely to repeat the offence, whereas a petty burglar or thief is likely to find it difficult to change his ways. It may be the only way of life he has ever known. Indeed, many are the most notable recidivists, in and out of prison most of their lives. But on the principle of rehabilitation a thief would receive a longer sentence than a murderer. And, moreover, as offenders would be confined until they are cured, presumably the incurable would receive a life sentence.

As you can see this seems to present us with a choice between two conflicting aims of punishment: rehabilitation or retribution. However, according to some philosophers, it may not be necessary for us to make this choice at all. For example, Antony Duff argues that they are both in fact quite compatible. Although those who advocate one or the other do so in terms suggesting there is a genuine contrast, especially in what actually goes on in the respective programmes designed to achieve each one, Duff argues that in fact rehabilitation or 'restoration' is not only compatible with retribution, but in fact requires it if it is to be effective. Both responses to crime, he insists, are right in their respective ways. We are right to demand that criminals pay for their offences and we are also right that they should be rehabilitated. But there is a coherent alternative in which both can be achieved.

The third objection is one we came across earlier in the context of R. D. Laing and Michel Foucault, and the questions they raise about what we regard as 'normality': whether we define it in terms of our failure to think in conformity with prevailing social beliefs and values. If this is the case, rehabilitation seems more like brainwashing or social conditioning into more socially acceptable patterns of behaviour. Society would be protecting itself by infringing the most basic of our human rights to our own personality and beliefs. If this is the case, we should, therefore, have the ultimate right to refuse such treatment and retain our anti-social behaviour, even though this would mean we will be punished and imprisoned.

The parallel to this is a state's operation of a mental health policy, which requires that it draws a careful and clear distinction between someone being eccentric and being insane. In Ken Kesey's famous novel, *One Flew Over the Cuckoo's Nest* (1962), and the film made from it, men are confined to a mental asylum against their will, and drugs and electroconvulsive therapy are used to control their eccentric behaviour. In Britain social workers who 'section' someone under the Mental Health Act are careful to distinguish harmful from merely eccentric behaviour. Even though neighbours might disapprove of a person's behaviour, perhaps even finding it offensive, this is not enough to confine people against their will.

The most sinister application of such treatment, of course, as we have seen, was in the Soviet Union's policy of confining dissidents to mental asylums. Here 'crime' was interpreted more broadly to include not just normal criminal offences, but offences against the state: political offences that derived from being outspoken critics of the ruling elite. Many were imprisoned for unspecified periods in hospitals and asylums for therapy and re-education, including mind-altering drugs, behavioural conditioning, and even surgical, chemical and electrical therapy. And all of this was justified on the grounds that such opposition posed a threat to the stability and security of the nation. Treatment was designed merely to 'cure' them of their opinions.

3.5 Protection

In contrast, our final theory has much less ambitious aims. At times of rising insecurity, when there seems to be overwhelming evidence of a significant increase in crime, the one thing we expect from a system of punishment is protection, a guarantee of public safety. Long prison sentences take people off the streets. Executions prevent them committing future crimes. The protection theory, therefore, has a simple goal of containing and isolating the offender.

But still this is not a theory of protection alone: it usually contains elements of other theories too. It would be unusual not to contain an element of retribution. We normally accept that legal punishment to protect society should be imposed only on lawbreakers, because they deserve punishment. If we were to apply it more widely we could no doubt protect society more effectively by imposing punishment on other groups that haven't broken the law. For example, it would protect society more effectively if we were to impose punishment on habitual late night revellers who regularly wake their neighbours and disturb their sleep. We could no doubt find other nuisances, too, who seriously damage the quality of our lives, but who don't actually break any law. Similarly, protection theories are frequently combined with deterrence theories. Actual punishment, as well as the threat of it, protects society by deterring criminals in general.

It seems, then, that, like the five criteria of responsibility, on its own no one of these theories is sufficient to achieve what we want to achieve from a system of punishment. We need two or more of them in combination.

■ 4. Conclusion

The problem we started with in Chapter 18 was that on the one hand it seems there is no other experience so deeply woven into the daily reality of our lives than that of being free to choose what to do, and yet with equal conviction, we all believe that things don't just happen, but that they happen because they're caused. We have now found that this has a direct bearing on the way we make sense of the connected notions of responsibility and punishment.

It is odd to say that everything I do is determined, even if it is by my own circumstances and psychological conditions. It makes us feel as if we were mere puppets, not responsible for what we do. And yet to be responsible at all for our actions it doesn't make sense if they are not determined. As Nagel explains, 'It's not clear what it means to say *I* determine the choice, if nothing about me determines it.' The question, then, is what is it about me that determines the choice I make?

If it is my character, is that determined by circumstances that were not of my choosing? Is it, then, my moral self, as Mill maintains, that chooses what to make of my character? But that in turn depends on my strength of will to do what I believe to be morally right and this might be the product of forces beyond my control. So, what is it that will rescue us from the fate of being mere 'conscious automata'? The answer you give to this will determine how responsible you believe people are for what they decide to do and what you believe we can effectively and morally set out to achieve through punishment.

■ Questions

1. 'The more thoroughly and in detail we know the causal factors leading a person to behave as he does, the more we tend to exempt him from responsibility.' (Hospers). Is Hospers right?

2. When should people be held responsible for acts which they did not intend?

3. 'If your actions are predictable, you cannot be held responsible for what you do.' Are we right in arguing this?

4. Discuss the view that smokers should be charged for medical treatment for smoking-related illnesses?

5. What reasons are there for not imposing the death penalty on one person for a parking offence if this will deter others from committing parking offences?

6. Are there any grounds for saying that it is wrong to stone adulterers, to cut off the hands of thieves, and to promise large rewards for killing those who have offended our religion?

7. Should justice always be done whatever the consequences?

■ Recommended reading

Bentham, Jeremy. *A Fragment on Government with an Introduction to the Principles of Morals and Legislation* (1789), (ed.) Wilfrid Harrison (Oxford: Blackwell, 1967).

Duff, Antony. Restoration and Retribution. In Andrew von Hirsch et al. (eds), *Restorative Justice and Criminal Justice: Competing or Reconcilable Paradigms?* (Oxford and Portland, Oreg: Hart Publishing, 2003), pp. 43–60.

Foucault, Michel. *Madness and Civilization: A History of Insanity in the Age of Reason* (London: Routledge, 1989).

Hospers, John. What Means This Freedom? In S. Hook (ed.), *Determinism and Freedom in the Age of Modern Science* (New York: Macmillan, Collier, 1961).

Kenny, A. *Freewill and Responsibility* (London: Routledge, 1987).

Milgram, Stanley. *Obedience to Authority* (London: Tavistock, 1974; New York: Harper and Row, 1974).

  The note structure to accompany this chapter can be downloaded from our website.

PART III

Understanding our Relations with Others

In Part II we were concerned with how we understand ourselves and whether we can genuinely regard ourselves and the choices we make as free. Only when we have some answer to these problems can we begin to consider the extent to which we can be held responsible for our actions. Now, in Part III, we are left with what often seems to be the most complex problem of them all: how we are to understand and manage our relations with others. Each day we are presented with problems that call for us to make choices which affect others and in each of these it seems we accept some degree and type of responsibility, whether that is moral or legal.

But before we can make informed choices that affect these relations we need to know the nature of these responsibilities and obligations, and how we are to meet them. It must seem odd to you as it does to me that, although almost at every turn we seem to face the moral implications of our actions, many of which have serious and long-lasting consequences, we are never taught how we are to think morally, as we are taught how to think mathematically and logically. Of course, this assumes that morality is not just a matter of opinion; that there is something in it which is absolute, as there is in mathematics and logic. Without this there would be no point in discussing moral matters, if our aim is to settle differences. If it were just a matter of taste, there would be nothing to argue about; it would just be your opinion against mine. But as we know all of us do continue to discuss moral matters, so either we are sadly mistaken about the nature of moral reasoning, or there is indeed something absolute in it.

Although we might find it uncomfortable to believe that most of us are indeed mistaken, as we have discovered in philosophy this shouldn't deter us from exploring the idea. Everyday we meet people who are willing to argue for this point of view: that morality is just relative, a matter of individual feelings or the social culture in which we were brought up and live. If this is true, if what we believe to be morally right is just a matter of emotions or a product of the society in which we live, all discussion of moral matters is futile, except with someone within our own culture who we think has simply got that culture wrong. Beyond this there is nothing either of us can appeal to in order to settle our differences.

Others believe that the purpose of moral discourse is not cognitive at all: it is not to exchange facts about a situation that involves a moral choice or to reason through it to reach some conclusion, which we can all agree on as if it were a mathematical or logical problem. Nor is it, similarly, to describe accurately the features of any situation as if all moral disagreement is the result of merely getting the description wrong. Rather, these philosophers believe that moral discourse has an altogether different purpose: it is non-cognitive. When we say that to do X is wrong or Y is a bad person, all we are actually expressing is our own emotional reaction to the situation or the person. It is like sighing with relief when your plane lands safely, or exclaiming 'Wow!', when you hear a particularly impressive piece of music the first time. Others say that it doesn't so much express your emotions as tell someone that they must or must not do something: you are *prescribing*, rather than *describing* something. When you say lying is bad, what you're really saying is 'Don't lie!'

If these people are right, it is indeed futile to discuss morality, because we could never find agreement over such things. It simply does not involve propositions, which we could discuss as a means of finding some solution to our differences. Even so, the fact is we still do continue to talk about moral matters. We argue with friends and acquaintances, even though they have strong opinions that have been shaped by radically different social experiences than ours. We discuss the moral implications of events we see on the evening news that occur in other parts of the world to people of quite different cultures, political systems and religious faiths. So we *do* seem to assume there is some point in discussing moral matters, that we can settle something, or at least push the discussion on towards some resolution. But if this is the case and we do in fact believe there is something absolute about it, what are these absolute features and where are we to find them?

One way of answering this question is to ask yourself: what is it about a moral problem that is to count most, the motives of the people involved, the consequences of their actions, or certain moral principles? You might argue that your actions are morally right if you act out of the best of motives or respect certain deeply held principles. But still they can result in harm to others, which provides reasonable grounds for believing that in fact they were not morally right. And, by the same token of course, most of us would not take much convincing that we should have serious doubts about whether an action is morally right, which we justify on the grounds that it benefits many people at the cost of sacrificing the life of an innocent individual. We would no doubt point out that it offends a principle we hold deeply: that all individuals have the right to life, that they are sacrosanct and cannot be sacrificed for the greatest good. So perhaps the answers to these questions lie in the type of people we are, rather than the decisions we reach, on the assumption that good people rarely do bad things. In the following chapters we will examine each of these three positions and the arguments of those philosophers who support them.

But what if the differences between us are due not so much to these factors as to different styles of moral thinking, in particular a fundamental difference between the way men and women think morally? Where men emphasize reason, abstract principles and justice, women are inclined to emphasize emotions, concrete personal relations and supporting people. Indeed, feminists argue, not only are male and female ethics different, but we should be deeply concerned about the male ethic with all its violent and destructive consequences for human life and for the planet itself.

Some argue that the reason for these differences is that the male nature and masculinity is linked to aggressive and destructive tendencies, while the female nature is less aggressive, more gentle, nurturing and cooperative. Others argue these differences are not so much the result of nature as of nurture; the life experiences of women are just very different from men. For example, the fact that they are more deeply involved in the experiences of child-rearing means that there is likely to be a significant difference in their reaction to the waste of lives in war. In contrast to the way men think about moral issues, the female ethic is likely to emphasize different values, virtues and priorities that support, repair and enrich relationships to help people fulfil their potential.

Running parallel with these claims, as we will see later in Chapter 24, is the argument that there exists in society an underlying set of power relations in which men have power over women; a patriarchal style of government with men deciding between themselves how they will control women for their own ends. Many feminists believe there exists an 'original pact', as Carole Pateman describes it, an agreement among men to dominate women prior to the creation of any form of democratic government.

At the heart of this lies the belief that we should not restrict our view of politics to public affairs involving governments, representative institutions and elections. Modern feminists argue 'the personal is the political.' Politics doesn't just stop at the front door: it is part of every aspect of men's relations with women. Oppression exists in many aspects of life, much of which originates in the family itself with the processes of socializing children into their respective masculine and feminine sexual roles. Indeed, feminists argue that the patriarchal family lies at the heart of a system of male domination, reproducing patriarchalism in education, at work and in politics.

As you can see this brings us to a different type of obligation, our political obligation to obey the state and comply with its laws. We need to ask whether there are any conceivable circumstances in which we would be justified in refusing to obey the law, or does this pose an even greater problem as people pick and choose what laws they will and will not obey? The answer to this is likely to be found in what we accept as the grounds for our political obligation: that we have freely chosen to accept it in regular elections, or that as we have benefited from the state we owe it our loyalty in return.

Whichever it is, it is likely to depend on the form of government and how it settles two problems: the extent of its power and whether it has taken too much; and whether the government uses these powers in a legitimate way. This will mean, of course, that we will examine not only the different forms of government and the ways in which they settle these issues, but also the key concepts we use – concepts like authority, power, legitimacy, force and influence. With this behind us we can then turn our attention to the political theories that use these forms of government to achieve their goals – theories like liberalism, conservatism, fascism, nationalism and communism.

In all of this we confront the moral and political realities of our everyday lives: whether a government, in its fight against rising crime, is right to introduce powers to gather more information on individuals; whether we are right to ignore the wishes of an elderly relative, who wants to keep her independence, in order to get her the help she needs; and whether a young woman can be blamed for selling her body, when her actions are driven by her need for the drugs to which she is addicted. They are the type of issue none of us can lightly refuse to consider.

You may find it helpful to have copies of the note structures for the following chapters by your side as you read them. These can be downloaded from our website at www.palgrave.com/foundations/greetham.

Metaethics

Contents

Key issues

▶ Is all moral discussion futile, because our moral beliefs are just a matter of taste? Or is there something absolute in morality, as there is in mathematics and logic, something which we can learn so that we can become better moral thinkers?

▶ Are moral beliefs just relative judgements, which relate just to us as individuals or to the social culture in which we were brought up and live?

▶ When I say that something is 'good', is this an objective characteristic that I can find in the real world in the same way that I can describe an object as having the characteristic of being blue?

▶ When we make moral judgements are these like statements of fact, which can be shown to be true or false?

▶ Perhaps they are just a way of giving vent to our emotions and feelings as we respond to some event or person in the same way you might sigh with relief when you are told that a medical scan on you has come back clear?

▶ Or perhaps they disguise our actual intention to tell people how they should behave, so that they are in fact imperatives or commands?

If our actions are free in any sense, are we free to do as we like? The simple answer, of course, is no: we live in societies that have laws prohibiting certain kinds of behaviour. In Chapters 24 to 27 we will examine different systems of government and political theories that legitimize such invasions into our freedom. But this still leaves the moral norms and values that we live by in our private lives as we interact with others. And, it seems, we are far from clear what legitimizes the influence of these self-imposed restrictions on our behaviour. Even though moral choice is deeply woven into the daily reality of our lives, most of us are still unclear about the basis on which we make these choices.

This is the study of ethics. We are concerned with how we should live; how we should relate to one another; what we may expect from others; and the limits we and others should impose on our behaviour. We set out to find justifications for the limits we set on our desires and actions: what we ought and ought not to do. But it is useful to distinguish between two types or levels of study in ethics: normative ethics, which we will explore in the next two chapters, and metaethics. The difference between the two can best be explained through the practice of philosophers of language who distinguish between the first-order language, in which we all communicate with one another, and the second-order language, in which we attempt to understand, analyse, and clarify the nature and meaning of first-order discourse. Thus normative ethics is first-order discourse, while metaethics is second-order.

Normative ethics, then, is more familiar to most of us. It involves all those activities we engage in at one time or another, frequently or infrequently, consciously or unconsciously. We make moral judgements that a certain action or type of action is right or wrong. These we justify by using broad principles and theories of moral obligation about what kinds of actions are morally right or permissible. We might use a utilitarian principle to justify our decision, arguing that actions are right in so far as they promote the greatest happiness of the greatest number. Or we might simply assert that everyone should look after themselves. We might find justification in the principle that we must devote ourselves to the service of God. Alternatively we might insist that actions are right as long as people have the right motives or comply with certain moral rules. Beyond these concerns, we also make judgements about what makes good or bad characters or dispositions. Known as 'virtue ethics' in philosophy, it is the concern we have to know the sort of features we should promote in ourselves and others that result in good moral characters.

However, by contrast, metaethics is concerned about what's going on in such first-order discourse: its meaning, the nature and status of such moral judgements and the degree to which we can justify them. In particular we are concerned about the meaning of ethical terms, like 'good', 'bad' and 'right'. When I say that something is 'good', is this something I can find in objects, so that I can see clearly that some have it and others don't? Is it something like a colour that I can see, or a taste, like sweetness? We want to know about the logical status of moral judgements that use such terms: whether they purport to be statements of fact, which we can show are true or false, or whether they are expressions or reports of feelings, attitudes and emotions, just a matter of taste, beyond truth and falsehood. And if they are subjective in this way, how can we justify any discussion about moral matters? If you say you like the colour green and I say I like the colour red, this leaves no room

for discussion: there is no purpose to it. Indeed, all discussion seems futile, you have your tastes and I have mine. So metaethics is concerned about the nature of the justifications, the moral reasoning, we give to support our moral judgements.

Perhaps the most useful way of distinguishing between the two lies in the fact that metaethics, unlike normative ethics, does not deal with substantive ethical theories or moral judgements, but rather with questions about the nature of these theories and judgements. The independence of the two is best illustrated by William Paley, the eighteenth-century theologian, who, in terms of metaethics, held similar views to Martin Luther on the nature of morality, believing that right and wrong are determined by the will of God. Yet, on the normative and substantive level, because he believed that God wills the happiness of his creatures, unlike Luther, he was a utilitarian. His normative ethical judgements were governed by the principle that whatever increases happiness is right and whatever decreases it is wrong. So, normative ethics is concerned with the content of our moral judgements, while metaethics is concerned with their nature.

You can see this distinction clearly in the main preoccupations of metaethics during the twentieth century. Perhaps the main one has been whether ethics is objective or subjective. In fact this is a controversy that dates back to Plato in the fourth century BC. Plato believed that 'good' refers to an idea or property having an objective existence quite apart from anyone's attitudes or desires, whereas the Sophists argued, as Protagoras famously put it, 'Man is the measure of all things.' But the positions we take in metaethics over whether ethics is objective or subjective do not tell us what we ought to do. That task is the province of normative ethics.

Another issue that has preoccupied twentieth-century philosophers has been the extent to which reason can bring about agreed decisions on what we ought to do. Frequent attempts have been made to show, in the face of considerable scepticism, either that it is in one's own interests to do what is good or that, even though this is not necessarily in one's own interests, it is the rational thing to do. There has been a similar concern over just what goodness and the standard of right and wrong might be and whether it is proper to refer to moral judgements as true and false. But again none of these concerns tell us what we ought to do.

■ 1. Relativism

Many of us are tempted to find the answers to these questions by asking where our moral values come from. For relativists this is the key question. They argue that as each of us acquires our moral values from radically different sources – different societies, social classes and individual experiences – we cannot hope to have any discourse between them. For this to occur there would have to exist absolute standards of good and bad, right and wrong, in terms of which we can discuss and evaluate these different value systems. Relativists simply deny that any such set of absolute standards exists: there are only different, insulated systems of values between which no discourse is possible.

Stimulated by the advances in anthropology and the sociology of knowledge in the late nineteenth and early twentieth centuries, it recognizes the sort of fact observed by Aristotle in *Nicomachean Ethics* that 'Fire burns both in Hellas and in Persia; but men's ideas of right and wrong vary from place to place.' There might be uniformity in experience from one society to another, but not in the value judgements we make about them. The relativist recognizes the importance of two things: the social environment in determining the content of beliefs about both what is and what ought to be the case, and the possible diversity of such social environments. They claim there are no sound procedures for justifying one moral code or one set of moral judgements as against another.

However, we ought to avoid a common confusion between this and ethical scepticism, which denies that knowledge or even rational belief is possible. Ethical sceptics believe that no one can ever say with any justification that something is good or bad, right or wrong. That's not to say that some actions may not be right and others wrong, there's just no way of knowing which is which. Thus the sceptic does leave open the possibility that some actions or principles are right or wrong, but claims simply that we can never be in a position to know that this is so. Relativism, by contrast, is a doctrine about truth and may very well be a response aimed at avoiding scepticism. The relativist argues we can know that some actions are right and others wrong, but only within a particular culture with its own particular set of moral values.

In effect this amounts to the claim that something is wrong or blameworthy if either the person herself, or the group to which she belongs, thinks it is. And, of course, the group can be defined in numerous ways as social class, culture, religion, profession, even clubs, societies and peer groups. As this makes clear there are two positions the relativist can hold. The first is the popular belief that we are free to invent our own morality: that if an individual *thinks* it is right, then it *is* right. But if this is to work it must overcome two problems. First, if it is taken to mean that what someone *thinks* is right is *really* right for her, it is circular and probably absurd. *Thinking* that something is right is to be convinced that it really *is* right. Drawing this distinction adds nothing.

Second, it implies there is no point in debating with someone what is right for her to do, unless she is in doubt herself. The relativist argues that if she *believes* that it is right, then it *is* right, at least for her. But we do generally believe there is some point in arguing about what is right to do, even when someone is in no doubt. One of your tutors may tell you on the first day of the course that he has decided and is in no doubt about the final grades he will give each member of the class, and no one gets more than a D. It is unlikely that you will take this lying down, even though he is in no doubt what you deserve. You will talk to him and anyone else who has influence over him to change his mind.

In the second position the individual takes her moral values from the group. If the moral principles recognized, say, by the society of which she is a member makes clear that it is wrong to wear shorts in public, then it *is* wrong for her to wear shorts in public. In effect it is saying that a person should only act in conformity with the moral standards of her group or society. Here again there are obvious problems. We can all recognize the type of situation in which the individual's personal moral obligations to friends and relatives outweigh any obligation decreed by her group or society.

For example, if you were a citizen of Germany in 1935 you would have been subject to the Nuremberg Laws. These were the culmination of a process that disenfranchised German Jews, effectively depriving them of their German citizenship, prohibiting marriage or relationships with the Aryan German population, and purging various professions of Jews, including the civil service, the judiciary, the universities, and the German medical establishment. So if you had been taught by a Jewish teacher or been cared for since birth by the family doctor, who happened to be Jewish, you were required to turn your back on them, even engage in actively denouncing them and their families. But many ordinary individuals were unable to go along with this. The film *The White Rose* tells the true story of a group of students at the university in Munich who challenged Nazism on moral grounds even at the risk of their lives, while other ordinary people found hiding places, provided forged documents and raised funds all at the risk of their lives.

Indeed this is not at all strange to most of us. We are all reluctant just to accept without evaluation what we have been taught by our parents, because we acknowledge that morality is not just blind obedience, but a question of doing what's right regardless of what some authority might say. Kant's moral philosophy is built around the central, defining characteristic of morality: our autonomy, our ability to think for ourselves. Since the Nuremberg Trials at the end of the Second World War we are not so willing to accept the defence that someone bears no responsibility for their actions, because they were merely following orders. The various international tribunals held since have recognized there is a higher moral obligation to humanity itself, and anyone can be held liable for crimes against humanity, irrespective of the orders they were following.

The same issue is taken up in Plato's dialogue *Euthyphro*. In it Socrates asks Euthyphro whether actions are right because God commands them, or whether God commands them because they are right. If he chooses the former any action God commands must be right regardless of what we may think of it, and for all we know God may be capricious and arbitrary, wielding his infinite power not for justice and mercy, but to satisfy his own desires and thirst for revenge. Yet still, if he were to command us to torture innocent children on these grounds, it would be right to do so. But whether or not anyone commands it, it is morally wrong to torture innocent children, which shows that actions are not good solely because God commands them. What God says is right is not reason in itself to think it is right.

So, it seems the answer to Socrates' question lies in the second part of the dilemma. In the religious context ethics is concerned with whether or not God's commands are justified. What he commands may indeed be right, but we need to determine it independently of God: we need an independent criterion by which we can judge the commands of God and indeed God himself. If we are to comply with God's commands we must know that he is good. In effect this means there must be a criterion even higher than God, against which his and our moral judgements can be evaluated. We cannot be moral without knowing what morality is in the first place. And this seems to lead us back to the absolutists and their belief that there exist absolute unchanging moral rules and standards, irrespective of different cultures, societies and circumstances.

■ 2. Metaethical theories: objectivism and subjectivism

So it seems relativism does not give us a way of side-stepping the problem of how we are to justify our moral judgements. Unlike the first part of the *Euthyphro* problem, they cannot be arbitrary and capricious, accepted without reason or justification. We need to know on what grounds they are made. And when we disagree with others we also need to be clear about the nature of this disagreement and if there is anything we can do to resolve it. This is no longer a question of where our values come from and whether we can compare one with another, but how we justify our moral judgements. The dilemma is elegantly put by a character in Aldous Huxley's novel *Point Counter Point* (1928), when he declares:

> One should be loyal to one's tastes and instincts. ... What's the good of a philosophy with a major premise that isn't the rationalization of your feelings? ... But one's tastes and instincts were accidents. There were eternal principles. ... Justice was eternal; charity and brotherly love were beautiful.

2.1 Objectivism

Where subjectivists believe our moral judgements are nothing more than an expression of our own thoughts and feelings with no means of resolving disputes, objectivists believe there is a moral reality of values and truths existing independently of human wishes and beliefs. And the objectivist believes that there are independent ways of establishing certain truths and answering questions of value. A moral judgement is objective if, and only if, it is either true or false and if its truth or falsity does not depend on the peculiarities of the person who makes the judgement or on the culture to which he belongs, but on a rational agent.

For example, Plato held that moral judgements are true or false in exactly the same sense that mathematical propositions are. He believed that a moral statement, like 'This is good', is not about anyone's psychology, but about the real world, in particular a feature of the real world called 'goodness'. There are, he believed, moral facts in the real world and goodness is one of them. This is an example of moral realism which sees moral truth as grounded in the nature of things and not as subjective and variable human reactions to things.

But still it seems inappropriate to talk about truth and falsity in relation to value judgements. Non-evaluative, factual statements can be proved true or false either necessarily, by analysis or definition, or empirically, but there are no ethical characteristics, like goodness, whose existence can be proved by definition or by direct or indirect observation. Take an objective theory, like utilitarianism. Its supporters would argue that all moral statements can be reduced to scientific statements about the real world that can be verified by empirical evidence. So, for example, statements like 'It is right to act in this way', means 'This act will produce an excess of pleasure over pain.' And, although this is about psychological factors, such as pleasure and pain, it is not just a statement about the speaker's psychology alone, but about the psychology of a number of people and, at times, all people. But it doesn't measure goodness itself, but redefines it as happiness in terms of pleasure and pain and sets out to measure that.

Nevertheless, even though moral judgements do not correspond to self-evident truths or objective facts, they may still be proper candidates for being true or false. This too has become known as moral realism, although for some it makes moral judgements true or false at the cost of taking objectivity out of the notion of truth. A statement or judgement is true if it can gain publicly warranted endorsement by informed, reasonable, reflective and careful observers. It must be endorsed by some publicly determinable procedure in virtue of which we can come to accept it. The supporters of this notion make their case by pointing out, by contrast, that if I were to say that an action is right because it arouses in me personally a feeling of approval, this does not count as an objective theory, because the truth of an ethical sentence like this will always

depend upon who uses it. In this sense a publicly determinable procedure gives warranted endorsement to moral judgements in a way not dissimilar to Kuhn's account of the way we call upon an informed, reflective community of observers to endorse theories in the natural and social sciences.

In summary, then, objective theories claim that moral statements are propositional: they are analogous to scientific statements in that we can show them to be true or false.

2.2 Subjectivism

In contrast, subjectivists argue there is simply no way of rationally resolving moral disputes, because moral judgements and principles cannot correctly be said to be true or false independently of the attitude of at least some people. For example, Thomas Hobbes is usually considered to be a subjectivist because he argued that moral judgements, like 'This is good', can be analysed into a statement, like 'I desire this', which is about my internal psychology, my preferences and my state of mind. Thus what is morally right is a mere matter of taste or personal opinion.

But this is not the only sense in which subjectivism is held. Some believe that what appear to be objective truths or ethical rules are really disguised commands, so that when I say 'Lying is wrong!' I am not stating an objective fact or value, but really issuing the command or imperative 'Never lie!' Others believe they are really expressions of attitudes or feelings. In this case, when I say 'Lying is wrong!' I am merely giving expression to my hostility to lying; in effect I am saying 'Lying! I hate it!' or 'I hate liars!' And still another version holds that all I am doing is not so much giving expression to such feelings as reporting that I have them. In this sense moral utterances are autobiographical reports that the speaker or people in general have these feelings and attitudes. 'Lying is wrong' would then mean 'I, or perhaps people in general, disapprove of lying.' The parallel to this in epistemology, as we have seen, is Berkeley's subjective idealism, which holds that physical objects are really ideas in the mind.

Yet despite these differences two elements characterize a theory as subjectivist:

◆   if the theory holds that ethical judgements are non-propositional – that they do not make statements that can be proved either true or false

◆ or, if the theory does hold that ethical judgements *are* propositional and can, therefore, be shown to be either true or false, but are about the psychology of the person or people who utter them and only them.

The implication of these principles is that there is no way of settling disputes: either moral judgements represent nothing more than statements of mere taste, between which nothing can adjudicate, or they are statements about my own state of mind that only I can verify through introspection. This means that discussion of moral issues is futile, even though it's an activity in which we all engage in the belief that we can, at least in principle, resolve conflicts and differences of opinion. It would be as absurd as arguing over our conflicting preferences for certain wines. The most we are doing is attempting to change someone's mind by getting them to abandon their criterion of a good wine in favour of ours. We are not trying to establish the truth because this would involve the assumption that there already exists a commonly agreed criterion. When this exists the whole function of argument changes. If we were to disagree about the distance between home and college, there would be some point in the argument, because there exists an objective, commonly accepted standard of measurement, for settling such disputes.

■ 3. Metaethical theories: cognitivism and non-cognitivism

As you can see, much of our discussion so far has been about whether morality is a feature of the real world and whether our moral judgements are propositional. This last characteristic provides another useful means of distinguishing between answers to metaethical questions. Concerned with what we are doing when we use moral language, it asks you whether there are any formal requirements which all moral judgements have; things you expect irrespective of the judgements' substantive content. When we examined the formal requirements of scientific explanations we found that they must be universal, empirical and yield testable consequences, which provide us the means by which we can attempt to falsify them. The question, then, is: do moral judgements have similar formal requirements?

In what we are about to discuss, keep in mind four requirements that may or may not be necessary to all moral judgements. First consider objectivity, that moral judgements are cognitive propositions, capable of being shown to be true or false. Second, and less controversial, moral judgements must be universal: if it is right for X to do Y in certain circumstances, then it is right for anyone to do Y in all relevantly similar circumstances. Third, non-cognitivists maintain that moral discourse is action-guiding or at least attitude-moulding. When we make moral judgements we are not just affirming that something *is* the case, but criticizing, appraising or *making* something the case. And finally consider the claim that morality is an autonomous mode of discourse: that is, no moral claim can be derived from purely nonmoral statements alone. Those who stress this as a formal requirement argue that we can never discover what we ought to do from knowledge of nonmoral facts alone, including facts about human nature and conduct.

So, to summarize:

Consider four possible requirements of moral judgements:

1. Objectivity.

2. Universalism.

3. Action guiding or attitude moulding.

4. Autonomous mode of discourse.

3.1 Cognitivism

Among twentieth-century philosophers, those defending the objectivity of ethical judgements have most often been naturalists or intuitionists. Both agree that moral language is cognitive, that moral claims can be known to be true or false, but they disagree on how this knowing is to be achieved. Naturalists hold either that these claims can be adequately justified by reasoning from statements employing only nonmoral terms or that moral terms themselves can be defined in nonmoral or factual terms. Intuitionists deny both of these positions and hold that moral terms are *sui generic* (literally 'of its own kind'), that moral statements are autonomous in their logical status and cannot be translated or reduced into other terms.

3.1.1 Naturalism

Ethical naturalists, then, are those who employ some form of argument in which they assume that moral terms are completely definable in nonmoral terms and that moral judgements are simply a subspecies of empirical judgements. Put simply they assume that moral terms stand for purely natural characteristics. Consider, for example, the difference between these two statements:

1. On 6 August 1945 a US B-29 bomber dropped an atomic bomb which destroyed the Japanese city of Hiroshima resulting in the immediate deaths of 130,000 people.

2. Dropping the atomic bomb on Hiroshima was a morally good thing.

The first is a factual statement, which can be verified or falsified by evidence. The second is a value judgement, which the naturalist believes can be verified in much the same way.

More specifically, ethical naturalism is most widely understood as the belief that ethical thinking can be exhaustively understood in terms of the natural propensities of human beings without having to resort to a belief in moral intuitions, conscience or even divine guidance. So, utilitarianism and evolutionary ethics can both be regarded as naturalistic in that they believe that moral judgements are just disguised ways of making psychological assertions. One argues, as in the second statement above, that moral good is defined by the individual's need to maximize his happiness and the other by his need to ensure his survival.

In another version of naturalism it is argued that all ethical statements are nothing more than statements that we have certain feelings of approval or disapproval, both personal and general. It's worth noting a subtle and important distinction here. If these were 'expressions' of these feelings, this would be a form of expressivism, which is usually described as subjectivism, but not naturalism. But as we are discussing ethical statements as 'statements' that we have certain feelings, this can be described as a naturalistic and subjectivist theory in the sense defined in our second principle above. In other words, it holds that ethical judgements are propositional, not just expressions of feelings, and can be

shown to be either true or false by reference to the psychology of the person or people who utter them.

For example, in contrast to what has already been said, the statement 'Dropping the atomic bomb on Hiroshima was a morally good thing', says nothing about the nature of the event or its consequences, but merely means that 'I approve of dropping the atomic bomb on Hiroshima', or 'The majority of people approve of dropping the atomic bomb on Hiroshima.' Both statements can be verified or falsified by reference to my, or the majority's, psychological response to this event: they can both be tested by examining me or by taking an opinion poll.

Of the numerous objections to this argument two are worth noting. First, it seems more than plausible to argue that such statements of approval or disapproval are evoked by prior judgements as to whether an action is right. I feel approval for an action, because I have already assessed the evidence and come to the judgement that it is right. After I have assessed the evidence of the likely consequences of dropping the bomb I come to the judgement that it is the right thing to do. But if we approve of an action because we judge it to be right, our thinking that it is right cannot be identical with our approving of it.

Second, such a theory seems to preclude any possibility of our settling, or even engaging in, moral disputes. If the theory is true that my moral judgements are nothing more than statements about my feelings of approval or disapproval, all I need do to settle any moral doubt is look within at my own feelings. But then my judgement can never be wrong, except when I misread my feelings, and it is very difficult, if not impossible, for anyone to be wrong about their feelings, whereas it is all too easy to make a mistake about whether an action is right. This theory precludes any possibility that our judgement can be disputed by another person, because all I have to say to be right is that I approve of it.

Even more, any judgement I might make is logically compatible with any judgement that I, or someone else, might subsequently make. Every judgement depends upon who makes it, at what time, and in what circumstances. If you say that it was wrong to drop the bomb on Hiroshima and I say that it wasn't, the two statements are not incompatible because they are merely different statements about different dispositions. And even if I make this judgement only to come to the opposite judgement some time later, my conflicting judgements are not incompatible, because they are merely reporting my feelings at different times. At this point you are no doubt coming to the conclusion that this sounds absurd: if I now say that it was wrong to drop the bomb, I am bound to say that earlier, when I said it was right, I was mistaken.

Indeed, even if we were to discover factual evidence that makes my position false and the other person's true and I change my mind accordingly, my original judgement would still be correct as a statement about my feelings at that particular time. Suppose I say that the bomb should have been dropped because I wrongly believe that dropping it would have saved more lives by bringing the Second World War in the Pacific to an end. According to this theory all I mean when I say this is that the thought of dropping the bomb aroused in me feelings of approval, and since it does this my statement that it ought to have been dropped is true, even though it is clear that I was mistaken about the facts. And I am under no obligation to withdraw my original judgement when I discover my mistake.

And, indeed, it makes no difference if moral judgements state what a *community* feels: the same criticisms still apply as to the 'private reaction theory' above. If one person belonging to one community comes to a judgement that conflicts with the judgement of another person from a different community, their statements will be perfectly compatible. Likewise, there is no contradiction if opposing statements are supported by the community at different times, regardless of how ignorant or mistaken it is about the facts. And there is no need for the individual to withdraw an opposing statement made at an earlier time, provided that the attitude of the community to which he belongs has changed accordingly during the interval.

However this version suffers from two additional flaws as you can no doubt already see. First, we have all had the experience of judging that some action was wrong, even though we know it was not disapproved of by the community. If you lived in the southern states of America in the 1950s, you might disapprove of the practice of segregation even though it was widely supported by the community. And, second, even when we know that a community is seriously mistaken or misinformed about a certain practice, which it holds to be right, we are still bound to approve of the practice as long as the community does. The community might wrongly believe that it is good for the baby's development if a woman regularly smokes crack cocaine during pregnancy.

Despite these failings it's obvious why naturalism has held such an appeal for philosophers particularly in the eighteenth and nineteenth centuries when hopes were high of following the example of natural science and discovering a science of morals and politics. If it were correct, ethical theory would become merely an empirical science with a perfectly objective method for confirming or disconfirming moral judgements. Moral knowledge would be empirical knowledge with conflicts resolved rationally and objectively as in science. To realize this, though, naturalists must show that all moral terms are equivalent in meaning to terms standing purely for empirical characteristics. Moral qualities or relations must be observable directly or indirectly by empirical methods.

Such an assumption famously came under the sustained attack of the intuitionist G. E. Moore in his *Principia Ethica* (1903). In it Moore rejects all forms of naturalism on the ground that they commit the 'naturalistic fallacy'. Goodness, he argued, is a unique, unanalysable, non-natural property and, therefore, all attempts to define it in terms of any natural property must be mistaken. However, as you can no doubt see, within this argument there are at least two important, though different, issues. Moore is arguing not just that it is a fallacy to define goodness, which is indefinable, but also that it is a fallacy to define it in terms of natural properties.

The first issue raises what has been described as the 'open-question argument'. For example, a naturalist may define 'moral good' as 'that which leads to the greatest happiness of the greatest number', but we can still ask without contradiction, 'Is that which leads to the greatest happiness of the greatest number good?' If 'good' and 'the greatest happiness of the greatest number' did in fact mean the same, by definition, we would not be able to do this. It would be a closed question. It would be like asking 'But are all bachelors unmarried men?' or 'Do all triangles have three sides?' The property denoted by the words 'three sides' represents a necessary condition for anything being a triangle. So, these are meaningless questions: by asking them we accept the possibility of denying the very meaning of the concept we use.

But it is not meaningless to ask if the pursuit of the greatest happiness of the greatest number, or that which promotes human survival (say, cannibalism or incest) is good. These are open questions. The property denoted by the words 'human survival' does not represent a necessary condition for anything being good. In these cases a negative answer is not plainly self-contradictory, thus the definition cannot be right. In answer to the question 'Do all triangles have three sides?' I cannot say 'No' without self-contradiction, but I can say 'No' without self-contradiction to the question 'Does moral good mean anything that promotes human survival?' Moore concludes that a definition is correct when the question asked is closed and incorrect when it is open. Asking an open question, in other words, means that the two expressions being used do not mean the same. This shows that such moral terms as 'good' or 'right' are not equivalent to empirical terms.

Before reading my comments on the following quote, see if you can spot what Moore would argue is wrong with the argument. In his essay, 'Utilitarianism' (1861), John Stuart Mill sets out to show there is a simple empirical test for what is 'desirable'. He explains,

> The only proof capable of being given that an object is visible, is that people actually see it ... and so of all the other sources of our experience ... the sole evidence it is possible to produce that anything is desirable, is that people do actually desire it.

But, as Moore was later to point out, 'desirable' does not mean 'able to be desired' as 'visible' means 'able to be seen'. 'Mill', he argues, 'has made as naïve and artless a use of the naturalistic fallacy as anybody could desire.' Things can be seen by virtue of our sight alone, but things are not desirable by virtue of the fact we desire

them alone. The word 'desirable' presupposes a criterion by which we judge them, which means not everything that is desired is, in fact, desirable. As long as we can continue to ask the open question without self contradiction, Mill's proposition still remains unproved. I might desire to smoke a cigarette, but I can still ask if it is desirable and as long as I can do that without self-contradiction 'desire' and 'desirable' are not conceptually the same.

As you can see the definitions of the kind Moore criticizes fail to capture all we ordinarily mean by the term 'good'. Nevertheless, naturalists defend themselves by arguing that moral terms have many contextually dependent meanings and it is this that the open-question argument shows up, not the impossibility of naturalism. Indeed, a question may only *appear* open when in fact it is closed. Beneath all the contextual meaning the two terms might be synonymous, particularly when the accurate definition is complex.

The naturalist might argue, therefore, that while he accepts that the definition fails to capture all we ordinarily mean by the term, this only shows that ordinary usage is muddled and needs revising. Such a defence has become known as the 'error theory' after J. L. Mackie's defence of subjectivism. Mackie argues that everyday thought in some areas has become sufficiently infected by mistaken philosophical views to be widely in error and in need of revision. Indeed, Moore acknowledged that the open question argument doesn't do anything to show that pleasure, for example, is not the sole criterion of the goodness of an action. It shows only

---

Brief lives
Mackie, J. L.

Dates: 1917–1981
Born: Sydney, Australia
Best known for: His contributions to metaethics, particularly his defence of moral subjectivism. He is also known for his defence of atheism and for maintaining that the problem of evil makes the main monotheistic religions untenable.

Major works: *Truth, Probability and Paradox* (1973), *Ethics: Inventing Right and Wrong* (1977), *The Miracle of Theism: Arguments for and against the Existence of God* (1982).

that this cannot be known to be true by definition, and so, if it is to be known at all, it must be known by some other means.

This brings us, then, to the second issue: that the naturalistic fallacy is not just a fallacy of *defining* goodness, but defining it in terms of natural properties and, therefore, implying that it is itself a natural property. One of the problems that strikes both naturalism and Moore's account concerns the nature of moral discourse. Moore argues that if goodness cannot be defined in terms of natural properties this must mean that it is not itself a natural property. But this may not be the only possible reason. It may be due to the fact that goodness is not a property at all. In normal moral discourse, when we say something is good, we probably no more attribute a property to it than when we respond to tasting milk that has gone off by exclaiming 'Ugh!' As non-cognitivists argue it may simply be a means of expressing our attitudes or emotions, or an attempt to evoke similar attitudes in others.

And even if goodness is a property it still doesn't follow from the fact that it's not definable in terms of natural properties that it must, therefore, be a non-natural property. Even though they don't possess identical meanings, ethical properties might still be identical with natural properties. The chemical formula H_2O and 'water' are the same, even though the two terms mean something different. What's more, certain properties simply cannot be defined in terms of other properties. The colour yellow can't be defined as round, large, with a rough texture, and so on, but this doesn't mean that it must be a non-natural property. It might simply be an indefinable property. Goodness, then, could be like any colour, just an indefinable property.

Over the years Moore's argument has retained a consistent appeal for many, largely because of the widespread, popular belief that there are two quite distinct classes of terms – ethical and non-ethical – and we can't define ethical properties in terms of non-ethical properties. But this doesn't rule out the possibility of defining ethical properties. All it means is that if we *can* define goodness, say in terms of the greatest happiness of the greatest number, or anything that promotes human survival, then this is an ethical property. Indeed, we can wonder why we should make it the definition of a non-ethical property that no ethical property can be defined in terms of it. This would be like arguing that biological terms cannot be defined in terms of non-biological terms.

It seems, then, that despite the effectiveness of Moore's criticism in many ways, naturalism has still not been decisively refuted. In terms of our four hypothetical formal requirements it does indeed demonstrate the objectivity and universality of moral discourse. But it fails to account successfully for the practical nature of moral discourse as action-guiding or attitude-moulding, and it denies the autonomy of moral claims.

3.1.2 Non-naturalism: intuitionism

Moore's theory, on the other hand, does appear to meet the requirements of objectivity and universality, and, most notably, it establishes the autonomy of moral claims. If ethical language cannot be reduced to factual statements, they cannot be regarded as true or false on the basis of empirical evidence. But, Moore argues, this doesn't mean that they cannot be considered true or false. We possess another method of verification: we can show their truth or falsehood through moral intuition.

It is clearly self-evident to us that some things and some persons are good and others not. Although we cannot demonstrate the truth or falsity of the statement 'Dropping the atomic bomb on Hiroshima was a morally good thing', we can see immediately that the property of moral goodness does not belong to an action that kills thousands of innocent individuals. This is an intuitive truth. It is both necessary and synthetic. To say that we intuit it is to say we have direct, non-sensory, cognitive awareness of the necessary truth of certain moral claims.

In this way Moore argues that morality is autonomous, and to establish this he must show that there is at least one primitive ethical term that is the vehicle for a non-natural quality, relation or concept. He argues that ethical terms are definable in terms of the word 'good', whereas 'good' is indefinable, because goodness is a unique, simple, unanalysable quality. The reality it stands for is an objective reality, which we must apprehend directly. We cannot prove such a reality exists by empirical observation; we're either directly aware of it or we're not. And in this way we gain our fundamental knowledge of good and evil. We can recognize when somebody or some action possesses it. Moore explains it is like a colour, a 'simple notion', you cannot explain to anyone the colour yellow, who does not already know it. Yet still yellow is a naturalistic quality that can be observed, whereas goodness cannot be so perceived, it is a non-natural quality the presence of which can only be known intuitively. He explains:

> The most important sense of 'definition' is that in which a definition states what are the parts which invariably compose a certain whole; and in this sense 'good' has no definition because it is simple and has no parts. It is one of those innumerable objects of thought which are themselves incapable of definition, because they are the ultimate terms by reference to which whatever is capable of definition must be defined.

But, as Moore acknowledges himself, his argument applies not just to attempts to define goodness in natural terms, but to any attempt to define goodness in terms of something else, including something metaphysical or supernatural, like 'what God wills'. It brings us back to the point we considered earlier that Moore is arguing not just that it is a fallacy to define goodness in terms of natural properties, but that it is a fallacy to define it at all, because it is indefinable. By arguing that goodness is just indefinable he casts the net wide to include theories that might otherwise be described as non-naturalistic.

Plato's and Christian ethical theory are both non-naturalistic. Plato believed that the world contains moral entities, like goodness and rightness, in the same way it contains natural entities. Moral judgements, therefore, are true or false in terms of these entities; they cannot be reduced to natural entities. In the same way Christian ethics regard moral judgements as expressions of the divine will. These are true or false, but not by empirical observation. The key issue that marks the difference between naturalistic and non-naturalistic theories is whether morality is autonomous.

As you can see there are problems with intuitionism, not least knowing what we are looking for. If 'good' is a non-natural property that cannot be identified through the normal method of observation, what is it that Moore claims to know through intuition? He hasn't given us an intelligible description of what it is we must apprehend in order to apprehend a non-natural quality or relation. He can't argue if we fail to apprehend some non-natural quality that he believes to be necessarily good that we're just morally blind. Unlike colour blindness or tone deafness there is neither an agreed-upon criterion for moral blindness, nor,

unlike the other two, is there a method of testing for it.

This, of course, is important as many of our intuitions turn out to be wrong, while others are notoriously difficult to choose between. Where there is a clash of intuitions we need to know how to settle it. We can't rely on the subsequent events to do this, because this would be to rely upon sense experience and not intuition. Moore's only answer is to insist that the right answer is self-evident. But it is not the case that we see as self-evidently true that we should not kill innocent individuals in the same way that we see that 2 plus 2 equals 4. There is nothing analogous between the two: mathematical and logical truths are analytic and can be demonstrated, while moral judgements, as the intuitionists insist, are synthetic.

As some philosophers have suggested intuitionism seems to have all the defects of a theory whose main purpose is to criticize another metaethical theory, naturalism. Yet they both share the same problems, which develop out of their conception of how moral language functions. Both assume that language is only meaningful if it stands for something: natural characteristics for the naturalist and non-natural characteristics for the intuitionist. But not all words are property-ascribing in this way. As we saw earlier, the way we use words like 'good' and 'right' suggests they don't stand for things in this way, or at least this is not the only thing they do.

Similarly, naturalism and intuitionism fail to account for the practical functions of moral discourse – their action-guiding or attitude-moulding role. When we judge morally we aim to guide our behaviour or someone else's, to change conduct. To know what we ought to do is at the same time to set ourselves to do it. There is a conative, not just a cognitive aspect to it. When I say that it is wrong to kill innocent individuals, I am not just saying what *is* the case, but what *ought* to be the case, what you, I and everyone else ought to do, that is, not kill innocent individuals. This is not just a *descriptive* statement ascribing some property to the act of killing innocent individuals, but a *prescriptive* statement aimed at changing behaviour. Indeed, if knowledge that it was wrong to do this were simply a process of understanding that something *is* the case, it would remain quite inexplicable why to know that we ought not to do this is to know that we must, if we are moral agents, *try* not to do it.

3.2 Non-cognitivism

In direct contrast, non-cognitivists, as the name indicates, stress different formal requirements. They deny that moral statements are simply, or sometimes even at all, cognitive, and that moral terms simply or at all stand for characteristics. Ethics is not a form of knowledge, and ethical language is not descriptive. Moral judgements cannot be verified nor can fundamental moral conflicts be resolved by empirical methods alone. It would remain at least a logical possibility that we might agree about all the facts, yet still disagree about what we ought to do or about what is good or worth having for its own sake.

Fundamental moral claims are not matters of knowledge, but expressions of attitudes, decisions of principle, or declarations of intentions. The intention behind moral language is not simply to *describe* what is the case, but to *prescribe* what ought to be the case or to evaluate something. Indeed, they warn of the problems that result from confusing fact-stating and normative discourse, insisting that what makes a statement normative is that it guides action and moulds or alters attitudes. In general non-cognitivists have fallen into two camps: emotivism and prescriptivism.

3.2.1 Emotivism

A number of twentieth-century philosophers, like A. J. Ayer, C. L. Stevenson, and Rudolph Carnap, who support the emotive theory of ethics, deny that moral utterances are cognitive, holding that they consist in emotional expressions of approval or disapproval, or attempts to arouse similar feelings in others, or to stimulate actions, primarily through commands. While moral judgements are about one's feelings, they are not descriptions of them, indeed they are not assertions or descriptions of anything, so they cannot be verified or falsified. They are expressions of feeling, much as you might groan with disappointment if your team misses a goal, or you might sigh with pleasure after a good meal. Since we would not say that a groan or a sigh are true or false, it is a mistake to say that moral judgements, which express feelings in a similar way, are true or false. This distinguishes emotivism from ethical naturalism, where the speaker was stating that she or her community had or did not have a certain attitude, which could be scientifically tested. Here all that is being expressed is the feeling

Brief lives
Ayer, Sir Alfred Jules

Dates: 1910–1989
Born: London, England
Best known for: Introducing logical positivism to the English-speaking world.

Major works: *Language, Truth and Logic* (1936), *The Foundations of Empirical Knowledge* (1940), *The Problem of Knowledge* (1956), *The Central Questions of Philosophy* (1973).

itself or the desire to evoke the same feeling in others.

But this is not the only similarity with ethical naturalism. If ethical statements make no cognitive claims, emotivism is open to the criticism, like ethical naturalism, that there can be no contradiction between conflicting claims, no genuine moral disagreements. And this, as we saw earlier, runs counter to all our experiences. Some philosophers, notably C. L. Stevenson in his book *Ethics and Language* (1944), have attempted to meet this objection by arguing that such disagreements are possible because they are often 'disagreements in attitude' that are themselves the product of 'disagreements in belief', which can be resolved by evidence.

For example, you might express the attitude that 'It was morally right to drop the bomb on Hiroshima', which is based on your belief that the US government's assessment of the number of lives that would be saved by ending the war earlier is correct. If, however, I can show you that these figures were in fact wrong, that they were grossly inflated, there is a chance that you will change your mind and withdraw the claim you originally made. So Stevenson's point is that the difference between conflicting moral statements is not always just a difference in approval, neither of which can be invalidated. In many cases our moral attitudes are based on a belief about the evidence, which can be shown to be wrong.

However, if the emotivists are right that for a moral utterance to be moral it must be attitude-expressing or attitude-evoking, how do we know this to be true? If this is an empirical claim it wouldn't show what makes an utterance moral; all that it would give us is information that a certain attitude was expressed. A car goes by blaring out loud music, while you wait at a bus stop. The stranger next to you turns and says, 'Disgusting!' Is he expressing a moral attitude, or does he just dislike the music or all loud noise?

If it is an analytic claim, then it must be necessarily true, which presumably means that when I make a moral utterance I am expressing an attitude about something I believe is right or wrong. As Stevenson maintains it is my *belief* that dictates my attitude and my attempt to get others to hold the same belief as myself by expressing this attitude. Yet we have all come across people who express certain attitudes, but believe in something quite different. I can say about someone, without any apparent self-contradiction, that 'He has the attitudes and emotional reactions of a wife-beater, but he knows that wife-beating is wrong.' If this were an analytic truth I should not be able to say this without self-contradiction. But we do not know of a rule which says that any utterance must be attitude-expressing to be moral. There is a strong link between our attitudes and strong feelings and morality, but this still allows for a cognitivist metaethic.

It's not even possible to argue that a moral dispute is at an end when, and only when, there is agreement in attitude between the parties. Two people might share the same attitude to wife-beating, in that they strongly disapprove of it. But they might still disagree morally about the issue because their reasons for disapproving of it are different. One might believe nobody should be subject to physical violence, whereas the other believes that physical violence is acceptable in some circumstances, but not in this one where husband and wife have jointly promised to trust and care for each other.

What's more not every consideration that leads us to adopt the same attitude as someone else will thereby count as a morally relevant reason for adopting that attitude. Emotional appeals and forms of non-rational persuasion are irrelevant to moral reasoning: they deny you your freedom to make moral choices by coercing and manipulating you. As a result you are more likely to act as *though* you were moral for non-moral reasons. In moral thinking justification and motivation, what we believe and what we desire, are two quite different things. A smoker might believe she should give up smoking cigarettes, but desires to do quite the opposite. You might believe you should go to the dentist to ensure your dental health, but this is the last thing you want to do. So, what motivates us to act in a certain way or adopt some attitude may or may not justify us in acting this way. And, conversely, what justifies us in doing it may or may not motivate us to do it.

3.2.2 Prescriptivism

The same problems are taken up by the British philosopher R. M. Hare and other exponents of prescriptivism, who argue that when we make moral judgements we are prescribing a course of action or inaction, rather than making statements of fact about the world. In *Moral Thinking* (1981) Hare argues that in making moral judgements we are not merely describing features of the external world, we are '…purporting to commend or condemn actions or people because they have some properties which make them right or wrong, good or bad.' We are not just making judgements that are logically grounded in statements of fact, but preferring one course of action, or one person, to another. A moral utterance is prescriptive because it contains an imperative: its function is to tell us to do something, to guide our actions. When we express the moral judgement that 'Lying is bad', this entails the imperative 'Don't lie!'

Yet, unlike emotivists, Hare maintains that moral judgements are not purely non-cognitive. They contain a cognitive element too: non-moral facts, that is, facts about people's preferences. Moral judgements are not just universal in the sense that they contain no individual constants (I, me, you, your) and start with a universal quantifier (all, everyone), they are also universal in the sense that we must treat other people's prescriptions as if they

Brief lives
Hare, Richard M.

Dates: 1919–2002
Born: Backwell, England
Best known for: His theory that all moral judgements are universal prescriptions which are ultimately expressions of preferences.

Major works: *The Language of Morals* (1952), *Freedom and Reason* (1963), *Moral Thinking: its Levels, Methods, and Point* (1981).

were our own. And, he believes, prescriptions, because they contain imperatives, are nothing more than the expression of our desires, our preferences.

This explains the importance of non-moral facts in the form of preferences. But to understand it completely you must take on board two key ideas. First, Hare argues prescriptivity is a characteristic of imperatives, so moral judgements are prescriptive in so far as imperatives can be derived from them. And, second, imperatives are the proper vehicle for expressing preferences. For example, if you want to park your car and my bike is occupying the parking space, I will have the preference 'I prefer not to have my bike moved', which is expressed as the prescription, 'You ought not to move my bike', which is prescriptive because it contains the imperative, 'Don't move my bike!', which in turn expresses my original preference.

In such a situation, to resolve the conflict between your preferences and mine you will have to put yourself imaginatively into my position, experiencing my preferences and the strength with which I hold them, and then set these against your own preferences. Whichever is the strongest should prevail. So if you believe my preference for not moving my bike is weaker than your preference to move it, then you should move it.

A moral judgement, then, is prescriptive, but it is based upon a cognitive element involved in weighing up conflicting preferences. Hare criticizes non-cognitivism for failing to recognize that a cognitive element is necessary. If we say 'Lying is wrong', we must be able to show that in avoiding lying we maximize preference satisfaction. Whether it does or not can be shown factually. Most non-cognitivist theories, by comparison, undermine the objectivity of moral judgements.

The minimum requirement for objectivity is for a moral judgement to be interpersonally validated: that is, it must be accepted by every rational, sincere agent, who is apprised of all the nonmoral facts. But if moral judgements are essentially resolutions to act in a certain way, expressions of attitude, decisions of principle or declarations of intentions, they don't call for such interpersonal agreement. Someone may decide after careful reflection, even as a matter of principle, to do what no one else would do or even contemplate, and yet there is nothing logically inappropriate about his decision. And this implies, as we found earlier, that there are no means of settling moral disputes and no point to moral discourse. If we had the opportunity to make Hitler accountable for the Holocaust, nothing would be achieved: no one could claim to have right on their side. All that it would amount to is an exchange of expressions of attitude none more valuable than any other.

But, equally serious, non-cognitivism fails, according to Hare, because all moral judgements are universal. They are not just expressing attitudes of individual approval. They are guides to conduct in that we are not just saying that it is right for X to do Y in circumstances C, but that it is right for all people to do Y in circumstances that are relevantly similar to C. As we have seen moral judgements are universal in that they contain no individual constants and start with a universal quantifier. So when you say it is right to move my bike so you can park your car, you are saying that everyone in similar relevant circumstances should move a bike blocking their parking spot. These are not just private reasons relating to this situation. Your judgement has universal implications.

Nevertheless, the problem with Hare's argument is whether we can indeed claim that prescriptions are simply expressions of preferences. Hare believes if I think something ought to be the case, then I must prefer it to be the case. Yet we all know circumstances in which what we believe we ought to do is not what we prefer to do and what we prefer to do is not what we believe we ought to do. Indeed we have already cited examples, like smoking and going to the dentist, which illustrate these common dilemmas. Not all moral judgements need be prescriptive in Hare's sense as expressing preferences. When I say I ought to do something I may be expressing a belief-statement which contains no corresponding preference. It may express a duty or an obligation of some kind, which may or may not go against my preferences. I might believe 'I ought to go with a UN agency to a war-torn country to relieve the effects of famine.' This expresses the imperative 'Go with the UN agency to relieve famine.' But my preference might be that I not go, because I fear my life will be in danger.

◼ 4. Is all moral discourse futile?

4.1 The is–ought gap

Hare's account illustrates how we might resolve one part of a problem that runs throughout our discussion of cognitivism and non-cognitivism. As the diagram below illustrates there are two gaps in our moral thinking between what we believe to be the case and what we desire to do; between our beliefs and our disposition to act. The first is what is commonly known as the 'is–ought gap' between our beliefs about what *is* the situation described in terms of certain nonmoral facts and our moral judgement about what we *ought* to do based on those facts.

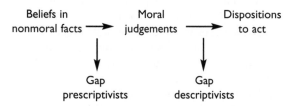

Then, given our moral judgement, we are faced with the second gap between this and our disposition to act. Though we may agree that we ought to do something, we might still not have the will to do it. Hare's account attempts to bridge this gap by arguing that the prescription entailed in our moral judgement is nothing more than the expression of our preferences, our desires, what we want to do. In other words they are nothing more than our dispositions to act. But this leaves prescriptivists like Hare with no means of accounting for how we bridge the is–ought gap, the logical gap between our *description* of the facts and our *prescription* based on those facts.

If the non-cognitivists are right this means all moral discourse is futile: there is no means of interpersonal validation through which we can resolve moral conflict. Moral judgements are merely imperatives or expressions of attitudes particular to the individual. This strikes at one of our most deeply held intuitions that there is some point in moral discourse and that certain facts make good reasons for certain moral judgements.

It has been commonly thought that the classic statement revealing this unbridgeable gap between a fact and a value is to be found in a famous passage in Hume's *Treatise of Human Nature*, although some philosophers now doubt whether indeed Hume was intent on showing that it was unbridgeable at all. In what has become known as 'Hume's Law' he argues that no value judgement can be deduced from any set of premises which does not itself contain a value judgement. As we

saw in Chapter 3, the requirement of a strict deductive argument is that nothing should be drawn out by way of a conclusion that is not already contained implicitly or explicitly in the premises. This leads Hume to argue that if a value judgement is not already contained within the premises, we cannot draw a conclusion that contains a value judgement. So, for example, from the major premise 'All bachelors are unmarried men', and the minor premise 'Tom is a bachelor', we cannot draw the conclusion 'Tom is unattractive.'

When we ignore this requirement we commit what Moore describes as the 'naturalistic fallacy'. In Mill's case he drew from the factual premise, 'I desire A', the value judgement, 'A is desirable.' Yet we saw that 'desirable' does not mean 'that which can be desired' and this can be revealed by the 'open question'. As long as I can ask without self-contradiction the question 'Is what I desire desirable?', 'desire' and 'desirable' are not analytically connected.

However, while accepting this, cognitivists and non-cognitivists have radically different interpretations of the 'is–ought problem'. For a very thorough account of this and the way it has developed read Chapter 6 of W. D. Hudson's *Modern Moral Philosophy* (1970). In it he notes what we have already discovered, that intuitionists see this distinction as one between properties. Natural properties we describe in statements of fact, like 'I want to cheat on my girlfriend' or 'I like to help people', whereas non-natural properties are described in terms of moral judgements, like 'It is wrong to cheat on your girlfriend', or 'It is good to help people.' The two properties are distinct from one another: what is said in terms of one can never be translated without loss or change of meaning into terms of the other. If we do attempt to do this we commit the naturalistic fallacy.

By contrast, as we have seen, emotivists and prescriptivists think of the 'is–ought problem' in different terms: as the different kinds of uses to which language can be put. Whereas factual statements *describe* things, moral judgements *evaluate* them. Emotivists believe that when we use moral language we use it to express attitudes of approval and disapproval. Prescriptivists, too, believe we use it to express these attitudes, but in addition, because moral judgements entail imperatives, we use it to guide actions and influence choices.

Two kinds of language

Facts	Values
Statements	Commands
Descriptions	Prescriptions
Verification	Evaluation

However, this is not the only difference in the way they interpret the 'is–ought problem.' Both see the gap between factual statements and evaluations in terms of a difference of meaning. Intuitionists believe no factual statement means exactly the same as a moral judgement. But still a logical connection can be made between certain factual statements and certain moral judgements. If I were to make the factual statement 'B promised to return,' although a straightforward factual statement, it still follows that 'B is under an obligation to return.' In other words, we can conclude from a factual statement the moral judgement that 'B ought to return.' We perceive this necessary connection between the factual statement and the moral judgement through our ethical intuition, which is one way in which we use our reason. Moral judgements, then, result from factual statements and to think morally is to intuit this connection.

By contrast, while emotivists and prescriptivists agree that 'is' and 'ought' differ in meaning, they also believe, unlike intuitionists, that 'ought' cannot be deduced from 'is'. Although it is normal for us to give factual statements as reasons to support our moral judgements, this cannot be ascribed, as intuitionists do, to some moral necessity, which belongs to the nature of things. Rather, it can be explained in terms of us invoking certain moral standards, which we and the society in which we live have set up. Thus, in contrast to intuitionists, emotivists and prescriptivists refuse to believe that moral judgements are consequential upon factual statements.

4.2 Descriptivism

However this leaves us with two answers to our question, 'What is to count as a good reason for a moral judgement?', neither of which is likely to furnish a publicly warrantable criterion that will rescue moral discourse from futility. One suggests a mysterious ability to intuit connections between facts and values, while the other maintains we derive our moral judgements from certain moral standards that are an accident of circumstance. Yet still, there is an alternative explanation proposed by a diverse group who are united by their opposition to prescriptivism. Known as 'descriptivists', they argue that the meaning of an evaluative term is given without an element of command, approval or pressure to act. Instead moral evaluations are logically grounded in certain descriptions of fact or supposed fact.

So, for a descriptivist what counts as good reasons for a moral judgement, bridging the 'is–ought gap', are those grounded in some description of human wants, or in some conception of man's true end or function, or those invoking the moral traditions of the society within which the judgement is made. Hudson suggests typical examples of such descriptions of supposed fact might be 'All men want to be free from physical injury,' 'This will be a courageous thing to do', or 'This will enable us to attain our true end, or fulfil our proper function as human beings' or, as we saw above, just the use of a word like 'promise' in a description of someone's behaviour as in 'B promised to return.'

As Hudson argues, from all these points of view not just anything can be spoken of as right or wrong, but only that which can be described in a certain way. If I were to describe someone's behaviour as 'courageous', the word contains certain conventional meaning which commits us, when we use it, to endorse certain patterns of behaviour and condemn others. In the same way, when we use the word 'promise', we are committed to the moral judgement that it is 'good' to keep promises. Whenever we use such terms to describe a situation, we are endorsing the conventional meaning of the word and all its demands. Indeed both the descriptive use and the endorsement of the moral implications of the word commonly occur in close combination and any attempt to single them out is not only implausible, but probably an incorrect analysis of ordinary moral language.

Once we have accepted the facts described using these terms, it may appear common sense, even logical, to draw the value judgement they appear to imply. And this may be true even without committing us to some form of naturalism and without denying the subjectivist case that one cannot either demonstratively prove or inductively establish fundamental moral claims. In so far as the description of the facts constitutes good, compelling reasons for doing something it appears to bridge the gap between a fact and a value, leaving us unsure whether there really is such a clear logical distinction between the two.

Not surprisingly Hare believes this account is mistaken, and he sets himself the task in *Moral Thinking* of dispelling the lure of descriptivism, which, he believes, so firmly grips our thinking that we are unable to think critically about moral issues. The unquestioning way in which we hold our everyday moral intuitions tempts us to assume that they amount to objective characteristics of the external world, and all that is necessary to defend or evaluate our decisions is to resort to the descriptivist strategy of appraising each decision we make to see how well it matches up to our descriptive account of these supposedly objective characteristics. This he describes as the 'descriptive fallacy': we believe our moral judgements are logically grounded in descriptions of fact. As a result we struggle to get beyond our intuitions, many of which amount to baseless opinion and mere prejudice.

Moreover, the descriptivists are faced with the equivalent problem to the prescriptivists who explain how to bridge one gap only to be left with the other. Using our diagram again, we said that Hare is able to deal with the gap between our moral judgements and our dispositions to act by arguing that prescriptions are nothing more than expressions of preferences, our desires. And if we desire something we are disposed to act to bring it about. But this leaves him and other prescriptivists with the is–ought gap between our beliefs, expressed in descriptions of nonmoral facts, and our judgements.

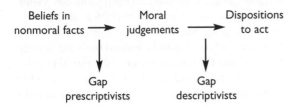

By contrast, the problem for the descriptivist is reversed. While he can explain how to bridge the is–ought gap, as we have just seen, he is left with the gap between our judgements and our dispositions to act. This is what philosophers describe as the conative problem. While descriptivists can explain how we come to our moral judgement about what we ought to do, this still leaves us with the problem of explaining why we are disposed to act in accordance with some moral judgements and not others.

■ 5. Conclusion

As you can see these are not problems that can easily be solved and you may think that the cognitivists and non-cognitivists can equally lay claim to part of the solution. As we discuss normative ethics in the next chapter you will have the opportunity to explore for yourself the nature of moral judgements and the principles we use to underwrite them. What these principles are and how we choose between them is the business of normative ethics. But as you explore these keep in mind the issues raised in this chapter. Once you have determined what type of principles these are, it will be easier to see how we are to evaluate them.

■ Questions

1. A: Keeping promises is right, because God commands it.

   B: This is not true. God commands us to keep promises because it is morally right to do so.

   What position should a believer in God adopt?

2. a) What is the 'is–ought' gap?

   b) Can it be bridged?

3. Is it naïve to judge other societies by our own moral standards, like the Greeks who kept slaves or the Mayans who made human sacrifices to the gods?

4. Is it true that something is morally right simply because we all approve of it? For example, if everyone approved of torture, would it be morally acceptable?

5. If I say to someone that she ought to do something is this just another way of telling her to do it?

6. If I say harming others is wrong, am I just expressing an emotion?

7. 'All sentences containing value judgements can be translated, without loss, into sentences that do not contain value judgements.' Discuss.

8. Are we right to believe that arguing about moral matters is futile?

9. 'Values must be relative: a thing only has value if someone values it, but we all value different things.' Critically evaluate this argument.

10. If moral judgements were just matters of taste, moral argument would be impossible. But we do engage in moral argument, so moral judgements cannot just be a matter of taste. Is this right or are we just all mistaken about the purpose of moral argument?

■ Recommended reading

Hare, R. M. *Moral Thinking* (Oxford: Clarendon, 1981).

Hudson, W. D. *Modern Moral Philosophy* (London: Macmillan, 1985), Chapter 6, The Derivation of 'Ought' from 'Is'.

Mackie, J. L. *Ethics: Inventing Right and Wrong* (Harmondsworth: Penguin, 1990).

Moore, G. E. *Principia Ethica* (Cambridge: Cambridge University Press, 1982).

Plato, 'Euthyphro' in *The Last Days of Socrates*, trans. Hugh Tredennick and Harold Tarrant (Harmondsworth: Penguin, 1993).

Williams, Bernard. *Ethics and the Limits of Philosophy* (London: Fontana, 1985).

 The note structure to accompany this chapter can be downloaded from our website.

Normative Ethics: Deontology

Contents

Key issues

▶ What is it about a moral judgement that is to count most: the motives of the people involved, the consequences of their actions, or certain moral principles?

▶ Should our only consideration be whether or not, in contrast to all the alternatives, our action produces the greatest balance of good over bad? Or are there certain features of the act itself which determine whether it is right or wrong, which means that even though it produces good consequences it is still wrong?

▶ Is it always wrong to do a bad act for the sake of good consequences, but permissible to do a good act even though you know that it will have bad consequences?

▶ Is acting morally a simple question of looking after your own interests?

▶ Perhaps it is not so much the action itself we ought to worry about but the motive behind it. For example, are all actions right if they are done in the service of God?

▶ Does the most reliable test as to whether our actions are right or not lie in the special feelings we all have for helping others?

▶ And are there fundamental differences between the way men and women think morally?

▶ Are feminists right that whereas men emphasize reason, abstract principles and justice, women are inclined to emphasize emotions, concrete personal relations and the importance of supporting people? Indeed, should we be deeply concerned about the violent and aggressive nature of the male ethic compared with the more gentle, nurturing and cooperative female ethic?

In contrast to metaethics, normative ethics is much closer to home, to those decisions we make every day about our behaviour and that of others. Was I right to break the confidence of a friend to protect his reputation? Should I have ignored the wishes of an elderly relative to be left alone, so that I could get her some help? Was the supermarket right to insist on prosecuting the unemployed father of three for shoplifting, when it was his first offence? In each of these our concern is to find some guide for making moral judgements.

But what type of thing are we searching for? Is it a theory about ethics made up of certain standards or rules, which we can appeal to whenever we have a moral problem to solve? Or perhaps we're after a different type of solution, one that's not so much about finding certain standards or rules, but just about being a good person, a virtuous character. In the next chapter we will examine the ideas of those who believe the answer lies here in 'virtue ethics', in discovering what makes virtuous characters who can be better relied upon to make the best moral judgements.

■ 1. Teleological and deontological ethics

But first we must consider the possibility that there are certain standards to which we can appeal to settle moral problems. Try to put yourself in the position of, say, a police official in charge of a province in Nazi occupied Europe. The German occupiers expect you to round up and 'interrogate' those of your fellow countrymen suspected of being members of the underground. They believe you are more likely to get useful intelligence from them than if they were to do it. If you refuse you will lose your job and your place will be taken by Nazi officials who are much less likely to treat suspects with the sort of compassion and understanding you would. So, do you refuse to have anything to do with it and give up your job, or do you stay on, believing you can make it easier for those you interrogate than if they were to face Nazi officials?

If you're a person of principle you are likely to refuse the job regardless of the consequences, justifying your decision by emphasizing your sense of justice, fairness, and your own personal integrity. You couldn't contemplate inflicting wanton suffering on anyone. Alternatively, you might be the sort of person who believes it should always be more important to try to reduce suffering, your own and other's. Even so, despite the importance you attach to that, in this case it has to be admitted that by taking the job you would be promoting not just the good of the whole community, but your own too, otherwise you would be unemployed. What's more, to complicate it still further, by working for the occupying regime you might in fact be lending it credence to do even more harm to your community. Whether you should put your own interests ahead of the community's is one of a number of

familiar dilemmas that arise in moral decision-making. Indeed if you are a person of principle you will have to tackle a dilemma of your own: whether you should put abstract principles ahead of the actual suffering of others.

Nevertheless, this illustrates the two contrasting positions we all adopt from time to time when we set about tackling moral problems. The first is a deontological theory of ethics and the second a teleological theory. To take the teleological theory first, a teleologist argues that the only thing we must know for an action or decision to be right is whether or not, in contrast to all the alternatives, it will produce the greatest balance of good over bad. And the measure of its goodness and badness, it's important to note, is the *nonmoral* value (happiness, survival, etc.) that is brought about. If it were otherwise we would be saying that the moral value of an act should be measured in the moral consequences it brings about, which is clearly circular.

But, as you know, people have very different views about whether a particular result is good or bad, which accounts for the variety of teleological theories. Many teleologists have been hedonists, identifying a good act with pleasurable consequences and a bad one with pain, whereas non-hedonists have identified goodness with a variety of things, including power, knowledge, self-fulfilment, perfection, survival and so on.

The other important distinction between teleologists, as it is among deontologists, is whose good one ought to try to promote. 'Ethical egoists' believe one should always promote one's own greatest good: an act is right if and only if it promotes the greatest balance of good over bad for oneself in the long run, compared with all other alternatives, and wrong if it doesn't. Alternatively those who believe the ultimate end should be the greatest general good and not just your own are 'ethical universalists', usually known as utilitarians. They believe an act is right if and only if it is likely to produce the greatest balance of good over bad for all. In line with the distinction we made in the last paragraph there are different forms of utilitarianism reflecting the different theories of value. Some, like John Stuart Mill and Jeremy Bentham, support the 'hedonist' position believing that the measure of value should be the amount of pleasure produced, whereas 'ideal utilitarians' place their faith in the different theories of value we listed above.

So, to summarize:

Teleologists

1. Consequences in nonmoral value:
   1.1 Hedonists – pleasure v pain.
   1.2 Non-hedonists – variety of things e.g. power, knowledge, survival.
2. Whose good?
   2.1 Ethical egoists – one's own.
   2.2 Ethical universalists – the good of all:
      2.2.1 Hedonistic utilitarians.
      2.2.2 Ideal utilitarians.

The deontologist, however, believes that the rightness or wrongness of actions and decisions does not depend solely on the consequences and the value they bring about, since there may be certain features of the act or decision itself which determines whether it is right or wrong. Some believe we should take into account the motive behind the act, while others believe it is right if it conforms to certain absolute rules, like 'Never tell lies' or 'Always keep promises.' Deontologists like W. D. Ross, A. C. Ewing and H. Prichard maintain that the rightness or wrongness of an act depends solely on the kind of act it is. If you keep a promise you have made, your actions are right irrespective of their consequences or your motives for doing them, because a promise by its very nature commits you to an obligation to carry it out. The stress deontologists place on notions of 'obligation' and 'duty', has led to the theory being described as 'duty ethics'. Effectively it means placing exclusive emphasis on the rules, laws or principles that we seem to believe are a part of morality.

In the case above you might refuse the job, regardless of whether you would have been able to make it better for those you interrogated, because you believe your primary obligation is to uphold the principles of justice. For the deontologist the principle of maximizing good over bad consequences is either not a moral criterion at all, or at least not the only one. It means that he is quite willing to accept the principle of 'double effect': that it is always wrong to do a bad act for the sake of good consequences, but permissible to do a good act even though you know that it will have bad consequences. In other words, an act might be right even though it doesn't maximize good over bad, because some other fact about it makes it right. In summary,

then, while the teleologist always looks *forward* to the consequences of his actions, the deontologist looks *back* at the nature of the act itself.

Still there is a fundamental question they both must address: what is good in itself irrespective of its consequences? At the final count we must know what is 'intrinsically' good for its own sake and not just 'extrinsically' good in that it brings about something else. Even the teleologist, who judges actions extrinsically, on their ability to achieve results, must ultimately judge such results in terms of what he believes is intrinsically good. For example, John Stuart Mill, one of the most famous consequentialists and utilitarians, argues in his essay 'Utilitarianism' (1861) that 'Whatever can be proved to be good, must be so by being shown to be a means to something admitted to be good without proof.' For the utilitarian it might be happiness, for a deontologist, like Kant, it is duty.

To give you a firmer grasp of this, when you have a moment read Arthur Koestler's novel *Darkness at Noon* (1940). Set in the Soviet Union in 1938 at the time of the 'Great Purge', when many of the original Bolsheviks were sentenced to death for treason after public show trials, it tells the story of the interrogation of Nikolai Bukharin (Rubashov in the novel). Like many he has moral doubts about Stalin's policies, in particular those involving the exile and execution of more than five million kulaks, the wealthy peasants, in order to finance the industrialization of the Soviet Union. These are presented as a conflict between two rival ethical theories, one teleological, the other deontological.

The first Koestler describes as 'vivisection morality', in that it justifies the sacrifices people are forced to make by citing the improved standards of living future generations will enjoy. In this theory the ends justify the means: it is right to experiment on the present generation in order to bring about benefits in the future. Rubashov says, 'Each wrong idea we follow is a crime committed against future generations.' The intrinsic value in this system is happiness: the collective happiness of the community. Ivanov, Rubashov's interrogator, justifies the basic principle of this system by arguing that 'a collective aim justifies all means, and not only allows, but demands, that the individual should in every way be subordinated and sacrificed to the community – which may dispose of it as an experimentation rabbit or a sacrificial lamb. ... [I]f these people had their say, we would have no serums against cholera, typhoid, or diphtheria.'

By contrast, the anti-vivisection morality places intrinsic value in the individual, who is sacrosanct. The individual has dignity. He cannot be sacrificed as a mere means to achieve some other end however noble. He is not a 'grammatical fiction' as the vivisectionists maintain; the romantic leftover of nineteenth-century liberal ethics of 'fair play'. The individual is an end in himself and our dealings with him are governed by certain inviolable rules. This is what Rubashov describes as 'Cricket morality' as opposed to the 'Consequential logic' of the vivisectionists. As in cricket there are rules that must guide us in all our dealings with individuals.

As you can see this is almost like two different vocabularies, two different ways of talking about ethics. Facts relevant to one, like those describing how we minimize the suffering of future generations, are considered irrelevant to the other, which considers relevant a different set of facts, like the innocence and motives of an individual. While the vivisectionist concedes, 'We admitted no private sphere, not even inside a man's skull. ... For us the question of subjective good faith is of no interest', the anti-vivisectionist counts for nothing facts about improving the conditions of life for future generations, even though this might mean generations being forced to endure poverty unnecessarily.

■ 2. Deontological ethics, Kant and rational rules

According to the deontologist, therefore, an action is right if it respects certain rights or is in accordance with our moral duty. What these are can be found not by looking at consequences, but by looking at ourselves and the world: certain norms are inherent in the world; they are part of its fabric.

Immanuel Kant derives the moral law from a consideration of man's rational nature. He denies any moral worth that can be derived from our empirical natures, from our inclinations and desires. His is a purely formal proof: it is derived from our rational natures alone. The only unconditional good for Kant is a good will, a will that involves acting in accordance with duty. Kant maintains, 'The first proposition of morality is that to have moral worth an action must be done from duty.' Human beings are free and rational. We should not, therefore, sacrifice this freedom by acting according to the dictates of our desires or inclinations. To act morally is to act out of duty in response to self-imposed obligations.

But these must meet the rational demands of the 'categorical imperative.' In other words they must be universal and they must treat people as ends and never as mere means.

But we need to explain this in a little more detail. Morality by its very nature involves choice, so any obligation cannot be imposed on the individual from outside her own will, nor can it be internally imposed as the expression of some compulsion or need, some inner desire that craves for satisfaction. In all these cases the individual's will would be unfree and the resulting decisions no longer moral. As Aristotle points out, a moral person acts voluntarily, and is not the slave of her passions.

Kant argues that it is this freedom that distinguishes man from other creatures or from mere things. The behaviour of other creatures is determined by laws of nature that are beyond their control. They are driven by desires, needs and inclinations over which they exercise no choice. In contrast humans are free to choose, but this does not mean that we are free from laws. Freedom is not the absence of laws, but acting according to self-imposed laws: imposed not through our desires or other inclinations, but through the freedom of our own reason. In this lies the importance of reason: the individual's capacity not just to impose laws on her own behaviour, but to act for reasons that are implicitly universal.

So, if a choice is to be moral it must be free, but if it is free it must be the result of our reason, not dictated by compulsive desires and inclinations. Reason results in objective laws, whereas our desires and inclinations are subjective. The distinctive characteristic of reason is that it is universal, unlike our desires, inclinations and emotions, which are particular to each of us. Reason imposes a form that is universal to us all: our self-determined, objective laws must meet the universal, non-relative standards imposed by our rational natures.

Therefore, in any particular situation I might produce a 'maxim', a rule which I want to follow, but for this to be moral I must ensure that it is a maxim I could will to be a universal law. In other words I must want all people finding themselves in similar circumstances to act in accordance with the same rule. Every action should be judged in the light of how it would appear if it were to be a universal code of behaviour. By imposing rational, objective laws on my will, rather than acting on my own subjective inclinations and desires, I do so only on the basis that the same laws should also be imposed on all other rational natures in the same circumstances.

Indeed, the only way we can be sure that our will is in fact determined by itself is if our maxims are universalizable. We transform our maxims into universal laws through the application of our reason. If they are not universalizable, then either they are determined by others, like the 'vivisectionists' in *Darkness at Noon*, who treat us as mere means to meet *their* needs and inclinations, or they are subjective: done as a result of *our* inclinations, our needs and desires determined for us by nature. These are natural, rather than rational laws. To treat individuals as ends in themselves is to accept that they are self-determining: that they are the makers of their own universal self-imposed laws. And a rational will can only be free and self-determining if it acts on universalized maxims. This is Kant's 'categorical imperative': 'Act only on that maxim through which you can at the same time will that it should become a universal law.'

For our maxims to become moral judgements, therefore, they must pass the test of universal willing: we must be able to will them without contradiction in either concept or will. Take the first test: conceptual contradiction. Kant explains: 'Some actions are so constituted that their maxim cannot even be *conceived* as a universal law of nature without contradiction, let alone be *willed* as what *ought* to become one.' In his second of four examples he asks whether we can will as a universal law that everyone should make promises they have no intention of keeping in order to get what they want. He argues we can't because such a law is clearly self-contradictory: a law that everyone was able to do it would result in a world where nobody trusted promises and in such a world it can't be rational to make promises. But he makes his point clear that this is not just a question of the law being *self-defeating*. It could not exist at all because it is simply *self-contradictory*: if there were such a law there would *be* no promises, but the law itself entails that there *are* promises.

The second test involves seeing whether the maxim involves us in consistent willing. In Kant's view moral questions are not merely about what we can think, but what we can will. A wrong act involves not just a theoretical contradiction, but the opposition of an inclination with a rational will. This is best illustrated by Kant's fourth example, the Samaritan dilemma, in which he asks whether I could make into a universal the maxim that I will not give aid and assistance to someone in distress.

In this there is no conceptual contradiction: I can *conceive* of a world in which people are indifferent to the distress of others. But Kant believes there is a contradiction of the *will*, because I cannot will the universal adoption of such a universal law and with it the sort of world this would bring about.

Indeed, he believes, it harbours two contradictions of will. As a rational agent I necessarily will the means that I need to achieve my ends and there are many occasions on which I find I need the help of others to do this. Therefore it would be irrational of me on simple grounds of prudence to exclude such help, although this would involve a contradiction not with a categorical imperative, but merely with a hypothetical imperative of the form, 'If I want to achieve X, then I must do Y.' Prudential concerns, those things it would be rational to do to achieve our ends, find their proper expression in hypothetical imperatives, whereas moral concerns are expressed in categorical imperatives. So, far more significant for Kant is that he believes it also involves the clearest contradiction of will in the categorical imperative that this should be willed as a universal law. If I were to do this I would be willing that others help me when I need help, but that no one help others when they need it – a clear case

So, to summarize:

Kant's theory: summary

1. Morality involves free choices.

2. We are not free if our choices are dictated by others, who treat us as mere means, or by our own compulsive desires and inclinations.

3. They can only be free if they are the result of our reason.

4. Reason produces objective moral law, because it imposes a universal form on our maxims – certain non-relative (absolute) standards common to all our rational natures.

5. Therefore, maxims can only be made into moral law if they meet the rational demands of the categorical imperative – if they can be universalized to apply to all people in relevantly similar circumstances.

6. For this they must pass the test of universal willing – there must be no contradiction in concept or will.

of inconsistent willing. Therefore I cannot *will* its universal adoption because a will in conflict with itself is self-contradictory.

It's not difficult to see the attractions of this theory. No matter how difficult the circumstances and the moral dilemmas we face, the ultimate good lies within us all, if we do the rational thing and act out of respect for the moral law. Despite the confusing chaos of life moral order can be found in the world, if only we test our maxims against the categorical imperative and apply only universalizable maxims that treat humans as ends and not as mere means.

Moreover, such hopefulness is matched by the theory's appeal to apparent common sense. We all recognize that consequences alone do not constitute morality: motives and intentions also matter. A doctor who bungles an operation might have been inefficient, but he is not necessarily immoral. And again, we all recognize that not just any motivation counts as moral. Those that stem from desires and inclinations offer no guarantee of their moral worth. As we saw in the last chapter we frequently desire things that we ought not to. A serial killer has a strong, even irresistible, desire to kill innocent people. Only when we act out of duty, against our own inclinations, do we regard ourselves as acting morally. This too reflects an experience familiar to us all of having to set aside our subjective desires and inclinations to do what is right in terms of our objective moral duties. And, likewise, we believe that such moral duties must be universal. We believe that to behave morally we must behave consistently: we must be able to universalize our behaviour.

Nevertheless, despite its common-sense appeal, there are many who are far from convinced. One common criticism of Kant's theory is that, whether he likes it or not, he is forced to smuggle in consequences to decide whether an act is right or wrong. When he considers the effect of not behaving in accordance with the categorical imperative, his claim that this involves inconsistent willing is nothing more than a judgement about the likely effects of doing this. If we break promises, when universalized, this would simply make life impossible. But this is a consequential judgement.

However, this seems to be based on a misreading of Kant's argument. If you go back to what we said above you will see that Kant is in fact arguing that one cannot even *will* that such a maxim as that involving breaking promises should be universally acted upon, because in so doing it would involve a contradiction of will: we would be simultaneously willing that it be possible to make promises and that we should all be free to break them. This is self-defeating, because if we did indeed all break our promises when we want to there would be no practice of promise-keeping – nobody would be making promises that in all likelihood would be broken. So, we cannot even will such a maxim to be universally acted upon, not because the consequences would be bad, but because the results are self-defeating.

Now consider the Samaritan example. Here it is not difficult to imagine someone so well-off that they can consistently will that nobody help others who are in distress, because with their wealth and access to all sorts of help they are never in any danger of being in need of the benevolence of others. This poses a more severe test to Kant's notion of inconsistent willing. But to understand the problem it's necessary to keep in mind three notions of universalism that are being used by Kant and his critics.

The weak sense implies just the formal demand for consistency: the maxim must apply to all people equally, that is it must start with a universal quantifier ('All', 'Every', etc.), and it must contain no individual constants, like 'me', 'my' or 'you'. In contrast the strong sense of universalism, as Jesse Kalin points out, involves a consensus of values, which are or ought to be common to everyone. It is a substantive concept, one that involves some notion of what is good and bad, say in terms of its capacity to promote pleasure, which cannot be derived from its rational basis alone. This is the sense used here by Kant's critics. They argue that Kant's case is that it would be inconsistent not to help others, because they would not help you when you need help, and this you regard substantively as a good thing in itself. It entails a judgement of what is good and bad, hence Kant smuggles in considerations of consequences.

However, between these two senses, neither substantive nor simply restricted to the weak logical sense of universal consistency, is the Kantian sense of universal willing. Still formal, because it begs no substantive questions, it is, nevertheless, interested in results: it forces us to ask, 'Can I will something consistently, or will it result in a situation that frustrates my own will?' This sense says nothing about what should be the substantive content of that will: its concern is just for the consequences of me willing this as defined by the principle itself.

Thus, while in the weak sense of consistency it is consistent to argue, as the ethical egoist would, that 'Everyone ought to maximize their own interests and disregard those of other people', this might not amount to consistent willing if it is clear that I can ensure I would be better off if we were all to cooperate with each other, because if this were true I would no longer be maximizing my interests by disregarding the interests of others. This sense goes beyond mere logical consistency with certain formal requirements and forces us to consider the results of us holding such principles and whether it frustrates or promotes our will, but it says nothing about the substantive content of this will. It says nothing about what consequences are good or bad.

But if Kant's theory can be defended on this charge it fares less well against others. One persistent problem is what we do when there is a conflict of duties. Kant regards all duties as absolute, and he doesn't foresee the possibility that they may come into conflict with one another and we will have to choose between them. In Plato's *Republic*, Socrates cites the example of someone who *promises* to return a weapon to a man bent on *harming someone*. Clearly the duty of keeping promises conflicts with the duty to prevent harm to others and there is no higher law determining which takes precedence. Although we all have an intuitive sense of which is the more important duty in most situations, it's not always easy to resolve these conflicts. In the United States, 'First Amendment' lawyers routinely uphold the right to freedom of expression, even when this is likely to result in the loss of life. And, as crime rates have risen, fear has driven many people to accept the installation of CCTV cameras in public spaces, even though this represents a significant invasion of their privacy.

In all these examples there are inveterate problems that we cannot so easily dismiss on the basis of our intuitions, yet Kant gives us no way of choosing. He rules out any appeal to consequences and, say, the calculation of the balance of pleasure over pain, even though we do need to be able to balance our principles in some way to determine which is overriding in a particular situation. For Kant's account to succeed we must be able to argue either that principles don't in fact conflict, in which case we need a way to account for the apparent conflict and resolve it, or, if they do conflict, we need a way to choose between them. Either we need some set of exceptionless rules that have all the necessary exceptions built into them, like 'We ought to keep

our promises, except when they cause harm to others', or some way to rank them in a hierarchy so they never conflict. But this then implies some higher law of prioritization, an exceptionless principle acting as the final arbiter.

Alternatively, perhaps it is just that Kant is urging too strong a claim. The problem of conflict comes about as a result of accepting laws, like 'Never tell lies' and 'Never break a promise', on the grounds that there can never be an exception to them. Those who argue for a form of 'moderate objectivism' believe the answer lies not in exceptionless categorical propositions, but in moral rules that are more like generalizations. In other words they are obligations one should keep as long as there are no other overriding factors present. W. D. Ross draws the distinction between 'actual' duties, those that we actually ought to do in a particular situation, and 'prima facie' duties, exceptionless duties that we have all things being equal. In other words, it is an actual duty as long as other moral considerations don't intervene. So, the duty never to break a promise is a *prima facie* duty in that it is always something we must take into consideration, even though there may be other considerations, which, on occasions, outweigh it or take precedence over it.

However this is no answer to our problem of conflict, since it still allows *prima facie* duties to come into conflict in actual situations. For this Ross needs what we suggested above, some means of ranking *prima facie* duties so that we know which takes precedence, but he doesn't believe this is possible. Moreover, he doesn't give us a criterion by which we can tell what our *prima facie* duties actually are. He merely argues that those he has chosen are self-evident and no criterion is necessary, which leaves him open to the charge that his choice is merely arbitrary. We need some means of justifying our choice, if our resulting moral judgements are not to be regarded similarly as merely arbitrary.

One way around this, as Frankena suggests, might be to have a small number of abstract, highly general rules, like the 'Golden Rule' ('Do unto others as you would have them do unto you'). Then, by applying these we can reach more concrete rules and particular conclusions, like Kant's categorical imperative, the principle that all moral judgements must be universalizable. But still it is doubtful whether this alone can furnish us with a method of determining what our duties might be. Universalizability is only a *necessary* condition of morality, not a *sufficient* condition. It doesn't tell us what is right and wrong, but only how we are to act: in other words, in an impartial way, treating other people as one would like to be treated oneself. It doesn't tell us which duties to accept as universally valid.

And, moreover, not all rules we may use in our personal lives can be regarded as universal moral duties. Yet Kant doesn't tell us how we are to determine which of our maxims are moral. In our personal lives we may govern our behaviour where relevant according to the principle 'Always wear bright clothing when you are riding your bicycle', but we wouldn't regard this as a universal moral duty. Indeed, Kant accepts this: he doesn't regard all maxims we can will to be universal as moral duties. He only maintains that those maxims we cannot will to be universal laws are immoral or wrong to act on.

Therefore, we are left with the conclusion that the concepts of rationality and freedom seem just too thin, too general, to guide us as to which duties to accept in our morality. We need more than this. As Henry Sidgwick and H. Rashdall point out, on their own they may not be enough: they may require other principles, indeed teleological principles, like the Principle of Prudence or Rational Egoism and the Principle of Beneficence or Utility.

More recently Peter Strawson and others have identified what they believe to be the basic principles people need to live harmoniously. First, they argue, we need to abide by the Principle of Non-maleficence: our obligation to refrain from harming others. On its own, however, this is not enough. We also need to abide by the Principle of Beneficence and agree to take positive actions to help others. If society is to work we must cooperate both to protect and support each other when necessary, and to provide health care, education and other essential services. But again this too is not enough on its own. It's still possible for us to apply such a principle selectively, helping some while ignoring others. So we also need to abide by the Principle of Justice, treating people fairly the same way under similar circumstances. Yet again even this is not enough for society to survive, if people cannot trust each other to keep their promises and fulfil their side of agreements not to harm each other, to help each other and do it in a just way. So, if we are to live in stable and harmonious societies we must also abide by the Principle of Non-deception, to keep promises and be honest.

Beyond these basic principles we live in a complex web of principles and obligations, of which Kant's theory takes no account. Our personal and professional relationships, like those between parents and children, teachers and students, doctors and patients, and friends and lovers, generate their own responsibilities and obligations. In these relationships we do things for our parents, children, students, patients, friends and lovers which we don't see strictly as our duty or as rules that should be followed by others. Even so, these are still moral actions and responsibilities in that our main concern is to promote the well-being of others and our harmonious relationship with them.

It seems, then, that Kant is right to assert the importance of universalizability in morality; otherwise we are left with arbitrariness. Similarly he is right to emphasize the notion of respect for individuals, that we must always treat them as ends and never as mere means. They are the makers of their own self-imposed moral laws. But, on its own, this does not lead us to a full account of how we are to determine which of our maxims are moral. Nor does it resolve the problem of what we are to do when our moral rules come into conflict and this drives us back in search of some higher law of prioritization, an exceptionless principle acting as the final arbiter.

■ 3. Egoism and altruism

No matter what our views on morality it seems that at the heart of moral thinking, common to us all, is the important assumption that it is possible for us to take into consideration the interests of others and we ought to do so. Indeed, the one thing that distinguishes prudential actions (actions in pursuit of our own self-interests) and moral actions is the motive that lies behind them. If a successful businessman were to contribute a large sum to charity we would applaud his benevolence as a moral thing to do. But if we were later to discover that he was in fact making this contribution to improve his own public image, to promote his business interests or to put him in line for a public honour, we would no longer consider this to be a moral action. The effects of the contribution would serve a moral purpose, but his action is motivated by prudential concerns to promote his own interests and not the interests of others. Only if our actions are motivated by a concern for others do we consider it moral.

But now, if Kant's theory is too thin to give us a full account of how we are to determine which of our maxims are moral, doesn't this leave open the possibility that these maxims might just be egoistic, concerned exclusively with promoting our own self-interests? Even accepting the importance Kant attaches to our being able to universalize our maxims, can't the egoist still consistently universalize the maxim, 'I will maximize my own interests and not those of other people', to conclude that, 'Everyone ought to maximize their own interests and disregard those of other people'?

3.1 Psychological egoism

First, though, we need to be clear what egoists say. An egoist argues that we ought to maximize our own long-term good; that the one and only obligation we have is to promote our own self-interests. We might do favours for others, but we should only do them for ulterior motives: we might expect favours in return, or rewards in heaven, or we might do them just to avoid a sense of guilt or to enjoy a sense of self-satisfaction. However for psychological egoists things are even more restricted. They argue that human beings are simply incapable of doing anything that doesn't promote their own self-interest. The only reason we are honest with people, or kind towards them, or generous, is to promote our own interests.

As you will have noticed, the important characteristic of this theory is that it is an empirical account of human nature, a psychological theory of human behaviour and human motivation. It's not an ethical theory: it *describes* what it believes *is* the situation, rather than *prescribe* what *ought* to be the case. But if it's true any ethical theory that calls upon us to do something that isn't in our self-interests must be unworkable, indeed not even an ethical theory. All ethical theories assume that we can in fact do what they argue we ought to do; that we have freedom to choose and act without which we would not be capable of acting morally by definition. But if we cannot do as they ask, then no matter how hard we try we don't have a choice and there is no sense in saying we ought to do it. In effect it challenges the very possibility of morality. Psychological egoism maintains that,

1. To say that we ought to do X entails that we are capable of doing X.

2. But if all we are capable of is promoting our own self-interests,

3. then all that we ought to do entails that we promote our own self-interests.

4. Therefore, egoism must be true.

However, for such a theory to be true there must be no evidence of altruistic acts; no evidence of an act not done out of self-interest, but just to help others. Such evidence would falsify the theory. But then how can psychological egoists be so certain of our motives that they can claim we never act altruistically, but always to promote our own interests? For example, the psychological egoist would argue that someone who loses their life trying to save someone from drowning or someone like Albert Schweitzer, who turned his back on a promising international career as a musician to work as a medical missionary in Africa, only do these things for their own self-interests. How can we possibly know this to be the case? Whether you believe this is likely to be the case or not, we simply can never know enough about their motivation to exclude the possibility of altruism. And as long as the psychological egoists cannot exclude this possibility, this alone is enough to refute their theory that *all* humans act in the way they describe.

Even so, or perhaps because of this, psychological egoism, like many pseudo-scientific theories, doesn't allow itself even the possibility of being falsified. No evidence is allowed to count against it. If we find that the theory doesn't conform to the evidence, then the evidence is made to conform to the theory. Say you are walking in a park next to a large lake. Suddenly you hear screams and you see two young girls shouting for help as their boat capsizes. You are a strong swimmer and you can help. If you refuse to help because you don't want to get your clothes wet, the psychological egoist would say this clearly demonstrates that her theory is correct. Alternatively, if you do help, still the psychological egoist will see this as evidence that supports her theory: your motives must be selfish, because you are human and all humans act in this way. So, it is not the evidence that demonstrates the theory, but the definition of 'human', which precludes any falsification of the theory.

3.2 Ethical egoism

Nevertheless, you don't have to believe in psychological egoism to be an egoist. Unlike psychological egoism, ethical egoism is not concerned with the motives we actually have, but with those we *ought* to have. An ethical egoist may deny the claims of psychological egoists and accept that people do often happen to act against their self-interest, but still maintain that we ought always to act in our own self-interests. The Greek philosopher Epicurus gives the classic statement of ethical egoism when he argues that the only measure of whether an action is right is the avoidance of pain and the promotion of pleasure. Similarly, the seventeenth-century English philosopher Thomas Hobbes argues in *Leviathan* (1651) that 'Good and evil are names that signify our appetites and aversions.' The individual rescues himself from the insecurity of a 'state of nature', in which everyone is at war with everyone else, by submitting himself to the rule of an all-powerful ruler. His obligation to obey the law, therefore, is based on a concern for his own self-interest.

But it is Plato who most famously sets out the problem posed by ethical egoism in the form of a fable, 'The Ring of Gyges', in Book II of *The Republic*. In Lydia a shepherd named Gyges was watching his sheep, when a chasm opened up in front of him. Being adventurous, he climbed down inside it where he found many fantastic things, including a bronze horse inside which he discovered a corpse larger than human size. On the corpse's finger he found a gold ring, which he took and placed on his own finger. Later, to his surprise, he found that when he turned the bezel of the ring towards himself he became invisible. As a result he was able to do all sorts of things without fear of being found out and held morally responsible. So, he got himself onto a deputation to the king, where he seduced the queen, murdered the king with her help, seized the throne and reigned gloriously for many years.

The point of the story is that as the ring makes him invisible so that he can act in any way he likes to maximize his own self-interest without being found out and being held responsible, does he still have reason to abide by moral rules? If he doesn't, morality is little more than an external device for controlling people, keeping them within social bounds. In such circumstances the selfish person will always fare better than the moral person. So, prudentially it doesn't seem to make sense to act morally, unless staying within social bounds benefits you more in the long run. Either way it seems we ought to act as the ethical egoist maintains to maximize our own self-interest.

But if this is an ethical and not a prudential 'ought', the egoist must deal with Kant's assertion that the reasons for abiding by moral rules are not external, but part of the very nature of practical reason, of thinking morally. Gyges can, of course, just adopt the amoralist position and refuse to think morally at all. But if he is an ethical egoist he poses the moral question, 'Should I act in my own self-interests or consider the interests of others?' In other words, he thinks morally, which necessarily involves being able to universalize our maxims. And this brings us back to our original question: can the egoist consistently universalize the maxim, 'I will maximize my own interests and not those of other people', to conclude that, 'Everyone ought to maximize their own interests and disregard those of other people'?

As an egoist the obvious disadvantage of endorsing such a universal principle is that it condones actions by others in pursuit of their own interests that are likely to damage yours. It's a clear case of inconsistent willing if, by willing your own interests, you will that others act in such a way that, in fact, restricts your own interests. As Brian Medlin points out, the egoist appears to be acting contrary to the egoistic principle: 'It cannot be to his advantage to convince them, for seizing always their own advantage they will impair his. Surely if he does believe what he says, he should try to persuade them otherwise.' But then if he doesn't persuade them to adopt the moral principle and behave as he plans to behave himself, he is no longer a universal egoist. Indeed G. E. Moore makes an even stronger point: if pursuing my own interests is a good absolutely that I have it, then not only does everyone else have as much reason for wanting it as I do, but they have 'as much reason for aiming at *my* having it, as I have myself.'

To avoid such inconsistent willing the egoist must retreat into individual egoism, where the principle would then become, 'Everyone ought to help me maximize my interests, but I ought to disregard their interests.' However, although this is now a consistent egoistic principle, which will allow the egoist to pursue his interests more effectively, it is unlikely to succeed in persuading anybody. To succeed the egoist's interests must be to me of absolute value and the individual egoist's principle a principle of absolute value in its own right, in which case it must be universalizable. In other words, *everyone* else must have an equal reason in pursuing it. As G. E. Moore explains, if something that belongs exclusively to one particular person is of absolute value, an end in itself, then if it is rational for him to pursue it, it is also rational for all to pursue it. And this means the egoist must persuade me that I should look after him regardless of myself and my interests. If he cannot argue this without enlarging his principle, so that everyone's interests are to themselves of absolute value, he has no doctrine at all.

So, the implausibility of persuading people of this leaves us with the only alternative: to enlarge the principle so that *each* person's interests are of absolute value to themselves alone, the sole end for themselves. But then it fails as a universal principle. If my interests are of absolute value to me, then everyone's interests are of absolute value to them. It is the only thing anyone ought to aim at. But then this leaves us with a number of different things each of which is of absolute value, the sole end of moral reasoning. G. E. Moore describes this as 'the fundamental contradiction of Egoism – that an immense number of different things are, *each* of them, *the sole good*.' Thus, he concludes, no possible meaning can be given to the phrase that a person's 'own happiness is the ultimate rational end for himself,' that will allow the egoist to escape the implication that his own happiness is an absolute value at which all should aim.

In summary, then, the only consistent ethical egoist appears to be an individual egoist. The only alternative to avoid the problem of inconsistent willing in universal egoism is to revert to individual egoism and attempt to dissuade people from doing what he knows to be in their interests, but which is not in his interests. As Medlin concludes, the egoist 'must behave as an individual egoist, if he is to be an egoist at all.' But this carries no implication for anyone else's behaviour, so I cannot, at least not successfully, promulgate it as I need to if this is to be regarded as a moral principle and not just as a personal attitude. But this can then no longer be described as an ethical theory, in so far as it does not set out to persuade others of a universal doctrine.

If this is the case, it means the individual egoist cannot promulgate it, at least successfully, without enlarging it, allowing others to enjoy the same benefits as he himself enjoys. But then he cannot do this without inducing others to pursue their interests in ways that conflict with his own and this gets us back to our starting point, that the egoist cannot argue his case in Kant's sense of universalism as consistent willing. To argue that 'Everyone ought to have as

their ultimate end their own happiness', is at the same time to put in jeopardy that very happiness as everyone else pursues theirs.

3.3 Altruism

As you can see egoism struggles to meet one of the key demands of moral judgements: that they be universalizable. The egoist judgement that 'Everyone ought to maximize their own interests and disregard those of other people' meets the demands of the weak sense of universalism, that our maxims must start with a universal quantifier and contain no individual constants. But it fails to meet the demands of universalism in any other sense, in particular the Kantian sense of universal willing. It ignores, therefore, an essential feature of morality: that moral principles are meant for everyone equally. Individuals have no privileges not enjoyed by everyone else. We cannot, therefore, set aside the interests of others in pursuit of our own.

But does this mean that altruism (acting for the sake of other people's interests) fares any better? Like its opposite, altruism, too, takes on two different forms: psychological and ethical, one descriptive the other prescriptive. Psychological altruism insists that people naturally act for each other's sakes, whereas ethical altruism argues they *ought* to act with each other's interests in mind. The 'Golden Rule' is typically seen as the standard statement of ethical altruism: 'Do unto others as you would have them do unto you.' But, while we all know that many actions are based on self-interest and are selfish, are there any that are *not* based on self-interest?

As we've seen the psychological egoist argues that all our actions are based on our desire to maximize our self-interest. A famous story involving Abraham Lincoln explains the challenge that psychological egoism poses for altruism. While travelling with a friend on a coach Lincoln was attempting to justify psychological egoism, when he spotted a mother pig on the bank of a river frantically watching as her piglets drowned in the river. He immediately stopped the coach, rushed over to the river and saved the piglets. When he returned to the coach his friend insisted that what he had just seen was a clear case of altruism. Lincoln, however, disagreed. He explained, 'Why that was the very essence of selfishness. I should have had no peace of mind all day had I gone on and left that suffering old sow worrying over those piglets. I did it to get peace of mind, don't you see?' If Lincoln is right this is true of all our actions and none of them can be described as altruistic.

Joseph Butler, the eighteenth-century English bishop, gave probably the definitive answer to the sort of problem posed by Lincoln's story. While he accepts the distinction between, on the one hand, 'private good and a person's own preservation and happiness' and, on the other, 'respect to society and the promotion of public good and the happiness of society', he argues they are not, as egoists argue, always in conflict; to the contrary, they are almost always in perfect harmony. The psychological egoist's account, represented here by Lincoln's argument, hangs on a few significant fallacies or misconceptions.

Two distinctions are worth making, both connected as you can see in the structure below. There is a difference between self-interest and selfishness, and between interests and desires. First, self-interest should not be confused with mere selfishness. Acting in a way that has some benefit to

yourself does not mean this is a selfish act. A brave man who rescues a person from a burning house is not usually regarded as acting selfishly, yet he may be self-interested in that he gives his interest (say, in enjoying a sense of personal pride for his action) preference over other people's (say, his wife and children, who could have lost him). And the same applies to Lincoln's example: he may have given his self-interest in enjoying peace of mind preference over all other people's interests, but this alone doesn't mean his action was selfish. Even if we agree that an act gives us some benefit, like peace of mind or a sense of personal pride, it may still be to the benefit of someone else. Moreover, even if this sort of personal benefit follows a virtuous action this doesn't mean that our *motivation* was selfish. The satisfaction that accompanies good acts is not necessarily itself the motivation for the act.

This brings into view the other distinction between interests and desires. What you desire is not necessarily what's in your interests. A drug

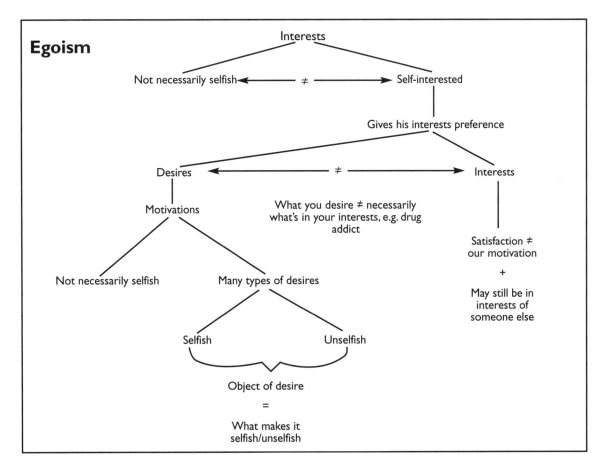

addict may get what she wants when she buys heroin, but it is not in her interests. A desire is what motivates you to do something and there are many types of desire, some selfish, like the drug addict who steals from her friends to buy drugs, some unselfish, like the brave man who puts his life on the line to save others. What makes one desire, or motivation, selfish and another unselfish is the object of desire not merely that it was acted upon. All actions are in some sense based on desires and some of these serve someone else's interests.

Therefore it seems, to answer our original question, there are actions that are not based on self-interest. Some actions can be described as altruistic as some can be described as selfish. Contrary to Lincoln's conclusion, self-interest does not necessarily imply selfishness. It seems, then, that his act in rescuing the piglets was indeed altruistic after all. His satisfaction at rescuing them and the peace of mind he enjoyed as a result was not the motive of the act, but its consequence, and although it benefits his self-interest, it is not a selfish act.

◼ 4. Morality and sentiment: Hume and Rousseau

We saw in Kant's moral theory that the key to the moral autonomy of the individual, our capacity to reveal for ourselves what is morally right or wrong, lies in our use of reason. But this is not the only answer to the question how we find within ourselves what is morally right and wrong. David Hume and the French philosopher Jean-Jacques Rousseau held a radically different view. They argue that we all possess personal feelings of a special moral kind to help our fellow men.

This offers us a very tidy solution to the problem that constantly presents itself as we have seen in our discussion of egoism and altruism: how to square our own personal interests with moral principles that enjoin us to consider the interests of others. The strong moral feelings, to which Hume and Rousseau refer, are in themselves a particular kind of personal interest, so we can satisfy our personal feelings and the demands of morality at the same time. Even so, we all know there are other feelings – greed, envy, jealousy, vanity – that are anything but moral feelings and work against the sort that Hume and Rousseau have in mind. The key to their moral philosophies lies in the concepts of

'sentiment' ('feeling') and 'sympathy' or 'fellow feeling', the feeling of pity for others and the willingness to take their interests into account. In *Enquiry Concerning the Principles of Morals* (1751) Hume explains, 'morality is determined by sentiment. It defines virtue to be whatever mental action or quality gives to a spectator the pleasing sentiment of approbation; and vice the contrary.'

4.1 Hume

Running throughout Hume's thoughts on morals is the distinction between those who see morality as a function of reason and those who see it as a matter of sentiment and passion. In a frequently quoted statement he says, 'reason is, and ought to be, the slave of the passions.' Feelings not only give us direct access to what is morally right, but they motivate us to pursue goodness in ways reason cannot, and they alone can answer the question 'What is of ultimate value?'

All those propositions we come to believe are true after we have reviewed all the evidence are still nevertheless subject to dispute. Even proofs we know to be true as a result of our own reasoning only come to be known as true after careful deliberation. But our feelings need no evidence and no proof: they are known immediately as true without question. Hume argues, 'Truth is disputable, not taste: what exists in the nature of things is the standard of our judgement: what each man feels within himself is the standard of sentiment.' In geometry we can prove propositions, but 'the harmony of verse, the tenderness of passion, the brilliance of wit must give immediate pleasure.'

But feelings are not just a more reliable and immediate source of answers to our cognitive moral questions; they are also the only solution to the conative aspects of moral judgements. In moral education, Hume argues, reason is of no use in motivating people. It has no hold on our affections. Echoing the thoughts of the character in Aldous Huxley's *Point Counter Point* (1928), when he wonders what is the point of a morality that isn't the rationalization of your own feelings, Hume argues similarly, 'where the truths which they (our reasoning) discover are indifferent and beget no desire or aversion, they can have no influence on conduct and behaviour.' Whereas what we regard as honourable, fair or generous 'takes possession of the heart and animates us to embrace and maintain it'.'

Moreover our moral feelings are natural and universal. The final sentence that judges some actions as praiseworthy and others as blameworthy, 'depends on some internal sense of feeling which nature has made universal in the whole species.' And unlike reason this is a source of ultimate values or ends. Reason works prudentially showing us the most effective way of getting what we want, but it is incapable of telling us what we ultimately want. It is concerned with knowledge, truth and falsehood, but taste and sentiment judge values, which ultimately depend on pleasure and pain.

Hume challenges us to ask someone why they exercise. They will say because they want to maintain their health. If you then ask them why they desire health, they will say because sickness is painful. If you push them still further and ask why they hate pain, they cannot give you an answer, because 'This is an ultimate end and is never referred to any other object.' There must be something of ultimate value and this is the avoidance of pain and the maximization of pleasure. He explains, 'Something must be desirable on its own account and because of its immediate accord or agreement with human sentiment and affection.'

As you've no doubt already realized, it's not difficult to make the connection between this part of Hume's account and his insistence that there is a clear and distinct difference between a fact and a value; between an 'ought' and an 'is'. As we saw earlier when we discussed 'Hume's Law', he insists that any notion of value or what we ought to do cannot be derived from a statement of fact. What we ought to do depends on sentiment and feeling. Reason excludes nothing; it is no guide to what we ought to do. It would not be irrational, he argues, to prefer the death of half the world to the pricking of his little finger. Nothing in reason forbids it.

4.2 Rousseau

Like Hume, Rousseau too rejects detached reason as any form of guide for moral judgements, although he does argue that sentiment is tied to a kind of 'natural reason'. But the key element in this is 'conscience', a powerful moral feeling that has its own kind of divine reason. To understand this and the significance of Rousseau's contribution to the development of Western thought, it's important to set it in context.

Rousseau's work is often described as the first attack of Romanticism on the dominance of the Enlightenment and rationalism in the eighteenth century. As we have seen, the Enlightenment had elevated reason, analysis and the scientific method as the only reliable tools for discovering truth. Its atomistic philosophy, breaking nature down into its elementary particles the behaviour of which were governed by laws of nature that could only be discovered through the application of reason, pictured nature as some vast machine working predictably according to natural laws.

Set against this mechanistic philosophy Romanticism presented a radically different vision that drew on the importance of spontaneous, unfettered, and emotional responses. Ultimate truth came from subjective, emotional, intuitive absorption in nature unfettered by civilization and intellect. William Blake in his *Songs of Innocence* (1789) and *Songs of Experience* (1794) compared the spontaneous innocence and imagination of the child with the adult corrupted by the experience of a mechanistic, industrial world that diminished him to a mere machine minder. At the heart of this, as in so much of romantic writing, was the analogy between humanity of the pre– and post-industrial worlds, with the latter corrupted by the regimentation of industrial processes, and intellectually and emotionally divorced from nature.

Into this stepped Rousseau with two of the most influential texts in western philosophy, *Du Contrat Social* (*The Social Contract*) and *Emile*, both published in 1762. The publication of *Emile*, a revolutionary work on education, was a sensation; indeed it is difficult to overestimate its influence even in our own day. It was a bestseller overnight and became one of the major textbooks of the French Revolution and of European Romanticism. The French writer, Chateaubriand, sometimes described as the founder of Romanticism, said of it, 'If one could read no more than five works in the whole of literature, *Emile* would be one of them.' It is said that Kant, who, as we saw in an earlier chapter, resolutely ran his life according to strict routines, refusing to work in the afternoons, nonetheless broke his regime when he was reading *Emile*, so reluctant was he to put it down.

In it Rousseau outlines a key distinction that runs throughout Romanticist literature between nature and society. He contrasts the natural goodness of man with the evil of society, which has perverted humanity. The evil found in the world has its origin in society. He argues, 'there is no original perversity in the human heart. ... [T]he whole duty of education is to discover human nature ... and be guided by its dictates.' Education should not curb or discipline the natural tendencies of the child, but encourage them to grow and blossom. And love and sympathy, not rules and punishments, are the tools for this task.

The answers, then, to our most important questions in ethics lie in allowing our natural moral feelings to flourish, not in disciplining them. Rousseau insists that man is by nature sociable, but he can only be so if he shares with others innate feelings common to his kind. That he often doesn't see that he shares these feelings with others is the result of the corrupting influence of society. In this way Rousseau finds the same solution as Hume to the problem of how to square our own personal interests with moral principles that enjoin us to consider the interests of others: he reconciles 'self-love' and 'moral goodness' as ultimately having the same goals. He explains:

> we do not learn to seek what is good for us and avoid what is bad for us, but get this desire from nature, in the same way the love of good and the hatred of evil are as natural to us as our self-love. The decrees of conscience are not judgements but feelings. Although all our ideas come from without, the feelings by which they are weighed are within us.

To exist at all is to feel, and we had feelings before we had ideas. Such feelings ensured our preservation. They are true to our nature and essential to our survival: feelings like self-love, fear, pain, the dread of death, the desire for comfort and our sociability, our need to cooperate with others to ensure our survival. Out of this sociability has come the power of conscience to motivate man to embrace what is good. It is derived from the moral system, which in turn is the product of a two-fold relationship with ourselves and with our fellow men. Rousseau insists, 'To know good is not to love it; this knowledge is not innate in man; but as soon as his reason leads him to perceive it his conscience impels him to love it; it is this feeling which is innate.' This is the force of conscience, the result of our nature, quite independent of reason. 'Conscience! Conscience!', he declares, 'Divine instinct, immortal voice from heaven; sure guide for a creature ignorant and finite indeed; yet intelligent and free; infallible judge of good and evil, making man like to God.'

Nevertheless this leaves us with a number of unanswered questions that reflect the concerns we had in the last chapter with subjectivist theories. Even if we all agree about what is morally right to do in a situation, how do we know our consciences or feelings are right? And if we disagree, whose conscience or feelings should we accept? Moral theories, like Hume's and Rousseau's, leave us with no means of settling such disputes. All we can do is examine our consciences or reflect on what our feelings are telling us. But if we have carefully reflected upon such things, it is very difficult to be mistaken about them; after all they are *our* conscience and *our* feelings; who better to know them than ourselves? Even so, this doesn't match up with our normal experiences with moral problems, where all too frequently we are mistaken about what action we should take in any situation. And, as a result, none of us are unfamiliar with the remorse that comes from not making the right decision.

The fact is that feelings often contradict, not just between people, but within one person. There are very few people who don't believe that someone who murders and tortures other people is committing evil deeds. This seems to be an objective moral statement, not a statement about personal feelings. When we say that the Holocaust, which resulted in the deaths of six million Jews, was an evil deed, we are talking about the act of killing these people, not our feelings about it. If we were to try to settle the issue by reference to our feelings, no doubt Hitler, Himmler and Heydrich would all defend themselves by arguing that their feelings strongly pointed to the rightness of such a policy. To this we are likely to respond by arguing that such people simply lack moral understanding, or if they do have such understanding, they simply ignored it at the time and acted immorally regardless.

But even within one person there are frequently conflicting feelings about a situation. There is nothing unusual in this. At the end of the Second World War one of Germany's most beautiful cities, Dresden, was destroyed by Allied planes dropping incendiaries designed to do as much damage to property as possible. Full of refugees fleeing the destruction elsewhere Dresden was no strategic military or industrial target. It was hit with the intent of destroying civilian morale with the hope that this would hasten the end of the war.

Today this is what we condemn terrorists for doing: they routinely set out to kill ordinary people selected randomly in order to deliver a message of fear and to destroy civilian morale, both of which they expect will bring pressure upon governments. The random nature of such killing strikes at the heart of one of our most deeply held moral commitments, that we are never justified in attacking the innocent and defenceless, whether they are the elderly war veteran mugged for his pension, the young child brutalised by uncaring parents, the trusting animal confined and tormented within its small prison, or unsuspecting shoppers or office workers maimed and killed on the streets of Belfast, Tel Aviv or New York.

But now how do feelings help us resolve such problems? On the one hand if the bombing of Dresden almost certainly shortened the war saving even more lives than were lost in the bombing, we are likely to feel that it was indeed justified. On the other hand, if we consider the fact that 100,000 innocent people lost their lives, and were deliberately and randomly targeted, rather than being the regrettable cost of war, we are likely feel that it was not justified. Are we to process each conflicting feeling, weighing each one and setting them against each other so that the strongest wins out? This is not a strategy that Hume or Rousseau have in mind. For them the brute feeling is enough to settle the issue.

And anyway, what we seem to have here are feelings evoked by a prior judgement about whether the action was right. If we come to the judgement that it was right because it saved lives, then this will result in feelings that support the action. Whereas if we judge it in terms of randomly taking innocent lives, we are likely to feel strongly that it was wrong. *Thinking* it wrong is different from *feelings* of disapproval. The wrongness of an act doesn't lie in the fact that it repels us; something about the act itself is wrong and the realization of this repels us.

■ 5. Female ethics: the ethic of care

Whether or not you agree with these arguments or with Kant's you can see that both adopt a similar strategy to answer the question how we find within ourselves what is morally right and wrong. Both search for some universal capacity within us to settle these issues – either our capacity to reason or to have feelings of a special moral kind. But what if there were not so much universal capacities as just styles of moral thinking, in particular a fundamental difference between the way men and women think morally?

Although we live in an age when we are more willing to accept such cultural diversity, at first glance it still seems odd to say that virtue is gendered. But the idea is not new. It first appeared in Rousseau's *Emile* (1762), where he argues that women become virtuous by being subordinated within marriage as wives and mothers. It was this that Mary Wollstonecraft attacked in her *A Vindication of the Rights of Women* (1792), arguing that virtue should mean the same for a woman as for a man. Today it's not uncommon for feminists to turn the tables and argue there are not only male and female ethics, but we should be deeply concerned about the male ethic with all its violent and destructive consequences for human life and the planet itself, particularly in its support for war, a conflict style of politics and capitalist economic activity.

But in what sense is it sensible to talk of a male or female ethic? Do we mean by this an essentialist argument, as some contemporary feminists do when they argue that the male nature and masculinity are linked to aggressive and destructive tendencies, while the female nature is less aggressive, more gentle, nurturing and cooperative? The problem is that we can never divorce individuals from their environments to identify what is the result of socialization and what is natural, so any argument that suggests certain attitudes are natural is bound to be indefensible. But if we believe that the 'nature' of men and women is not fixed by nature but created largely through the influence of the societies and times in which we

---

Brief lives
Wollstonecraft, Mary

Dates: 1759–1797
Born: London, England
Best known for: Her advocacy of women's rights. The *Vindication* (1792), in which she challenges Rousseau's assumptions of feminine inferiority, is widely regarded as the founding document of modern feminism. She died giving birth to her daughter, the future Mary Shelley.

Major works: *Thoughts on the Education of Daughters* (1787), *A Vindication of the Rights of Men* (1790), *A Vindication of the Rights of Women* (1792).

live, can we spell out clearly enough male and female ethics without resorting to some form of essentialism?

Just such an attempt was made by Carol Gilligan in her influential book, *A Different Voice: Psychological Theory and Women's Development* (1982). She takes the example of two 11-year old children, Jake and Amy, who are given a moral dilemma to resolve. A woman is near death from a special kind of cancer. There is one drug that the doctors think might save her, a form of radium that a druggist in the same town has recently discovered. But the drug is expensive to make, and anyway the druggist is charging ten times what it costs to make. The sick woman's husband, Heinz, goes to everyone he knows to borrow the money, but he can only raise half what the druggist wants. He tells the druggist that his wife is dying and asks him to sell it cheaper or let him pay later, but the druggist refuses, saying that he discovered the drug and he intends to make money from it. So, in desperation Heinz breaks into the man's store to steal the drug for his wife. The children were asked 'Should he have done that?'

Jake argues that Heinz should steal the drug for his wife, while Amy argues that the best strategy is for Heinz to take out a loan, because if he were sentenced to a term of imprisonment for burglary he would not be able to care for his wife. Gilligan concludes that this illustrates the typical differences in the way men and women think about moral issues and that we are wrong to think that female moral reasoning is somehow deficient or inferior.

Men see moral problems in terms of rights, abstract principles and impartiality. Those involved in any moral situation have certain obligations and duties that they have accepted much like a social contract. The aim of this is to ensure justice and fairness, which is seen as the ultimate value. In line with the tradition that runs through Kant, Rawls and Hare, morality is a matter of logic, rules and principles. Individuals are separate, isolated and autonomous. They are free to do as they like as long as they don't interfere with others. When they do come into conflict or when the principles themselves conflict, they must be ranked into a hierarchy to settle the issue. And this, it seems, is exactly what Jake does in this case. There is a conflict between the right to life and the right to property, which he settles by placing the right to life higher on the hierarchy of rights.

In contrast, the female ethic of care sees moral problems as conflicts of responsibility. Situations are not seen in terms of rights and principles, but as concrete situations involving relationships between people with all their complex emotions and feelings. Rather than abstract impartiality, morality involves caring and bonding with particular individuals to get a full measure of their feelings before you can settle the conflict and repair the damage done to relationships. Nel Noddings argues that it is a misrepresentation of moral decision-making to reduce it to a 'desert-island dilemma' stripped of all the situational and contextual knowledge, which alone can offer a solution. In this, she argues, lies the distinctive nature of female moral thinking. It has as its ultimate aims inclusion and protection from harm.

Gilligan's account is similar in that she believes the female ethic involves moral agents as caregivers. The key to understanding morality is emotional and personal relationships, which involve, rather than impersonal detached reason, sympathy and identification with the feelings and needs of others. The core relationship in morality is not a self-centred one involving individuals asserting abstract rights and obligations, but a caring relationship in which the caregiver is concerned with the feelings and needs of others in order to help them grow and fulfil themselves. The basis of a more general morality lies in extending to others the way we conduct personal relationships with those we know. Such a morality does not consist of rules for moral actions, but guidelines to help us become more sensitive to the needs and feelings of others, doing what we can to help them and avoiding actions that cause them harm.

The problem, as many feminists see it, is that feminist values have been systematically devalued in western societies in favour of male values. According to Alison Jaggar supposedly male values, like independence, autonomy, intellect, will, hierarchy, domination, culture, war and death, have been regarded as more important than female values, like interdependence, community, connection, sharing, emotion, trust, joy and peace. And much of this devaluation has come about because women's moral experience itself has been devalued. Yet the supposedly universal, impartial standpoint that male values occupy, which gives them their prominence in moral thinking, is nothing of the sort, accordingly to Jaggar. In fact it reflects a culturally specific perspective, which is systematically biased against women and members of other subordinated groups.

Of course, as you can see, at the heart of this lies two interrelated questions: first, whether there is a real difference between male and female ethics; and, second, if so, are the different values the result of a natural difference between men and women or merely a reflection of the way they have been taught to think about ethics and value certain things.

If the assumption that there is a real difference is based upon what we believe to be our common experience of the way men and women reason, we can always point to exceptions: men and women who do not reason in the way we would expect and who place importance on different values than they would if this were true. If this is the case we would have grounds for doubting the claim that we can describe some values, like autonomy, intellect and will, as masculine and others as feminine. Still, as we have seen previously, although we can find exceptions to inductive generalizations this might not call for us to abandon them. If Kuhn is right, the point at which we abandon them is when systematic exceptions rob us of the confidence we have in them.

Indeed Jean Grimshaw argues there may not be a difference between how the sexes reason about ethics at all; it might be just that they have different ethical priorities: 'what is regarded as an important principle by women (such as maintaining relationships) is commonly seen by men as a *failure* of principle.' And this should not surprise us given that the life experiences of women are very different from men. As a result their ethical priorities are bound to be different. The fact that they are more closely involved in the experience of child-rearing means that there is likely to be a significant difference in their reaction to the waste of lives in war. Indeed, such different priorities, with their emphasis on supporting, repairing and enriching relationships to support people in fulfilling their potential, can usefully inform and challenge the prevailing male ethic.

However, by the same token, if we can throw doubt on the claim that the sexes *think* differently about ethics, we can probably also throw doubt on the claim that there is a coherent set of distinctly female values. As Virginia Held points out, not all feminists agree that there are distinctive feminist virtues and values, not only because it might play into the hands of those who want to confine women to traditional roles, but because all claims about women are divided by class, race and sexual orientation, which make any conclusion about 'women's experience' dubious.

Whatever our values they are always influenced by our culture and situation. Social class, race, whether or not we live in a state of poverty or in relative comfort, all these factors are likely to shape our values in ways which cut across so-called women's values. As Jean Grimshaw points out, if you were a women growing up in Nazi Germany your view of motherhood might have been heavily influenced by government propaganda that it was every woman's responsibility to the 'Fatherland' to have as many Aryan children as possible. Similarly, a woman in America today is likely to value individuality and freedom of choice in contrast to a woman in India or Pakistan, who is likely to place more emphasis on community and interpersonal relations.

Changing times also make an obvious difference. Women's experience has traditionally been in the home, while men's has been out in the public world of work. But now more women work, while many men accept a greater share of domestic responsibilities. The differences in experience explain why we so often detect differences in our perception of moral values and priorities as much *within* genders as between them. It seems, then, that it is difficult to sum up the differences with any confidence in generalizations about men and women.

Well, what is the answer then? Gilligan does seem to have a point that there seem to be different styles of moral thinking, one very broadly associated with women and the other with men. And, as Virginia Held argues, there do appear to be three questionable aspects about the way we approach moral thinking: the legacy from Descartes of the concept of self constructed largely from a male point of view; the split between reason and emotion, and the devaluation of emotion; and the public/private distinction and the relegation of the private to the natural.

One answer might be to avoid attributing sexual stereotyping to males and females altogether, and just see them as evidence of the diversity in the ways we see and think about moral values. The Swiss psychiatrist, Carl Jung, argues that every viewpoint has its shadow figure. So every male has his female side and every female has her male side. Rather than polarized stereotypes we might in fact have a continuum with so-called male values at one end and female values at the other. Nature or nurture might simply predispose us to one or the other; either to tackling moral problems by resorting to reason, rights and abstract principles, or to emotions, care and concrete relationships.

Picking up the same idea Sandra Bem suggests that we might depict masculine and feminine traits along axes: one registering low to high masculinity, the other low to high femininity. Each individual can then be plotted somewhere in the geometric space, with traditional males high in masculinity and low in femininity, and traditional females high in femininity and low in masculinity. It would enable us to get away from the stark stereotypes and depict more realistically the balance between what we describe as male and female values in each individual.

However, this still leaves us with the problem of how we combine these two radically different approaches to ethics. Is there a supreme principle, like justice, as John Rawls believes? Or are we inclined to recognize this as such only because we have grown up within male-dominated societies in the Western tradition of philosophy? Alison Jaggar argues that feminists are naturalists: they begin by acknowledging that our insights and moral beliefs are always conditioned by our social experiences and locations. Such a view abandons any claim that there are foundations in philosophy: ultimate principles on which our moral reasoning depends. Instead our approach to moral problems should reflect the same shift in thinking that we have seen with postmodernism and T. S. Kuhn in the philosophy of science. The most we can do is to chart the differences in styles of moral thinking through empirical and multidisciplinary studies involving disciplines like psychology, economics and the social sciences.

Alternatively, if we believe it is possible to escape such moral relativism by revealing the foundations of moral thinking, we are left with the problem of how to combine these two radically different approaches. Is there one principle, like Rawls' principle of justice, that trumps all others in any situation? Or should we redefine such concepts to take into account the values, virtues and insights of an ethic of care? A form of moral thinking drawing exclusively on reason, rights and abstract principles to settle moral problems can appear at times to produce anything but justice. Our search for the foundations of moral thinking might lie in combining the insights of both, enlarging the traditional view of moral thinking with a greater understanding of the context, the feelings and interrelations of those involved.

■ 6. Conclusion

We began this chapter by comparing two different ways of looking at ethics: two different moral vocabularies. The deontological view argued that we could find what is morally right by looking at ourselves or the world; that rights and duties are inherent in our very nature. We might find them in our rationality or in our feelings, a simple matter of conscience. This is what Koestler describes as 'Cricket morality', the anti-vivisectionist morality that sees the individual as sacrosanct.

In the next chapter we will examine the other view, which Koestler describes as 'Vivisection morality'. This emphasizes the importance of the consequences of our actions and whether they maximize the good defined in non-moral terms, like happiness and survival. But we will also examine a third view, 'Virtue Ethics', which is not so much concerned about finding certain standards or rules, as about being a good person, a virtuous character.

■ Questions

1. Is it morally better to have acted out of duty and resisted the temptation to do evil, or never to have acted out of duty, instead doing the right thing out of natural inclination?

2. 'There is no such thing as a really altruistic action; for everything a person does is done for the pleasure she gets from satisfying her own desires.' Discuss.

3. A: 'If everyone were to break their promises as you do, the effect would be that we would no longer be able to rely upon anyone's word.'

   B: 'But everyone will not do as I do, so it doesn't matter if I do it.'

   Discuss.

4. If the knowledge that I have a terminal illness would make the rest of my life less happy than if I hadn't been told, would it be wrong to inform me of my condition?

5. Are we right to think it is important that our moral judgements should be universalizable? Is this a moral or a rational obligation, or both?

6. Are there any kinds of action that can never be justified under any circumstances?

7. Are feminists right that we should be deeply concerned about the violent and aggressive nature of the male ethic compared with the more gentle, nurturing and cooperative female ethic?

■ Recommended reading

Butler, J. *Fifteen Sermons Upon Human Nature* (London: Macmillan, 1900). Arguments against egoism, particularly sermon XI.

Frankena, W. K. *Ethics* (Englewood Cliffs, NJ: Prentice-Hall, 1973).

Gilligan, Carol. *A Different Voice: Psychological Theory and Women's Development* (Cambridge, Mass: Harvard University Press, 1982).

Hume, David. *Enquiry Concerning the Principles of Morals* (La Salle, Ill: Open Court, 1912).

Nagel, T. *The Possibility of Altruism* (New York: Oxford University Press, 1970).

Paton, H. J. (Trans.) *The Moral Law: Kant's Groundwork of the Metaphysic of Morals* (London: Hutchinson, 1948). Paton's introduction is especially useful.

Plato. *The Republic*, trans. H. D. P. Lee (Harmondsworth: Penguin, 1971), 'The Ring of Gyges' in Book II.

Rousseau, Jean-Jacques. *Emile* (New York: Dutton, 1970).

The note structure to accompany this chapter can be downloaded from our website.

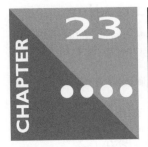

23 | Normative Ethics: Consequentialism and Virtue Ethics

Key issues

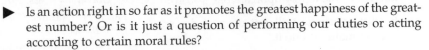

▶ Is an action right in so far as it promotes the greatest happiness of the greatest number? Or is it just a question of performing our duties or acting according to certain moral rules?

▶ If we are to judge an act entirely on its good or bad consequences, what is it about the consequences that make an act good or bad?

▶ Is our principal concern in everything we do to maximize our pleasure?

▶ But then what about friendship, knowledge, beauty, health, courage, love, fairness, all things we seem to desire for themselves and not for the pleasure they bring us?

▶ Perhaps the answers to these questions lie in the type of people we are, rather than the decisions we reach, on the assumption that good people rarely do bad things?

Koestler's *Darkness at Noon* may have left you thinking that any moral theory which diminishes the individual to a mere means for bringing about consequences that are good for the majority is seriously flawed. Yet deontological ethics is not without similar problems. Here too individuals can be diminished, in this case dwarfed by the overbearing importance of duties and rules. The double effect has it that a bad act that produces good consequences can never be condoned, whereas a good act done in the full knowledge that bad consequences will ensue is quite permissible.

This is the position in which most ordinary SS officers and officials found themselves, when they became involved in the Nazi's 'Final Solution' for the extermination of Jews. At his trial in 1961 in Israel Adolf Eichmann defended his actions in just these terms. He was doing no more than his duty as Kant had insisted. He had obeyed orders and the law without exception. Hannah Arendt, the German-born US philosopher, describes this as the 'banality of evil' in her book *Eichmann in Jerusalem* (1963): average, even normal, people simply following orders doing routine bureaucratic jobs.

Like many at this level of responsibility, Eichmann was not driven by evil, but by the desire to do a good job. He was responsible for arranging the transport of Jews from occupied territories, which he prided himself he did without compromise, shortcuts, intrusion of personal feeling and without favour. His conscience was clear; he had done an honest bureaucratic job. As Arendt argues, this uncompromising attitude towards the performance of his murderous duties in his own eyes justified him: 'No exceptions – this was the proof that he had always acted against his "inclinations," whether they were sentimental or inspired by interest, that he had always done his "duty".'

■ 1. Consequentialist theories: utilitarianism

In the light of this it's not surprising that many philosophers are convinced the most important moral consideration of any action is its consequences. The American philosopher William Frankena makes a comparison between the theories we have examined so far by arguing that deontological theories take people seriously, but do not take the promotion of good seriously enough, whereas egoism takes the promotion of good seriously, but does not take other people seriously enough. Utilitarianism, the most popular and influential of all consequentialist theories, remedies both of these defects at once. It not only takes the results of our actions seriously, but individuals too, at least in the form of their happiness or preferences.

This raises the key distinction we saw earlier between deontological and teleological theories. While deontologists argue that an act is intrinsically wrong in terms of the nature of the act itself, for the consequentialist an act is wrong extrinsically, in terms of something other than the act, found in the nature of the consequences. A theory is described as

consequentialist if it holds that the rightness or wrongness of an act depends entirely upon its good or bad consequences. The right action is that which produces the best overall result. But this leaves us with the problem of what it is about the consequences that makes them good or bad. And this, as we saw in the last chapter, must be defined in non-moral terms; otherwise we will be left with the circular argument that an act is morally right because it produces consequences that are morally right. As the utilitarian John Stuart Mill points out, 'Whatever can be proved to be good, must be so by being shown to be a means to something admitted to be good without proof.'

The answer to this question produces broadly two types of consequentialist theory: hedonistic and agathistic theories. In those described as hedonistic the rightness or wrongness of an act depends upon its consequences measured in terms of pleasure and pain. In contrast, agathistic theories hold that goodness cannot be identified this way. It is something unique, just as a colour, like redness, is unique and cannot be reduced to anything else. In chapter 21 we saw that G. E. Moore maintains that the rightness or wrongness of an act depends upon the amount of goodness or badness the act produces.

Of all consequentialist theories, the hedonistic theory of utilitarianism is the most influential. Utilitarians argue that actions are right in so far as they produce the greatest possible happiness for all concerned. John Stuart Mill, whose father, James Mill, and Jeremy Bentham were the architects of modern utilitarianism, defines the 'Greatest Happiness' principle at the heart of the theory in his essay 'Utilitarianism' (1861) in these words:

> Actions are right in proportion as they tend to promote happiness, wrong as they tend to produce the reverse of happiness. By happiness is intended pleasure and the absence of pain; by unhappiness, pain and the privation of pleasure.

1.1 Act and rule utilitarianism

This sounds straightforward enough, but as with many things the devil is in the details. In particular how are we to calculate the pleasure and pain resulting from an action; what are we to take into account? One answer, known as 'act utilitarianism,' restricts the calculation to a particular action in

John Stuart Mill (1806–1873)

John Stuart Mill was not only the most influential British philosopher of the nineteenth century, but thought by many to be the most intelligent man of his time. Educated by his father, James Mill, he was reading Greek at the age of three and Latin at eight. At 12 he began a thorough study of scholastic logic and by 14 he had mastered the basics of economic theory. But at 20 this intense education, strictly in line with the principles of Bentham's associationist psychology, left him in crisis without any cultivation of his feelings.

His salvation lay in a radically different tradition: the romanticism of Wordsworth, Carlyle and Coleridge. Along with the influence of French thinkers, notably Saint-Simon and Auguste Comte, this gave him a more developed understanding of the historical and collective forces shaping ideas and societies. In 1830 Mill met and later married Harriet Taylor, whom he described as crucial to his intellectual and moral development. After she died in 1858 in Avignon he spent six months of each year there to be near her grave. In 1873 when he too died in Avignon he was buried next to her. His influence continues to be felt today through works like *A System of Logic* (1843), *Principles of Political Economy* (1848), *On Liberty* (1859), *Utilitarianism* (1861) and *The Subjection of Women* (1861).

particular circumstances, judged in terms of the pleasure and pain of just those directly involved. It does not consider the effect of everyone learning from my example and everyone doing likewise in similar circumstances. In other words, it does not involve a universal prescription: it legislates just for this particular act in these particular circumstances. Today, we would call this a form of 'situation ethics': the view that ethical judgements apply just to existing whole situations and do not involve abstracting features of a situation which might then be applied to future possible situations.

Still this arbitrarily excludes from the calculation the impact of my actions on the general balance of happiness, which might be significant if others, say, follow my example and refuse to keep their promises or tell the truth. What's more, there are many situations in which we have neither the time nor the information necessary to make a good decision, when we do need a generalization, a rule, informing us what is most likely to maximize happiness in

this particular type of situation and, therefore, what we should do.

To answer these two problems 'rule utilitarians' argue that we should not consider particular actions in isolation, but sorts of actions. Like deontological theories, rule utilitarianism is universally prescriptive; we commit ourselves to obeying rules irrespective of the consequences in any particular case. Yet still it is consequentialist in that our calculations are directed towards the consequences of adopting some general rule, like 'Always keep promises' or 'Never tell lies.' If the consequences of its general adoption are better than those of the general adoption of some other rule, then we are justified in adopting it. Unlike deontological ethics we must always decide what these rules are to be by asking which ones will produce or are likely to produce the greatest general good for everyone. This means, of course, in some circumstances it might be right to comply with a law, like always keeping promises, because it is very useful to have the rule generally adopted, even though in this particular case keeping a promise will not result in the best consequences.

Two further distinctions are worth making at this point. Unlike rule utilitarianism, act utilitarianism lends itself to being interpreted as both an egoistic and non-egoistic theory. It depends upon whether the good consequences we must consider in any situation relate just to us or to mankind in general. If it is just to us, then this is 'egoistic utilitarianism', if it is to all mankind it is 'universalistic utilitarianism'. As we saw in the last chapter, since what is good for me is unlikely to maximize the happiness of everyone, the two are incompatible with each other. However, this has not always been acknowledged by utilitarians. In the nineteenth century they tended to adopt the assumption of *laissez-faire* advocates, with whom they were theoretically close, that society was just a loose collection of isolated individuals, the sum of its parts. Therefore, as each individual maximizes his happiness, society too, as the aggregate of individuals, will maximize its happiness.

The other distinction worth noting, that between 'hedonistic' and 'ideal' utilitarianism, cuts across both act and rule utilitarianism. As we have seen 'hedonistic utilitarianism' holds that the goodness or badness of consequences depends upon their capacity to promote pleasure and avoid pain. Indeed Bentham maintained there was no difference in the quality of pleasure; they all counted equally; pushpin (a child's game), he said, is as good as poetry. Ideal utilitarianism, however, does accept this difference in quality. It is an agathistic theory in that it holds that the goodness or badness of a certain state of consciousness depends not just on its pleasant or unpleasantness, but also on various intellectual and aesthetic qualities, knowledge and the contemplation of beautiful things. This leaves open the possibility that certain pleasant states of mind can be intrinsically bad, while some unpleasant ones can be intrinsically good.

John Stuart Mill took an intermediate position between these two, due largely to what he describes as his 'mental crisis' at the age of 20 in 1826. At the hands of his father he had undergone a rigorous utilitarian education. Widely regarded as the most brilliant man of his generation, he was taught Greek at the age of three, Latin at seven, logic at 12 and political economy at 13. But it left him with what he describes as his inveterate habit of analysis, which had a 'tendency to wear away the feelings', reducing everything of value to mere quantities of pleasure, leaving nothing indissolvable, resistant to its corrosive influence. Through 'associationist psychology' whatever he regarded as good he had learnt to do so by associating it with pleasurable feelings and whatever was bad with unpleasant feelings. That there was nothing of value he hadn't learnt to associate in this way through effective conditioning left Mill in despair of ever finding something that could be a solid foundation of value in his life. He says, despairingly,

> the habit of analysis has a tendency to wear away the feelings. ... My education ... had failed to create these feelings in sufficient strength to resist the dissolving influences of analysis, while the whole course of my intellectual cultivation had made precocious and premature analysis the inveterate habit of my mind.

Luckily he found Wordsworth's poetry, and later Coleridge and Carlyle, romantic philosophers who relied more on imagination and intuition than analysis. Not surprisingly, then, Mill maintains that although pleasure is a necessary condition for goodness, the intrinsic goodness of a state of mind could depend on things other than pleasure. In other words, in contrast to Bentham, he argues there are in fact higher and lower pleasures. Indeed in his essay 'Utilitarianism', he declares, 'It is better to be a human being dissatisfied than a pig satisfied; better to be Socrates dissatisfied than a fool satisfied.'

However, with these two distinctions aside, it appears rule utilitarianism is a closer approximation to what we have in mind when we make moral judgements. First, it avoids the practical problem of act utilitarianism that we would have to be incessant calculators weighing up the balance of pleasure and pain in every situation before we could come to a judgement, when in fact we might not have sufficient information, time or the inclination to do this.

Second, it avoids the danger of elevating expediency to the status of our most important moral principle. An act utilitarian believes anything that is truly expedient, anything at all that is effective in maximizing happiness, must, therefore, be right. In such circumstances it would be right to lie, break promises or bear false witness against the innocent. But then it is difficult in these circumstances to see how we could rely on other people's honesty or trustworthiness. At least rule utilitarianism mitigates this by calculating that our compliance with certain rules, say against lying or about promise-keeping, are likely to maximize happiness, leaving us with enough reason to trust the honesty and trustworthiness of others.

It raises a common objection to act utilitarianism and, indeed, all forms of consequentialism. Many of our actions which we would normally regard as wrong are right under act utilitarianism. And even if utilitarians do decide that such an action is wrong, the wrongness depends upon inappropriate factors: in other words, it is the right decision, but for the wrong reason. For example, we would agree that bearing false witness is wrong, but not because of the overall consequences if people generally did this, but simply because it is unjust.

This suggests that we believe an act may be made right or wrong by facts about it other than the amount of good produced. Butler and Ross demonstrate this in a simple, yet effective, way by citing a situation in which it is possible to do one of two acts, A and B. In terms of their consequences both will bring about the same balance of good over bad. But A involves breaking a promise, whereas B does not. An act utilitarian would say that there is nothing to choose between the two, because they both bring about the same amount of good. Yet without much doubt we would all argue that B is preferable, because it doesn't involve breaking a promise. So it seems something other than their consequences makes some acts right.

Still, while we might find it difficult to endorse unqualified the underlying act utilitarian principle that if ever these obligations conflict with the general obligation to promote happiness they should be subordinated to it, we would not dispute the claim that it is right to break a promise in order to save a life or to avoid a disaster. In consequentialist terms what we achieve by breaking the promise outweighs what we could have achieved by keeping it. But the advantage has to be significant: if there were only a slight advantage to be gained, we are likely to argue that the obligation to keep our promises comes first. The balance is between what Bentham describes as first and second-order evil. First-order evil, which outweighs obligations like promise-keeping, involves pain caused to particular individuals, whereas second-order evil is the harm done to the community in general by shattering public confidence in institutions like promise-keeping.

Yet perhaps the most telling defence that an act utilitarian, indeed all consequentialists, can mount to deal with the suggestion that an act may be made right or wrong by facts about it other than the amount of good produced, is to challenge us to defend these moral intuitions. If our intuitions conflict with a utilitarian account of why breaking a promise in a certain situation is right, the utilitarian might well respond as J. J. C. Smart does, when he says, 'well so much the worse for our moral intuitions!' Our moral intuitions are not sacrosanct; indeed they may be wrong and in need of critical examination.

R. M. Hare argues in *Moral Thinking* that our intuitions are just a general guide, a set of *prima facie* principles that help us make our daily moral decisions without the necessity of coming to utilitarian calculations in every situation. They are chosen on the high probability that if we follow them they will maximize the good in all similar situations. But we only arrive at which intuitions to maintain and which to discard by critical moral thinking in which we evaluate them in utilitarian terms on their capacity to maximize the good. When we convince ourselves that they are inviolable and sacrosanct, we are no longer seeing them for what they are. As you can appreciate this has proved to be a resilient defence against most deontological criticisms.

1.2 Happiness

Even Bernard Williams, a long-time critic of utilitarianism, concedes that it has four important attractions for moral thinking. First, he says, it is

> **Brief lives**
> **Williams, Bernard**
>
> Dates: 1929–2003
> Born: Westcliff-on-Sea, England
> Best known for: Arguing against Kantian and utilitarian ethics particularly their emphasis on the impersonal factors involved in moral decision making, when so much of our practical moral lives is concerned with personal projects.
>
> Major works: *Morality: An Introduction to Ethics* (1972), *Descartes: the Project of Pure Inquiry* (1978), *Moral Luck* (1981), *Ethics and the Limits of Philosophy* (1985), *Shame and Necessity* (1993).

'non-transcendental': it does not make any appeal to religious authorities that lie outside human life. We need make no appeal to a supreme authority, as in the Euthyphro problem, to underwrite our moral convictions. Second, it is 'minimally problematical' in that whatever else we believe we all accept it is reasonable to aim at our own happiness. In this sense, he argues, it is a 'minimum commitment morality': given the minimum commitment for being in the moral world, that we should be willing to consider other people's concerns, utilitarianism can get going as a moral theory on this assumption alone.

Third, its attraction for many lies in its empirical nature and the belief that all moral issues can finally be settled by the empirical calculation of consequences. Any moral obscurity that remains, therefore, is due solely to the technical limitations of actually making the empirical calculations. And fourth, he argues, it provides a common currency of moral thought, in which all our conflicting moral claims can be cashed. It provides a solution to the deontological problem we all face at times of accepting two conflicting moral claims on us, both of which are valid and irreconcilable, so that whatever we do involves doing something wrong. Such a conflict to the utilitarian is incoherent in that there is the common measure in the Greatest Happiness Principle that can always settle it.

For the moment, putting aside until later in this chapter the question whether happiness is really the aim of all human life and the ultimate appeal for all ethical questions, we need to know what exactly is meant by happiness and how it can be made to work for utilitarianism. The simplest answer, of course, is the hedonistic view that happiness is the balance of pleasure over pain and all other things are valuable only as means to that. The problem for the hedonist, as you can see, is how we measure the quantity of pleasure or pain involved and how we compare them. How are we to know that one pleasure or pain outweighs another and by how much? For this Jeremy Bentham developed his 'hedonic' or 'felicific calculus' through which he argues we can calculate units of happiness as units of pleasure. They are valued according to their intensity, duration, their certainty or uncertainty, and their propinquity or remoteness, the total providing an objective framework for valuing and comparing different courses of action.

If we were to conceive of a system for calculating such things, no doubt this is roughly how we would expect it to look. But is it theoretically and practically feasible? In theory our problem would be to calculate all the possible consequences of an action and then measure them using these four criteria. But one action can have a rippling effect on things long after the event and not just on those directly involved. Tracing all these and valuing them seems an impossible task. And then, even if we managed that, we would still need to overcome the problem of commensurability: that is, we would need a non-arbitrary measure with which to compare one pleasure or pain with another. We can compare one length with another, because in inches, feet, centimetres and metres we have non-arbitrary measures for comparison. Similarly, we can compare the temperature of one thing to another, because we have temperature scales. But we have no common non-arbitrary scale by which we could measure and compare different pleasures and pains.

Equally serious, in practical terms we would have to become incessant calculators, weighing up each action in terms of its likely direct and indirect effects on others and the consequences of these in terms of pleasure and pain. We could not prescribe in advance what we ought to do in such situations until we have all the facts in front of us and have had time to evaluate the likely consequences of all the alternative courses of action. So, unless we restrict it to rule utilitarianism, such a theory fails to meet two of the key requirements of all moral theories, that they should be universally prescriptive and action-guiding. To overcome this we would have to adopt something like Hare's *prima facie* principles; a set of moral intuitions that can guide our routine, everyday decision making.

However, beyond these two considerations there is a third that has troubled utilitarians and non-utilitarians alike. To argue that our principle concern is to maximize our pleasure, and that all our actions, including our self-sacrifices, even martyrdom, our struggle for ideals, and our love of poetry, music and fine art, are nothing more than units of pleasure no different from playing a video game or watching a football match, seems a banal description of the limitless forms that our activities take. It seems to ignore a radical difference in quality between one form and another. There is a distinctive range and variety of human happiness. To many it seems incomprehensible that we could describe the experience of listening to Tchaikovsky's Violin Concerto or Eric Clapton's guitar on *Crossroads* in the same terms as playing a video game, as just units of pleasure.

Even J. S. Mill, who was deeply committed to making utilitarianism work, after his crisis saw this as the major deficiency in his father's and Bentham's theory. Both seemed shackled by a limited understanding of the variety and range of human happiness. Indeed Mill said of Bentham that he was possessed 'both of remarkable endowments for philosophy and of remarkable deficiencies for it,' his 'lot was cast in a generation of the leanest and barrenest men whom England had yet produced and he was an old man before a better race came in.'

Mill rejects a simple quantitative assessment of pleasure, because he argues that while humans experience 'lower' pleasures as animals do, they are capable of certain 'higher' pleasures. There is, therefore, a difference in the quality and not just the quantity of pleasure. He says, 'It is quite compatible with the principle of utility to recognize the fact that some *kinds* of pleasure are more desirable and more valuable than others.' Yet this, it seems, is to embrace ideal utilitarianism and admit tacitly that there is something else, apart from pleasure, which is intrinsically good: other things, like truth, beauty and love that are good in themselves as well as pleasure. To say that some kinds of pleasure are more valuable than other kinds is not the same as saying they will yield greater pleasure. This leads him to argue, as we've seen, that 'It is better to be a human being dissatisfied than a pig satisfied; better to be Socrates dissatisfied than a fool satisfied.'

But to be able to come to this sort of decision, we must appeal to those who have experienced both higher and lower pleasures. In fact Mill believes those who have indeed experienced both 'give a marked preference to the manner of existence which employs their higher faculties.' So poetry is after all more valuable than pushpin. Nonetheless, while he may believe it is simply *inconceivable* that an educated person should choose lower pleasures, this does not make it *impossible*. And even if he were to find a majority did in fact choose higher pleasures, this does not make it right anymore than a majority of scientific opinion makes a scientific theory right.

Perhaps the most we can rely on is our own sense of what we would normally regard as human life. Bernard Williams challenges us to consider whether we would choose to spend our lives in a 'hedon machine', a machine that can give us constant, unremitting pleasure whenever we want it. Beyond our need for food and other essentials to maintain life, we could spend every waking hour enjoying pleasure, like an unlimited supply of some euphoric drug. But is this what we regard as human life? Is this the limit of the challenges we accept that make our lives worthwhile?

And one further thought before we leave this subject, if we were to satisfy our cravings for pleasure in this direct way, would this make us happy, or does happiness come indirectly from pursuing other things? This is what Henry Sidgwick, the nineteenth-century English utilitarian, describes as the 'Paradox of Hedonism, that the impulse towards pleasure, if too predominant, defeats its own aim.' The problem arises, he maintains, because we cannot achieve the highest degree of pleasure as long as we keep these pleasures as our main focus. J. S. Mill, too, describes the same problem in his *Autobiography* (1873), when he says

> Aiming thus at something else, they find happiness by the way. The enjoyments of life ... are sufficient to make it a pleasant thing, when they are taken *en passant*, without being made a principal object. Once made them so, and they are immediately felt to be insufficient. ... Ask yourself whether you are happy, and you cease to be so. The only chance is to treat, not happiness, but some end external to it, as the purpose of life.

So, only by pursuing other things, like knowledge, friendship, love, or projects that help others, are we likely to achieve happiness as opposed to the pleasure we might get from spending our days in a hedon machine.

1.3 Preference utilitarianism

With all these problems perhaps we should dispense with such a contentious notion as happiness and think instead of what we all prefer, irrespective of what that is and whether it promotes pleasure. Preference utilitarianism is grounded in the assumption that the individual is rational and knows his own interests best. In this form of utilitarianism the good is that which is subjectively desired, the satisfaction of such desires being the goal of all moral actions. This is a hard-headed democratic approach in which we simply set out to maximize the satisfaction of the preferences people have chosen. The only way to know which outcome is better overall is to count how many desires are satisfied; this is the ultimate standard. In this way it dispenses with the contentious questions about what is intrinsically valuable and how we measure and compare pleasures and pains. There is no need for a theory that ranges across individuals. The only thing that matters is what we want, and about this it is completely impartial.

Nevertheless, to make it work we need some method of determining how many people have a preference for something. If this is a simple method of arithmetically counting the people who have preferences for X as against Y, we are likely to reach decisions that resemble what Mill describes as 'the tyranny of the majority': we maximize preference satisfaction by ignoring the preferences of the minority. This might not be quite so bad if we could ensure that we make some people better off and nobody worse off, but this is not usually the case. More often than not we make some people better off, while others are worse off.

If this is true of most cases, we now have the problem of how we are to lay off the disadvantage to some against the advantage to others. As you can see this is a question of justice, in this case distributive justice. Although it's a problem for all moral systems, it poses a particular difficulty for utilitarianism, because utilitarians are tied to the notions of maximization and utility or welfare. For utilitarians to recognize the problem of justice is to accept that we do have certain special responsibilities that do not necessarily derive from the fact that they increase the sum total of human happiness. When justice and other special responsibilities, like promise-keeping, conflict with our obligation to promote the general good, utilitarians should argue they should be subordinated to it. Utilitarians are committed to the rule of expedience: the end justifies the means.

In *Moral Thinking* Hare poses a problem that bears upon our special responsibilities to friends, family and loved ones. If an aircraft crashed and you were only able to save one person, your son or a world-renowned surgeon, who, if he were saved, would no doubt go on to save many lives in the future, which should you save? The preference utilitarian would have to urge us to save the surgeon, but most of us would find it difficult to accept such advice. We believe we have a special responsibility to our friends, family and loved ones that outweighs any moral claim a stranger may have on us.

Another example will illustrate the problem utilitarians have with justice as a similar special responsibility. Let's say good consequences might result from punishing an innocent person, if he is generally thought by the community to be guilty, say, of paedophile offences. If he is acquitted riots may break out. This is an example of Bentham's second-order evils – harm done to the community, which now feels insecure and less confident that the judicial system can protect its children. But most of us think it wrong to punish the innocent, even if the second-order evil could be avoided in doing so. Although utilitarianism can claim to be just in the sense that it involves no special pleading or bias to oneself, it is still willing to trade off one person against others, or a minority against a majority.

So, an action may maximize the amount of good, but be unjust in the way it distributes it. It seems, then, that utility alone is not enough; it needs to be supplemented by a deontological principle about justice, which establishes that a just distribution is a good thing in itself. But this means there will be occasions when justice overrules utility and maximization, which suggests utilitarianism cannot be right. One outcome may be preferable to another because it is more just, and utility can say nothing about this.

One answer is to refine the notion of preference counting so that we are not just counting how many people want X, but measuring the strength of their competing preferences. R. M. Hare argues for a winner-takes-all strategy, in which those with the strongest preferences win. This at least seems to ameliorate the problem by setting the strong preferences of an individual against the weaker preferences of the majority. But now we need a more complex strategy for counting up preferences and assessing their strength, so that we can reach a total of preference satisfaction for each alternative we consider. Hare argues that we do this by putting ourselves imaginatively in someone else's position and experiencing for ourselves how much we would or would not want the same thing to happen to us. In this way we transform an interpersonal problem (a problem between different people) into an intrapersonal one (a problem within oneself) and settle it in the same way we settle all our problems involving our conflicting preferences.

Even so, this still only ameliorates the problem of justice: it still allows the majority's weak, trivial preferences to outweigh the strong preferences, the needs, of the few. What's more, it allows in preferences that are widely regarded as immoral, yet are held with such strength that they outweigh the aggregate preferences of all those involved. Someone might be a paedophile and have a very strong, indeed an overwhelming, preference to molest children. If we were to transfer those preferences and make them our own, as Hare suggests, we would have to condone the paedophile's behaviour, because it is driven by the strongest preference.

Of course, you might argue that these preferences are quite likely to be outweighed by the preferences of all those in society who disapprove of it. But then this too is likely to result in the tyranny of the majority. We would find ourselves unable to approve of any behaviour of which the majority disapproves. Moreover, we would then have a problem of what to include in our calculations; not just the preferences of those directly involved, but those indirectly involved and those with just 'external preferences' for things other than experiences of the preferrer, someone who might know nothing of the case, but just campaigns for the rights of children. Then the calculation would become impossibly difficult. We would have to discount the preferences of those only indirectly involved, reducing them, say, by 50 per cent and those even more remote by another 25 per cent, perhaps having a sliding scale right down to those with only external preferences. But how we decide on these percentages would appear to be quite arbitrary.

To avoid this utilitarianism would need a supplementary criterion of value in addition to preferences, to exclude immoral preferences. But then this poses the same problem as special responsibilities, like justice, in that at times, as in the paedophile case, it would have to overrule utility and maximization. The same issues are raised with the problem of needs and whether they should count for more than mere preferences. A large number of people may have 'mere' preferences, say for a second car, but should this outweigh the very strong preferences that a smaller number have for their needs, like food and shelter, if preference maximization dictates this?

We all easily recognize that some preferences, like food and shelter, are just more fundamental and we ought to satisfy these before mere preferences, like the convenience of having more than one car. But utilitarianism has no special place for needs and the priority of meeting them first. It is simply a

question of adding up preferences and if preference maximization dictates that other preferences should be met instead, then that is the moral thing to do. It cannot even account for our intuition about the importance of needs by arguing that these are our strongest preferences. We can have strong preferences for things that are not fundamental to survival or to alleviate suffering, but which outweigh our preferences for things that are.

We cannot even argue that if we enjoy it when we get it, that's what we 'really' want; implying that in some sense this is what we need. It may be our desire for it is merely the effect of being in that state that this thing puts us in. A heroin addict wants his next fix more than anything he can imagine, but, although a very strong desire, we can argue without contradiction that this is not what he 'needs'. To take it is to want it strongly: the state it creates in turn creates the desire. Someone who belongs to a religious sect that demands strict conformity and heavily indoctrinates its members is being made to want to be a member of the sect by belonging to it.

As you can see there are different notions at work here; different things we need to consider:

not just 1. what we *want* – preferences;
   but   2. what we *think* we want;
          3. what we would want if we knew all the *facts*;
          4. what is in our best *interests*;
   and   5. what we *need*.

Any solution to the problems preference utilitarianism creates needs to be able to take these distinctions into account. But to do so involves a radical departure from narrowly conceived preference utilitarianism. It would mean no longer just accepting 'brute' preferences, but instead some form of preference management, a means of processing them to see what they 'really' mean. In effect we would get behind preferences and maximization and again evaluate them in terms of a supplementary criterion of value. Bernard Williams describes this as 'Government House Utilitarianism', in that we no longer just accept preferences on their face value, but evaluate them paternalistically.

By now it will be clear that, although preference utilitarianism accounts for an important part of what we ordinarily do when we think morally, it still leaves untouched much of what we normally regard as morality. We ought to try to maximize as many preferences as possible in any situation, but this is not all there is to it. Moral behaviour can occur on two levels. On the ordinary or obligatory level certain actions are morally required: for example, that we should not steal or kill others. But on the extraordinary or 'supererogatory' level people do things because they make things better, even though they are not morally required to do so: for example, a person might risk her life to save another. Many supererogatory acts are driven by moral ideals that don't hold for everyone. They are not obligatory. So, the difference between obligatory and supererogatory moral behaviour can be said to rest on four key characteristics.

1. Supererogatory actions are optional – neither prohibited nor prescribed by ordinary morality.

2. They exceed the expectations of ordinary morality.

3. They are intended to promote the welfare of others.

4. And they are morally good actions.

As preference utilitarianism is driven by the need to maximize preference satisfaction, it finds it difficult to account for such behaviour. Even so, there are those who do in fact argue that such behaviour poses no problem at all for preference utilitarianism, because supererogatory actions are merely the maximization of the preferences of all. There is no reason why we should regard preference utilitarianism from an egoistic point of view as just maximizing our own preferences. It can and perhaps rightly should be seen as a universalistic doctrine.

But then this poses another problem. The preference utilitarian cannot make a distinction between what is morally required of us and what is a supererogatory action. Ultimately they are the same in that they both merely aim to maximize preference satisfaction. But this means whenever we see the possibility of maximizing preference satisfaction we are *obligated* to so act and this may involve what we would normally regard as supererogatory actions. As the Australian philosopher Peter Singer argues, for example, we must give away our income to famine relief charities until we reach the point when our marginal suffering – the suffering we will experience when we donate the next penny – is equal to the marginal suffering of the recipient.

Brief lives
Singer, Peter

Dates: 1946–
Born: Melbourne, Australia
Best known for: The major influence he has exerted in promoting the cause of animal rights. He argues that speciesism is no different from racism or sexism in that all identify morally irrelevant characteristics as the basis for discrimination.

Major works: *Animal Liberation* (1975), *Practical Ethics* (1979), *How Are We To Live* (1995), *Rethinking Life and Death: The Collapse of Our Traditional Ethics* (1996), *One World: The Ethics of Globalization* (2002).

In other words, morality is driven by marginal utility: only when the marginal utility of the donator is equal to the marginal utility of the recipient do we maximize utility or preference satisfaction.

But for most people this seems to be an impossible moral obligation. Preference utilitarianism simply appears to be demanding too much. It has made supererogatory actions into our everyday moral obligations. Peter Singer, however, would argue that this assessment is wrong. It may only *seem* impossible, when in fact it is just *difficult*, and nobody said that moral behaviour was going to be easy.

1.4 Moral pluralism

It seems, therefore, that preference utilitarianism is rather like Goldilocks' porridge: either it is too narrow, excluding much that we normally regard as morality, or it is too wide, demanding that we accept supererogatory actions as our normal moral obligations. It has the advantage of sidestepping many of the problems posed by hedonism, but it does so by leaving us with an account of moral thinking that is not completely persuasive.

But if hedonistic and preference utilitarianism struggle to work satisfactorily because they are grounded in something (pleasure and preferences) that is not rich enough to account for all our moral behaviour, then perhaps we ought to look at the broader more inclusive ideas of ideal utilitarianism represented in the theory of moral pluralism. This maintains there is no single goal or state constituting the good. There are many values besides happiness that possess intrinsic worth: friendship, knowledge, beauty, health, courage, love, fairness. All of these are good in themselves, independent of any pleasurable consequences. With this the principle of utility dictates that an action's rightness or wrongness should be assessed in terms of the greatest aggregate good produced, which is determined by multiple intrinsic goods. As G. E. Moore argues, one outcome is better overall than another when it contains a greater amount of intrinsically valuable things than another.

One of the apparent advantages of this is that it seems to solve the problem of justice. Equality or just distribution can be seen as an intrinsic good to be promoted for its own sake. But as Frankena points out, this may be to confuse 'rightness' with 'goodness'. Fairness may not be a good in itself, like beauty, knowledge or pleasure, but simply the right state to bring about, in this case a fair distribution of what is good. And this points to a more general problem with this theory: it is difficult to agree on what is objectively valuable. Different people find value in different things.

Indeed, it's doubtful whether we can in fact claim that anything is objectively valuable; if it were there is every reason to expect science to have discovered it already. For example, we might argue that beauty is objectively or intrinsically valuable, but not if nobody sees it. And as long as its value depends upon its effects on people, it can no longer be described as objectively valuable. Can knowledge be intrinsically valuable or is this too dependent upon the effects upon someone who has it or on the world in terms of what we can do with it? This explains the popularity of the two previous theories in that we are inclined to think what is of value is getting what we want. Pleasure is good because and only because we want it; beauty is good because and only because we want it.

Finally, in practical terms this theory gets us back to our original problems with hedonistic utilitarianism. Each action can be justified by reference to radically different utilities, so how are we to measure and compare these? To compare the actions of two different people we need some non-arbitrary, interpersonal measure, otherwise we are no farther forward than the same problems we faced in measuring and comparing pleasures and pains.

■ 2. Virtue ethics

This brings us back to a question we put aside earlier, whether happiness is really the aim of all human life and the ultimate appeal for all ethical questions. In deontological ethics we saw just how difficult it is in any complex situation to specify the relevant principles and then decide which of them is overriding when they come into conflict. In consequentialism we have seen how difficult it is to identify all the consequences of an action and then to measure and weigh one set against another. So, it seems, all we can do is rely upon our own moral characters to come to the best moral decision in any situation. At least this is the conclusion of those philosophers who have embraced virtue ethics.

Coming to the best moral decision involves taking a look at our moral characters and trying to develop them in accordance with the most important virtues. So the primary moral question is not about performing one's duty, nor about maximizing the greatest possible good in any situation, but one of character: acting as a good person ought to; living up to the best of what we are. The important questions, therefore, are,

1.   What sort of persons are we, or are we becoming?

2.   Which virtues ought to take precedence?

3.   How do we show these virtues ourselves or bring them forth in others?

In virtue ethics the notion of character involves a set of stable traits that affect our judgements and actions. These can be cultivated in us. A virtue is a trait of character which is valued by the society in which we live. They are, as Beauchamp and Childress describe it, 'habituated character traits', dispositions to act in accordance with one's moral goals. Nevertheless, it is not enough that these character traits or virtues should merely be valued by society, they must be supported by moral reasons: they must be justifiable in terms of morally acceptable values. Although Aristotle thought the classical virtues (courage, justice, temperance, wisdom and prudence) depended on the social context, he believed all rational beings will always admire them.

In the medieval Christian world there were seven cardinal virtues – faith, hope, charity, prudence, temperance, justice and fortitude – along with seven deadly sins – pride, wrath, envy, lust, gluttony, avarice and sloth. These have been added to in the modern world as a result of the rise of capitalism in the nineteenth century and the influence of the Protestant work ethic and the 'self-help philosophy' of writers like Samuel Smiles. Consequently, we are inclined to emphasize virtues like independence, self-reliance, responsibility, self-discipline, hard work, prudence, fortitude, perseverance, pride and courage. In the twentieth century no doubt the rise of the Welfare State promoted a different set of virtues, like compassion, benevolence, sensitivity, generosity, charity, patience, nurturing and honesty. Out of this some have argued there is a central core of virtues that make up a virtuous character: compassion, discernment (sensitivity), trustworthiness, integrity (having a coherent, integrated set of core convictions and being actively faithful to them) and conscientiousness.

But whatever the core virtues might be, this is not incompatible with the deontological notions of duty and obligation. A person with a morally good character needs to be guided by moral rules. Goodness without the tools necessary for analysis and insight is not enough to reach the right decision in any complex situation. But, whereas for the consequentialist and deontologist virtue is only a means serving certain ends, enabling us to bring about good consequences or perform certain duties, in virtue ethics the relationship is reversed. Virtue is the result of, and is the source of ultimate reasons for, happiness, duty and practical reason. Virtue is the end, not the means.

This view of ethics can be traced back to the ancient Greeks, particularly Plato in *The Republic* and Aristotle in *Nicomachean Ethics*. However, although Aristotle is often regarded as a typical model, his is not the purest of models for modern supporters of virtue ethics, for whom, as we have seen, virtue is the source of ultimate reasons for happiness, duty and practical reason. For Aristotle the fundamental concept is '*eudaimonia*', or human flourishing. When, as in some modern accounts, the equation between flourishing and virtue is broken, when virtue alone is the single fundamental concept, the approach is different. Nevertheless, Aristotle's theory does give us the fullest, most developed account of what we would expect a theory of virtue ethics to look like.

According to the ancient Greeks the good life is a life of virtue and any action is right only when it is in accordance with virtue. The foundation of ethics, therefore, lies in what constitutes the good life for man, with the content of ethics being the virtues that such a life entails. So the key problem is how we determine what the good life is for a man. Once we know this we can address our central concern, the character of human agents and the virtues it should possess. One answer, of course, is that the good life is one full of happiness. Aristotle describes happiness as the most desirable of all good things. It is the end at which all actions are aimed. Final and self-sufficient it depends upon nothing else for the justification of its importance.

But to Aristotle happiness means more than mere pleasure. Pleasure comes from the satisfaction of desires: getting what you want and wanting what you get. But happiness comes from the fulfilment of the person. And what is good for a thing, what leads to its fulfilment, depends upon what type of thing it is. So for the good life we must know what type of thing we are. We all have needs, desires and appetites. We pursue goals. We have ambitions and ideals. And we share with other things similar capacities. Like plants and animals we have nutritive capacities: we ingest and process nutrients. We also share with other animals appetitive capacities: desires for food, water and sex. But what sets us apart from nature is our capacity to make free and conscious choices. What is unique and peculiar to us, higher than all other capacities, is our capacity to reason. Reason is nature functioning at the highest level. It is characteristic of us and our highest capacity. Therefore, the good life, the life of fulfilment, is the life of excellence in this capacity. And this is what we call the life of virtue.

As you can see the key elements of Aristotle's argument reflect what most of us believe. We generally believe that our fulfilment is not to be found in the bodily or animal side of our nature, but in our rational side. Indeed we define fulfilment in just these terms. We don't merely *do* things, we have a *conception* of what we do and why, and of ourselves as doing it. We regard ourselves as fulfilled when we approve of ourselves and the qualities we possess, which are usually those we most admire in others.

But still why should this involve leading a good life, a life of virtue? The answer, according to Aristotle, is simple: because 'virtuous activities or their opposites are what constitute happiness or the reverse.' Happiness is 'an activity of the soul in accordance with virtue.' Therefore, only the virtuous are happy. As for why we should want to be happy, Aristotle argues this is an ultimate end, the goal to which all else is a means. But while you can aim directly at pleasure, you cannot aim directly at happiness. This, as we saw earlier, is what is described as the 'Paradox of Hedonism'. John Stuart Mill argues, you can experience it *en passant* in the process of pursuing other things – personal goals, values, ideals. Happiness comes when you don't aim at it directly, when you're content with what you have done and who you are.

But what does this mean in practical terms? After all, ethics is not just concerned with theory; it is practical reason concerned with questions about how we should act in any particular situation. If our ultimate goal is happiness and this only comes through acting virtuously, we must learn how to do this. Aristotle argues that moral virtues are not given us by nature; we acquire them by first exercising them, through proper training in which we develop certain habits and the right dispositions to act in virtuous ways. We become virtuous by acting virtuously. He explains, 'states of character arise out of like activities.'

So, we must examine the nature of our actions because these determine the nature of our character. We must learn to exercise our character traits in a virtuous way. For this there are some general principles, the most important of which is the 'Golden Mean' – the key to using our practical reason. This is the principle that the virtuous nature of our actions and therefore our character can be destroyed by a deficiency or excess of any particular character trait. Excess and deficiency in these both constitute a vice, while the mean between them is a virtue. While eating and drinking is good for our health, too little destroys it as does too much. It is good to keep fit, but too much fitness training can destroy our health just as easily as too little. And this applies equally to all those actions that affect our moral characters. Temperance is a good thing, but too much pleasure results in self-indulgence, while too much abstinence results in insensitivity. Likewise, too little courage results in cowardice, too much in rashness. All such virtues are destroyed by excess and deficiency, but preserved by the mean. And when we have pleasure in acting virtuously in this way, this is a sign that the virtuous disposition has been acquired.

The focus of this, then, is how we manage our passions and our faculties when we act. These are given us by nature: we're not praised or blamed for our capacity to feel strong passions. But we *acquire* our moral character ourselves, and we are praised and blamed for the way our character controls our passions. We can be blamed if we feel anger violently or too weakly, and praised if we feel it moderately. In this way we let our anger work the way it should. Aristotle says, 'every virtue or excellence both brings into good condition the thing of which it is the excellence and makes the work of that thing be done well.'

Moral virtues, therefore, are concerned with feeling passions, like fear, confidence, appetite, anger, pity, not too much and not too little. Anyone can give and spend money, but to do this to benefit the right person, to the right extent, at the right time, with the right motive, and in the right way is the mean, the intermediate, the virtuous. Virtue, then, is a kind of mean; it aims at what is intermediate. It is possible to fail in many ways, but only possible to succeed in one way. To miss the mark is easy; to hit it is difficult. Aristotle says, 'men are good in but one way, but bad in many.'

In the following table you can see the mean for many of our passions and faculties, along with the many ways we can miss the mark.

Table 23.1   Missing the mark

Deficiency	Mean	Excess
Cowardice	Courage	Rashness
Self-indulgence	Temperance	Insensitivity
Prodigality or waste	Liberality or charity	Meanness or stinginess
Niggardliness	Magnificence or extravagance of living	Tastelessness or vulgarity
Humility	Pride	Vanity
Irascibility or bad temper	Anger or good temper	Too easy going a nature
Lying	Truthfulness	Boastfulness
Quarrelsomeness or surliness	Friendliness	Obsequiousness or flattery
Boorishness	Wittiness	Buffoonery
Bashfulness	Modesty	Shamelessness

Virtue ethics has certain obvious advantages over the other theories we have examined. It is not so concerned with just one aspect of moral decision making – the consequences of what we do or the principles according to which we act – but with the whole individual and the judgement we exercise. It promotes an understanding of the way we manage those passions which so often feature in situations and which most of us get wrong at least some of the time: passions like temperance, pride, courage and temper. In complex situations, where it is difficult to work out all the consequences of actions or decide between conflicting principles, it may be that all we can rely upon is our judgement and skills in managing these things.

Nevertheless, we still need to know how a virtuous moral agent thinks when she considers a course of action, without it being in terms of consequences or duties, either of which would then become pre-eminent. When we have dealings with a person we don't know well, we should both probably take seriously the sort of rights and procedures the other two theories advocate. We cannot rely upon the other person's character, which we know nothing about, so the only thing we can both rely upon is our shared belief in these interpersonal rules and procedures. What's more, good characters can always make mistakes, so we all need rules and procedures to guide our judgements. Aristotle gives us the example of anger. He says it is not always easy to determine how, with whom, on what provocation and for how long, to be angry, because we sometimes praise those who fall short of the mean and call them good-tempered, while at the same time we praise those who get angry and call them manly.

Yet perhaps the most difficult of all problems lies in a paradox of which we, and indeed the ancient Greeks, are all acutely aware. Even though Aristotle argues that a life of virtue is the highest goal for mankind, a life in which we flourish as the kind of being we are, we all know that the cheat who ignores all this seems to prosper at the expense of the good man. Those who cheat and swindle their way to wealth, power and success seem to have all we could possibly need to be happy, while those who trudge the moral path are likely to be taken advantage of as they strive for justice and treat others as they would like to be treated themselves. Nevertheless, what appears to escape us as we hustle about our lives with little time to reflect, is that, as Aristotle argues, cheating destroys the very thing that makes happiness possible – our self-respect. Who can genuinely respect a victory won by foul means? Least of all can we convince ourselves, when we reflect on it, that what we have done deserves our own respect.

What's more, those with virtuous characters, who commit themselves to others, deal fairly with those they meet, stand up for justice and good causes, and are temperate in their ways, are more likely to be surrounded by long-lasting, durable relationships. For them relationships are about genuine respect and affection, not about what they can get out of them, to be discarded as soon as they are spent. They are prepared to commit themselves for the long-term and are rewarded for that.

And perhaps more important still, while they may be more vulnerable to those who seek to exploit and take advantage of them, they are much better able to cope with this. Those who take the easiest and most lucrative path, say the coward who avoids all dangers, returning from war to tell his tales, or the businessman who carefully calculates his way out of a difficult situation, cheating others as he goes, ending up with his vast fortune intact, fail to develop the qualities that enable them to survive bad luck. As Roger Scruton points out, 'The courageous person is likely to surmount the dangers which might also destroy him; whatever his luck, he is better placed to emerge from trials in a happy frame of mind than the coward who avoids them.' The virtuous character has indeed inculcated the dispositions which will lead to fulfilment while at the same time leaving him vulnerable to exploitation, but only by developing the means of overcoming this. As Scruton suggests, the clue to moral education for us as it was for Aristotle is that while 'We cannot guarantee good luck for our children ... we can do our best to ensure that bad luck will not destroy them.'

■ 3. Conclusion

In each of these approaches to ethics – deontology, consequentialism and virtue ethics – we have seen different ways of answering the problem of how we are to lead moral lives. Each one you may think answers part of the question, some more complete than others. You may think rational egoism, or Kantian ethics, or Hume's and Rousseau's theories have the greater part of the answer. Alternatively, you may be convinced that the thing that matters above all in moral matters is consequences. In this case you may be keen to embrace the approach advocated by hedonistic utilitarians, or moral pluralists, like G. E. Moore, or preference utilitarianism of the kind developed by R. M. Hare. Failing this you may believe the virtue ethicists, like Aristotle, have the answer. But whichever you side with,

Timeline:

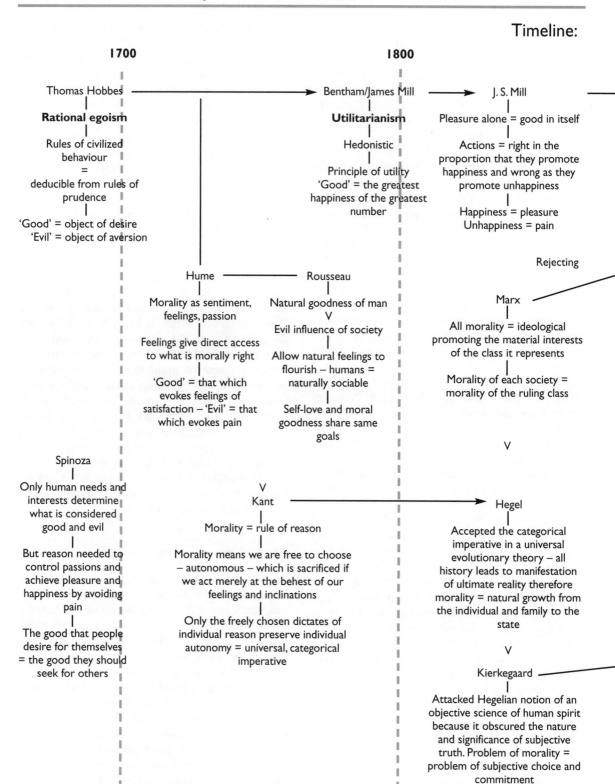

1700

1800

Thomas Hobbes ⟶ Bentham/James Mill ⟶ J. S. Mill

Rational egoism

Rules of civilized
behaviour
=
deducible from rules of
prudence

'Good' = object of desire
'Evil' = object of aversion

Utilitarianism

Hedonistic

Principle of utility
'Good' = the greatest
happiness of the greatest
number

Pleasure alone = good in itself

Actions = right in the
proportion that they promote
happiness and wrong as they
promote unhappiness

Happiness = pleasure
Unhappiness = pain

Rejecting

Hume ⟶ Rousseau

Morality as sentiment,
feelings, passion

Feelings give direct access
to what is morally right

'Good' = that which
evokes feelings of
satisfaction – 'Evil' = that
which evokes pain

Natural goodness of man
V
Evil influence of society

Allow natural feelings to
flourish – humans =
naturally sociable

Self-love and moral
goodness share same
goals

Marx

All morality = ideological
promoting the material interests
of the class it represents

Morality of each society =
morality of the ruling class

V

Spinoza

Only human needs and
interests determine
what is considered
good and evil

But reason needed to
control passions and
achieve pleasure and
happiness by avoiding
pain

The good that people
desire for themselves
= the good they should
seek for others

V
Kant ⟶ Hegel

Morality = rule of reason

Morality means we are free to choose
– autonomous – which is sacrificed if
we act merely at the behest of our
feelings and inclinations

Only the freely chosen dictates of
individual reason preserve individual
autonomy = universal, categorical
imperative

Accepted the categorical
imperative in a universal
evolutionary theory – all
history leads to manifestation
of ultimate reality therefore
morality = natural growth from
the individual and family to the
state

V

Kierkegaard

Attacked Hegelian notion of an
objective science of human spirit
because it obscured the nature
and significance of subjective
truth. Problem of morality =
problem of subjective choice and
commitment

Ethics

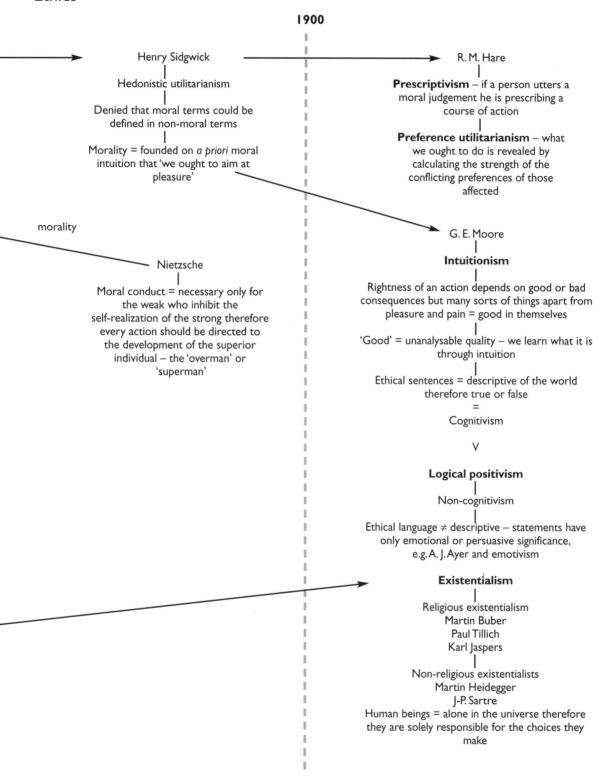

1900

Henry Sidgwick

Hedonistic utilitarianism

Denied that moral terms could be defined in non-moral terms

Morality = founded on *a priori* moral intuition that 'we ought to aim at pleasure'

morality

Nietzsche

Moral conduct = necessary only for the weak who inhibit the self-realization of the strong therefore every action should be directed to the development of the superior individual – the 'overman' or 'superman'

R. M. Hare

Prescriptivism – if a person utters a moral judgement he is prescribing a course of action

Preference utilitarianism – what we ought to do is revealed by calculating the strength of the conflicting preferences of those affected

G. E. Moore

Intuitionism

Rightness of an action depends on good or bad consequences but many sorts of things apart from pleasure and pain = good in themselves

'Good' = unanalysable quality – we learn what it is through intuition

Ethical sentences = descriptive of the world therefore true or false
=
Cognitivism

V

Logical positivism

Non-cognitivism

Ethical language ≠ descriptive – statements have only emotional or persuasive significance, e.g. A. J. Ayer and emotivism

Existentialism

Religious existentialism
Martin Buber
Paul Tillich
Karl Jaspers

Non-religious existentialists
Martin Heidegger
J-P. Sartre
Human beings = alone in the universe therefore they are solely responsible for the choices they make

let it not obscure your role in all this. You may be new to the theory, but not to the subject. You have your own experiences of moral life, which yield new and valuable insights for improving our understanding of moral thinking. Your contribution is as valuable as any.

■ Questions

1. 'We should never let our conscience get in the way of doing the right thing.' Discuss.

2. Can we argue that some people are morally better than others, or are they just different?

3. Are utilitarians right to argue that the only measure of right and wrong is the greatest happiness of the greatest number?

4. Should we keep our promises even when doing so would be worse than the consequences of breaking them?

5. As we can never really know the full consequences of an action, does this mean that we are wrong to judge whether it is right or wrong on the basis of its consequences?

6. If you can treat 50 geriatric patients for the cost of one heart transplant, wouldn't it be more humane to care for the 50 rather than the one?

7. Am I right always to choose to benefit a friend just because she is a friend, rather than a stranger, when I have the choice to do the same amount of good to either, but not both of them?

■ Recommended reading

Aristotle. *Nicomachean Ethics*, trans. W. D. Ross (Oxford: Oxford University Press, 1925).

Beauchamp, T. L. and J. F. Childress. *Principles of Biomedical Ethics* (Oxford: Oxford University Press, 2001). See Chapter 2 for virtue ethics.

Frankena, W. K. *Ethics* (Englewood Cliffs, NJ: Prentice-Hall, 1973).

Hare, R. M. *Moral Thinking* (Oxford: Clarendon, 1981).

Mill, J. S. Utilitarianism. In *Utilitarianism, On Liberty and Considerations on Representative Government* (London: Dent, 1972).

Smart, J. J. C. and Bernard Williams. *Utilitarianism For and Against* (Cambridge: Cambridge University Press, 1973).

The note structure to accompany this chapter can be downloaded from our website.

Politics: Legitimacy and the State

CHAPTER 24

Key issues

▶ What sort of obligation do we have to obey the state and comply with its laws? What justifies us in accepting this obligation and in giving a government power over us?

▶ What do we mean by 'obligation' and how does this differ from being 'obliged' to do something?

▶ We claim that governments are 'legitimate', but what do we mean by this and how do we ensure that they exercise their powers 'legitimately'?

▶ Are there any conceivable circumstances in which we would be justified in refusing to obey the law?

▶ Does there exist in society an underlying set of power relations in which men have power over women?

▶ Are feminists right to believe that politics doesn't just stop at the front door: it is part of every aspect of men's relations with women?

Contents

In the last three chapters our focus has been on the restrictions to our freedom we voluntarily accept as part of our moral responsibilities to those with whom we live. These are internal, self-imposed obligations and duties. But, as we all know, we have other obligations and duties, which are political, imposed on us externally by the state. Politics is concerned with the study of the power and authority states have to do this: the limits, sources and goals of political power, the relationships between rulers and ruled, and the sources and justification of authority. In the next four chapters we will consider the different forms of government, the aims and purposes that politicians claim to be the paramount concern of the state, and the different political theories that go to justify their use of power to achieve these aims.

But first, to avoid all manner of common confusion it is worth drawing a distinction between forms of government and political theories. Put simply, forms of government are concerned with the *way* governments are organized, rather than what they are organized *for*, what they set out to achieve. In other words, forms of government are concerned with issues like the relationship between the rulers and the ruled, the rights of individuals, the distribution of power and authority, the extent of power and how it is controlled and legitimized.

In contrast, political theories are concerned with the ideals, values and ultimate aims of governments, and these are shaped by their underlying philosophical assumptions about issues like the nature of man, equality, welfare, freedom and what is thought to be the ideal, in some cases, the 'utopian' society. We might say that while forms of government are the engine, the locomotive, the means of achieving political goals, political theories are the map describing the route the locomotive must take and its destination. It's not surprising, therefore, to find political theories with very little in common, like communism and fascism, adopting the same form of government.

With that bit of housekeeping behind us we can examine what exactly we mean by a 'form of government'. As a concept it combines two ideas: not just the extent of power held by those in government, but the legitimacy of their possession of that power and the way they use it. Each form of government reflects the way they deal with these two issues. In democracies, for example, governments legitimize their use of power by appealing to popular consent, while autocracies see popular consent as broadly irrelevant. As for the extent of power, liberal states restrict the power of governments, believing the state to be a necessary evil, while totalitarian states mobilize total power with no distinction between public and private matters, believing that all power is beneficial to improving the condition of citizens.

As you can see from the figure below, combining these two issues in this way allows us to group governments into four forms of government:

a) liberal democracies

b) totalitarian democracies

c) liberal autocracies

d) totalitarian autocracies.

In the following chapters we will examine each of these forms of government in more detail. But first we need to examine the issues raised by the legitimacy and the extent of a state's power.

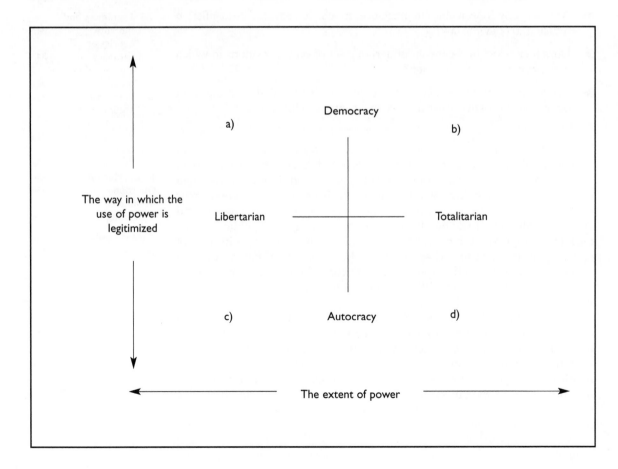

■ 1. Authority, power, legitimacy, force and influence

In Chapter 2 when we analysed the concept of authority we found that it doesn't simply amount to the possession of power alone. We use the word 'power' to describe somebody as having 'force', the capacity to compel us to do something against our wishes. A police officer has this sort of power, but so too does a mugger. The difference is that the police officer also exercises this power 'rightfully': he has the authority to exercise it. We talk about such people as being *in* authority, possessing institutional power. They have been given the authority to exercise such power in a 'legitimate' way, say, by those who have been elected and have democratic legitimacy. We often describe this as having *de jure* or rightful authority.

But we also found that some people, like the art collector, possess a different type of authority. Though she has no power to force us to do something, she is *an* authority, what is often described as having *de facto* authority – authority 'in fact'. We could say she has a 'right' to her authority, although it's a different sense of right from that exercised by the police officer. It's the right that has been *earned* rather than been *given*. In her case it has been earned through long years of study and dedication to her profession. It's also different from the authority of the elected representative, although they can both be described as being 'an' authority.

It also suggests that through the 'force' of her arguments and her 'power' of persuasion, she has the ability to secure voluntary compliance to her way of seeing things without the use of threats or force in the other sense, because she has earned her authority. We could say that we have good 'moral'

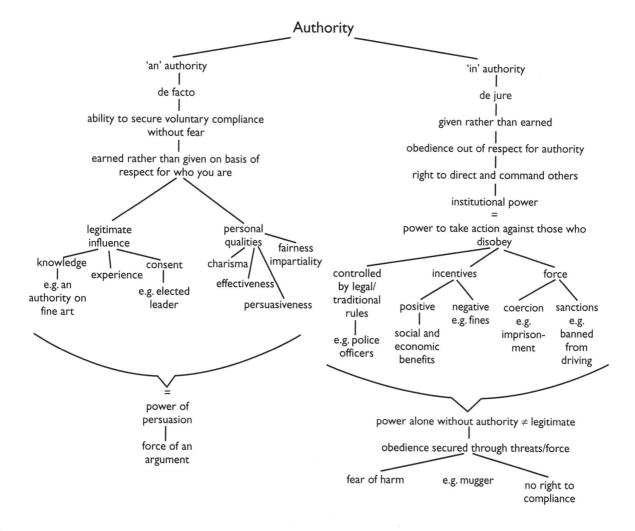

reasons for complying with this sort of authority: that is, we have reasons that convince us to act in this way as a matter of our own free will. Rather than having power in the normal sense, she has 'influence', like so many specialists and those with unique abilities, skills and experience.

In contrast, when we comply with orders of those who are *in* authority, we do so not necessarily because we have any moral reason, that we respect them as individuals or their knowledge and expertise, but because we know that it would be 'prudent' to do so. In this sense we are 'obliged' to obey in much the same way we would be if a mugger threatened to harm us. But the one difference between the mugger and those in authority is that the latter have a rightful authority to issue us with orders and we have an 'obligation' to obey. We have no 'obligation' to obey the mugger, because such threats are not backed by any right to make such orders. We are just 'obliged' to.

■ 2. Legitimacy

As this shows, although the state is the ultimate source of political power, on its own, power is not enough. It must hold that power and use it in a legitimate way. When it does, it can claim to have a right to use its power. It has authority: the rightful exercise of power. Power alone means only that we are 'obliged' to obey. To have an 'obligation' is to accept an order issued by those who have a right to issue it. But what gives this right? What makes the giving of this order legitimate? To answer these questions we must be clear about what we mean by legitimacy and the grounds on which we accept we have a political obligation.

Legitimacy is the process or principle which indicates the public's acceptance of a person who occupies a particular political office, or of the way power is used by a government. We accept that such a process or principle confers authority on individuals or groups, or sanctions the use of power, either generally or in a specific instance. But the normative standards by which we make this judgement arise in a complex way involving various things – conventions, traditions, customs, consent. We will see later in this chapter that there are different theories that justify these standards; some on the grounds of expediency, that stable life would not be possible unless some individual or body exercised such power; some

on the grounds of popular consent; and some arguing that the state is legitimized in its exercise of power because it pursues moral objectives, like justice or the welfare of all. But the normative standards by which we make a judgement are far from simple, as Tony Benn, the British politician and former Labour cabinet minister, demonstrates when he urges us to ask five questions of any powerful person:

1. What power do you have?

2. Where do you get it from?

3. In whose interests do you exercise it?

4. To whom are you accountable?

5. How can we get rid of you?

In liberal democracies we assume the answers to these questions, and the accepted procedure by which governments and their policies are legitimized, lie in elections. But this is not always the most reliable guide. The electoral system might heavily distort the public's sentiments, perhaps because it is dominated by large, influential and wealthy pressure groups. This, in turn, might be compounded by the electorate's disillusionment with the system, which encourages a large proportion to stay away from the polls, leaving a government with the expressed support of only a small minority. If this is the case other empirical indicators can be employed, as they are in autocracies, although these too vary in their degree of reliability. Among them might be the level of coercion that is necessary to implement policies, the number and effectiveness of attempts to overthrow the government or the leader of the government. Other indicators might include the occurrence of civil disobedience, rebellion, civil war and similar disruptions aimed at the government generally or at particular policies, either of which might be considered to lack legitimacy.

2.1 Legitimacy and legality

As you can see from this, legitimacy should not be confused with legality. If they have a majority in the legislature governments can usually pass whatever law they like. But regularly they find themselves passing and implementing what has been described controversially as 'bad' law: that is, law that turns out to be unworkable, because it doesn't command general agreement among the people whom it most affects. For example, many trade unionists defied the industrial relations legislation passed by the British government (1970–74), because they felt it lacked legitimacy. Similarly, the decision of the British government in 1984 to ban trade unions from GCHQ, the centre for electronic surveillance operations, was seen, even by their own supporters, as lacking legitimacy, not only because it denied a minority its fundamental rights, but because the government, by refusing to negotiate and seek a compromise, had ignored accepted procedures that confer legitimacy within democracies.

Of course, the problem that governments face in their interpretation of public opinion is that it is constantly changing. Usually this is imperceptible and sometimes quite rapid, leaving governments seriously out of step with the public. In the late 1960s and early 1970s the American public's support for their government's involvement in Vietnam fell away dramatically, leaving many politicians out of step with public opinion. Large numbers no longer felt the war was legitimate, even though it was still 'legal' in that the Congress had supported it and the South Vietnamese government had invited the American troops in. Similarly, in the early nineteenth century it was both legitimate and legal to sell slaves in Britain, but, as the century progressed, such a practice lost its legitimacy, even though it still retained its legality.

2.2 Legitimacy and consent

But we should not conclude from this that legitimacy is merely synonymous with consent. Although consent is important, (indeed it might be central to every interpretation of the concept), there are other factors that have a strong claim to be considered as a source of legitimacy. Moreover, we can talk of different levels of consent, each with a stronger or weaker claim as a source of legitimacy.

Ultimately all political systems, from democracies to autocracies, depend upon some form of consent, whether it's expressed through elections or in mere acquiescence, the quiet acceptance of injustices or exploitation without organized opposition or civil disobedience. It's true that some regimes, like military dictatorships, have survived principally through their control of the military and the police, but they are usually short-lived. Where

they do survive for longer periods, it could be argued that discontent is not sufficiently strong to produce an organized opposition on a scale large enough to destabilize the regime, which can, therefore, claim to have maintained sufficient legitimacy.

Moreover, we all realize that the importance of consent explains why political parties invest so heavily in 'image consultants', psephologists who can identify the 'target voters' the party needs to convince, and 'spin doctors' who can project the right image. Since the 1960 US presidential election politicians have realized the importance of paying careful attention to how they package and sell themselves on TV. Those who *saw* the televised debate between Nixon and Kennedy in 1960 thought Kennedy had won a close contest, while those who only *listened* on the radio were convinced Nixon had won hands down.

2.3 Other sources of legitimacy

But if consent is not the whole picture, and if there are various levels or forms of consent ranging from clear expressions of opinion to mere acquiescence, we must consider other criteria that are accepted as a source of legitimacy. In aristocratic forms of government the customary deference for traditional authority promotes unquestioning respect for so-called natural leaders, like the military, along with acquiescence in the status quo, even though this might mean limited opportunities for the many and poverty in the midst of great wealth.

Similarly, there are religious and theoretical justifications that have the effect of insulating governments from accountability to popular consent. Theories of kingship, like the 'Divine Right of Kings', which were once important in European systems of government, can be matched in the twentieth century by theocracies, like Iran and other Islamic states. Religious inspiration, rather than popular consent, is the source of legitimacy here. The politics of other states have been guided by what we might describe as theoretical sources of legitimacy. Fascist and communist ideologies both justify government policies and actions by reference to a theory of history interpreted by a natural, charismatic leader, who alone chooses the course the state should follow. In *Darkness at Noon* Koestler describes such a leader, in this case Stalin, as 'the infallible pointsman'.

Even so, we could argue that it is only because

people are persuaded by such theories, traditions and religious authorities that they agree to allow these alternative sources of authority to supplant popular consent. In times of national emergencies, like war or when there is serious internal conflict, people are similarly persuaded to surrender their freedoms 'temporarily' in order to give their leaders the power necessary to cope effectively with the situation. And, of course, most governments are not beyond exploiting a serious situation or manufacturing such concern. In this way they can free themselves of criticism and accountability, which they can claim would only endanger national interests. In George Orwell's *Nineteen Eighty-Four* each day the public are made aware of the threat posed by enemy forces that are constantly on the point of invading. The country is always supposedly at war with some foreign power. There are even suspicions that the government has launched attacks on its own people just to keep up their commitment to the war effort, which leaves no room for criticism and accountability of the government.

To accept such a plea to give governments unaccountable powers to tackle a national emergency in this way is to legitimize, albeit on a temporary basis, an autocratic system of government. Writing just after the English Civil War (1642–51), Thomas Hobbes presents the most celebrated justification of such a government in *Leviathan*. He argues that the major threat to the peace and security of society is the antisocial, aggressive nature of the warring individuals that compose it. The only solution, therefore, is to give unconstrained power to a leader to secure stability and order.

In *The Prince* (1513) Niccolò Machiavelli, the Italian Renaissance politician and author, argues for a similar form of government, but in response to different types of problems. He argues that such a concentration of unconstrained power is justified in order to reform corrupt states. In the modern era this justification has displayed remarkable adaptability, from the overthrew of the Shah in Iran in 1979, supposedly corrupted by decadent western values, to the McCarthyite purges of the 1950s, designed to eradicate all values that were seen as 'un-American'. Similar examples can be found in the Chinese Cultural Revolution of 1966–69, the purges of the 1930s in the Soviet Union, and even the military coup in Nigeria in 1985, where the military overthrew the civilian government, because of the corruption that was evident throughout

government departments, involving ministers and officials. Determined to eradicate it, the military government introduced its anti-corruption campaign WAI ('War Against Indiscipline').

All these arguments attempt to legitimize on the grounds of efficiency a policy of giving the government unaccountable power to tackle problems. It is argued that this is the only effective way of dealing with the emergency. A similar argument can be seen in the acceptance of science and technology in modern government. In the eyes of some this is transforming democracies into technocracies or bureaucracies. As more and more of modern government is dominated by theoretical approaches, in areas like economic management and military planning, power shifts from the elected government to the new technocratic elite. Governments, and therefore the electorates, surrender decisions to the technocrats, the guardians of the new theoretical knowledge, 'the new priesthood' as Ralph Lapp describes them. Efficiency demands that the experts, not the unqualified elected amateurs, make such complex, technical decisions.

In the past a similar argument has been made for gerontocracies: that power should reside with the elderly who have more experience and a wealth of wisdom denied the young and the majority of the community.

So, to summarize:

As you can see we have identified a number of criteria upon which legitimacy might be based:

1. Popular consent.
2. Tradition.
3. Political and religious theories:
   3.1 Theories of kingship e.g. the Divine Right of Kings.
   3.2 Theories of history e.g. fascism and communism.
   3.3 Religious authority e.g. Islamic states.
4. Efficiency:
   4.1 In times of crisis.
   4.2 To reform corrupt states.
   4.3 Technocracy – technocratic expertise.
   4.4 Gerontocracy – the wisdom of the elderly.

2.4 Legitimacy and morality

But to say that this is all there is to the components that make up legitimacy would be to overlook important moral factors, which are usually thought to have a significance that transcends all other criteria. Irrespective of the form of government and the source of legitimacy, we would still argue that a government's policies are not legitimate if they ignore certain moral absolutes, certain rights that are held to be fundamental to all individuals, like the right to representation or to family life. For example, if a government were convinced by the latest scientific findings that it could improve the health of the community by preventing marriage and breeding between all those who fail government-imposed tests that measure their physical fitness and intelligence, such a policy, we would no doubt argue, infringes accepted moral values and rights, and therefore lacks legitimacy.

Equally, as we saw in the GCHQ example, the procedures that a government adopts, the way it acts, can raise similar moral objections. If it acts capriciously or arbitrarily without treating all sections of society with equal fairness; if it deliberately conceals its actions; if it lies or even if it just fails to reveal crucial information that is unfavourable to it; or if it fails to allow for adequate representation and pursues confrontation, rather than compromise; in all these cases, regardless of whether the policies are popular or not, we are likely to conclude the government's policies lack legitimacy.

No matter how popular a policy may be, if it discriminates against a minority, or denies individuals their human rights, or withholds information in order to conceal its actions, we would argue that it lacks legitimacy. The democratic and popular Nazi Government of the Third Reich passed the Nuremberg Laws in 1935, which discriminated against Jews, denying them their rights to marry, to work in certain professions and to exercise human freedoms which we now consider to be inviolable. Although the laws appear to have been supported by the majority, we are still likely to argue that they lacked legitimacy, and that those who opposed them in order to rescue Jews, or resorted to civil disobedience and other forms of protest, were right to do so, because the laws unfairly discriminated against a minority.

■ 3. Theories of legitimacy

Unless we've chosen to become members of a state by becoming naturalized citizens, we have no choice about whether or not to obey its laws. It is natural, therefore, to ask why I should obey the rules that govern the way the state goes about its business, when I have not freely chosen to do so. As we have seen, power alone is not enough to describe the state: it must have legitimate power; it must have authority. But where and how does it get this? This is no longer just a question about particular governments and their policies, but whole systems of government to which we are subject the moment we are born without having any say in it.

So, a central issue in political philosophy concerns the grounds of political obligation: 'Why should I accept political obligation to a state?'; 'What makes a state's power legitimate?'; 'What gives it its authority?' Like three concentric circles, there are three levels of generality on which we can examine the problems of legitimacy and authority. The first is how a particular government is shown to be legitimate in the policies it pursues. A second and higher level of generality is how a certain form of government is legitimate: say, a liberal democracy or a totalitarian democracy. And third, on the highest level, lies the question of the legitimacy of the state itself.

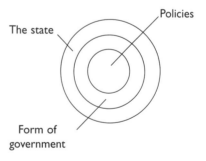

So far we have been largely concerned with legitimacy on the first level: whether a government's policies are legitimate and on what grounds. We must now turn our focus onto the other two levels: to the legitimacy of particular forms of government and of the state. In particular we must ask why it is legitimate for the state to demand and expect us to accept the obligation to comply with its laws when all that has happened is that we have been born within its territory. We can gather the different theories that give us an answer to this question into four main groups: divine right theory, force theory, voluntary acceptance theories, and moral purpose theories.

3.1 Divine right theory

In the medieval world the church taught a Christian cosmology that depicted a divinely ordered, hierarchically system. At the centre of the universe was the earth surrounded by concentric circles or crystalline spheres inhabited by the planets and the constellations of stars, along with divine beings – angels, archangels and seraphim – reaching up into heaven and to God himself. From antiquity a theory of classification of all things, known as 'The Great Chain of Being', had depicted a world in which all natural things could be arranged into a single vertical chain, with each ascending link one degree superior to the former in its attributes.

The same hierarchical cosmology was replicated in the political and social hierarchy. Kings, bishops, lords and peasants each occupied their appropriate places ordained by God. Kings, queens and emperors were God's representatives, their authority coming directly from Him. Moreover, as it was believed that morality depended on the will of God, to say that the King was divinely invested with authority was at the same time to say that his was moral and not just legal authority. His power, therefore, held its own legitimacy. We saw earlier that when we search for reasons why we should consider someone *an* authority or, as in this case, why we should obey the commands of a political leader or acknowledge the authority of the state, we look for moral reasons. But if the sovereign is the representative of God, the fountain of all moral wisdom, we need look no further.

However, in our own more secular world, where it is no longer thought plausible to argue that the sovereign is the manifestation of the will of God, some other way is needed to give moral justification for political authority. It is interesting that in the twentieth century the rise of totalitarian forms of government included a similar idea of a leader with charismatic authority and superior moral judgement, which qualified him alone to guide the nation towards its moral goals. His use of power had likewise its own in-built

moral justification, in that he was the one person capable of attaining the highest moral ends.

3.2 Force theory

Although Thomas Hobbes was not writing in a secular age, the theory he develops in *Leviathan* defines the problem in secular terms. It is for this reason, no doubt, that he was blamed for causing the Great Fire of London and the Great Plague, and was refused permission to print works on human conduct in Britain again. As a result, it's not surprising to find that he was buried beneath a stone slab that says simply, 'Thomas Hobbes – a famous and original philosopher, known abroad.' He was born in 1588 at the time when fear gripped the land with the coming of the Spanish Armada. This gave him, he said later, an intense desire for peace, because 'he and fear had been twins.' The preservation of peace, he believed, was the primary goal of politics which alone justified the use of power and gave sovereigns their authority.

As we saw earlier, writers like Hobbes and Machiavelli believe that the essence of a state is power, and that political events are determined by the struggle for power. Individuals are forced through the fear of uncontrolled aggression of others to accept the authority of an absolute ruler, whose primary obligation is to preserve peace and security. Both confront the moral dilemma of a world in which a just and innocent individual can be destroyed unless he acts to preserve himself. In a state of nature men are in a desperate condition; they are perpetually at war with each other; he says, 'there is always war of every one against every one.' If two men desire something they cannot both have, they become enemies and set about destroying or subduing each other. In his famous description he says, life is 'solitary, poor, nasty, brutish, and short.'

This is in sharp contrast to the ideas of John Locke, whose *Two Treatises of Government* (1690) had significant influence in shaping government in Britain after the Glorious Revolution of 1689, which effectively brought about a constitutional monarchy and the first stirrings of a modern democracy. Locke believes man has certain natural rights founded in property, which are inviolable, inalienable and beyond the meddling of governments. In contrast, Hobbes refuses the pretence of discovering political solutions in the highest, unquestionable authority of nature. He argues there are no rights prior to the creation of the state. All rights are created through its authority. Government cannot be created as a result of reason, consent and respect for individual rights. Individuals do not bind themselves together to form a state as a result of consenting to a form of government, but consent because they are *obliged* by their interests. In other words, they do not agree to be obliged out of consent, but consent because they are obliged.

Once you accept Hobbes' account of the nature of man as acquisitive, aggressive and antisocial you are driven to accept the conclusion that there can be no peace and stability unless individuals are compelled through necessity and fear for their lives to surrender their right of self-protection to a third party, a leviathan, a supreme lawgiver with the power to suppress all conflict. 'Covenants, without the sword', he insists, 'are but words, and of no strength to secure a man at all.'

As a result the individual cannot seek protection from the sovereign by appealing to his inalienable rights. Each act of the sovereign is, by virtue of the transference of my right to the sovereign, *my* act. So there can be no safeguards or limits on state authority, no bill of rights or separation of powers. To set such safeguards would mean we would have to create a power greater than the sovereign. Any adequate account of the state must include only one concentrated power of the last resort, supreme, unified, encompassing all legal and political authority. This is a contract made between individuals who are in a state of war and in desperate need of a common authority to maintain peace.

From the eighteenth to the twentieth century our preoccupation has been with how we are to limit the power of governments through separation of powers, checks and balances, and declarations of individual rights. So our attitude to Hobbes depends largely on where we think the real danger lies: in the state that rules us or in our fellow citizens, Hobbes' warring individuals. For Hobbes the state is a precarious construction, an outgrowth of our warring natures designed not for truth, nor even justice, but to maintain peace and stability. Only if everyone accepts the rules of the sovereign, guaranteed by force, can there be peace. As more than one philosopher has pointed out, although this may seem alien to our liberal democracies with their carefully honed constitutions, this still has important

implications for international relations, which often appear to resemble a state of nature, and for the role of bodies, like the UN, in maintaining peace.

3.3 Voluntary acceptance theories

Although it is used to justify and explain the origins of a very different form of government, Hobbes' account shares with other theories the belief that the relationship between rulers and ruled is a form of mutual and voluntary contract, a 'social contract'.

3.3.1 Social contract theory

However, according to these theories the individual willingly submits to authority, not out of fear and coercion, but out of self-interest: he recognizes that he can maximize his self-interest more effectively within society. Locke in *Two Treatises of Government*, Rousseau in *The Social Contract (Du Contrat Social)*, and Plato in *The Republic* and the *Crito* dialogue, all argue that societies arise and are maintained by individuals voluntarily making a contract among themselves for their mutual benefit. The contract is freely and rationally entered into if each individual benefits from it. Nevertheless, there will be times when our obedience to the rules simply does not pay on an individual level. The contract, therefore, entails the obligation that we must comply with the rules at all times and not just when it suits us.

Nowhere in the literature of philosophy is this more dramatically illustrated than in Plato's *Crito*, set in Socrates' cell after he has been sentenced unjustly to death. Crito, a friend and student of Socrates, attempts to convince him that he can escape from his cell and his unjust fate with the help of his friends to enjoy a long and peaceful life in another country. However, to Crito's surprise Socrates refuses such help, resigning himself to his fate, on the grounds that he has agreed to abide by the laws of Athens and, like all citizens, has benefited from them for many years by being educated and brought up well in peace and freedom. He cannot now renege on this agreement just because things are not going his way.

Whether any of us would have argued similarly might depend upon whether we recognize that we have indeed agreed to a contract committing us to these sorts of obligations. The only citizens who can genuinely be said to have agreed such a contract are those who have migrated from one country to

Brief lives
Socrates

Dates: 469–399BC
Born: Athens, Greece
Best known for: Developing the 'Socratic method', a form of dialogue in which he used a series of probing questions to reveal the meaning and implications of concepts, like virtue, wisdom and knowledge.

Major works: Although he wrote nothing, his ideas were recorded in the works of Plato, Xenophon and Aristotle.

another and become naturalized citizens in the country of their choice. No doubt they have weighed up the pros and cons and agreed to accept the obligations that citizenship entails. Indeed, they take an oath of allegiance to that effect and accept that their citizenship is held on condition of good behaviour. Like any contract the benefits of citizenship can be withdrawn if the contract is broken.

However, this doesn't apply to natural-born citizens. The theory presupposes the freedom to accept or reject the contract, but they had no opportunity to agree to anything before they became citizens. Their citizenship was granted automatically as a result of their birth in the country. So their privileges of citizenship cannot be withdrawn in the same way. The state cannot rightfully withdraw something that has not been granted in the first place.

Nevertheless, the rules of any society are very much like a social contract as a set of principles agreed to in advance as the best way of setting up social life to the benefit of all. Of course, except for those states like the USA and modern France that began life with a signed constitution or bill of rights, to talk of a social contract being signed by all is a historical fiction. And even those states that have a written constitution signed by their founders still bind those members of subsequent generations who have taken no part in the negotiations and have signed nothing. So the idea of a social contract seems to be more a way of generating moral reasons for our continuing commitment to the state and its laws and institutions. If we accept the idea of a social contract we accept that we have made promises, which we have a

stringent moral obligation to keep. As we haven't rationally and voluntarily entered into any such promise, talk of a social contract seems to be an analogous device to generate the continuing commitment of subsequent generations.

3.3.2 The theory of consent

An alternative, watered-down version of the social contract that is closer to our own experience in modern democracies is the theory of consent. This is most closely associated with John Locke, who argues in *Two Treatises of Government*, that 'no one can be ... subjected to the political power of another, without his own consent' and that a person remains in a state of nature outside civil society 'till by their own consents they make themselves members of some politic society.'

Yet in Locke's theory to consent is to make a promise, so this still involves a social contract and the problem we have just examined, that most people cannot strictly be said to have promised anything. Locke's way of meeting this objection is the view that if anyone acquiesces in the laws that are imposed upon him, or someone who has been born within a particular state chooses not to leave, then it can be said that they have consented to those laws and agreed to accept the obligation of abiding by them. Indeed, Plato presents a similar argument in *Crito*.

The question we need to ask, therefore, is whether consent, particularly in this form, can amount to a promise – a commitment to impose a certain obligation on oneself? We make promises and sign contracts, because we have a reason for doing so. Implicit in signing a contract is the promise that we will get something in return, some future benefit. But the mere failure to protest against the state or resist its demands does not seem to amount to a promise. It may be an *indication* of your willingness to accept the social contract, but on its own it gives no reason why you would be willing to do so. You may not agree with the state having the powers it does, but merely fear the consequences of resisting or protesting against it. Or you might simply be too apathetic to consider alternatives. Either way, you could not really be said to have a reason for accepting obligations to the state. Of course, we could say that you have made a 'tacit' promise, but even this fails to work, unless we have good reasons for why you can be supposed to have undertaken the promise.

This is not to say that consent is unimportant. It has a vital role to play, but not it seems in determining whether or not we are obligated to obey the state. It draws attention to the point that we should be free to choose whether or not we will accept the obligation, and not coerced into it. But it doesn't in itself provide the grounds for that obligation, unless consent is to be understood to mean that we are also making a promise, which seems to go beyond what we normally believe to be involved when we consent to something.

3.3.3 The theory of the general will

So we are still left with the problems of a social contract – that members of subsequent generations are bound by it even though they have taken no part in framing it and have made no promise to obey the laws of the state. The only answer appears to lie in some notion of the will of the people that transcends the collection of individual wills of this and all generations, and to which we are obligated though we may not know it. This is precisely the answer found in Rousseau's *The Social Contract*. He maintains that the state is subject to what he calls the 'general will', which is more than simply the sum of individual wills. When we talk about 'the spirit of the age', 'the spirit of the revolution' or 'the discontent of the workers' we are talking not just about the collection or the aggregate of individual spirits or discontents, but something more. In the same way, he agues, all communities have a spiritual identity, which represents the community's 'real' interests as opposed both to the interests of individuals somehow aggregated to represent the interests of the majority and to the interests of powerful sectional groups.

Still, we need to know exactly what Rousseau means by this. It cannot be the will of all citizens, because if everybody wanted the same thing we would have no problem to solve. The problem arises because the demands of the state go beyond the wishes of the individual. As Rousseau says, it's not a question of the state doing what we all want; it sorts through our conflicting wants with a clear eye for what we 'really' want. Giovanni Gentile argues similarly that 'the state is the will of the individual himself in its universal and absolute aspect', and therefore 'since legitimate authority cannot extend beyond the actual will of the individual, authority is resolved completely in liberty.'

Jean-Jacques Rousseau (1712–1778)

Rousseau was born in Geneva and spent most of his life wandering from one place to another and from one job to another. But his immense influence on philosophy comes from the fact that his is the first expression of the revolt of Romanticism against reason and the Enlightenment. Consequently, echoes of Rousseau can be heard throughout the nineteenth century as the various themes of Romanticism are picked up and developed by others: the importance of feelings over reason, the innocence of childhood, the unity of nature with humankind, and the stages human history must go through to achieve true freedom.

The two most influential of Rousseau's writings, *The Social Contract* and *Emile*, both appeared in 1762. *Emile*'s influence on education can still be found today, particularly Rousseau's insistence that the natural tendencies of the child should be fostered and encouraged, not disciplined and regimented. *The Social Contract* too starts from similar premises that the natural tendencies of the individual are good; that individuals are only distorted and deprived of their freedom by the influence of society. As a single individual, if left to her own self-governance, will not 'forge fetters' for herself, so, too, society, as one organic unity, will not enslave itself if its will is acted upon.

Equally it cannot be the will of the majority. Why should the majority be free to impose its will on the minority? We might argue that a majority is closer to what we all want and is more likely to be right. But this is not always the case. A minority can be more experienced and wiser judges of what we want. And anyway the individual can normally be expected to know what he wants without the intervention of the majority.

What's more, the will of the majority carries the very real danger of 'moral populism', what John Stuart Mill describes as 'the tyranny of the prevailing opinion and feeling.' In the history of most nations majority opinion has at times asserted itself arrogantly as right, intolerant of any dissenting opinion. In the 1980s the 'Moral Majority' is reported to have targeted all literature that expressed 'un-American' sentiment, including many of the finest works in the English language. With remarkable prescience for our own time Mill warns in 'On Liberty' that such tyranny of the majority 'practises a social tyranny more formidable than many kinds of political oppression, since, though not usually upheld by such extreme penalties, it leaves fewer means of escape, penetrating much more deeply into the details of life, and enslaving the soul itself.'

The general will, then, is not the sum of all individual wills, or even the will of the majority. Nor is it the product of a non-moral individual simply out for her own interests as in Locke's account. Rousseau conceives it as the product of moral volition, of man as a moral agent. Cast your mind back to the last chapter and you will notice that Rousseau seems to tackle the same problem we saw in Hare's theory of preference utilitarianism. Rousseau sets out to show that what we 'really' want is what we ought to want in the same way that Hare believes he has shown that what we ought to do is what we most prefer to do. Rousseau has an optimistic view of human nature: he believes man is 'naturally good'. It is only contemporary society that has made him selfish and destructive. The function of the state, therefore, is to enable people to develop the 'natural goodness' that they already possess in the absence of any state.

But, as you can also see from this, in aiming to achieve what we 'really' want the state is, in effect, getting us to do what we want to do. This is the key message of The Social Contract: that man must regain his freedom. Rousseau begins with his most famous assertion that 'Man is born free; and everywhere he is in chains.' He can regain his freedom by wanting to do what is good for society. This is what he 'really' wants, because of his natural goodness. The selfish and destructive individual, consumed by what he wants for himself, is in chains. He must, therefore, be taught to want what he 'really' wants. In his 'freedom paradox', one of the most contentious statements in The Social Contract, Rousseau declares that 'Man must be made to be free.'

But what are these 'real' wants? Well, the simple answer is something we want with complete wisdom; otherwise we are quite likely to want something that is not good for us. For Rousseau this means anything that is harmonious with the rest of our wants and with the interests of all. Because the conflict of interests is harmful, the harmony of interests of all is the aim of each citizen. So, the common good is in the general interest of all individuals – it is the 'rational' will, the real or general will. The rational, enlightened individual will realize that his good and the good of each individual lie in the harmony of interests of all. Since the state's aim is to secure the common good, the state and the law are the expression of the general will. If an individual doesn't understand what he 'really' wants and is unwilling to comply, then the state is justified in forcing him to comply.

The paradox inherent in this has coloured the way many have viewed Rousseau's political philosophy. On the one hand his is rightly seen as one of the most important liberal and revolutionary theories of the modern age. He emphasizes the importance of individual freedom and rights even above the state itself. Indeed both Marx and Mill acknowledge their debt to him. Yet his emphasis on the state as an entity in itself with the individual subservient to it has led some to see in his work the origins of totalitarianism.

In truth Rousseau can rightly be described as an advocate of democracy, though not liberal democracy. The source of the paradox lies in the concept of the general will as more than the sum of individual wills, representing the 'real' interests of citizens. Legitimacy, then, is given to the state by the general will, not by each individual. So someone who does not agree with the general will may find himself forced to comply with the state. As Rousseau points out, 'whoever refuses to obey the general will shall be compelled to do so by the whole body. This means nothing less than that he will be forced to be free.'

Whether you believe Rousseau's theory is

successful will depend at least partly on whether you believe we are as individuals naturally the same – that we want the same things – and governments can know what we really want, while we ourselves can be mistaken about it. It would be foolish to deny that there is a fair amount of common ground in our fundamental needs, like education, health, employment and security. But we are immensely complex beings whose nature we have barely scratched the surface of. And, while governments can possess the expertise necessary to solve the efficiency problems of how best to meet many of these fundamental needs, they lack the necessary expertise or superior wisdom to decide how we should best rank these needs in importance or whether we should use our scarce resources to pursue them and not others.

However perhaps the most serious problem is Rousseau's assumption, similar to Hare's, that what we *ought* to do is what we *want* to do. This accounts for political obligation in much the same way that Hare accounts for our moral dispositions. It solves the problem of why we voluntarily agree to accept our obligations to the state by converting it into a prudential obligation – we agree to it because it is in our interests. This presents no problem as long as we all have the same obligations to serve other people's interests as well as our own. But it rests on the unlikely assumption that we all want the same. Moreover, it assumes we can only be obliged to do something if it is in our interests – if it is a means of getting what we want. For most of us this seems a distorted and over-simplified account of human motivation.

3.3.4 Feminism and social contract theory

However before we leave the voluntary acceptance theories and particularly social contract theory, we must examine a fundamental challenge that strikes at all these different attempts to tie consent to obligation. Feminists and racial theorists both criticize in similar ways the viability and adequacy of social contract theory. Feminists argue that there is in fact a more fundamental 'contract' that lies behind all these forms of voluntary acceptance: men's relation with women.

Socialist feminists argue that behind the political and legalistic terms of a social contract there lies a reality defined by the productive relations in capitalist society. This requires women to be bred to perform a certain role as private property and

certain functions, like child rearing. Freedom, then, lies in eliminating the social structure that makes such functional discrimination necessary. In contrast, radical feminists argue that it is inevitable that men dominate women, because men have an unavoidable tendency to set up social relations and create institutions that work in their favour. Sexual oppression, they believe, is the most fundamental feature of society; other forms of injustice, like racial and class discrimination, are secondary.

As you can see behind both forms of feminist thinking there lies the belief that there exists an 'original pact', as Carole Pateman describes it in her book *The Sexual Contract* (1988): a prior agreement among men to dominate women. Although the social contracts of Hobbes, Locke and Rousseau are between equals freely consenting, this only has a bearing on men's relationship to one another; it doesn't change men's power relations over women. Behind the contract lies the question of modern patriarchalism: who has control over women? All that changes as we enter into more democratic forms of government is that more men have this control. In tyrannies or oligarchies only one or a few respectively exercised this control, but in democracies every man possesses it. He has entered a contract with other men and part of that contract involves control over women.

One of the most interesting facets of this argument and a key insight that has inspired feminism around the world is what we can legitimately regard as 'political' and what is merely 'personal'. While the latter concerns our moral and private relations with others, which are usually out of bounds to governments, the former involves public claims of inequality and oppression of an individual or group. In the 1960s and 1970s, when feminist writers, like Betty Friedan (*The Feminine Mystique*, 1963), Kate Millett (*Sexual Politics*, 1969) and Germaine Greer (*The Female Eunuch*, 1970), publicly discussed a range of issues affecting women, including aspects of the personal side of their lives, the personal became the political. Kate Millett redefined politics to include the 'politics of the personal' by arguing that any relationship is political if it is a 'power-structured relationship, the entire arrangement whereby one group of people is governed by another, one group is dominant and the other subordinate.'

According to this novel account of politics and political relationships, what is political is not just that which is restricted to the affairs of government and public bodies, but includes private life, involving personal, family and sexual conduct. While 'first wave feminism' in the first half of the twentieth century focused on achieving women's political rights, like the right to vote and stand for representative office, 'second wave feminism' found its voice with this new direction and the cry went up 'the personal is the political.'

Politics doesn't just stop at the front door: it is part of every aspect of men's relations with women. Modern feminists argue that oppression exists in many aspects of life, much of which originates in the family itself. The 'politics of everyday life' includes things like the conditioning of children through the process of socializing them to masculine and feminine sexual roles. Indeed, feminists argue that the patriarchal family lies at the heart of a system of male domination, reproducing patriarchalism in education, at work and in politics.

According to Carole Pateman modern patriarchy is found in at least three paradigmatic contracts: the prostitution contract, the contract for surrogate motherhood, and the marriage contract. In each control is granted to men in general over women or one man over one woman. For example, in most US states a husband is given through the marriage contract the right of sexual access, thereby excluding the possibility of rape in marriage. Pateman concludes that a contract, far from being a means of guaranteeing freedom and equality, in fact serves only to uphold patriarchy and strengthen the means of controlling and dominating women.

But if the nature of the contract is one way in which feminists criticize the idea of a social contract, another opens up the moment you think about who it is that are supposed to be parties in the contract. Although the individual at the heart of the social contracts envisaged by Hobbes, Locke and Rousseau, and indeed by modern social contract theorists like the American philosophers John Rawls and David Gauthier, is presented as a universal model representing all individuals, an abstract general account of humanity, feminist and racial theorists argue that he is anything but. Each individual is found in a particular social context, located in a specific period in history. And, they believe, in almost every case the individual is the same: rational, educated, white, male and middle class. The same figure features as the central character in all political theories that have developed out of the Western liberal tradition.

In *Configurations of Masculinity* (1991), Christine

Di Stefano argues that most contract theorists have developed their theories in the context of a certain type of modern masculinity. In Hobbes' social contract the primary model is an individual who is a solitary figure living in a liberal society conceived in atomistic terms as a loose collection of isolated individuals. This modern concept of the individual is most clearly represented in Daniel Defoe's 'Robinson Crusoe', someone abandoned to his own devices and personal resources, a self-reliant individualist. In just the same way Rousseau's 'Noble Savage' is also someone who is thrown into the world. Free of the influence of anyone else, including the culture of his society and the age in which he is born, like Robinson Crusoe, he still possesses intact all the moral and intellectual characteristics of his age.

The same can be said of Adam Smith's notion of 'economic man', which has also served as a model for many contractarians. Virginia Held argues that once the liberal individual in this form is placed at the heart of the contract, certain male values and experiences are also placed at the heart of the contract, while female interests are ignored. The primary aim of economic man is to maximize his own self-interests; indeed it is his only reason for agreeing to the contract in the first place.

But this is not a universal model of the individual; it doesn't represent all people at all times and in all places. In particular it doesn't represent women, whose role has always been to care for others and not to maximize her own self-interests. It also fails to represent those, like children, who depend upon the caregiver. Enshrining such philosophical ideals as autonomy, reason and self-reliance in the contract has excluded feminine ideals and given maleness a privileged position, making it the standard by which sameness and difference are to be judged.

Still, beyond these concerns there is a third line of criticism. So far we have examined two grounds upon which feminists criticize social contract theorists: the nature of the contract itself and the type of individuals involved. But contracts are also concerned with the relationships between those individuals. Feminists like Virginia Held and Annette Baier believe that in defining these relationships contract theory fails as an adequate account of our social and moral responsibilities. It merely lays down our rights and obligations, but this fails to account adequately for what it is to be a moral person and how we are to manage our relations with others, particularly when these involve dependency of one form or another.

Baier is convinced that in this lies a crucial flaw in social contract theories. In particular she is critical of Gauthier's claim that the affective bonds between people, like those between friends, are non-essential and voluntary, which she believes fails to capture anything near a complete understanding of human motivations and psychology. Indeed, as Gauthier conceives them, such bonds are parasitical of the normal relations between people from which the contracts seek to release us. As Gauthier says, we might indeed be freer if we could conceive our affective relations with others as voluntary, but, Baier argues, these are the very relationship, like those between mothers and children, that have in the first place allowed us to develop the characters and abilities on which contract theory places so much value. Only if we have had such experience are we likely to become the sort of people that are capable of entering such contracts.

Baier believes this flaw in contract theory points to the more general shortcomings of any system of ethics based solely on justice. A solution might lie in supplementing such a system with the ethic of care, drawn from the perspective and experience of caregivers who fulfil our emotional needs to be attached to something. The reciprocal nature of any contract involving individuals who enjoy equal status fails to fulfil this. Contract theories involving liberal individuals freely agreeing to accept certain obligations in return for the freedom to maximize their interests is not only, as Virginia Held describes it, 'an impoverished view of human aspiration', but fails to capture the attachment to others that people need.

First, they envisage agreement and interaction between equals, whereas caring relationships are more often between unequals: doctors and patients, parents and children, teachers and students. Second, the liberal nature of a social contract means that it is designed to guarantee only the minimum of protection consistent with the maximum freedom of opportunity for the individual. It cannot, therefore, protect the powerless or promote the capacities necessary for an ethic of care and responsibility. And third, liberal social contract theory regards action as free, but, as Baier points out, such a theory 'cannot regard concern for new and future persons as an optional charity left for those with a taste for it. If the morality the theory endorses is to sustain itself, it must provide for its own continuers.' It must be for all people, men, women and children alike. A mother cannot simply opt out and choose to neglect her children.

Nevertheless, despite the force of these arguments we are still left wondering exactly what sort of relationship would be adequate to reflect the complexity of needs and interests of all those involved, while at the same time meeting the feminist objections to patriarchy and the inequality of women. Equality in the present situation would mean sharing what men have and being like them, being 'male identified'. However, although feminists want to overthrow the patriarchy, few want to do so in a way which involves adopting the same aggressive and competitive behaviour they attribute to men. For most, if not all, feminists liberation must mean being 'woman identified': achieving what it is to be a woman.

So settlement of the issues in any form must achieve two things: it must abolish patriarchy and allow women to achieve their fulfilment as women. However, to achieve the first we need to understand the nature of patriarchy, how it originated and how it functions. As we know it can be found in vastly different areas of our lives: in the family and the process of conditioning that goes on within it; in the physical intimidation by men to control women; in the cultural stereotypes of women as housewives, mothers and sex objects; and in the employment system that makes it difficult for women to reach senior positions in most organizations.

The question we need to be able to answer, though, is how much of this is due to nature and how much to nurture: how much to innate natural differences, which cannot be changed, and how much to the social and cultural attitudes, which can. The evidence of female achievement as a result of greater opportunities in the twentieth century suggests that much of it is due to the latter.

As to the second problem of how to ensure women have the conditions in which they can achieve their fulfilment as women, there is more disagreement among feminists. Most accept that equality should not mean merely being like men, but this still leaves two options: to achieve some form of 'personhood' abolishing all gender differences, or accepting that there are crucial differences between the sexes that must be acknowledged in any resolution to the problem.

Radical feminists tend to adopt the first position arguing that the true nature of the sexes means that in all essential characteristics they are identical and therefore should be treated equally.

Such a resolution would be based on some androgynous, sexless nature incorporating characteristics of both sexes. Other feminists argue that such a resolution ignores the fact that there are fundamental differences in the essential natures of men and women. They argue that women should celebrate the distinctive characteristics of the female sex, rather than embrace some androgynous nature. Supporters of the 'pro-woman' position among feminists argue that the very notion of equality is misguided and undesirable. Women should seek liberation as developed and fulfilled women, recognizing and embracing the bonds that bind them to other women. Indeed, rather than equality they argue that women possess superior qualities to men in their creativity, caring and sensitivity.

3.4 Moral purpose theories

In our discussion so far we have seen that the problem all forms of the voluntary acceptance theory struggle to solve is how to demonstrate that we do indeed consent and promise to comply with the demands made by the state. This is quite independent of the aims and consequences of government. But if we cannot convincingly show that we voluntarily commit ourselves in any form more than mere acquiescence, perhaps we should consider the aims and consequences of government as an alternative means of providing grounds for political obligation. This is what 'moral purpose' theories set out to show, particularly the 'theory of justice' and the 'general interest' or 'utility theory'. Both argue that we have moral obligations to pursue certain moral ends. We must seek justice for everyone and to maximize the greatest good for all. To achieve this we are obliged to adopt any means. Therefore, as the state is the means of fulfilling these moral ends, we are obliged to obey the state.

3.4.1 The theory of justice

In this form our moral obligation is to secure justice for all. Our political obligation, therefore, is based on the fact that the state's laws are intended to secure this. The most influential version of this appears in Locke's *Two Treatises of Government*, in which Locke argues that we have certain 'natural rights', certain absolute moral rights that the state must ensure are protected from all infringement.

In Locke's view these are life, liberty and property, although there is little 'natural' about the latter. It appears to be more a reflection of the needs of the time in which Locke lived and the type of property-owning democracy that was evolving. Nevertheless, he makes a spirited attempt to defend it, arguing the 'labour theory of value' that all value I create through my own labour becomes my property. Therefore, everything I, or my servant, or even my horse, mix our labour with becomes my property. Even so, he was uncomfortable with property as a natural right. So, too, were the founding fathers who wrote the American Declaration of Independence. Although they were strongly influenced by Locke, they famously substituted the right to the pursuit of happiness for the natural right to property.

Nonetheless, it seems odd to describe rights as 'natural', implying that they are God-given or given by the natural law in the same way that we have been given our mental and physical attributes. But then this was more a way of distinguishing moral principles and rights, those we have independently of anyone giving them to us, from those that are artificially created by the state – man-made laws and rights. In contrast to so-called 'natural law' this is described as 'positive law'. It includes all those rights that wouldn't exist without the state: the right to an education, the right to a state pension, and, in some countries, the right to free health care. In contrast the rights to life and liberty do not depend in the same way on the state.

Still this may not be all there is to what we mean by justice. It seems to be more than just a matter of defending our fundamental rights. Justice entails, in addition, a notion of fairness, of equal treatment between people. Given both of these elements we may say that our political obligation to support the state is in essence a moral obligation, because the state is the necessary means of securing these moral ends. Locke sees our political obligation as a form of trust. As long as the state pursues justice the trust is maintained, but as soon as it fails in its duty and becomes unjust in its dealings with individuals it forfeits this trust and has no right to our obedience. The individual is then justified in resorting to rebellion to replace the state with another that does aim at the moral end of justice.

Although this effectively sidesteps the problems we confronted in the previous theories, it has still been criticized on three main grounds. First, as we have already suggested, we can question whether any right is 'natural' and therefore absolute.

However, if we put aside the difficult implications of any right being 'natural' and, as D. D. Raphael suggests, talk instead about 'stringent moral obligations' that other people owe us and we owe them to respect things like their right to life and liberty, then we can maintain the same argument. As for rights being absolute, likewise there is no need to argue this. Locke accepts that an individual will forfeit his natural rights if he breaches the natural rights of others. If a gang were to abduct and imprison someone, the state would have the power to imprison them for infringing the other person's right to liberty. The same is the case if someone steals your property, and in some countries, of course, taking a life entails forfeiting your own.

The same applies to the argument that these rights are 'inalienable'. There is, as Raphael points out, no need to argue this when all that is being maintained is that moral rights cannot be lost by legal enactment, that is, the law cannot morally deprive someone of their natural rights for non-moral reasons. If I deprive you of your liberty by imprisoning you in my cellar, the law has a moral reason for depriving me of my liberty in response, but it cannot simply deprive me of my liberty, because I have blonde hair or because my name begins with 'G'. To say that certain rights are 'natural' and 'inalienable' is just to say that there is a difference between such rights and the 'artificial' rights created by the government's legal enactments in the form of positive law. All that is being pointed out is that so-called natural rights are moral, rather than legal. As such they do not depend upon law, rather our legal obligations must depend upon our moral reasons to be morally acceptable.

The second criticism focuses on the use of the term 'rights'. It is argued that this is a legal term denoting legal rights, so it is inappropriate to talk about 'moral rights'. Strictly speaking this is correct, although, as Raphael points out, if in fact what we are referring to when we talk about moral rights is 'stringent moral obligations', the analogy with rights serves a useful purpose. Not only are these obligations stringent, but we owe them to others, so that if I accept that I have a stringent moral obligation to respect your liberty in effect this means you have a moral right to liberty. My stringent obligation to you corresponds to your moral right as your stringent obligation to me corresponds to my moral right. In other words, our stringent moral obligations correspond with the moral

rights of others in the same way our legal obligations correspond to the legal rights of others.

Indeed talk of rights might serve another purpose. If this simply means that we have a moral obligation to support the state, because it is the necessary means of ensuring we fulfil the stringent moral obligations we have to others, then this is often a way of saying such moral rights should indeed be given the support of the legal system by being turned into legal rights. This is often the case when it has been shown that moral rights have been systematically ignored. At the end of the Second World War as evidence came to light of the systematic abuse and extermination of Jews and members of other minority groups in Nazi Germany, along with evidence of the abuse of prisoners in Japanese POW camps, demands for better protection of such human rights resulted in the UN Declaration of Human Rights, The European Convention on Human Rights and Fundamental Freedom, and the International Court of Justice.

However, the third and perhaps the most interesting criticism comes from utilitarian philosophers, who argue that the aims of a theory of justice and the notion of natural rights can be subsumed under the more comprehensive moral principle of promoting the common good or utility. Ultimately justice and concern for natural rights are just ways of fulfilling the aims of the theory of utility, that of maximizing the happiness of all.

3.4.2 The utility or general interest theory

Just as utilitarianism in moral theory argues that actions are right in so far as they promote the greatest happiness of the greatest number, so in political theory it argues that the state is legitimate as long as it promotes the general happiness. As all our moral obligations depend on their capacity to promote the general happiness or interest, and as the state is the most important element in achieving this, we have an obligation to obey it as a vital condition of us fulfilling our obligations. However, by the same token, if the state were to demonstrate it was no longer capable of promoting the general happiness it would lose its claim to our obedience.

Despite the obvious appeal of this as a theory of political obligation, the reluctance of those living in western democracies to embrace it lies largely in the need we feel for such obligations to be voluntarily undertaken, even though, as we have seen, most citizens cannot be said to have voluntarily undertaken any such commitment. But our reluctance is also due to the problems the utility theory confronts when the need to promote individual happiness conflicts with the need to promote the general happiness. We saw in Koestler's *Darkness at Noon* clear examples of justice being sacrificed for the general good. 'Vivisection morality' demanded that the state sacrifice one generation's happiness for the happiness of all future generations and one group's happiness, the kulaks', for the rest of society.

Yet utilitarians claim the principle of utility already provides for all the functions of justice – that utility is just a more comprehensive principle encompassing all the moral aims of justice. Utility demands that the state protect the *rights* of individuals in order to prevent harm to individuals, while at the same time *fairness*, the other element of justice, is also accounted for in the redistribution of rights necessary to promote general happiness. This demonstrates, according to John Stuart Mill, that only utility can give the abstract notion of justice some concrete basis in human life. Eventually the notion of justice must be cashed in terms of the well-being of individuals and the community.

So, how do utilitarians defend this argument when they are confronted by the sort of cases we saw in *Darkness at Noon*, when an individual's or a minority's well-being is sacrificed for the general well-being or, indeed, when the general well-being is sacrificed for an individual's – say, in a case where a paedophile is freed into the community as a result of a technicality? David Hume argues that we need to distinguish between the utility of a single act and the utility of the overall system. Although a specific act of justice might go against the individual or against the community's interests, the system of justice will necessarily be in the general interest. So a single unjust act must not be seen in isolation, but in the context of a general set of rules and principles serving the ends of justice and the general well-being.

This is an argument we have all come across before. Nevertheless, in these sorts of cases, even though the general well-being is promoted, we are still left with the conviction that justice has not been served. And as long as this persists, as long as we can believe that something can both promote utility and be unjust, it seems utility cannot account for all the ideas of justice. It needs to be combined in some way with other principles. Perhaps the most successful attempt to achieve this can be found in the work of the American political philosopher

John Rawls (1921–2002)

Born in Baltimore, Rawls was educated at Harvard and Oxford before teaching at Princeton, Cornell and from 1959 at Harvard. His major work, *A Theory of Justice* (1971), is widely regarded as one of the major works in twentieth-century Anglo-American political philosophy, which it effectively revitalized.

Rawls argues that utilitarianism with its emphasis on maximizing the overall aggregate happiness inadequately protects freedom and the fundamental political value of justice as fairness. Employing the notion of a social contract he envisages a hypothetical 'original position' in which citizens as rational people would choose under conditions of impartiality the basic institutions and principles of society. Under a 'veil of ignorance' they would have no knowledge of their own position in society, so they would be unable to pursue selfish interests or choose conditions that favour a particular type of person.

From this 'original position' Rawls contends that free persons would agree to a liberal egalitarian conception of 'justice as fairness', comprising two principles. First, certain basic liberties are so important that they take precedence over other social values, such as economic efficiency and improving the welfare of the poor. And second, although all social values, like liberty and opportunity, and wealth and income, would be distributed equally, under certain specific conditions inequalities may nevertheless be justified. In particular they may be justified if they are to the greatest benefit of the least advantaged and if they are 'attached to offices and positions open to all under conditions of fair equality of opportunity.'

John Rawls, particularly in his very influential book *A Theory of Justice* (1971). In this he combines recognition of the desirability of promoting the public interest with a concern for justice conceived in terms of individual rights rather than utility. This is similar to the approach adopted by Kant, who, as we have seen, defended notions of 'duty' and 'obligation' as morally basic to any concern for utility.

Rawls proposes two principles in order of priority. In the first he argues that in terms of our personal freedom we all have certain basic and equal rights. He explains, 'each person participating in a practice, or affected by it, has an equal right to the most extensive liberty compatible with a like liberty for all.' In the second he argues that, although we cannot expect everyone to be equal economically and socially in terms of their wealth, health and opportunities, we should insist that all inequalities are to the advantage of everyone. Again, he explains, 'inequalities are arbitrary unless it is reasonable to expect that they will work out for everyone's advantage, and provided the positions and offices to which they attach, or from which they may be gained, are open to all.'

His justification for these principles lies in what he describes as 'the original position.' He argues that if we were to put ourselves in the sort of position envisaged in Hobbes' state of nature and begin to create a society from its roots without any knowledge of the part we will play in it or of our abilities, talents and interests, the principles according to which we would run society would be these, because they are the fairest. If we were unsure of what role and position we would have, he argues, the only rational thing to do would be to enact laws that would treat all people equally.

In this way he combines the importance of promoting utility with other principles for a more complete account of justice. He argues, 'These principles express justice as a complex of three ideas: liberty, equality, and reward for services contributing to the common good.' As a result they exclude the sort of strategy we saw in *Darkness at Noon* of laying off the disadvantages to one group against the greater advantages to another. Any inequality must be to the advantage of *everyone*. 'This rather simple restriction,' he argues, 'is the main modification I wish to make in the utilitarian principle as usually understood.'

Although simple the modification is important. Like Hume, who argues that justice should be characterized not just by the structure of society and everyone's place in it, but by the interests and well-being of each and every individual, Rawls too ties justice to equality. But it is not the socialist notion of equality as the fair distribution of wealth and income. Nor is it the sort favoured by nineteenth-century liberalism and forms of conservatism today. This restricts all talk of equality to political equality, to legal rights and freedom of opportunity, excluding rights to social benefits and services, and a basic material standard of living. Where Mill and other nineteenth-century utilitarians would argue that all such considerations must pass the test of

utility – they must show they promote the greatest happiness of the greatest number – Rawls is more Kantian, arguing it is our obligation to help the worst-off members of society irrespective of the collective effects on the community.

With this he provides a much more complex understanding of the notion of justice, its relation with utility, and how they provide grounds for political obligation. The question we need to ask is whether in this form utility and justice together can provide a convincing account of political obligation.

As each of these four theories has shown, the grounds of our willingness to accept the legitimacy of the state and our political obligation to it are likely to be more complex than any one theory. Each of them no doubt identifies some fragment of the whole picture. Hobbes and Machiavelli are right to the extent to which we do accept our obligations to the state because it can ensure peace and security. But this entails only prudential reasons, which is no different from the mugger, with whom we first started this chapter. We accede to his demands because it is the prudent thing to do, but this means we are only 'obliged' to obey his commands: we have no obligation to him and, therefore, he has no right, no authority to issue commands. Hobbes' leviathan leaves us in the same state: we are obliged to obey for fear of the consequences of living in a state of nature if we don't. Without moral grounds, in the form of a promise, consent or the moral purposes of the state, we cannot be said to have an obligation.

But, then, the fact that the state pursues moral ends does not in itself seem to oblige us to give it our support. We may believe we have a moral obligation to contribute to famine relief, but we are not obliged to do so. The only grounds on which it might be said we have an obligation *and* are obliged to support the state is if we have, by virtue of our nature, moral obligations, which are primary to all other obligations, and the state is a necessary means of our fulfilling them. But then we have seen the difficulties of establishing this assumption in the last three chapters.

Failing that we are left with promise-making as the moral basis for political obligation, or some form of consent. Certainly this is closer to what we ordinarily understand that we are doing when we authorise someone to do something. But as we have seen it is difficult to establish any convincing case for arguing that we do explicitly or implicitly authorise the state in any recognizable way.

■ 4. Conclusion

In this chapter we have considered one of the key questions for any form of government: whether or not, and on what grounds, we believe a state is legitimate. In the next we will consider the other key question: how much power should a government have to meet its responsibilities? Like legitimacy, this too raises the question of what we should do when a government breaks our trust and extends its powers further than we have allowed.

■ Questions

1. 'Ultimately the authority of the state rests in its possession of force.' Does this adequately explain what we understand by political obligation?

2. (a) What does it mean to say that laws are the expression of the general will?

   (b) How intelligible is the notion of the general will?

3. 'To accept authority is to refrain from exercising one's own judgment.' Discuss.

4. Distinguish between authority, power, legitimacy and force.

5. If a government's policy is popular does this mean it is legitimate?

6. Are feminists right when they argue that a) there is an underlying set of power relations in all societies in which men dominate women, and b) the real situation is obscured because we believe politics ends at the front door?

7. Why do feminists criticize social contract theory? Are they right?

■ Recommended reading

Locke, J. *Two Treatises of Government* (Cambridge: Cambridge University Press, 1962; New York: New American Library, 1965).

Machiavelli, Niccolò. *The Prince*, trans. C. Detmold (New York: Airmont, 1965).

Pateman, Carole. *The Sexual Contract* (London: Polity, 1988).

Plato. *The Republic*, trans. H. D. Lee (Harmondsworth: Penguin, 1955; New York: Random, 1983).

Plato. Crito. In *The Last Days of Socrates*, trans. Hugh Tredennick and Harold Tarrant (Harmondsworth: Penguin, 1993).

Rawls, J. *A Theory of Justice* (Cambridge, Mass: Harvard University Press, 1971; London: Oxford University Press, 1972).

Rousseau, Jean-Jacques. *The Social Contract* (New York: Dutton, 1950).

 The note structure to accompany this chapter can be downloaded from our website.

Politics: The Extent of Power

CHAPTER 25

Key issues

▶ How much power should a government have to meet its responsibilities? What should we do when a government breaks our trust and extends its powers further than we have allowed?

▶ If it is not possible to have complete liberty and complete authority, how are we to establish the right balance to ensure both freedom and security?

▶ Or is there no problem at all? Is Rousseau right that the individual has nothing to fear from the state? If democracy is self-government and individuals are unlikely to enslave themselves, any limit placed on the state's powers will restrict the ability of individuals to liberate themselves using the powers of the state.

▶ What do we mean by 'freedom': is it freedom 'from' some restraint or freedom 'to' do certain things, like develop our potential?

▶ Does freedom consist in learning to want only those things you can have?

▶ If we decide that governments should intervene to protect us from 'harm', what do we mean by this? Physical, psychological, economic or even moral harm?

Contents

For over three hundred years the main concern for most Western political philosophers has been how to balance the liberty of the individual and the powers of the state that are necessary for it to do its job effectively. As we have seen, Hobbes argued that we must radically restrict the liberty of individuals so that we can enjoy the benefits of stability and peace. The state of war can only be brought to an end by men surrendering all their rights to a common authority, a sovereign. In contrast Locke and Mill believed that the state must be limited to allow as much room as possible for individuals to enjoy their liberties. But what they were all agreed on was that liberty and the authority of the state conflict; that it is not possible to have complete liberty and complete authority.

And yet there is another tradition of political thought that argues the two do not conflict. On the contrary complete liberty can only be achieved by giving the state complete powers. Rousseau argues that the state represents the general will and so is a form of self-government. And as the individual, in governing himself, will not 'forge fetters' for himself the state poses no danger. Thus, if he has nothing to fear from the state, there can be no case for limiting its powers. To do so would be to restrict the ability of the individual to liberate himself through the powers of the state. Those who stubbornly refuse to see the liberty they can enjoy through the state must be 'forced to be free'.

These are the two traditions that roughly divide political theory on the extent of government: one arguing that liberty is best promoted by insulating the individual from the effects of the state – the liberal view; the other arguing it can best be done by the individual surrendering himself to the state – the totalitarian view.

1. Theories of human nature

As you can see, on one level whether you believe the state should have more or less power depends on your view of human nature. If, like Hobbes, you hold a pessimistic view, believing that the individual is basically selfish, aggressive, acquisitive and egoistic, living in a perpetual state of war with others, in a fierce, uncontrolled, competitive struggle to maximize self-interest, then you are more likely to agree to give greater powers to the state to control the anti-social activities of the individual which threaten peace and stability.

If, however, you believe as a liberal thinker does that man is basically sociable and can confidently be left to govern his own affairs unimpeded, you are more likely to argue to restrict the powers of the state, leaving the individual free to govern his own affairs in accordance with his natural sociability. In its modern form this is developed by the American philosopher Robert Nozick in his *Anarchy, State and Utopia* (1974). He sets out the 'entitlement theory', in which he argues for the 'minimal state'. He explains,

---

Brief lives
Nozick, Robert

Dates: 1938–2002
Born: New York City, USA
Best known for: His contributions to political philosophy and his defence of libertarianism and the 'minimal state'.

Major works: *Anarchy, State and Utopia* (1974), *Philosophical Explanations* (1981).

Our main conclusions about the state are that a minimal state, limited to the narrow functions of protection against force, theft, fraud, enforcement of contracts, and so on, is justified; that any more extensive state will violate persons' rights not to be forced to do certain things.

Alternatively, if, like Rousseau, you also hold an optimistic view of human nature, believing that the individual is basically good and cooperative, but, unlike liberals, you believe his nature is constrained by the social institutions of the society into which he is born ('Man is born free; and everywhere he is in chains'), then you are more likely to argue for the state to have unlimited powers to liberate the individual from these constraints.

There is, of course, no way of evaluating these competing views, because there is no way of separating 'natural man' from the influence of his environment. The idea of a 'state of nature', or of some pre-social 'human nature', has been used by countless writers, not as a historical argument, but as an analytical device, an ideal concept, against which to assess political systems in theory and practice.

2. Freedom

The same can be said of the different concepts of liberty that we hold, although here our competing views of the nature of the individual are not merely conceptual, analytical devices; they are more closely related to the empirical evidence of the condition of the individual. If he is seen as self-reliant, independent, educated and healthy, then any extension of state authority is likely to result in the diminution of his freedom to govern his own affairs. However, if the empirical evidence suggests a different picture of someone who is restricted by social forces that prevent him from developing his abilities and maximizing his liberty, if he is ill-educated, poor, unemployed and suffering from ill-health, then the extension of the state's powers would enlarge the individual's liberty, if it led to the removal of these inhibiting influences.

In these two accounts of the individual lie the roots of two concepts of liberty: negative and positive. But first, before we go any farther, we ought to lay down some simple markers. Although the two terms, freedom and liberty are usually interchangeable, there is a useful distinction to be drawn between them. 'Freedom' is usually the generic term including all types of unfettered behaviour: freedom of choice, the sort of freedom we discussed in our examination of the issues surrounding determinism, and freedom of action. 'Liberty', however, usually refers to freedom of action – social and political freedom.

2.1 Negative liberty

In his famous essay 'Two Concepts of Liberty' Isaiah Berlin describes 'negative liberty' as the sense in which we are free to the degree to which no one interferes with our activities. It is negative in that there is an absence of constraint: we are free 'from' legal and social constraints, like censorship or similar restrictions on, say, gambling or drinking. It is this sense that Hobbes means, when he says that 'Freedom is the silence of the law', and 'A free man is he that ... is not hindered to do what he hath the will to do.' It is a conceptual type of liberty in that if you were to analyse the concept of the individual this would entail, among other things, certain natural rights and freedoms. The individual is free by definition without any intervention by the state. Thus, any extension of the powers of the state necessarily leads to the restriction of these freedoms: the state gaining power as individuals surrender it.

Under this concept of liberty the individual's freedoms cannot be enlarged, because they are natural, absolute and inalienable. The individual has certain natural rights, which are distinct from those he sacrifices to create a state in which he can live peacefully. Natural rights are inalienable since they are an essential part of what it is to be a human being. They are given by nature and nothing can be done to alter them. The individual has certain natural desires and the state should leave him an area of personal freedom to satisfy them. So the concept of the individual in which this is grounded is one who is rational and self-interested, willing to cooperate with others when it suits him in his quest to satisfy his desires. And the negative definition of freedom that develops from this is the power lastingly to satisfy these desires.

2.2 Positive liberty

In as much as negative liberty is freedom 'from' constraints, positive liberty is the freedom 'to' do certain things. It consists in being free to pursue full

self-realization; to live within social and cultural conditions that allow you to choose what you want to be and achieve self-mastery. It sets out the sort of life worthwhile for free agents, which is not always easy to achieve, and is not simply a matter of being given the freedom to satisfy certain natural desires. Berlin explains, 'I wish to be a subject, not an object; to be moved by reasons, by conscious purposes, which are my own, not by causes which affect me, as it were, from outside.' The contrast he strikes is between a human nature driven by desires that are given us by external forces (nature), and a human nature in which we conceive our own goals and policies and set about to realize them. He says, 'I wish, above all, to be conscious of myself as a thinking, willing, active being, bearing responsibility for my choices and able to explain them by references to my own ideas and purposes.'

As you can see he has two sides of our nature in mind. On the one side, that envisaged by negative liberty, there is the self driven by the need to satisfy the 'empirical bundles of desires and passions.' This is our 'lower nature' driven by 'irrational impulse, uncontrolled desires ... the pursuit of immediate pleasure ... swept by every gust of desire and passion.' On the other side is our 'higher nature', driven by reason and our pursuit of self-mastery. We calculate and aim for what will satisfy us in the long term as expressions of our 'real' or 'ideal' self.

By controlling our immediate desires and aiming at a concept of ourselves which we ourselves have fashioned, we not only achieve self-mastery by bringing about what we really want to be, but we gain a 'higher freedom'. T. H. Green, one of the British idealists whose work was built around the

Brief lives
Green, Thomas Hill

Dates: 1836–1882
Born: Birkin, Yorkshire, England
Best known for: Being one of the most influential of the British idealists, who were responsible for spreading the influence of Kant and Hegel in England against the prevalent trends of empiricism and utilitarianism.

Major works: *Prolegomena to Ethics* (1883), *Principles of Political Obligation* (1895).

concept of positive freedom, argues, 'The ideal of true freedom is the maximum of power for all the members of human society alike to make the best of themselves.' In other words, if you were not to aim for what was the best in yourself, but instead sought merely to satisfy an immediate desire, you would not be experiencing true freedom.

In practical terms the negative concept of liberty restricts the role of government to certain limited and negative powers to remove obstacles to the individual's desires and nothing more. With positive liberty the state is a facilitator, progressively liberating the individual through its policies and the collective achievements of the community it is able to promote. This means that, as Berlin argues, it is at times justifiable to coerce individuals to pursue things, like justice or public health, which they would pursue without coercion if they were more enlightened.

The other useful contrast to draw between the two concepts is that negative liberty is a static, absolute notion of rights that cannot be maximized but only preserved and protected from invasions by the state, whereas positive liberty is an idealistic and progressive concept. In the light of this the sort of rights and freedoms supporters of the concept of negative liberty usually talk about are more often just potential. They are actualized through social policies and government intervention, which liberate the individual from the limitations that constrain the development of his talents, abilities and choice. Berlin asks, 'What is freedom to those who cannot make use of it?'

The only measure of liberty, therefore, is not the simple absence of restraints, but the empirical evidence that the individual can and indeed does actually exercise his freedoms. Freedoms are not just defined into existence, but made manifest by governments whose goal is to progressively liberate the individual. This explains why the concept of positive liberty appears in theories, like Marxism and nationalism, which have at their centre a theory of history in which individuals progress towards an ideal society in which they are able to maximize their liberty.

Advocates of positive liberty argue that those who accept negative liberty are willing to tolerate inequality in the exercise and possession of rights and freedoms. Those who have the means, through wealth and influence, to exploit and actualize potential, negative freedoms enjoy greater liberty than those who do not have the means to exploit them. An individual has the negative freedom to own property, but if she does not have the means to buy property then she can hardly be said to have that freedom. Similarly you may have the right of expression, but if you have no right to information or to an education that would enable you to use your freedom effectively, it seems misleading to argue that you have that freedom. And, indeed, it is even more misleading to maintain that you have the same freedom as someone who has been able through wealth to acquire a good education and through influence in high places to get access to useful information. For example, it would be absurd to argue that you have the same freedom of expression as the editor of a national newspaper.

Consequently, most theories that embrace the positive concept of liberty argue that it is the community's duty to ensure its poorest and most vulnerable members have equal means of enjoying and actualizing their freedoms. This involves a commitment to the ideal of equality of freedom and of liberating all individuals from the natural, material, social and individual limitations that enslave them. The community is the source of freedom and the individual achieves it through his commitment to the community and his acceptance of the duties he owes it. T. H. Green argues that freedom is not the absence of duties, but the recognition of self-imposed duties. But what are these limitations that enslave the individual? Berlin identifies three.

2.2.1 Natural limitations

In this sense, largely historical, man is liberated progressively from the constraints derived from his dependence upon nature. But this is only achieved as a result of social, rather than individual, effort and organization. Individuals share in the benefits of advances in technology, science and medicine, achieved by others in a cumulative collaboration over many generations.

In the eighteenth century, for example, our dependence upon nature as a source of power, principally in the form of water power to drive textile mills, restricted the individual to a pattern of work dictated by the seasons. For long periods in the summer there might not be sufficient water to drive the mills. But the invention of means of producing power, like steam and electricity, which was within the control of man, liberated him from the tyranny of nature. The same can be said of the development of new chemicals, fertilizers and machinery, which improved agricultural productivity, thereby liberating the individual from the fear of bad harvests, famine and poor diet.

The examples, of course, are almost limitless. The air of inevitability in this historical, progressive account of the development of man's freedom has promoted the popularity of those political theories, more often totalitarian, like communism, fascism and nationalism, which are founded upon a theory of history as the sole criterion for judging what is politically right.

2.2.2 Social and political limitations

The same could be said of the process through which we have been liberated socially and politically from the tyranny of authoritarian government. Herbert Butterfield in 1931 coined the phrase the 'Whig interpretation of history' to identify a tendency among historians to describe the past as a conflict between those representing progressive democratic ideas and those seeking to maintain the privileges they enjoy in authoritarian forms of government. In this interpretation the Whigs, the progressive champions of democracy, inevitably triumphed.

Although this account of history is oversimplified, liberation has come about as the result of individuals committing themselves to group action in the form of revolution or radical movements for social and political reform. The Glorious Revolution in Britain in 1689, the French Revolution in 1789 and the Russian Revolution in 1917 all brought about change in the form of government that brought greater equality and respect for individual freedoms. Marxists maintain that societies have universally developed through distinct stages in which the consciousness of the oppressed has been raised sufficiently to bring about revolution, each time taking society into new and more liberated stages.

2.2.3 The individual

In the third sense of limitation we can say that we are liberated from ourselves, from the tyranny of our own undeveloped skills, talents and abilities, by the state's provision of free public education. We are also liberated from the threat of poverty and ill-health, which limit our personal development, by the state's provision of unemployment and sickness benefits, pensions and free healthcare. What's more, through progressive direct taxation the state also redistributes wealth and income to the poor and needy, thereby creating greater equality of opportunity.

What should be clear from this analysis is that liberty is an ideological creation: throughout we are concerned not with how much liberty, but what type of liberty the individual enjoys, and this depends, as we have seen, on how the individual is conceived. As an ideological term – that is as part of a system of beliefs that promotes and protects the interests of a particular group or class – if the group is composed of self-reliant individuals, then liberty takes the negative form, if it is composed of individuals beset by social forces over which they have no influence, then it takes the positive form.

The concept of a neutral, basic, apolitical liberty is little more than the product of a creative imagination. Liberty is not a neutral commodity that may be quantified: the struggle is not for a desirable quantity of liberty, but between different concepts of liberty. This has been obscured in the debate by a confusion of means and ends, of theory and practice. For the liberal, individual liberty is an end in itself requiring no justification, existing as an absolute. Actions seeking to make that ideal more accessible and realistic are rejected should they violate traditional freedoms, even though these might only be the exclusive possession of the privileged few. In contrast, the socialist also desires individual liberty, but since freedom implies choice and choice implies opportunity, for the socialist a redistribution of opportunity (achieved through collective action) is a prerequisite of individual liberty. Socialists argue that collective action, which may at times impinge on the nebulous and generally unexercisable ideals of libertarianism, is a necessary means to achieve the higher end of genuine freedom – an equality of freedom. Such is the ideological debate.

▪ 3. The extent of state power

The question is how these different concepts of liberty translate into different theories that establish just how much power the state should have and how we are to control it. For those who accept the negative concept, like John Locke and John Stuart Mill, the problem is framed in terms of insulating the individual: setting a cordon around her that cannot be invaded by the state. The emphasis is on being free from legal and social constraints. Then, to support this, some mechanism to control governments needs to be created to keep them within the limits of their power.

In contrast, those who embrace the positive concept see no need to set up a cordon around the individual since the state is doing nothing more than what the individual wants anyway – maximizing her freedom. As we will see those idealist philosophers, who accept the Hegelian theory of the state, argue that the most important kinds of freedoms and opportunities can only exist in a structured society, therefore constraints on the individual are necessary to create such a society as the necessary means to these ends.

3.1 Insulating the individual

Those theories that set about insulating the individual assume that the state is a necessary evil designed with limited and negative powers to create a stable and peaceful environment in which the individual is free to maximize her own interests with only minimal interference. In their different ways these theories share three common assumptions. First, they are atomistic. They believe society is just a loose collection of isolated individuals; no more than the sum of its parts. Second, all individuals are ruled by two key characteristics: they are rational and self-interested. Therefore, they know their interests best, so it is better that they are left to themselves, pursuing their own interests according to their own judgement. William Ewart Gladstone, the British liberal prime minister and Chancellor of the Exchequer in the late nineteenth century, insisted that 'Money should be left to fructify in the pockets of the people.' In other words, the state

should not interfere and tax individuals in order to do what it thinks is right, but leave this up to the individual, who knows best how to use his wealth and income.

The third assumption follows from the first two. If society is no more than the sum of its parts (individuals) and as each of these parts is governed by certain rules of behaviour (they are rational and self-interested), then the behaviour of society itself is governed by simple laws derived from these, principally the laws of supply and demand. In other words, society is mechanistic, and as with any machine problems only develop when we interfere with its smooth and efficient running.

The Reverend Thomas Malthus, in his *Essay on the Principle of Population* (1798), gives us a good example of just how this theory might work. In what is known as the 'wage fund theory' he describes a simple mechanism for controlling population consisting of two facts: there is only so much in an economy that can go to wages and individuals cannot survive below a certain subsistence level. Given this, a free market will control population naturally without interference. As population rises the average wage will decline until it falls below the subsistence level. At this point the weakest will die, reducing the population. As a result the average wage will rise until it again reaches subsistence level. In this way this simple, natural mechanism will control population around the subsistence level. Any interference, say in the form of charity to the destitute, is immoral because it only worsens the problem by maintaining a larger population in a state of abject poverty than the wage fund can support.

3.1.1 John Locke

In *Two Treatises of Government* John Locke also bases his account on a theory of natural law. Reflecting the same atomistic assumption, it is a theory of society framed in terms of individual interests. He claims that there are certain innate, indefeasible rights inherent in each individual, of which private property is paramount. Government and society, therefore, exist merely to preserve these rights, their indefeasibility acting as a limitation on the authority of the state.

But this is not idealism; these are not ideals to which we must aspire. They are basic human needs and if a government fails to satisfy them, then it has no right to power. No ruler can retain office if he fails to protect life and liberty: if he kills or imprisons innocent men or allows those who attack others to go unpunished. Nor can he if he fails to protect the right to property: if he seizes a person's property, other than by a proper system of taxation, or allows others to seize property unpunished. While it's not unusual to recognize our right to our own body as fundamental, Locke takes it one step further, arguing that anything I have mixed the labour of my body with is now my property. This is the labour theory of value, out of which emerged the Protestant work ethic that has had such a powerful influence in modern western societies. Work and rights are interdependent: the former being our way of earning the latter.

The power of the ruler, therefore, is not absolute; it is held on trust and is revocable. The only basis for political obligation is consent, which means society has the right to rid itself of a ruler who betrays that trust. Locke's theory is remarkable, therefore, not just for its concern to protect the rights of the individual, but because it also enshrines the right to rebellion and revolution. While Locke thought he was presenting a theory dictated by the conservative intention to protect the individual from an over-powerful sovereign, he was in fact pioneering the right of revolution. And how do we decide when the ruler has betrayed our trust? Locke's answer is simple: when he no longer governs according to the settled processes of law but resorts to 'inconstant, uncertain, unknown, and arbitrary government.'

3.1.2 John Stuart Mill

But although this makes it clear *how* governments should rule – in a non-arbitrary manner – we still need to set clear limits to *what* they can do. For Locke in the seventeenth century this was not such a pressing problem as it was to be later. While the electorate was composed exclusively of members of the propertied, educated and responsible middle-class the powers of government were bound to remain limited: they would hardly be willing to allow the state to extend its powers to threaten their own interests. However, in late nineteenth century Britain things were different, particularly after the franchise was extended beyond property owners as a result of the Second and Third Reform Bills (1867 and 1884).

At the time when Mill wrote 'On Liberty' (1859), the concern among many was for the effects of mass democracy on governments. In 1869 Matthew Arnold published *Culture and Anarchy*, the title manifesting the fear that society might be moving from one to the other as a result of the extension of the vote beyond the property-owning elite. Mill's fears centred on the 'tyranny of the majority', which he believed held as many dangers as the 'tyranny of the magistrate': the tyranny of kings and oppressive rulers. The tyranny of mass opinion, he feared, would compel conformity and repress individuality. It would force everything into an unprogressive common mould, a 'collective mediocrity' that allows no room for 'eccentricity', which alone enriches society infusing it with excellence and inventiveness.

Moreover, as the government's popularity would depend more and more on the opinion of the propertyless classes, the poor and the unemployed, it would be more likely to attract support by extending its powers to provide social and material benefits and infringe the property rights of the middle classes by redistributing wealth and income through increased taxes like progressive direct taxation, death duties and taxes on unearned income.

One answer, of course, was to use education to convince the new working class voter to adopt a more 'enlightened' view. Reflecting the view of many liberals, Robert Lowe argued in support of the 1870 Forster Education Act 'We must educate our masters.' While supporting this, too, Mill rested his faith in a clear definition of a principle of insulation to restrict the powers of the state. He argues in a very famous passage from 'On Liberty':

The object of this Essay is to assert one very simple principle ... that the sole end for which mankind are warranted, individually or collectively, in interfering with the liberty of action of any of their number, is self-protection. That the only purpose for which power can be rightfully exercised over any member of a civilised community, against his will, is to prevent harm to others. His own good, either physical or moral, is not a sufficient warrant. ... The only part of the conduct of any one, for which he is amenable to society, is that which concerns others. In the part which merely concerns himself, his independence is, of right, absolute. Over himself, over his own body and mind, the individual is sovereign.

Although a utilitarian, in this principle Mill abandons the dictates of the principle of utility. More consistent utilitarians, like Bentham, argued that the only criterion we can use to decide whether or not a government should intervene is the principle of utility: if it can show that by doing so it will promote the greatest happiness of the greatest number, then it must intervene. The problem with this, of course, is that governments can always see ways of promoting the greatest happiness, so this could lead to the state possessing very extensive powers; the sort we saw in *Darkness at Noon*. But to act otherwise and erect a superior principle to utility, as Mill does, is to accept the logic of a social contract, which Bentham dismisses as 'nonsense on stilts'. In Mill's theory, whether or not a government should intervene is to be decided by a prior agreement to accept the un-utilitarian principle of 'harm'.

But that's not the only problem with Mill's principle as you can see from the diagram below. First, the notion of harm defies easy definition. Mill dismisses 'harm to oneself', although today governments do regularly pass laws, like seatbelt and crash helmet legislation, which are designed for our own good and involve no harm to others. But beyond that, how are we to define 'harm'? Physical harm poses no real problem. We all recognize that we should not punch other people and even the more contentious examples, like the harm from passive smoking, is generally accepted even among smokers.

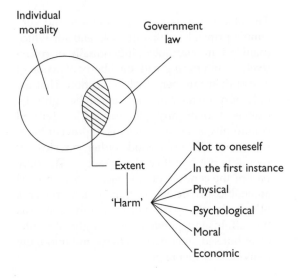

But what about 'psychological harm'? Today we have laws against inciting racial hatred. A broadcaster who hosts a show full of openly racist comments offends and causes distress to people. Should we have similar laws against discrimination and comment that cause distress to gays and other groups, or is such distress merely the price we must pay for free speech in democracies? Just as contentious, we could argue governments should have the power to prevent 'moral harm'. There is a strong movement of opinion supporting the censorship of movies and computer games that are violent or sexually explicit. In recent years one of the most strident advocates for extending the state's powers to prevent moral harm has been Lord Patrick Devlin, who argues in *The Enforcement of Morals* (1965):

> an established morality is as necessary as good government to the welfare of society. ... [H]istory shows that the loosening of moral bonds is often the first stage of disintegration so that society is justified in taking the same steps to preserve its moral code as it does to preserve its government and other essential institutions. The suppression of vice is as much the law's business as the suppression of subversive activities. ... [T]here can be no theoretical limits to legislation against immorality.

And then, of course, there are 'economic harms'. Should your employer be free to dismiss you when it suits him? Today we accept that governments should have the power to force employers to make redundancy payments to long-term employees whom they have sacked.

But Mill would not countenance the extension of the state's powers in any of these ways beyond the more obvious forms of physical harm. He draws the distinction between 'direct' and 'indirect' harm: he argues we should only be concerned with harm 'in the first instance'. And this brings us to our second problem. It is difficult if not impossible to distinguish between that part of a person's behaviour which only affects himself, in which the individual has unlimited liberty, and that part which affects others. Yet Mill has in mind three types of harm (harm to oneself, and 'direct' and 'indirect' harm to others), each drawing fine distinctions that are difficult to maintain:

So, to summarize:

1. Harm to oneself

2. Harm to others:

    2.1 Direct – 'in the first instance'.

    2.2 Indirect.

For example, Mill argues there should be the fullest liberty of expression as long as it does not cause 'direct' harm. He gives the example of a corndealer who keeps his corn back from the market so that the price will increase and his profits will be higher. If I were to publish an article accusing him of being a starver of the poor, no matter what harm he might suffer as a result, I would not be culpable because this would only be indirect harm. But if I were to say the same things to a crowd outside his house and the crowd were to turn on him, I would be culpable, because this is direct harm. In other words I should have the fullest liberty to say what I please as long as it makes no difference to others. Mill insists that I am free to say what I like about tyrannicide (the killing of tyrants), but if I instigate others to actually do it and an overt act occurs, then I am culpable.

But this means someone can hold a principle without having any intention of applying it, which raises the question whether they in fact hold it at all and are not just pretending to. You might argue that no one can genuinely claim to believe in a principle without taking some share of the responsibility if an overt act occurs. Even more, they have no right to persuade others if they are not themselves willing to accept their share of responsibility. And in practice, of course, it is difficult if not impossible to distinguish between someone who is merely expressing a belief in a principle and someone who is attempting to persuade others.

So, as you can see the distinction between direct and indirect harm is difficult to establish, leaving us wondering whether it's a useful distinction at all. If you were to see a programme on TV that filled you with moral disgust and outrage, we would not count this as evidence of harm, particularly if it was motivated by opinion voiced on the programme that conflicted with a deeply held view or moral principle of your own.

We would argue that we're all entitled to our moral opinions and to be offended by people expressing those we don't agree with is just the price of democracy.

But now, what if it produced more than this? Say it resulted in deeply unpleasant emotions of abhorrence, loathing, anger or repulsion. In the US town of Skokie in 1977 a number of neo-Nazis planned to demonstrate wearing swastikas and other reminders of the Third Reich. But Skokie is the home of a large Jewish community containing many survivors of the Holocaust, who would no doubt be made to feel horrified and fearful by such a display of Nazism on their streets. Yet do they have a right to be protected from being reminded of their experiences in the Nazi camps, or are these just people exercising their inalienable first amendment right of self expression?

Mill would no doubt argue this is indirect harm and, therefore, doesn't count. And this is the case even though we may be able to establish convincing grounds for believing there is a causal link between the demonstration and harm to individuals. Let's say there was a substantial rise in damage to private property and attacks on Jews following the demonstration. In Nazi Germany the mere public display of intolerance and violence towards Jews seemed to legitimize anti-Semitism and anaesthetize the perpetrators of violence to the moral implications of what they were doing.

Still, though, Mill would argue this is indirect harm and doesn't count, even though we can establish a causal link. So it seems to be less an empirical distinction based on whether we can establish a causal link and more a conceptual distinction grounded in Mill's atomistic assumptions that society is nothing more than a loose collection of *isolated* individuals. In our own societies we see such assumptions commonly reflected in the arguments of those who seek to defend their rights and interests. Those who profit from the making of violent films defend their interests on first amendment grounds, even though there may be mounting evidence suggesting a link between the desensitizing effects of such films and the incidence of violence. In the same way we argue in the West that we cannot be held responsible for the effects our over-consumption of the world's resources has on the developing world, since this too is only indirect harm.

3.2 The state as the actual will of the individual

However, in Chapter 19 we saw a radically different picture to this in the 'objective idealism' of the German philosopher Hegel. Unlike atomistic and mechanistic theorists, he argues we cannot understand what any part is without first seeing how it fits into the whole. He rejects any philosophy that denies the ultimate reality of relations – any one that sets out to understand the parts distinct from the whole – on the grounds that it is not possible to 'know' anything in isolation. Reason lies at the heart of things and each stage through which the nation develops is a manifestation of the 'Spirit' (*Geist*) or 'Mind', the source of rational intelligibility. Only by committing ourselves to this, and to its highest manifestation in the state, can we regard ourselves with complete objectivity and be liberated from our petty prejudices into absolute freedom.

In the late nineteenth century, idealism spread from Germany to Britain. The British school, consisting of philosophers like T. H. Green, F. H. Bradley and David Ritchie, shared among other things a concern for liberty defined in terms quite different from the negative concept of Locke and Mill. Theirs was the positive concept. Although not all of the same opinion, idealists are committed to the ethical theory of self-realization, that ultimate freedom lies in fulfilling the end of human life to realize one's 'true' or 'higher' self. Set against this is the bondage of life tied to satisfying mere desires and meeting the needs of our 'lower' selves. Mere freedom to do as we want, free of all duty with the state safely cordoned off, doesn't represent real or true freedom. Indeed, that someone should consider their duty a restraint on their freedom is evidence of their enslavement to their lower selves and their need to satisfy their desires. Perfect freedom can only be found in our higher selves, where there is no longer tension between our duty and our desires; where we have discovered a harmony between our conscience and our desires.

In this most of us will recognize an important insight. Freedom does not just consist in being able to do as you want to without constraints. It is not just a matter of satisfying all our present desires, but of striving to achieve all the potentialities of human nature. Someone who is satisfied to meet just his present desires without striving to get more out of himself by putting aside such gratification seems to have missed something important. A contented slave can hardly be described as free.

Thomas Hill gives us the example of the 'Deferential Wife': 'This is a woman who is utterly devoted to serving her husband. She buys clothes *he* prefers, invites the guests *he* wants to entertain, and makes love whenever *he* is in the mood.' She defers to her husband and is happy to do so, because this is the role she believes a wife should adopt. She doesn't have ideas, interests or values of her own. And when she does voice an opinion, she counts it as less important than her husband's. But she is not unhappy in this role. Indeed, she believes this is the proper role for a woman and much of her happiness comes from her belief that she serves her husband and her family well: 'No one is trampling on her rights, she says, for she is quite glad, and proud, to serve her husband...'

She is free in the sense that she is able to satisfy all her present desires, but set against that is the freedom to explore all her potential. No doubt prior to the emancipating impact of the First World War many women considered themselves perfectly free, but all subsequent generations of women look back in the light of the wealth of opportunities and freedoms they now enjoy and have no doubt that they are far freer today. Someone who fears meeting other people has all her desires satisfied if she can live her life within the walls of her own home, but few of us would doubt that she would be freer if she could overcome her fears through counselling and begin to explore all the possibilities the world offers her. Then at least she would be making a free choice between seclusion and the outside world.

This suggests two ways of testing whether people are free. We can either liberate them by making them aware of all the possibilities that are open to them and giving them the confidence to pursue them, or we can make sure they are free just to do what they want to do. If we adopt the latter, there are two things we can do: we can either remove the obstacles to them pursuing what they want or simply change the wants. We are accustomed to think in the west that the first option is best served by the market system in which people are free to satisfy their desires, whereas the latter is more closely associated with totalitarian regimes. Yet even in the west we have our desires engineered in the most efficient way by the combined talents of advertising agencies, large corporations and the media.

It's customary for us to associate such strategies with the totalitarian regimes described in novels like George Orwell's *Nineteen Eighty-Four* and Aldous Huxley's *Brave New World*. In both the individual is made to want just what the system could satisfy. As a result, although the obstacle might still exist, it is no longer an obstacle to the individual's happiness, because she no longer desires it.

However, to a degree such social engineering may be essential to all political systems and not just totalitarian regimes. All need to manage the desires citizens can have, if they are to control the level of dissatisfaction with the system. As Aldous Huxley says in the 1946 Foreword to *Brave New World*, 'Round pegs in square holes tend to have dangerous thoughts about the social system and to infect others with their discontents.' Even so, there is still something odd about saying that someone like Winston Smith in *Nineteen Eighty-Four* is now free because he has been brainwashed into not wanting what he cannot have. The contented slave is still not free, even though he gets what he wants and wants what he gets. We suspect that if he, like women before the First World War, were given a taste of emancipation he would prefer that rather than enslavement.

Yet the oddness of this claim disappears if the individual's freedom to choose is only an apparent freedom: if the choices that make up this freedom are determined by desires he hasn't chosen. If we were to change the desire of a drug addict for his next fix, so that he no longer desired it, we could genuinely argue he is now free in a real and not just an apparent sense. He would no longer be driven by his addiction, his overpowering desire, but could make reasoned choices about whether to steal off his friends and family.

**Brief lives
Gentile, Giovanni**

Dates: 1875–1944
Born: Castelvetrano, Italy
Best known for: Being the philosopher of fascism. His philosophy of 'actual idealism', or the 'theory of the spirit as pure act', denied the existence of individual minds and of any distinction between theory and practice, subject and object, past and present.

Major works: *The Reform of Education* (1920), *The Philosophy of Art* (1931), *My Religion* (1943), *Genesis and Structure of Society* (1946).

This lies at the core of the argument of those, like Rousseau and the twentieth-century Italian philosopher Giovanni Gentile, who argue that the state has a legitimate role in changing our desires to 'force' us to be free. When it does so, it is simply releasing us from bondage to our desires that, like the drug addict, we are not free to choose. While our actions are motivated by such desires we cannot claim to be genuinely free. Only those choices made on the basis of reason constitute 'real' freedom. In pursuing the 'general' or 'real' will, the state is pursuing just this: what we really want, our rational desires.

In *Genesis and Structure of Society* (1946) Gentile argues that in pursuing the general will the totalitarian state does not swallow the individual, as it is normally assumed, but quite the reverse. The state represents the general will, the rational will of the individual 'in its universal and absolute aspect.' This is not a mere aggregate of millions of individual desires, but the rational and universal will of the individual representing what we all really want. Consequently, it is the individual that swallows the state: the will of the individual *is* the will of the state.

In one stroke the two problems we started out with (legitimacy and the extent of power) are resolved in totalitarian regimes. Not only is the state legitimate in what it does, but it has no need to limit its powers. He explains:

> since legitimate authority cannot extend beyond the actual will of the individual, authority is resolved completely in liberty. Lo and behold, absolutism is overturned and appears to have changed into its opposite, and the true absolute democracy is not that which seeks a limited state but that which sets no limit to the state that develops in the inmost heart of the individual, conferring on his will the absolutely universal force of law.

Why limit the powers of the state when it is only a form of self-government? As Rousseau points out the individual will not voluntarily 'forge fetters' for himself. But it has to be the general will, not the pursuit of private or partial interests. To pursue our private wants is to pursue our apparent will. This is want we *think* we want, not what we *really* want. Although we might think we are free, we are not actually free. We are enslaved by our desires for our particular interests, whereas when the state forces us to pursue the general will we are pursuing our actual freedom, what we really want.

The problem with this argument, as I'm sure you can see, is that not all our desires are compulsive like those driven by addictions for drugs or cigarettes. We have a whole range of desires we would be reluctant to describe as addictive. We might have a desire for a new pair of shoes or to go to the theatre, but we wouldn't describe these as compulsive. Even so, as our knowledge advances we are inclined to describe more and more things as addictive, anything from food to sex. So what is the difference between a compulsive and a rational desire?

We can probably find an answer by drawing an analogy between two different types of shoppers. One walks down the high street, sees a pair of red shoes, and knows immediately she must have them, so she goes in and buys them. The other knows she must have a pair of red shoes to go with her dress for the party next week. All her other shoes are either too old, the wrong shade of red or need to be repaired. She may even have decided that, because she has been working hard lately without a break, she deserves a reward to lift her spirits and buying a new pair of shoes will do the trick.

The first shopper has no choice over her desire, or its strength in relation to other desires. It often seems that our desires choose us; we don't choose them. You might have a desire for honey, while others cannot stand the stuff, but you would be hard pressed to give reasons for your desire or how you developed it. Though not addictive, these sorts of desires involve very little, if any, freedom. When the desire takes hold, you reach for the spoon and the jar of honey; you don't consider the reasons for wanting it or the beneficial consequences; you just want it.

But the second shopper does appear to exercise her freedom: she does weigh up, measure and balance her reasons. She needs a new pair of shoes, but can she afford it and can she make do with what she has got? She considers all the evidence and evaluates the arguments that support or weaken the case for doing what she proposes to do. Whatever your view of liberty and the role of the state, it is likely to reflect the type of people you think we are or should be; whether we are or should be like the first or second type of shopper.

4. Conclusion

As we suggested earlier this may ultimately be an ideological judgement. The problem is we all have widely different notions about human nature and what a suitable life is for it. If, like those who argue for negative liberty, the sort of individual you have in mind is self-reliant with no need to depend on the state, then any extension of state power restricts his liberty in order to increase the liberty of others. Rational and self-interested he willingly cooperates with others only when it suits him. Liberty for him is defined negatively as a lack of obstacles to him fulfilling his desires. If this is what you mean by liberty you must ask whether life is simply a matter of satisfying as many desires as possible. If it is then the state should indeed be restricted to a minimum.

If life is more than this, then the answer is not so simple. Those who believe in positive liberty and the state's role in promoting it, have in mind a certain kind of life that is suitable to a free individual. But if this is what you believe you must come clean about what sort of life this is.

Questions

1. 'The enforcement of morals is not a proper concern of the law.' Discuss.

2. '[T]he only purpose for which power can be rightfully exercised over any member of a civilised community, against his will, is to prevent harm to others. His own good, either physical or moral, is not a sufficient warrant.' Critically assess Mill's defence of this claim.

3. By placing so much importance on individuality, does Mill overlook the disintegrating effects of his theory on society?

4. Is it always a good thing to have unfettered freedom of speech?

5. 'Those who find a book or magazine offensive should just avoid reading it, rather than try to prevent its publication.' Do you agree?

6. The evidence suggests that hidden cameras reduce the incidence of crime. If this is true, shouldn't we have as many as possible in every public place?

7. If a person chooses to shorten his life by taking

drugs, isn't that his business and nothing to do with the state?

■ Recommended reading

Berlin, I. *Four Essays on Liberty* (Oxford and New York: Oxford University Press, 1986), particularly 'Two Concepts of Liberty'.

Feinberg, J. *Social Philosophy* (Englewood Cliffs, NJ: Prentice-Hall, 1973).

Gentile, Giovanni. *Genesis and Structure of Society* (1946) (Urbana: University of Illinois Press, 1960).

Locke, J. *Two Treatises of Government* (Cambridge: Cambridge University Press, 1962; New York: New American Library, 1965).

Mill, J. S. On Liberty. In *Utilitarianism, On Liberty and Considerations on Representative Government* (London: Dent, 1972).

Nozick, R. *Anarchy, State and Utopia* (Oxford: Blackwell, 1974; New York: Basic Books, 1974).

Rousseau, Jean-Jacques. *The Social Contract* (New York: Dutton, 1950).

 The note structure to accompany this chapter can be downloaded from our website.

Politics: Forms of Government

CHAPTER 26

Contents

Key issues

▶ Can we genuinely argue that we live in democracies when most individuals lack the time and expertise to keep themselves informed about the complex issues of modern government?

▶ Doesn't the right to vote in private at elections merely result in the accumulated self-interest of the majority and have a tendency to promote short-term policies that damage the community in the long term?

▶ As more and more of the responsibilities of modern government fall into the hands of scientists and technocrats, aren't all modern governments technocracies, rather than democracies?

▶ How can we claim we live in a *liberal* democracy when governments have such extensive powers, and how *democratic* is it when there are so few parties that can genuinely aspire to government, political leadership is drawn largely from the same exclusive pool of talent and opinion is expertly managed by the parties and the media?

▶ Is it best to judge democracies by the progress they make towards democratic goals like equality and the relief of poverty, rather than by the frequency of elections?

▶ If the law compels you to do something that offends your moral conscience, should your conscience take precedence over your moral obligation to keep your promise to obey the law?

Over the last two chapters we have examined the two key questions that all forms of government must answer: first, how to ensure that governments use their power legitimately and, second, how to determine the amount of power they should have. Now we can bring what we have learned together to see the practical consequences in the different forms of government.

We saw in Chapter 24 that when we combine these two concepts – the legitimacy and the extent of power – this gives us four forms of government, as shown opposite.

■ 1. The extent of power

Along the axis representing the differing views about the extent of government power various positions are held, some grounded in a particular account of

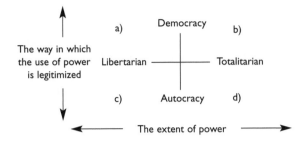

human nature, like anarchism, which entails an optimistic view, believing that individuals can be left to themselves to govern their own affairs without the intrusion of authority. Others are grounded in particular views about the nature of the influence of government, some believing that it is inherently good, like totalitarianism, others that it is inherently bad, like *laissez-faire* conservatism. And it's worth noting that these do not necessarily correspond to the 'left–right' continuum of political ideas: theories like totalitarianism and anarchism may both take a 'left-wing' or 'right-wing' form. In anarchism the left wing commune, with its democratic decision-making and non-sexist approach to work, contrasts with the right-wing survivalist community, bristling with modern armaments behind which there exists authoritarian government replete with military discipline and courts martial.

1.1 Totalitarian

So, at one end of the axis there is the totalitarian form of government, in which the state has total control throughout society, recognizing no distinction between public and private matters. This means that actions are not just private and moral, but public and political. To criticize the government within the privacy of your own home among your own family and friends is a political act, a matter of concern to the state. One of the most popular jokes in Moscow in the 1930s concerned a hostess who had invited ten of her closest friends for a dinner party. Aware of her moral and political obligations to the state, she submitted the names to the secret police for their approval, fully expecting the list to be returned with two names added – the secret police needed their observers to be present to record who said what to whom. But to her dismay the list was returned unamended – there was no need to add two of their own. Unknown to her they were already there, among her own trusted friends.

1.2 Libertarian

Towards the other end of the axis there are forms of government that seek to protect the individual from the effects of government, which is believed to be harmful to the individual who for the most part is capable of governing his own affairs. The classical liberalism of the nineteenth century advocated the restriction of state intervention to protect the individual's negative liberty, whereas modern liberalism accepts moderate state intervention to enhance the positive liberty of individuals. In the twentieth century the mantle of classical liberalism has been taken up by *laissez-faire* conservatism, the supporters of which argue for minimum intervention necessary for the preservation of the state. This, they argue, represents strong, though limited, government.

At the extreme end of this axis lies anarchism, whose followers argue that all authority represents forms of coercion which pervert man's natural sociability, his intuitive sense of right and wrong, what the nineteenth century French anarchist Pierre Joseph Proudhon describes as man's 'immanent sense of justice'. Anarchists argue that as all authority denies individuals their sovereignty over their own affairs, it is by definition undemocratic.

■ 2. Legitimacy

On the other axis, representing the different ways in which governments and their use of power are legitimized, there are those who accept degrees of authoritarian rule as legitimate, because they believe their leaders either are uniquely qualified in some way or need unconstrained authority to do those things necessary to develop the nation, and others who insist on some measure of popular expression to legitimize a government's policies.

2.1 Autocracy

Whether liberal or totalitarian, autocracy is a form of government in which decisions are made by a minority without the majority having any participation in the decision making or any influence over events. One person or a group with a clearly identifiable leader exercises power without effective legal or traditional restraints and without any responsibility to an electorate or any other political body.

Although based upon orders backed by uncompromising threats of punishment for disobedience, such power is exercised legitimately if there is reason to believe that the regime is not maintained wholly by coercion. Usually it embraces the belief that the ruler's authority is its own justification. His actions and policies are accepted by his subjects without consultation or persuasion, because of the authority vested in him by religious authority (a theocracy), by tradition (an aristocracy), by a theory of history (as in the cases of Stalin, Hitler and Mao Tse-Tung), or because of the recognition of some form of necessity, like a national emergency or domestic unrest, when the nation needs an efficient, powerful government unrestrained by tradition or democratic procedures.

Beyond these circumstances autocracy is more often found in countries with low literacy rates, or with impatient leaders eager to bring about change quickly. In China, during the period 1957–60, Mao embarked unsuccessfully on the ambitious programme of forced, rapid industrialization, known as the 'Great Leap Forward'. This mirrored a similar strategy in the Soviet Union where Stalin forced through the reconstruction of agriculture to allow resources to be shifted to the industrial sector in the five-year plans of the 1930s. But perhaps the most inveterate factor making it difficult to establish and maintain democratic institutions and procedures is a strong tradition of submissiveness. In societies where there is a strong pattern of dominance and submission maintained under the influence of traditional institutions, like the church and the military, the prospects for long-lasting democratic political relations are weakened.

Nevertheless, there are exceptions. Although literacy is vital for informed discussion in democracies, in Germany in the 1930s the Weimar Republic, founded on what was hailed as one of the most democratic constitutions in history, was voted out of existence by a highly educated and literate electorate in favour of the totalitarian autocracy of Nazism. In his famous work, *Escape from Freedom* (1941), Erich Fromm argues that it is a feature of modern societies that occasionally people are prepared to 'escape from freedom': to throw off the responsibilities and the right to rule themselves in order to submit to the direction of a leader they perceive as some form of father figure to the nation.

**Brief lives
Fromm, Erich**

Dates: 1900–1980
Born: Frankfurt am Main, Germany
Best known for: His belief that psychology and society interact so that psychoanalytical principles could be effective in curing social and cultural ills.

Major works: *Escape from Freedom* (1941), *The Sane Society* (1955), *The Art of Loving* (1956), *To Have or To Be* (1976).

2.2 Democracy

In contrast, democracy can be described as a form of government in which the members of society act either as policy makers (direct democracy), or are represented by a small number, who make policy on their behalf (indirect democracy).

2.2.1 Direct democracy

The clearest examples of direct democracies (sometimes known as 'classical democracies') were found in some small Greek city-states, like Athens in the fourth century BC, and in the seventeenth and eighteenth century New England 'town meetings'. In both the number of citizens was sufficiently small to enable them to meet together and make governmental or policy decisions without the need for representatives.

Such a system has clear advantages over the indirect systems of modern times. First, citizens have direct influence over decisions by casting their individual vote. Unlike modern democracies they are not expected to vote for a candidate who most nearly approximates to what they believe, when it's unlikely the match will be anything more than a very weak approximation. And, second, votes are cast in the presence of the rest of the community. Therefore, citizens are more likely to be influenced by the wider needs, opinions and interests of others, rather than voting solely for their own self-interest as they are likely to when they enter the polling booths of indirect democracies and cast their votes in private.

Nevertheless, given the public nature of the voting system, voters are more open to intimidation and influence. Before the Secret Ballot Act of 1872 in

Britain the 'hustings' – the raised stage on which voters would cast their vote – was notorious for the bribes offered, and threats made, to influence voters. In recent times legislation has been passed to ensure that when a trade union votes for industrial action each individual member does so by secret ballot and not by the mass assemblies where individual workers can feel intimidated to vote one way or another.

But as you can see legislating in this way involves sacrificing one of the key advantages of direct democracies: that individuals are less likely when they vote in public to vote merely for their own self-interest, resulting in the accumulated self-interest of the majority. While direct democracies can guarantee both advantages, all forms of indirect democracies must choose between one or the other, and in this lies the key difference, as we will see, between liberal and totalitarian democracies.

So, to summarize:

Direct democracy:

1. Individual vote, and

2. Exercised in the context of the community.

Indirect democracy:

Either   1. Elections and individual secret ballot
           – Liberal democracy

             – representative democracy

             – responsible democracy.

Or   2. The 'general will' – the context of the community – Totalitarian democracy.

2.2.2 Indirect democracy

However, in the modern era a number of fairly obvious factors have combined to make direct democracy impractical. The growth in the populations of modern societies has meant they are far too large for direct democracy. Modern states embrace much larger areas made possible by better communications. Moreover, governments have assumed much greater responsibilities, which produce a stream of issues requiring prompt decision and action, from international trade, the economy and defence to health, social policies and education. In contrast to those societies that were able to run their affairs through systems of direct democracy,

government has become much more complex, leaving the average citizen inadequately qualified, in any practical sense, to take decisions. Indeed, the same could be said of elected representatives and ministers, who are amateurs themselves and are, therefore, dependent on the specialist help and opinion of their advisers. And, given that the average person leads a much busier life, it's not surprising that the large majority neither want to nor can devote much time to political participation.

Nevertheless the impracticality of direct democracy in national politics, with the exception of the occasional referendum or plebiscite, exacts a significant price in the form of one or other of the benefits listed above. If, as in liberal democracies, the community's will is expressed through elections, in which voters express their preferences in private, the chances are this will produce just the accumulated self-interest of individuals who make up the majority as well as a commitment to short-term immediate interests at the cost of long-term interests.

The first is what J. S. Mill describes as 'the tyranny of the majority', in which minority interests are not only neglected, but actively discriminated against. This 'intolerant consensus' trivializes, if not censors, all opinion, which is thought not to represent the norm. Long before environmental issues became the concern of mainstream politics, the public were encouraged by a largely partisan press to see pressure groups like Greenpeace and Friends of the Earth as faintly ridiculous, irresponsible and even unpatriotic.

This has also taken the form of what has been described as 'moral populism': the intolerance of the majority for the moral values of those who dissent from what is thought to be majority opinion. In the 1980s 'Moral Majority', the US evangelical movement led by Jerry Falwell, campaigned to censor what the public could read, pressuring many states into removing from the shelves of school and public libraries all those texts that fail to support what they believed to be the 'American way of life'. According to reports this resulted in the censorship of major texts, including most Shakespearean plays in some states, along with best-sellers, like *To Kill a Mockingbird, Catcher in the Rye, Of Mice and Men, Catch 22, The Diary of Anne Frank, One Flew over the Cuckoo's Nest* and many others. Indeed, one story maintains that Moral Majority even sought to censor all dictionaries with entries for the word 'bed' as a verb as well as a noun, along with a little known text entitled

Making it with Mademoiselle, only to discover later that it was in fact a French cookery book.

The other benefit of direct democracy listed above, which we are in danger of losing in indirect democracies, is our willingness to sacrifice our short-term interests to achieve long-term goals that will ultimately benefit us and our children more. This is likely to generate less efficient government. It would be reasonable to argue that one of the principal goals of government is to achieve a high and sustainable standard of living for all its citizens. But if it were to satisfy voters' short-term interests for, say, cheap petrol, this might lead to the exhaustion of the declining oil reserves and bring about a fall in the standard of living before alternatives can be found. At present most governments are reluctant to take the measures that seem necessary to deal with the long-term problems posed by climate change for fear of losing popular support by introducing policies that might raise the cost of living.

Some democracies have weakened the impact of these problems by adopting a form of *responsible* as opposed to *representative* democracy. At one end of a spectrum depicting the degree to which elected representatives are free to use their own judgement to decide how to vote on individual issues lies the 'delegate'. She is most constrained in the use of her own judgement, even receiving instructions from those she represents about which way they want her to vote on each issue. At the other end in liberal democracies lies responsible democracy, in which elected representatives are free to use their best judgement about how best to vote, putting the nation's interests ahead of their constituents' and long-term ahead of short-term interests. Somewhere in the middle lies representative democracy.

Representative democracy

In representative democracy elected leaders govern in accordance with the expressed wishes of the electorate, to whom they are accountable. In the past the British Labour Party has been committed to the 'Mandate Theory', that all governments should be bound to enact the policies laid out in their manifestos, upon which the electorate voted. At its conference in 1979 it passed an amendment to its constitution, stipulating that all Labour MPs should be reselected at least once in the lifetime of a parliament. This was designed to ensure that MPs would have to explain and defend their voting record

before local party members and in competition with other candidates for selection when the next general election came around. Clearly the danger was that if they had not voted in a way that accorded with local views they would be out of a job at the next election.

While this tackled the problem of representatives being elected for safe seats with large majorities, who were free to vote as they wished without regard for local views, because they would never be in any danger of losing the seat, it was not the complete answer. It didn't so much make the representative accountable to the electorate, or even to all those who voted for her, but just to the local party members. In the event it gave an opportunity to extreme Trotskyists in the party to gain influence within the local party and get one of their number elected in place of the sitting MP, who would be deselected. Such a strategy is known as 'entryism'.

Responsible democracy

By contrast, in responsible democracies elected leaders govern in what they believe to be the best interests of the electorate. The wishes of the electorate are interpreted and frequently ignored by representatives, if they believe them to be unwise or opposed to long-term or national interests. Edmund Burke, one of the major contributors to Conservative thinking in Britain, makes this clear in his address to the electors of Bristol in 1776. He describes the role of the MP by pointing out to his electorate that 'Your representative owes you not his industry only, but his judgement; and he betrays instead of serving you if he sacrifices it to your opinion.'

Conservative parties on the right of the political spectrum are most likely to hold this view. The British Conservative Party has long held the view that there are natural leaders endowed with natural ability and wisdom to govern in the best interests of the community. Policy decisions are the prerogative of the party leader, and although the annual conference debates resolutions it has no authority. Indeed the party leader used to 'emerge' through a process shrouded in mystery, though usually it involved consultation among senior members of the party. But since 1965 the leader has been elected by Conservative MPs, who are expected to 'consult' constituency associations before making a decision.

The 'general will' and totalitarian democracies

You might argue that even further along our spectrum depicting the degree to which elected representatives are free to use their own judgement, beyond even responsible democracy, lies totalitarian democracy and the notion of the general will. Totalitarian leaders with all their charismatic authority to shape the will of the people and guide the nation towards its historical destiny are the least constrained of all by the expressed wishes of the people. As there is only one will, not many, and as the leader alone is thought to possess the intuitive skills to interpret it accurately, there is no room for accountability to the people. The community is one organic being with one vote. The 'head' of this organic being, the natural leader that history throws up, is the only one with the special gifts necessary to interpret the will of the community and the course of history.

In contrast to liberal democracy and the importance it attaches to the first benefit we listed above, totalitarian democracy emphasizes the second benefit – the importance of the community as one whole entity at the expense of elections and the individual's right to vote at least meaningfully for what she believes. The advantage of this form of democracy is, of course, that it avoids the accumulated self-interest of individuals and, therefore, it is less inclined to sacrifice long-term goals to short-term interests. For example, this process of subduing all sectional interests to achieve the goals of the wider community enabled the Soviet Union to suppress the interests of the kulaks while it developed rapidly from a semi-feudal state in 1917 to an advanced industrial state just thirty years later. Given this, totalitarian democracies should be better able to achieve similar idealistic goals that demand sacrifices from the community, like the fairer distribution of wealth and the eradication of poverty.

However the price paid for these advantages is, of course, elections and the freedom to choose between competing candidates. In liberal democracies parties and pressure groups compete for influence and ascendancy in promoting their interests. In totalitarian democracies the belief that there is one general will implies that if natural leaders are indeed 'natural', there need only be one party: it is pointless to have more than one interpretation of the general will, when that one is 'correct'. Indeed,

to have competing parties is merely to compound the error by promoting unnecessary divisiveness that can only weaken the self-confidence of society and jeopardize its progress.

The interpretation of the general will by the leader must, by definition, be correct, otherwise he cannot be the natural leader. And if he's not accountable to the electorate he can only be accountable to results, to history. If his decisions fail to produce the expected results, then clearly his status as the infallible natural leader is jeopardized. In *Darkness at Noon* Koestler describes this as 'consequential logic' and the leader as 'the infallible pointsman'. This is the means and ends criterion: his policies are legitimized by the consequences. If the means fail to bring about the ends, the leader has no claim to infallibility. This goes a long way towards explaining why totalitarian leaders, like Stalin, consistently resorted to rewriting history in order to square the results retrospectively with the original decisions and projections. George Orwell draws attention to the same thing in *Nineteen Eighty-Four*: Winston Smith's role in the Ministry of Truth is to rewrite old articles, in which forecasts were made, so that, in retrospect, they reflect accurately the actual results.

■ 3. Forms of government

We said earlier that by combining these two concepts – the extent of power and legitimacy – we end up with four possible forms of government: liberal democracies, totalitarian democracies, liberal autocracies and totalitarian autocracies. Of these liberal autocracies are least likely to be found today. In them the individual enjoys considerable freedom, but has no power to make the government accountable or challenge the authority of the ruling elite. Decision making is monopolised by a small elite, which makes little or no reference to public opinion. But examples are difficult to find. Probably Britain prior to the 1832 Reform Act is the closest we get. The government had only limited powers and was accountable to only a small percentage of the population. Today perhaps the best examples are to be found in Islamic regimes and those countries, like Kuwait and Saudi Arabia, that are ruled by a small elite around the royal family but who possess only limited powers.

The problem is that any government which is not accountable to the people is unlikely to rest easy with only limited powers, so liberal autocracies all too easily become totalitarian autocracies. As Lord Acton, the British historian, maintained, 'Power tends to corrupt, and absolute power corrupts absolutely.' In this form government is by a small unaccountable elite, who take extensive powers to control almost every aspect of people's lives, so that the distinction between private and public largely disappears. Individuals are politicized in that their actions are no longer private and moral but public and political.

But these, too, are difficult to find, or perhaps more accurately there are few states prepared to admit that their form of government is a totalitarian autocracy. In an age of democracy nobody wants to admit they are not democratic, that is with the exception of Islamic states who see no value in acceding to public opinion, when only religious leaders have access to what is true and morally right. Just a few years ago the overwhelming majority of the members of the United Nations were not democratic, but by 1996 Freedom House was reporting that 118 of the 191 member countries were claiming to be democracies. In fact this number had more than doubled in just twenty-five years.

The most interesting questions, therefore, are raised by the two remaining forms of government. How liberal are modern liberal democracies with all their powers to manage the economy, compulsorily purchase property, determine the content of the education in schools and monitor the movements and transactions of their citizens? And just how democratic are they when there are so few parties who can genuinely aspire to government, political leadership is drawn largely from the same exclusive pool of talent and opinion is expertly managed by the parties and the media? In his essay, 'Segregation of Dissent', E. P. Thompson describes modern liberal democracies as 'tautocracies' in which politics is largely a game at the top:

> with the media conditioning public attitudes to which politicians adjust their 'images' in the hope of floating the marginal voter their way. From image to echo and back to image, it is a system of political tautology into which principle need not enter.

Such a system of self-reinforcing opinion, which defines itself in its own terms, is likely to be intolerant to any opinion that violates the vicious circle.

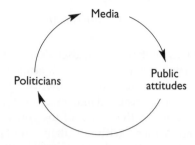

As for totalitarian democracies, how can we describe any system as democratic which allows for little or no participation and genuine accountability, and in which the protection of minority rights and civil liberties is not regarded as a priority?

Underlying many of these issues there seem to be two competing definitions of democracy. As a concept democracy seems to be one of those we previously described as 'open'. Although one part of it seems closed in its definition as government in accordance with the popular will, beyond this everything appears open. The form it takes seems to depend on the social conditions to which it needs to adapt. Western liberal democracies, based on the belief that democracy implies one-man-one-vote, regular elections, secret ballots, multi-party politics and freedom of expression, are just one adaptation of the concept.

In *The Real World of Democracy* (1966) C. B. Macpherson argues democracy emerged only after liberalism had established itself as the ruling, economic orthodoxy. Consequently, in the West it was made to serve the needs of a liberal society, which emphasized the importance of individualism, competition, free trade and consumer sovereignty. Adapting to these social conditions it matched the economic characteristics of liberalism with its own equivalent political characteristics, like the secret ballot, free competition between political parties, and the sovereignty of the electorate.

However, under different social and cultural conditions democracy has taken on different forms, ranging from what Macpherson describes as the 'underdeveloped variant' to the 'communist variant'. In these, accountability, participation, multi-party politics, even regular elections and voter sovereignty, are much less important. More significant is the progress that is being made towards achieving democratic goals like the eradication of epidemic diseases, alleviation of poverty, improvement in literacy, even industrialization. The achievement of these goals, rather than voter approval at elections, is more likely to be accepted as evidence of the democratic nature of government.

So there are here two quite different concepts of democracy, one narrow the other broad. The narrow definition of liberal democracy describes a system of government, a certain set of institutional mechanisms. There must be equal participation in regular, free elections: every vote should count the same as every other vote. The qualification to vote must not arbitrarily exclude sizeable minorities, but be based on universal franchise. And, to ensure elections are free, 'improper' influence must be kept to a minimum, which means among other things that voters must be free to vote in secret.

But still, all this would be meaningless without choice, so the system emphasizes the importance of multi-party politics. Competing parties present themselves to the electorate as viable alternative governments with a set of national policies. Although parties representing sectional interests or those campaigning on one issue are common, there must be genuine competition between parties that can form alternative governments. Importance is attached to the rule of law, that everyone is equal before the law, which is administered not in an arbitrary, but a regular, manner with clear procedures and regular courts. Likewise there are mechanisms to protect minority rights and civil liberties, with laws guaranteeing freedom of speech, information, assembly and so on. All of this amounts to a set of institutional mechanisms we commonly describe as government *for* and *by* the people.

But the broad sense, represented by totalitarian democracies and Macpherson's 'communist' and 'underdeveloped' variants, describes a form of democracy that is *for*, though not *by*, the people. Rather than a *system of government*, a mechanism, this describes a *type of society*, one in which certain social and economic conditions are met or at least governments are working to meet. Supporters of this form of democracy argue that changes in economic and social relationships only found in these types of society are essential prerequisites to equal participation of all citizens in politics. Governments must work towards reducing poverty, increasing agricultural production and improving the education system, particularly the levels of literacy. In Cuba in 1959, after the revolution that brought Fidel Castro to power, the new government sent out many educated middle-class people from the cities into the rural areas. Known as the 'Alphabet Army', their task was to raise the levels of literacy among the uneducated peasant population to equip them to take part in the political process.

If you go back to our discussion of legitimacy and the grounds for political obligation, each sense of democracy reflects one of the two sources of legitimacy grounded in either consent and promise-keeping or the government pursuing avowedly moral ends. Liberal democracies can be said to meet the standard of legitimacy grounded in theories of consent in that they give a mandate to governments through the popular vote at elections. It can also be said the converse of this (and the other source of legitimacy) is that governments in their turn promise to keep their campaign pledges and enact the policies the electorate have approved.

In contrast, totalitarian democracies and those who view democracy as less a system of government and more a type of society seem to base their claim to legitimacy on the grounds that governments are pursuing avowedly moral ends – the reduction of poverty, greater equality, eradication of disease and hunger and so on. The test for their legitimacy is not the creation of the machinery of government, the institutions and processes necessary for participation and accountability, but the empirical evidence that governments are actually achieving these moral ends.

Both these senses of democracy raise concerns about modern government that we all share to a large degree. Can leaders be far-sighted with clear long-term visions of where they believe the country should go, while at the same time being responsible to the public? It hardly seems sensible that leaders be influenced by what might be passing currents of opinion, when they are dealing with issues that affect all-important questions like national security and the future wealth and well-being of the country.

And this raises the broader question whether the public can be trusted to select leaders who have the judgement and capacity for leadership. A person elected to office because he is popular might not possess the qualities necessary for running an efficient government. From the voter's point of view there often appears to be a conflict between their opinions and those of leaders who take advice from permanent professional advisers. It seems that while the latter make the decisions the former provide the democratic facade. Nevertheless as voters we're not beyond willingly embracing the leadership of unelected technocrats in the hopeful belief that they know best how to achieve improvements in living standards or effective measures to combat crime. As Bernard Crick points out, there is a certain endurable attraction to voters of those who promise through their technocratic skills and knowledge to 'rescue mankind from the lack of certainty and the glut of compromises in politics.'

As for liberal democracies in particular, most voters have no doubt questioned whether a vote once every four or five years is a meaningful form of political participation. Even party activists at the centre of power may find themselves without any influence on policy, since parties are said to be run behind the scenes by small powerful groups, party bosses and 'spin doctors'. The most effective influence appears to be exercised by pressure groups, who may simply focus attention on their particular interests to the detriment of the public at large. In the United States the way Congress votes is largely the result of behind-the-scenes trading between lobbyists representing powerful interests and elected representatives. Under such circumstances policies seem to be a reflection of warring pressure groups, rather than the opinion of the constituencies, which have little sense of cohesion to influence the votes cast in their name.

In any case, as we saw earlier with Thompson's concept of 'tautocracy', the information on which voters depend to make their judgements and choose representatives is likely to have been carefully managed and presented by the media to deliver the results they most favour. And even if voters were to be given full and untarnished information to make their decisions, as we saw with direct democracy there is still concern about the capacity of citizens to make judgements on complex issues relating to national and international policies. Not only is this technical in nature, but there are doubts about whether we can retain the sense of detachment which allows us to separate what's in the public interest from what's in our own private and selfish interests.

As for totalitarian democracies and all those systems of government that lack the same mechanisms for making leaders accountable, there is very little preventing leaders pursuing their own interests or that of their own social or religious group. This tends to manifest itself in two ways. First the immense personal fortunes built up by leaders even in the poorest of countries, in many cases points to systematic corruption. And, second, poorly repre-

sented minorities and political opponents have in many cases suffered not only from systematic discrimination, but the loss of their liberties and even their lives as those in power attempt to eradicate their influence altogether.

■ 4. Protest, civil disobedience and our moral and legal obligations

Given these problems and the inadequacy of periodic elections in making governments realistically accountable, what are we to do? As we have seen in the last two chapters John Locke argues that our political obligation is a form of trust. As long as the state pursues justice the trust is maintained, but as soon as it fails in its duty and becomes unjust in its dealings with individuals it forfeits this trust and has no right to our obedience. The power of the ruler, therefore, according to Locke, is not absolute; it is held on trust and is revocable. As one of the earliest theories laying the groundwork for a modern theory of democracy Locke's theory is quite remarkable, not just for its concern to protect the rights of the individual, but because it also enshrines this right to rebellion and revolution.

But we have to be clear on what grounds this allows for not so much lawful protest, which is not the problem, but unlawful protest, like civil disobedience. This involves deliberately breaking the law, usually on moral grounds, and willingly accepting the consequences. John Rawls describes it as a:

> public, nonviolent, conscientious act contrary to law usually done with the intent to bring about change in the policies or laws of the government ... where arrest and punishment are expected and accepted without resistance.

4.1 Law and morality

As this suggests the grounds for civil disobedience are more often seen to be bound up with our competing moral and legal obligations. If the government breaks our trust, our political obligations to obey the law seems to conflict with our moral obligation to resist all those who break promises and fail to live up to the trust invested in them. So, the question we need to answer is whether our political obligation to obey the law, which seems to be at heart a moral obligation to fulfil our promise of obedience, should hold sway over our other moral obligation to comply with the dictates of our moral conscience?

The authoritarian answer is that law and morality are the same. Machiavelli says we learn our morality from the prince, the lawgiver. In other words, our morality comes from the law, so that our primary obligation must be to obey it rather than our moral conscience. Indeed, we have already seen Lord Devlin express a similar view that morality is as much the law's business as is subversion and that to allow for 'moral disintegration', is to accept the possibility of the disintegration of society itself.

For anarchism too, law and morality are the same, although here the precedence is reversed: it is the individual's morality that gives legitimacy to the law. When the law no longer reflects the moral consensus of the community there is no longer an obligation to obey it. Law and authority represent a distortion of man's natural sociability. They can only reflect our moral beliefs at any one time. They cement it in legislation, while the moral consensus continues to evolve. So law and authority can never accurately reflect the moral consensus; it is by definition always a form of tyranny forcing individuals to abandon their natural morality, what Proudhon describes as man's 'immanent sense of justice'.

As for totalitarian theory, here law and morality are quite separate. Hans Kelsen makes clear in *The Pure Theory of Law* (1934) that for moral problems there are moral solutions and for legal problems there are legal solutions. So we should never search for answers to our moral problems by challenging the law. Nevertheless, as we've already seen, in totalitarian regimes the difference between private and public, between moral and political, has largely disappeared. So although different, much of what we believe is moral and private in totalitarianism regimes is in fact just public and political. Our political obligations grow larger as our moral obligations recede.

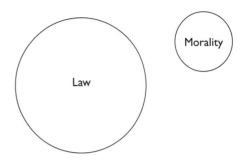

But in liberal democracies things are not so simple. Law and morality intersect. Some of our obligations are purely moral while others are purely legal. However, with a significant number of our obligations, which we might otherwise have considered to be private, the law has been extended to dictate to us what we should do. As we saw with J. S. Mill the degree of this overlap, the extent of a government's legal powers over us, is determined by the notion of 'harm': the judgement as to whether our actions are likely to cause harm to others. But how are we to define 'harm' and set the limits to legislation designed to prevent it? Earlier we analysed the different types of harm governments might legislate against from 'harm to oneself', like seat belt and crash helmet legislation, to 'harm to others', including physical, psychological, economic and moral harm. How are we to decide which harms are to count and when governments have extended their powers too far?

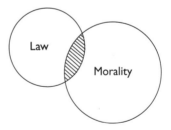

4.2 Civil disobedience

We are left, then, with two issues to consider: how far should this overlap go, how far should the government be able to dictate to us in areas we might want to regard as private; and, when they do conflict, which takes precedence, our obligation to obey the law or our moral conscience? If this does justify resorting to civil disobedience, we have found justification for unlawful protest on the grounds of the *extent of government* powers; that the government has exceeded the limits we set on its powers. But we may also find grounds in terms of the other element of forms of government that we have been examining, the *legitimacy of government*. If a government has broken the trust we place in it by using these powers in ways that lack moral legitimacy – if it has acted unjustly towards a minority or simply acted in ways that lack popular support – this too might provide grounds for civil disobedience.

We ought to dispense first with the simpler cases when it is thought civil disobedience is justified. Perhaps the most obvious is when government actions appear to lack legitimacy in the sense that they disregard popular opinion. In autocratic regimes, for instance, the interests of the majority might be sacrificed unjustly to promote the interests of a privileged minority. So, in cases like South Africa under apartheid, where the black majority had their freedoms severely curtailed for the benefit of the white minority, deliberately breaking laws upholding apartheid, like the Pass Laws that restricted the movement of members of the black population, was widely accepted by the international community as justified.

Less straightforward are the cases in which governments appear to act legitimately on the basis of majority will, but in doing so they tyrannize a minority. In Germany in the 1930s the democratically elected Nazi Government passed the Nuremberg Laws that deprived Jews of their civil rights, prevented them from working in certain professions and criminalized sexual relations between Jews and 'Aryans'. Then and later, when the lives of Jews were threatened in the 'Holocaust', individuals set about systematically rescuing Jews and giving them protection, even though they knew they were deliberately breaking the law at the risk of their own lives.

Similarly, in the United States the policy of racial segregation in many of the southern states created white-only restaurants, park benches and other public amenities, and separated the races on public transport. In the 1960s Martin Luther King justified civil disobedience against such discrimination on the grounds that the laws were unjust. He argues that there are two characteristics by which we can identify unjust laws: if 'a code that the majority inflicts on the minority ... is not binding on itself'; and if the 'minority had no part in enacting or creating (it), because that minority had no vote.' Those who commit themselves to civil disobedience do so

on the realization that there are just and unjust laws. He insists that these are not anarchists with no respect for the laws, on the contrary,

> They believe that there are laws which must be followed; they do not seek to evade the law. ... [T]he individual who disobeys the law, whose conscience tells him it is unjust and who is willing to accept the penalty by staying in jail until that law is altered, is expressing at the moment the very highest respect for law.

But what if Martin Luther King's standard is met and the minority has had the opportunity of voting on legislation and it applies equally to the majority as well as the minority, can we still oppose laws with which our moral conscience forbids us to comply? This is the most difficult of cases. Quakers who refuse to pay a proportion of their income tax, which represents what the government will spend on nuclear weapons, do so on the dictates of conscience alone, not on any question of this being an unjust law. Henry David Thoreau, the nineteenth-century American advocate of civil disobedience, argues similarly: 'If a thousand men were not to pay their tax-bills this year, that would not be a violent and bloody measure, as it would be to pay them, and enable the State to commit violence and shed innocent blood.' Thoreau argues the anarchist case that the dictates of conscience must always hold sway over our obligations to the state. He asks,

> Why has every man a conscience, then? I think that we should be men first, and subjects afterwards. It is not desirable to cultivate a respect for the law, so much as for the right. The only obligation which I have a right to assume, is to do at any time what I think right. ... Law never made men a whit more just; and, by means of their respect for it, even the well-disposed are daily made the agents of injustice.

However, even though we may want to argue that individuals putting their consciences first, even at the cost of their own liberty, have been the cause of many socially necessary reforms, which could not have been brought about in any other way, like votes for women and the campaign against slavery, still this may not be enough to counter the danger that this may allow individuals to pick and choose what laws they will and won't obey. It would mean the weakening of the rule of law: there would no longer be one objective arbiter ensuring equality and justice before the law. It would simply leave each individual to decide on the dictates of her own conscience.

However, the authoritarian answer fares little better. To argue that the individual's primary obligation is to obey the law from which she learns her morality ignores her moral sense, her capacity to make her own moral judgements. By simply complying with rules that are not of her own making she acts as *though* she is moral. This takes us back to the *Euthyphro* problem we discussed in Chapter 12. If all that makes actions right is that God commands them, then we have no freedom to exercise our own moral judgements and decide for ourselves. We simply obey commandments and comply with moral rules, whether or not we see adequate reason to and without considering whether we believe it is in fact morally right to do so.

And if we don't exercise our moral judgement we cannot develop it. We are left like poorly developed adolescents with lives blighted by moral blindness. The alternative, which allows for moral conscience, is to argue that God commands these actions because they are right. Now we have room to exercise our moral judgement and decide for ourselves the reasons God commands these actions. There is an independent criterion by which we can judge God's commands.

What's more, when we comply with laws without exercising our moral judgement in this way, it is more than likely that it is fear of the consequences, rather than the need to be virtuous, that is guiding our behaviour. Our motives are more likely to be prudential, not moral. It is in our interests not to be punished for breaking the law and it is this, rather than a will to be moral, that drives our decisions. And in this climate, of course, there is nothing preventing those in authority from using their powers in an arbitrary manner to flout the principles of justice to promote their own interests and exact revenge for presumed wrongs.

4.3 Solutions

So it seems we are left with two ways of solving the problem of whether we are always obligated to obey the law and not resort to unlawful protest, like civil disobedience. We can argue the utilitarian/empirical case of philosophers like Hume and Bentham, that the government has authority to the extent that it enjoys the allegiance of its subjects. In this case the reasons for our allegiance are more important than any promise we are said to have made by way of a social contract. And, as we have seen, these reasons are ethical. As long as the government continues to successfully pursue ethical goals we have every reason to give it our allegiance. But this is only a *prima facie* obligation as Locke's notion of trust suggests. Whatever our reasons for obeying the law, there may be stronger reasons against doing so in particular cases.

However, the problems with this are all too obvious. Such allegiance is only provisional and dependent on circumstances. It means that individuals are free to withdraw it whenever it seems they can better pursue moral objectives by doing so. Moreover, from the government's perspective its obligation is to promote the greater good whenever it sees the possibility and by whatever means. But this can lead to governments with very extensive powers with only a limited obligation to protect individual and minority rights, as we know from the history of the twentieth century and those countries, like the Soviet Union, that were guided by an ideology that focused the state's power on achieving certain ideal moral goals.

But if not the utilitarian/empirical case, then we could argue for the alternative account that we must comply with the law irrespective of our moral conscience, because the individual has implicitly agreed to the social contract. Despite his utilitarian allegiance, we have seen Mill advance this model through his principle of insulation that commits us to a similar contract with the state, which, he maintains, should only intervene if an individual's actions cause harm to others. Indeed, this is the way most of us understand the government's power to intervene in our lives. Nevertheless, the classic statement of this account, as we've seen, is in Plato's *Crito* dialogue. In this our obligation is derived from our implicit acceptance of the benefits the state provides and which we have willingly accepted. Socrates argues that he cannot make his escape from execution because the state has educated him and provided him safety and stability throughout his life, so he has a moral obligation to keep his side of the bargain and obey its judgements.

However, this too suffers from serious drawbacks. As we saw in Chapter 24 it presupposes we all have the freedom to accept or reject the contract, when natural-born citizens have never made such a deliberate choice. It also binds the next generation who, similarly, have never voluntarily agreed. If we water down the theory to allow agreement to mean mere acquiescence, as Socrates does in his argument with Crito, we are left with the problem that if consent no longer implies a promise, as it doesn't in the form of acquiescence, then it is difficult to see how it can impose an obligation. Mere failure to protest or resist the government's use of power, or our willingness to accept the benefits that this brings, does not imply an obligation. It may be an *indication* that we have accepted its authority, but it doesn't indicate *why* we have: it doesn't make clear our reasons. And a contract does involve the giving of reasons. In a contract we accept we will do something in return for certain anticipated benefits.

Mere acquiescence, then, fails to make clear why we have supposedly undertaken an obligation, when we might merely fear the consequences of resisting authority, or we might just be apathetic, or we might simply have not considered the alternatives. Given these possibilities we cannot say for certain that a person has a reason and, therefore, we cannot say he has made a promise.

But perhaps more serious still, the notion of a contract between two equal partners, the individual and the state, seriously misconceives modern power relations. In modern states the struggle for influence over the government is between the organized opinion of pressure groups and lobbyists, those who have interests to promote and protect. It is an ideological system in which social, professional and political groups inside and outside government seek to promote their interests through the close contacts they have in departments or, if they are outsiders, through the media in an attempt to influence the government indirectly through popular opinion.

In this system the individual rarely has the opportunity to exert influence. The only hope he has is to raise funds and create his own pressure group, but then new pressure groups are unlikely to be successful, particularly when they confront the established groups with close inside links to ministers and their officials. Even then it's doubtful whether liberal democracies should expect citizens to go this far to have an influence on governments. As Macpherson maintains, an effective liberal democracy should not depend upon requiring individuals to commit themselves beyond what is reasonable.

■ 5. Conclusion

As you can see this brings us back full circle to issues concerning the reasons we can give to explain why we should accept our political obligations to a form of government and how we are to legitimize a government and its use of power. When we began this section on political philosophy we used the analogy of an engine or locomotive to describe forms of government in contrast to political theories, which we described as the map setting out the destination and the route the engine must take. Now that we have examined the *way* governments are organized, we must turn our attention to political theories and what governments are organized *for*, what they set out to achieve.

In the next chapter we will examine what an ideology is and the ideals, values and ultimate aims of some of the most important. We will see the way in which they have been shaped by certain underlying philosophical assumptions about issues like the nature of man, equality, welfare, freedom and what is thought to be the ideal, in some cases, the 'utopian', society. In the process we will see the way content and form are married to produce some of the most influential political systems that have shaped our world.

■ Questions

1. In any conflict between your moral conscience and your political obligation to obey the law, do you have the moral right to disobey the law?

2. In a democracy how can we best protect liberty against the tyranny of the majority?

3. In modern democracies we entrust power to unqualified voters, but we wouldn't dream of allowing ourselves to be operated on by an unqualified surgeon. Is this criticism of democracy fair?

4. What is the definition of civil disobedience? Do you think it can ever be justified?

5. Is the claim 'all men are equal' just meaningless?

6. Can a one-party state be democratic?

7. 'If people are free to pursue their own self-interests, they will rapidly become unequal.

The only way to prevent this involves a considerable invasion of individual liberty. This shows that equality and liberty must be incompatible goals.' Discuss.

8. What is meant by 'representative democracy'? Discuss the problems involved in ensuring its effectiveness?

■ Recommended reading

King, Martin Luther, Jr. *A Testament of Hope* (ed. James M. Washington). (New York: Harper and Rowe, 1986).

Laslett, P. and W. G. Runciman (eds.) *Philosophy, Politics and Society* (Oxford: Blackwell, 1964).

MacPherson, C. B. *The Real World of Democracy* (Oxford: Oxford University Press, 1972).

Pateman, C. *Participation and Democratic Theory* (Cambridge and New York: Cambridge University Press, 1975).

Plato. Crito. In *The Last Days of Socrates*, trans. Hugh Tredennick and Harold Tarrant (Harmondsworth: Penguin, 1993).

Thoreau, H. D. *Civil Disobedience and Other Essays* (New York: Dover Publications, 1993).

 The note structure to accompany this chapter can be downloaded from our website.

Politics: Political Theories

Contents

Key issues

▶ What do we mean by saying that a particular theory or statement is ideological?

▶ Even though this might mean we are less free to choose our own beliefs and attitudes, is some form of political socialization unavoidable in modern societies if we are to guarantee the system's survival?

▶ Does the way in which we view the nature of the individual determine our view of the role of the government and its use of power?

▶ Does freedom ultimately lie in the complete abolition of government and all forms of authority as anarchists believe or must we settle for just limiting the power of the state?

▶ In democracies is it wiser to depend upon the wisdom of past generations than draw exclusively upon the limited experience of the present generation?

▶ Do we systematically confuse nationalism with patriotism?

▶ Is the state merely the means of oppression of one class by another?

We have now examined the characteristics we can find in any form of government: the nature and extent of their power and the different ways in which we legitimize the authority we give to our rulers. All this awaits those who seek to take the reins of power to pursue certain ideals, values and ultimate goals they believe to be important. What these are and how they justify them by emphasizing certain underlying philosophical assumptions about issues, like the nature of man, equality, welfare, freedom and what is thought to be the ideal society, is generally what we mean by a political theory.

Nevertheless this still leaves us with a curious distinction between those theories we describe as scientific, which we generally believe to be objective, dealing in facts and certainties, and political theories, which we hold in either deep suspicion or sublime reverence. One way of explaining the difference between the two is to say that one is ideological the other not. But what do we mean by this? It's a word we all use, but often find difficult to pin down.

■ 1. Ideology

Most political theories, if not all, are described as ideologies, although there may be good reason for arguing that some theories are not ideological in one of the many senses of the word. In the modern era the concept of ideology can be traced to the seventeenth century and Francis Bacon's reference to the 'idols of the mind', by which he means the pattern of beliefs and ideas through which we interpret the world and our experiences. For Bacon this was always something we should free ourselves from if we were to pursue the inductive method and see the world accurately as it is without preconceptions. However, in the early nineteenth century the French philosopher Destutt de Tracy employed the concept in a distinctly modern sense to mean the 'science of ideas'. He believed that by studying language and the way meaning is shaped by our social life we could reveal the sources of our biases and prejudices.

Although, as we will see, this is one of the senses in which we still use the concept today, it has also developed other implications. It is most commonly used to describe any comprehensive religious or political belief system: in other words, any system of related ideas, beliefs and values, which we may use both to understand and interpret events and comments, *and* to guide and direct actions towards specific goals. So it can identify, as Destutt de Tracy maintains, a method of revealing those biases and prejudices that shape the way we understand the world, but it can also mean, and most often does, those political ideals and goals we believe to be important.

In some cases these might constitute clear, conscious commitments to political programmes and policies, like those of communism, fascism, conservatism or liberalism. Or they might just be the product of political socialization: in other words, they might be habitual responses and interpretations adopted as a result of living and being educated within a certain type of society. We might find we have unconsciously adopted beliefs, ideas and values, which we now hold to be certain and unquestionable, as a result of legitimating forces in society which constantly reinforce them; forces like the media, the education system, and institutions like the judiciary. Alternatively, a political ideology may be so strongly and consciously held as to constitute almost a secular religion, promoting levels of commitment that involve self-sacrifice, even martyrdom.

1.1 The end of ideology debate

In Britain in the early days of the Labour Party there was quite a clear distinction between the ideas and programmes of the Labour and Conservative parties. But in the 1950s and 60s commentators noted a growth in 'consensus politics', with the two parties shedding many of their ideological differences and following quite similar policies when in government. It led some writers, most notably Daniel Bell in *The End of Ideology* (1962), to believe that they were witnessing the decline and disappearance of strong belief systems in the politics of western industrial societies – the end of ideology.

This was a popular view during the post-war economic boom, when voters appeared to choose between parties less on ideological grounds or on class loyalty, and more on their assessment of the party's ability to improve standards of living for all. The parties realized that the way to get elected in such a climate was to target the same set of voters: the undecided voters in the marginal constituencies. This meant both parties promoting the same type of policies to meet the needs and preferences of the same group. Inevitably, then, their policies seemed to be very much alike. But this theory has been less persuasive during recessions, when governments have not had the benefits of an expanding economy bringing full employment. In these circumstances they are confronted by the contentious problem of shifting wealth from one group or class to another.

However, in more general terms the history of the twentieth century can in fact be seen as 'the age of ideology'. Only the twentieth century offered the means by which governments could manipulate opinions and indoctrinate whole populations into a particular ideology, whether communism, fascism or liberal democracy. And of equal importance, the twentieth century was the age of mass democracy with universal suffrage, public education and higher levels of literacy forcing governments to persuade vast populations, rather than resort to the coercive measures employed by the autocratic governments of previous centuries.

1.2 Political socialization

Indeed, such political socialization might be unavoidable in modern societies. All individuals have to learn to adapt to the system in which they are living and, in turn, every system, if it is to survive, must encourage this process of adaptation. Thus, everyone from a relatively early age holds some sort of ideology or political belief system, even if it is only a very vague and unthinking acceptance of the status quo. Sometimes, of course, this process amounts to open indoctrination, but usually there are more subtle and effective methods. The family, the mass media, school and work, peer groups and religion all play their part. In this way in the West we come to define the concept 'democracy' purely in terms of the representative, liberal variant. In the United States most are taught from an early age to see communism as one of the more obvious manifestations of evil.

Of course, the way we are presented with knowledge of competing ideologies and the limits set on this knowledge are themselves important elements in the socialization process. The unnoticed choice of words describing political activists to conceal positive or negative value judgements is the most common and subliminal method of shaping beliefs. Someone is a 'hardliner' or 'extremist' if we disapprove of their views, but a 'committed person of principle' if we approve of them. At times of crisis ideologies show an even more intense concern to protect themselves in this way and by limiting our access to knowledge about other ideologies. Those who seek a more objective, fuller understanding are presented as unpatriotic, even seditious, a danger to national security. Examples abound in most ideologies from Stalin's purges of the 1930s to McCarthyism and the work of the Committee for Un-American Activities in the 1950s.

1.3 Interpretations of ideology

The description of ideology so far developed can be analysed into three interpretations that commonly underlie our use of the concept.

1.3.1 Karl Marx: ideology as 'false consciousness'

In *The German Ideology* (1845) Marx argues that all ideas are the product of specific economic and social systems. All thought is socially determined: individuals are not autonomous in their ideas; they are not free to determine their own beliefs and attitudes. Instead, they are socialized from birth into a certain pattern of values, beliefs and attitudes depending on their class position in society. Marx argues:

> the production of ideas, of conceptions, of consciousness, is at first directly interwoven with the material activity and the material intercourse of men, the language of real life. ... Consciousness can never be anything else than conscious existence, and the existence of men is their actual life-process. ... We set out from real, active men, and on the basis of their real life-process we demonstrate the development of the ideological reflexes and echoes of this life-process. ... Morality, religion, metaphysics, all the rest of ideology and their corresponding forms of consciousness, thus no longer retain the semblance of independence. ... [M]en, developing their material production and their material intercourse, alter, along with this their real existence, their thinking and the products of their thinking. Life is not determined by consciousness, but consciousness by life.

But this doesn't mean that man is impotent, unable to think for himself and change his world. The circumstances that shape and form consciousness are not independent of human activity. Marx argues that men are both the products and the potential changers of circumstances. Living within a capitalist society man is imbued with unquestioning faith in the values of capitalism: in the 'natural' justice and inviolability of the central tenets of capitalism, like the pursuit of self-interest, profit, private property, the division of labour and inequality. But, Marx argues, as capitalism develops, the inequality, injustice and exploitation of such a system will become more apparent to the individual worker, who will join with his fellow workers to overthrow and change the system. Out of their experience of living and working within capitalist society workers will develop their own ideology reflecting their own interests and class consciousness. In opposition to this, the ruling class will seek to preserve the status quo, within which lies their interests, by promoting the ruling class ideology – a 'false consciousness', which seeks to blindfold the worker to the reality of his situation.

This class-based picture of the world that ideology presents is, therefore, partial and incomplete. It is composed of justifications which mask the specific interests of any particular class. Thus, for Marx, ideology is a subjective and distorted set of ideas and beliefs which corresponds to the interests of a particular class. It amounts to 'false consciousness', because it presents itself as a true, undeniable and total picture of society.

In all class societies the dominant class has the capacity to impose its own set of ideas and values upon subordinate classes as a means of defending its own position and interests. In contemporary capitalist society, according to the Marxist argument, the bourgeoisie spreads its ideology throughout society by virtue of its ownership and control of the mass media and the major institutions of society – political, judicial, military, industrial, educational and religious. Except in times of crisis, this is not a conscious or deliberate effort to mislead other classes, but a necessary and inevitable consequence of the economic and social relationships in a class society.

So, in every class society there is a 'dominant ideology', which favours the maintenance of the status quo and continued rule by the dominant class. Marx explains:

> The ideas of the ruling class are in every age the ruling ideas: i.e. the class which is the ruling *material* force of society is at the same time its ruling *intellectual* force. The class which has the means of material production at its disposal has control at the same time over the means of mental production.

And his collaborator, Friedrich Engels, extends this picture to show how history moves through distinct class stages with one ruling class replacing another:

> As society has hitherto moved in class antagonism, morality was always a class morality; it has either justified the domination and the interests of the ruling class, or as soon as the oppressed class become powerful enough, it has represented the revolt against this domination and the future interests of the oppressed.

Ideology in this sense, therefore, can only be eliminated with the abolition of all classes and with it

class rule: in other words, with the establishment of a classless society or communism.

1.3.2 Karl Mannheim: ideology as a system of beliefs

In *Ideology and Utopia* (1929), Karl Mannheim endorses Marx's argument that people's ideas are shaped by the social context in which they live. Like Marx he maintains that ideology is the thought system of a dominant ruling group, and 'utopia' is the conflicting thought system of an oppressed or subordinate group. But, in contrast to Marx, Mannheim's concept of ideology could be said to have a broader application. He argues that ideologies are different 'styles of thought', systems of beliefs characteristic of a particular class or group, which promote and protect their interests. These he describes as 'particular' ideologies; they could be, say, the ideology of small businessmen or the ideology of the professions. They constitute, he explains, 'more or less conscious disguises of the real nature of the situation' which may range from unconscious self-deception to conscious lies.

In striking contrast to this he identifies another type of ideology: a 'total' ideology or a *weltanschauung*, the world-view of a whole class or age. It promotes more than just the interests of a particular class or group; instead it seeks to generate a complete commitment to a certain way of life. It seeks to convert more of the world to its beliefs and through this exercise more influence in the protection of its own interests. During the Cold War of the 1950s and 1960s, and more recently in the 1980s with Reagan and Thatcher on one side and Brezhnev on the other, two competing world-views

---

Brief lives
Mannheim, Karl

Dates: 1893–1947
Born: Budapest, Austria-Hungary
Best known for: Helping to establish the sociology of knowledge. He emphasized the importance of the role played by ideology in shaping knowledge.

Major works: *Conservatism: A Contribution to the Sociology of Knowledge* (1925), *Ideology and Utopia* (1929), *Man and Society in an Age of Reconstruction* (1940).

(Western Capitalism and Soviet Communism) sought to control certain areas of interest and influence in the world. Peace and stability in this context depended on a balance of power and influence in an atmosphere of 'ideological warfare'.

In contrast to the narrow sense of ideology, total ideologies might not be a matter of deceit or even interests, but rather an expression of the outlook of a whole social group, a way of life. And in this, according to Mannheim, lies the strength of Marxism, in that it fuses both of these conceptions of ideology into one.

1.3.3 Lionel Trilling: ideology as 'emotional safety'

In comparison with the other two Lionel Trilling in *The Liberal Imagination* (1950) identifies a different, though important, aspect of the concept. He defines ideology as:

> the habit or the ritual of showing respect for certain formulas to which, for various reasons having to do with emotional safety, we have very strong ties of whose meaning and consequences in actuality we have no clear understanding.

As you can see this stresses our unconscious acceptance of the effects of socialization and our need to conform with, and be accepted by, the wider social group. Ideology in this sense gives us a familiar conceptual framework through which we can reinterpret unfamiliar experiences and arguments into familiar terms. In this way arguments, opinions and evidence that might otherwise seem threatening are robbed of their force, thereby preserving our 'emotional safety'. Like Mannheim's 'particular' ideologies, it emphasizes the importance of accepting a common core of values and beliefs as part of the process of belonging to a particular group. So we might argue that groups like vegetarians, feminists, even accountants, real-estate agents and second-hand car salesmen all have their own distinct ideologies.

But there is one note of caution before we leave these three interpretations. It would be too simplistic to assume that there are just three straightforward, uncontentious definitions of ideology: that the concept can be wrapped up in a simple list of meanings. As we have already discovered, concepts rarely have just one meaning: in a sense they don't have meaning in their own right at all, but only in so far as people use them in different ways. So, as we found in Chapter 2, it is probably more accurate to say that our task is to analyse concepts by mapping out their actual or possible uses and applications. The concept of ideology is no exception to this.

Indeed, it reveals the complexity and often contradictory nature of this task. There are no right answers, although clearly some are better than others. For example, all three of the definitions appear to point to contradictions within the uses and applications of the concept. On the one hand ideology suggests that the individual, through his beliefs and ideas, distorts reality to reflect his preconceptions, whereas, on the other hand, it implies that reality distorts the individual by shaping his language, through which he attempts to understand the world. Both of these implications will reappear repeatedly as we examine particular political ideologies.

■ 2. Classifying political theories

As we have seen in the last few chapters, politics is concerned with the study of power and authority; the limits, sources and goals of political power; the relationships between rulers and ruled; and the sources and justification of authority. The range of political ideas and theories, that address these issues, can be variously classified according to their views on certain key issues, notably,

1. The use and limits of power.

2. Human nature.

3. The left and right wing spectrum.

4. The concept and role of the state.

2.1 The use and limits of power

The first we have examined in previous chapters, particularly in our analysis of libertarian and totalitarian theories, both of which in their different ways set the limits to government power and the mechanisms by which we can gauge whether governments are using their powers legitimately. The same could be said for our understanding of human nature, although we have not examined this as systematically as it deserves.

2.2 Human nature

In one way or another all political theories have as their central concern the liberty of the individual, whether that liberty is seen as best promoted by the individual surrendering himself to the state, or by being insulated from the effects of it. But the implications of this concern depend upon how the individual is conceived. Earlier we pointed out that if the individual is seen, for example, as self-reliant, independent, educated, and healthy, any extension of state authority is likely to result in the diminution of his freedom to govern his own affairs. But, if he is restricted by social forces that prevent him from developing his abilities and maximizing his liberty, if he is, for example, poorly educated, dependent on social benefits, unemployed, and suffering from ill-health, any extension of the state's powers is likely to enlarge his liberty, if it leads to the removal of these inhibiting influences.

What's more, earlier we found this not only suggested the two concepts of liberty – negative and positive – but that the very concept of liberty was itself ideological. We are not so much concerned with the quantity of liberty as with the concept of liberty that best promotes the interests of a certain group made up of certain types of individual. If we envisage society as largely made up of self-reliant individuals, we are likely to argue for the negative concept of liberty because, in Mannheim's sense of ideology, this promotes and protects the interests of the group made up of people like this. And, by the same token of course, if it is made up of individuals dependent upon the state, then it is the positive concept of liberty we choose, in this case an ideological concept promoting and protecting the interests of this group.

But in passing we have also seen views of human nature influence political ideas in yet another way. Some political philosophers, like Hobbes, hold a pessimistic view of the nature of man, believing that he is basically selfish, aggressive, acquisitive and egoistic. Consequently, he lives in a perpetual state of war with others: in a fierce, uncontrolled, competitive struggle to maximize self-interest. Others, like Rousseau, hold an optimistic view, believing that man is basically good and cooperative, but his nature is constrained by the social institutions of the society into which he is born: 'Man is born free; and everywhere he is in chains.' Still others, like Mill and most other liberals, believe that man can live without too much intervention by the state. Like Rousseau they believe he is sociable, but, unlike Rousseau, they don't believe the individual is enslaved and needs the state to relieve him from bondage. Rather they believe he is already in a state of freedom and can be left confidently to sort out his own affairs without interference.

Of course the consequences of this are obvious. If you believe in the pessimistic account of human nature you are likely to believe that effective government demands strong authoritarian controls exerted by the state over the individual to restrain his anti-social nature, to prevent 'the war of all against all.' In contrast, if you are convinced by the optimistic account, then you are likely to argue for limited state powers, which leave the individual free to govern his own affairs in accordance with his natural sociability.

But now add to this pessimistic/optimistic split another and you can see an interesting and, at times, helpful way of classifying political theories. Some political philosophers, like Hobbes, Locke and most classical liberals in the nineteenth century, view the individual in static, mechanistic terms. The state can take no role in developing the individual, whose nature and state are fixed from birth. All the state can do is to provide the right environment in which the individual can live in freedom and stability: in Hobbes' account an authoritarian regime that will contain his aggressive instincts; in the liberal account a limited government that will allow him to live according to his own desires, maximizing his own self-interest. Other philosophers, like Rousseau, Gentile and those who advocate more totalitarian systems of government, adopt a dynamic concept of the individual, who is full of potential and can be developed towards greater self-realization and freedom.

Put both of these classifications together – the optimistic/pessimistic split with the static/dynamic split – and we have a broad classification of political theories into three types, shown overleaf.

2.3 The left and right wing spectrum

The terms 'left' and 'right' were first used politically during the French Revolution, when the

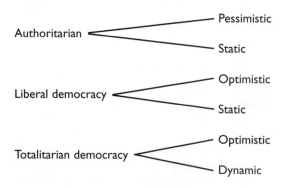

parliamentary deputies were seated in a semi-circle from the most reactionary (backward-looking) on the right to the most radical (forward-looking) on the left. In the broad sense the term 'right wing' applies to those who support and defend the existing system, while the term 'left wing' applies to those who challenge the existing system and seek progressive changes. A shift to the right, or a desire to return to a previous situation, is described as 'reactionary', while a shift to the left, or a desire to move forward, is described as 'radical' or 'revolutionary' depending on the degree and speed of change.

Even so, this broad classification must be treated with some caution. With the progress achieved by the left in politics and particularly with the advance of liberalism and socialism since the Industrial Revolution, it is not unusual to refer to the 'radical right'. Although this appears to be self-contradictory, it refers to those who adopt radical policies and extreme political methods in order to return to a pre-socialist, pre-liberal state of affairs, which existed before the Industrial Revolution. Mussolini, for example, said of himself 'I am a reactionary and a revolutionary.' This is in contrast to the traditional right, who merely approach change cautiously.

In economic terms 'right wing' is usually associated with supporters of private ownership, and 'left wing' with advocates of collective ownership. There are, of course, obvious reasons for this: supporters of private ownership tend to be the wealthier members of society who have vested interests in the status quo. Those on the left, therefore, tend to see the left–right struggle as one of class conflict over the

distribution of wealth, power and status in society. But, again, some caution is needed before we assume that 'left' and 'right' corresponds to extensive and limited government involvement in the economy and society. Collective ownership may take the form of self-government in small local regions or in communes, and private ownership may take the form of totalitarian fascism.

In terms of values and ideals the right wing emphasizes the importance of preserving the status quo or returning to the values of the past, consequently they are likely to support policies that seek to maintain tradition, inequality and nationalism or patriotism. In contrast the left stresses progressive social change, radical reform or revolution, equality, internationalism, humanity and toleration. But still these labels take on new meanings as circumstances change. The 'radical left' were distinguished in the nineteenth century by their demands for universal suffrage, which is no longer viewed as a radical demand. They are also relative to their context. In the political culture of some countries, those parties regarded as the radical left are nothing more than the representatives of centre-left politics in others, while those who are regarded as centre-right in other countries are the advocates of extreme right wing values.

2.4 The concept and role of the state

However, one of the more interesting ways of classifying political theories cuts across the left–right spectrum. This classifies political theories according to the way in which the state as both a society and as a system of government is conceived, either organically or mechanistically. This is useful in that it allows us to identify more clearly what a particular political theory is likely to see as the role and functions of the state given that it is either an organic or mechanistic theory.

2.4.1 Organic theory: the natural state

This likens the state to a living organism, like the human body. Indeed, philosophers have long used the term 'body politic' to describe the state. But once it is conceived in this way certain things follow. Like

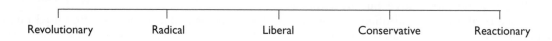

the human body, in which every part has its appropriate place and function, in society every individual and every institution too has its appropriate place and function, its natural social role. And each part as it performs this is dependent upon every other part within the harmonious organic whole. It follows, therefore, that theories adopting this concept accept that there is a natural inequality between individuals and groups, each with their own role to play within a hierarchy of social orders. While some are natural leaders (the brain in the organic analogy), others have more subordinate roles as mere workers (the hands). So, there is limited upward social mobility, which, of course, would be unnatural according to this concept. This is no meritocracy in which talent competes to rise up the social scale. Natural leaders 'emerge': either they are chosen by history to fulfil the nation's destiny or they emerge from an aristocracy who have been bred over the centuries for leadership.

Extend the analogy still further and you find that since the parts are dependent on the whole for their continued existence, the whole is therefore more important than any group or individual within it. The state is natural and prior to the individual, who exists to serve the state. The state is greater than the sum of its parts. And, like all organic things that grow and develop through time, it is the product of past experience, history and tradition, encapsulated within institutions which have through the ages soaked up the unique wisdom and personality of a particular community of people. Each nation is quite unique, as each individual is unique; the product of its own particular set of experiences. Because of this, history, tradition and the institutions that symbolise them attract reverence and respect.

In the nineteenth century nationalist philosophers, like Hegel and Mazzini, employed the organic analogy to develop political theory as a theory of history. More than just a theory of the past, or tradition, as in conservatism, this depicted the nation, like an individual, with a particular character and temperament which gradually reveals itself through history according to distinct laws of history. As individuals have talents and personal characteristics which only emerge as the individual grows, so too has the state. But laws of history that govern this growth are not just a means of interpreting the past; they also determine the way in which the nation will develop in the future as it fulfils its destiny. They alone legitimize a leader's decisions; they are the final arbiter of what is politically right.

Hegel maintained that the nation-state represented 'the march of God through history'.

Equally important, as the state progresses through history towards greater and greater enlightenment and freedom, so too will the individual. It follows, then, that to achieve this freedom individuals can do nothing else but submit themselves to the inevitability of the laws of history and, in turn, to the state. It means, as Hegel argues, that freedom lies in the recognition of necessity. Indeed, to do otherwise amounts to little more than the illusion of freedom, like the prisoner on the deck of a ship, who is free to crawl eastward as the ship travels westward.

This explains why organic political theories, like conservatism and nationalism, are suspicious of the value of democracy and expressions of the popular will. Rather than representative democracy, in which rulers are guided, even compelled, to implement the wishes of the electorate revealed through elections, conservatism favours responsible democracy, in which the wishes of the electorate are subordinate to the judgments of natural leaders. They alone are qualified to interpret history and tradition, because they have privileged access to what Edmund Burke in *Reflections on the Revolution in France* (1790) describes as the accumulated wisdom of the ages. At the heart of this lies the assumption that individuals are only made civilized through the influence of institutions and natural leaders, both of whom over the centuries have soaked up this wisdom.

Finally, by the very nature of an organic analogy, conflict within the body politic can never be a good thing: it must be a sign of ill-health and disorder. All forms of conservatism believe in natural consensus and harmony, unlike Marxism, for example, which sees conflict as the driving force of human progress. Indeed, in the British Conservative Party members have been denounced for their willingness to use the language of social 'class', because of the implication of social conflict. Any conflict and disharmony within the body politic calls for strong medicinal measures, usually in the form of new laws, higher sentences and increased police powers, to bring it back into line and restore the health of society.

As in any organic body the well-being of society depends upon maintaining the good health of the community, which means maintaining its harmony and stability. Social conflict, therefore, is usually an indication that groups or individuals have temporarily lost sight of their duties and responsibilities. The solution lies not in reforming society to appease social grievances, as the radical liberals and socialists would demand, but in re-educating individuals, improving their sense of social responsibility. The fault lies not with society, but with the individuals and groups that compose it. It explains the importance conservatives place upon law and order, resistance to change and the national interest above that of individuals and groups.

2.4.2 Mechanistic theory: the artificial state

In contrast, mechanistic theories see the state as an artificial creation, a machine designed by humans to meet their needs, with each part, each individual, equal, autonomous and free to move beyond the social class into which they were born. Individuals, therefore, are more important than the group or the state, which exists to serve their needs. It also follows that it is the wishes of the present, rather than the wisdom of past generations and natural leaders that determine policies. To reflect current opinion with any accuracy calls for representative, rather than responsible, democracy. The machine operates in regular, predictable ways unaffected by our understanding of the past. It is ideally designed to meet the needs of individuals, so it must reflect these needs and nothing more: not the past nor the opinions of a traditional elite.

As you can see, this is an atomistic theory: the state is no more than the sum of its parts. It is merely a loose collection of isolated individuals, whose behaviour, and that of the state's, is governed by certain natural laws. Supporters of political theories of this kind tend to argue that as states are all merely the sum of isolated individuals and as these individuals are universally the same, in that they are thought to be rational and self-interested, then states everywhere are universally alike.

This sort of thinking was at the heart of much of the missionary zeal of late nineteenth-century imperialism, with governments seeking to bring parliamentary democracy to all nations across the world, regardless of their unique culture and traditions. Their optimistic belief in progress strengthened their confidence in the present generation which had in many respects advanced beyond all previous generations. According to the mechanistic analogy, to respect tradition and the wisdom of the past is unprogressive, amounting almost to superstition. Regardless of tradition and customs, states should assume the same universal pattern, in which government is conducted in accordance with the aggregate of individual wills and natural,

particularly economic, laws are allowed to operate freely without government interference.

Of course, the claim that all states are universally alike is in marked contrast to the organic theory, which argues that each one is quite unique as a result of its particular historical experiences. It also underlines the importance that supporters of the mechanistic model attach to rationalism in politics. The natural laws that govern the behaviour of the state as a machine can only be revealed through the application of reason. Reason is universal. It alone can provide the guarantees necessary for the protection of freedom and equality. Surrendering to emotions only threatens democracy, along with the rights and liberties of individuals. It gives free rein to our strongly held prejudices about certain groups and, in turn, lends support to policies and actions that discriminate against individuals and treat them as unequal. Only the universal dictates of reason can protect us from this.

In contrast, the organic theory emphasizes the unique national temperament and the importance of affective factors in politics, like emotions and feelings. Emotive appeals to national fervour in nationalism, fascism and conservatism, and to the love of the leader in totalitarian regimes, endorse the importance that systems modelled on the organic analogy find themselves placing on these affective factors in politics and in turn on their suspicion of rationalism in politics.

Lastly, all those theories adopting the mechanistic analogy argue for a strategy of non-interference. In the last chapter we saw that supporters of liberalism tend to see society as a machine which must be left without interference to operate freely according to certain natural laws that govern the behaviour of the individual. Like any machine it must be left to run as smoothly as possible without interference. The only role for the government, therefore, is to remove obstacles that might affect its efficiency and the individual's freedom to maximize his own self-interests. The government's powers are, therefore, limited and negative. Only in this way, they argue, through *laissez-faire* economic policies and limited government involvement in the affairs of individuals, can they ensure economic efficiency and social justice.

Early advocates of *laissez-faire* policies and limited government, like Adam Smith, argued that leaving entrepreneurs to make their own decisions about things which directly affect their interests will guarantee efficient distribution and use of economic resources. With their own interests at stake they are bound to make the best use of them, which will in turn promote the interests of the community. In *The Wealth of Nations* (1776) he argues,

> By pursuing his own interests he frequently promotes that of the society more effectually than when he really intends to promote it. I have never known much good done by those who affected to trade for the public good.

The same compatibility between individual and community interests lies at the core of the utilitarian arguments of Jeremy Bentham and James Mill, who also supported the mechanistic model of limited government. As each individual exploits her freedom to maximize her own interests, by definition, in view of the fact that society is seen as merely the sum of its parts, the happiness of society as a whole will be maximized. The well-being of society is represented by nothing more than the arithmetical calculation of the aggregate individual happinesses.

What's more, they warn that government interference beyond these limits is likely to infringe the natural rights of individuals. In contrast to the emphasis in organic theories, mechanistic theories, like liberalism, emphasize the importance of *rights*, rather than *duties*. By analysing man and society into their parts, each governed by natural laws, they ascribe to each individual equivalent natural rights which they regard, like natural laws, to be inviolable.

As you've no doubt realized already it is possible and quite useful to draw up two comparative lists of the characteristics of each theory. The list below is by no means comprehensive, so, as you develop your understanding of

different political theories, you will be able to add your own characteristics to them.

3. Political theories

Now that we have ways of classifying political theories we can examine them individually. Although limited space prevents us exploring them as thoroughly as we would like, it will give us the opportunity to explore their individual assumptions, to see how they fit into the methods of classifying them that we have seen above and ask in what sense each of them can be described as an 'ideology'.

In the structure overleaf you can see the broad distinction between mechanistic and organic theories. As the United Nations figures indicated, most modern states claim to be democracies, so they must answer in one way or the other the questions John Locke poses in *Two Treatises of Government*: how are we to set the limits to a government's power and how are we to ensure that it uses that power in a legitimate way, that is to say in a way which reflects the popular will. As you can see there are two ways in which these questions can be answered, by appealing either to individuals or to the community, assuming that it is one harmonious entity with one clear voice.

The first way is perhaps the most familiar, at least to those of us who live in the West. This is the libertarian view that societies are just loose collections of isolated individuals, and so to get a clear reflection of the popular will we need only ask individuals through elections, referendums and wherever possible through systems of direct democracy. But in such systems the individual and her interests need to be made sovereign: she must not be dwarfed by large centralised institutional structures of government.

3.1 Anarchism: order without authority

Anarchism presents the most extreme, although most consistent, expression of this argument. It advocates the complete abolition of the state, indeed all forms of authority and their replacement by free, voluntary association and cooperation between individuals and groups. Anarchists are not opposed to all forms of law, but just to that which is not self-imposed. Paul Goodman describes them as

So, to summarize:

Mechanistic	Organic
Atomistic	Holistic
Individual	Community
Arithmetical	Traditional
Representative	Responsible
Meritocratic	Elitist
Reason	Emotion
Rationalism	Romanticism
Rights	Duties
Equality	Hierarchy
Universalism	Uniqueness

Political theories

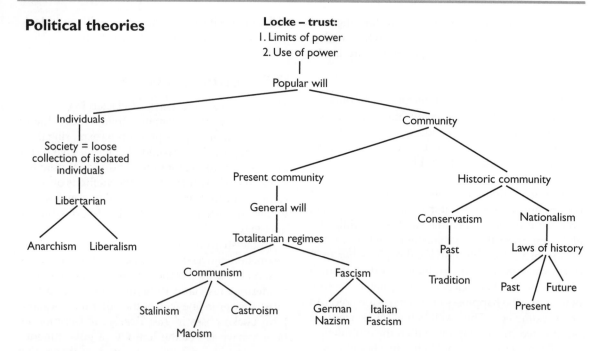

Locke – trust:
1. Limits of power
2. Use of power

Popular will

Individuals

Society = loose collection of isolated individuals

Libertarian

Anarchism   Liberalism

Community

Present community

General will

Totalitarian regimes

Communism

Stalinism   Castroism

Maoism

Fascism

German   Italian
Nazism   Fascism

Historic community

Conservatism   Nationalism

Past   Laws of history

Tradition

Past / Future

Present

believing in 'local power, community development, rural reconstruction, decentralist organization. ... They prefer a simpler standard of living. ... [T]hey do not trust the due process of administrators and are quick to resort to direct action and civil disobedience.'

Indeed they view all authority as a form of tyranny in that it has a stultifying effect, crystallizing the status quo, cementing it in law for the foreseeable future, when in fact the moral consensus, social customs and mutual agreements are continually evolving and adjusting. Failure to reflect this amounts to tyranny in that individuals are forced to do things they otherwise would not choose to do. For the same reason, as Goodman points out, they are committed to a simple life. They are opposed to the complex technology, materialism and wealth of modern society, because it dictates to the individual and enslaves him in the process.

It may also seem surprising that they are opposed not just to aristocracy, which they see as rule by an unrepresentative elite, but also to parliamentary democracy. The reason is that the aim of parliamentary democracy is to give sovereignty to 'the people', whereas, according to anarchists, there are only individuals. The collective term merely diminishes the importance of the individual, which should in fact be the central concern. On similar grounds they reject parliamentary institutions,

because they represent the individual abdicating her sovereignty to representatives. This underscores their insistence that all individuals must take full, individual, moral responsibility for their actions and the decisions they make. In direct action and civil disobedience, the individual acts herself, she doesn't delegate to others, and she accepts the consequences.

So, while anarchism is clearly on the mechanistic side of our structure, it does not seem to be ideological, at least in the Mannheim sense as a system of beliefs that promote and protect the interests of a particular group or class. However, it cuts across the left–right spectrum. On the left there are the 'communalist anarchists', like Pierre Proudhon and Peter Kropotkin, the Russian anarchist who was imprisoned by the Tsar, who advocate individuals committing themselves to communal living on socialist principles, involving the smallest loss of individual sovereignty. On the right there are the extreme laissez-faire individualists who advocate, as Nozick describes it, only a 'minimal state'.

3.2 Liberalism: minimizing the state

Beyond what we have already said about liberalism, although, unlike anarchism, it doesn't advocate the abolition of the state but accepts it as a necessary evil, the extent of government it accepts as necessary largely depends on the type of individual it is legislating for. In other words, this is ideological in the sense that anarchism is not, in that it seeks to promote the interests of a group made up of a certain type of individual.

For example, classical liberalism in the early nineteenth century in Britain sought a system of limited government, *laissez-faire* economics and free competition, which met the needs of middle-class entrepreneurs, who received the vote in 1832. But at the end of the nineteenth century Victorian society discovered, largely through the work of social reformers like Charles Booth and Seebohm Rowntree, that poverty and unemployment were not the individual's problems, the products of personal failings and idleness. The Great Depression (1874–96) brought the realization that the capitalist system has a habit of periodically falling into a recession through no fault of the individual worker, a growing number of whom were now able to vote.

With this new type of individual in their sights, and through the work of philosophers like David Ritchie whose book, *Natural Rights* (1895), brought the concept of positive liberty to the notice of a wider number, liberals began to talk about positive, rather than negative liberty. And to promote this it was necessary to give governments greater powers to tax the rich, through direct progressive income tax, inheritance tax and taxes on unearned income to redistribute wealth to the poor, and to set up systems of unemployment benefit and state pensions.

From this two distinct types of liberalism have survived. One maintains the commitment to positive liberty, supporting the welfare state along with government intervention in the economy, while at the same time promoting competition and free markets. This is broadly the position of the Liberal Democrats, who occupy a position at the centre of the left–right spectrum of British politics. The other, modelled on classical liberalism, is now a key element in conservative thinking, particularly in the British Conservative Party and the American Republican Party. Advocating leaner governments, reduction in welfare payments and support for the poor, free markets and a low-tax economy, it conflicts with the paternalistic element in conservatism, which develops out of the organic nature of conservative political theory. This side of conservative thinking has long maintained that the price natural leaders pay for their privileges is their responsibility to maintain the health of the community by aiding the poor and unemployed when they need help.

3.3 Totalitarianism: constant mobilization

The other way of answering Locke's two questions, as we suggested above, is to appeal to the community, assuming that it is one harmonious entity with one clear voice. But then we need to know what we mean by 'community'. There are two ways in which we can answer this: either it means the present community that exists in the society in which we live, or it refers to a historic community, not just the present but the past and the future. This means we have a responsibility to think not just about this generation but the legacy of the past and the interests of future generations.

Those political theories that claim to be able to identify clearly the will of the present community, communist theories like Stalinism, Maoism and Castroism, and fascist theories like German Nazism and Italian Fascism, have all adopted the totalitarian form of government. Each is grounded in the assumption that history throws up a leader with rare intuitive abilities to interpret accurately the general will and the course the nation should take. This is thought to be, as Gentile describes it, 'the will of the individual himself in its universal and absolute aspect'. By reflecting this the leader's will is made legitimate; it is the will of the individual writ large.

In effect, supporters of this type of regime maintain it is merely a form of self-government, and, as the individual is unlikely to enslave himself – as Rousseau says, he is unlikely to 'forge fetters for himself' – there is no point in limiting the power he has to liberate himself. This is what Gentile describes as 'absolute democracy' as opposed to liberal democracy. Unlike liberal democracy it is not static and limited, it is dynamic with total power. Those theories adopting totalitarianism have as their goal the destiny of the nation. In the process they claim to liberate the individual; as Rousseau puts it, 'Man must be made to be free.'

The peculiar dynamism that drives these regimes means that although the leader is the head of a state composed of the usual institutions of government, he must successfully subjugate them to his own personal will, otherwise he would be restricted to using his powers as the institutions dictate. To avoid this sort of accountability and give himself the freedom to use his powers according to his own dictates, the leader must keep everything around him moving: he must maintain 'mass mobilization'. Unlike liberal democracies, where, during times of emergencies like wars, there is temporary mass mobilization of effort to achieve the ultimate goal of defending the nation successfully, in totalitarian regimes this is permanent, what Hannah Arendt describes as 'permanent impermanence'.

She argues that totalitarian leaders are driven by 'perpetual motion mania' to keep everything around them in a process of constant change and uncertainty so as to secure and enhance their power. In this way the leader can guarantee uncritical acceptance of his policies and the sacrifices he demands from his people. In communist and fascist regimes, two types of ultimate goal have been used to generate and justify mass mobilization. The first, the achievement of certain ideal goals like social equality or rapid industrialization, was used to justify the worsening economic and social conditions. The leader argued that if there were to be jobs for all, free education and health care, and improvements in living standards, sacrifices had to be made – present consumption had to be cut to invest in the future. With everyone working to achieve such noble ideals, uncritical acceptance of the leader's policies was virtually guaranteed.

But probably the most popular pretext was national defence. This could take two forms: the external and the internal aggressor. In either case it was frequently fictitious. With the external aggressor it was argued that the nation faced a serious threat to its survival from a foreign power, although this could change with the most bewildering about-turns, as occurred in 1939 when Soviet Russia signed the non-aggression pact with Nazi Germany. Like the external aggressor, the pretext of the internal aggressor could be equally fictitious. People were constantly reminded that the nation was under continual threat from the ruthless activities of counter-revolutionaries within the state, who were dedicated to forcing them into slavery, into the servitude of other nations. Their agents were supposed to be everywhere – working on the next bench in the factory, sitting next to you in the works canteen, or living in the apartment opposite.

In this way the totalitarian leader could keep everything around him moving, in a state of constant uncertainty, leaving people more willing to depend blindly on his supposed infallibility. As a result, he could avoid being trapped within the fixed rules and systems of accountability of institutional government which would have ensured the regular use of power and authority. Under these conditions to talk about the state is fundamentally misleading: there *was* no state. As Leonard Schapiro says about the term 'totalitarian state', it is a contradiction in terms.

3.4 Conservatism: the rule of tradition

As to the second way of interpreting community, as 'historic community', this in turn might mean two things: either a theory of the past, as in conservatism, or a theory of history, embracing the past, present and the future.

At the risk of repeating what we have already said about conservatism as a theory resembling the organic analogy, this is an approach that places inordinate value on the wisdom to be found in the past. It is reluctant to accept, as liberalism does, that the present generation alone offers sufficient knowledge and ability to make the right decisions. Suspicious anyway of all rational approaches to politics, and traditionally anti-intellectual, it would rather depend upon the wisdom found in tradition. In Edmund Burke's account it is better to rely upon the accumulated wisdom of the many past generations of natural leaders than to depend just upon the slender stock of wisdom of the present generation. He says:

> We are afraid to put men to live and trade each on his own private stock of reason; because we suspect that this stock in each man is small, and that the individuals would do better to avail themselves of the general bank and capital of nations, and of ages.

Society, he declares, is a contract:

> It is a partnership in all science; a partnership in all art; a partnership in every virtue, and in all perfection. As the ends of such a partnership cannot be obtained in many generations, it becomes a partnership not only between those who are living, but between those who are living, those who are dead, and those who are to be born.

This stress on tradition and the pragmatic, responsive and empirical way in which it approaches political problems make it more difficult to say exactly in what way conservatism can be said to be ideological. In terms of espousing a certain set of consistent principles it is often difficult to pin down. Nevertheless, on many issues, like law and order and respect for authority, conservatives demonstrate a stubborn, principled approach: they are predictable in their unwillingness to compromise on them. However, it is more clearly ideological in the Mannheim sense of promoting and protecting the interests of a particular class. So is it in the Trilling sense of ideology as a science of ideas, a way of interpreting the world stemming from, and sympathetic to, the experiences of a particular social class. It has always been a party of the propertied classes, which today include more than just the landed classes.

3.5 Nationalism: pre-political homogeneity

However, beyond this interpretation of 'historic community' in terms of tradition, there are those theories, like nationalism, fascism, and communism (in the special sense of Marxism), that define it in terms of theories of history. Nationalism in its broadest sense is the feeling of belonging to a group that is united by certain common ties – racial, linguistic, cultural or historical. But, in its ideological sense, it extols the virtues of the nation insisting that it has an overriding claim on all those who are members of it.

In its earliest form in the nineteenth century it reflected the broad sense above. The Italian nationalist Giuseppe Mazzini argued that individual nations were merely sub-divisions of the larger world society. The German romantic philosopher Johann Gottfried von Herder argued similarly that nations have their own individual characters and cultures, which, like individuals, develop and reveal themselves through time. As each nation reaches its fulfilment it contributes to the pool of world culture, bringing greater understanding and peaceful co-existence. But with Hegel a line of thought began which stressed both the need for purity of national cultures and the recognition that some cultures were superior and would dominate others.

Today it might not have the same stress on purity and superiority, although these are rarely far away. As Eli Kedourie argues, nationalism holds that 'humanity is naturally divided into nations, that nations are known by certain characteristics that can be ascertained and that the only legitimate type of government is national self-government.' In other words it is the belief that there exists, prior to becoming a nation, some form of homogeneity among people, some form of pre-political unity. This can be based on language, race, history, culture, even religion. But it is better if these distinctions are natural and not a matter of choice. If they are based on will and not nature, this amounts to a definitional defeat. The distinction most often made is between the state, which is based on consent, and the nation, which is a natural distinction.

Despite this, even though nationalists present the political struggle as one of a homogeneous society threatened by outside oppressors, more often than not the politics comes first in the form of the political ambitions of a few, and the national culture is constructed later as a means of achieving these aspirations. Kenneth Minogue describes the claims of nationalists as mere 'rhetoric', 'a form of self-expression by which a certain kind of political excitement can be communicated from an elite to the masses. These ideas are chameleons that take on the colour of the locality around them.'

The national struggle becomes an ingenious device for ruling a country which has been persuaded by the national rhetoric that homogeneity is essential to a state. Ernest Gellner argues similarly that 'Nationalism is not the awakening of nations to self-consciousness: it invents nations where they do not exist.' So, more often than not nationalism is not a spontaneous popular phenomenon. Many see it as an ideological device to promote the interests of a certain class or group. The masses are mobilized to exert pressure by middle-class professionals (lawyers, doctors, teachers, army officers, etc.), who are professionally frustrated because their advancement is blocked by an aristocratic or foreign elite.

For those who do not benefit in this way this poses a significant threat to individual liberty. As Lord Acton warns, 'Whenever a single definite object is made the supreme end of the state ... the state becomes for a time inevitably absolute.' Even so, despite this threat, commitment to the nationalist cause can seem attractive. Indeed it was one of the most powerful political forces of the twentieth century. In part this may be due to the confusion

Timeline: political theories

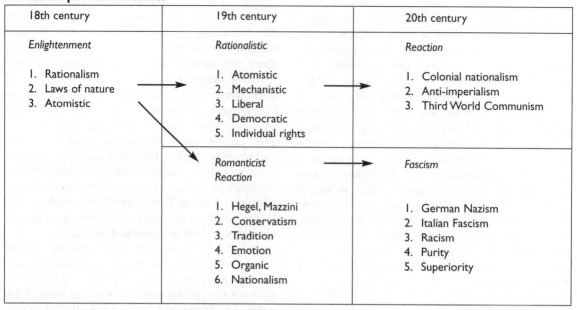

18th century	19th century	20th century
Enlightenment 1. Rationalism 2. Laws of nature 3. Atomistic	*Rationalistic* 1. Atomistic 2. Mechanistic 3. Liberal 4. Democratic 5. Individual rights	*Reaction* 1. Colonial nationalism 2. Anti-imperialism 3. Third World Communism
	Romanticist Reaction 1. Hegel, Mazzini 2. Conservatism 3. Tradition 4. Emotion 5. Organic 6. Nationalism	*Fascism* 1. German Nazism 2. Italian Fascism 3. Racism 4. Purity 5. Superiority

between patriotism and nationalism. While the attachment to the nation is natural – it is something we are born with rather than choose – patriotism has been described as the development of the instinct of self-preservation into a moral duty. Our willingness to defend others in this way is achieved by the state, which cannot be identified with the nation in any natural sense, although it often is. The success of many nationalist leaders and movements has depended upon the confusion between these two.

3.6 Fascism: reversing the forces of history

As you can see from the timeline in the diagram above, fascism shares many of the same characteristics as nationalism. Like nationalism it represents a romanticist reaction to the rationalism of the Enlightenment and the confidence of the heirs of the Enlightenment – liberalism and socialism – in reason and the inevitability of progress. But fascism is the political expression of a much larger ferment of ideas at the end of the nineteenth century, which was the basis of not only fascism but radical changes in modern art, music, literature and psychology. It presents itself as the 'Third Way', the only effective alternative to socialism and liberalism for all those who were disadvantaged by these two.

The Industrial Revolution seemed to indicate

that order and reason were natural to man's inevitable progress. The rational, ordered exploration of the natural world by scientists and engineers increased industrial and agricultural production to unprecedented levels and opened up markets with new forms of mechanised transport. Such progress not only seemed inevitable, but to be accelerating. In contrast fascism, as part of the romanticist reaction, emphasized the unpredictability of the individual; it was obsessed with the creative potential of irrationalism. Nietzsche attacked the moral values of Christianity and the political values of liberalism and socialism. The Christian man, he maintained, was the product of a slave mentality, producing a sickly civilization, which denied life and suppressed all true feelings and emotions. The only solution was to turn inward and become a complete person. The will to achieve this he called 'the will to power': a creative irrational impulse, which liberates the passions and gives them direction.

To this heady mix of ideas was added the work of Joseph Gobineau in his *Essay on the Inequality of Human Races* (1855). Along with the developments in evolutionary theory, this enabled the supporters of the Third Way to extend the arguments of nationalism into Social Darwinism. Nations are no different from species, they argued. They evolve towards more adapted and superior forms with the more advanced being superior intellectually, physically and morally. Gobineau argues that races are permanently unequal; those that are superior owing their superiority to the purity of their blood. And, in fact, there is only one pure race, the Aryan race. It was a short step from this to argue that for the health of mankind nations should protect their purity and promote breeding between the superior races, while doing all they can to prevent breeding between the inferior.

From this it's not difficult to see why fascism should be so attractive to all those groups whose privileged position in the old order was now being threatened by industrialization and the growth in influence of liberalism and socialism. Groups who stood to lose most, like small businessmen and shopkeepers, the self-employed, civil servants, white-collar workers, army officers, and peasant farmers, flocked into the Nazi Party. In 1930, for example, white-collar workers represented 25.6 per cent of its membership and the self-employed 20.7 per cent, when they only represented 12 per cent and 9 per cent respectively of German society as a whole. Their representation in the Nazi Party was more than double their size as a proportion of the national population.

From liberalism they feared the impact of free markets and open competition, with international companies and supermarkets robbing shopkeepers and small businessmen of their traditional customers. From socialism the fears were even greater. The steady advance of the welfare state meant a steady increase in taxes, while the influence of large well-organized trade unions meant that wage costs were steadily increasing too. For those like clerical workers, civil servants and teachers, who had enjoyed a privileged status as the lower-middle class, the aristocracy of the labour force, they too were threatened by the growth in power and influence of the large trade unions. If they failed to join these unions they would fall behind in terms of wages with a steady decline in their standard of living. But if they were to join, then they would lose their status and become just another group in the ranks of the proletariat.

Fascism offered them a way out. This is the radical right: revolutionary, not traditional conservatism. It resorts to the sweeping and dynamic politics of systematic terror and total control to reverse the historical forces of liberalism and socialism, and return to a pre-industrial social system. To do this it had to convince the lower middle class that their problems were not social and economic, but racial, brought about by a Jewish, liberal, Bolshevik conspiracy. This enabled them to channel the anti-capitalism of the lower-middle class into anti-Semitism and sidestep the social and economic analysis of their problems which would have resulted in concrete economic and social reforms, and in turn would have leant support either to socialist or liberal solutions to the problems. Fascism was a convenient way of explaining social and cultural differences without acknowledging that they were socially conditioned and may be ameliorated by progressive social legislation.

This doesn't mean that the radical right are always anti-Semitic, but normally and perhaps necessarily they are racist. Fascism cannot recognize the social and historical reasons why conservative values are threatened by change in rapidly modernizing societies. To do so would be to surrender to the left. It must find a group it can present as absolute villains and conspirators who are genetically incapable of changing their character and opinion.

3.7 Socialism and communism: dialectical history

It is not difficult to see how fascism fits into the left–right spectrum, the organic/mechanistic distinction and into our three interpretations of ideology. The same can be said of socialism and communism, and particularly of Marxism as we can see in its dialectical theory of history, 'Historical materialism'.

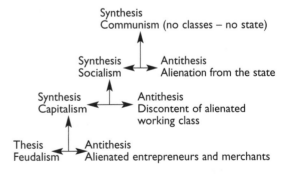

In contrast to organic theories like conservatism, nationalism and fascism, socialist and communist theories are built around the assumption that there are unavoidable underlying conflicts between social classes, each with their own interests that they seek to advance. Indeed, history and progress towards greater individual freedom are the products of such conflict as you can see in the diagram above. Hence Marx's theory, like Hegel's, is a dialectical theory in that it moves from one stage to another as a result of the conflict between the thesis, the interests of the ruling class, and the antithesis, the interests of the exploited class. This conflict resolves itself into a higher synthesis, which then becomes the new thesis with a new, more inclusive, ruling class.

But unlike Hegel, Marx believed it was not ideas that were the motive force behind historical change, but material forces: the way a society is organized economically and socially to meet its needs through production and distribution. As you can see in the diagram below, this is the substructure from which develop all the ideas, values, institutions of government and ideology in the superstructure. All ideas develop out of the way in which the means of production and distribution are organized and the social relations that develop from them. If the means of production and distribution are controlled by one class, the ideas and values of that society will reflect these.

In this lies 'false consciousness', the ideas of the ruling class, the guardian of which is the state with all its power and control to perpetuate the ruling ideology and protect the status quo in which lie the interests of the ruling class. In each stage of the dialectic, whether this involves a feudal, capitalist or socialist ruling class, the state is not objective and neutral: it is the means of oppression of one class by another. And all stages are dominated by the state with the exception of the last, the communist stage, in which there are no classes and, therefore, by definition, there can be no state.

So, for example, in pre-industrial times the means of production and distribution were based on landed property. Out of this developed the

Superstructure Consciousness	Ideology Class consciousness
↑ State of society ↑	Political relations ↑
	Social relations ↑
Substructure	Means of production and distribution

feudal system of government with feudal lords holding the allegiance of peasants, not through the free market and the forces of supply and demand, but through the customary relations of the feudal system. In return for the land he cultivates for his own family's needs, the peasant might be obliged to pay rent in goods or in labour services, like 'boon work' when the lord's harvest had to be brought in at the end of the summer.

But after the industrial revolution the means of production and distribution were based on mass industrial production by machines in mills and factories. The old allegiances were swept away in favour of the market and the laws of supply and demand. Wages were paid in terms of money, not goods, negotiated freely between the factory owner and the individual worker.

In this, as in all the stages (seven in all), a dialectic, a conflict, develops between the owners of the means of production and distribution, the capitalists, and the workers, who become increasingly discontented as they become more conscious of the degree to which they are exploited and alienated both from the product of their own labour and from their fellow workers. The ruling ideology of the capitalists attempts to mask this as the workers become more class conscious. Eventually, as capitalism continues to develop along with the workers' exploitation, a crisis will develop and a revolution will usher in a new stage. So dialectical materialism will continue to develop through each stage until it reaches communism, where there are no more classes and no more conflict.

Nevertheless Marx insists that each stage of the dialectic must achieve full maturity for the subsequent revolution to be successful. Capitalism must have developed to the point where it has become international and imperialistic with multinational corporations exploiting the workers of all nations. Otherwise they can just move or threaten to move their production into another country, playing one set of workers off against another. Fearful of losing their jobs one country's workers might be willing to accept lower wages if they thought the company might move somewhere else.

This accounts for the distortions of Marxism seen in Stalinism in the Soviet Union, Maoism in China and Castroism in Cuba. In each the socialist revolutions were forced through in unmarxist conditions: they came before each country had even gone through a capitalist stage. In Russia industrialization had begun in the 1880s, but by 1917, when the Russian Revolution took place, the industrial workers, the proletariat, still only represented 7 per cent of the working population. Stalin, therefore, assumed all the power of a totalitarian state to force through rapid industrialization in the 1930s as we have seen at the cost of five million kulaks. Similarly in China industrialization had hardly begun at all when the revolution took place. As in Russia in 1917, in 1949 it was a world war that brought matters to a head. Subsequently Mao, like Stalin, assumed totalitarian powers to force through industrialization in the Great Leap Forward (1957–60) and to re-educate the consciousness of workers in the disastrous Cultural Revolution of 1966–9.

By contrast in Europe in the 1970s western communist parties came to the realization that a Marxist revolution was unlikely to come about in the way Marx describes, particularly with the deep-rooted system of parliamentary democracy in post-war Europe. So a new form of Marxism, 'Eurocommunism', was developed by Marxist politicians, who argued that modern western communist parties could only survive as normal parliamentary parties within the parliamentary system. They had to repudiate their commitment to revolution, accept they must work within the parliamentary system and disavow the leadership of the Soviet Communist Party in the international revolutionary struggle. In other words, they accepted capitalism, parliamentary democracy and their place within it.

■ 4. Conclusion

As you can see all of these political theories describe more than just the means of achieving certain ends. They describe the form governments should take, the power they should be given, how they should be legitimized and the relationship between the ruler and the ruled. And they are concerned with ultimate ends, the values and ideals they believe should be the overwhelming concern of politics. But beyond even these important issues, each in its own way describes a whole way of life and a political language that determines not only what should, but what can, be said. It is a language that not only communicates a certain kind of political excitement from leaders to their followers, but, as Trilling says, brings emotional safety, enabling their followers to understand and put into some sensible form events and ideas that might otherwise seem bewildering and fearful.

■ Questions

1. 'The ruling ideas of each age have ever been the ideas of its ruling class.' Discuss.

2. Is nationalism an anachronism or a liberating force?

3. Do you agree that all political doctrines are simply the self-interest of some group?

4. Explain and discuss the different meanings attached to the term 'ideology'. Why are we so suspicious of theories described as 'ideologies'?

5. What was meant by the 'end of ideology' thesis? Do you think there could ever be an end to ideology?

6. Why have conservatives claimed that conservatism should not be based on ideology or abstract principles?

7. To what extent do liberals and anarchists differ in the way they defend individuality and freedom?

8. 'The idea of total control and transformation is the key to totalitarianism.' Discuss.

9. Is fascism anything more than racialism?

■ Recommended reading

Bell, D. *The End of Ideology* (Glencoe, IL: Free Press, 1960).

Kedouri, E. *Nationalism* (London: Hutchinson, 1985).

Laqueur, W. (ed.) *Fascism: A Reader's Guide* (Harmondsworth: Penguin, 1979; Berkeley: University of California Press, 1979).

Mannheim, Karl. *Ideology and Utopia* (London: Routledge and Kegan Paul, reprint 1968).

Marx, K. and F. Engels. *The German Ideology* (London: Lawrence and Wishart, 1982).

McLellan, D. *The Thought of Karl Marx: An Introduction* (London: Macmillan, 1971).

Schapiro, L. *Totalitarianism* (London: Macmillan, 1972).

Trilling, Lionel. *The Liberal Imagination* (Harmondsworth: Penguin, 1970), pp. 280–300.

 The note structure to accompany this chapter can be downloaded from our website.

Conclusion

We started this book by examining what it is to philosophize. Since then we have explored among other things what it is to 'know' something; what we mean when we say something is true; whether we are minds or just bodies; if we can genuinely say that our decision to do something is a free decision; the nature of moral thinking; and how we are best able to preserve our political freedom. As you look back on all this you may think that although you are clearer about the nature of these questions and the complex issues they raise, you are now no more certain about them than when we started. Indeed you may be a great deal more uncertain.

Although this might sound glib and dismissive, in one important sense this is a good result. Doubt is a sign of growth. Moreover, as we found out at the beginning of our quest this is an important part of what philosophy should teach us. We ought to be able to accept doubt and still function. We quoted Bertrand Russell earlier and his assertion that 'To teach how to live without certainty and yet without being paralysed by hesitation is perhaps the chief thing that philosophy, in our age, can do for those who study it.'

But still, like many teachers of this fascinating subject, I have been asked: 'Why complicate the issue by studying some long dead philosopher, whose ideas have been shown to be just plain wrong by subsequent research?' After all, that is the nature of all forms of learning: each subsequent generation is able to stand on the shoulders of those who went first and see further. As Sir Isaac Newton famously said, 'If I have seen further it is by standing on the shoulders of giants.' You might ask, 'Is there any use in studying Locke's atomistic theory of perception when we know from modern gestalt psychologists that perception cannot really be like this?' Or you might reasonably question the value of studying political philosophers like Karl Marx, when he was writing about a time that was in very

many ways quite different economically and socially from our own.

The simple answer is that these philosophers show us what it is to recognize a problem and how to set about solving it. They teach us to ask the right questions, those about things we are all too willing to accept without question. Take the time to look closely at the work of philosophers, like Hume, Kant and Marx, whose vision and courage were awe-inspiring, and ask yourself how much strength of character and uncompromising determination it took to overturn the weight of accepted opinion as they did.

Not for nothing does A. J. Ayer believe that Hume was 'the greatest of all British philosophers'. After all he had the audacity to ask, if all we can be sure about is the evidence of our senses, our perceptions, how can we talk about the 'self' or 'causes', when we can see neither? Surely, all we see is 'nothing but a bundle or collection of different perceptions, which succeed each other with an inconceivable rapidity, and are in a perpetual flux and movement.' No wonder such talk attracted the ridicule of all those who couldn't bear to question such commonplace assumptions. Without them all other certainties might just collapse.

And what about Kant, who was awoken by Hume from his 'dogmatic slumber'? Just think how much courage and vision it took to reverse the accepted order of things and see that necessary connections come from the mind of the knower and not from the known. It is us and the very structure of our minds that invests necessity in what we see, otherwise without these laws of thought we could know nothing of the world at all. It seems simple enough for us in retrospect, but at the time it took all the power of a most exceptional creative imagination to overturn what had been for centuries one of the pillars of certainty holding up the whole edifice of philosophy.

And what of Marx? By turning Hegel upside down, by insisting that it is not ideas but material forces, the way societies are organized to meet their needs, that generate ideologies and drive historical change, he challenged an inveterate assumption of his time – and of ours, come to that. How can unconscious inanimate forces bring about political change? As a result, he overturned the whole weight of German philosophy and set in train a revolution in ideas, the impact of which is still rippling through not just philosophy, but sociology, history, politics and literature.

Moreover, in the summer of 1845 as he worked on *The German Ideology* he saw with a rare clarity what now seems so obvious to us, that the 'mechanistic materialists' could not be right that ideas and individuals are simply the product of material forces, otherwise there could be no change. In other words, if this were true, if we were nothing more than passive products of circumstances, we would only be capable of thinking in ways dictated by the material forces. This could only lead to fatalism. We would be unable to think outside the forms and structures of the stage of the dialectic in which we live. And our capacity to do this was essential if we were to envisage change.

In this was born the most unique insight of Marx's theory, 'Praxis' or 'revolutionary practice', that individuals are not only the products of circumstances, but also their potential changers. And with this came the revolutionary potential of Marxism. As he says in the *11th Thesis on Feuerbach*, 'The philosophers have only *interpreted* the world, in various ways; the point is to *change* it.'

So, to put it rather grandly, what we learn from each of these philosophers is to think the unthinkable – to question the obvious, and not to flinch at what seems ridiculous. If you can do this; if you can have doubts about those things you usually take for granted, and the whole weight of opinion takes for granted, and you are still able to function, then you too have the capacity to see the problem, define it, and have the imagination to devise a solution. You, too, can make a real contribution to this great venture, this quest to discover the true nature of things.

Answers to Questions

Chapter 2

Necessary and contingent propositions:

1. 1
2. 1
3. 3
4. 2
5. 1
6. 2
7. 1
8. 2
9. 3
10. 1
11. 2
12. 1
13. 2
14. 1
15. 3
16. 2
17. 1
18. 1
19. 2
20. 2

Olics: answers to the questions on page 18

1. The olics are numbers 1, 4, 5, 7, 11 and 12.
2. You could have chosen your three
   characteristics from any of the following:
   * a long rectangular base
   * a circle at the centre
   * a triangle surrounding the circle
   * a rectangle surrounding the circle and
     intersecting the triangle.

Chapter 3

Fallacious arguments

1. Affirming the consequent.
2. Denying the antecedent.
3. Affirming the consequent.
4. Denying the antecedent.
5. Equivocation.
6. Division.
7. Equivocation on 'creators'.
8. Composition.

The concept 'revolution': see the structured notes opposite.

Revolution

English Rev. 1649/French Rev. 1789

Russian Rev. 1917/Hungarian Rev. 1956

Why 'revolutions' and not just 'revolts' or 'rebellions' like Jack Cade's Rebellion 1450 or Peasants' Revolt 1381?

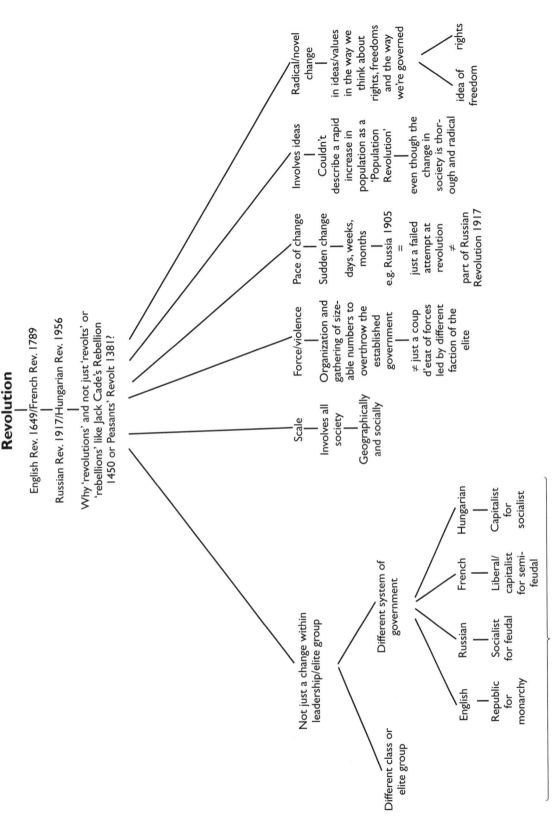

Radical/novel change

in ideas/values in the way we think about rights, freedoms and the way we're governed

idea of freedom — rights

Involves ideas

Couldn't describe a rapid increase in population as a 'Population Revolution'

even though the change in society is thorough and radical

Pace of change

Sudden change

days, weeks, months

e.g. Russia 1905 = just a failed attempt at revolution

≠ part of Russian Revolution 1917

Force/violence

Organization and gathering of sizeable numbers to overthrow the established government

≠ just a coup d'etat of forces led by different faction of the elite

Scale

Involves all society

Geographically and socially

Not just a change within leadership/elite group

Different class or elite group

Different system of government

English — Republic for monarchy

Russian — Socialist for feudal

French — Liberal/capitalist for semi-feudal

Hungarian — Capitalist for socialist

Reflects deep-seated social change

Glossary

Accidental generalizations

Some generalizations, although they are universal in form, cannot support counterfactual or subjunctive conditionals and cannot, therefore, serve as scientific generalizations. In effect there is nothing analogous about the relationships they describe. The most popular example is suggested by William Kneale who asks if all the men in the next room were playing poker, would this mean that if the Archbishop of Canterbury were to enter the room he too would be playing poker? Similarly, if I were to find that the generalization is true that 'All the coins in my pocket are dated 1990', this does not allow me to support a subjunctive conditional to the effect that if I were to put another coin in my pocket this too would be dated 1990. Neither of these examples can support counterfactual and subjunctive conditionals, even though they are universal generalizations. They are merely accidental generalizations.

See also counterfactual and subjunctive conditionals.

Analytic/synthetic

If a proposition is true analytically it is true by virtue of itself alone: it is not necessary to refer to anything beyond its own terms. In contrast synthetic propositions are formed as a result of pulling together different bits of empirical evidence. Unlike analytic propositions, they go beyond the terms that make them up to say something about the real world. Being an analytic or synthetic truth has to do with the logical structure of the sentence and the meaning of the words it uses. The logic of analytic statements is self-contained. They are self-referential, whereas synthetic statements are not: they depend upon the way the world is.

Antimonies and paralogisms

Kant argues that antimonies and paralogisms result from the error of assuming that our modes of perception and conception, like space, time and causation, are external and independent of the mind; that they are features of the noumenal world, whereas, in fact, they are the structure of our own experience, the conditions that regulate our phenomenal world. As

such they can never tell us if the noumenal world is similarly governed by space, time and causation. There is no way of knowing whether this mental apparatus can be extended beyond the phenomenal world to build a bridge to the noumenal world.

Any attempt to accomplish this, he believes, ends either in elementary logical fallacies or in contradictory results, in 'paralogisms' or in 'antinomies'. For example, if a scientist were to ask whether the universe had a beginning, this would result in an antinomy, something that can be both proven and disproven. Paralogisms, errors in our reasoning, result from the same cause: the mistaken attempt to use our modes of perception and conception to prove what lies beyond the phenomenal world. Among these are the attempts of religion to establish the existence of the soul, free will beyond the confines of cause and effect, and the alleged proofs of the existence of God, particularly the ontological argument.

See also the noumenal and phenomenal worlds; Forms of intuition and understanding.

a posteriori
See epistemology.

a priori
See epistemology.

Argument by analogy

When we argue by analogy we use an analogy to connect the premises to the conclusion. We assert that things which resemble each other in some respects will resemble each other in some further respect. We might conclude from the fact that A, B and C all have characteristics x and y, and A and B in addition have characteristic z, that C too will probably have characteristic z. However, the fallacy of false analogy is often committed when we ignore differences and push similarities beyond what is reasonable.

Begging the question

Begging the question occurs when you accept as an

assumption what you are supposedly arguing for as a conclusion.

See Chapter 2.

Biconditional propositions

In biconditional propositions the two parts of the conditional proposition are connected by 'if and only if'. In this case the relation holds both ways: the two terms are said to be identical in that each part is a necessary *and* sufficient condition for the truth of the other.

Categorical and conditional propositions

Categorical propositions assert relationships between two groups of objects or two classes of people or things (All As are Bs, Some As are Bs, Most As are Bs), whereas conditional or hypothetical propositions are marked by their distinctive 'if/then' structure (If A, then B). The 'if' clause is known as the antecedent, and the 'then' clause as the consequent.

Category mistakes

The influential British philosopher Gilbert Ryle developed the view of philosophy according to which its function was to identify and correct the misunderstandings that arise from what he described as 'category mistakes'. This is the mistake of talking about the facts of something as if they belong to one logical type or category when in fact they belong to another.

Conation, cognition and affection

This is a useful way of classifying different aspects of the mind. Conation or volition covers those aspects associated with the initiation of actions, including willing, motivation, intending, endeavour, effort and so on. Cognition covers all those aspects involving the acquisition of beliefs, learning, knowing and reasoning. By contrast affection covers all those aspects of the mind associated with feeling and emotion.

Contingent

A factor is contingent if it is a non-necessary attribute. In other words it just happens to be an attribute, but things could have been different. Similarly, a proposition is contingent if its truth depends upon evidence that could go either way. Unlike propositions that are necessarily true, it can be asserted or denied without self-contradiction.

See also necessary truth.

Conversion

Conversion is the process of interchanging the subject and the complement of a sentence. It follows from the proposition 'No Xs are Ys' that 'No Ys are Xs.' The subject (X) and the predicate (Y) can be interchanged: that is, the converse is also true. But while total exclusion is a reversible relation, total inclusion is not. We cannot similarly argue that given 'All Xs are Ys', then 'All Ys are Xs'. While we can argue that 'All dogs are animals', we cannot reverse this and argue that 'All animals are dogs'. This would be an example of illicit conversion. Nevertheless, partial inclusion is reversible. We can argue not only that 'Some accountants are businessmen', but also that 'Some businessmen are accountants.'

Counterfactual and subjunctive conditionals

If a theory is to be considered scientific it must support unfulfilled conditionals, otherwise there would be no way of testing it. We generally talk about two types of conditionals: counterfactual and subjunctive. The first is perhaps more usually associated with historians who ask what would have happened if something else had occurred rather than that which did in fact occur. So, counterfactual conditionals have the form: 'If A had been the case, then B would have occurred.' For example, you might suggest 'If the First World War had not occurred, industry would have developed along different lines.' With subjunctive conditionals the question is forward looking, in that we ask what will happen if we do something: 'If A should occur, then so would B.' For example, we might posit 'If the water freezes, the pipes will burst.'

Decentring the subject

To 'decentre' the subject is to undermine the primacy, the importance, of the individual, particularly in theories about the self, and in epistemological, moral and political theories. For example, both Freud and Marx can be said to 'decentre' the conscious, rational self by pointing to influences that undermine its primacy – in the case of Freud, the forces of instinct, and for Marx, the conditioning effects of society.

Deductive and inductive arguments

Deduction is a form of argument in which the conclusion is already contained within the premises. It can therefore be described as 'conclusive reasoning', because the conclusion never states more than is contained in the assumptions that make up the argument, whereas an inductive argument always does. In an inductive argument we start with singular observation statements that certain events, all similar in some important respect, have occurred, and then we derive a universal generalization that applies to all events of this type, observed and unobserved, past, present and future.

Deism and theism

Deism is the belief that God created the world and left it to run by itself, while theism is the belief that not only did he create the world, but he continues to exercise an influence over it. Most modern religions are theistic.

Disjunctive or alternative propositions

A disjunctive or alternative proposition brings two ideas together in an 'either/or' relationship. It is valid only when a categorical premise contradicts one of the disjuncts. If we were merely to affirm the truth of one of them, this would not imply the falsehood of the other: both can in fact be true. This occurs because of the *inclusive* sense of 'or', which allows both disjuncts to be true. It would be different if both disjuncts were *exclusive*.

See Chapter 3.

The double effect

Supporters of the double effect argue that a bad act that produces good consequences can never be condoned, whereas a good act done in the full knowledge that bad consequences will ensue can be.

Dualism

See monism.

Empirical

An empirical proposition is one that is based wholly or in part on the evidence of our senses.

Empiricism

An empiricist believes that for a proposition to amount to knowledge it does not have to be absolutely certain. Such certainty is restricted to limited areas, in particular mathematics and analytic truths. Beyond that our knowledge of the outside world depends on the evidence of our senses. Indeed some empiricists accept that certain types of direct evidence of the senses have primitive authenticity, that is, they are immediately known to be true and certain, because they have not been processed through our reason and imagination, which would make them prone to error. They argue there are no grounds to doubt that your senses do in fact register a certain colour or smell. However, beyond this, empiricists accept that the general laws we derive from the evidence of our senses can only be justified inductively. For this there can only be qualified assurance.

The Enlightenment

The Enlightenment elevated reason, analysis and the scientific method as the only reliable tools for discovering truth. In line with its atomistic methods philosophers sought to break nature down into its elementary particles, the behaviour of which were governed by laws of nature that could only be discovered through the application of reason. Philosophers pictured nature as some vast machine working predictably according to natural laws.

Societies were no different: they were universally alike and, like nature, no more than just the sum of their parts, a loose collection of isolated individuals. So in the same way that the universal laws of physics were revealed through the analytical methods of modern science, breaking nature down into its elementary particles, societies too could be broken down into individuals and individuals in turn into their elementary drives and needs. And once the laws governing the behaviour of individuals in terms of these drives and needs were revealed, then, as societies were no more than the sum of their parts, the universal laws of societies would be revealed. The science of society would be born.

Individuals appeared to be possessed of two dominant characteristics: they were rational and self-interested – they sought to maximize their pleasure and minimize their pain. As Bentham described it, 'nature has placed mankind under the governance of two sovereign masters, pain and pleasure.' It followed, then, that they are the best judge of not only their own interests, but the best way of maximizing them. So if the new science of society were to improve the freedom and condition of individuals living in all modern societies, it was clear that governments should allow the natural order to function freely without interference. They should have only limited and negative powers just to remove the obstacles restricting the capacity of individuals to maximize their own self-interest. As Adam Smith advocated, wherever possible the 'invisible hand' of the market should rule.

See also romanticism.

Entailment

This is the relationship between premises and conclusion, in which the conclusion necessarily follows or can be validly inferred from the premises. If the premises are true then so too is the conclusion. It amounts to a sufficient condition for the conclusion to be true.

Epiphenomenalism

Epiphenomenalists believe the mind cannot causally affect the body, but that the body can causally affect the mind. Mental events are merely some kind of by-product of certain complex physical processes in the brain and nervous system. Consciousness is an 'epiphenomenon', literally an event which occurs 'after' the physical process.

Epistemology

An issue is described as 'epistemological' if it is concerned with the theory of knowledge: with the nature and scope of knowledge, how we come by it, and the reliability of our claims to knowledge. So, for example, both *a priori* and *a posteriori* refer to the epistemological issue of the way we come by the truth of a proposition: whether or not it can be known to be true or false without consulting experience. We come by the truth of an *a priori* proposition by means of reason or by some direct intuition, and not by consultation with the outside world. Indeed an *a priori* proposition is such that we can conceive of nothing that would count as evidence against it. This contrasts with an *a posteriori* proposition (meaning that the truth 'comes after' we have consulted experience), the truth of which we can only establish by reference to experience.

Error theory

The term 'error theory' developed out of J. L. Mackie's defence of subjectivism. Mackie argues that everyday thought in some areas has become sufficiently infected by mistaken philosophical views to be widely in error and in need of revision.

Essentialism

Essentialism is the view that an entity has certain attributes without which it would not be that kind of entity. The problem is: on what grounds do we decide what these essential attributes are? One answer, the nominal solution (*see* nominalism), is to argue that they arise from the different ways of describing things, that is to say they are conventional and linguistic. Another view is suggested by John Locke: that things have real and not just nominal essences that underlie and explain all their other characteristics.

This has been the focus of attack by both existentialists and Marxists. Jean-Paul Sartre argues against all forms of determinism, including the form of natural determinism assumed by essentialist arguments. He argues that 'existence precedes essence', that individuals are free to 'invent' themselves. Marx, too, attacks it on the grounds that it is a form of natural hierarchy, used to justify all forms of social inequality. Instead Marx argues that all social stratification is the result of the economic and social organization of society. All forms of essentialism, then, are nothing more than expressions of the ruling class ideology, through which the ruling class seeks to obscure the truth and promote and protect its own interests.

Some feminist philosophers, too, have employed essentialist arguments to draw the distinction between male and female natures: the former is typified by the insistence upon rules, rights and justice, manifesting itself in aggressive, selfish behaviour, while the latter is characterized by its emphasis on nurturing and caring. In contrast some put such differences down to the different life experiences of males and females, and the accidental factors of social and cultural forces, rather than to essential differences.

Forms of intuition and understanding

In the *Critique of Pure Reason* Kant argues that as we process sense experience through the mind we impose certain *a priori* characteristics, which he describes as 'forms of intuition' and 'forms of understanding'. Forms of intuition consist of two types of *a priori* characteristics: temporal and geometric features, like space and time; and the truths of mathematics. Forms of understanding consist of those principles and concepts through which we organize data to create intelligible information. Kant identifies three categories: quantity (all, some, many, none, etc.); quality (positive, negative); and 'categories', like causation, through which we impose a general conceptual scheme on data to order and relate them.

See also antinomies and paralogisms; the noumenal and phenomenal worlds.

Holism

This is the argument that we cannot, as in much of modern science, reduce systems atomistically into their elementary particles to discover the laws that govern the behaviour of each part and from there reveal the laws governing the whole. The whole is more than the sum of the parts. Structuralism is a form of 'holism'.

Hypothetical syllogisms: pure and mixed

Pure hypothetical syllogisms contain hypothetical propositions exclusively, whereas a mixed hypothetical syllogism has a hypothetical proposition as its major premise and a categorical premise as its minor premise.

See Chapter 3.

Idealism

The philosophical doctrine that reality is in some sense mental: that it is either a reflection of the mind or the mind coordinates ideas so that reality as we understand it can never be anything but a reflection of the workings of the mind. The conflict within idealism raged in the nineteenth century over whether the mind in question was within the individual (*see* Subjective idealism) or outside the individual in the form of nature itself or God (*see* Objective idealism). Idealism is usually contrasted with realism and materialism.

Illicit conversion
See conversion.

Inductive arguments
See deductive arguments.

Loaded language
This is language that carries with it more than what it means descriptively, usually an emotional content, which manipulates our responses without us being aware of it.

See Chapter 2.

Logical fallacies
The *fallacy of equivocation* occurs where the terms used change their meaning or application throughout the argument.

The *fallacy of division* is committed whenever someone argues that something, which is true only for the whole, is also true of its parts taken separately.

The *fallacy of composition* occurs when we assume that what is true of the part is also true of the whole.

The *fallacy of the undistributed middle term* occurs when we do not distribute the middle term in a syllogistic argument and, consequently, we can no longer validly deduce the conclusion

The *fallacy of illicit process of major or minor term* – in this fallacy it is not so much that the terms have not been distributed correctly, but that they have been badly processed. In effect, the conclusion asserts more than the premises will allow.

See Chapter 3.

Logical positivism
This is the term given to the movement that developed in the 1920s out of the Vienna Circle, an informal discussion group at the University of Vienna presided over by Moritz Schlick. They maintained that the only meaningful propositions are those that can be verified empirically. Metaphysics, religion, ethics and aesthetics are therefore meaningless. The most prominent member of the Circle was Rudolph Carnap, although other well known philosophers were associated with it, including Karl Popper, A. J. Ayer and Ludwig Wittgenstein. Their meetings finally came to an end in 1936 with the murder of Schlick and with the events in Nazi Germany which sent the majority of its members into exile in Britain and the United States.

Materialism
This is the view that the world is composed entirely of matter. Today philosophers are inclined to talk about 'physicalism', because modern science has shown us that there are even more basic constituents of the world in the energy and forces that make up matter.

Metaphysics
This is the branch of philosophy Aristotle called 'first philosophy', because it deals with first principles. Literally 'metaphysics' means 'the subject that follows or transcends physics'. Thus the questions it is concerned with are those about reality that go beyond factual or scientific questions about the world. Traditionally the issues that have been raised are those relating to questions about mind and body, free will, causation, substance and ontology.

See also ontological, substance.

Modus ponens and *modus tollens*
There are two forms of valid argument for mixed hypothetical syllogisms. The first is *modus ponens* (Latin: 'mood that affirms'), which means that to argue validly we must affirm the antecedent of the hypothetical major premise. The second is *modus tollens* (Latin: 'mood that denies'). Unlike *modus ponens* this form is valid because it denies the consequent. If the valid forms of the argument are to affirm the antecedent and deny the consequent, the fallacies are the reverse: to deny the antecedent and affirm the consequent.

See Chapter 3.

Monism
This is the term used to describe any doctrine which maintains that reality is made up of only one substance. The alternative doctrine is dualism, which divides reality into two substances, mind and matter. The Dutch philosopher Baruch Spinoza saw the one substance as God or Nature. In political philosophy the term is sometimes used to describe any political system that only allows one political party to operate, in contrast to pluralist states where the political system involves different political parties competing with each other to gain power through elections.

Necessary and sufficient conditions
A condition is sufficient if its truth is all that is required for a belief to be true, or a certain event to occur. When an assumption is a sufficient condition for a belief to be true it is said to entail that belief. In other words, given the assumption, the belief necessarily follows, so that if the assumption is true, then so too is the belief.

An assumption is a necessary condition if it *must* be true in order for another belief to be true or an event to occur. When a proposition X necessarily cannot be true unless another proposition Y is true, then the truth of Y is by definition a logically necessary true condition for X. When a proposition like this must be true for the theory to be true it is said to be a presupposition of the theory. Necessary assumptions are entailed by the theory they presuppose; therefore, if you can show them to be false, you have disproved the theory.

See Chapter 4.

Necessary truth

If something is true necessarily it is a logical truth. A proposition is said to be necessarily true if and only if its denial would involve a self-contradiction. If I were to deny the truth of propositions like 'All bachelors are unmarried men' or 'Either this is a pen or it is not a pen', it would mean I have made a logical mistake. Either I do not understand the meaning of the concept 'bachelor' or I have not understood the logical implications of using truth-functional connectives like 'either' and 'or'. Such propositions express beliefs about what must be the case, or what cannot be the case.

See also contingent.

Nominalism

This is the belief that those things identified by the use of a term share nothing in common except this very fact – their common term. So, all those objects we identify by using the word 'table' have nothing else in common but the fact that we identify them with the word 'table'. Importantly this view regards universals as merely names for the group of individual particulars that are subsumed by the universal, in contrast to philosophers like Plato, who believe that universals are the unchanging world of reality, the object of knowledge, while appearances and contingency are merely partial and misleading representations of them. Nominalism is usually associated with the belief that all that exists are particular individuals – there are no such things as universals.

The noumenal and phenomenal worlds

In the *Critique of Pure Reason* Kant describes the noumenal world as the real world, consisting of 'things in themselves', which can never be known to us. In contrast, the phenomenal world, or the world as known by the mind, is a product of experience and the *a priori* conditions supplied by the mind. So while the noumenal world is independent of us and unknowable in itself, the phenomenal world is known to us, because it is a product of our own active processing of sense data.

See also antimonies and paralogisms; forms of intuition and understanding.

Objective idealism

A term used to describe the philosophy of those who believe that reality lies in ideas, but that these ideas are the product of a mind that lies outside the individual in the form of nature or God. The most influential form of this was 'absolute idealism' developed after Kant, most notably by Hegel, which became very influential among the 'British idealists' like T. H.

Green, J. M. E. McTaggart and F. H. Bradley in the years 1865 to 1925. Although there are numerous forms of absolute idealism, they all have as their central idea that there is only one ultimate reality or mind, the Absolute, which is spiritual in nature. All other phenomena are merely imperfect or partial manifestations of it.

Absolute idealists believe that anything short of the 'whole' can only aspire to degrees of the truth, sometimes described as 'degrees of the truth theory'. A single proposition can only be an approximation to the truth. Indeed Hegelian philosophers believe that we cannot understand what any part is without already seeing how it fits into the whole. To understand something it is not enough to understand it in isolation: we must also know all its manifold and complex relations with other things.

See also subjective idealism.

Obversion

This is the process of changing a proposition into its logical equivalent: from the affirmative to the negative form. The four basic forms are:

1. All As are Bs into No As are non-Bs.

2. No As are Bs into All As are non-Bs.

3. Some As are Bs into Some As are not non-Bs.

4. Some As are not Bs into Some As are non-Bs.

Illicit obversion occurs when it does not necessarily follow that those who are excluded from one class are also excluded from the other. To say that 'All golfers are competitive' is not the same as saying 'All non-golfers are non-competitive.' The fact that someone is not a golfer doesn't mean they are non-competitive.

Ockham's razor

This is the famous principle of William of Ockham (c. 1285–1349) 'Entia non sunt multiplicanda praeter necessitatem': that is, 'entities are not to be multiplied beyond necessity.' It is the argument that we should not postulate the existence of things unless we have to. In other words, the simpler theory that accounts for the facts is the better theory.

Ontological

Any argument can be said to be ontological which infers that something really exists. Ontology, from the Greek word meaning 'being', is the study of what exists. In philosophy there have been many arguments that the world must contain one kind of thing or another: material objects, minds, persons, universals and so on. The correspondence theory of truth is described as an ontological theory because it infers there exists an objective independent reality. In contrast the subjective, psychological or epistemic theories, like coherence or pragmatism, define truth in terms of a subjective belief state: truth is the quality of our subjective convictions. Knowledge is a special kind of mental state or a disposition.

Pantheism
This is the doctrine that regards all reality as divine and God and nature as one. All those metaphysical doctrines, like objective idealism, that make claims about the universe as one Unity tend towards a form of pantheism. Within these assumptions the universe must be greater than the sum of its finite parts and there can be no deity distinct from it. The most notable modern pantheistic philosophers include Baruch Spinoza, J. G. Fichte and G. W. F. Hegel.

Paradox
A paradox is usually composed of a pair of statements, each with strong reasons for accepting them, but which cannot both be true. So an absurd conclusion appears to result from perfectly acceptable ways of thinking. One of the most interesting examples which has troubled philosophers for centuries is the 'Liar's paradox'. If someone were to say 'I am lying', then if what he says is true, he is lying and what he says is, accordingly, false. Therefore the statement is both true and false at the same time: if what he says is true, he is speaking falsely; and if what he says is false, he is speaking truly.

Theories of perception
Those who believe in the 'causal theory of perception' maintain that if material things can be known at all, they must be inferred from the ideas they cause in us. Locke's 'atomistic theory of perception' is much the same: our understanding of what a table is is made up of isolated constituents of sense data, the whole being no more than the sum of its parts.

However, in the twentieth century more sophisticated neuro-physiology and Gestalt psychology have suggested that the unified whole, or 'gestalt', is greater than, or different from, the sum of its parts: it is a complete structure, which cannot be explained simply by analysing it into its constituent elements.

Phenomenalism
This is the view that denies that we must suppose that physical objects have an existence distinct from sensible appearances, ideas or 'phenomena'. Instead, as a theory of perception, phenomenalism argues that all statements about physical objects are logically equivalent to statements about sense data. The most useful slogan to remember is J. S. Mill's that a material thing is a permanent possibility of sensa-

tion, or even Russell's remark that a thing is the class of its appearances.

But this is very different from concluding from this, as Locke and Descartes do, that external objects really exist 'out there' apart from our sensations. If we have no way of proving their separate existence, the best and, perhaps, the only alternative is to deny it. Known as 'sensationalism' this is one form of phenomenalism, as a theory of knowledge, supported by philosophers like Hume, Russell and J. S. Mill, who maintain that nothing exists beyond appearances presented to our senses. Or, to put it another way, this is to argue simply that the object just is the name we give to a certain collection of ideas or sensations. Hume argues it is nothing else apart from these ideas: as Berkeley explains, 'In truth the object and the sensation are the same thing, and cannot therefore be abstracted from each other.' The alternative view of phenomenalism, supported by Kant and known as 'agnosticism', maintains that although we cannot infer the character of what lies beyond our sense experience we can at least infer there is something out there.

Phenomenology
Literally the study of appearances, in Edmund Husserl's hands it became the description of consciousness and experience in the abstract, stripped of all presuppositions, particularly intentional content. Such immediate conscious experience Husserl believed was intuited by the mind and, therefore, the role of phenomenology was to 'bracket' the world, all these preconceptions, until the only thing that was left was pure conscious experience, 'pure subjectivity'. Phenomenology led on to the study of being, associated with existentialism. Husserl's influence can be seen in the work of modern existentialists, like his former student, Heidegger, and in turn Sartre.

Philosophical scepticism
Philosophical scepticism ends only when a belief is true beyond any *conceivable* doubt: that is, not just practical doubt, but any doubt that could be imagined. It sets out by identifying a set of beliefs which we accept as basic to our view of the world and whose truth we normally accept without question. Then it lays out all the possible grounds for such beliefs and sets out to show that these do not justify the beliefs.

Platonic forms
Plato believed that for statements to be true they must be so in virtue of an unchanging 'reality', not by convention or agreement. In other words, such a reality could not be located in any particular place or time; it could only be found, he believed, in unchanging 'forms' or universals, pure ideas outside space and time, which could only be grasped by reason. While

the senses could tell us all about the shadows, only reason could tell us about the causes of those shadows. Plato believed that there were two kinds of information derived from two distinct worlds: the world of appearances and the world of forms or universals.

Positivism

In its original form in the nineteenth century this was associated with the French philosopher, Auguste Comte, who believed the only genuine form of knowledge was scientific knowledge, which describes the world using sensory phenomena. His account is of three stages of human belief: the metaphysical, the theological and, finally, the scientific, so-called because it confines itself to what is given positively and avoids all speculation. However, in the wider sense the term positivism is used to apply to all those who believe that the only legitimate way of acquiring genuine knowledge is to avoid all forms of speculation and adopt scientific methodology of devising law-abiding explanations, which can then be tested through observation and experiment. For example some positivists have maintained that historians can only genuinely claim to have explained a historical event if their explanation can subsume those events under natural laws of human behaviour.

See also logical positivism.

Postmodernists

Postmodernists ask not whether a theory is true, but what its cultural roots are. All knowledge, they believe, is socially constructed; all experience mediated by language and culture. Whatever the nature of theories, whether they are scientific, historical or religious, none are inherently better or worse that any other. Experience can only be evaluated by asking how interesting and edifying the theory is in terms of certain cultural agendas or how well it serves human needs, and not ranked in terms of a hierarchy of some supposed objective truth.

Post-structuralism

Like other forms of postmodernism it rejects all concepts of objectivity, reality and truth. In particular it rejects the search for scientific objectivity. Derrida and the deconstructionists challenged the structuralist claim to have uncovered the hidden unconscious structures behind surface meanings, arguing instead that language is irreducible, involving a multiple play of meaning. Rather than reducing human behaviour to certain laws or generalizations, the sort associated with deterministic systems like Marxism, the post-structuralists emphasize instead the spontaneous, the formless and subjective.

See also structuralism.

Pragmatism

This is an almost exclusively American movement, most notably associated with Charles Peirce, John Dewey and William James. James believes that the truth of a statement can be defined in terms of the utility, the practical usefulness, in accepting it. Something is true if it allows us to accomplish what we set out to accomplish, if it helps us achieve our objectives.

Predicate

A predicate is what is said about a subject: what is 'predicated' of it. We might say 'The sky is blue' or 'The grass is green.' In both of these sentences, known as subject/predicate sentences, the subject is 'sky' and 'grass', and the predicate is 'is blue' and 'is green', respectively. A predicate connects one or more terms, expressing a condition that the things referred to are thought to satisfy. In the case of the sky we believe it satisfies the condition of being blue.

Premises

An argument is a set of sentences one of which is the conclusion and the others, called premises, are offered as the grounds for the conclusion. The premises are said to imply or entail the conclusion.

See also syllogism.

Proposition

A proposition is an indicative sentence, which can be true or false, as opposed to a question or a command. It can also be distinguished from the sentence itself in that a proposition is the meaning of the sentence. So, two sentences can be quite different linguistically, yet contain the same proposition.

Rationalism

Rationalists place their primary trust in reason to reveal and justify truth. Genuine knowledge, as in mathematical and logical truths, requires certainty. All such truths are derived deductively from a relatively small number of axioms and definitions known to be self-evidently true. Philosophers like Leibniz, Spinoza and Descartes believe that genuine knowledge about the world can only be acquired through the application of reason in this way and experience in the normal sense is at best misleading, if not irrelevant.

See also empiricism.

Realism

To be a realist is to insist on the reality of any entity, object or thing that exists essentially independently of a mind or any human activity, both of which suggest the role of a person with certain presuppositions, intentions and purposes. So a materialist is a realist if she insists that material objects exist 'essentially' independently of any mind. In other words, although its existence may be the result of human activity, this is not essential to its existence: it could have come into existence without it. The same is true of those who insist that propositions or universals exist essentially independently of any mind. Others are realists in the sense that they oppose the arguments of those who reject talk about objects in favour of talk about words (nominalism), or ideas (idealism), or logical constructions (phenomenalism).

See also idealism, nominalism and phenomenalism.

Reductio ad absurdum

As you can see, literally this means to reduce to absurdity. It is any process of reasoning from a certain set of assumptions that results in a contradiction, with the conclusion that the set as a whole is untenable.

Reductive fallacy

When two things always occur together we are often tempted to reduce one to the other; to argue that one is nothing but the other. This is the reductive fallacy – the nothing-but fallacy. In effect it is an attempt to deny the existence of something by using the word in a particular restricted way. In an age of science, perhaps not surprisingly, the fallacy is found most commonly in the form of materialism. In Arthur Koestler's novel *Arrival and Departure*, a character suggests that heroism is nothing more than an overactive thyroid gland.

Romanticism

Set against the mechanistic philosophy of the Enlightenment, romanticism presented a radically different vision that drew on the importance of spontaneous, unfettered, and emotional responses. Ultimate truth came from subjective, emotional, intuitive absorption in nature unfettered by civilization and intellect. At the heart of this, as in so much of romantic writing, was the analogy between humanity of the pre- and post-industrial worlds, with the latter corrupted by the regimentation of industrial processes, and intellectually and emotionally divorced from nature. The same themes were picked up in the wave of romanticism at the end of the nineteenth and early twentieth century when the political expression of a ferment of ideas that captured the revolt against industrial mechanization and capitalism took the form of fascism.

Even so the key analogies in romanticism were born much earlier, at the end of the eighteenth and early nineteenth century, when the forces of conservatism and nationalism rose up against the universal system of government that swept across Europe under Napoleon, the heir of the Enlightenment. Romantic philosophers and poets insisted nature was organic, not mechanistic, and so were nations. Like individuals, they were the product of their own history and temperament. They had grown and developed according to their own unique qualities and characteristics and in response to their own unique experiences.

See also the Enlightenment.

Semantics and syntax

A sentence is semantic in the sense that in establishing its truth we are concerned with the relation between the words used in the proposition and what those words signify in the real world. In contrast, a sentence, like an analytic proposition, is syntactical in that in establishing its truth we are concerned with the words and the relations between themselves alone. Semantics is concerned with the relations between the symbols we use and what they represent in the world, whereas syntax is only concerned with the relations between the symbols and can be dealt with independently of what they represent.

Situation ethics

This is the view that ethical judgements apply just to existing whole situations and do not involve abstracting features of a situation which might then be applied to future possible situations.

Solipsism

This is the belief that only oneself and one's experience exists. Supporters of this view argue that once you accept that your sense impressions are mind-dependent it is difficult to argue validly for a mind-independent world.

Sound arguments

An argument is sound if and only if it is a valid argument and has true premises. Therefore, we can challenge the soundness of an argument either by criticizing it for being invalid, or by arguing that one or more of its premises are untrue.

See also validity.

Structuralism

The key element in the structuralist approach is the belief that we can only understand the phenomena of human life through the underlying structures which determine the way in which systems of social organization develop. The only way to make such phenomena intelligible is through their interrelations, and these form common structures that lie behind the surface phenomena. Even though different societies display a range of diversity, these local variations only disguise the underlying laws of abstract structure.

Although it began as a linguistic theory under the influence of Saussure, the movement known as structuralism extended this approach beyond language to social and cultural phenomena more generally. The more general claim being made is that we should not treat these phenomena as the intentional products of human subjects, but as structured systems of elements with specific rules of combination and transformation. It is these structured systems that now determine the meaning of social and cultural phenomena.

See also post-structuralism.

Subjective idealism

Subjective idealism is the belief that all we can know to exist are ideas in the largest sense (feelings, sense impressions, memories, ideas and so on), and other minds. It is a term used to describe the views of those who believe not only that reality lies in ideas, but that these ideas are the product of the human mind. The term is most often used to describe the philosophy of Berkeley, although he preferred to describe his philosophy as 'immaterialism'. In contrast to objective idealism, subjective idealists believe that what we describe as 'reality' can only be appearances and products of the mind.

See also objective idealism.

Substance

A term used in philosophy to indicate some underlying reality, that in which qualities reside. For example, in the *Second Meditation* Descartes argues that wax has specific qualities: it is dull, yellow, plastic (when warm), adhesive, impressible and so on. Take these away and what you're left with is substance or that in which qualities reside. The mind, for example, has the qualities to think, perceive, remember, imagine and the like. If we take these away we are left with an immaterial substance, indivisible and immortal. There are, then, according to Descartes, two substances: two underlying realities that support certain qualities or properties. One is matter, an extended substance, in which resides certain physical properties like shape, size and weight. The other is mind, a non-spatial, conscious substance, in which reside mental properties like the capacities to think, perceive, remember, and imagine.

Syllogism

One of the most common forms of deductive reasoning, a syllogism is an argument that moves from the most general premise, known as the major premise, to the particular premise, known as the minor premise, and finally to the conclusion, which follows logically from the first two premises and forms a valid argument.

See also deductive arguments.

Synthetic *a priori* propositions

A synthetic *a priori* proposition is not shown to be true merely as a result of the analysis of its constituent words or its logical form. It explains something about the world of experience, and yet is known to be true independently of experience: we accept no experience as a refutation of it. And yet, at the same time, the negation of a synthetic *a priori* truth is not self-contradictory: in other words, it is not analytic.

Tautology

When propositions say nothing about how things are in the real world and are true independently of the way things are, they are said to be tautologies. Literally it means saying the same thing. We see this most clearly in the form of analytic truths, like 'All bachelors are unmarried men.' But the term has a wider application. Tautologies are also true solely by virtue of the logical operators or the 'truth-functional connectives' ('and', 'or', 'if-then') used to construct them, rather than because things are in the real world as they are said to be in the proposition. So, the proposition, 'Either this is a pen or it is not a pen', is true solely by virtue of the truth-functional connectives 'either' and 'or'. Tautologies are not refutable because they are in fact trivially true. Whatever the content, and they may have no content at all, it is irrelevant to their truth, which is established by the logical form involved.

Universal generalizations

Universal generalizations assert the relationship between all the members of one group and those of another. In universal affirmative generalizations all of one class of things or people are contained in the class of another, whereas in universal negative generalizations all the members of one class of things or people are totally excluded from another. In contrast partial generalizations state that one class of things or people is partially included in another.

Validity

When we examine the validity of a deductive argument we are concerned with its form, not with its truth, the substance of the argument. Validity is a way of ensuring that if we do have true premises then we also guarantee that our conclusion is true. When an argument is valid it is not possible for its premises to be true, while its conclusion is false. It can have false premises and a false conclusion, but never true premises and a false conclusion. An argument is valid if and only if it is not possible for its premises all to be true and its conclusion to be false.

See also deductive arguments.

Bibliography

In this bibliography my aim has been to cover those texts you might find helpful in tackling your assignments, while at the same time organizing it in such a way that you can use it effectively. To help you in this I have broken it up into groups of chapters so that you can more easily access the most useful texts for the topic you are studying.

General introduction

Ayer, A. J. *The Central Questions of Philosophy* (Harmondsworth: Penguin, 1976).

Blackburn, S. *Think* (Oxford: Oxford University Press, 1999).

Burr, J. and M. Goldinger (eds). *Philosophy and Contemporary Issues* (London: Macmillan, 1988).

Emmet, E. R. *Learning to Philosophize* (Harmondsworth: Penguin, 1968).

Flew, A. *Thinking about Thinking (Or, Do I sincerely want to be right?)* (London: Fontana, 1976).

Malcolm, A. *Making Names: An Idea of Philosophy* (Oxford: AKME, 1993).

Nagel, Thomas. *The View from Nowhere* (Oxford: Oxford University Press, 1986).

Nagel, Thomas. *What Does It All Mean? A Very Short Introduction to Philosophy* (New York: Oxford University Press, 1989).

Nozick, R. *Philosophical Explanations* (Oxford: Oxford University Press, 1984).

Pinchin, C. *Issues in Philosophy* (London: Macmillan, 1990).

Russell, B. *The History of Western Philosophy* (London: Allen and Unwin, 1967).

Warburton, N. *Philosophy: The Basics* (London: Routledge, 1992).

Chapters 2–4

Carney, James, D. and Richard K. Scheer. *Fundamentals of Logic* (New York: Macmillan, 1974; London: Collier Macmillan, 1974).

Cohen M. and E. Nagel. *An Introduction to Logic* (London: Routledge and Kegan Paul, 1963).

Conway, D. and R. Munson. *Elements of Reasoning* (Belmont, Calif: Wadsworth, 2003).

Copi, Irving. *Introduction to Logic* (New York: Macmillan, 1978).

Copi, Irving. *Symbolic Logic* (New York: Macmillan, 1986).

Copi, Irving and Carl Cohen. *Introduction to Logic* (New York: Macmillan, 1997).

Gorovitz, Samuel, Merrill Hintikka, Donald Provence and Ron G. Williams. *Philosophical Analysis* (New York: Random House, 1979).

Hurley, Patrick J. *A Concise Introduction to Logic* (Belmont, Calif: Wadsworth, 1985).

Jeffrey, R. *Formal Logic* (New York: McGraw-Hill, 1967).

Lemmon, E. J. *Beginning Logic* (London: Nelson, 1965).

Mates, Benson. *Elementary Logic* (New York: Oxford University Press, 1965).

Quine, W. V. O. *Methods of Logic* (New York: Holt, Rinehart and Winston, 1959).

Russell, B. *The Problems of Philosophy* (Oxford: Oxford University Press, 1987).

Salmon, Wesley C. *Logic* (Englewood Cliffs, NJ: Prentice-Hall, 1973).

Skyrms, Brian. *Choice and Chance: An Introduction to Inductive Logic* (Encino and Belmont, Calif: Dickenson, 1975).

Teays, Wanda. *Second Thoughts: Critical Thinking for a Diverse Society* (New York: McGraw-Hill, 2002).

Wilson, John. *Thinking with Concepts* (Cambridge: Cambridge University Press, 1976).

Chapter 5 Knowledge

Audi, Robert. *Epistemology: A Contemporary Introduction to the Theory of Knowledge* (London: Routledge, 1998).

Aune, Bruce. *Knowledge, Mind and Nature: An*

Introduction to the Theory of Knowledge and the Philosophy of Mind (New York: Random House, 1967).

Ayer, A. J. *The Problem of Knowledge* (Harmondsworth and Baltimore: Penguin, 1990).

Carr. B. and D. J. O'Connor. *Introduction to the Theory of Knowledge* (Hemel Hempstead: Harvester Wheatsheaf, 1982).

Dancy, J. *Introduction to Contemporary Epistemology* (Oxford: Blackwell, 1985).

Hamlyn, D. W. *The Theory of Knowledge* (Garden City, NY: Doubleday, 1971).

Nagel, E. and R. Brandt (eds). *Meaning and Knowledge* (New York: Harcourt Brace Jovanovich, 1965).

Pears, David. *What is Knowledge?* (New York: Harper and Row, 1971).

Phillips Griffiths, A. (ed.). *Knowledge and Belief* (Oxford: Oxford University Press, 1967).

Plato. Theaetetus. In Irwin Edman (ed.), *The Works of Plato* (New York: Tudor, 1927).

Plato. Meno. In *Plato: Protagoras and Meno*, trans. W. K. C. Guthrie (Harmondsworth: Penguin, 1956).

Russell, B. *The Problems of Philosophy* (Oxford: Oxford University Press, 1987).

Trusted, J. *An Introduction to the Philosophy of Knowledge* (London: Macmillan, 1982).

Woozley, A. D. *Theory of Knowledge* (London: Hutchinson, 1949).

Chapter 6 Truth

Austin, J. L. *Philosophical Papers*, edited by J. O. Umson and G. J. Warnock (Oxford: Oxford University Press, 1990).

Blanshard, Brand. *Nature of Thought* (New York: Macmillan, 1941).

Grayling, A. C. (ed.). *Philosophy: A Guide Through the Subject* (Oxford: Oxford University Press, 1998).

Guyer, Paul (ed.). *The Cambridge Companion to Kant* (Cambridge: Cambridge University Press, 1992), Chapter 5.

Hamlyn, D. W. *The Theory of Knowledge* (Garden City, NY: Doubleday, 1971), Chapter 5.

Hume, D. *A Treatise of Human Nature* (1739–40) (London and New York: Dent and Dutton, 1966).

James, William. *Pragmatism: A New Name for Some Old Ways of Thinking* (New York: Longmans, Green, 1907).

Kant, I. *Critique of Pure Reason* (1781) (London: Dent, 1993).

Kemp, J. *The Philosophy of Kant* (London: Oxford University Press, 1968).

Kirkham, R. *Theories of Truth* (Cambridge, Mass: Massachusetts Institute of Technology Press, 1992).

Kripke, Saul. *Naming and Necessity* (Oxford: Oxford University Press, 1980).

O'Connor, D. J. *The Correspondence Theory of Truth* (London: Hutchinson, 1975).

Plantinga, A. *The Nature of Necessity* (Oxford: Oxford University Press, 1974).

Quine, W. V. O. *Philosophy of Logic* (Englewood Cliffs, NJ: Prentice-Hall, 1970).

Rorty, Richard. *Philosophy and the Mirror of Nature* (Princeton, NJ: Princeton University Press, 1979).

Rorty, Richard. Pragmatism, Davidson and Truth. In R. Rorty, *Objectivity, Relativism and Truth: Philosophical Papers I* (Cambridge: Cambridge University Press, 1991).

Strawson, P. F. Truth and A Problem about Truth. In P. F. Strawson, *Logico-Linguistic Papers* (London: Ashgate, 1994).

Walker, Ralph. *The Coherence Theory of Truth* (London: Routledge, 1990).

Warnock, G. J. Kant. In D. J. O'Connor (ed.), *A Critical History of Western Philosophy* (New York: Free Press, 1964).

White, Alan R. *Truth* (New York: Doubleday, Anchor, 1970).

Chapter 7 Scepticism

Ayer, A. J. *The Problem of Knowledge* (Harmondsworth: Penguin, 1984).

Burnyeat, Myles. (ed.). *The Skeptical Tradition* (Berkeley, Calif: University of California Press, 1983).

Chisholm, R. M. *Theory of Knowledge* (Englewood Cliffs, NJ: Prentice-Hall, 1988), Chapters 1, 2, 3, 10.

Curley, E. M. *Descartes Against the Skeptics* (Cambridge, Mass: Harvard University Press, 1978).

Descartes, R. Discourse on Method. In *Discourse on Method and other Writings*, trans. F. E. Sutcliffe (Harmondsworth: Penguin, 1970).

Descartes, R. Meditations on First Philosophy. In *Discourse on Method and other Writings*, trans. F. E. Sutcliffe (Harmondsworth: Penguin, 1970).

Hume, David. *An Enquiry Concerning Human Understanding*, edited by L. A. Selby-Bigge (Oxford: Oxford University Press, 1902).

Hume, David. *A Treatise of Human Nature* (1739–40) (London and New York: Dent and Dutton, 1966).

Kant, I. *Prolegomena* (New York: Hackett, 1977).

Malcolm, Norman. *Dreaming* (London: Routledge and Kegan Paul, 1954).

Moore, G. E. *Selected Writing* (London: Routledge, 1993).

Pollock, J. *Contemporary Theories of Knowledge* (Lanham, MD: Rowman and Littlefield, 1991).

Popkin, R. H. *The History of Scepticism from Erasmus to Spinoza* (Berkeley, Calif: University of California Press, 1980).

Putnam, Hilary. *Reason, Truth and History* (Oxford: Oxford University Press, 1984).

Quine, W. V. O. and J. S. Ullian. *The Web of Belief* (New York: Random House, 1970).

Slote, Michael A. *Reason and Scepticism* (London: Allen and Unwin, 1973).

Stroud, Barry. *The Significance of Philosophical Scepticism* (Oxford: Oxford University Press, 1984).

Unger, Peter. *Ignorance* (London: Oxford University Press, 1975).

Chapters 8 and 9

Armstrong, D. M. *Perception and the Physical World* (London: Routledge and Kegan Paul, 1961).

Ayer, A. J. *Language, Truth and Logic* (1936) (Harmondsworth: Penguin, 1946).

Ayer, A. J. *The Problem of Knowledge* (Harmondsworth and Baltimore: Penguin, 1990), Chapter 3.

Berkeley, G. A Treatise concerning the Principles of Human Knowledge (1710). In T. E. Jessop (ed.), *Berkeley, Philosophical Writings* (Austin Tex: University of Texas Press, 1953).

Berkeley, G. *Three Dialogues between Hylas and Philonous*, edited by R. M. Adams (Indianapolis, Ind: Hackett, 1979).

Cottingham, J. *Rationalism* (London: Paladin Granada, 1984).

Dancy, J. (ed.). *Perceptual Knowledge* (Oxford: Oxford University Press, 1988).

Descartes, R. Second Meditation (1641). In *Discourse on Method and other Writings*, trans. F. E. Sutcliffe (Harmondsworth: Penguin, 1970).

Foster, J. *The Case for Idealism* (London: Routledge and Kegan Paul, 1982).

Hamlyn, D. W. *The Psychology of Perception* (London: Routledge and Kegan Paul, 1979).

Hamlyn, D. W. *The Theory of Knowledge* (Garden City, NY: Doubleday, 1971), Chapter 6.

Hirst, R. J. (ed.). *Perception and the External World* (Problems in Philosophy Series) (London: Macmillan, 1965).

Hirst, R. J. *The Problems of Perception* (London: George Allen and Unwin, 1959).

Hume, David. *An Enquiry Concerning Human Understanding*, edited by L. A. Selby-Bigge (Oxford: Oxford University Press, 1902).

Hume, David. *A Treatise of Human Nature* (1739–40) (London and New York: Dent and Dutton, 1966).

Kant, I. *Critique of Pure Reason* (1781) (London: Dent, 1993).

Locke, J. *An Essay Concerning Human Understanding* (1690) (London: Fontana, 1973).

Merleau-Ponty, M. *The Phenomenology of Perception* (London: Routledge and Kegan Paul, 1962), Preface and Chapter 3.

Plato. Meno. In *Plato: Protagoras and Meno*, trans. W. K. C. Guthrie (Harmondsworth: Penguin, 1956).

Plato. *The Republic*, trans. H. D. P. Lee (Harmondsworth: Penguin, 1971).

Plato, Theaetetus. In Irwin Edman (ed.), *The Works of Plato* (New York: Tudor, 1927).

Quine, W. V. O. Two Dogmas of Empiricism. In W. V. O. Quine, *From a Logical Point of View* (Cambridge, Mass: Harvard University Press, 1953).

Russell, B. *The Problems of Philosophy* (Oxford: Oxford University Press, 1987), Chapters 1 and 2.

Sturrock, J. *Structuralism* (London: Fontana, 1993).

Warnock, G. J. (ed.). *The Philosophy of Perception* (2 vols) (Oxford: Oxford University Press, 1967).

Chapters 10 and 11

Agassi, J. and R. S. Cohen (eds). *Scientific Philosophy Today* (Dordrecht, Holland: D. Reidel, 1981).

Ayer, A. J. *Language, Truth and Logic* (1936) (Harmondsworth: Penguin, 1946).

Benhabib, Seyla, Judith Butler, Drucilla Cornell, Nancy Fraser and Linda J. Nicholson. *Feminist Contentions: A Philosophical Exchange* (New York: Routledge and Kegan Paul, 1995).

Braithwaite, R. B. *Scientific Explanation* (Cambridge: Cambridge University Press, 1953).

Bunge, M. *Causality and Modern Science* (New York: Dover Publications, 1980).

Burtt, E. A. *Metaphysical Foundations of Modern Science* (London: Routledge and Kegan Paul, 1963).

Campbell, Norman. *What is Science?* (New York: Dover Publications, 1952).

Carnap, R. *An Introduction to the Philosophy of Science* (New York: Dover, 1995, reprint of 1966 edition).

Chalmers, A. F. *What is this thing called Science?* (Milton Keynes: Open University Press, 1982).

Churchland P. and C. Hooker (eds). *Images of Science* (Chicago: University of Chicago Press, 1985).

Cohen, Morris R. and Ernest Nagel. *An Introduction to Logic and Scientific Method* (Safety Harbor, Fla: Simon Publications, 2002).

Doyle, L. and R. Harris, *Empiricism, Explanations and Rationality* (London: Routledge, 1986).

Duhem, P. *The Aim and Structure of Physical Theory*, trans. P. Wiener (Princeton, NJ: Princeton University Press, 1953), Chapter 6.

Earman, J. *Bayes or Bust* (Cambridge, Mass: Massachusetts Institute of Technology Press, 1992).

Feigl, H. and N. Brodbeck (eds). *Readings in the Philosophy of Science* (New York: Appleton-Century-Crofts, 1953).

Feyerbend, P. *Against Method* (London: Verso, 1975).

Fricker, Miranda, and Jennifer Hornsby (eds). *The Cambridge Companion to Feminism in Philosophy* (Cambridge: Cambridge University Press, 2000).

Gardner, M. *Fads and Fallacies in the Name of Science* (New York: Dover Publications, 1957).

Garry, Ann and Marilyn Pearsall. *Women, Knowledge and Reality* (Boston: Unwin Hyman, 1989).

Goodman, N. *Fact, Fiction and Forecast* (Cambridge, Mass: Harvard University Press, 1983).

Harding, Sandra. *Whose Science? Whose Knowledge? Thinking from Women's Lives* (Ithaca, NY: Cornell University Press, 1991).

Harré, R. *The Philosophies of Science: An Introductory Survey* (Oxford: Oxford University Press, 1976).

Hempel, C. G. *Philosophy of Natural Science* (Englewood Cliffs, NJ: Prentice-Hall, 1966).

Hempel, C. G. The Logic of Explanation. In H. Feigl and N. Brodbeck (eds), *Readings in the Philosophy of Science* (New York: Appleton-Century-Crofts, 1953).

Hempel, C. G. Studies in the Logic of Confirmation. In *Aspects of Scientific Explanation and Other Essays in the Philosophy of Science* (New York: The Free Press, 1965).

Hesse, M. Duhem, Quine and the New Empiricism. In H. Morick (ed.), *Challenges to Empiricism* (Indianapolis, Ind: Hackett, 1980).

Horwich, P. *Probability and Evidence* (Cambridge: Cambridge University Press, 1982).

Hospers, John. What is Explanation? In A. Flew (ed.), *Essays in Conceptual Analysis* (London: Macmillan, 1956).

Howson, C. and P. Urbach. *Scientific Reasoning: The Bayesian Approach* (La Salle, Ill: Open Court, 1993).

Jaggar, Alison M. and Iris Marion Young (eds). *A Companion to Feminist Philosophy* (Oxford: Blackwell, 1999).

Kneale, W. *Probability and Induction* (Oxford: Oxford University Press, 1949).

Kuhn, T. S. *The Structure of Scientific Revolutions* (Chicago: University of Chicago Press, 1970).

Kukla, A. *Studies in Scientific Realism* (Oxford: Oxford University Press, 1998).

Lakatos, I. and A. Musgrave (eds). *Criticism and the Growth of Knowledge* (Cambridge: Cambridge University Press, 1970).

Laudan, L. *Science and Hypothesis* (Dordrecht, Holland: D. Reidel, 1981).

Longino, Helen. *Science as Social Knowledge* (Princeton, NJ: Princeton University Press, 1990).

Mayo, D. *Error and the Growth of Experimental Knowledge* (Chicago: University of Chicago Press, 1996).

Medawar, P. B. *Induction and Intuition in Scientific Thought* (London: Methuen, 1969).

Medawar, P. B. *The Art of the Soluble* (London: Methuen, 1967).

Millett, K. *Sexual Politics* (London: Virago, 1977; New York: Simon and Schuster, 1990).

Nagel, E. *The Structure of Science: Problems in the Logic of Scientific Explanation* (New York: Harcourt, Brace and World, 1961; London: Routledge and Kegan Paul, 1970).

O'Hear, Anthony. *An Introduction to the Philosophy of Science* (Oxford: Clarendon, 1989).

Popper, K. *Conjectures and Refutations: Growth of Scientific Knowledge* (London: Routledge and Kegan Paul, 1969).

Popper, K. *The Logic of Scientific Discovery* (London: Hutchinson, 1968).

Putnam, H. *Philosophical Papers* (Cambridge: Cambridge University Press, 1975).

Russell, B. *Mysticism and Logic and Other Essays* (London: Longmans, Green, 1918).

Salmon, W. C. *Four Decades of Scientific Explanation* (Minneapolis, Minn: University of Minnesota Press, 1990).

Swinburne, J. (ed.). *The Justification of Induction* (London: Oxford University Press, 1974).

Taylor, D. M. *Explanation and Meaning: An Introduction to Philosophy* (Cambridge: Cambridge University Press, 1970).

Toulmin, S. *The Philosophy of Science* (London: Hutchinson, 1953).

Trusted, J. *Inquiry and Understanding* (London: Macmillan, 1987).

Wright-Mills, C. *The Sociological Imagination* (Oxford: Oxford University Press, 2000).

Chapters 12 and 13

Abraham, W. J. *Introduction to the Philosophy of Religion* (Englewood Cliffs, NJ: Prentice-Hall, 1985).

Anselm, *Proslogium*, trans. M. J. Charlesworth (Oxford: Clarendon, 1965).

Auden, W. H. *The Living Thoughts of Kierkegaard* (Bloomington, Ind: Indiana University Press, 1963).

Cahn, S. (ed.). *Philosophy of Religion* (New York: Harper and Row, 1970).

Collins, J. *The Mind of Kierkegaard* (Chicago: Regnery, 1953).

Copleston, F. C. *Aquinas* (Harmondsworth: Penguin, 1967).

Davies, B. *Introduction to the Philosophy of Religion* (Oxford: Oxford University Press, 1993).

Descartes, R. Meditations. In *Discourse on Method and other Writings*, trans. F. E. Sutcliffe (Harmondsworth: Penguin, 1970), particularly the third (Of God: That He Exists) and the fifth (the ontological argument).

Flew, A. *God and Philosophy* (Loughton, Essex: Prometheus, 2005).

Flew, Antony and Alasdair MacIntyre. *New Essays in Philosophical Theology* (London: SCM Press, 1969).

Freud, Sigmund, *The Future of an Illusion*, trans. W. D. Robson-Scott (New York: Doubleday, Anchor, 1953).

Gaskin, J. C. A. *The Quest for Eternity* (Harmondsworth: Penguin, 1984).

Geach, P. T. *God and the Soul* (New York: Schocken, 1969).

Geach, P. T. *Providence and Evil* (New York: Cambridge University Press, 1977).

Hick, J. *Arguments for the Existence of God* (London: Macmillan, 1970).

Hick, J. *Evil and the Love of God* (London: Macmillan, 1966).

Hick, J. *Faith and Knowledge* (Ithaca, NY: Cornell University Press, 1966).

Hick, J. (ed.). *Faith and the Philosophers* (New York: St Martin's Press, 1964).

Hick, J. *Philosophy and Religion* (Englewood Cliffs, NJ: Prentice-Hall, 1989).

Hume, David. *An Enquiry Concerning Human Understanding*, edited by L. A. Selby-Bigge (Oxford: Oxford University Press, 1902), Section X, Of Miracles.

Hume, David. *Dialogues Concerning Natural Religion*, edited by J. M. Bell (Harmondsworth: Penguin, 1990).

James, William. *The Varieties of Religious Experience* (New York: Longmans, Green, 1902).

James, William. *The Will to Believe and Other Essays in Popular Philosophy* (New York: Longmans, Green, 1897), Chapter 1.

Kant, Immanuel. *Critique of Practical Reason* (New York: Bobbs-Merrill, 1956), Book II, Chapter II.

Kant, Immanuel. *Critique of Pure Reason* (1781) (London: Dent, 1993), B611–670, The Ideal of Reason.

Kenny, A. *The Five Ways* (London: Routledge and Kegan Paul, 1969). Translation, analysis and criticism of Aquinas' five arguments.

Kenny, A. *What is Faith? Essays in the Philosophy of Religion* (Oxford: Oxford University Press, 1992).

Kierkegaard, S. *Concluding Unscientific Postscript* (1846), trans. D. F. Swenson (Princeton, NJ: Princeton University Press, 1941).

Leibniz, Gottfried. *New Essays Concerning Human Understanding* (Cambridge: Cambridge University Press, 1981).

Leibniz, Gottfried. *Theodicy* (1710), trans. D. Allen (Ontario: Dent, 1966).

Lewis, C. S. *The Problem of Pain* (New York: Macmillan, 1962).

Mackie, J. L. *The Miracle of Theism: Arguments For and Against the Existence of God* (Oxford: Oxford University Press, 1982).

Marx, Karl. Economic and Philosophical Manuscripts (1844). In *Early Writings*, trans. T. Bottomore (New York: McGraw-Hill, 1963).

Marx, K. and F. Engels. *The German Ideology* (London: Lawrence and Wishart, 1982).

Mill, J. S. *Three Essays on Religion* (Loughton, Essex: Prometheus, 1998).

Mitchell, B. (ed.). *The Philosophy of Religion* (London: Methuen, 1971).

Nietzsche, F. *On the Genealogy of Morals* (1887), trans. Francis Golffing (New York: Doubleday, 1956).

Nietzsche, F. The Anti-Christ. In *The Viking Portable Nietzsche*, trans. Walter Kaufmann (New York: Viking, 1959).

O'Hear, A. *Experience, Explanation and Faith: An Introduction to the Philosophy of Religion* (Aldershot: Gregg Revivals, 1992).

Pascal, Blaise. *Pensées* (Harmondsworth: Penguin, 1966).

Pike, N. (ed.). *Good and Evil* (Englewood Cliffs, NJ: Prentice Hall, 1964).

Plantinga, A. *God and Other Minds* (Ithaca, NY: Cornell University Press, 1967).

Plantinga, A. *God, Freedom and Evil* (London: Allen and Unwin, 1975).

Plato. Euthyphro. In *The Last Days of Socrates*, trans. Hugh Tredennick and Harold Tarrant (Harmondsworth: Penguin, 1993).

Rundle, Bede. *Why There is Something Rather Than Nothing* (Oxford: Oxford University Press, 2004).

Spinoza, Benedict. *The Collected Works of Spinoza*, trans. Edwin Curley, Vol. 1 (Princeton, NJ: Princeton University Press, 1985), Short Treatise on God, Man and His Well-being. Part I, Chapter 1.

Smart, N. (ed.). *Historical Selections in the Philosophy of Religion* (New York: Harper and Row, 1962).

Swinburne, R. *Faith and Reason* (Columbia, SC: Columbia University Press, 1983).

Swinburne, R. *The Coherence of Theism* (New York: Oxford University Press, 1993).

Swinburne, R. *The Existence of God* (Oxford: Oxford University Press, 1991).

Tillich, P. *Systematic Theology* (Chicago: University of Chicago Press, 1953–64).

Tillich, P. *The Dynamics of Faith* (New York: Harper, 1958).

Chapters 14 and 15

Borst, C. V. (ed.). *The Mind–Brain Identity Theory* (New York: St Martin's Press, 1970).

Campbell, K. *Body and Mind* (Chicago: University of Notre Dame Press, 1985).

Carruthers, P. *Introducing Persons: Theories and Arguments in the Philosophy of Mind* (London: Routledge, 1990).

Churchland, P. M. *Matter and Consciousness: A Contemporary Introduction to the Philosophy of Mind* (Cambridge, Mass: Massachusetts Institute of Technology Press, 1988).

Descartes, R. Meditations. In Meditations on First Philosophy in *Discourse on Method and Other Writings*, trans. F. E. Sutcliffe (Harmondsworth: Penguin, 1970).

Descartes, R. The Passions of the Soul (1649) and Principles of Philosophy. In *The Philosophical Writings of Descartes*, trans. J. Cottingham, R. Stoothoff and D. Murdoch (Cambridge: Cambridge University Press, 1985), Vol. I. for his classic statement of dualistic interactionism.

Dewey, J. *The Quest for Certainty* (New York: Minton Blach, 1929).

Flew, A. *A Rational Animal* (Oxford: Clarendon, 1978), chapters 5,6,7 and 8.

Flew, A. (ed.). *Body, Mind and Death* (New York: Crowell-Collier, 1964).

Flew, A. *The Logic of Mortality* (Oxford: Blackwell, 1987).

Freud, S. *Five Lectures on Psychoanalysis* (Harmondsworth: Penguin, 1983).

Glover, J. (ed.). *The Philosophy of Mind* (Oxford Readings in Philosophy) (Oxford: Oxford University Press, 1977).

Hobbes, T. *Leviathan*, edited by C. B. Macpherson (Harmondsworth: Penguin, 1968; Buffalo, NY: Prometheus, 1988).

Husserl, S. *Ideas: General Introduction to Pure Phenomenology*, trans. W. R. Boyce Gibson (New York: Macmillan, 1931).

Huxley, Thomas. *Animal Automatism and Collected Essays* (New York: reprinted Greenwood Press, 1968).

Kripke, S. *Naming and Necessity* (Oxford: Oxford University Press, 1980).

Leibniz, Gottfried, *The New System and Associated Contemporary Texts*, edited by R. S. Woolhouse and R. Francks (Oxford: Clarendon, 1997). Parallelism.

Leibniz, G. W. *Discourse on Metaphysics and the Monadology*, trans. R. Montgomery (Loughton, Essex: Prometheus, 1992).

Lovejoy, A. *The Revolt Against Dualism* (La Salle, Ill: Open Court, 1955).

Malcolm, N. *Problems of Mind: Descartes to Wittgenstein* (London: Allen and Unwin, 1971).

McGinn, Colin. *The Character of Mind* (Oxford: Oxford University Press, 1982).

McGinn, Colin. *The Problem of Consciousness* (Oxford: Oxford University Press, 1991).

Merleau-Ponty, M. *Phenomenology of Perception*, trans. C. Smith (New York: Humanities, 1962; London: Routledge and Kegan Paul, 1962).

Nagel, T. *Mortal Questions* (Cambridge: Cambridge University Press, 1991), Chapter 12, What is it like to be a bat?

O'Connor, J. (ed.). *Modern Materialism: Readings on Mind–Body Identity* (New York: Harcourt, Brace and World, 1969).

Parfit, D. *Reasons and Persons* (Oxford: Oxford University Press, 1986).

Perry, J. (ed.). *Personal Identity* (Berkeley: University of California Press, 1975).

Plato, Phaedo. In *The Last Days of Socrates*, trans. Hugh Tredennick and Harold Tarrant (Harmondsworth: Penguin, 1993). Plato's views on the soul.

Rescher N. (ed.). *Studies in the Philosophy of Mind* (Oxford: Blackwell, 1972).

Rosenthal, D. (ed.). *Materialism and the Mind–Body Problem* (Englewood Cliffs, NJ: Prentice Hall, 1971).

Rosenthal D. (ed.). *The Nature of Mind* (New York: Oxford University Press, 1991).

Ryle, G. *The Concept of Mind* (Harmondsworth: Penguin, 1990), Chapters 1, 2 and 5.

Ryle, G. *Dilemmas* (Cambridge: Cambridge University Press, 1964).

Sartre, J-P. *Existentialism and Humanism* (1946) (London: Methuen, 1948).

Searle, J. R. *Minds, Brains and Science* (Harmondsworth: Penguin, 1992).

Searle, J. R. *The Rediscovery of the Mind* (Cambridge, Mass: Massachusetts Institute of Technology Press, 1992).

Shaffer, J. A. *The Philosophy of Mind* (Englewood Cliffs, NJ: Prentice Hall, 1968).

Shoemaker, Sydney. Functionalism and Qualia. In *Identity, Cause and Mind* (Cambridge: Cambridge University Press, 1984).

Skinner, B. F. *About Behaviourism* (London: Cape, 1975).

Smart, J. J. C. *Philosophy and Scientific Realism* (London: Routledge and Kegan Paul, 1963).

Smith P. and O. R. Jones. *The Philosophy of Mind* (Cambridge: Cambridge University Press, 1986).

Spinoza, B. *Ethics*, trans. A. Boyle (London: Dent, 1993). The dual-aspect theory.

Taylor, C. *The Explanation of Behaviour* (London: Routledge and Kegan Paul, 1980).

Trilling, L. *Sincerity and Authenticity* (London: Oxford University Press, 1972), Chapter 6.

Vesey, G. N. A. *Body and Mind* (London: George Allen and Unwin, 1964).

White, A. R. *The Philosophy of Mind* (Westport, Conn: Greenwood Press, 1978).

Chapters 16 and 17

Beauvoir, S. de. *The Second Sex* (1949), trans. H. M. Parshley (Harmondsworth: Penguin, 1972).

Derrida, Jacques. *Of Grammatology* (Baltimore: Johns Hopkins University Press, 1976).

Derrida, Jacques. *Speech and Phenomena* (Evanston: Northwestern University Press, 1973).

Derrida, Jacques. *Writing and Difference*, trans. A. Bass (London: Routledge and Kegan Paul, 1978).

Descartes, R. Meditations of First Philosophy. In *Discourse on Method and other Writings*, trans. F. E. Sutcliffe (Harmondsworth: Penguin, 1970).

Foucault, Michel. *Discipline and Punish* (Harmondsworth and New York: Penguin, 1979).

Foucault, Michel. *History of Sexuality, volume 1: An Introduction*, trans. R. Hurley (Harmondsworth: Penguin, 1978).

Foucault, Michel. *The Care of the Self: The History of Sexuality*, vol. 3, trans. R. Hurley (Harmondsworth: Penguin, 1984).

Frankl, Viktor E. *Man's Search for Meaning* (New York: Washington Square Press, 1984).

Freud, S. *The Ego and the Id*, trans. James Strachey (London: W. W. Norton, 1990).

Glover, J. *The Philosophy and Psychology of Personal Identity* (Harmondsworth: Penguin, 1991).

Hume, D. *A Treatise of Human Nature* (1739–40) (London and New York: Dent and Dutton, 1966), Of Personal Identity, Vol. I, Part IV, Section 6 and Appendix.

Kant, I. *Critique of Pure Reason* (1781) (London: Dent, 1993).

Kierkegaard, S. *Fear and Trembling and the Sickness unto Death*, trans. W. Lowrie (Princeton: Princeton University Press, 1974).

Laing, R. D. *The Divided Self* (Harmondsworth: Pelican, 1960).

Laing, R. D. *The Politics of Experience and The Bird of Paradise* (Harmondsworth: Penguin, 1967).

Lloyd, Genevieve. *The Man of Reason: 'Male' and 'Female' in Western Philosophy* (Minneapolis: University of Minnesota Press, 1984).

Locke, J. Of identity and diversity. In his *An Essay Concerning Human Understanding* (1690) (London: Fontana, 1973), Book II, Chapter 27.

Macquarrie, J. *Existentialism* (Harmondsworth: Penguin, 1986).

Marcuse, H. *Eros and Civilisation* (London: Sphere, 1969).

Marcuse, H. *One-Dimensional Man* (London: Sphere 1968).

Marx, K. and F. Engels. *The German Ideology*, edited by C. J. Arthur (London: Lawrence and Wishart, 1977).

Nietzsche, F. *Beyond Good and Evil* (1887), trans. R. J. Hollingdale (Harmondsworth and New York: Penguin, 1973).

Perry, J. (ed.). *Personal Identity* (Berkeley, Calif: University of California Press, 1985).

Piaget, J. *Structuralism*, trans. C. Maschler (London: Routledge and Kegan Paul, 1971).

Sartre, J-P. *Being and Nothingness* (1943) (London: Methuen, 1984).

Sartre, J-P. *Existentialism and Humanism* (1946) (London: Methuen, 1948).

Sartre, J-P. *Transcendence of the Ego* (New York: Noonday, 1957).

Shoemaker, Sydney. *Self-Knowledge and Self-Identity* (Ithaca, NY: Cornell University Press, 1963).

Skinner, B. F. *About Behaviourism* (London: Cape, 1975).

Sturrock, J. *Structuralism* (London: Fontana, 1993).

Warnock, Mary. *Existentialist Ethics* (New York: St Martin's Press, 1967).

Warnock, Mary. *The Philosophy of Sartre* (London: Hutchinson, 1966).

West, David. *An Introduction to Continental Philosophy* (Cambridge: Polity, 1997).

Chapters 18–20

Bentham, Jeremy. *A Fragment on Government with an Introduction to the Principles of Morals and Legislation* (1789), edited by Wilfrid Harrison (Oxford: Blackwell, 1967).

Berofsky, Bernard (ed.). *Freedom and Responsibility* (Stanford, Calif: Stanford University Press, 1961).

Berofsky, Bernard (ed.). *Free Will and Determinism* (New York: Harper and Row, 1966).

Brandt, R. B. *Ethical Theory* (Englewood Cliffs, NJ: Prentice-Hall, 1959), Chapter 20.

Burke, Edmund. *Reflections on the Revolution in France* (1790) (Harmondsworth: Penguin, 1969).

Campbell, C. A. On Selfhood and Godhead. In Arthur Minton (ed.), *Philosophy: Paradox and Discovery* (New York: McGraw-Hill, 1976).

Dilthey, W. *W. Dilthey: Selected Writings*, edited by H. P. Rickman (Cambridge and New York: Cambridge University Press, 1976).

Duff, Antony. Restoration and Retribution. In Andrew von Hirsch, Julian Roberts, Anthony Bottoms, Kent Roach and Mara Schiff (eds). *Restorative Justice and Criminal Justice: Competing or Reconcilable Paradigms?* (Oxford and Portland, Oreg: Hart Publishing, 2003), pp. 43–60.

Edwards, Paul and Arthur Pap (eds). *A Modern Introduction to Philosophy* (New York: Free Press, 1965).

Feinberg, Joel and Russ Shafer-Landau (eds). *Reason and Responsibility* (London: Wadsworth, 2002).

Foucault, Michel. *Discipline and Punish* (Harmondsworth and New York: Penguin, 1979).

Foucault, Michel. *Madness and Civilization: A History of Insanity in the Age of Reason* (London: Routledge, 1989).

Hegel, G. W. F. *Phenomenology of Spirit*, trans. A. V. Miller (Oxford and New York: Oxford University Press, 1977).

Hegel, G. W. F. *Reason in History*, trans. R. Hartman (New York: Bobbs-Merrill, 1953), the introduction.

Hobbes, T. *Leviathan*, edited by C. B. Macpherson (Harmondsworth: Penguin, 1968; Buffalo, NY: Prometheus, 1988), Chapter 21.

Hook. S. (ed.). *Determinism and Freedom in the Age of Modern Science* (New York: Macmillan, Collier, 1961).

Hospers, John. *Human Conduct* (New York: Harcourt Brace Jovanovich, 1961), Chapters 9 and 10.

Hospers, John. What Means This Freedom? In S. Hook (ed.), *Determinism and Freedom in the Age of Modern Science* (New York: Macmillan, Collier, 1961).

Hume, David. *An Enquiry Concerning Human Understanding*, edited by L. A. Selby-Bigge (Oxford: Oxford University Press, 1902), section 8.

Hume, D. *A Treatise of Human Nature* (1739–40) (London and New York: Dent and Dutton, 1966), Book II, Part iii, sections 1–3.

James, William. The Dilemma of Determinism. In W. James (ed.), *The Will to Believe and Other Essays in Popular Philosophy* (New York: Longmans, Green, 1897).

Kane, Robert. *The Significance of Free Will* (New York: Oxford University Press, 1996).

Kant, Immanuel. *Critique of Practical Reason* (New York: Bobbs-Merrill, 1956), Book I, Chapter 3.

Kenny, A. *Freewill and Responsibility* (London: Routledge, 1987).

Kierkegaard, S. *Fear and Trembling and the Sickness unto Death*, trans. W. Lowrie (Princeton: Princeton University Press, 1974).

Körner, Stephen. *What is Philosophy? One Philosopher's Answer* (London: Penguin, 1969), Part IV.

Lehrer, Keith. (ed.). *Freedom and Determinism* (New York: Random House, 1966).

Lévi-Strauss, Claude. *Structural Anthropology*, trans. C. Jacobson and B. G. Schoepf (Harmondsworth: Penguin, 1986).

Locke, J. *An Essay Concerning Human Understanding* (1690) (London: Fontana, 1973), Book II, Chapter 21.

Marx, Karl. *Communist Manifesto* (1848), trans. S. Moore (Chicago: Regnery, 1969).

Marx, Karl and F. Engels. *The German Ideology* (1846) (London: Lawrence and Wishart, 1982).

Milgram, Stanley. *Obedience to Authority* (London: Tavistock, 1974; New York: Harper and Row, 1974).

Mill, J. S. *A System of Logic* (London: Longmans, 1965), Book IV, Chapter 2.

Mill, J. S. On Liberty (1859) in *Utilitarianism, On Liberty and Considerations on Representative Government* (London: Dent, 1972).

Morgenbesser, Sidney and James Walsh. *Free Will* (Englewood Cliffs, NJ: Prentice-Hall, 1962).

O'Connor, D. *Free Will* (London: Macmillan, 1972).

Paton, H. J. (trans.). *The Moral Law: Kant's Groundwork of the Metaphysic of Morals* (London: Hutchinson, 1948).

Pears, D. F. (ed.). *Freedom and the Will* (New York: St Martin's Press, 1963; London: Macmillan, 1963).

Samenow, Stanton. *Inside the Criminal Mind* (New York: Random House, 1983).

Sartre, J-P. *Being and Nothingness* (1943) (London: Methuen, 1984).

Sartre, J-P. *Existentialism and Humanism* (1946) (London: Methuen, 1948).

Schopenhauer, A. *Prize Essay on the Freedom of the Will* (1841), trans. E. F. J. Payne (1960) (Cambridge Texts in the History of Philosophy) (Cambridge: Cambridge University Press, 1999).

Schopenhauer, A. *The World as Will and Representation*, trans. E. F. J. Payne (New York: Dover, 1966).

Spinoza, B. *Ethics*, trans. A. Boyle (London: Dent, 1993), Part III.

Sturrock, J. *Structuralism* (London: Fontana, 1993).

Taylor, Richard. *Metaphysics* (Englewood Cliffs, NJ: Prentice-Hall, 1975), Chapter 4.

Watson, G. (ed.). *Free Will* (Oxford: Oxford University Press, 1982).

Chapters 21–23

Almond, B. *Moral Concerns* (New York: Humanities Press, 1987).

Arendt, Hannah. *Eichmann in Jerusalem: A Report on the Banality of Evil* (Harmondsworth: Penguin, 1979).

Aristotle. *Nicomachean Ethics*, trans. W. D. Ross (Oxford: Oxford University Press, 1925).

Aune, B. *Kant's Theory of Morals* (New Jersey: Princeton University Press, 1979).

Ayer, A. J. *Language, Truth and Logic* (1936) (Harmondsworth: Penguin, 1946).

Baier, A. C. *Moral Prejudices* (Cambridge, Mass: Harvard University Press, 1994).

Beauchamp, T. L. and J. F. Childress. *Principles of Biomedical Ethics* (Oxford: Oxford University Press, 2001), see Chapter 2 for virtue ethics.

Bentham, Jeremy. *A Fragment on Government with an Introduction to the Principles of Morals and Legislation* (1789), edited by Wilfrid Harrison (Oxford: Blackwell, 1967).

Blackburn, S. *Being Good: A Short Introduction to Ethics* (Oxford: Oxford University Press, 2003).

Brandt, Richard. *Ethical Theory* (Englewood Cliffs, NJ: Prentice Hall, 1959).

Brandt, Richard. *Value and Obligation* (New York: Harcourt Brace Jovanovich, 1961).

Broad, C. D. *Five Types of Ethical Theory* (London: Kegan Paul, Trench, Trubner, 1934; New York: Harcourt, Brace, 1934).

Butler, J. *Fifteen Sermons Upon Human Nature* (London: Macmillan, 1900), arguments against egoism – particularly sermon XI.

Foot, Philippa. *Theories of Ethics* (Oxford: Oxford University Press, 1986).

Frankena, W. K. *Ethics* (Englewood Cliffs, NJ: Prentice-Hall, 1973).

Gilligan, Carol. *A Different Voice: Psychological Theory and Women's Development* (Cambridge, Mass: Harvard University Press, 1982).

Grimshaw, Jean. *Feminist Philosophers: Women's Perspectives on Philosophical Traditions* (Brighton: Wheatsheaf, 1986).

Guyer, Paul (ed.). *The Cambridge Companion to Kant* (Cambridge: Cambridge University Press, 1992).

Hare, R. M. *Freedom and Reason* (Oxford: Oxford University Press, 1963).

Hare, R. M. *Moral Thinking* (Oxford: Clarendon, 1981).

Hare, R. M. *The Language of Morals* (Oxford: Clarendon, 1952).

Hobbes, T. *Leviathan*, edited by C. B. Macpherson (Harmondsworth: Penguin, 1968; Buffalo, NY: Prometheus, 1988), particularly Part I.

Hudson, W. D. *Modern Moral Philosophy* (London: Macmillan, 1985), Chapter 6.

Hudson, W. D. *The Is/Ought Question* (New York: Macmillan, 1969).

Hume, David. *An Enquiry Concerning the Principles of Morals* (La Salle, Ill: Open Court, 1912).

Hume, David. *A Treatise of Human Nature* (1739–40) (London and New York: Dent and Dutton, 1966).

Jaggar, Alison M. and Paula S. Rothenberg (eds). *Feminist Frameworks* (New York: McGraw-Hill, 1993).

Kant, Immanuel. *Lectures in Ethics*, trans. L. Infield (New York: Harper and Row, 1963).

Kaufmann, Walter. *Nietzsche* (Princeton, NJ: Princeton University Press, 1950).

Körner, S. *Kant* (Baltimore: Penguin, 1955), particularly Chapter 6.

Mabbott, J. D. *An Introduction to Ethics* (London: Hutchinson, 1969).

MacIntyre, A. C. *After Virtue* (London: Duckworth and University of Notre Dame Press, 1981).

MacIntyre, A. *A Short History of Ethics* (New York: Macmillan, 1966).

Mackie, J. L. *Ethics: Inventing Right and Wrong* (Harmondsworth: Penguin, 1990).

McCracken, Janet. *Thinking About Gender: A Historical Anthology* (Fort Worth: Harcourt Brace, 1997).

Midgley, Mary. *Can't We Make Moral Judgements?* (New York: St Martin's Press, 1991).

Mill, J. S. *Autobiography of John Stuart Mill* (1873) (New York: Signet, 1964).

Mill, J. S. Utilitarianism. In *Utilitarianism, On Liberty and Considerations on Representative Government* (London: Dent, 1972).

Moore, G. E. *Principia Ethica* (Cambridge: Cambridge University Press, 1982).

Moravscik, J. (ed.). *Aristotle* (New York: Doubleday, Anchor, 1966).

Nagel, Thomas. *Mortal Questions* (Cambridge: Cambridge University Press, 1979).

Nagel, T. *The Possibility of Altruism* (New York: Oxford University Press, 1970).

Nietzsche, F. *Beyond Good and Evil* (1887), trans. R. J. Hollingdale (Harmondsworth and New York: Penguin, 1973).

Noddings, N. *Caring: A Feminine Approach to Ethics and Education* (Berkeley, Calif: University of California Press, 1978).

Paton, H. J. *The Categorical Imperative* (New York: Harper Row, 1964).

Paton, H. J. (trans.). *The Moral Law: Kant's Groundwork of the Metaphysic of Morals* (London: Hutchinson, 1948). Paton's introduction is especially useful.

Plamenatz, J. *Man and Society* (2 Vols) (London and New York: Longman, 1992), Vol. 1 chapters on Hobbes, Locke, Hume and Rousseau; Vol. 2 chapters on Hegel and Marx.

Plato, Euthyphro. *In The Last Days of Socrates*, trans. Hugh Tredennick and Harold Tarrant (Harmondsworth: Penguin, 1993).

Plato. *The Republic*, trans. H. D. P. Lee (Harmondsworth: Penguin, 1971), The Ring of Gyges, In Book II.

Plato. *The Works of Plato*, edited by Irwin Edman (New York: Simon and Schuster, 1928).

Quinton, A. *Utilitarian Ethics* (London: Duckworth, 1989).

Rachels, James. *The Elements of Moral Philosophy* (New York: McGraw Hill, 1993).

Raphael, D. D. *Moral Philosophy* (Oxford: Oxford University Press, 1981).

Raphael, D. D. *The Moral Sense* (London: Oxford University Press, 1947).

Ross, W. D. *Aristotle* (New York: Meridian, 1959), Chapter 7.

Ross, W. D. *Kant's Ethical Theory* (London: Oxford University Press, 1954).

Rousseau, Jean-Jacques. *Emile* (New York: Dutton, 1970).

Rousseau, Jean-Jacques. On the Origins of Inequality. In *The Social Contract* (New York: Dutton, 1950).

Ryan, A. *J. S. Mill* (London: Routledge and Kegan Paul, 1974).

Scheffler, Samuel (ed.). *Consequentialism and its Critics* (Oxford: Oxford University Press, 1988).

Sen, A. and B. Williams. (eds). *Utilitarianism and Beyond* (Cambridge: Cambridge University Press, 1982).

Sidgwick, Henry, *The Methods of Ethics* (1874) (London: Macmillan, 1962).

Singer, P. (ed.). *A Companion to Ethics* (Oxford: Blackwell, 1993).

Singer, P. *Practical Ethics* (Cambridge: Cambridge University Press, 1993).

Singer, P. *The Expanding Circle* (Oxford: Oxford University Press, 1983).

Smart, J. J. C. and Bernard Williams. *Utilitarianism: For and Against* (Cambridge: Cambridge University Press, 1973).

Spinoza, B. *Ethics*, trans. A. Boyle (London: Dent, 1993).

Stevenson, C. L. *Ethics and Language* (New Haven: Yale, 1944).

Stevenson, C. L. *Facts and Values* (New Haven: Yale, 1963).

Toulmin, S. E. *An Examination of the Place of Reason in Ethics* (London: Cambridge University Press, 1952).

Trusted, J. *Moral Principles and Social Values* (London: Routledge, 1987).

Urmson, J. O. *The Emotive Theory of Ethics* (London: Hutchinson, 1968).

Walsh, J. and H. Shapiro (eds). *Aristotle's Ethics* (Belmont, Calif: Wadsworth, 1967).

Warnock, G. L. *Contemporary Moral Philosophy* (London: Macmillan, 1974).

Warnock, Mary. *Ethics since 1900* (Oxford: Oxford University Press, 1979).

Warnock, Mary. *Existentialist Ethics* (New York: St Martin's Press, 1967).

Williams, Bernard. *Ethics and the Limits of Philosophy* (London: Fontana, 1985).

Williams, Bernard. *Morality: an Introduction to Ethics* (London: Cambridge University Press, 1982).

Wollstonecraft, M. *A Vindication of the Rights of Women* (1792), edited by C. W. Hagelman (New York: Norton, 1967).

Chapters 24–27

Arendt, H. *Origins of Totalitarianism* (New York: Meridian Books, 1958).

Aristotle, *Politics*, trans. T. A. Sinclair (Harmondsworth: Penguin, 1977).

Beauvoir, S. de. *The Second Sex*, trans. H. M. Parshley (New York: Bantam, 1968).

Bell, D. *The End of Ideology* (Glencoe, Ill: Free Press, 1960).

Benhabib, Seyla, Judith Butler, Drucilla Cornell, Nancy Fraser and Linda J. Nicholson. *Feminist*

Contentions: A Philosophical Exchange (New York, London: Routledge, 1995).

Benn, S. I. and R. S. Peters. *Social Principles and the Democratic State* (London: Allen and Unwin, 1965).

Bentham, Jeremy. *A Fragment on Government with an Introduction to the Principles of Morals and Legislation* (1789), edited by Wilfrid Harrison (Oxford: Blackwell, 1967).

Berki, R. N. *Socialism* (London: Dent, 1975; New York: St Martin's Press, 1975).

Berlin, I. *Four Essays on Liberty* (Oxford and New York: Oxford University Press, 1986), particularly Two Concepts of Liberty.

Berlin, I. *Karl Marx* (London: Oxford University Press, 1978).

Bracher, K. D. *The Age of Ideologies* (London: Methuen, 1985).

Bryson, V. *Feminist Political Theory* (London: Macmillan, 1992).

Burke, Edmund. *Reflections on the Revolution in France* (1790) (Harmondsworth: Penguin, 1969).

Burnham, J. *The Managerial Revolution* (Harmondsworth: Penguin, 1945; Bloomington, Ind: Indiana University Press, 1960).

Carter, A. *The Political Theory of Anarchism* (London: Routledge and Kegan Paul, 1982).

Carter, A. *The Politics of Women's Rights* (London and White Plains NY: Longman, 1988).

Devlin, P. *The Enforcement of Morals* (Oxford: Oxford University Press, 1968).

Di Stefano, Christine. *Configurations of Masculinity* (Ithaca, NY: Cornell University Press, 1991).

Dworkin, R. *Taking Rights Seriously* (London: Duckworth, 1978).

Dworkin, R. (ed.). *The Philosophy of Law* (Oxford: Oxford University Press, 1986).

Edwards, Stuart (ed.). *Selected Writings of P-J. Proudhon* (London: Macmillan, 1969).

Elshtain, J. V. *Public Man, Private Woman* (Oxford: Martin Robertson, 1981; Princeton: Princeton University Press, 1981).

Evans, J. and J. Hills (eds). *Feminism and Political Theory* (London and Newbury Park, Calif: Sage, 1986).

Feinberg, J. *Social Philosophy* (Englewood Cliffs, NJ: Prentice-Hall, 1973).

Friedan, Betty. *The Feminine Mystique* (New York: Dell, 1974).

Friedan, B. *The Second Stage* (London: Michael Joseph, 1982; New York: Summit, 1981).

Fromm, E. *Escape from Freedom* (New York: Avon, 1941), Chapters. 1, 2, 4 and 7, also published as *The Fear of Freedom* (London: Ark, 1984).

Fromm, E. *To Have or To Be* (London: Abacus, 1979).

Gauthier, David. *Moral Reason: Contract, Ethics and Reason* (Ithaca, NY: Cornell University Press, 1990).

Gellner, Ernest. *Thought and Change* (Chicago: University of Chicago Press, 1965), especially Chapter 7.

Gentile, Giovanni. *Genesis and Structure of Society* (1946) (Urbana: University of Illinois Press, 1960).

Gobineau, Joseph. *Essay on the Inequality of Human Races* (1855) (New York: reprint Howard Fertig, 1999).

Golding, M. P. *Philosophy of Law* (Englewood Cliffs, NJ: Prentice-Hall, 1975).

Graham, K. (ed.). *Contemporary Political Philosophy: Radical Studies* (Cambridge: Cambridge University Press, 1982).

Gray, J. *Liberalism* (Milton Keynes: Open University Press, 1986; Minneapolis, Minn: University of Minnesota Press, 1986).

Green, T. H. *Prolegomena to Ethics: Lectures on the Principles of Political Obligation* (Cheltenham: Nelson Thornes, 1986).

Greer, Germaine. *The Female Eunuch* (London: Flamingo Harper Collins, 1999).

Hart, H. L. A. *Law, Liberty and Morality* (Oxford: Oxford University Press, 1968).

Hart, H. L. A. *The Concept of Law* (Oxford: Oxford University Press, 1976), particularly Chapter 8.

Hegel, G. W. F. *Philosophy of Right*, trans. S. W. Dyde (Loughton, Essex: Prometheus, 1996).

Heywood, Andrew. *Political Ideologies* (London: Macmillan, 1992).

Hitler, A. *Mein Kampf* (London: Hutchinson, 1969; Boston, Mass: Houghton Mifflin, 1973).

Hobbes, T. *Leviathan*, edited by C. B. Macpherson (Harmondsworth: Penguin, 1968; Buffalo, NY: Prometheus, 1988).

Hook, S. *From Hegel to Marx* (Ann Arbor, Mich: University of Michigan Press, 1962).

Hume, D. *A Treatise of Human Nature* (1739–40) (London and New York: Dent and Dutton, 1966), Book III, section 2.

Jaggar, Alison M. and Iris Marion Young (eds). *A Companion to Feminist Philosophy* (Oxford: Blackwell, 1999).

Kamenka, E. (ed.). *Nationalism: The Nature and Evolution of an Idea* (London: Edward Arnold, 1976; New York: St Martin's Press, 1976).

Kedouri, E. *Nationalism* (London: Hutchinson, 1985).

King, Martin Luther, Jr. *A Testament of Hope*, edited by James M. Washington (New York: Harper and Row, 1986).

Kittay, Eva Feder. *Love's Labor: Essays on Women, Equality, and Dependency* (London: Routledge, 1998).

Kolakowski, L. *Main Currents of Marxism*, trans. P. S. Falla (Oxford and New York: Oxford University Press, 1982).

Laqueur, W. (ed.). *Fascism: A Reader's Guide* (Harmondsworth: Penguin, 1979; Berkeley: University of California Press, 1979).

Laslett, P. and W. G. Runciman (eds). *Philosophy, Politics and Society* (Oxford: Blackwell, 1964).

Lively, J. *Democracy* (Oxford: Blackwell, 1975).

Lloyd, D. *The Idea of Law* (Harmondsworth: Penguin, 1987).

Locke, J. *Two Treatises of Government* (Cambridge: Cambridge University Press, 1962; New York: New American Library, 1965).

Löwith, K. *From Hegel to Nietzsche* (New York: Holt Rinehart Winston, 1964).

Lucas, J. R. *On Justice* (Oxford: Oxford University Press, 1989).

Lukes, S. *Individualism* (Oxford: Blackwell, 1974).

Lyons, D. *Ethics and the Rule of Law* (Cambridge: Cambridge University Press, 1983).

Machiavelli, Niccolò. *The Prince*, trans. C. Detmold (New York: Airmont, 1965).

MacPherson, C. B. *The Real World of Democracy* (Oxford: Oxford University Press, 1972).

Mannheim, Karl. *Ideology and Utopia* (London: Routledge and Kegan Paul, reprint 1968).

Marx, Karl and F. Engels. *Selected Works* (London: Lawrence and Wishart, 1968).

Marx, Karl. *Communist Manifesto*, trans. S. Moore (Chicago: Regnery, 1969).

Marx, Karl. *Early Writings*, trans. T. Bottomore (New York: McGraw-Hill, 1963).

Marx, Karl and F. Engels. *The German Ideology* (London: Lawrence and Wishart, 1982).

McLellan, D. *Ideology* (Milton Keynes: Open University Press, 1986; Minneapolis, Minn: University of Minnesota Press, 1986).

McLellan, D. *Marx after Marxism* (London: Macmillan, 1979).

McLellan, D. *Marx before Marxism* (Harmondsworth: Penguin, 1970).

McLellan, D. *The Thought of Karl Marx: An Introduction* (London: Macmillan, 1971).

McLellan, D. *The Young Hegelians and Karl Marx* (New York: F. A. Praeger, 1969).

Mill, J. S. On Liberty. In *Utilitarianism, On Liberty and Considerations on Representative Government* (London: Dent, 1972).

Millett, K. *Sexual Politics* (London: Virago, 1977; New York: Simon and Schuster, 1990).

Minogue, K. R. *Nationalism* (London: Batsford, 1967).

Mitchell, J. *Women's Estate* (Harmondsworth: Penguin, 1971).

Nicholson, Linda (ed.) *The Second Wave: A Reader in Feminist Theory* (London: Routledge, 1997).

Nietzsche, F. *Thus Spoke Zarathustra*, trans. R. J. Hollingdale (Harmondsworth: Penguin, 1961; New York: Random, 1982).

Nisbet, Robert. *Conservatism: Dream and Reality* (Minneapolis: University of Minnesota Press, 1986).

Nozick, R. *Anarchy, State and Utopia* (Oxford: Blackwell, 1987; New York: Basic, 1974).

Oakeshott, M. *Rationalism in Politics and Other Essays* (London: Methuen, 1962; New York: Routledge Chapman and Hall, 1981).

Olafson, F. (ed.). *Justice and Social Policy* (Englewood Cliffs, NJ: Prentice Hall, 1961).

Pateman, C. *Participation and Democratic Theory* (Cambridge and New York: Cambridge University Press, 1988).

Pateman, Carole. *The Sexual Contract* (London: Polity, 1988).

Plato. *The Republic*, trans. H. D. Lee (Harmondsworth: Penguin, 1955; New York: Random, 1983).

Plato. Crito. In *The Last Days of Socrates*, trans. Hugh Tredennick and Harold Tarrant (Harmondsworth: Penguin, 1993).

Popper, K. *The Open Society and its Enemies*, 2 vols. (London: Routledge and Keegan Paul, 1962).

Randall, V. *Women and Politics* (London: Macmillan, 1987).

Raphael, D. D. *Problems of Political Philosophy* (London: Macmillan, 1979).

Rawls, J. *A Theory of Justice* (London: Oxford University Press, 1972; Cambridge, Mass: Harvard University Press, 1971).

Rousseau, Jean-Jacques. *The Social Contract* (New York: Dutton, 1950).

Schapiro, L. *Totalitarianism* (London: Macmillan, 1972).

Seliger, M. *The Marxist Conception of Ideology: A Critical Essay* (London: Allen and Unwin, 1977).

Singer, Peter. *Democracy and Disobedience* (Oxford: Clarendon, 1973).

Singer, Peter. *Marx* (Oxford: Oxford University Press, 1986).

Skinner, B. F. *Beyond Freedom and Dignity* (New York: Knopf, 1971).

Stacey, M and M. Price. *Women, Power and Politics*

(London: Tavistock, 1981; New York: Routledge Chapman and Hall, 1981).

Thoreau, H. D. *Civil Disobedience and Other Essays* (New York: Dover Publications, 1993).

Trilling, Lionel. *The Liberal Imagination* (Harmondsworth: Penguin, 1970), pp. 280–300.

Vazquez, A. S. *The Philosophy of Praxis* (London: Merlin, 1977).

Wollstonecraft, M. *A Vindication of the Rights of Women*, edited by C. W. Hagelman (New York: Norton, 1967).

Woodcock, George. *Anarchism* (Harmondsworth: Penguin, 1963).

Woodcock, George. *The Anarchist Reader* (London: Fontana, 1977).

Index